T0202845

Lecture Notes in Computer Science

Lecture Notes in Artificial Intelligence   14327

Founding Editor

Jörg Siekmann

Series Editors

Randy Goebel, *University of Alberta, Edmonton, Canada*
Wolfgang Wahlster, *DFKI, Berlin, Germany*
Zhi-Hua Zhou, *Nanjing University, Nanjing, China*

The series Lecture Notes in Artificial Intelligence (LNAI) was established in 1988 as a topical subseries of LNCS devoted to artificial intelligence.

The series publishes state-of-the-art research results at a high level. As with the LNCS mother series, the mission of the series is to serve the international R & D community by providing an invaluable service, mainly focused on the publication of conference and workshop proceedings and postproceedings.

Fenrong Liu · Arun Anand Sadanandan ·
Duc Nghia Pham · Petrus Mursanto ·
Dickson Lukose

Editors

PRICAI 2023:
Trends in
Artificial Intelligence

20th Pacific Rim
International Conference on Artificial Intelligence, PRICAI 2023
Jakarta, Indonesia, November 15–19, 2023
Proceedings, Part III

Springer

Editors
Fenrong Liu (ID)
Tsinghua University
Beijing, China

Arun Anand Sadanandan
SEEK Limited
Cremorne, NSW, Australia

Duc Nghia Pham (ID)
MIMOS (Malaysia)
Kuala Lumpur, Malaysia

Petrus Mursanto (ID)
Universitas Indonesia
Depok, Indonesia

Dickson Lukose (ID)
Tabcorp Holdings Limited
Melbourne, VIC, Australia

ISSN 0302-9743   ISSN 1611-3349 (electronic)
Lecture Notes in Artificial Intelligence
ISBN 978-981-99-7024-7   ISBN 978-981-99-7025-4 (eBook)
https://doi.org/10.1007/978-981-99-7025-4

LNCS Sublibrary: SL7 – Artificial Intelligence

This Springer imprint is published by the registered company Springer Nature Singapore Pte Ltd.
The registered company address is: 152 Beach Road, #21-01/04 Gateway East, Singapore 189721, Singapore

Paper in this product is recyclable.

Preface

Greetings and welcome to 20th Pacific Rim International Conference on Artificial Intelligence (PRICAI 2023). It was an honor to convene this significant event in a hybrid format in Jakarta, Indonesia. It was indeed a privilege for the Faculty of Computer Science at Universitas Indonesia to undertake the role of hosting these pivotal discussions that reach beyond the academic realm, advancing societies and economies across the Pacific Rim and Oceania.

This year, we received a remarkable 422 submissions: 354 for the Main track and 68 for the AI-Impact track. Every submission underwent a rigorous double-blind review process, receiving a minimum of 3 reviews, and in some cases up to 6. Throughout the process, the program committee (PC) members engaged in discussions, with additional reviews sourced as needed, prior to finalizing recommendations. The program chairs then assessed the reviews and comments, calibrating discrepancies in individual reviews and ratings to maintain decision consistency. The collective effort of the entire program committee, including chairs, 409 PC members, and 91 external reviewers, was monumental in ensuring a fair and consistent selection process. We ultimately accepted 95 regular papers and 36 short papers for oral presentation, resulting in a 22.51% acceptance rate for regular papers and an overall acceptance rate of 31.04%. Additionally, a comprehensive quality control procedure was introduced for camera-ready papers. The aim was to prompt authors to incorporate the feedback provided by PC members and reviewers into their final submissions. Content similarity checks were also performed to ensure that the similarity rate did not exceed 15%.

The technical program was comprehensive and intellectually engaging, featuring five workshops, nine tutorials, two panel discussions, and the main conference sessions. All regular and short papers were orally presented over three days in parallel and in topical program sessions. We were honored to have some of the brightest minds in AI to share their insights and enrich our collective understanding: Thomas Anton Kochan (Massachusetts Institute of Technology, USA), Hanna Kurniawati (Australian National University, Australia), Anand Rao (Carnegie Mellon University, USA), and Geoff Webb (Monash University, Australia).

A heartfelt thanks was expressed towards the organizing committee for their tireless and unwavering efforts that facilitated the success of this event. A special recognition to Adila Alfa Krisnadhi for his leadership on local arrangements. We would also like to acknowledge our workshop and tutorial organizers, who formed the core of our technical program. These dedicated individuals brought a diverse range of expertise that promised to deepen our exploration of AI technologies.

We would like to thank our advisory board members for their invaluable guidance during the planning stages. A special recognition to Abdul Sattar for his extraordinary contribution towards planning, execution, and a conference site visit that contributed to the success of PRICAI 2023. Furthermore, we extend our gratitude to the PRI-CAI Steering Committee for entrusting us with the privilege of hosting this impactful conference.

We would not have been here without the support of our sponsors, whose commitment enabled us to keep pushing boundaries. To them, as well as all participants in this event, thank you.

As we delved into the various topics that PRICAI 2023 had to offer, let us remind ourselves that our deliberations have a lasting impact on the future of AI in the Pacific Rim and beyond. We genuinely hope that our time spent at PRICAI 2023 will pave the way for innovations that are both groundbreaking and beneficial.

November 2023

Fenrong Liu
Arun Anand Sadanandan
Duc Nghia Pham
Dickson Lukose
Petrus Mursanto

Organization

PRICAI Steering Committee

Steering Committee

Quan Bai	University of Tasmania, Australia
Tru Hoang Cao	University of Texas Health Science Center at Houston, USA
Xin Geng	Southeast University, China
Guido Governatori	Reasoning Research Institute, Australia
Takayuki Ito	Kyoto University, Japan
Byeong-Ho Kang	University of Tasmania, Australia
M. G. M. Khan	University of the South Pacific, Fiji
Sankalp Khanna	CSIRO Australian e-Health Research Centre, Australia
Fenrong Liu	Tsinghua University, China
Dickson Lukose	Tabcorp Holdings Ltd., Australia
Hideyuki Nakashima	Sapporo City University, Japan
Abhaya Nayak	Macquarie University, Australia
Seong Bae Park	Kyung Hee University, South Korea
Duc Nghia Pham	MIMOS Berhad, Malaysia
Abdul Sattar	Griffith University, Australia
Alok Sharma	RIKEN, Japan & University of the South Pacific, Fiji
Thanaruk Theeramunkong	Thammasat University, Thailand
Zhi-Hua Zhou	Nanjing University, China

Honorary Members

Randy Goebel	University of Alberta, Canada
Tu-Bao Ho	Japan Advanced Institute of Science and Technology, Japan
Mitsuru Ishizuka	University of Tokyo, Japan
Hiroshi Motoda	Osaka University, Japan
Geoff Webb	Monash University, Australia
Albert Yeap	Auckland University of Technology, New Zealand
Byoung-Tak Zhang	Seoul National University, South Korea
Chengqi Zhang	University of Technology Sydney, Australia

Conference Organizing Committee

General Chairs

Dickson Lukose	Tabcorp Holdings Ltd., Australia
Petrus Mursanto	Universitas Indonesia, Indonesia

Program Chairs

Fenrong Liu	Tsinghua University, China
Arun Anand Sadanandan	SEEK, Australia
Duc Nghia Pham	MIMOS Berhad, Malaysia

Local Organizing Chair

Adila Alfa Krisnadhi	Universitas Indonesia, Indonesia

Workshop Chairs

Evi Yulianti	Universitas Indonesia, Indonesia
Takahiro Uchiya	Nagoya Institute of Technology, Japan

Tutorial Chairs

Fariz Darari	Universitas Indonesia, Indonesia
M. A. Hakim Newton	University of Newcastle, Australia

Publicity Chairs

Panca Hadi Putra	Universitas Indonesia, Indonesia
Md Khaled Ben Islam	Griffith University, Australia

Advisory Board

Abdul Sattar	Griffith University, Australia
Hammam Riza	KORIKA; University of Syiah Kuala, Indonesia
Patricia Anthony	Lincoln University, New Zealand
Jirapun Daengdej	Merlin's Solutions International, Thailand
Seong Bae Park	Kyung Hee University, South Korea
M. G. M. Khan	University of the South Pacific, Fiji

Qingliang Chen	Jinan University, China
Takayuki Ito	Kyoto University, Japan
Tru Hoang Cao	University of Texas Health Science Center at Houston, USA
Sankalp Khanna	CSIRO Australian e-Health Research Centre, Australia
Stéphane Bressan	National University of Singapore, Singapore
Hideyuki Nakashima	Sapporo City University, Japan

Program Committee

Tooba Aamir	Data61, CSIRO, Australia
Azizi Ab Aziz	Universiti Utara Malaysia, Malaysia
Taufik Abidin	Universitas Syiah Kuala, Indonesia
Kiki Adhinugraha	La Trobe University, Australia
Martin Aleksandrov	Freie Universität Berlin, Germany
Hissah Alotaibi	University of Melbourne, Australia
Sagaya Amalathas	University of Southampton, Malaysia
Galia Angelova	Bulgarian Academy of Sciences, Bulgaria
Patricia Anthony	Lincoln University, New Zealand
Ryuta Arisaka	Kyoto University, Japan
Mohammad Arshi Saloot	MIMOS Berhad, Malaysia
Siti Liyana Azman	International Islamic University Malaysia, Malaysia
Mohamed Jaward Bah	Zhejiang Lab, China
Quan Bai	University of Tasmania, Australia
Thirunavukarasu Balasubramaniam	Queensland University of Technology, Australia
Arishnil Kumar Bali	University of the South Pacific, Fiji
Vishnu Monn Baskaran	Monash University, Malaysia
Chutima Beokhaimook	Rangsit University, Thailand
Pascal Bercher	Australian National University, Australia
Ateet Bhalla	Independent Technology Consultant, India
Hanif Bhuiyan	Monash University, Australia
Ran Bi	Dalian University of Technology, China
Thomas Bolander	Technical University of Denmark, Denmark
Chih How Bong	Universiti Malaysia Sarawak, Malaysia
Aida Brankovic	CSIRO, Australia
Chenyang Bu	Hefei University of Technology, China
Agus Buono	Bogor Agriculture University, Indonesia
Xiongcai Cai	University of New South Wales, Australia

Jian Cao	Shanghai Jiao Tong University, China
Tru Cao	University of Texas Health Science Center at Houston, USA
Sixian Chan	Zhejiang University of Technology, China
Narayan Changder	National Institute of Technology Durgapur, India
Hutchatai Chanlekha	Kasetsart University, Thailand
Kaylash Chaudhary	University of the South Pacific, Fiji
Bincai Chen	Dalian University of Technology, China
Gang Chen	Victoria University of Wellington, New Zealand
Liangyu Chen	East China Normal University, China
Qi Chen	Victoria University of Wellington, New Zealand
Rui Chen	Nankai University, China
Siqi Chen	Tianjin University, China
Songcan Chen	Nanjing University of Aeronautics and Astronautics, China
Tingxuan Chen	Central South University, China
Weitong Chen	University of Adelaide, Australia
Weiwei Chen	Sun Yat-sen University, China
Wu Chen	Southwest University, China
Yakun Chen	University of Technology Sydney, Australia
Yingke Chen	Northumbria University, UK
Wai Khuen Cheng	Universiti Tunku Abdul Rahman, Malaysia
Yihang Cheng	Tianjin University, China
Boonthida Chiraratanasopha	Yala Rajabhat University, Thailand
Cody Christopher	Data61, CSIRO, Australia
Jinmiao Cong	Dalian University of Technology, China
Dan Corbett	University of Sydney, Australia
Zhihong Cui	Shandong University, China
Jirapun Daengdej	Assumption University of Thailand, Thailand
Li Dai	Zaozhuang University, China
Fariz Darari	Universitas Indonesia, Indonesia
Iman Dehzangi	Rutgers University, USA
Zelin Deng	Changsha University of Science and Technology, China
Chandra Kusuma Dewa	Universitas Islam Indonesia, Indonesia
Sarinder Kaur Dhillon	Universiti Malaya, Malaysia
Shiyao Ding	Kyoto University, Japan
Zheng Dong	Baidu, China
Shyamala Doraisamy	University Putra Malaysia, Malaysia
Ellouze Ellouze	University of Sfax, Tunisia
Uzoamaka Ezeakunne	Florida State University, USA
Lei Fan	University of New South Wales, Australia

Priyanto Hidayatullah	Politeknik Negeri Bandung, Indonesia
Linlin Hou	Zhejiang Lab, China
Shuyue Hu	Shanghai Artificial Intelligence Laboratory, China
Jiwei Huang	China University of Petroleum, China
Victoria Huang	National Institute of Water and Atmospheric Research, New Zealand
Xiaodi Huang	Charles Sturt University, Australia
Nguyen Duy Hung	Thammasat University, Thailand
Huan Huo	University of Technology Sydney, Australia
Habibi Husain Arifin	Assumption University of Thailand, Thailand
Du Huynh	University of Western Australia, Australia
Van Nam Huynh	Japan Advanced Institute of Science and Technology, Japan
Masashi Inoue	Tohoku Institute of Technology, Japan
Md Khaled Ben Islam	Griffith University, Australia
Md. Saiful Islam	University of Newcastle, Australia
Takayuki Ito	Kyoto University, Japan
Sanjay Jain	National University of Singapore, Singapore
Mehrdad Jalali	Karlsruhe Institute of Technology, Germany
Fatemeh Jalalvand	Data61, CSIRO, Australia
Wojtek Jamroga	Polish Academy of Sciences, Poland
Wisnu Jatmiko	Universitas Indonesia, Indonesia
Jingjing Ji	Huazhong University of Science and Technology, China
Liu Jiahao	Southwest University, China
Guifei Jiang	Nankai University, China
Jianhua Jiang	Jilin University of Finance and Economics, China
Ting Jiang	Zhejiang Lab, China
Yuncheng Jiang	South China Normal University, China
Nattagit Jiteurtragool	King Mongkut's University of Technology North Bangkok, Thailand
Rui-Yang Ju	Tamkang University, Taiwan
Imah Kamkar	Deloitte, Australia
Hideaki Kanai	Japan Advanced Institute of Science and Technology, Japan
Rathimala Kannan	Multimedia University, Malaysia
Natsuda Kaothanthong	Thammasat University, Thailand
Jessada Karnjana	National Electronics and Computer Technology Center, Thailand
Shohei Kato	Nagoya Institute of Technology, Japan
Natthawut Kertkeidkachorn	Japan Advanced Institute of Science and Technology, Japan
Nor Khalid	Universiti Teknologi MARA, Malaysia

Jane Jean Kiam	Universität der Bundeswehr München, Germany
Huan Koh	Monash University, Australia
Kazunori Komatani	Osaka University, Japan
Sébastien Konieczny	French National Centre for Scientific Research, France
Harindu Korala	Monash University, Australia
Fajri Koto	Mohamed bin Zayed University of Artificial Intelligence, United Arab Emirates
Adila A. Krisnadhi	Universitas Indonesia, Indonesia
Alfred Krzywicki	University of Adelaide, Australia
Charles Kuan	Tabcorp Holdings Limited, Australia
Li Kuang	Central South University, China
Dinesh Kumar	University of the South Pacific, Fiji
Shiu Kumar	Fiji National University, Fiji
Young-Bin Kwon	Chung-Ang University, South Korea
Ho-Pun Lam	Independent Researcher, Australia
Davide Lanti	Free University of Bozen-Bolzano, Italy
Roberto Legaspi	KDDI Research, Japan
Dazhu Li	Chinese Academy of Sciences, China
Gang Li	Deakin University, Australia
Guángliang Li	Ocean University of China, China
Guoqiang Li	Shanghai Jiao Tong University, China
Ren Li	Chongqing Jiaotong University, China
Tianrui Li	Southwest Jiaotong University, China
Weihua Li	Auckland University of Technology, New Zealand
Yicong Li	University of Technology Sydney, Australia
Yuan-Fang Li	Monash University, Australia
Xiubo Liang	Zhejiang University, China
Ariel Liebman	Monash University, Australia
Alan Wee-Chung Liew	Griffith University, Australia
Donghui Lin	Okayama University, Japan
Chanjuan Liu	Dalian University of Technology, China
Di Liu	Inner Mongolia University, China
Fenrong Liu	Tsinghua University, China
Guanfeng Liu	Macquarie University, Australia
Hao Liu	Hong Kong University of Science and Technology, China
Jinghui Liu	University of Melbourne, Australia
Kangzheng Liu	Huazhong University of Science and Technology, China
Xinpeng Liu	Dalian University of Technology, China
Yang Liu	Dalian University of Technology, China

Yue Liu	Data61, CSIRO, Australia
Sin Kit Lo	Data61, CSIRO, Australia
Emiliano Lorini	French National Centre for Scientific Research, France
Qinghua Lu	Data61, CSIRO, Australia
Dickson Lukose	Tabcorp Holdings Limited, Australia
Jieting Luo	Zhejiang University, China
Sreenivasan M.	International Institute of Information Technology, India
Chuan Ma	Zhejiang Lab, China
Hui Ma	Victoria University of Wellington, New Zealand
Pathum Chamikara Mahawaga Arachchige	Data61, CSIRO, Australia
Michael Maher	Reasoning Research Institute, Australia
Vikash Maheshwari	Universiti Teknologi PETRONAS, Malaysia
Rohana Mahmud	Universiti Malaya, Malaysia
Eric Martin	University of New South Wales, Australia
Sanparith Marukatat	National Electronics and Computer Technology Center, Thailand
Atiya Masood	Iqra University, Pakistan
Nur Ulfa Maulidevi	Bandung Institute of Technology, Indonesia
Alan Mccabe	Griffith University, Australia
Md Humaion Kabir Mehedi	BRAC University, Bangladesh
Qingxin Meng	University of Nottingham - Ningbo, China
Jian Mi	Yangzhou University, China
Lynn Miller	Monash University, Australia
Muhammad Syafiq Mohd Pozi	Universiti Utara Malaysia, Malaysia
Kristen Moore	Data61, CSIRO, Australia
Fernando Mourao	SEEK, Australia
Lailil Muflikhah	Universitas Brawijaya, Indonesia
Ganesh Neelakanta Iyer	National University of Singapore, Singapore
M. A. Hakim Newton	University of Newcastle, Australia
Phi Le Nguyen	Hanoi University of Science and Technology, Vietnam
Thanh Thi Nguyen	Deakin University, Australia
Nianwen Ning	Henan University, China
Hussain Nyeem	Military Institute of Science and Technology, Bangladesh
Kouzou Ohara	Aoyama Gakuin University, Japan
Nurul Aida Osman	Universiti Teknologi PETRONAS, Malaysia
Takanobu Otsuka	Nagoya Institute of Technology, Japan
Abiola Oyegun	Birmingham City University, UK

Maurice Pagnucco	University of New South Wales, Australia
Shirui Pan	Griffith University, Australia
Anum Paracha	Birmingham City University, UK
Anand Paul	Kyungpook National University, South Korea
Pengfei Pei	Chinese Academy of Sciences, China
Shengbing Pei	Anhui University, China
Songwen Pei	University of Shanghai for Science and Technology, China
Tao Peng	UT Southwestern Medical Center, USA
Arif Perdana	Monash University, Indonesia
Laurent Perrussel	University of Toulouse, France
Duc Nghia Pham	MIMOS Berhad, Malaysia
Ioannis Pierros	Aristotle University of Thessaloniki, Greece
Chiu Po Chan	Universiti Malaysia Sarawak, Malaysia
Thadpong Pongthawornkamol	Kasikorn Business-Technology Group, Thailand
Surya Prakash	University of the South Pacific, Fiji
Mauridhi Hery Purnomo	Institut Teknologi Sepuluh Nopember, Indonesia
Ayu Purwarianti	Bandung Institute of Technology, Indonesia
Qi Qi	Hainan University, China
Shiyou Qian	Shanghai Jiao Tong University, China
Jianglin Qiao	Western Sydney University, Australia
Chuan Qin	Baidu, China
Lyn Qiu	Shanghai Jiao Tong University, China
Joel Quinqueton	Laboratoire d'Informatique, de Robotique et de Microélectronique de Montpellier, France
Teeradaj Racharak	Japan Advanced Institute of Science and Technology, Japan
Jessica Rahman	CSIRO, Australia
Mohammad Shahriar Rahman	United International University, Bangladesh
Srikari Rallabandi	Vidya Jyothi Institute of Technology, India
Tian Ran	Northwest Normal University, China
Annajiat Alim Rasel	BRAC University, Bangladesh
Mahmood Rashid	Griffith University, Australia
Md Saifullah Razali	University of Wollongong, Australia
Farid Razzak	New York University, USA
Karuna Reddy	University of the South Pacific, Fiji
Fenghui Ren	University of Wollongong, Australia
Jiankang Ren	Dalian University of Technology, China
Yongli Ren	RMIT University, Australia
Yuheng Ren	Jimei University, China
Mark Reynolds	University of Western Australia, Australia
Jia Rong	Monash University, Australia

Yi Rong	Wuhan University of Technology, China
Liat Rozenberg	Griffith University, Australia
Ji Ruan	Auckland University of Technology, New Zealand
Filip Rusak	CSIRO, Australia
Arun Anand Sadanandan	SEEK Limited, Australia
Khairun Saddami	Universitas Syiah Kuala, Indonesia
Payel Sadhukhan	TCG CREST, India
Sofia Sahab	Kyoto University, Japan
Chiaki Sakama	Wakayama University, Japan
Ario Santoso	Independent, The Netherlands
Muhamad Saputra	Monash University, Indonesia
Yunita Sari	Universitas Gadjah Mada, Indonesia
Anto Satriyo Nugroho	National Research and Innovation Agency, Indonesia
Abdul Sattar	Griffith University, Australia
Thanveer Shaik	University of Southern Queensland, Australia
Lin Shang	Nanjing University, China
Nandita Sharma	Australian Government, Australia
Dazhong Shen	University of Science and Technology of China, China
Yifan Shen	University of Illinois Urbana-Champaign, USA
Chenwei Shi	Tsinghua University, China
Kaize Shi	University of Technology Sydney, Australia
Xiaolong Shi	Guangzhou University, China
Zhenwei Shi	Beihang University, China
Kazutaka Shimada	Kyushu Institute of Technology, Japan
Yanfeng Shu	CSIRO, Australia
Harvinder Singh	Torrens University, Australia
Ronal Singh	Data61, CSIRO, Australia
Patrick Chin Hooi Soh	Multimedia University, Malaysia
Chattrakul Sombattheera	Mahasarakham University, Thailand
Insu Song	James Cook University, Australia
Xin Song	Hebei University, China
Pokpong Songmuang	Thammasat University, Thailand
Lay-Ki Soon	Monash University Malaysia, Malaysia
Bela Stantic	Griffith University, Australia
Markus Stumptner	University of South Australia, Australia
Guoxin Su	University of Wollongong, Australia
Ruidan Su	Shanghai Jiao Tong University, China
Xingchi Su	Zhejiang Lab, China
Jie Sun	Nanjing Xiaozhuang University, China
Xin Sun	Zhejiang Lab, China

Ying Sun	Hong Kong University of Science and Technology, China
Yongqian Sun	Nankai University, China
Boontawee Suntisrivaraporn	DTAC, Thailand
Thepchai Supnithi	National Electronics and Computer Technology Center, Thailand
Chang Wei Tan	Monash University, Australia
David Taniar	Monash University, Australia
Thitipong Tanprasert	Assumption University of Thailand, Thailand
Xiaohui Tao	University of Southern Queensland, Australia
Sotarat Thammaboosadee	Mahidol University, Thailand
Truong Thao Nguyen	National Institute of Advanced Industrial Science and Technology, Japan
Bui Thi-Mai-Anh	Institut de la Francophonie pour l'Informatique, Vietnam
Michael Thielscher	University of New South Wales, Australia
Hung Nghiep Tran	National Institute of Informatics, Japan
Jarrod Trevathan	Griffith University, Australia
Bambang Riyanto Trilaksono	Institut Teknologi Bandung, Indonesia
Bayu Trisedya	SEEK, Australia
Eric Tsui	Hong Kong Polytechnic University, China
Shikui Tu	Shanghai Jiao Tong University, China
Ayad Turky	University of Sharjah, United Arab Emirates
Takahiro Uchiya	Nagoya Institute of Technology, Japan
Khimji Vaghjiani	Torrens University, Australia
Hans van Ditmarsch	University of Toulouse, France
Miroslav Velev	Aries Design Automation, USA
Agustinus Waluyo	La Trobe University, Australia
Biao Wang	Zhejiang Lab, China
Chao Wang	HKUST Fok Ying Tung Research Institute, China
Chen Wang	National Institute of Water and Atmospheric Research, New Zealand
Hao Wang	Monash University, Australia
Hao Wang	Nanyang Technological University, Singapore
Li Wang	Henan University, China
Shuxia Wang	Northwestern Polytechnical University, China
Weiqing Wang	Monash University, Australia
Xiangmeng Wang	University of Technology Sydney, Australia
Xinxhi Wang	Shanghai University, China
Yuxin Wang	Dalian University of Technology, China
Zhen Wang	Zhejiang Lab, China
Ian Watson	University of Auckland, New Zealand

Xian Wei	East China Normal University, China
Xiao Wei	Shanghai University, China
Manuel Weiss	SEEK, Australia
Paul Weng	UM-SJTU Joint Institute, China
Derry Wijaya	Monash University Indonesia, Indonesia
Tri Kurniawan Wijaya	Huawei Ireland Research Centre, Ireland
Arie Wahyu Wijayanto	Politeknik Statistika STIS, Indonesia
Wayne Wobcke	University of New South Wales, Australia
Daphne Wong-A-Foe	Leiden University, The Netherlands
Sartra Wongthanavasu	Khon Kaen University, Thailand
Brendon J. Woodford	University of Otago, New Zealand
Huiwen Wu	Ant Group, China
Ou Wu	Tianjin University, China
Shiqing Wu	University of Technology Sydney, Australia
Xing Wu	Shanghai University, China
Yutong Wu	CSIRO, Australia
Pierre-Henri Wuillemin	LIP6, Sorbonne University, France
Zhanhao Xiao	Guangzhou University, China
Zhuoyu Xiao	Hunan Industry Polytechnic, China
Kaibo Xie	University of Amsterdam, The Netherlands
Ming Xu	Xi'an Jiaotong-Liverpool University, China
Shuxiang Xu	University of Tasmania, Australia
Yongxiu Xu	Chinese Academy of Sciences, China
Zenghui Xu	Zhejiang Lab, China
Hui Xue	Southeast University, China
Chao Yang	University of Technology Sydney, Australia
Chunming Yang	Southwest University of Science and Technology, China
Fengyu Yang	Nanchang Hangkong University, China
Haoran Yang	University of Technology Sydney, Australia
Liu Yang	Central South University, China
Tianle Yang	Osaka University, Japan
Yi Yang	Hefei University of Technology, China
Yuan Yao	University of Nottingham - Ningbo, China
Roland Yap	National University of Singapore, Singapore
Xuefei Yin	Griffith University, Australia
Dianer Yu	University of Technology Sydney, Australia
Hang Yu	Shanghai University, China
Ting Yu	Zhejiang Lab, China
Youren Yu	Beijing Information Science and Technology University, China

Weiwei Yuan	Nanjing University of Aeronautics and Astronautics, China
Lin Yue	University of Newcastle, Australia
Evi Yulianti	Universitas Indonesia, Indonesia
Intan Nurma Yulita	Padjadjaran University, Indonesia
Nayyar Zaidi	Deakin University, Australia
Chengwei Zhang	Dalian Maritime University, China
Daokun Zhang	Monash University, Australia
Du Zhang	California State University, USA
Haibo Zhang	Kyushu University, Japan
Haijun Zhang	Harbin Institute of Technology, China
Huan Zhang	China University of Geosciences, China
Le Zhang	University of Science and Technology of China, China
Leo Zhang	Griffith University, Australia
Liying Zhang	China University of Petroleum, China
Min-Ling Zhang	Southeast University, China
Mingyue Zhang	Southwest University, China
Peng Zhang	Shandong University, China
Qi Zhang	University of Science and Technology of China, China
Shenglin Zhang	Nankai University, China
Wei Emma Zhang	University of Adelaide, Australia
Wen Zhang	Beijing University of Technology, China
Xianhui Zhang	Hangzhou Normal University, China
Xiaobo Zhang	Southwest Jiaotong University, China
Xinghua Zhang	Chinese Academy of Sciences, China
Yuhong Zhang	Hefei University of Technology, China
Yunfeng Zhang	Shandong University of Finance and Economics, China
Zili Zhang	Deakin University, Australia
Dengji Zhao	ShanghaiTech University, China
Ruilin Zhao	Huazhong University of Science and Technology, China
Yijing Zhao	Chinese Academy of Sciences, China
Jianyu Zhou	Nankai University, China
Shuigeng Zhou	Fudan University, China
Xin Zhou	Nanyang Technological University, Singapore
Yun Zhou	National University of Defense Technology, China
Enqiang Zhu	Guangzhou University, China
Guohun Zhu	University of Queensland, Australia

Jingwen Zhu	Nankai University, China
Liang Zhu	Hebei University, China
Nengjun Zhu	Shanghai University, China
Xingquan Zhu	Florida Atlantic University, USA
Yanming Zhu	Griffith University, Australia

Additional Reviewers

Angelov, Zhivko
Azam, Basim
Burgess, Mark
Cao, Xuemei
Chan, Chee-Yong
Chandra, Abel
Chen, Xiaohong
Clifton, Ava
Duan, Jiaang
Ebrahimi, Ali
Fang, Han
Fei, Wu
Fodor, Gabor Adam
Folkman, Lukas
Geng, Chuanxing
Guo, Ruoyu
Guo, Siyuan
Hammond, Lewis
Han, Xin
Hao, Chen
Haruta, Shuichiro
He, Haoyu
He, Tao
He, Zhengqi
Hu, Han Wen
Hua, Qin
Hua, Yuncheng
Huang, Renhao
Hung, Nguyen
Jiang, Zhaohui
Li, Jingyang
Li, Xiang
Liga, Davide
Lin, Songtuan
Liu, Chuan

Liu, Hongquan
Liu, Yongchang
Liu, Yutao
Liu, Zhaorui
Ma, Jiaxuan
Mataeimoghadam, Fereshteh
Mayer, Wolfgang
Mezza, Stefano
Mohamed Muzammil, Mohamed
 Mufassirin
Mu, Chunjiang
Nikafshan Rad, Hima
Nwe, Hlaing Myat
Pan, Chaofan
Peng, Lilan
Perera, Isuri
Rahman, Julia
Reddy, Emmenual
Ren, Siyue
Ren, Yixin
Schwenker, Friedhelm
Selway, Matt
Semenov, Ivan
Shiri, Fatemeh
Singh, Priyanka
Singh, Satyanand
Smith, Jeff
Song, Zhihao
Soni, Bhanu Pratap
Tan, Hongwei
Tang, Jiaqi
Viriyavisuthisakul, Supatta
Wang, Luzhi
Wang, Mengyan
Wang, Xiaodan

Wang, Yunyun
Wei, Tianpeng
Wu, Lingi
Wu, Shixin
Xia, Boming
Xu, Dalai
Xu, Rongxin
Xu, Weilai
Yang, Yikun
Yao, Naimeng
Yin, Yifan

Yuan, Zixuan
Zaman, Rianon
Zhang, Denghui
Zhang, Junyu
Zhang, Lin
Zhang, Yunfei
Zhang, Zhenxing
Zhao, Zijun
Zheng, Xin
Zheng, Yizhen
Zhou, Zheng

Contents – Part III

AI Impact

Vision and Perception

A Multi-scale Densely Connected and Feature Aggregation Network for Hyperspectral Image Classification

Jian Zhu[1], Yi Liu[1]([⊠]), Jiajie Feng[1], and Caihong Mu[2]

[1] School of Electronic Engineering, Xidian University, Xi'an 710071, China
yiliuxd@foxmail.com
[2] School of Artificial Intelligence, Xidian University, Xi'an 710071, China

Abstract. Convolutional neural networks have been widely used in the field of hyperspectral image (HSI) classification due to their excellent ability to model local regions, and have achieved good classification performance. However, HSI classification still faces challenges such as insufficient representation of spectral-spatial features and inadequate fusion of multi-level features. To address these issues, we propose a Multi-scale Densely Connected and Feature Aggregation Network (MSDC-FAN) for HSI classification. The network mainly consists of a Spectral-Spatial Feature Extraction (SSFE) module, three Multi-scale Feature Extraction (MSFE) modules, and a Multilevel Feature Aggregation Module (MFAM). Firstly, the SSFE module is carried out to extract more comprehensive spectral-spatial features. Secondly, three MSFE modules are used in sequence to extract multi-scale features and highlight significant features, thus further improving the model's performance. Finally, the MFAM is designed to aggregate features at different levels, enhancing the model's feature representation ability. Experimental results on two commonly used hyperspectral datasets demonstrate the superiority of the proposed method.

Keywords: Hyperspectral image · Multi-scale feature · Dense connection

1 Introduction

Hyperspectral images (HSIs), containing abundant spectral-spatial information, have been widely used in environmental monitoring [1], mineral exploration [2], precision agriculture [3] and other fields. Early HSI classification methods only considered spectral features, such as support vector machine [4], k-nearest neighbor [5], and random forest [6], which had certain limitations. To simultaneously consider spectral-spatial information, methods such as sparse representation [7] and Markov random field [8] were proposed. However, spectral-spatial feature extraction and fusion still face challenges.

Convolutional neural networks (CNNs) have been widely used in HSI classification tasks due to their excellent ability to model local regions [9, 10]. Zhong et al. [11] designed spectral and spatial residual blocks to learn discriminative features and

F. Liu et al. (Eds.): PRICAI 2023, LNAI 14327, pp. 3–15, 2024.
https://doi.org/10.1007/978-981-99-7025-4_1

alleviate the problem of accuracy degradation in deep networks. Song et al. [12] constructed a very deep network to extract more discriminative features and fused low-level, mid-level, and high-level features by addition to improve performance. Yu et al. [13] introduced an image-based global learning framework into HSI classification to fully utilize global information and achieved good classification results. Shi et al. [14] designed spectral feature extraction branch and spatial feature extraction branch to fully exploit the spectral-spatial information of HSIs and further improve the classification performance.

In addition, redundant information and noise in HSIs can interfere with model classification decisions, so it is important to extract effective information. To address this issue, attention mechanisms have been introduced into HSI classification [15] to help the model focus on more important features and regions. Zhu et al. [16] designed a spectral attention module and a spatial attention module to emphasize useful bands and pixels, achieving good classification results. In addition, the Transformer has been introduced into HSI classification tasks due to its excellent global feature modeling ability [17]. Sun et al. [18] introduced the Transformer for global features modeling, achieved good classification results and improved computational efficiency. Mei et al. [19] significantly improved the HSI classification accuracy by introducing a grouped pixel embedding module and constructing the Transformer in a hierarchical manner.

These networks have improved the HSI classification performance to some extent. However, limited by the fixed size of the CNN's convolutional kernel, the local features it extracts are limited, resulting in insufficient spectral-spatial feature representation. Additionally, multi-level features that are complementary and correlated have not been fully fused and utilized, and the classification performance needs to be further improved. To address the above issues, we propose a Multi-scale Densely Connected and Feature Aggregation Network (MSDC-FAN) for HSI classification. The main contributions of this paper are summarized as follows.

(1) A spectral-spatial feature extraction (SSFE) module is devised to capture the spectral-spatial features of HSIs more comprehensively. Firstly, features of different scales are extracted by dilated convolution, and then concatenated and fused by skip connections.
(2) A multi-scale feature extraction (MSFE) module is designed to fully extract HSI features. The multi-scale branch is adopted to extract multi-scale features, and the residual branch is carried out to make the information flow between the shallow layer and the deep layer. Then the cross-attention module is employed to enhance the feature fusion of the two branches, thus improving the model's performance.
(3) A multi-level feature aggregation module (MFAM) is proposed to enhance the model's feature representation ability. Three MSFE modules are used in sequence to extract multi-scale features at different levels, which are then aggregated through the top-down channel to enhance the feature representation.

The rest of this paper is organized as follows. Section 2 provides a detailed introduction to the MSDC-FAN method. Section 3 presents the experimental results and analysis. Section 4 concludes the paper.

2 Proposed Method

In this section, we will introduce in detail our proposed MSDC-FAN for HSI classification, the overall framework of which is shown in Fig. 1. Firstly, the SSFE module is adopted to extract features from the dimension-reduced HSI after principal component analysis (PCA), in order to acquire the spectral-spatial information effectively. Then, the two-dimensional (2D) convolution is used to unify the number of channels. Secondly, multi-scale and multi-level features are extracted by stacking three MSFE modules in sequence, and features of different levels are aggregated by the MFAM module to obtain the final feature representation for classification. Finally, the aggregated features are fed into the linear layer for classification.

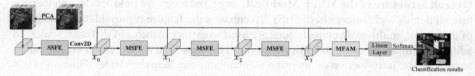

Fig. 1. Overall framework of the proposed MSDC-FAN

2.1 Spectral-Spatial Feature Extraction Module

The three-dimensional (3D) convolution can move simultaneously in both spectral and spatial dimensions, making it more effective to extract the spectral-spatial features of HSIs. Therefore, we construct the SSFE module to capture the features in HSIs more comprehensively, and the specific structure of the SSFE module is shown in Fig. 2.

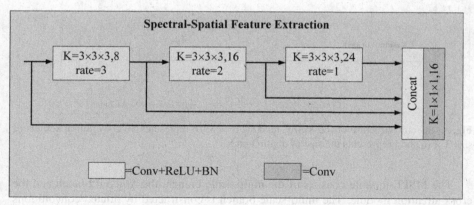

Fig. 2. Specific structure of the SSFE module. Conv, ReLU and BN represent convolution operation, ReLU activation function and batch normalization, respectively. $K = 3 \times 3 \times 3$, 8 represents eight convolution kernels of size $3 \times 3 \times 3$. Rate and Concat represent the dilation rate and the concatenation operation, respectively

The SSFE module mainly consists of dilated convolutions and skip connections. By increasing the dilation rate (i.e., rate in Fig. 2), the receptive field of the convolution kernel can be expanded while keeping the kernel size fixed, thereby improving the network performance. Skip connections can fully utilize the multi-level features extracted by the module, enhancing the feature representation capability of the network. Firstly, three convolution kernels are cascaded for multi-scale feature extraction. Then, the features extracted by each kernel are concatenated along the channel dimension through skip connections. Finally, the channel number is unified to 16 by a convolution kernel of size $1 \times 1 \times 1$.

2.2 Multi-scale Feature Extraction Module

Overall Structure of the MSFE Module. Using fixed receptive field, CNNs cannot capture all details and features in the HSI. To enhance the feature representation capability of the model, multi-scale convolutions are used to extract features of different scales. In addition, redundant and noisy information in HSI may lead to decreased classification accuracy. The introduction of attention mechanisms can help the model focus on pixels and spectral bands with important information, thereby improving classification accuracy and performance. Therefore, we propose the MSFE module to extract multi-scale features and highlight significant features, and the specific structure of the MSFE module is shown in Fig. 3.

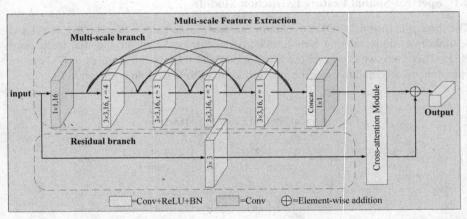

Fig. 3. Specific structure of the MSFE module. 3×3, 16 represents 16 convolution kernels of size 3×3, and r represents the size of dilation rate

The MSFE module consists of the multi-scale branch, the residual branch and the cross-attention module. The multi-scale branch is constructed by dilated convolutions and dense connections. The dilated convolutions extract features of different scales by cascading convolution kernels with different dilation rates. The dense connections connect the features of all previous layers to the input of the current layer, increasing the reusability of features and avoiding information loss. The residual branch uses skip connections to allow shallow and deep features to complement each other, improving the ability of the model to represent the features. The cross-attention module aims to highlight the significant features and enhance the feature fusion of the two branches, thereby improving the performance of the model.

As shown in Fig. 3, MSFE first uses 1×1 convolution kernel to unify the channel number of the input feature $x_i \in R^{s \times s \times c}$ to 16, denoted as $x_{i,0} \in R^{s \times s \times 16}$. Secondly, four convolution kernels are cascaded and dense connections are used to extract multi-scale features, where the size and number of the four convolution kernels are 3×3 and 16, and the dilation rates (i.e., r in Fig. 3) are 4, 3, 2 and 1, respectively. In dense connections, for the lth layer, it receives $x_{i,0}$ and all the previously extracted features, denoted as $x_{i,0}, x_{i,1}, x_{i,2}, \cdots, x_{i,l-1}$, and uses them as input to calculate the output, as shown in Eq. (1):

$$x_{i,l} = BN\left(\delta\left(Conv\left(\left[x_{i,0}, x_{i,1}, x_{i,2}, \cdots, x_{i,l-1}\right]\right)\right)\right), l = 1, 2, 3, 4 \qquad (1)$$

where BN and δ represent the batch normalization and ReLU activation functions, respectively. $[\cdot]$ represents concatenation operation, $Conv$ represents 3×3 convolution operation. Then, the input feature $x_{i,0}$ and the output feature $x_{i,l}$ of each convolutional layer are concatenated along the channel dimension, and the output is unified to have the same channel number as x_i by a 1×1 convolution. In addition, in the residual branch, a 3×3 convolution kernel is used to convolve the input feature x_i.

Cross-Attention Module. The cross-attention module aims to combine the complementary information from two different-level features to better highlight the effective information and enhance the feature fusion of the two branches, and the specific structure is shown in Fig. 4. It mainly consists of the spectral attention block and the spatial attention block. The former aims to generate band weights to recalibrate the importance of each band and adjust the correlation of each band, while the latter aims to enhance spatial information of pixels that have the same class as the center pixel and suppress pixels from other classes. The specific implementation of the cross-attention module is described as follows.

The features M and N extracted by the residual and the multi-scale branches have the shape of $H \times W \times C$. The feature $F_{spe} \in R^{H \times W \times C}$ is obtained by adding and fusing the two features element-by-element and sent to the spectral attention.

In spectral attention, firstly, the input features are processed by the global average pooling and max pooling operations in two branches, respectively, to obtain $F_{spe,avg}$ and $F_{spe,max}$, whose shapes are $1 \times 1 \times C$. Then, they are passed through the multilayer perceptron (MLP) to obtain features $F'_{spe,avg}$ and $F'_{spe,max}$. Finally, the two obtained features are added and normalized using the Softmax function to obtain the band weight $W_{spe} \in R^{1 \times 1 \times C}$. The operations above are described as shown in Eqs. (2)–(4):

$$F'_{spe,avg} = \delta\left(W_1 * \delta\left(W_0 * F_{spe,avg}\right)\right) \qquad (2)$$

$$F'_{spe,max} = \delta\left(W_1 * \delta\left(W_0 * F_{spe,max}\right)\right) \qquad (3)$$

$$W_{spe} = \sigma\left(add\left[F'_{spe,avg}, F'_{spe,max}\right]\right) \qquad (4)$$

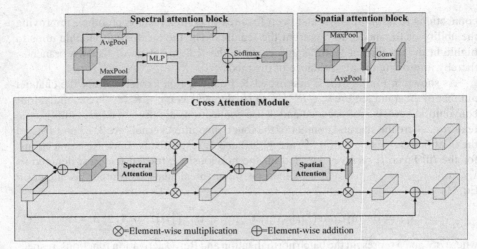

Fig. 4. Specific structure of the cross-attention module

where $*$ represents the convolution operation, $add[\cdot]$ represents element-wise addition, σ and δ represent the Softmax normalization function and ReLU activation function, respectively. W_0 and W_1 are the weight parameters of the two fully connected layers sharing weights.

Then, the obtained band weights W_{spe} are used to recalibrate the bands of features M and N to highlight the informative bands. Next, we additively fuse the calibrated features to obtain the feature $F_{spa} \in R^{H \times W \times C}$, which is fed into the spatial attention.

In spatial attention, firstly, the input features are subjected to global average pooling and max pooling operations in the two branches, respectively, to obtain $F_{spa,avg}$ and $F_{spa,max}$, whose shapes are both $H \times W \times 1$, and they are concatenated along the channel dimension to obtain $F_{avg,max} \in R^{H \times W \times 2}$. Then, it is fed into a two-dimensional convolution to obtain the spatial weight W_{spa}. The operations above are described as shown in Eq. (5):

$$W_{spa} = \sigma \left(W_0 * cat[F_{spa,avg}, F_{spa,max}] \right) \qquad (5)$$

where $*$ represents the convolution operation, $cat[\cdot]$ represents concatenation along the channel dimension, σ represents the Sigmoid activation function, and W_0 represents the weight parameter of a 3×3 convolution kernel.

Then, the resulting spatial weight W_{spa} is used to recalibrate the spatial information of the features to highlight the useful information. Next, we add the original features through the skip connections and the features passed through the attention blocks to avoid the loss of information of features with lower weights.

2.3 Multi-level Feature Aggregation Module

In deep neural networks, shallow features contain spatial details such as edges and textures, whereas they are lacking of semantic information. Conversely, deep features have stronger semantic information but lose spatial details. Therefore, fusing complementary information between features at different levels can further improve the performance of HSI classification. In this paper, by stacking MSFE modules, features at different levels can be extracted. To fully utilize these features, we construct the MFAM module, the specific structure is shown in Fig. 5.

Firstly, MFAM aggregates all levels of features through a top-down channel to enhance the feature representation, as shown in Eq. (6).

$$x_i = \delta\big(W_i * add\big[x_i, x_{i+1}\big]\big), i = 0, 1, 2 \tag{6}$$

where $*$ and δ represent convolution operation and ReLU activation function respectively, W_i represents the weight parameter of a 3×3 convolution kernel, and $add[\cdot]$ represents element-wise addition. Then, the enhanced features of each level are concatenated along the channel dimension, and the 3×3 convolution kernel is used to unify the channel number.

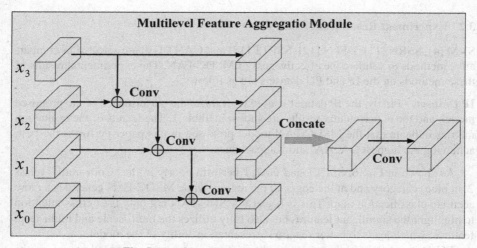

Fig. 5. Specific structure of the MFAM module

3 Experiment and Analysis

3.1 Dataset Description and Experiment Setup

Dataset Description.   To evaluate the performance of the proposed method, two classic datasets are selected for the experiments: Indian Pines (IP) and Pavia University (PU). IP dataset is a hyperspectral remote sensing image with a size of 145×145. It contains 200 available spectral bands and 16 classes of land cover with a total of 10,249 labeled samples. The PU dataset is a hyperspectral remote sensing image with a size of 610×340. It contains 103 available spectral bands and nine classes of land cover with a total of 42,776 labeled samples.

Evaluation Metrics. Overall accuracy (OA), average accuracy (AA), and Kappa coefficient are used as evaluation metrics. OA indicates the ratio of the number of correctly classified samples to the total number of samples. AA represents the average of the accuracy values with which the samples of each class are classified. Kappa coefficient can measure the consistency of classification results.

Experiment Setup. The Pytorch deep learning framework is used to train the network in the experiments, and epoch and batch_size are set to 100 and 32, respectively. The learning rate is set to 0.001, and Adam is selected as the optimization method for the experiment. Each group of experiments is performed five times independently, and the average values are taken as the experimental results, and the standard deviations about three metrics are also provided.

The patch sizes (Patch_Size) in IP and PU are set to 21 and 15, respectively, and the numbers of the principal components of PCA (PCA_Components) is set to 32. The percent of the training samples are set to 10% and 5%, respectively.

3.2 Experiment Results and Analysis

SVM [4], SSRN [11], DFFN [12], SSFTT [18] and GAHT [19] are selected as comparative methods to validate the effectiveness of MSDC-FAN. The experimental results of these methods on the IP and PU datasets are as follows.

IP Dataset. Firstly, the IP dataset is used to evaluate the performance of the proposed model, and the experimental results are shown in Table 1. The results of the evaluation metrics indicate that the MSDC-FAN model proposed in this paper performs the best, achieving the highest OA, AA, and Kappa values.

As shown in Fig. 6, SSFTT and GAHT perform poorly in the "Corn-notill" (class 2, in blue) category and at the edges of the region, while MSDC-FAN generates a more accurate classification map. This is because MSDC-FAN not only uses cross-attention to highlight the significant features but also fully utilizes the multi-scale and multi-level features, which leads to better feature representation ability of the model.

PU Dataset. We further evaluate the performance of the proposed model on the PU dataset, and the experimental results are shown in Table 2. The PU dataset has a large number of samples and relatively balanced sample sizes for each land cover category, so the classification results of each method are relatively ideal. The evaluation data shows that MSDC-FAN performs the best and has relatively uniform accuracy on each category. As shown in Fig. 7, several comparative methods perform poorly in the "Gravel" (class 3, in orange) category, while MSDC-FAN improves the accuracy of "Gravel" by 6.45% and 3.38% compared to SSFTT and GAHT, respectively, achieving 99.85%. This indicates that MSDC-FAN has a better ability to represent spectral-spatial features and can distinguish spectrally similar classes well.

3.3 Parametric Analysis

Impact of Patch_Size and PCA_Components on OA. We analyze the impact of Patch_size and PCA_Components on classification performance on IP and PU datasets.

Table 1 Classification results of IP dataset obtained by different methods

Class	SVM	SSRN	DFFN	SSFTT	GAHT	MSDC-FAN
1	38.10	98.54	93.17	99.02	98.05	96.59
2	77.84	93.21	86.40	95.22	96.17	99.47
3	70.41	86.96	92.34	96.17	93.82	99.12
4	45.79	98.97	99.25	99.53	96.43	99.15
5	90.80	98.80	95.36	98.67	97.43	99.17
6	96.19	99.82	99.21	99.79	99.12	99.06
7	76.92	87.20	84.80	99.20	99.20	100
8	96.29	99.95	99.91	100	99.49	100
9	27.78	78.89	75.56	81.11	93.33	92.22
10	71.78	94.40	92.46	95.59	98.29	98.19
11	83.67	95.82	94.34	96.99	97.90	99.10
12	68.54	86.85	90.60	90.64	94.61	97.79
13	94.05	100	88.76	100	96.54	99.78
14	93.77	99.81	97.70	99.68	99.75	100
15	56.03	88.59	93.78	91.30	94.87	99.31
16	85.71	95.71	95.71	97.62	78.81	98.10
OA	80.81 ± 0.01	95.04 ± 1.01	93.67 ± 3.52	96.82 ± 0.24	97.19 ± 0.31	**99.13 ± 0.09**
AA	73.35 ± 0.01	93.97 ± 1.64	92.46 ± 6.50	96.28 ± 0.70	95.86 ± 0.32	**98.57 ± 0.29**
Kappa	78.05 ± 0.01	94.33 ± 1.15	92.78 ± 4.04	96.38 ± 0.27	96.80 ± 0.35	**99.01 ± 0.11**

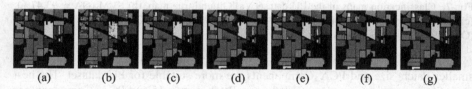

(a)	(b)	(c)	(d)	(e)	(f)	(g)

Fig. 6. Classification maps of the IP dataset. (a) Ground-true map. (b) SVM (OA = 80.81%). (c) SSRN (OA = 95.04%). (d) DFFN (OA = 93.67%). (e) SSFTT (OA = 96.82%). (f) GAHT (OA = 97.19%). (g) MSDC-FAN (OA = 99.13%)

Among them, the Patch_size increases in the range of [11,21], and PCA_Components are among [32,128] and [32,112] on IP and PU datasets, respectively. It can be seen from Fig. 8(a) that the impact of Patch_size and PCA_Components on the OA values of IP dataset fluctuates slightly, and a local maximum region can be obtained by selecting appropriate Patch_size and PCA_Components. As can be seen from Fig. 8(b),

Table 2 Classification results of PU dataset obtained by different methods

Class	SVM	SSRN	DFFN	SSFTT	GAHT	MSDC-FAN
1	93.37	97.61	98.43	99.40	99.58	99.86
2	98.04	99.58	99.96	99.89	99.95	99.96
3	72.53	86.13	97.28	93.40	96.47	99.85
4	94.40	95.29	92.17	98.83	94.59	97.36
5	98.36	99,98	99.77	100	99.66	100
6	87.02	94.31	99.94	99.65	99.98	100
7	83.23	97.58	99.92	99.70	100	99,95
8	90.82	92.64	99.21	98.92	99.37	99.43
9	99.89	99.31	86.49	99.62	90.71	96.98
OA	93.47 ± 0.02	97.03 ± 0.18	98.66 ± 0.63	99.30 ± 0.15	99.08 ± 0.07	**99.65 ± 0.04**
AA	90.85 ± 0.01	95.82 ± 0.36	97.02 ± 0.85	98.82 ± 0.24	97.81 ± 0.17	**99.27 ± 0.04**
Kappa	91.31 ± 0.01	96.06 ± 0.24	98.22 ± 0.83	99.07 ± 0.20	98.78 ± 0.10	**99.53 ± 0.05**

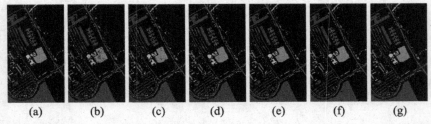

(a)   (b)   (c)   (d)   (e)   (f)   (g)

Fig. 7. Classification maps of the PU dataset. (a) Ground-true map. (b) SVM (OA = 93.47%). (c) SSRN (OA = 97.03%). (d) DFFN (OA = 98.66%). (e) SSFTT (OA = 99.30%). (f) GAHT (OA = 99.08%). (g) MSDC-FAN (OA = 99.65%)

smaller Patch_size and PCA_Components are more suitable for PU dataset. The best classification performance is obtained when Patch_size is 15 and PCA_Components is 32.

OA of Different Models Using Different Percentages of Training Samples. Figure 9 shows the OA values of different models that use different percentages of training samples. From Fig. 9, it can be seen that the OA values of all methods increase as the percentages of training samples increase. Among them, the OA values of SSFTT and

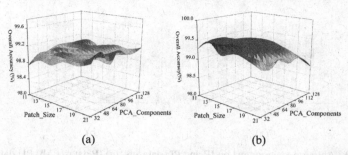

Fig. 8. Impact of Patch_Size and PCA_Components on OA. (a) IP dataset. (b) PU dataset

GAHT are close to our MSDC-FAN, demonstrating their good classification performance. On the whole, MSDC-FAN achieves the best results in almost all cases and it can obtain good performance even with extremely few training samples.

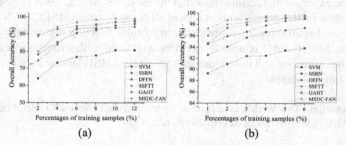

Fig. 9. OA of different models using different percentages of training samples. (a) IP dataset. (b) PU dataset

3.4 Ablation Experiments

We conduct ablation experiments about SSFE and MFAM modules on the IP and PU datasets. Three variants of MSDC-FAN are compared with MSDC-FAN, among which Base represents the network constructed only by MSFE. The experimental results are shown in Fig. 10. The Base network has the worst classification performance on IP and PU datasets. When SSFE or MFAM is added, there is a significant improvement in classification performance compared to the Base network, which verifies the effectiveness of SSFE and MFAM. The MSDC-FAN network has the best classification performance, which reflects that using two modules at the same time can not only fully extract spectral-spatial features, but also make full use of multi-level features, which further enhances the ability of the network to represent the features, thus contributing to the improvement of classification performance.

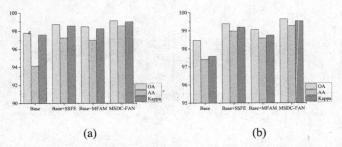

(a)   (b)

Fig. 10. Ablation experiments on IP and PU datasets. (a) IP dataset. (b) PU dataset

4   Conclusion

In this paper, we propose a Multi-scale Densely Connected and Feature Aggregation Network (MSDC-FAN) to improve the performance of hyperspectral image (HSI) classification. The experimental results show that the proposed MSDC-FAN performs better than several state-of-the-art methods in almost all cases, because MSDC-FAN has better ability of spectral-spatial feature representation by fully utilizing multi-scale and multi-level features. MSDC-FAN is able to perform well even with extremely few training samples. In the future, we will investigate how to improve HSI classification performance further with limited samples.

Acknowledgements. This work was supported by the National Natural Science Foundation of China (Nos. 62077038, 61672405, 62176196 and 62271374).

References

1. Zhang, X., Liu, L., Chen, X., Gao, Y., Jiang, M.: Automatically monitoring impervious surfaces using spectral generalization and time series Landsat imagery from 1985 to 2020 in the Yangtze River Delta. Remote Sens. **2021** (2021).
2. Avtar, R., Sahu, N., Aggarwal, A. K., et al.: Exploring renewable energy resources using remote sensing and GIS—A review. Res. **8**(3), 149(2019)
3. Weiss, M., Jacob, F., Duveiller, G.: Remote sensing for agricultural applications: a meta-review. Remote Sens. Environ. **236**, 111402 (2020)
4. Ye, Q., Huang, P., Zhang, Z., Zheng, Y., Fu, L., Yang, W.: Multiview learning with robust double-sided twin SVM. IEEE Trans. Cybern. **52**(12), 12745–12758 (2021)
5. Cariou, C., Chehdi, K.: A new k-nearest neighbor density-based clustering method and its application to hyperspectral images. In: 2016 IEEE International Geoscience and Remote Sensing Symposium (IGARSS), pp. 6161–6164(2016).
6. Zhang, Y., Cao, G., Li, X., Wang, B., Fu, P.: Active semi-supervised random forest for hyperspectral image classification. Remnote Sens. 11(24), 2974 (2019)
7. Cui, B., Cui, J., Lu, Y., Guo, N., Gong, M.: A sparse representation-based sample pseudo-labeling method for hyperspectral image classification. Remote Sensing, 12(4), 664 (2020)
8. Cao, X., Xu, Z., et al.: Spectral-spatial hyperspectral image classification via robust low-rank feature extraction and Markov random field. Remote Sens. **11**(13), 1565 (2019).

9. Liu, J., Yang, Z., et al.: Hyperspectral remote sensing images deep feature extraction based on mixed feature and convolutional neural networks. Remote Sens. **13**(13), 2599 (2021).
10. Li, Y., Zhang, H., Shen, Q.: Spectral–spatial classification of hyperspectral imagery with 3D convolutional neural network. Remote Sens. **9**(1), 67 (2017)
11. Zhong, Z., Li, J., Luo, Z., Chapman, M.: Spectral–spatial residual network for hyperspectral image classification: A 3-D deep learning framework. IEEE Trans. Geosci. Remote Sens. **56**(2), 847–858 (2017)
12. Song, W., Li, S., et al.: Hyperspectral image classification with deep feature fusion network. IEEE Trans. Geosci. Remote Sens. **56**(6), 3173–3184 (2018)
13. Yu, H., Zhang, H., et al.: Dual-channel convolution network with image-based global learning framework for hyperspectral image classification. IEEE Geosci. Remote Sens. Lett. **19**, 1–5 (2021)
14. Shi, H., Cao, G., Zhang, Y., Ge, Z., Liu, Y., Fu, P.: H2A2 Net: a hybrid convolution and hybrid resolution network with double attention for hyperspectral image classification. Remote Sens. **14**(17), 4235 (2022)
15. Yang, K., Sun, H., et al.: Cross-attention spectral–spatial network for hyperspectral image classification. IEEE Trans. Geosci. Remote Sens. **60**, 1–14 (2021)
16. Zhu, M., Jiao, L., et al.: Residual spectral–spatial attention network for hyperspectral image classification. IEEE Trans. Geosci. Remote Sens. **59**(1), 449–462 (2020)
17. Hong, D., et al.: SpectralFormer: rethinking hyperspectral image classification with transformers. IEEE Trans. Geosci. Remote Sens. **60**, 1–15 (2021)
18. Sun, L., Zhao, G., et al.: Spectral–spatial feature tokenization transformer for hyperspectral image classification. IEEE Trans. Geosci. Remote Sens. **60**, 1–14 (2022)
19. Mei, S., Song, C., et al.: Hyperspectral image classification using group-aware hierarchical transformer. IEEE Trans. Geosci. Remote Sens. **60**, 1–14 (2022)

A-ESRGAN: Training Real-World Blind Super-Resolution with Attention U-Net Discriminators

Zihao Wei[1,2(✉)], Yidong Huang[1,2], Yuang Chen[1,2], Chenhao Zheng[1,2], and Jingnan Gao[2]

[1] University of Michigan, Ann Arbor, MI 48109, USA
zihaowei@umich.edu
[2] Shanghai Jiao Tong University, Shanghai 200240, China
{owenhji,cyaa,neymar}@umich.edu; gjn0310@sjtu.edu.cn

Abstract. Generative adversarial networks (GANs) have recently made great progress in blind image super-resolution (SR) with their superiority in learning mappings between manifolds, which benefits the reconstruction of image's textural details. Recent works have largely focused on designing more realistic degradation models, or constructing a more powerful generator structure but neglected the ability of discriminators in improving visual performances. In this paper, we present A-ESRGAN, a GAN model for blind SR tasks featuring an attention U-Net based, multi-scale discriminator that can be seamlessly integrated with other generators. To our knowledge, this is the first work to introduce attention U-Net structure as the discriminator of GAN to solve blind SR problems. And the paper also gives an interpretation of the mechanism behind multi-scale attention U-Net that brings performance breakthrough to the model. Experimental results demonstrate the superiority of our A-ESRGAN over state-of-the-art level performance in terms of quantitative metrics and visual quality. The code can be find in https://github.com/stroking-fishes-ml-corp/A-ESRGAN.

Keywords: Blind Super Resolution · Generative adversarial networks · attention mechanism · Multi-scale · U-Net

1 Introduction and Motivation

Image super-resolution (SR) is a low-level computer vision problem aiming to reconstruct a high-resolution (HR) image from a distorted low-resolution (LR) image. Blind super-resolution, specifically, refers to the idea of restoring LR images suffering from unknown and complex degradation, as opposed to the traditional assumption of ideal bicubic degradation.

By the competition of generator and discriminator, the networks are encouraged to favor solutions that look more like natural images. The state-of-the-art methods using generative adversarial network includes ESRGAN, RealSR, Real-ESRGAN and BSRGAN [6, 20, 22, 25].

© The Author(s), under exclusive license to Springer Nature Singapore Pte Ltd. 2024
F. Liu et al. (Eds.): PRICAI 2023, LNAI 14327, pp. 16–27, 2024.
https://doi.org/10.1007/978-981-99-7025-4_2

Recent works in super-resolution GANs have largely focused on simulating a more complex and realistic degradation process [20] or building a better generator [22], with little work trying to improve the performance of the discriminator. However, the importance of a discriminator can not be ignored since it provides the generator with the direction to generate better images, similar to a loss function. In this work, we construct a new discriminator network structure: **Multi-scale Attention U-Net Discriminator** and incorporate it with the existing RRDB based generator [22] to form our GAN model A-ESRGAN. Our model shows superiority over the state-of-the-art real-ESRGAN model in sharpness and details (see 7b). According to our ablation study, this result owes to the combination of attention mechanism and U-Net structure in our proposed discriminator. The U-Net structure in discriminator can offer per-pixel feedback to the generator [17], which can help the generator to generate more detailed features, such as texture or brushstroke. Meanwhile, the attention layer can not only distinguish the outline of the subject area to maintain the global coherence but strengthen the lines and edges of the image to avoid the blurring effect (this is demonstrated in the attention map analysis section in our paper). Therefore, the combination of U-Net and Attention is very promising. Besides, to increase the perception field of our discriminator, We use two attention U-Net discriminators that have an identical network structure but operate at different image scales as our final discriminator, which is called multi-scale discriminator. Extensive experiments show that our model outperforms most existing GAN models both in quantitative NIQE performance metric and qualitative image perceptual feelings.

In summary, the contributions of our work are:

1. We propose a new multi-scale attention U-Net discriminator network. To the best of our knowledge, it is the first work to adopt attention U-Net structure as a discriminator in the field of generative adversarial networks. This modular discriminator structure can be easily ported to future work.
2. We incorporate our designed discriminator with the existing RRDB based generator to form our generative adversarial network model A-ESRGAN. Experiments show that our model outperforms most state-of-the-art models in image super-resolution tasks.
3. Through detailed analysis and visualization about different layers of our network, we provide convincing reasons why a multi-scale attention U-Net discriminator works better than existing ones in image super-resolution tasks.

2   Related Work

2.1   GANs-Based Blind SR Methods

GANs-based SR methods have better perceptual results than CNN-based SR methods, because GANs are more competitive in learning mapping between manifolds, which benefits in reconstructing local textures [10]. Recent state of the art methods have raised a perceptual-driven perspective to improve GANs by better modeling the perceptual loss between images [9, 22]. The ESRGAN [22], as a representative work, proposed a practical perceptual loss function as well as a residual-in-residual block(RRDB) generator network, and produces synthesized HR images with convincing visual quality. Another perspective is to solve the intrinsic problem of blind SR that the LR images used for training are synthesized from HR images in the dataset. Most existing methods are based on bicubic downsampling [3, 8, 16] and traditional degradations [24, 26], while real-world degradations are far more complicated. To produce more photo-realistic results, the real-ESRGAN [20] proposed a practical high-order degradation model and achieved visually impressive results as well as state-of-the-art NIQE [12] performance.

2.2   Discriminator Models

Some remarkable attempts have been made to improve the discriminator model [15, 17, 19]. To synthesize photo-realistic HR images, two major challenges are presented: the discriminator needs a large receptive field to differentiate the synthesized image and the ground truth(GT), requiring either deep network or large convolution kernel [19]. Besides, it's difficult for one discriminator to give precise feedback on both global and local features, leading to possible incoherence in the synthesized image such as twisted textures on a building wall [20]. To resolve these issues, Wang et al. [19] proposed a novel multiple discriminator architecture. By using several discriminators taking different scale down-sampled synthesized images as input, the new discriminator can learn from different receptive fields. Another pioneer work [17] introduces U-Net based discriminator architecture into GANs-based blind SR tasks. The U-Net discriminator model can provide per-pixel feedback to the generator while maintaining the global coherence of synthesized images.

3   Method

The overall architecture of A-ESRGAN is shown in Fig. 1, which contains a Generator composed of residual-in-residual dense blocks (RRDBs) [22] and a multi-scale attention U-net discriminator.

Attention U-Net Discriminator. Inspired by [14, 17], we propose the attention U-Net discriminator structure, which is shown in Fig. 2. It is composed of a down-sampling encoding module, an up-sampling decoding module and several attention blocks. The structure of the attention block in Fig. 3 is modified from attention gate, which is used by [14] in 3D medical graphs. By utilizing attention blocks, we want the generator to put more emphasis on important regions during super resolution, which also conforms to how people evaluate a graph as they would focus more on the region where their attention locates. A detailed analysis of how the attention mechanism works is carried out during the experiment. In order to stabilize the training process, we also apply spectral normalization regularization [13] to the attention U-net.

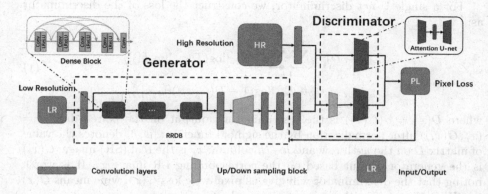

Fig. 1. The overall architecture of the A-ESRGAN. The generator of A-ESRGAN is using RRDB and the discriminator of A-ESRGAN is a multi-scale attention U-net structure.

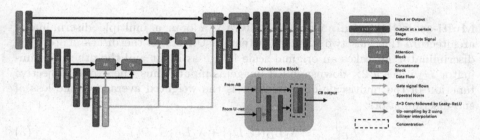

Fig. 2. The architecture of a singe attention U-Net Discriminator. F, W, H represents output channel number of the first convolution layer, height of the image and width of the image respectively.

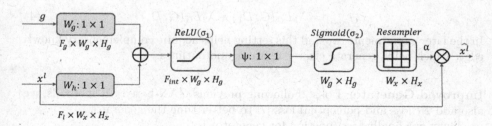

Fig. 3. The architecture of the attention block (AB). Here x^l is the input features from the U-Net and g is the gating signal. F_{int} is a super parameter denoting the output channels of the one by one convolution in the AB. In the AB, x^l is scaled by attention coefficient α.

For a single U-net discriminator, we construct the loss of the discriminator as:

$$L_D(G, D) = \sum_{w=1}^{W} \sum_{h=1}^{H} (-E_{x_r}[\log(D(x_r)[w, h])]) \\ - E_{x_i}[\log(1 - D(G(x_i))[w, h])]) \tag{1}$$

where $D(x) = \sigma(C(x))$ is the discriminator's output on the paired data $x = (x_r, G(x_i))$ after normalization by the sigmoid function; $[w, h]$ denotes the value of matrix D on the w-th row and $h - th$ column; x_r is the real (SR) image; $G(x_i)$ is the generator output based on the corresponding LR image x_i. It is worth noting that the discriminator will give us pixel-wise loss $C(x)$, whic means $C(x)$ is a $W \times H$ matrix with the same size as the $G(x_i)$.

Similarly we can derive the adversarial Generator Loss as:

$$L_G(G, D) = \sum_{w=1}^{W} \sum_{h=1}^{H} (-E_{x_i}[\log(D(G(x_i))[w, h])]) \tag{2}$$

Multi-scale Discriminator. A-ESRGAN adopts a multiple discriminator architecture that has two identical attention U-Nets as the discriminator.One discriminator D_1 takes an original scale image as input and the other discriminator D_2 takes a 2× downsampled image as input. Thus, the overall objective function of the multiscale discriminator is the weighted average of the loss of sub-discriminators:

$$L_{D_{multi}} = \lambda_1 L_D(G, D_1) + \lambda_2 L_D(G, D_2) \tag{3}$$

where λ_1 and λ_2 are the weight coefficients which denote how much each discriminator contributes to the overall loss.

Likely the overall generator loss is

$$L_{G_{multi}} = \lambda_1 L_G(G, D_1) + \lambda_2 L_G(G, D_2) \tag{4}$$

In the later experiments, we find this setting helps acquire complementary knowledge, which helps generate clearer textures and outlines.

Improved Generator Loss. Following previous GAN-based SR methods, we also add L_1 loss and perceptual loss [7] to better tune the generator.

Thus, our finally loss function for generator is:

$$L_{G_{Total}} = L_{precep} + \eta L_1 + \lambda L_{G_{multi}} \tag{5}$$

where λ, η are the weight coefficients for each loss.

Overall Objective. With the above discussions, our full objective is to solve the following task:

$$(D_1, D_2), \quad G = \arg\min_{D_1, D_2} L_{D_{multi}}, \quad \arg\min_{G} L_{G_{Total}} \tag{6}$$

where D_1, D_2 and G are trained simultaneously.

4 Experiments

4.1 Implementation Details

To compare the functionality of multi-scale mechanism, we build two A-ESRGAN models: A-ESRGAN-single and A-ESRGAN-multi. The difference is that A-ESRGAN-single features one single attention U-Net discriminator, while A-ESRGAN-multi features multi-scale network, i.e. two identical attention U-Net discriminator operating at different image scale.

We trained with our A-ESRGAN on DIV2K [1] dataset. For better comparison with Real-ESRGAN, we follow the setting of generating degradation images of Real-ESRGAN [20] and load the pre-trained Real-ESRNET to the generator of both networks. The training HR patch size is 256. We train our models with one NVIDIA A100 and three NVIDIA A40 with a total batch size of 48 by using Adam optimizer.

The A-ESRGAN-Single is trained with a single attention U-Net discriminator for $400K$ iterations under 10^{-4} rate. The A-ESRGAN-Multi is trained for $200K$ iterations under 10^{-4} learning rate. For both A-ESRGAN-Single and A-ESRGAN-Multi, the weight for L1loss, perceptual loss and GAN loss are $\{1, 1, 0.1\}$. In A-ESRGAN-Multi, the weight for GAN loss of D_1 and D_2 is $\{1, 1\}$.

4.2 Testsets and Experiment Settings

In prior works, blind image super-resolution tasks are usually tested on synthesized LR images from HR images. However, the human simulated degraded images can hardly reflect the low-resolution image coming from degradation in real world, which usually features complicate combinations of different degradation processes. Besides, there is no real dataset which provides real-world LR images. Therefore, we choose to use real-world images directly as our test dataset and see their performance.

In this paper, we use the real-world images in the seven standard benchmark datasets, Set5 [2], Set14 [23], BSD100 [11], Sun-Hays80 [18], Urban100 [5], OST300 [21] and General100 [4]. These seven datasets contain images from manifold groups, such as portraits, scenery and buildings. We argue that a good general super resolution model should achieve good performance on the overall seven datasets.

4.3 Comparing with the State-of-the-Arts

We compare the proposed A-ESRGAN-Single and ESRGAN-Multi with several state-of-the-art(SOTA) generative based methods, i.e. ESRGAN [22], RealSR [6], BSRGAN [25], Real-ESRGAN [20] . Note that the architecture of the generators of ESRGAN, RealSR, BSRGAN and Real-ESRGAN are the same as ours, which can help verify the effectiveness of our designed discriminator.

Table 1. The NIQE results of different methods on Set5, Set14, BSD100, Sun Hays80, Urban 100, OST300 and General100 (The lower, the better). The best and second best results are high lighted in red and blue, respectively.

NIQE	Bicubic	ESRGAN	BSRGAN	RealESRGAN	RealSR	A-ESRGAN-Single(Ours)	A-ESRGAN-Multi(Ours)
Set5	7.8524	5.6712	4.5806	4.8629	3.5064	3.9125	3.8480
Set14	7.5593	5.0363	4.4096	4.4978	3.5413	3.4983	3.5168
BSD100	7.3413	3.1544	3.8172	3.9826	3.6916	3.2948	3.2474
Sun-Hays80	7.6496	3.6639	3.5609	2.9540	3.3109	2.6664	2.5908
Urban100	7.1089	3.1074	4.1996	4.0950	3.9290	3.4728	3.3993
OST300	7.3801	3.4689	3.2931	2.7919	3.0364	2.6778	2.5751
General100	8.0730	4.7717	5.0998	5.7158	4.5357	4.5585	4.3992

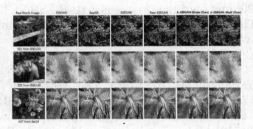

Fig. 4. Visual comparison of our method with other ×4 super resolution methods. Zoom in for the best view.

Since there is no ground-truth for the real-world images of the dataset, so we adopt the no-reference image quality assessment metrics NIQE [12] for quantitative evaluation. NIQE indicates the perceptual quality of the image. A lower NIQE value indicates better perceptual quality. As can be seen from the Table 1, our method outperforms most of the SOTA methods in NIQE metrics. Meanwhile, we can find it is more robust and has stronger generalization ability, since it achieves high score in all kinds of datasets. From visual comparison (some examples are shown in Fig. 4), we observe our methods can recover sharper edges and restore better texture details.

4.4 Attention Block Analysis

To verify the effectiveness of attention gate in our discriminator, We visualize the attention weights in the attention layer from test images during our training process. An example is shown in Fig. 5. Initially, the attention weights are uniformly distributed in all locations of the images. As the training process goes on,

Fig. 5. The figure shows the weight in the third attention layer across the training process from iteration 5000 to 285000 at an interval of 20000. The example image is picked from Urban100 [5]. It clearly shows at first the attention is uniformly distributed. Then the attention is gradually updated and begins to focus on the edges. Zoom in for the best view.

we can observe that the attention weight is gradually updated and begin to focus on "particular regions", which are the edges where color changes abruptly. Meanwhile, by visualizing attention map at different layers, we argue that different attention layers recognize the images at different granularity. The lower attention layers that are coarse-grained and give rough edges of the patches while the upper attention layers are fine-grained and focus on details such as lines and dots.

4.5   Multi-scale Discriminator Analysis

We study the output image generated by the two attention discriminators propose that the two discriminators play different roles in identifying the properties of the images. The normal discriminator, which is also used in the single version, emphasizes more on lines. In contrast, the downsampled inputs with blurred edges force the other discriminator to focus more on larger patches. As shown in Fig. 6, the output image of the normal discriminator judges the edges while the dowsampled discriminator judges thicker blocks, such as textures on the branches of the tree.

Input   Normal Discriminator   Down-sampled Discriminator

Fig. 6. The figure shows Unet output of the two discriminators. The example image is picked from BSD100 [11]. The example shows the normal discriminator(first) would focus on lines in the image while the discriminator that parse the downsampled input will focus on patches. The brighter a pixel is, the more likely it is a real picture.

4.6   Ablation Study

Effectiveness of Attention U-Net Discriminator. The key factor of A-ESRGAN surpassing the existing models is our designed attention U-Net discriminator. In the ablation study, we compare the results of Real-ESRGAN model with A-ESRGAN-Single model. The only difference between these two networks is that Real-ESRGAN uses a plain U-Net as discriminator, while A-ESRGAN applies an attention U-Net discriminator.

As shown in Table 1, A-ESRGAN-Single achieves better NIQE in all tested datasets. By taking a close look at the result, we could find since plain U-Net uniformly gives weight to each pixel, it can't distinguish between the subject area and background of images. However, as shown in Sect. 4.4, the attention U-Net is able to put more efforts on the edges than on ordinary pixels. We believe this will bring at least two benefits. First, the result image will give sharper and clearer details as shown in 7a. Second, when up-sampling process is based on the main edges of the image, there will be less probability of distortion (like shown in 7b).

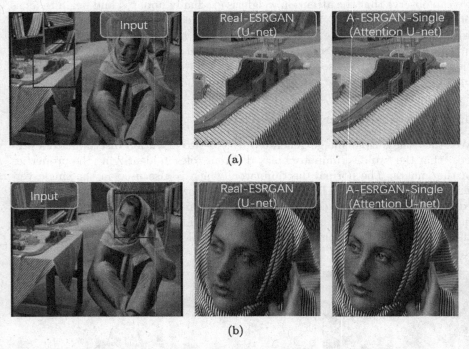

Fig. 7. Ablation on the discriminator design.

Effectiveness of Multi-scale Discriminator. The multi-scale discriminator enables our model to focus not only on the edges but also on more detailed parts such as textures. In the ablation study, we compare the results of the A-ESRGAN-single and the A-ESRGAN-multi. The latter has the same generator as the former·while it possesses two discriminators, which are a normal one and a downsampled one.

As shown in Table 1, the A-ESRGAN-multi surpasses the performance of A-ESRGAN-single in all dataset except Set14. By analyzing the output images of the two models, we conclude that the A-ESRGAN-multi does much better in showing the texture of items than A-ESRGAN-single. Like the images shown in Fig. 8, the A-ESRGAN-single poorly performs on rebuilding the texture of the branches and the sea creature. In contrast, because the downsampled discriminator focuses on patches, it can rebuild the texture and give shaper edge details.

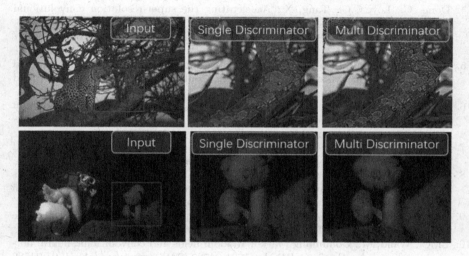

Fig. 8. Ablation on the multi-scale design.

5   Conclusions

In this paper, a multi-scale attention U-Net discriminator is proposed to train a deep blind super-resolution model. Based on the new discriminator, we trained a deep blind super-resolution model and compared it with other SOTA generative methods by directly upscaling real images in seven benchmark datasets. Our model outperforms them in both NIQE metrics and visual performance. By systematically analyzing how the attention coefficient changes across time and space during the training process, we give a convincing interpretation of how the attention layer and multi-scale mechanism contribute to the progress in SR problems. We fully believe that other super-resolution models can benefit from our work.

References

1. Agustsson, E., Timofte, R.: NTIRE 2017 challenge on single image super-resolution: dataset and study. In: 2017 IEEE Conference on Computer Vision and Pattern Recognition Workshops (CVPRW), pp. 1122–1131 (2017). https://doi.org/10.1109/CVPRW.2017.150
2. Bevilacqua, M., Roumy, A., Guillemot, C., Alberi-Morel, M.-L.: Low-complexity single-image super-resolution based on nonnegative neighbor embedding. In: Proceedings of the British Machine Vision Conference, pp. 1–10. BMVA Press (2012). https://doi.org/10.5244/C.26.135
3. Dong, C., Loy, C.C., He, K., Tang, X.: Image super-resolution using deep convolutional networks. CoRR abs/1501.00092 (2015). arxiv.org/abs/1501.00092
4. Dong, C., Loy, C.C., Tang, X.: Accelerating the super-resolution convolutional neural network. In: Leibe, B., Matas, J., Sebe, N., Welling, M. (eds.) ECCV 2016. LNCS, vol. 9906, pp. 391–407. Springer, Cham (2016). https://doi.org/10.1007/978-3-319-46475-6_25
5. Huang, J.B., Singh, A., Ahuja, N.: Single image super-resolution from transformed self-exemplars. In: Proceedings of the IEEE Conference on Computer Vision and Pattern Recognition, pp. 5197–5206 (2015)
6. Ji, X., Cao, Y., Tai, Y., Wang, C., Li, J., Huang, F.: Real-world super-resolution via Kernel estimation and noise injection. In: 2020 IEEE/CVF Conference on Computer Vision and Pattern Recognition Workshops (CVPRW) (2020)
7. Johnson, J., Alahi, A., Fei-Fei, L.: Perceptual losses for real-time style transfer and super-resolution. CoRR abs/1603.08155 (2016). arxiv.org/abs/1603.08155
8. Lai, W.S., Huang, J.B., Ahuja, N., Yang, M.H.: Deep Laplacian pyramid networks for fast and accurate super-resolution. In: Proceedings of the IEEE Conference on Computer Vision and Pattern Recognition, pp. 624–632 (2017)
9. Ledig, C., et al.: Photo-realistic single image super-resolution using a generative adversarial network. CoRR abs/1609.04802 (2016). arxiv.org/abs/1609.04802
10. Li, C., Wand, M.: Combining Markov random fields and convolutional neural networks for image synthesis. CoRR abs/1601.04589 (2016). arxiv.org/abs/1601.04589
11. Martin, D., Fowlkes, C., Tal, D., Malik, J.: A database of human segmented natural images and its application to evaluating segmentation algorithms and measuring ecological statistics. In: Proceedings Eighth IEEE International Conference on Computer Vision, ICCV 2001, vol. 2, pp. 416–423. IEEE (2001)
12. Mittal, A., Fellow, I.E.E.E., Soundararajan, R., Bovik, A.C.: Making a "completely blind" image quality analyzer. IEEE Sig. Process. Lett. **20**(3), 209–212 (2013)
13. Miyato, T., Kataoka, T., Koyama, M., Yoshida, Y.: Spectral normalization for generative adversarial networks. In: International Conference on Learning Representations (2018). www.openreview.net/forum?id=B1QRgziT-
14. Oktay, O., et al.: Attention U-Net: learning where to look for the pancreas (2018)
15. Park, S.-J., Son, H., Cho, S., Hong, K.-S., Lee, S.: SRFeat: single image super-resolution with feature discrimination. In: Ferrari, V., Hebert, M., Sminchisescu, C., Weiss, Y. (eds.) ECCV 2018. LNCS, vol. 11220, pp. 455–471. Springer, Cham (2018). https://doi.org/10.1007/978-3-030-01270-0_27
16. Sajjadi, M.S., Scholkopf, B., Hirsch, M.: EnhanceNet: single image super-resolution through automated texture synthesis. In: Proceedings of the IEEE International Conference on Computer Vision, pp. 4491–4500 (2017)
17. Schonfeld, E., Schiele, B., Khoreva, A.: A U-Net based discriminator for generative adversarial networks. In: Proceedings of the IEEE/CVF Conference on Computer Vision and Pattern Recognition (CVPR) (2020)

18. Sun, L., Hays, J.: Super-resolution from internet-scale scene matching. In: 2012 IEEE International Conference on Computational Photography (ICCP), pp. 1–12. IEEE (2012)

19. Wang, T.C., Liu, M.Y., Zhu, J.Y., Tao, A., Kautz, J., Catanzaro, B.: High-resolution image synthesis and semantic manipulation with conditional GANs. In: Proceedings of the IEEE Conference on Computer Vision and Pattern Recognition (CVPR) (2018)

20. Wang, X., Xie, L., Dong, C., Shan, Y.: Real-ESRGAN: training real-world blind super-resolution with pure synthetic data. In: 2021 IEEE/CVF International Conference on Computer Vision Workshops (ICCVW), pp. 1905–1914 (2021). https://doi.org/10.1109/ICCVW54120.2021.00217

21. Wang, X., Yu, K., Dong, C., Loy, C.C.: Recovering realistic texture in image super-resolution by deep spatial feature transform. In: IEEE Conference on Computer Vision and Pattern Recognition (CVPR) (2018)

22. Wang, X., et al.: ESRGAN: enhanced super-resolution generative adversarial networks. In: Leal-Taixé, L., Roth, S. (eds.) ECCV 2018. LNCS, vol. 11133, pp. 63–79. Springer, Cham (2019). https://doi.org/10.1007/978-3-030-11021-5_5

23. Yang, J., Wright, J., Huang, T.S., Ma, Y.: Image super-resolution via sparse representation. IEEE Trans. Image Process. **19**(11), 2861–2873 (2010)

24. Zhang, K., Li, Y., Zuo, W., Zhang, L., Van Gool, L., Timofte, R.: Plug-and-play image restoration with deep denoiser prior. IEEE Trans. Pattern Anal. Mach. Intell. **PP**, 1 (2021)

25. Zhang, K., Liang, J., Van Gool, L., Timofte, R.: Designing a practical degradation model for deep blind image super-resolution. In: Proceedings of the IEEE/CVF International Conference on Computer Vision (ICCV), pp. 4791–4800 (2021)

26. Zhang, Y., Li, K., Li, K., Wang, L., Zhong, B., Fu, Y.: Image super-resolution using very deep residual channel attention networks. In: Ferrari, V., Hebert, M., Sminchisescu, C., Weiss, Y. (eds.) ECCV 2018. LNCS, vol. 11211, pp. 294–310. Springer, Cham (2018). https://doi.org/10.1007/978-3-030-01234-2_18

AI-Based Intelligent-Annotation Algorithm for Medical Segmentation from Ultrasound Data

Tao Peng[1]($\boxtimes$), Yaogong Zhang[2], Yan Dong[3], Yiwen Ruan[1], Rui Jin[1], Zhaorui Liu[1], Hongzhuang Wu[1], Yuling Shen[1], and Lei Zhang[2]($\boxtimes$)

[1] School of Future Science and Engineering, Soochow University, Suzhou, China
tpeng@suda.edu.cn
[2] Medical Physics Graduate Program and Data Science Research Center,
Duke Kunshan University, Kunshan, Jiangsu, China
lei.zhang@dukekunshan.edu.cn
[3] Department of Ultrasonography, The First Affiliated Hospital of Soochow University,
Suzhou, China

Abstract. The management of prostate cancer, a prevalent source of mortality in men, calls for meticulous delineation of the prostate in transrectal ultrasound (TRUS) images for effective treatment planning. This paper introduces a hybrid artificial intelligence approach for prostate delineation, leveraging prior information from experts, a machine learning model, and a quantum-inspired evolutionary network to augment the accuracy of prostate segmentation. The approach incorporates three novel elements: 1) limited prior information from expert and adaptive polygon tracking (APT) module for initial segmentation; 2) a novel historical storage-based quantum-inspired evolutionary network (HQIE) mechanism to search for the optimal neural network and enhancing solution diversity and capacity to address unimodal and multimodal challenges, and 3) a unique mathematical formulation denoted by parameters of the neural network is used to achieve smooth prostate periphery. The method was evaluated across various noise conditions and against several state-of-the-art methods using a multi-center dataset. In addition, an ablation study was performed to evaluate the efficacy of each component. The results demonstrated the superior performance of the hybrid AI method (Dice index: 96.4 ± 2.4%) against state-of-the-art deep learning methods (e.g., UTNet, Dice index: 90.1 ± 5.7%). The hybrid method also showed higher robustness to image noise than traditional methods. This study suggests new insights and technical approaches in the field of prostate segmentation using hybrid artificial intelligence methods.

Keywords: segmentation · hybrid artificial intelligence (AI) method · deep learning · ultrasound · medical image

1 Introduction

Prostate cancer, a significant health concern for men, is a prominent source of death related to cancer [1]. Optimal management of this disease relies heavily on accurately extracting prostate contours from medical images, including transrectal ultrasound

(TRUS) images. The segmentation process is crucial for both the cancer diagnosis process of insertion of biopsy needles [2] and the cancer treatment process of image-guided radiotherapy. However, accurate and robust delineation of the prostate in ultrasound images is a challenging task. The difficulties primarily stem from the intrinsic nature of ultrasound images, where the boundaries of organ-of-interest (e.g., prostate) and surrounding tissues may not be apparent or affected by image artifacts. In addition, significant differences in patient anatomy have made automated prostate contouring more difficult. Therefore, it calls for more accurate and robust ultrasound prostate segmentation methods. The performance of state-of-the-art ultrasound image automatic prostate segmentation techniques is around 0.9 in the Dice index (DI) [3, 4]. To enhance the model's performance, this study presents a novel hybrid artificial intelligence strategy for prostate segmentation in TRUS images.

1.1 Contributions

Our work incorporates several innovative components to achieve the aim, summarized as follows:

- A model was designed to combine the inherent advantages of the principal curve in finding the initial boundary and the AI model's advantage in minimizing model deviation.
- Different from current Closed Polygon Tracking (CPT) model [5], an Adaptive Polygon Tracking (APT) model was introduced to automatically determine the principal curve's segment number, and data radius. Additionally, we integrated a normalization scheme to deal with the medical data more effectively.
- In pursuit of an optimal neural network, a Historical Storage-based Quantum-inspired Evolutionary Network (HQIE) was developed. This system integrates a historical storage-based quantum evolution mechanism and a Cuckoo Search (CS) module [6], coupled with the fusion of a new mutation technique. This not only preserves the solution diversity within the population but also enhances the ability to address both unimodal and multimodal problems. The HQIE model was adopted to hunt for the initialization of the optimal neural network.
- An interpretable mathematical model which is embodied by the parameters of the neural network was developed. This function is used to enhance the smoothness of initial segmentation of prostate.

1.2 Related Work

In the realm of clinical applications, the demand for completely automated segmentation from TRUS prostate images is on the rise. A deep learning architecture for prostate TRUS image segmentation was formulated by Vesal et al. [7], tackling transfer learning problems by integrating a distillation loss function. The robustness of the model could be augmented further through data augmentation tactics. Meanwhile, Orlando *et al.* [3] modified the U-Net segmentation model, employing transpose convolution to replace conventional convolution and improve model prediction. Yet, the method may suffer from the lack of multi-expert calibration and varied radiologist evaluations. He et al. [8] established a cooperative learning framework that capitalized on image-based and voxel-metric segmentation sub-networks to refine segmentation and feature space. Similarly, Zavala-Romero et al. [9] sought to advance the U-net model by integrating batch normalization and a 20% dropout rate post-convolution, though the model's performance may vary depending on the dataset's diversity. On the other hand, semi-automatic models utilize radiologist expertise during the segmentation processes. Xu et al. [10] developed a shadow-consistent learning model that harnessed both fully annotated and unlabeled data to augment model training. A worthy direction for future studies could be the effect of annotated and unlabeled data ratios on the model's performance. Zhou et al. [11] proposed a UNet + + for medical image segmentation, while combing the multiscale features to assist the prediction. To boost the useful features while decreasing the attention to the useless features, Gao et al. [12] developed the Transformer-based UTNet method for medical image segmentation. Considering the influence of improving the segmentation accuracy of region of interest (ROI) during the brachytherapy, Peng et al. [13] designed a hybrid method, named H-SegMed, which integrated the principal curve and neural network for achieving the high-accuracy ROI contour. Zeng et al. [14] used a statistical shape method to gather magnetic resonance imaging priors, though the model could benefit from the evaluation of segmentation discrepancy based on surrounding tissue landmarks. A similar approach by Godley et al. [15] made use of contours from previous days for accurate prostate segmentation, although the amount of available data may restrict the model. Finally, Karimi et al. [16] used prior shape details to handle uncertainties during training, but the model's generalizability could be challenging due to the sourcing of images from single ultrasound system.

2 Methodology

2.1 Workflow

Our approach of high-performance prostate segmentation is composed of three fundamental phases, which summarize with three stages:

(1) *Principal curve-based stage*: In the initial stage, the APT model is employed to yield a prostate boundary constituted of segments, with sequence-ordered vertices. This is assisted by a limited number of prior points to assist accurate ROI identification (Sect. 3.2).
(2) *Evolution-based stage*: The subsequent stage involves the utilization of the HQIE model to procure the ideal initial model of the adaptive learning-rate backpropagation neural network (ABNN), helping avoid local minima during the training process (Sect. 3.3).
(3) *Mapping stage*: In the final stage, the aim is to discover a suitable mapping function (articulated through parameters of the ABNN model) that reflects a smooth boundary (Sect. 3.4). The comprehensive structure of our model is demonstrated in Fig. 1.

2.2 Adaptive Polygon Tracking (APT) Model

The pioneering concept of the principal curve was first introduced by Hastie et al. [17], succeeded by the development of the PT model by Kégl et al. [18, 19] in pursuit of

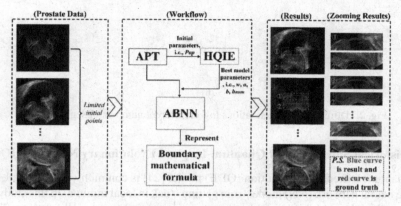

Fig. 1. Workflow of our hybrid model

the K-segment principal curve. To enhance the efficiency of the PT model in describing closed datasets, Peng et al. designed the Closed Polygon Tracking (CPT) model [20], later refining it with the optimized closed polygon tracking (OCPT) model [21], which improved the resilience of the CPT model. We developed an adaptive polygon tracking (APT) model in this study. This model incorporates an innovative normalization method and a smart data radius judgment scheme with the CPT model, thereby optimizing the trade-off between precision and efficiency on a global scale.

Innovation and Enhancement

Normalization: In contrast to Jain *et al.* employing a min-max normalization approach [22], this study incorporates a different normalization technique [23]. This method starts with the calculation of the average μ (depicted in Eq. (1)) and variance σ (displayed in Eq. (2)) of the p_i coordinates. Following this, an update is performed on the x- and y-axis coordinates of p_i as outlined in Eq. (3).

$$\mu_x = \frac{1}{n}\sum_{i=1}^{n} x_i \, \mu_y = \frac{1}{n}\sum_{i=1}^{n} y_i \tag{1}$$

$$\sigma_x = \sqrt{\frac{1}{n}\sum_{i=1}^{n}\left[(x_i - \mu_x)^2\right]} \, \sigma_y = \sqrt{\frac{1}{n}\sum_{i=1}^{n}\left[(y_i - \mu_y)^2\right]} \tag{2}$$

$$x_i = \frac{x_i - \mu_x}{\sigma_x} \, y_i = \frac{y_i - \mu_y}{\sigma_y} \tag{3}$$

Data radius r's automatic determination: r affects the number of segments $N_s = \beta * n^{\frac{1}{3}} * r * (\Delta_n(f_{N_s,n})^{-\frac{1}{2}})$. Different selections of the N_s determine different shapes of the f, shown in Fig. 2. An optimal outcome is showcased in Fig. 2(a). As per Fig. 2(b), a small N_s value inadequately represents the true character of the function f, necessitating a larger N_s. Conversely, as illustrated in Fig. 2(c), the use of an excessively large N_s results in an unnecessary addition of vertices, leading to longer computation time and compromised accuracy.

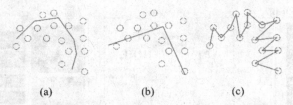

(a)   (b)   (c)

Fig. 2. Different characterizations to f at different numbers of segments *is*.

2.3 Historical Storage-Based Quantum-Inspired Evolutionary Network (HQIE)

The Quantum Differential Evolution (QDE) model [24] is commonly employed to prevent the neural network (NN) model from getting stuck in local minima. In this study, we substantially enhanced this model by incorporating several novel modifications. These include 1) a quantum evolution mechanism underpinned by historical data storage, 2) a novel mutation method, and 3) the implementation of the cuckoo search (CS) model.

Historical Storage-Based Quantum Evolution Mechanism. This mechanism seeks to preserve the optimal mutation Factor F and Crossover Rate CR from the preceding cycle, which are subsequently repurposed as initial values for the next cycle. The optimization of both F and CR values is achieved by utilizing the succeeding formulas,

$$F = (1 - val) \times F + rand(0, 1) \times Average_L(S_F) \tag{4}$$

$$CR = (1 - val) \times CR + rand(0, 1) \times Average_L(S_{CR}) \tag{5}$$

where S_F and S_{CR} respectively denote acceptable probabilities of mutation and crossover and the adjustment parameter *val* is within $(0, 1)$. The tuning parameter, *val*, ranges between 0 and 1. Guided by the Lehmer average approach [25], the optimum values for F and CR are computed as per Eqs. (6) and (7).

$$Average_L(S_F) = \frac{\sum_{F \in S_F} F^2}{\sum_{F \in S_F} F} \tag{6}$$

$$Average_L(S_{CR}) = \frac{\sum_{F \in S_F} CR^2}{\sum_{F \in S_F} CR} \tag{7}$$

Mutation Technique. Typical mutation procedures applicable to the QDE model add various advantages to optimization problems. For instance, DE/rand/1 and DE/rand/2 are exploration-based schemes [26], effectively addressing a wide spectrum of optimization challenges. On the other hand, DE/best/1 and DE/best/2 are exploitation-based schemes, which excel in handling a variety of unimodal problems. In the context of our research, we devised a fresh mutation method that amalgamates the features of both the mentioned schemes, described by,

$$vec_i^g = a_{best}^g + F \times \left(a_{i2}^g - a_{i3}^g\right) \tag{8}$$

$$a_{best}^g - math.floor\left(a_i^g \times NI\right) \tag{9}$$

$$a_{best}^g = \lambda \times a_{i1}^g + (1 - \lambda) \times a_{best}^g \tag{10}$$

where λ is defined as,

$$\lambda = \left(\frac{g_{\max} - g}{g_{\max}} \right)^2 \tag{11}$$

When λ equals 1, the DE/best scheme corresponds to the DE/rand/1 scheme via mathematical deduction (among Eq. (8) to Eq. (10)). When λ equals 0, the DE/best scheme corresponds to the DE/best/1 scheme.

Cuckoo Search (CS) Model [6] : This model is inspired by natural processes and excels at pinpointing the optimal candidate. The solution a_{best}^{g-1} at *(g-1)-th* iteration is adopted to optimize a new solution a_{best}^g, which is updated by the Levy flight scheme, as indicated by,

$$a_{best}^g = a_{best}^{g-1} + Levy(ap) \tag{12}$$

With *ap* functioning as the independent variable, Levy flight essentially provides a random shift when random steps are acquired from a Levy distribution for a significant leap.

$$Levy(ap) = g^{-ap}, 1 \le ap \le 3 \tag{13}$$

Finally, a novel mutant vector $nvec_i^g$ can be derived, as exhibited by,

$$nvec_i^g = rand[0, 1] \times a_{best}^g + (1 - rand[0, 1]) \times vec_i^g \tag{14}$$

2.4 Mathematical Model-Based Contour Detection

Our work also designs an interpretable smooth mathematical model to derive a smooth outline. Utilizing a three-layer architecture, our ABNN incorporates Sigmoid and Exponential Linear Unit (ELU) activation functions in the forward propagation phase. The output variables of the ABNN model, represented by $o(x)$ and $o(y)$, correspond to the representation formulas $o(x(t))$ and $o(y(t))$, respectively. In this context, the vertex sequence t serves as the independent variable.

$$(o(x(t)), o(y(t))) = \left(\frac{1}{2 \times \left(e^{\sum_{i=1}^H \frac{1}{1+e^{-(tw_{1i}-a_i)}} w_{2i,1}-b_1-1} \right)}, \frac{1}{2 \times \left(e^{\sum_{i=1}^H \frac{1}{1+e^{-(tw_{1i}-a_i)}} w_{2i,2}-b_2+1} \right)} \right) \tag{15}$$

The purpose of this stage is using the model parameters of a neural network to explain the boundary contour so that to aim the purpose of smoothing the contour. The thresholds in the hidden and output layers are represented by ai $(i = 1,..., H)$ and bi $(i = 1, 2)$, respectively. The weights in the hidden and output layers are denoted by $w1$ and $w2$, respectively.

After training is concluded, a smooth mathematical depiction of the boundary can be conveyed as,

$$f(t) = (x, y) = \left(\frac{2 \times o(x(t)) + 1}{2 \times o(x(t)) + 2}, \frac{2 \times o(y(t)) + 1}{2 \times o(y(t)) + 2} \right) \tag{16}$$

The resulting boundary's vertex coordinates along the x and y axes are denoted by x and y, respectively.

3 Experiment Setup and Results

3.1 Databases

In this study, we evaluate the model using two clinical databases of transrectal ultrasound prostate images from two hospitals respectively: the Tsinghua Changgung Hospital (TCH) and the Jiangsu Province Hospital of Chinese Medicine (JPHCM). By segregating and then amalgamating these databases, we formed a new'Combined' collection. The distribution of groups within the Combined database is detailed in Table 1.

Table 1. The group proportion of all the mentioned databases. All the training, validation, and testing data was randomly selected for evaluation.

Total group		Training group (raw + augmentation)	Validation group	Testing group
TCH	945	675	146	124
JPHCM	393	215 (raw) + 430 (aug)	70	108
Combined database	–	1320	216	232

The performance of our proposed model was evaluated using three metrics: the Dice index (DI) [27], Jaccard index (OMG) [28], and accuracy (ACC) [28], on the 'Combined' database.

$$\Omega = \frac{TP}{FP + TP + FN} \tag{17}$$

$$DSC = \frac{2TP}{2TP + FP + FN} \tag{18}$$

$$ACC = \frac{TP + TN}{TP + FN + FP + TN} \tag{19}$$

where TP, FP, FN, and TN represent true positive, false-positive, false-negative, and true negative, respectively.

3.2   Performance on the Testing Dataset Disturbed by Noise

Our study employed varying intensities of salt and pepper noise, specifically, a signal-to-noise ratio (SNR) of either 0.8 or 0.6, to disturb the testing images. The simulated data was then utilized to test the model's resilience to noise. Additionally, to measure the rate of overlap between the histograms of original (*RawH*) and disturbed (*DisturbH*) data, we employed an overlap metric, defined by,

$$overlap = \frac{|Rawh \cap DisturbH|}{RawH} \qquad (20)$$

Table 2 reveals that as SNR decreased from 1 to 0.6, the average DI, OMG, and ACC metrics reduced by 4.21%, 4.82%, and 4.34%, respectively. Despite slight increases in standard deviation (SD) for all metrics as SNR decreases, the mean and SD for each metric demonstrated minimal fluctuation under various SNRs. Our model showed robust segmentation performance under original and noise-disturbed scenarios. Figure 3 illustrates diverse segmentation results using our hybrid model.

Table 2. Evaluation outcomes under various degrees of salt and pepper noise. After using the original training and validation for training, we used the corrupted testing data for final evaluation.

DI ± SD (%)		OMG ± SD (%)	ACC ± SD (%)
Clean set	96.4 ± 2.4	95.5 ± 2.9	96.1 ± 2.5
SNR = 0.8	94.9 ± 3.1	93.4 ± 3.2	94.4 ± 3.3
SNR = 0.6	92.5 ± 3.6	91.1 ± 4.1	92.1 ± 3.2

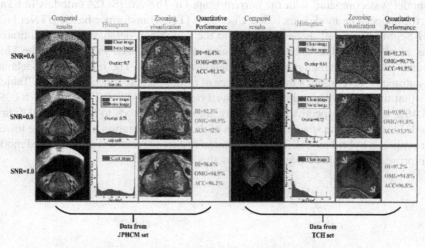

Fig. 3. Model capability on different degrees of salt and pepper noise.

3.3 Ablation Study

A range of ablation experiments were conducted to evaluate the impact of individual modules in this hybrid model. The results of these experiments are detailed in Table 3. Serving as the benchmark, Model 1 delivered a performance with a DI of $91.6 \pm 4.1(\%)$, OMG of $90.5 \pm 4.3(\%)$, and an ACC of $91.4 \pm 4.1(\%)$. With the integration of various modules such as QDE, APT, HQIE, and ABNN to boost performance, the average DI, OMG, and ACC increased by 0.98% –5.24%, 1.32% –5.52%, and 1.09% –5.13%, respectively. Among all, the final model (Model 5) delivers the highest performance. Figure 4 visually demonstrates the results of the ablation experiments.

Table 3. Ablation evaluation outcomes. (BNN: backpropagation neural network)

Structure		DI ± SD (%)	OMG ± SD (%)	ACC ± SD (%)
Model 1	CPT + BNN (baseline)	91.6 ± 4.1	90.5 ± 4.3	91.4 ± 4.1
Model 2	CPT + QDE + BNN	92.5 ± 3.3	91.7 ± 3.7	92.4 ± 3.5
Model 3	APT + QEN + BNN	94.1 ± 2.9	92.6 ± 3.5	93.5 ± 3.1
Model 4	APT + HQIE + BNN	95.8 ± 2.4	94.1 ± 3.1	95.2 ± 2.6
Model 5	APT + HQIE + ABNN (our model)	96.4 ± 2.4	95.5 ± 2.9	96.1 ± 2.5

3.4 Comparison with State-Of-The-Art (SOTA) Models

Our model was compared with the current State-Of-The-Art (SOTA) models in terms of performance. The models included Unet + + [11], Transformer-based UTNet [12], and H-SegMod [27], all assessed based on the Combined database. The quantitative results of all the models under consideration are summarized in Table 4. The Unet + + and Transformer methods are completely automated. The other two models are semi-automatic, leveraging a limited number of prior points to guide the model. Table 4 shows that the DI, OMG, and ACC improved between 5.54% –7.7%, 5.18% – 8.03%, and 5.46% –7.85%, respectively, from fully automatic methods to the proposed hybrid method. In addition, the standard deviation of the three-evaluation metrics is the lowest in our proposed hybrid model. These evaluation results suggest that our proposed model had improved performance over existing methods.

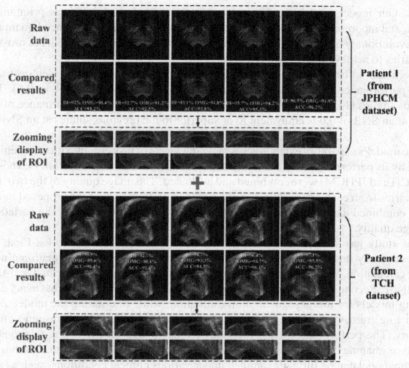

Fig. 4. Visual demonstration of ablation experiment results. Red line shows the ground truth, while the blue line shows model-generated results.

Table 4. Comparison with SOTA segmentation models

Paper	Method	DI ± SD (%)	OMG ± SD (%)	ACC ± SD (%)
[11]-2020	Unet + +	89.5 ± 6.4	88.4 ± 6.6	89.1 ± 6.1
[12]-2021	UTNet	90.1 ± 5.7	88.7 ± 6.1	89.7 ± 6.1
[27]-2022	H-SegMod	95.1 ± 3.3	93.3 ± 3.7	94.6 ± 3.5
Proposed model	Hybrid	96.4 ± 2.4	95.5 ± 2.9	96.1 ± 2.5

4   Conclusion

Segmentation of the prostate in TRUS images is inherently challenging, especially using fully automatic methods. A hybrid artificial intelligence segmentation method was developed to improve the accuracy and robustness of prostate segmentation in ultrasound images. Our model used limited sonographer-determined seed points as prior information, and incorporated an enhanced polygon tracking system, an advanced quantum-based evolutionary network, and a smooth, interpretable mathematical model of prostate boundaries to achieve improved performance.

The noise influence on images was critically evaluated. Our model demonstrated robust performance even at lower signal-to-noise ratio scenarios (SNR = 0.6). The previous studies [13, 29] examined SNR values of down-to 0.8. The performance of our model at an SNR of 0.6 is equivalent to or superior to the previous studies at an SNR of 0.8.

The model's capability extends across varying levels of task complexities, as demonstrated by its performance in a combined database. Ultrasound datasets from two hospitals (TCH and JPHCM) were combined and evaluated. The image quality of the two hospitals varies from each other. However, the superior performance of the proposed model on the combined database demonstrated the model's capability to adapt the variations in image quality.

Our study has some limitations that can be improved in future works. First, the model currently has three major components, contributing to the computational need during calculation. We will optimize the model by compressing it for potential real-time clinical use. Second, we hope to transit the model to a fully automatic format using deep learning models for initial segmentation estimation, while fine-tuning the model using the existing framework. Third, the model is currently examined on ultrasound image modality. The performance of the method on other image modalities, e.g., magnetic resonance imaging (MRI), or computed tomography (CT) could be studied. Last but not least, the model can be further examined under various clinical conditions, such as age, demographics, prostate zone, and changes in prostate shape and position over treatment periods, to improve its range of clinical applications.

By enhancing and broadening the model's application in these ways, we hope to contribute to the advancements in medical imaging, disease diagnostics, and treatment, bringing us closer to a future where precise, efficient, and robust ultrasound image segmentation is a reality.

References

1. Swami, U., McFarland, T.R., Nussenzveig, R., Agarwal, N.: Advanced prostate cancer: treatment advances and future directions. Trends in Cancer. **6**, 702–715 (2020)
2. Peng, T., Wu, Y., Zhao, J., Zhang, B., Wang, J., Cai, J.: Explainability-guided mathematical model-based segmentation of transrectal ultrasound images for prostate brachytherapy, In: IEEE 16th International Conference on Bioinformatics and Biomedicine (BIBM), pp. 1126–1131 (2022)
3. Orlando, N., Gillies, D.J., Gyacskov, I., Romagnoli, C., D'Souza, D., Fenster, A.: Automatic pros tate segmentation using deep learning on clinically diverse 3D transrectal ultrasound images. Med. Phys. **47**, 2413–2426 (2020)
4. Lei, Y., et al.: Ultrasound prostate segmentation based on multidirectional deeply supervised V-Net. Med. Phys. **46**, 3194–3206 (2019)
5. Peng, T., Wang, Y., Xu, T.C., Shi, L., Jiang, J., Zhu, S.: Detection of lung contour with closed principal curve and machine learning. J. Digit. Imaging **31**, 520–533 (2018)

6. Cobos, C., Muñoz-Collazos, H., Urbano-Muñoz, R., Mendoza, M., León, E., Herrera-Viedma, E.: Clustering of web search results based on the cuckoo search algorithm and Balanced Bayesian Information Criterion. Inf. Sci. **281**, 248–264 (2014)
7. Vesal, S., et al.: Domain generalization for prostate segmentation in transrectal ultrasound images: A multi-center study. Med. Image Anal. **82**, 102620 (2022)
8. He, K., et al.: MetricUNet: Synergis tic image- and voxel-level learning for precise prostate segmentation via online sampling. Med. Image Anal. **71**, 102039 (2021)
9. Zavala-Romero, O., et al.: Segmentation of prostate and prostate zones using deep learning: A multi-MRI vendor analysis. Strahlenther. Onkol.. Onkol. **196**, 932–942 (2020)
10. Xu, X., Sanford, T., Turkbey, B., Xu, S., Wood, B.J., Yan, P.: Shadow-consistent semi-super vised learning for prostate ultrasound segmentation. IEEE Trans. Med. Imaging **41**, 1331–1345 (2022)
11. Zhou, Z., Siddiquee, M.M.R., Tajbakhsh, N., Liang, J.: Unet++: Redesigning skip connec tions to exploit multiscale features in image segmentation, IEEE Trans. Med. Imaging. **39**, 1856–1867 (2020)
12. Gao, Y., Zhou, M., Metaxas, D.: UTNet: a hybrid transformer architecture for medical image segmentation, in: International Conference on Medical Image Computing and Computer-Assisted Intervention, pp. 61–71 (2021)
13. Peng, T., Tang, C., Wu, Y., Cai, J.: H-SegMed: a hybrid method for prostate segmentation in TRUS images via improved closed principal curve and improved enhanced machine learning. Int. J. Comput. Vis.Comput. Vis. **130**, 1896–1919 (2022)
14. Zeng, Q., et al.: Segmentation in transrectal ultrasound using magnetic resonance imaging priors, Int. J. Comput. Assist. Radiol. Surg. **13**, 749–757 (2018)
15. Godley, A., Sheplan Olsen, L.J., Stephans, K., Zhao, A.: Combining prior day contours to improve automated prostate segmentation: combining previous contours for automated prostate segmentation, Med. Phys. **40**, 021722 (2013)
16. Karimi. D., et al.: Accurate and robust deep learning-based segmentation of the prostate clinical target volume in ultrasound images, Med. Image Anal. **57**, 186–196 (2019)
17. Hastie, T., Stuetzle, W.: Principal curves. J. Am. Stat. Assoc. **84**, 502–516 (1989)
18. Kegl, B., Krzyzak, A.: Piecewise linear skeletonization using principal curves, IEEE Trans. Pattern Anal. Machine Intell. **24**, 59–74 (2002)
19. Kegl, B., Krzyzak, A., Linder, T., Zeger, K.: Learning and design of principal curves. IEEE Trans. Pattern Anal. Machine Intell. **22**, 281–297 (2000)
20. Peng, T., Xu, T.C., Wang, Y., Li, F.: Deep belief network and closed polygonal line for lung segmentation in chest radiographs. Comput. J. (2020)
21. Peng, T., Wu, Y., Qin, J., Wu, Q.J., Cai, J.: H-ProSeg: hybrid ultrasound prostate segmentation based on explainability-guided mathematical model. Comput. Methods Programs Biomed. **219**, 106752 (2022)
22. Jain, A., Nandakumar, K., Ross, A.: Score normalization in multimodal biometric systems. Pattern Recognit. **38**, 2270–2285 (2005)
23. Kabir, W., Ahmad, M.O., Swamy, M.N.S.: A novel normalization technique for multimodal biometric systems. In: 2015 IEEE 58th International Midwest Symposium on Circuits and Systems (MWSCAS), pp. 1–4, IEEE, Fort Collins, CO, USA (2015)
24. Su, H., Yang, Y.: Differential evolution and quantum-inquired differential evolution for evolving Takagi-Sugeno fuzzy models. Expert Syst. Appl. **38**, 6447–6451 (2011)
25. Ali, M.Z., Awad, N.H., Suganthan, P.N., Reynolds, R.G.: An adaptive multipopulation differ ential evolution with dynamic population reduction. IEEE Trans. Cybern. **47**, 2768–2779 (2017)
26. Cui, L., Li, G., Zhu, Z., Wen, Z., Lu, N., Lu, J.: A novel differential evolution algorithm with a self-adaptation parameter control method by differential evolution. Soft. Comput.Comput. **22**, 6171–6190 (2018)

27. Peng, T., Zhao, J., Gu, Y., Wang, C., Wu, Y., Cheng, X., Cai, J.: H-ProMed: Ultrasound image segmentation based on the evolutionary neural network and an improved principal curve. Pattern Recognit. **131**, 108890 (2022)
28. Peng, T., et al.: Hybrid automatic lung segmentation on chest ct scans. IEEE Access. **8**, 73293–73306 (2020)
29. Benaichouche, A.N., Oulhadj, H., Siarry, P.: Improved spatial fuzzy c-means clustering for image segmentation using PSO initialization, Mahalanobis distance and post-segmentation correction. Digit. Signal Process. **23**, 1390–1400 (2013)

An Automatic Fabric Defect Detector Using an Efficient Multi-scale Network

Fei Gao[1]([⊠])[ID], Xiaolu Cao[1][ID], and Yaozhong Zhuang[2]

[1] College of Computer Science and Technology, Zhejiang University of Technology, Hangzhou 310023, China
feig@zjut.edu.cn
[2] Xinfengming Group Co., Ltd., Tongxiang 314513, China

Abstract. Efficient and accurate fabric defect detection can be beneficial to enhance the competitiveness of enterprises. Aiming at fabric defects with multi-scale characteristics, an Efficient Multi-scale Detector (EMSD) is proposed in this paper. Specifically, by combining Self-calibrated Convolution (SCConv) and Ghost Convolution (GhostConv), a novel feature extraction network is proposed to extract low-level spatial feature maps more accurately and efficiently. Then, a Dense-connected Spatial Pyramid Pooling - Fast (DCSPPF) module is designed to integrate local and global information of low-level spatial feature maps in a way that reduces the loss of defect information. Further, a feature fusion network is constructed to extract high-level semantic feature maps and integrate them with low-level spatial feature maps by skip connections to guide defects localization. Finally, three defect feature maps of different scales are sent into detection heads for large, medium and small defects detection respectively. Experiments are conducted on public Tianchi dataset and TILDA dataset to evaluate the effectiveness of EMSD. The results show that EMSD significantly outperforms all its variants and previous works with a more lightweight network architecture, and has better fabric defect detection capability.

Keywords: Fabric defect detection · Self-calibrated convolution · Ghost convolution · DCSPPF · Feature fusion

1 Introduction

There is a huge demand for the production of fabrics, which are widely used in all kinds of clothing and household goods, etc. Effective fabric defect detection is an important means to control the quality of fabrics and a key measure for manufacturers to enhance their competitiveness. Many textile mills still use manual visual inspection to detect defects, which is costly and inefficient, easy to cause missed and wrong detection. To this end, automatic fabric defect detection has become one of the research hotspots in the field of computer vision.

In practical applications, automatic fabric defect detection should be suitable for multi-scale defects, and ensure its applicability to the hardware platforms

F. Liu et al. (Eds.): PRICAI 2023, LNAI 14327, pp. 41–53, 2024.
https://doi.org/10.1007/978-981-99-7025-4_4

with limited resources. Therefore, researchers have made a lot of works, which can be roughly divided into two categories [10], traditional methods and deep learning methods. Traditional methods construct texture features through artificial analysis, which suffered from their low efficiency and poor performance. In recent years, with deep learning achieving best performance in many visual tasks by means of automatic feature extraction, more and more deep learning-based fabric defect detection methods have been proposed, which can be divided into two categories: (1) One-stage methods [7,11,22,23,25], and (2) two-stage methods [9,14,19–21]. One-stage methods output location information and categories of defects at the same time, which have higher detection efficiency with low accuracy. Two-stage methods separate location process from classification process, which have higher detection accuracy with low efficiency.

To achieve a balance between efficiency and accuracy, in this paper, an Efficient Multi-scale Detector (EMSD) for fabric defects is proposed. The main contributions are as follows:

1) A noval feature extraction network is designed to reduce the pollution of background information and improve the efficiency of feature extraction.
2) DCSPPF module is designed to reduce the loss of defect information, and integrate local and global features to improve model accuracy.
3) A feature fusion network is constructed to extract multi-scale high-level semantic feature maps and integrate them with low-level spatial feature maps through skip connections to guide defect location.

2   Related Work

One-stage detection methods treat all pixels as potential targets, regress categories and location information of defects at the same time, such as RetinaNet [12], YOLO [6] series, and EfficientNet [17], et al. Xie et al. [22] make some improvements to fit fabric defects based on RefineDet. Jin et al. [7] propose a defect detection method based on YOLOv5, which adopts teacher-student architecture for processing. Zhou et al. [25] propose an efficient defect fabric detector (EDD), which adopts EfficientNet as backbone network and conducts a new feature extraction structure to emphasize the importance of low-level features. In addition, Li et al. [11] propose a compact convolution neural network architecture, which is applicable to real-time detection. Xu et al. [23] propose a deformable defect detection network (D4Net) for non-rigid products with large patterns.

Two-stage detection methods adopt multi-phase scheme, output regional proposals first, and then classify them. Existing two-stage detection detectors include RCNN [3], Fast RCNN [2], Faster RCNN [16] et al. Wei et al. [20] propose a fabric defect detector based on Faster-RCNN. Wu et al. [21] design dilated convolution module with multi-scale kernels to enhance feature extraction capability of network. Beyond that, Liu et al. [14] train a multi-stage GAN model to synthesize reasonable defect samples and design a deep semantic segmentation network to detect fabric defects. Jun et al. [9] propose a two-stage architecture to detect local defects and global defects respectively by Inception-V1 model and LeNet-5 model. Wang et al. [19] propose a self-attention deep saliency network for defects with blurred or complex shapes.

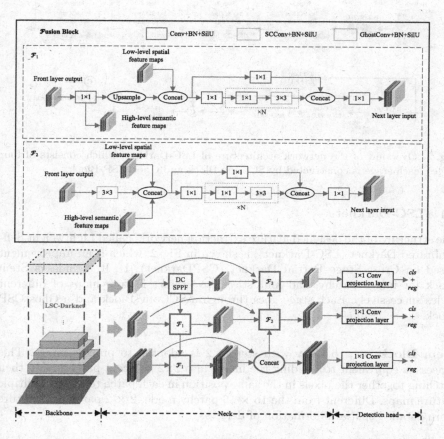

Fig. 1. Overview of the network architecture of EMSD. 1) LSC-Darknet as backbone to extract low-level spatial feature maps; 2) DCSPPF module is used to integrate global and local information; 3) LSG-PAFPN as neck to refine and fuse low-level spatial and high-level semantic feature maps; 4) A projection layer as detection head.

3 Proposed Model EMSD

Inspired by the outstanding performance of Ghost Convolution (GhostConv) [4], Self-calibrated Convolution (SCConv) [13] and Dense Connection [5] in various visual tasks, we cleverly transplant them into a unified architecture to explore an efficient multi-scale network for fabric defect detection. The overall architecture is shown in Fig. 1.

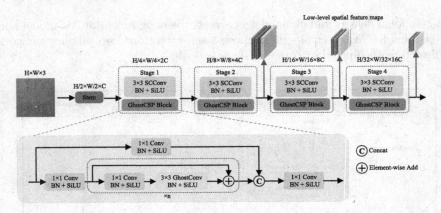

Fig. 2. Overview of the network architecture of LSC-Darknet, which consists of four stages, each stage is constructed by SCConv Block and GhostCSP Block.

3.1 LSC-Darknet

The structure of the designed feature extraction network, called Lightweight Self-calibrated Darknet (LSC-Darknet), is shown in Fig. 2, which is an improvement based on Cross Stage Partial Darknet (CSPDarknet) [1]. It includes a Stem Block for image patchy, and four stages to extract feature maps of different scales successively. Each stage goes through a SCConv Block and a GhostCSP Block.

Stem Block. 6×6 Conv with step of 2 is adopted to process image. This process is equivalent to dividing the image into 2×2 adjacent patches, and then stitching together the pixels in the same position in each patch to obtain multiple feature maps. Different from the 16×16 patchy mode, 2×2 patch can capture more detailed spatial information of defects.

SCConv Block. This structure is composed of SCConv, batch norm and SiLU activation function. Among them, SCConv is an improved convolution, which divides convolution kernels into four parts by channel, one part retains original spatial information, and the other parts guide the feature extraction through the lantent space after downsampling. Due to the shape characteristics of fabric defects, the detection boxes often contain redundant background information. Use SCConv can focus on the context information around the defects, avoid the information pollution of unrelated background, and can achieve more accurate defect location with nearly equivalent computation. Therefore, in each stage, 3×3 SCConv with step of 2 is adopted.

GhostCSP Block. This structure is improved based on Cross Stage Partial (CSP) [1]. The input feature maps X are divided into two parts $\{X_1, X_2\}$ by channel through 1×1 Conv. One part is jointed with another after passing through dense bottleneck structures, which are the key to affect the efficiency of feature extraction. This process produces abundant highly similar feature maps, bringing unnecessary calculation, as shown in Fig. 3(a).

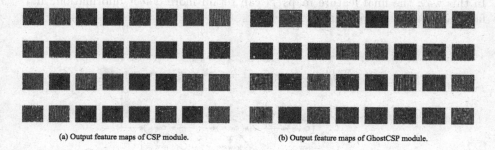

(a) Output feature maps of CSP module.   (b) Output feature maps of GhostCSP module.

Fig. 3. Output feature maps comparison of CSP module and GhostCSP module.

Therefore, we adopt GhostConv in bottleneck structure. Instead of directly generating all feature maps, it generates partial simple feature maps first, and then performs linear transformation to extend them to the expected number. The process of the improved GhostCSP can be formulated as:

$$X_s = Conv_{3\times3}(Conv_{1\times1}(X_2)) = \{x_1, x_2, \cdots, x_m\} \tag{1}$$

$$X_a = \Phi(X_s) = \{x_1, x_2, \cdots, x_m, x_{m+1}, x_{m+2}, \cdots, x_n\} \tag{2}$$

$$Y = Conv_{1\times1}(Concat(X_1, X_a+X_2))) \tag{3}$$

where X_s represents m simple feature maps, Φ represents linear transformation, X_a represents feature maps with expected number $(n \geq m)$, $Conv_{n\times n}$ represents convolution with $n \times n$ kernel size, and Y represents final output. GhostCSP can significantly improve efficiency by simplifying the process of feature extraction. For the same image, the comparison of the output feature maps of CSP and GhostCSP on the same layer is shown in Fig. 3. It can be seen that GhostCSP can achieve the same effect as CSP. Through the above structure, three scales of low-level spatial feature maps $\{f_1, f_2, f_3\}$ can be obtained in the last three stages for further network processing.

3.2 DCSPPF

To further improve model accuracy, f_3 is sent to Dense-connected Spatial Pyramid Pooling - Fast (DCSPPF) module based on SPPF to fuse local and global information. The structure is composed of serial 5×5 MaxPool layers to obtain multiple feature maps with the same size. However, since many fabric defects occupy only 1% of the image pixels, multi-layer MaxPool are prone to loss of defect information. To solve the problem, we adopt the idea of Dense Connection [5], as shown in Fig. 4. Every time the feature maps pass through a Maxpool layer, a concatenate operation is performed to fuse the feature maps of the front and back layers. In addition, feature maps that have not been processed by the Maxpool layer are fused each time to emphasize the original feature information. In this way, the final feature maps f_4 can retain more defect information, and facilitate feature propagation.

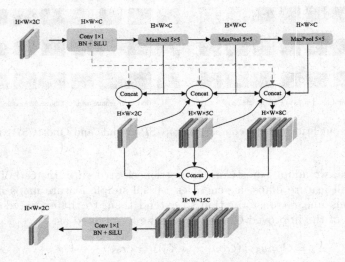

Fig. 4. The structure of DCSPPF module.

3.3   LSG-PAFPN

The Lightweight Self-guided Pixel Aggregation Feature Pyramid Network (LSG-PAFPN) are designed based on PAFPN [15] to fuse features of different scales, which adopts a bidirectional structure including bottom-up and top-down path. Due to the bidirectional scheme, the structure requires more computation, so SCConv and GhostConv are used in an intelligent way to simplify the network and improve the detection accuracy, as shown in Fig. 1.

Top-Down Path. The $\mathcal{F}_1$ module is used for the top-down path. Specifically, it first converts the input into high-level semantic feature maps through 1×1 Conv, then upsamples them to double size and concatenates them with low-level spatial feature maps. After that, feature maps are sent to a bottleneck structure, in which repeated part is executed by 3×3 GhostConv. Finally, after 1×1 Conv, the input of the next layer is obtained. After top-down fusion process, three scales of high-level sementic feature maps $\{f_4, f_5, f_6\}$ can be obtained.

Bottom-Up Path. This path adds three skip connections from backbone to enhance feature fusion and defects location guidance by low-level feature maps. The $\mathcal{F}_2$ module is used for the bottom-up path. Specifically, it first extracts feature maps from input by 3×3 SCConv, then concatenates them with low-level spatial and high-level semantic feature maps. After that, feature maps are sent to the same bottleneck structure and 1×1 Conv as top-down path to obtain the input of the next layer. After bottom-up fusion process, three scales of feature maps $\{f_7, f_8, f_9\}$ can be obtained and sent to detection heads for the detection of large, medium and small scale defects respectively.

3.4 Detection Head

Three detection heads are used for multi-scale fabric defects. Each detection head is a Fully Connected Mapping Layer, outputs the location information and categories of the detection boxes. The output length can be formulated as:

$$l_{output} = (n_{cls} + 4 + 1) \times n_{anchor} \tag{4}$$

where n_{cls} represents the number of categories, 4 represents the coordinates of detection box, 1 represents the confidence score, and n_{Anchor} represents the number of anchors at each pixel. To guide network output, the loss function consists of three parts, which can be formulated as:

$$Loss = \lambda_1 L_{cls} + \lambda_2 L_{obj} + \lambda_3 L_{loc} \tag{5}$$

where $\lambda_1, \lambda_2, \lambda_3$ represent balance coefficients, L_{cls} represents classification loss to calculate the classification correctness, L_{obj} represents confidence loss to calculate the confidence score of the network, L_{loc} represents location loss to calculate the error between the detection box and ground-truth box. The details are shown as follow:

$$\begin{cases} L_{cls} = BCE\left(c, c^{gt}\right), \\ L_{obj} = BCE\left(p, p^{iou}\right), \\ L_{cIoU} = 1 - IoU + \frac{\rho^2\left(b, b^{gt}\right)}{l^2} + \alpha v \end{cases} \tag{6}$$

where c and c^{gt} respectively represent the predicted category and ground-truth category, p and p^{iou} respectively represent the confidence score predicted by network and calculated by the IoU value between the detection box and ground-truth box, b and b^{gt} respectively represent the center point of the detection box and ground-truth box, ρ represents the Euclidean Distance between the two center points, l represents the diagonal distance of the minimum closure area that can contain both the detection box and ground-truth box, α is the weight coefficient, v represents the similarity of aspect ratio and is calculated as follow:

$$v = \frac{4}{\pi^2}\left(arctan\frac{w^{gt}}{h^{gt}} - arctan\frac{w}{h}\right)^2 \tag{7}$$

where w and w^{gt} respectively represent the width of the detection box and ground-truth box, h and h^{gt} respectively represent the height of the detection box and ground-truth box.

4   Experiments

4.1   Setup

Our implementation is based on Ubuntu18.04 system and Pytorch1.12 on four NVIDIA semantic RTX 2080Ti cards. SGD optimizer is used with a learning rate of 0.01. The batch size is 16 and 800 epochs are trained. Other methods compared in the experiments are trained on the same environment and datasets, the training parameters are the same as those published by the original method.

4.2   Datasets

To validate the effectiveness of EMSD in the task of fabric defect detection, two representative fabric defect datasets are used. One is the public dataset TILDA. As with other methods, four of the most common fabric defects: holes (e1), patches (e2), scratches (e3), lines (e4), and four fabric groups: unpatterned (C1), regular textured (C2), regular patterned (C3), complex irregular patterned (C4) are used. There are 1600 fabric defect images in total. The other dataset is Tianchi dataset provided by Alibaba Cloud in 2019 with a total of 5913 defect images, which contains 20 categories of defects. Compared with TILDA, Tianchi dataset is more challenging for the following reasons: Uneven distribution of object categories; Defects vary widely in size; Annotated bounding boxes contain a lot of background information. In the experiments, both datasets take 80% of all defect images as the training set and the remaining 20% as the test set.

4.3   Evaluation Metrics

mAP is used to evaluate the detection results, specifically calculated as follow:

$$\begin{cases} Precision = TP/(TP + FP), \\ Recall = TP/(TP + FN), \\ AP = \int_0^1 P(r)dr, \\ mAP = \sum_{i=1}^C AP_i/C, \end{cases} \tag{8}$$

where TP represents the positive sample with positive prediction, FP represents the positive sample with negative prediction, FN represents the negative sample with negative prediction, $P(r)$ represents the Precision-Recall (P-R) curve, AP is the region below the curve, C represents categories, and mAP is the average AP for each category. In addition, IoU represents the ratio of intersection and union between the detection boxes and ground-truth boxes. mAP@0.5 means setting the threshold of IoU to 0.5, the detection box is positive if IoU is greater than 0.5 and negative if IoU is less than 0.5. mAP@0.5:0.95 represents the average mAP at different IoU thresholds (from 0.5 to 0.95, step size is 0.05).

4.4 Comparison Experiment Results

Comparison experiment results on Tianchi dataset are shown in Table 1. (mAP refers to mAP0.5:0.95). It can be seen that the first three methods have large parameter amounts, which are difficult to meet the real-time requirements. Yolov5 and EDDs [25] achieve similar performance to the above methods with relatively few parameters. While EMSD achieves the best detection performance, mAP metric is significantly better than the other five methods, and the parameter amount is the least, realize a good balance between accuracy and efficiency.

Table 1. Metrics comparison of different methods on the Tianchi dataset.

Method	mAP	Params
Faster RCNN [16]	19.7	41.10M
EfficientDet-d3 [17]	19.9	14.28M
RetinaNet-R101 [12]	20.5	56.51M
EDDs-d3 [25]	20.9	7.07M
Yolov5s [8]	22.5	7.07M
EMSD(ours)	**26.3**	**7.05M**

Table 2. Metrics comparison of different methods on the TILDA dataset.

Method	P	R	mAP
Faster RCNN [16]	69.5	68.8	70.9
FCOS [18]	76.1	81.5	76.8
RefineDet [24]	74.3	85.0	77.7
YOLOv5 [8]	74.6	79.3	78.5
Xie et al. [22]	78.9	85.5	80.2
EMSD(ours)	**80.1**	**85.5**	**83.2**

In addition, the comparison experiment results on TILDA dataset are shown in Table 2. Since there is no public open source of manual annotated TILDA dataset, the annotation by authors of different methods will lead to a big difference in metrics, this paper only compares the methods with similar results.

Table 3. Comparison of EMSD variants on the Tianchi dataset.

Configurations	mAP@0.5	mAP@0.5:0.95	Params
baseline	48.3	22.5	7.07M
baseline+LSC-Darknet	50.5	24.9	6.34M
baseline+LSC-Darknet+DCSPPF	51.4	25.5	7.20M
Ours	**53.8**	**26.3**	**7.05M**

The performance of existing advanced detection methods on TILDA dataset is similar. The performance of Xie et al. [22] specifically designed for fabric defects is significantly superior to that of existing methods, while the EMSD performs better, and each metric is optimal for all methods, which proves the effectiveness of EMSD.

4.5   Ablation Experiments

In order to verify the contribution of each component in the EMSD network, a series of ablation experiments are conducted on the Tianchi dataset. The unimproved network structure is taken as the baseline, and components were replaced one by one. All of these variants are trained using the same training strategy, and the experiment results are shown in Table 3.

Fig. 5. Detection results of EMSD on the Tianchi dataset.

Each component contributes to the performance enhancement, and our EMSD network integrates all components to achieve the best detection results at a comparable computation. More specifically, LSC-Darknet improves mAP@0.5 by about 4.6%, and mAP@0.5:0.95 is significantly improved by about 10.7% with less computation. This means that LSC-Darknet pays more attention to the information around the defects, resulting in more accurate localization. Secondly, adding the idea of Dense Connection to the SPPF module also brings some gains, such as about 1.8% increase in mAP@0.5 and 2.4% increase in mAP@0.5:0.95, while the extra computation is negligible. In addition, LSG-PAFPN further improves the performance with less computing, mAP@0.5 increases by about 4.7%, mAP@0.5:0.95 increases about 3.1%, which verifies the validity of the low-level feature guidance and bidirectional structure.

4.6   Visualization of Detection Results

The visual detection results of EMSD on Tianchi dataset is shown in Fig. 5. For defects of any scale and shape, EMSD can predict accurate detection box location, even for defects that are hard to inspect with the naked eye.

Figure 6 shows the test results of EMSD on the TILDA dataset, covering four defects and eight fabrics. EMSD can be well adapted to multi-scale defects on fabrics with different textures and patterns. For some defects that are not clearly distinguished from the background, such as small holes, light-colored spots, slight scratches, etc., accurate detection boxes can also be predicted. In general, EMSD performs well on the common dataset TILDA.

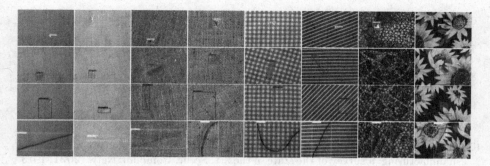

Fig. 6. Detection results of EMSD on the TILDA dataset.

5   Conclusion

In this paper, an efficient multi-scale network EMSD is proposed for the task of automatic fabric defect detection. EMSD can reduce the affect of background pollution and the loss of defect information, and enhance the feature fusion process. Compared with other methods, EMSD improves accuracy significantly with higher efficiency. It is suitable for multi-scale defects on different texture fabrics so that has strong application value. However, EMSD is less robust to small defects on complex patterned fabrics. In the future work, we plan to analyze more texture information to better apply to complex patterned fabrics.

Acknowledgements. This work is being supported by the National Key Research and Development Project of China under Grant No. 2020AAA0104001and the Zhejiang Provincial Science and Technology Planning Key Project of China under Grant No. 2022C01120.

References

1. Farhadi, A., Redmon, J.: Yolov3: An incremental improvement. In: Computer Vision and Pattern Recognition. vol. 1804, pp. 1–6. Springer, Berlin/Heidelberg, Germany (2018)
2. Girshick, R.: Fast R-CNN. In: Proceedings of the IEEE International Conference on Computer Vision, pp. 1440–1448 (2015)
3. Girshick, R., Donahue, J., Darrell, T., Malik, J.: Rich feature hierarchies for accurate object detection and semantic segmentation. In: Proceedings of the IEEE Conference on Computer Vision And Pattern Recognition, pp. 580–587 (2014)
4. Han, K., Wang, Y., Tian, Q., Guo, J., Xu, C., Xu, C.: Ghostnet: More features from cheap operations. In: Proceedings of the IEEE/CVF Conference on Computer Vision and Pattern Recognition, pp. 1580–1589 (2020)
5. Huang, G., Liu, Z., Van Der Maaten, L., Weinberger, K.Q.: Densely connected convolutional networks. In: Proceedings of the IEEE Conference on Computer Vision and Pattern Recognition, pp. 4700–4708 (2017)

6. Jiang, P., Ergu, D., Liu, F., Cai, Y., Ma, B.: A review of yolo algorithm developments. Procedia Comput. Sci. **199**, 1066–1073 (2022)
7. Jin, R., Niu, Q.: Automatic fabric defect detection based on an improved yolov5. Math. Probl. Eng. **2021**, 1–13 (2021)
8. Jocher, G., et al.: ultralytics/yolov5: v6. 2-yolov5 classification models, apple m1, reproducibility, clearml and deci. ai integrations. Zenodo (2022)
9. Jun, X., Wang, J., Zhou, J., Meng, S., Pan, R., Gao, W.: Fabric defect detection based on a deep convolutional neural network using a two-stage strategy. Text. Res. J. **91**(1–2), 130–142 (2021)
10. Li, C., Li, J., Li, Y., He, L., Fu, X., Chen, J.: Fabric defect detection in textile manufacturing: a survey of the state of the art. Secur. Commun. Netw. **2021**, 1–13 (2021)
11. Li, Y., Zhang, D., Lee, D.J.: Automatic fabric defect detection with a wide-and-compact network. Neurocomputing **329**, 329–338 (2019)
12. Lin, T.Y., Goyal, P., Girshick, R., He, K., Dollár, P.: Focal loss for dense object detection. In: Proceedings of the IEEE International Conference on Computer Vision, pp. 2980–2988 (2017)
13. Liu, J.J., Hou, Q., Cheng, M.M., Wang, C., Feng, J.: Improving convolutional networks with self-calibrated convolutions. In: Proceedings of the IEEE/CVF Conference on Computer Vision and Pattern Recognition, pp. 10096–10105 (2020)
14. Liu, J., Wang, C., Su, H., Du, B., Tao, D.: Multistage GAN for fabric defect detection. IEEE Trans. Image Process. **29**, 3388–3400 (2019)
15. Liu, S., Qi, L., Qin, H., Shi, J., Jia, J.: Path aggregation network for instance segmentation. In: Proceedings of the IEEE Conference on Computer Vision and Pattern Recognition, pp. 8759–8768 (2018)
16. Ren, S., He, K., Girshick, R., Sun, J.: Faster R-CNN: Towards real-time object detection with region proposal networks. In: Advances in Neural Information Processing Systems, 28 (2015)
17. Tan, M., Le, Q.: Efficientnet: Rethinking model scaling for convolutional neural networks. In: International Conference on Machine Learning, pp. 6105–6114. PMLR (2019)
18. Tian, Z., Shen, C., Chen, H., He, T.: Fcos: Fully convolutional one-stage object detection. In: Proceedings of the IEEE/CVF International Conference on Computer Vision, pp. 9627–9636 (2019)
19. Wang, J., Liu, Z., Li, C., Yang, R., Li, B.: Self-attention Deep Saliency Network for Fabric Defect Detection. In: Pan, L., Liang, J., Qu, B. (eds.) Bio-inspired Computing: Theories and Applications: 14th International Conference, BIC-TA 2019, Zhengzhou, China, November 22–25, 2019, Revised Selected Papers, Part II, pp. 627–637. Springer Singapore, Singapore (2020). https://doi.org/10.1007/978-981-15-3415-7_53
20. Wei, B., Hao, K., Tang, X., Ren, L.: Fabric defect detection based on faster RCNN. In: Wong, W.K. (ed.) AITA 2018. AISC, vol. 849, pp. 45–51. Springer, Cham (2019). https://doi.org/10.1007/978-3-319-99695-0_6
21. Wu, J., et al.: Automatic fabric defect detection using a wide-and-light network. Appl. Intell. **51**(7), 4945–4961 (2021)
22. Xie, H., Wu, Z.: A robust fabric defect detection method based on improved refinedet. Sensors **20**(15), 4260 (2020)

23. Xu, X., Chen, J., Zhang, H., Ng, W.W.: D4net: De-deformation defect detection network for non-rigid products with large patterns. Inf. Sci. **547**, 763–776 (2021)
24. Zhang, S., Wen, L., Bian, X., Lei, Z., Li, S.Z.: Single-shot refinement neural network for object detection. In: Proceedings of the IEEE Conference on Computer Vision and Pattern Recognition, pp. 4203–4212 (2018)
25. Zhou, T., Zhang, J., Su, H., Zou, W., Zhang, B.: EDDs: A series of efficient defect detectors for fabric quality inspection. Measurement **172**, 108885 (2021)

An Improved Framework for Pedestrian Tracking and Counting Based on DeepSORT

Yanxin Tao[1] and Jiping Zheng[1,2]([✉]) [ID]

[1] College of Computer Science and Technology, Nanjing University of Aeronautics and Astronautics, Nanjing, China
{draco,jzh}@nuaa.edu.cn
[2] State Key Laboratory for Novel Software Technology, Nanjing University, Nanjing, China

Abstract. Due to the rapid growth in the demand for crowd analysis and monitoring methods, there is an urgent need for pedestrian tracking and counting methods that are more efficient, accurate, and reliable. However, the existing trackers and counters rarely have the three characteristics of efficiency, accuracy and reliability simultaneously. Therefore, we propose a framework named FR-DeepSORT for tracking and counting pedestrians based on DeepSORT. FR-DeepSORT first selects the YOLOv5 network as the object detector. Then the Re-ID information is combined with IoU to construct a cost matrix to improve the tracker by introducing FastReID. Finally, FR-DeepSORT introduces vector cross product and combines the tracking results to monitor the pedestrian crossing dynamics. The experimental results on the MOT tracking benchmark datasets show that the accuracy of our tracker is 89.38%, and the IDF1 value is 82.45%, which are competitive and more reliable to existing tracking methods. The counter error rate is also superior in the real-time dynamic statistical accuracy of the crowd.

Keywords: Multi-object tracking · YOLOv5 · Fast re-identification · Intersection over union · FR-DeepSORT · Pedestrian counting

1 Introduction

As the global population increases, crowd surveillance in public places has become a hot topic. Due to the great interest in crowd-gathering events such as carnivals, sports [10], concerts and festivals [7], the increase in population has led to an increase in large-scale events. Crowded entrance and exit areas pose challenges for organizers to ensure safety and business health, and appropriate safety measures and crowd management are becoming increasingly important.

As important techniques in the field of computer vision, crowd analysis and monitoring have been widely used to estimate crowd density and track human activities in crowded areas [12]. They are still very challenging research directions

F. Liu et al. (Eds.): PRICAI 2023, LNAI 14327, pp. 54–66, 2024.
https://doi.org/10.1007/978-981-99-7025-4_5

due to the influence of occlusion [2], appearance and background/foreground object detection of different targets [13], crowded scenes, fast motion and other issues, attracting attentions of many researchers [1]. Crowd surveillance usually includes two parts, namely, pedestrian tracking and pedestrian counting [12], both of which have been studied to some extent.

In terms of multi-object tracking (MOT), tracking by detection is currently the most effective paradigm [17]. Bewley et. al [3] use Kalman filter to predict and update targets, and use Hungarian algorithms to match prediction parameters and detect frames with an overall framework, which can achieve accurate tracking without occlusions, but the tracking accuracy is poor with occlusions [4]. The accuracy of tracking in simple occlusion scenarios (measured by MOT accuracy, MOTA) is improved by using a single-target visual tracker in cases where no object detection is available [3], but the ID switch problem still exists. In order to improve the performance of the multi-object tracking algorithms with occlusions, the re-identification (Re-ID) feature is introduced to solve the ID switch problem of SORT [16]. However, it is noted that this feature may reduce the accuracy of tracking. In this regard, we improve the DeepSORT framework to solve the occlusion problem by combining the ReID information with IoU on the basis of [16], which is able to find a balance between the trackers' detection capabilities measured by MOTA and the trackers' abilities to maintain the correct identity over time measured by IDF1.

In terms of counting, Bewley et. al [9] propose an algorithm based on Gaussian process regression to improve the accuracy of pedestrian counting, but it is not suitable for the situation of a large number of pedestrians because of its large calculation amount and low efficiency [14]. The use of the frame difference method for target counting can speed up the calculation process, but the harsher environmental demands lead to that it cannot meet the requirements of pedestrian detection in public areas. Choosing too low thresholds cannot handle the background while too high ones will appear to be unable to identify pedestrians normally [15]. In [11], a counting method based on tracking using Kalman filter is proposed, which combines the detection results for head counting. Although it can improve real-time efficiency while ensuring counting accuracy, it is more dependent on the performance of the tracker because it only uses Kalman filter in the tracking part and is easy to lose the target when the moving target is blocked for a long time. In this regard, we introduce the vector cross product method for target counting based on the improved DeepSORT.

Our Contributions. We propose a modified DeepSORT-based pedestrian tracking and counting framework named FR-DeepSORT, which is competitive for pedestrian tracking on the MOT tracking benchmark datasets and has good performance in real-time dynamic statistical accuracy, and the main contributions of our work can be summarized as follows:

(1) We use YOLOv5 instead of the Faster R-CNN network in DeepSORT to perform detection resulting in a higher tracking rate. In the correlation part, the cost matrix is constructed by combining the FastReID information with IoU,

which not only improves the accuracy of the overall tracker, but also makes the detection and trajectory obtain a stable correlation, thereby reducing the number of ID switches.

(2) Based on the tracking results, we introduce the vector cross product method for target cross-line monitoring, which counts pedestrian flow faster and more accurately.

(3) Experiments on the MOT benchmark datasets verify that our proposed FR-DeepSORT framework is with high MOT and counting accuracy and a low number of ID switches.

2   FR-DeepSort for Pedestrian Tracking and Counting

We propose a method that exploits the advantages of FastReID and IoU to improve DeepSORT, and implement a framework for pedestrian tracking and cross-line counting on this basis. In this section, we first introduce the details of our proposed FR-DeepSORT framework, and then elaborate the pedestrian tracking and counting modules respectively.

2.1   The FR-DeepSORT Framework

There are four modules in DeepSORT for completing the target tracking task [16], namely, object detection, tracklet prediction, data association and trajectory generation. For the object detection module, DeepSORT adopts Faster R-CNN detector while for tracklet prediction, the Kalman filter is adopted to build a cost matrix based on Re-ID feature information. Then the Hungarian algorithm is used to match the detected frames and the predicted boxes. At last, the short tracklets are connected to form a trajectory.

However, in crowded scenarios, DeepSORT cannot work well for its inherent deficiencies. Since DeepSORT uses Faster R-CNN to detect targets in each frame which is a two-step object detection process, it is necessary to use area extraction technique to extract the area where the target is located, and then detect the target for a specific area. These cumbersome steps lead to slow detection, which further leads to a long time of the whole tracking process. In addition, the cost matrix of DeepSORT in the cascaded matching process only considers the Re-ID information, which is apt to reduce the accuracy of the final tracking results. Therefore our specific improvements to DeepSORT mainly include two aspects: a) YOLOv5 is used to replace the Faster R-CNN detector to improve the detection rate; b) FastReID was introduced and an approach combining the Re-lD and loU information is adopted to reduce the tracking error caused by occlusions and simplify the process. Figure 1 illustrates the FR-DeepSORT framework, where the modules shaded in dark cyan color depict the ones of DeepSORT. By these modules, matched and confirmed tracklets compose of trajectories. Our proposed modules for our FR-DeepSORT framework as shown in Fig. 1 are in dark yellow color which improve accuracy for tracking and reliability for counting of DeepSORT.

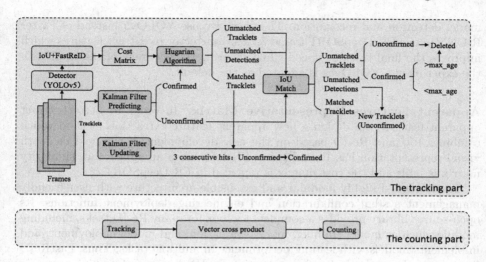

Fig. 1. The FR-DeepSORT framework.

2.2 Pedestrian Tracking

In the tracking part of FR-DeepSORT, we first use YOLOv5 to detect pedestrians, and then predict the possible positions of pedestrians in the next adjacent frames through Kalman filtering. Next, we introduce FastReID to obtain the Re-ID information and combine IoU and Re-ID to construct a pedestrian target cost matrix and adopt the Hungarian algorithm to associate the detected frames with the predicted boxes, and finally obtain the complete trajectory of different targets.

The Object Detection Network. False or missed detection of the object detection network will cause problems such as frequent switching of target ID or disconnection of the target trajectory, and its rate is also closely related to the speed of the entire tracking process. Thus, a target detection network needs to take into account both accuracy and speed which have a crucial impact on the overall performance of multi-target trackers. As the mainstream one-stage structure object detection network of deep learning, YOLO series detector [5] is a regression method based on deep learning differentiating from R-CNN, Fast-RCNN and other deep learning-based classification methods. Compared with the RNN series, the YOLO series network can see the information of the entire image in the whole process, and it can make good use of the context information when detecting targets. It is not easy to predict the wrong object information on the background, and the recognition and position are combined into one, which has the advantages of simple structure and fast detection speed. Among them, YOLOv5 is at present the most prominent one where most of the network components are optional resulting in reducing the computational cost and speeding up the inference process while guaranteeing the accuracy of model detection and recognition. Therefore, we use YOLOv5 instead of Faster R-CNN in our FR-DeepSORT framework as a detector to extract features which improves the final tracking speed while ensuring the accuracy of the results. In the experiments, YOLOv5s is adopted as the default.

Apparent Features Representative Matrix. In order to better extract apparent features, we design a new apparent feature extraction method which combines IoU and Re-ID based on the new development in the field of depth visual representation FastReID library, FR-IoU. Then an appearance similarity matrix is built and the cost matrix is replaced in FR-DeepSORT.

FastReID is a highly modular and extensible architecture with user-friendly management system configuration and engineering deployment functions. Its open-source library provides a complete toolbox for many Re-ID tasks, including modules such as model training, model evaluation, and model deployment, and implements models with leading performance in multiple tasks. Thus, FastReID is a commonly used solution for computing Re-IDs because of its high accuracy and efficiency in various pedestrian re-identification dataset tests. IoU is an important indicator in object detection, which generally refers to the ratio of the intersection over the union of the prediction and the detection boxes. IoU is adopted to measure the degree of overlap between the prediction box and the detection box, and is a standard for measuring the accuracy of detecting the corresponding object in the specified dataset. Let the intersection of the prediction bounding box and the detection bounding box be $Intersection$, and the union be $Union$, and its calculation formula is:

$$\text{IoU} = \frac{bbox_{prediction} \cap bbox_{detection}}{bbox_{prediction} \cup bbox_{detection}} = \frac{Intersection}{Union} \tag{1}$$

Combined with the above information, we construct a cost matrix. First, we define the average appearance state vector of the ith tracklet in the kth frame, expressed as e_i^k:

$$e_i^k = \frac{e_i^{k-1} + f_i^k}{k} \tag{2}$$

where f_i^k is the appearance vector of the currently matched detection target computed by FastReID. Because appearance features are susceptible to crowds, occlusions, and obscure objects, we only consider high-confidence detection to maintain correct feature vectors. In order to match the average trajectory appearance state e_i^k with the new detection appearance embedding vector f_i^k, we use cosine similarity to measure, and then construct the cost matrix.

Assuming that the minimum value of each element in the matrix can be used as the final value of the cost matrix C, the FR-IoU calculation process is expressed as:

$$\widehat{d}_{i,j}^{\cos} = \begin{cases} 0.5 \cdot d_{i,j}^{\cos}, \left(d_{i,j}^{\cos} < \theta_{\text{reid}}\right) \wedge \left(d_{i,j}^{\text{iou}} < \theta_{\text{iou}}\right) \\ 1, \text{ otherwise} \end{cases} \tag{3}$$

$$C_{i,j} = \min \left\{ d_{i,j}^{iou} , \widehat{d_{i,j}^{cos}} \right\} \tag{4}$$

where $C_{i,j}$ is the final value of the (i,j)-bit element of the cost matrix C, $d_{i,j}^{iou}$ is the IoU difference between the prediction bounding box of the ith tracklet and the jth detection bounding box, $d_{i,j}^{cos}$ is the cosine distance between the average appearance descriptor e_i^k of the ith tracklet and the appearance descriptor of the new detection j, and $\widehat{d_{i,j}^{cos}}$ is the obtained new appearance cost. θ_{iou} is the rejection threshold of IoU and is set to 0.5 which is used to reject the trajectory-detection pair with weak probability, and θ_{reid} is the Re-ID threshold, which is used to separate the positive correlation of the detection embedding vector from the trajectory appearance state and is set to 0.25. To find a balance between the IoU and Re-ID values, we set the weight of $d_{i,j}^{cos}$ to 0.5.

2.3 Pedestrian Counting

In the counting part, we use the counting line method to determine whether the line segment formed by the center point of the adjacent detection boxes intersects with the preset counting line of pedestrians in each independent tracking trajectory for two consecutive frames and complete the statistics of the number of pedestrians. First, the preset line is drawn in the middle of the video, and then the vector cross product method is further combined on the basis of Sect. 2.2 to decide whether the target crosses the line and the direction of the target crossing the line according to the intersection of the target center point and the preset lines.

To achieve the real-time dynamic judgment of pedestrians up and down, it is necessary to preprocess the position data of pedestrians obtained in Sect. 2.2 at different times to facilitate the next judgment operation. Taking target A for an example, the center points of the trajectory frame in frames $frame_t$ and $frame_{t+1}$ captured of A at moments t and $t+1$ are calculated separately, and the center coordinates of A in the two frames are obtained. Let the position value of target A at time t be expressed as (x, y, w, h), then m, n in the center point $midpoint(m, n)$ of A can be expressed as:

$$m = x + w/2 \tag{5}$$

$$n = y + h/2 \tag{6}$$

In the counting process, it is necessary to determine whether the pedestrian trajectory crosses the line, that is, to determine whether the center point connection line of the trajectory boxes of two consecutive frames intersects with the preset counting line, and we introduce vector cross product to judge.

$$\boldsymbol{a} \times \boldsymbol{b} = x_1 * y_2 - y_1 * x_2 \tag{7}$$

For two vectors $\boldsymbol{a} = (x_1, y_1)$ and $\boldsymbol{b} = (x_2, y_2)$, if $\boldsymbol{a} \times \boldsymbol{b} < 0$, it means that $\boldsymbol{b}$ is clockwise in $\boldsymbol{a}$ direction; if $\boldsymbol{a} \times \boldsymbol{b} > 0$, it means that $\boldsymbol{b}$ is counterclockwise in $\boldsymbol{a}$; if $\boldsymbol{a} \times \boldsymbol{b} = 0$, it means that $\boldsymbol{b}$ is parallel or collinear with $\boldsymbol{a}$.

The idea can be further generalized to two line segments AB and CD. Then the sufficient conditions for judging their intersection are: point A and point B are on both sides of the line segment CD, and points C and D are also on both sides of the line segment AB. When point C and point D are on both sides of the line segment AB, and points A and B are also on both sides of the line segment CD, it can be concluded that the two line segments intersect, that is, satisfying

$$\begin{cases} (\overrightarrow{AC} \times \overrightarrow{AB})(\overrightarrow{AD} \times \overrightarrow{AB}) < 0 \\ (\overrightarrow{CB} \times \overrightarrow{CD})(\overrightarrow{CA} \times \overrightarrow{CD}) < 0 \end{cases} \tag{8}$$

By Eqs. 5,6,7 and 8, it is easy to decide whether the center point connection line intersects with the preset center count line in the frames.

3   Experiments

To verify the effectiveness of the tracking and counting methods, we conduct experiments to evaluate our proposed method and the other ones on the MOTS and MOTSynth datasets. MOTS focuses on pedestrians in crowded scenes and is very challenging because it contains many occlusion situations. However, since there are no ground truth (gt) files, it is necessary to manually annotate the original video sequence in MOTS by the DarkLabel tool [8]. MOTSynth is a large, highly diverse synthetic dataset which can replace real datasets in tasks such as pedestrian detection, re-identification, segmentation and tracking, and can better simulate crowded and rapid pedestrian movement in real scenes [6]. To comprehensively evaluate the pedestrian tracking method, we use multi-metrics to evaluate various aspects of trackers, including the MOTA metric and IDF1 score. Among them, MOTA focuses on multi-target tracking accuracy, while IDF1 score focuses on association performance which can demonstrate how reliable the tracker is. To evaluate our pedestrian counting method, we used three metrics: mean absolute error (MAE), mean squared error (MSE), and mean absolute percentage error (MAPE).

3.1   Analysis of Pedestrian Tracking Results

To test the performance of the tracking methods, we conducted comparative experiments using SORT, DeepSORT, MOTS and FR-DeepSORT etc. as trackers to track pedestrians in each frame of the video. The accuracy is measured by comparing the results of these methods with those labeled by DarkLabel, and the experimental results on the test set of MOTS are shown in Table 1.

From Table 1, we can see that in the test sets of MOTS, FR-DeepSORT's tracking accuracy, i.e., MOTA value, is 89.38%, which is 9.8% higher than DeepSORT, 4.98% higher than ReMOTSv2, and 5.68% higher than EMNT. In addition, the ratio of correctly identified detections over the average number of ground-truth and computed detections. The total number of IDs for identity ID switches is 213, which has a significant decrease compared to DeepSORT and

Table 1. Experimental results of various algorithms on the test sets of MOTS.

	Year	MOTA↑	IDF1↑	IDs↓
DeepSORT	2017	79.58%	57.75%	364
ReMOTS	2020	84.40%	75.00%	231
ReMOTSv2	2022	84.40%	75.80%	229
EMNT	2022	83.70%	77.00%	261
FR-DeepSORT	2023	**89.38%**	**82.45%**	**213**

(a) DeepSORT

(b) FR-DeepSORT

Fig. 2. Comparison of experimental results on MOTS20-09.

others. It can be seen that the accuracy of the tracking with FastReID improved and the number of ID switches decreased.

The results of DeepSORT and our FR-DeepSORT framework for tracking on MOT-09 are shown in Fig. 2a and Fig. 2b, respectively. In Fig. 2a, pedestrian No. 4 was confirmed in frame 31 by DeepSORT but was misidentified as No. 6 in frame 57, while pedestrian No. 16 was also confirmed in frame 153 but was wrongly identified as No. 6 in frame 180. We can see that tracking by DeepSORT has serious identity ID switch problem. In Fig. 2b, it can be found that pedestrians No. 4 and No. 21 were confirmed by FR-DeepSORT in frame 149 and pedestrian No. 4 was blocked in frame 175. In frame 189, pedestrian No. 4 reappeared while pedestrian No. 21 was occluded. But both pedestrians reappeared in frame 192, and there was no ID switch problem for tracking by our FR-DeepSORT framework.

For the MOTSynth dataset, the results of DeepSORT and FR-DeepSORT are shown in Fig. 3a and Fig. 3b, respectively. In Fig. 3a, it can be found that pedestrians 28 and 6 were confirmed by DeepSORT in the first frame, but there were occlusions in the second frame, No. 28 was blocked by pedestrian No. 6, and the original pedestrian No. 28 reappeared in the third frame, but DeepSORT did not accurately identify pedestrian ID No. 28. Instead, the trajectory of pedestrian No. 28 in this frame is connected to pedestrian No. 6. That is, the trajectory

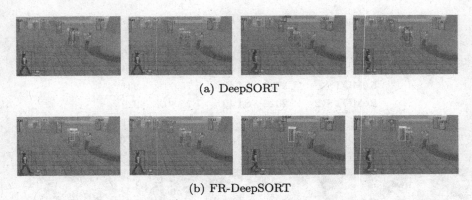

(a) DeepSORT

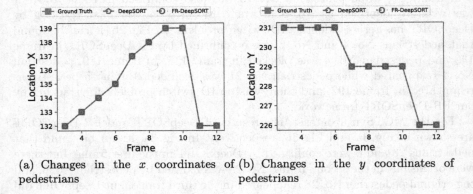

(b) FR-DeepSORT

Fig. 3. Comparison of experimental results on MOTSynth-515.

of pedestrian No. 28 is incorrectly marked as No. 6, and the original pedestrian trajectory of No. 6 is incorrectly marked as No. 28 in the fourth frame. We can see that there was a serious problem of mis-identification. In Fig. 3b, it can be found that pedestrians No. 29 and No. 6 were confirmed by FR-DeepSORT at the first frame, and occluded in the last 2 frames. Pedestrian No. 29 was occluded by pedestrian No. 6, and pedestrian No. 29 reappeared at the last frame. We also find that the pedestrians are accurately tracked by FR-DeepSORT, and there is no ID switch problem.

Next, experiments for tracking of FR-DeepSORT and DeepSORT on the MOTS dataset under different circumstances were conducted and the coordinates of pedestrians with the same identity in the ground truth files in random continuous frames were recorded. The tracking results representing the coordinates of the specified pedestrians in these continuous frames were reported compared to the coordinates in the gt files.

(a) Changes in the x coordinates of pedestrians

(b) Changes in the y coordinates of pedestrians

Fig. 4. The tracking effects in pedestrian coordinates of the two methods compared to the ground truth without occlusions.

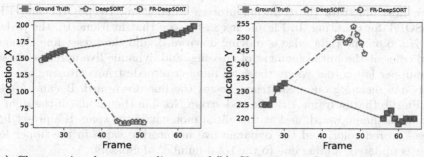

(a) Changes in the x coordinates of pedestrians

(b) Changes in the y coordinates of pedestrians

Fig. 5. The tracking effects in pedestrian coordinates of the two methods compared to the ground truth with occlusions.

Figure 4 and Fig. 5 show the effect in the pedestrian coordinates of Deep-SORT and FR-DeepSORT compared to the ground truth without/with occlusions respectively. In Fig. 4, the pedestrian coordinates of DeepSORT, FR-DeepSORT and the ground truth are almost the same. That is, DeepSORT and FR-DeepSORT are both with good performance when there are no occlusions. But in Fig. 5, the coordinates of DeepSORT and FR-DeepSORT differentiate a lot. When occlusions occur, in frames 52 to 65, the tracking results of Deep-SORT are missing and there is a large deviation from the ground truth in 30–52 frames, which may be caused by false detection or ID switch problem. For FR-DeepSORT, the results are the same with the ground truth which proves that FR-DeepSORT can better handle the target tracking problem with occlusions. The reason is that FR-DeepSORT can avoid false detection and solve the ID switch problem effectively.

3.2 Analysis of Pedestrian Counting Results

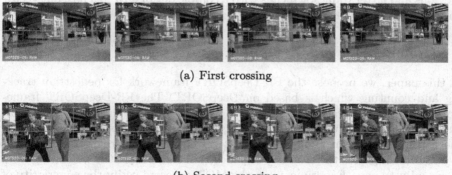

(a) First crossing

(b) Second crossing

Fig. 6. The illustration of FR-DeepSORT for counting on MOTS20-09.

We first illustrate the counting process when using DeepSORT and FR-DeepSORT for counting. In Fig. 6a, it can be seen that in frame 16, the pedestrian No. 6 on the right edge is moving downward, and the preset line changes to red color at the initial moment of crossing, and dynamic live updates are set in the upper left corner where the total number of pedestrians crossing the line is plus one meaning one pedestrian crosses the line downward. It can be seen from Fig. 6b that in frame 183, the pedestrian No. 5 in the middle of the right is crossing the line upward, and at the initial moment of the span, the preset line changes to red color, and the dynamic live monitoring value in the upper left corner is updated, adding one to the total number of crossers.

Table 2. Counting results of the two trackers on different datasets.

	MOTS-02			MOTS-06		
	MAE↑	MSE↓	MAPE↓	MAE↓	MSE↓	MAPE↓
DeepSORT	**0.76%**	1.12%	7.29%	1.07%	2.48%	19.67%
FR-DeepSORT	0.78%	**1.04%**	**7.09%**	**0.12%**	**0.14%**	**1.49%**
	MOTS-07			MOTS-09		
	MAE↑	MSE↓	MAPE↓	MAE↓	MSE↓	MAPE↓
DeepSORT	**0.87%**	1.57%	4.58%	37.28%	49.14%	5.16%
FR-DeepSORT	0.88%	**0.90%**	**4.51%**	**4.21%**	**4.21%**	**0.61%**

Table 2 shows the results of DeepSORT and FR-DeepSORT trackers, respectively, measured by MAE, MSE and MAPE of the counting results and their true values. We can see that our proposed FR-DeepSORT framework outperforms DeepSORT. In addition, since most of the previous pedestrian counting methods use Gaussian regression density map where the Gaussian kernel function runs slowly with an overall computational complexity $O(n^2) * O(nd)$. As a contrast, our vector fork multiplication method only needs to perform the computation for the line connecting the midline with the target centroid in the previous and latter frames, which is with a complexity of $O(n^2)$. Thus, our vector fork multiplication method is much faster than the density map method.

4   Conclusion

In this paper, we propose the FR-DeepSORT framework for pedestrian tracking and counting which is based on DeepSORT. The FR-DeepSORT framework improves the tracking and counting efficiency by replacing the detector, and also makes full use of the advantages of IoU and FastReID to improve the feature expression ability of the tracker. In addition, the counter of FR-DeepSORT improves the accuracy of pedestrian traffic statistics benefiting from above adjustments. Experiments on the MOT datasets verify the superiority of our method which can be applied to a variety of scenarios.

References

1. Akhter, F., Khadivizand, S., Siddiquei, H.R., Alahi, M.E.E., Mukhopadhyay, S.: Iot enabled intelligent sensor node for smart city: pedestrian counting and ambient monitoring. Sensors **19**(15), 3374 (2019)
2. Arif, A., Jalal, A.: Automated body parts estimation and detection using salient maps and gaussian matrix model. In: 2021 International Bhurban Conference on Applied Sciences and Technologies (IBCAST), pp. 667–672 (2021)
3. Bewley, A., Ge, Z., Ott, L., Ramos, F., Upcroft, B.: Simple online and realtime tracking. CoRR abs/1602.00763 (2016), arxiv.org/abs/1602.00763
4. Bochinski, E., Senst, T., Sikora, T.: Extending iou based multi-object tracking by visual information. In: 2018 15th IEEE International Conference on Advanced Video and Signal Based Surveillance (AVSS), pp. 1–6 (2018)
5. Diwan, T., Anirudh, G., Tembhurne, J.V.: Object detection using YOLO: challenges, architectural successors, datasets and applications. Multim. Tools Appl. **82**(6), 9243–9275 (2023)
6. Fabbri, M., et al.: Motsynth: How can synthetic data help pedestrian detection and tracking? In: 2021 IEEE/CVF International Conference on Computer Vision (ICCV), pp. 10829–10839 (2021)
7. Jalal, A., Kim, Y., Kim, Y.J., Kamal, S., Kim, D.: Robust human activity recognition from depth video using spatiotemporal multi-fused features. Pattern Recognit. **61**, 295–308 (2017)
8. Kletz, S., Leibetseder, A., Schoeffmann, K.: A comparative study of video annotation tools for scene understanding: Yet (not) another annotation tool. In: MMSys '19, pp. 133–144. Association for Computing Machinery, New York, NY, USA (2019)
9. Li, W., et al.: People counting based on improved gauss process regression. In: 2017 International Conference on Security, Pattern Analysis, and Cybernetics (SPAC), pp. 603–608 (2017)
10. Mahmood, M., Jalal, A., Sidduqi, M.A.: Robust spatio-temporal features for human interaction recognition via artificial neural network. In: 2018 International Conference on Frontiers of Information Technology (FIT), pp. 218–223 (2018)
11. Masoud, O., Papanikolopoulos, N.: A novel method for tracking and counting pedestrians in real-time using a single camera. IEEE Trans. Veh. Technol. **50**(5), 1267–1278 (2001)
12. Pervaiz, M., Ghadi, Y.Y., Gochoo, M., Jalal, A., Kamal, S., Kim, D.S.: A smart surveillance system for people counting and tracking using particle flow and modified som. Sustainability **13**(10), 5367 (2021)
13. Rafique, A.A., Jalal, A., Ahmed, A.: Scene understanding and recognition: Statistical segmented model using geometrical features and gaussian naïve bayes. In: 2019 International Conference on Applied and Engineering Mathematics (ICAEM), pp. 225–230 (2019)
14. Redmon, J., Divvala, S.K., Girshick, R.B., Farhadi, A.: You only look once: Unified, real-time object detection. CoRR abs/1506.02640 (2015), arxiv.org/abs/1506.02640
15. Shahzad, A.R., Jalal, A.: A smart surveillance system for pedestrian tracking and counting using template matching. In: 2021 International Conference on Robotics and Automation in Industry (ICRAI), pp. 1–6 (2021)

16. Wojke, N., Bewley, A., Paulus, D.: Simple online and realtime tracking with a deep association metric. In: 2017 IEEE International Conference on Image Processing (ICIP), pp. 3645–3649 (2017)
17. Zhang, Y., et al.: Bytetrack: Multi-object tracking by associating every detection box. In: Computer Vision-ECCV 2022, pp. 1–21. Springer (2022). https://doi.org/10.1007/978-3-031-20047-2_1

Bootstrap Diffusion Model Curve Estimation for High Resolution Low-Light Image Enhancement

Jiancheng Huang[1,2], Yifan Liu[1], and Shifeng Chen[1,2(✉)]

[1] ShenZhen Key Lab of Computer Vision and Pattern Recognition, Shenzhen
Institute of Advanced Technology, Chinese Academy of Sciences, Shenzhen, China
{jc.huang,yf.liu2,shifeng.chen}@siat.ac.cn
[2] University of Chinese Academy of Sciences, Beijing, China

Abstract. Learning-based methods have attracted a lot of research attention and led to significant improvements in low-light image enhancement. However, most of them still suffer from two main problems: expensive computational cost in high resolution images and unsatisfactory performance in simultaneous enhancement and denoising. To address these problems, we propose BDCE, a bootstrap diffusion model that exploits the learning of the distribution of the curve parameters instead of the normal-light image itself. Specifically, we adopt the curve estimation method to handle the high-resolution images, where the curve parameters are estimated by our bootstrap diffusion model. In addition, a denoise module is applied in each iteration of curve adjustment to denoise the intermediate enhanced result of each iteration. We evaluate BDCE on commonly used benchmark datasets, and extensive experiments show that it achieves state-of-the-art qualitative and quantitative performance.

Keywords: Low-light image enhancement · Diffusion model · High resolution image · Image processing

1 Introduction

Low-light image enhancement (LLIE) is a very important and meaningful task in computer vision. Images captured in environments with insufficient lighting often exhibit numerous issues, including diminished contrast, dark colors, low visibility, etc. Therefore, LLIE is often used to process these poor quality images, and the processed images can also be better suited for other downstream tasks.

J. Huang and Y. Liu—Contributed equally to this work.
This work is supported by Key-Area Research and Development Program of Guangdong Province (2019B010155003), the Joint Lab of CAS-HK, and Shenzhen Science and Technology Innovation Commission (JCYJ20200109114835623, JSGG20220831105002004).

F. Liu et al. (Eds.): PRICAI 2023, LNAI 14327, pp. 67–80, 2024.
https://doi.org/10.1007/978-981-99-7025-4_6

| Input | naive | w/o denoise | w/o diff | w/o self | BDCE |

Fig. 1. Visual results of ablation study. The naive DCE-based method can't denoise and obtain satisfactory result. w/o means without. Detail settings are provided in Sect. 4.4 and Table 3

The traditional LLIE method is mainly implemented based on histogram equalization [2,22] and Retinex model [30,42,51]. However, these methods still do not do a good job of detail and accurate color restoration. In the past few years, with the continuous development of deep learning, there are more and more LLIE methods based on deep learning [15,18,23,27,32,33,37,50,60–64,71,72]. Compared with traditional methods, these methods achieve better visual effects and are more robust.

Despite the progress of existing methods, two major problems remain: 1) The first problem is that LLIE on high resolution images is computationally too expensive. 2) The second problem is that simultaneous enhancement and denoising is unsatisfactory. Solving both problems is extremely challenging.

For the first problem, many LLIE methods [18,23,27,32,33,37,50,60–64,71] are not specifically designed for high resolution images, and these methods need to feed high resolution images into their networks, which is computationally expensive. The first problem can be solved using DCE-based methods [15], which achieve a small computational cost by downsampling the input image to a lower resolution, then predicting the Light-Enhancement curves (LE-curves) at the low resolution. However, DCE-based methods [15,72] tend to use lightweight networks, resulting in poor curve estimation, and their pixel-wise adjustment causes them to fail to denoise, so they are less effective on real data as shown in Fig. 1 (naive result).

Hence, while the first problem can be addressed using the existing DCE-based methods, the second problem remains unresolved. Some existing diffusion models [8–10,55] for image restoration also fail to solve these two problems, because they work on RGB pixel space, which makes them computationally expensive on high resolution images.

To deal with these two key problems, we proposes BDCE, an effective bootstrap diffusion model based high-resolution low-light enhancement and denoising method. The main contributions are summarized as follows:

– In BDCE, a bootstrap diffusion model is presented for model the distribution of optimal curve parameters, which can then be used for high resolution images.
– We set a denoising module into each iteration of curve adjustment for enhancement and denoising simultaneously.
– Extensive experiments on benchmark datasets demonstrate the superiority of BDCE over previous state-of-the-art methods both quantitatively and qualitatively.

2 Related Work

2.1 Learning-Based Methods in LLIE

Recently, there has been a notable surge in the development of deep learning solutions for addressing the LLIE problem [32,33,50,53,57,60,62,67–69,72]. Wei *et al.* [57] introduce a Retinex-based method that achieves superior enhancement performance in most cases while maintaining physical interpretability. DCC-Net [71] employs a collaborative strategy based on a strategy of partition and resolve to preserve information of color and retain a natural appearance. Zhang *et al.* [69] introduce KinD, which consists of three specialized subnetworks for layer decomposition and reflectance restoration, and illumination adjustment. LLNet [33] utilizes a multi-phase encoder for reducing sparse noise to enhance and denoise images captured under low-light conditions. Wang *et al.* [53] present LLFormer, a computationally efficient approach that leverages blocks employing multi-head self-attention along different axes and cross-layer attention fusion for computational reduction. Wu *et al.* [60] propose a novel approach where the Retinex decomposition problem is reformulated as a learnable network that incorporates implicit prior regularization. Liu *et al.* [32] employ a cooperative prior architecture search strategy along with a principled optimization unrolling technique. Liang *et al.* [31] propose a unique self-supervised approach that optimizes a separate untrained network specifically for each test image. SCI [37] utilizes a self-supervised approach to autonomously adjust the reflection component. EnGAN [23] takes an unsupervised learning approach to tackle the challenges of overfitting and limited generalization. Zero-DCE [15] performs pixel-level adjustments by leveraging a depth curve estimation network and a collection of non-reference loss functions. This combination allows for precise adjustments and improvements in image quality. Jin *et al.* [24] propose a specialized network designed to suppress light effects and enhance illumination in darker regions. However, these methods are still challenging to solve the two problems mentioned in Sect. 1.

2.2 Diffusion Models

Within the domain of computer vision, diffusion models have garnered significant attention as a category of generative models. These models are trained to reverse the sequential corruption process of data by utilizing Gaussian random noise. Two main types of diffusion models have emerged: score-matching based [21,49] models and diffusion-based models [44]. Notably, denoising diffusion probabilistic models [19,40] and score networks [11,38,46–48] conditioned on noise have shown great promise in generating high-quality images. In recent times, there has been a notable increase of interest in exploring the advantages of conditional forward processes in diffusion-based models. This exploration has demonstrated promising potential across diverse computer vision applications, including image synthesis [13,20,26,73], deblurring [59], and image-to-image translation [7,43,54]. Moreover, diffusion models have found applications in image restoration. For example, Ozan *et al.* [41] proposed a patch-based diffusion model for restoring images captured under challenging weather conditions. While many existing methods [8–10,55] in image restoration focus on solving inverse problems and require prior knowledge of the degradation models, several concurrent works [34,58] have specifically addressed blind restoration problems such as deraining, deblurring, denoising, and face restoration. Kawar *et al.* introduced DDRM [25] as a solution for linear inverse image restoration problems, but its applicability is limited to linear degradation. However, these diffusion based methods can't handle the first problems (high resolution image) mentioned in Sect. 1.

3 Methodology

In this section, we describe the details of BDCE given a low-light image $\mathbf{I}_l$. Firstly, we describe the curve estimation for high resolution image in Sect. 3.1. Then, we design the bootstrap diffusion model for curve estimation in Sect. 3.2. Finally, we describe the denoising module for real low-light image in Sect. 3.3.

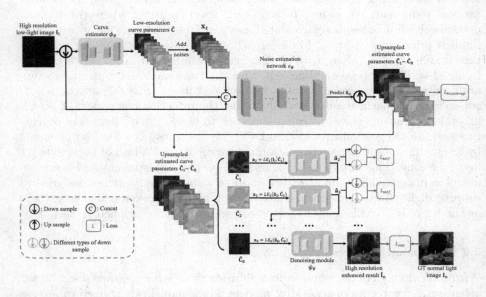

Fig. 2. The training pipeline of our BDCE. We first downsample the high resolution low-light image and use curve estimator to predict the low-resolution curve parameters $\bar{\mathbf{C}}$. Then diffusion model is applied to learn a more accurate distribution of $\bar{\mathbf{C}}$. The estimated $\hat{\mathbf{C}}$ is upsampled and we adopt our denoise module in each iteration of curve adjustments to get a denoised final result.

3.1 Curve Estimation for High Resolution Image

Deep Curve Estimation Network (DCE-Net) [15] is one of the most effective methods for enhancing low-light images since their adaptability to high resolution images. In DCE-Net [15], a network is designed to predict a set of

optimal Light-Enhancement curves (LE-curves) that match well with the input
low-light image. This method maps all pixels of the input image by progressively applying curves to achieve the ultimate enhanced image. DCE-Net uses
quadratic curves $LE(\mathbf{I}_l, \mathbf{C}) = \mathbf{I}_l + \mathbf{C}\,\mathbf{I}_l(1 - \mathbf{I}_l)$ for mapping, where $\mathbf{I}_l \in \mathbb{R}^{3 \times H \times W}$,
$\mathbf{C} \in [-1, 1]^{3 \times H \times W}$ and $LE(\mathbf{I}_l, \mathbf{C}) \in \mathbb{R}^{3 \times H \times W}$ denote the input image, the curve
parameters and the adjusted image, respectively. The curve parameters $\mathbf{C}$ are
per-pixel predicted by a CNN in DCE-Net.

The above procedure $LE(\mathbf{I}_l, \mathbf{C})$ represents only one iteration of curve adjustment, in fact 8 curve adjustments are used in DCE-Net and each iteration can
be denoted as

$$\mathbf{a}_{i+1} = LE_i(\mathbf{a}_i, \mathbf{C}_i) = \mathbf{a}_i + \mathbf{C}_i\,\mathbf{a}_i(1 - \mathbf{a}_i), \quad i = 1, ..., 8, \quad \mathbf{a}_1 = \mathbf{I}_l. \tag{1}$$

Then the total adjustment can be denoted by

$$LE(\mathbf{I}_l, \mathbf{C}) = LE_8(\mathbf{a}_8, \mathbf{C}_8), \; \mathbf{a}_8 = LE_7(\mathbf{a}_7, \mathbf{C}_7), \; ..., \; \mathbf{a}_2 = LE_1(\mathbf{a}_1, \mathbf{C}_1). \tag{2}$$

$\mathbf{C}_i \in [-1, 1]^{3 \times H \times W}$ and $\mathbf{C} = [\mathbf{C}_1, ..., \mathbf{C}_8] \in [-1, 1]^{24 \times H \times W}$. We express the
above adjustment by $\mathbf{C} = \phi_\theta(\mathbf{I}_l)$ and $\mathbf{I}_e = LE(\mathbf{I}_l, \mathbf{C})$, where ϕ_θ is a CNN network.

Based on the localised nature of the curve adjustment, DCE-Net can efficiently cope with high resolution input images. For a high-resolution input image
$\mathbf{I}_l$, DCE-Net first resizes to get a fixed low resolution image $\bar{\mathbf{I}}_l \in \mathbb{R}^{3 \times \bar{H} \times \bar{W}}$ where
$\bar{H}$ and $\bar{W}$ are always set to 256, then uses the curve estimation described above
$\bar{\mathbf{C}} = \phi_\theta(\bar{\mathbf{I}}_l)$ to get a curve $\bar{\mathbf{C}} \in [-1, 1]^{24 \times \bar{H} \times \bar{W}}$ at the low resolution, then upsamples that curve $\bar{\mathbf{C}}$ to the original high resolution $\mathbf{C} \in [-1, 1]^{24 \times H \times W}$, and per-
forms curve adjustment at high resolution. For any high resolution image, the
computational cost of network is the same.

3.2   Bootstrap Diffusion Model for Better Curve Estimation

In order to make BDCE adaptable to arbitrary high resolution images, BDCE is
very different from other diffusion model based methods, where other diffusion
model based methods learns the distribution of target images, while our BDCE
learns the distribution of curve parameters $\bar{\mathbf{C}} \in [-1, 1]^{24 \times \bar{H} \times \bar{W}}$. Because the
target image $\mathbf{I}_n$ (the normal-light image in our task) may have a high resolution
such that $\mathbf{I}_n \in \mathbb{R}^{3 \times H \times W}$, the learning burden of $\mathbf{I}_n$ will be much bigger than it
of $\bar{\mathbf{C}}$ if $H \gg \bar{H}$.

The forward process in DDPMs aims to learn the distribution of $\mathbf{x}_0$, i.e.,
$\bar{\mathbf{C}}$ (curve parameters) in our BDCE. However, the values of $\bar{\mathbf{C}}$ are unknown
at the beginning of training. To solve this, first we enter resized $\bar{\mathbf{I}}_l$ into curve
estimator ϕ_θ to get a curve estimation $\bar{\mathbf{C}}$. Then, we denote $\mathbf{x}_0 = \bar{\mathbf{C}}$ as the data
distribution of our diffusion model. Specifically, the forward process of BDCE
can be described as follows:

$$q(\mathbf{x}_t \mid \mathbf{x}_0) = \mathcal{N}(\mathbf{x}_t; \sqrt{\bar{\alpha}_t}\,\mathbf{x}_0, (1 - \bar{\alpha}_t)\,\mathbf{I}). \tag{3}$$

$$\mathbf{x}_t = \sqrt{\bar{\alpha}_t}\,\mathbf{x}_0 + \sqrt{1 - \bar{\alpha}_t}\epsilon_t, \ \ \epsilon_t \sim \mathcal{N}(\mathbf{0}, \mathbf{I}) \tag{4}$$

With the same setting of $\tilde{\mu}_t(\mathbf{x}_t, \mathbf{x}_0)$ in [45], the reverse process from $\mathbf{x}_T$ to $\mathbf{x}_0$ is:

$$q(\mathbf{x}_{t-1} \mid \mathbf{x}_t, \mathbf{x}_0) = \mathcal{N}(\mathbf{x}_{t-1}; \tilde{\boldsymbol{\mu}}_t(\mathbf{x}_t, \mathbf{x}_0), \tilde{\sigma}_t^2 \,\mathbf{I}), \tag{5}$$

where $\mathbf{x}_0$ can be predicted by a noise estimation network $\epsilon_\theta(\mathbf{x}_t, \bar{I}_l, \bar{\mathbf{C}}, t)$:

$$\hat{\mathbf{x}}_0 = \frac{\mathbf{x}_t - \sqrt{1 - \bar{\alpha}_t}\epsilon_\theta(\mathbf{x}_t, \bar{I}_l, \bar{\mathbf{C}}, t)}{\sqrt{\bar{\alpha}_t}}. \tag{6}$$

As shown in Fig. 2, a U-Net similar to that in [66] is used as the noise estimation network ϵ_θ of BDCE. As for the curve estimator ϕ_θ, we adopt a lightweight network following [15]. In each step t of training, the given low-light image I_l and the curve parameters $\bar{\mathbf{C}}$ serve as the conditions in BDCE to model the distribution of $\bar{\mathbf{C}}$. L_{simple} defined in [39] is utilized as the supervision for ϵ_θ.

Note that the curve parameters $\bar{\mathbf{C}}$ estimated by ϕ_θ are not the optimal curve parameters for enhancement. Therefore, we adopt a bootstrap diffusion model for stable training and better optimization for learning the distribution of $\bar{\mathbf{C}}$. To achieve this, the following bootstrap loss is used:

$$\mathcal{L}_{bootstrap} = ||LE(\mathbf{I}_l, \hat{\mathbf{C}}) - \mathbf{I}_n||_2, \ \ \hat{\mathbf{C}} = \text{Upsample}(\hat{\mathbf{x}}_0), \tag{7}$$

where $\hat{\mathbf{C}} \in [-1, 1]^{24 \times H \times W}$ denotes the estimated curve parameters from $\hat{\mathbf{x}}_0$ in Eq. 6 upsampled to the original high resolution.

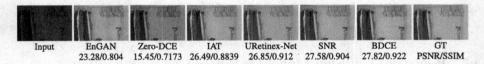

Input	EnGAN	Zero-DCE	IAT	URetinex-Net	SNR	BDCE	GT
	23.28/0.804	15.45/0.7173	26.49/0.8839	26.85/0.912	27.58/0.904	27.82/0.922	PSNR/SSIM

Fig. 3. Visual comparison on LOL-v1. BDCE yields less noise and more natural colors.

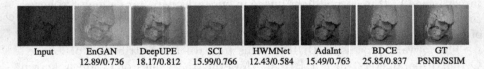

Input	EnGAN	DeepUPE	SCI	HWMNet	AdaInt	BDCE	GT
	12.89/0.736	18.17/0.812	15.99/0.766	12.43/0.584	15.49/0.763	25.85/0.837	PSNR/SSIM

Fig. 4. Visual comparison on MIT-Adobe FiveK. BDCE yields better colors.

3.3 Denoising Module for Real Low-Light Image

Because most of the real low-light images are degraded by real noises, LLIE always includes the demands of real image denoising. However, using only LE-curves is difficult to remove the real noises since curve adjustment is pixel-wise without localised smoothing, so all DCE-based methods suffer from the problem of real noises [15].

To solve this problem, we propose to combine enhancement and denoising in one model by applying a denoising module ψ_θ consisting of servel residual blocks. We implement the denoising during each iteration by refining the intermediate enhanced result $\mathbf{a}_i$ as following, given $\mathbf{a}_1 = \mathbf{I}_l$:

$$
\begin{aligned}
\mathbf{a}_2 &= LE_1(\mathbf{a}_1, \hat{\mathbf{C}}_1), \ \hat{\mathbf{a}}_2 = \psi_\theta(\mathbf{a}_2), \\
\mathbf{a}_3 &= LE_2(\hat{\mathbf{a}}_2, \hat{\mathbf{C}}_2), \ \hat{\mathbf{a}}_3 = \psi_\theta(\mathbf{a}_3), \\
&\ldots \\
\mathbf{a}_9 &= LE_8(\hat{\mathbf{a}}_8, \hat{\mathbf{C}}_8), \ \hat{\mathbf{I}}_n = \psi_\theta(\mathbf{a}_9),
\end{aligned}
\tag{8}
$$

where $\mathbf{a}_i$ denotes the intermediate enhanced result of the i-th iteration. The process described above can be briefly expressed as $\hat{\mathbf{I}}_n = LE_{de}(\mathbf{I}_l, \hat{\mathbf{C}})$. It can be understood as using the denoising module to denoise after each iteration of brightness adjustment before proceeding to the next iteration of brightness adjustment. After 8 iterations of brightness adjustment and denoising, the result is an enhanced output with less noise. To train ψ_θ, a full-supervised loss $\mathcal{L}_{sup}$ and a self-supervised loss $\mathcal{L}_{self}$ are used:

$$
\begin{aligned}
\mathcal{L}_{sup} &= ||\hat{\mathbf{I}}_n - \mathbf{I}_n||_2, \\
\hat{\mathbf{a}}_i^{d1} &= \text{Down}_1(\hat{\mathbf{a}}_i), \ \hat{\mathbf{a}}_i^{d2} = \text{Down}_2(\hat{\mathbf{a}}_i), \\
\mathcal{L}_{self} &= \sum_{i=1,\ldots,8} ||\hat{\mathbf{a}}_i^{d1} - \hat{\mathbf{a}}_i^{d2}||_2,
\end{aligned}
\tag{9}
$$

where Down_1 and Down_2 denote two types of downsampling way (randomly choose from max-pooling, average-pooling, nearest, bilinear, bicubic and lanczos interpolation), because the MSE between two different downsampling results $\hat{\mathbf{a}}_i^{d1}$ and $\hat{\mathbf{a}}_i^{d2}$ should be small for a denoised image.

| Input | Zero-DCE++ | Retinex-Net | RUAS | SCI | SSIENet | BDCE | Reference |

Fig. 5. Visual comparison on LSRW. BDCE yields natural colors with clear details.

Table 1. Results on LOL-v1, LOL-v2, MIT and LSRW. The best and second best are in bold and underlined, respectively.

				LOL-v1				
Method	KinD [69]	Retinex [57]	DRBN [64]	URetinex [60]	IAT [12]	SNR [61]	DCC-Net [71]	BDCE
PSNR ↑	20.87	18.23	19.55	21.32	23.38	<u>24.61</u>	22.72	**25.01**
SSIM ↑	0.800	0.720	0.746	0.834	0.809	<u>0.842</u>	0.810	**0.850**

				LOL-v2-real				
Method	KinD [69]	SID [5]	MIR-Net [67]	A3DLUT [52]	Retinex [57]	SNR [61]	Uformer [56]	BDCE
PSNR ↑	14.74	13.24	20.02	18.19	18.37	<u>21.48</u>	18.82	**22.70**
SSIM ↑	0.641	0.442	0.820	0.745	0.723	<u>0.849</u>	0.771	**0.851**

				LOL-v2-synthetic				
Method	KinD [69]	SID [5]	MIR-Net [67]	A3DLUT [52]	Retinex [57]	SNR [61]	Uformer [56]	BDCE
PSNR ↑	13.29	15.04	21.94	18.92	16.66	<u>24.14</u>	19.66	**24.93**
SSIM ↑	0.578	0.610	0.876	0.838	0.652	**0.928**	0.871	<u>0.929</u>

				MIT				
Method	LCDPNet [18]	DPE [6]	DeepUPE [50]	MIRNet [67]	HWMNet [14]	STAR [72]	SCI [37]	BDCE
PSNR ↑	23.23	22.15	23.04	23.73	<u>24.44</u>	24.13	20.44	**24.85**
SSIM ↑	0.842	0.850	0.893	**0.925**	0.914	0.885	0.893	<u>0.911</u>

				LSRW				
Method	Retinex-Net [57]	KinD [69]	Zero-DCE [15]	SSIENet [70]	Zero-DCE++ [29]	RUAS [32]	SCI [37]	BDCE
PSNR ↑	15.90	16.47	<u>17.66</u>	16.74	15.83	14.43	15.01	**20.10**
SSIM ↑	0.3725	<u>0.4929</u>	0.4685	0.4879	0.4664	0.4276	0.4846	**0.5308**

4 Experiments

4.1 Datasets Settings

In our supervised experiments, we utilize several datasets, including LOL-v1 [57], LOL-v2 [65], MIT-Adobe FiveK (MIT) [4] and LSRW [17]. The LOL-v1 dataset consists of 485 training pairs and 15 testing pairs of real low-light images. As for LOL-v2, it consists of two parts: LOL-v2-synthetic and LOL-v2-real images. LOL-v2-synthetic contains 900 pairs of synthetic low-light images for training and 100 pairs for testing, while LOL-v2-real comprises 689 pairs of real low-light images for training and 100 pairs for testing. The MIT dataset comprises 5,000 paired synthetic low-light and normal-light images. We adopt the same training and testing settings as previous methods [50, 72] for consistency. To assess the generalization ability of BDCE, we further evaluate its performance on unpaired real low-light datasets, including DICM [28], LIME [16], MEF [36], NPE [51], and VV [1].

4.2 Comparison with SOTA Methods on Paired Data

First, we assess the performance of our BDCE model through supervised training on paired datasets (LOL-v1, LOL-v2, MIT, LSRW). Subsequently, we evaluate

Table 2. Average results in terms of 5 NR-IQA metrics (NIQE, NIMA, BRISQUE, NRQM [35] and PI [3]) on the 5 unpaired real low-light datasets (DICM, LIME, MEF, NPE and VV).

Method	Retinex-Net [57]	KinD [69]	Zero-DCE [15]	EnGAN [23]	Zero-DCE++ [29]	SSIENet [70]	BDCE
NIQE ↓	4.85	4.09	4.93	4.27	5.09	4.50	**3.99**
BRISQUE ↓	27.77	26.87	24.78	18.97	21.11	21.08	**17.43**
NIMA↑	**4.24**	4.16	3.87	3.92	3.85	3.53	3.86
NRQM ↑	**7.86**	7.47	7.52	7.50	7.34	7.58	7.44
PI ↓	3.15	3.26	3.21	2.90	3.29	3.47	2.87

Input   Retinex-Net   EnGAN   RUAS   KinD   Zero-DCE   Zero-DCE++   BDCE

Fig. 6. Visual comparisons on unpaired real low-light images, and the example is from the NPE dataset.

the model's effectiveness by conducting testing on the corresponding test sets of these datasets.

LOL Dataset. Our BDCE is evaluated on LOL-v1 and LOL-v2 datasets. Results in the Table 1 demonstrate BDCE's superiority over other state-of-the-art methods. The PSNR and SSIM metrics for the compared methods are sourced from their respective papers. Visual comparisons in the Fig. 3 reveal that BDCE yields visually appealing results with reduced noise.

MIT Dataset. The performance of BDCE is assessed on the MIT dataset [4], and the obtained results in Table 1 indicate that it achieves the highest PSNR and SSIM scores. Figure 4 clearly demonstrates that our BDCE method effectively prevents color-shift in the enhanced images. In contrast, some of the compared methods tend to exhibit over-enhancement or under-enhancement.

LSRW Dataset. Among the evaluated methods, BDCE achieves the highest scores on PSNR and SSIM, as shown in the Table 1. Figure 5 presents a visual comparison of the results. While the images enhanced by other methods suffer from color shifts or appear under-enhanced, the images enhanced by BDCE exhibit a more natural appearance.

4.3 Comparison with SOTA Methods on Unpaired Data

Our BDCE approach's effectiveness is evaluated on various unpaired datasets, namely DICM, LIME, MEF, NPE, and VV datasets. The evaluation is conducted by directly testing our pretrained model on the test set of each dataset.

Table 3. Comparison of different settings in BDCE on LOL-v1. Bootstrap Diffusion Model: using the proposed bootstrap diffusion model for learning the distribution of curve parameters. Denoising Module: using the proposed denoising module in each iteration of curve adjustment. Self-supervised Loss: using self-supervised loss in Eq. 9. ✔: used. : ✗ not used.

Method	Bootstrap Diffusion Model	Denoising Module	Self-supervised Loss	PSNR	SSIM
naive	✗	✗	✗	18.51	0.721
w/o denoise	✔	✗	✗	22.15	0.809
w/o diff	✗	✔	✔	23.33	0.807
w/o self	✔	✔	✗	24.56	0.810
BDCE	✔	✔	✔	25.01	0.850

We compare the result of BDCE with other SOTA methods on these unpaired real low-light image datasets. The quantitative results in terms of 5 NR-IQA metrics are provided in a Table 2. Additionally, a visual comparison is presented in Fig. 6, demonstrating that the results obtained by the compared methods often exhibit unrealistic appearances, loss of fine details, or excessive enhancement. In contrast, BDCE consistently produces images with enhanced colorfulness and sharp details.

4.4 Ablation Study

We evaluate the performance of BDCE using various modules, presenting the results in Table 3 and providing visual comparisons in Fig. 1.

The absence of the bootstrap diffusion model makes it challenging to acquire desirable curve parameters, leading to noticeable deficiencies in color rendition and illumination quality.

Removing the denoising module results in severe noise in the enhanced output due to the inability of pixel-wise curve adjustment alone to effectively leverage the spatially local smooth prior for denoising.

The denoising module's performance is enhanced by our self-supervised loss, which enables it to focus on denoising during each iteration of curve adjustment. Consequently, the utilization of the self-supervised loss proves advantageous. Overall, the combination of the proposed components effectively enhances the LLIE performance.

5   Conclusion and Limitation

In this paper, we first analyse the problems of high computational cost in high resolution images and unsatisfactory performance in simultaneous enhancement and denoising. To mitigate these problems, we propose BDCE, a bootstrap diffusion model adapted to LLIE. For high resolution images, a curve estimation method is adopted and the curve parameters are estimated by our bootstrap diffusion model. At each iteration of curve adjustment, a denoise module is applied to denoise the intermediate enhanced result of each iteration. BDCE outperforms SOTA methods on LLIE benchmarks.

The main limitation of BDCE is its time cost, which is due to the multiple steps of the sampling process of the diffusion model. For future research, we aim to devise a more streamlined approach for acquiring the curve parameter distribution. In addition, finding a lightweight network design is also a consideration.

References

1. https://sites.google.com/site/vonikakis/datasets
2. Abdullah-Al-Wadud, M., Kabir, M.H., Dewan, M.A.A., Chae, O.: A dynamic histogram equalization for image contrast enhancement. IEEE Trans. Consum. Electron. **53**(2), 593–600 (2007)
3. Blau, Y., Mechrez, R., Timofte, R., Michaeli, T., Zelnik-Manor, L.: The 2018 PIRM challenge on perceptual image super-resolution. In: Leal-Taixé, L., Roth, S. (eds.) ECCV 2018. LNCS, vol. 11133, pp. 334–355. Springer, Cham (2019). https://doi.org/10.1007/978-3-030-11021-5_21
4. Bychkovsky, V., Paris, S., Chan, E., Durand, F.: Learning photographic global tonal adjustment with a database of input/output image pairs. In: CVPR (2011)
5. Chen, C., Chen, Q., Xu, J., Koltun, V.: Learning to see in the dark. In: CVPR (2018)
6. Chen, Y.S., Wang, Y.C., Kao, M.H., Chuang, Y.Y.: Deep photo enhancer: unpaired learning for image enhancement from photographs with GANs. In: CVPR (2018)
7. Choi, J., Kim, S., Jeong, Y., Gwon, Y., Yoon, S.: ILVR: conditioning method for denoising diffusion probabilistic models. arXiv preprint arXiv:2108.02938 (2021)
8. Chung, H., Kim, J., Kim, S., Ye, J.C.: Parallel diffusion models of operator and image for blind inverse problems. arXiv preprint arXiv:2211.10656 (2022)
9. Chung, H., Kim, J., Mccann, M.T., Klasky, M.L., Ye, J.C.: Diffusion posterior sampling for general noisy inverse problems. arXiv preprint arXiv:2209.14687 (2022)
10. Chung, H., Sim, B., Ryu, D., Ye, J.C.: Improving diffusion models for inverse problems using manifold constraints. arXiv preprint arXiv:2206.00941 (2022)
11. Chung, H., Sim, B., Ye, J.C.: Come-closer-diffuse-faster: accelerating conditional diffusion models for inverse problems through stochastic contraction. In: CVPR (2022)
12. Cui, Z., et al.: You only need 90k parameters to adapt light: a light weight transformer for image enhancement and exposure correction. In: BMVC (2022)
13. Dhariwal, P., Nichol, A.: Diffusion models beat GANs on image synthesis. In: NeurIPS (2021)
14. Fan, C., Liu, T., Liu, K.: Half wavelet attention on M-Net+ for low-light image enhancement. arXiv preprint arXiv:2203.01296 (2022)
15. Guo, C., et al.: Zero-reference deep curve estimation for low-light image enhancement. In: CVPR, pp. 1780–1789 (2020)
16. Guo, X., Li, Y., Ling, H.: Lime: low-light image enhancement via illumination map estimation. IEEE Trans. Image Process. **26**(2), 982–993 (2016)
17. Hai, J., et al.: R2RNet: low-light image enhancement via real-low to real-normal network. arXiv preprint arXiv:2106.14501 (2021)
18. Wang, H., Xu, K., Lau, R.W.H.: Local color distributions prior for image enhancement. In: Avidan, S., Brostow, G., Cissé, M., Farinella, G.M., Hassner, T. (eds.) Computer Vision – ECCV 2022. ECCV 2022. LNCS, vol. 13678. Springer, Cham (2022). https://doi.org/10.1007/978-3-031-19797-0_20

19. Ho, J., Jain, A., Abbeel, P.: Denoising diffusion probabilistic models. In: NeurIPS (2020)
20. Ho, J., Salimans, T.: Classifier-free diffusion guidance. arXiv preprint arXiv:2207.12598 (2022)
21. Hyvärinen, A., Dayan, P.: Estimation of non-normalized statistical models by score matching. JMLR **6**(4), 695–709 (2005)
22. Ibrahim, H., Kong, N.S.P.: Brightness preserving dynamic histogram equalization for image contrast enhancement. IEEE Trans. Consum. Electron. **53**(4), 1752–1758 (2007)
23. Jiang, Y., et al.: EnlightenGAN: deep light enhancement without paired supervision. IEEE Trans. Image Process. **30**, 2340–2349 (2021)
24. Jin, Y., Yang, W., Tan, R.T.: Unsupervised night image enhancement: when layer decomposition meets light-effects suppression. In: Avidan, S., Brostow, G., Cissé, M., Farinella, G.M., Hassner, T. (eds.) Computer Vision – ECCV 2022. ECCV 2022. LNCS, vol. 13697. Springer, Cham (2022). https://doi.org/10.1007/978-3-031-19836-6_23
25. Kawar, B., Elad, M., Ermon, S., Song, J.: Denoising diffusion restoration models. arXiv preprint arXiv:2201.11793 (2022)
26. Kawar, B., Ganz, R., Elad, M.: Enhancing diffusion-based image synthesis with robust classifier guidance. arXiv preprint arXiv:2208.08664 (2022)
27. Kim, H., Choi, S.M., Kim, C.S., Koh, Y.J.: Representative color transform for image enhancement. In: CVPR (2021)
28. Lee, C., Lee, C., Kim, C.S.: Contrast enhancement based on layered difference representation of 2D histograms. IEEE Trans. Image Process. **22**(12), 5372–5384 (2013)
29. Li, C., Guo, C.G., Loy, C.C.: Learning to enhance low-light image via zero-reference deep curve estimation. In: IEEE Trans. Pattern Anal. Mach. Intell. **44**, 4225–4238 (2021). https://doi.org/10.1109/TPAMI.2021.3063604
30. Li, M., Liu, J., Yang, W., Sun, X., Guo, Z.: Structure-revealing low-light image enhancement via robust Retinex model. IEEE Trans. Image Process. **27**(6), 2828–2841 (2018)
31. Liang, J., Xu, Y., Quan, Y., Shi, B., Ji, H.: Self-supervised low-light image enhancement using discrepant untrained network priors. IEEE Trans. Circuits Syst. Video Technol. **32**(11), 7332–7345 (2022)
32. Liu, R., Ma, L., Zhang, J., Fan, X., Luo, Z.: Retinex-inspired unrolling with cooperative prior architecture search for low-light image enhancement. In: CVPR, pp. 10561–10570 (2021)
33. Lore, K.G., Akintayo, A., Sarkar, S.: LLNeT: a deep autoencoder approach to natural low-light image enhancement. Pattern Recogn. **61**, 650–662 (2017)
34. Luo, Z., Gustafsson, F.K., Zhao, Z., Sjölund, J., Schön, T.B.: Image restoration with mean-reverting stochastic differential equations. arXiv preprint arXiv:2301.11699 (2023)
35. Ma, C., Yang, C.Y., Yang, X., Yang, M.H.: Learning a no-reference quality metric for single-image super-resolution. Comput. Vis. Image Underst. **158**, 1–16 (2017)
36. Ma, K., Zeng, K., Wang, Z.: Perceptual quality assessment for multi-exposure image fusion. IEEE Trans. Image Process. **24**(11), 3345–3356 (2015)
37. Ma, L., Ma, T., Liu, R., Fan, X., Luo, Z.: Toward fast, flexible, and robust low-light image enhancement. In: CVPR (2022)
38. Meng, C., et al.: SDEdit: guided image synthesis and editing with stochastic differential equations. In: ICLR (2021)

39. Nair, N.G., Mei, K., Patel, V.M.: AT-DDPM: restoring faces degraded by atmo-
    spheric turbulence using denoising diffusion probabilistic models. arXiv preprint
    arXiv:2208.11284 (2022)
40. Nichol, A.Q., Dhariwal, P.: Improved denoising diffusion probabilistic models. In:
    ICML (2021)
41. Özdenizci, O., Legenstein, R.: Restoring vision in adverse weather conditions with
    patch-based denoising diffusion models. arXiv preprint arXiv:2207.14626 (2022)
42. Park, S., Yu, S., Moon, B., Ko, S., Paik, J.: Low-light image enhancement using
    variational optimization-based Retinex model. IEEE Trans. Consum. Electron.
    63(2), 178–184 (2017)
43. Saharia, C., et al.: Palette: image-to-image diffusion models. In: ACM SIGGRAPH
    (2022)
44. Sohl-Dickstein, J., Weiss, E., Maheswaranathan, N., Ganguli, S.: Deep unsuper-
    vised learning using nonequilibrium thermodynamics. In: ICML (2015)
45. Song, J., Meng, C., Ermon, S.: Denoising diffusion implicit models. arXiv preprint
    arXiv:2010.02502 (2020)
46. Song, Y., Ermon, S.: Generative modeling by estimating gradients of the data
    distribution. In: NeurIPS (2019)
47. Song, Y., Ermon, S.: Improved techniques for training score-based generative mod-
    els. In: NeurIPS (2020)
48. Song, Y., Sohl-Dickstein, J., Kingma, D.P., Kumar, A., Ermon, S., Poole, B.: Score-
    based generative modeling through stochastic differential equations. arXiv preprint
    arXiv:2011.13456 (2020)
49. Vincent, P.: A connection between score matching and denoising autoencoders.
    Neural Comput. **23**(7), 1661–1674 (2011)
50. Wang, R., Zhang, Q., Fu, C.W., Shen, X., Zheng, W.S., Jia, J.: Underexposed
    photo enhancement using deep illumination estimation. In: CVPR (2019)
51. Wang, S., Zheng, J., Hu, H.M., Li, B.: Naturalness preserved enhancement algo-
    rithm for non-uniform illumination images. IEEE Trans. Image Process. **22**(9),
    3538–3548 (2013)
52. Wang, T., Li, Y., Peng, J., Ma, Y., Wang, X., Song, F., Yan, Y.: Real-time image
    enhancer via learnable spatial-aware 3D lookup tables. In: ICCV (2021)
53. Wang, T., Zhang, K., Shen, T., Luo, W., Stenger, B., Lu, T.: Ultra-high-definition
    low-light image enhancement: a benchmark and transformer-based method. arXiv
    preprint arXiv:2212.11548 (2022)
54. Wang, T., Zhang, T., Zhang, B., Ouyang, H., Chen, D., Chen, Q., Wen,
    F.: Pretraining is all you need for image-to-image translation. arXiv preprint
    arXiv:2205.12952 (2022)
55. Wang, Y., Yu, J., Zhang, J.: Zero-shot image restoration using denoising diffusion
    null-space model. arXiv preprint arXiv:2212.00490 (2022)
56. Wang, Z., Cun, X., Bao, J., Zhou, W., Liu, J., Li, H.: Uformer: a general U-shaped
    transformer for image restoration. In: CVPR (2022)
57. Wei, C., Wang, W., Yang, W., Liu, J.: Deep Retinex decomposition for low-light
    enhancement. In: BMVC (2018)
58. Welker, S., Chapman, H.N., Gerkmann, T.: DriftRec: adapting diffusion models to
    blind image restoration tasks. arXiv preprint arXiv:2211.06757 (2022)
59. Whang, J., Delbracio, M., Talebi, H., Saharia, C., Dimakis, A.G., Milanfar, P.:
    Deblurring via stochastic refinement. In: CVPR (2022)
60. Wu, W., Weng, J., Zhang, P., Wang, X., Yang, W., Jiang, J.: URetinex-Net:
    retinex-based deep unfolding network for low-light image enhancement. In: CVPR,
    pp. 5901–5910 (2022)

61. Xu, X., Wang, R., Fu, C.W., Jia, J.: SNR-aware low-light image enhancement. In: CVPR (2022)
62. Yang, C., Jin, M., Jia, X., Xu, Y., Chen, Y.: AdaInt: learning adaptive intervals for 3D lookup tables on real-time image enhancement. In: CVPR (2022)
63. Yang, C., Jin, M., Xu, Y., Zhang, R., Chen, Y., Liu, H.: SepLUT: separable image-adaptive lookup tables for real-time image enhancement. In: Avidan, S., Brostow, G., Cissé, M., Farinella, G.M., Hassner, T. (eds.) Computer Vision – ECCV 2022. ECCV 2022. LNCS, vol. 13678. Springer, Cham (2022). https://doi.org/10.1007/978-3-031-19797-0_12
64. Yang, W., Wang, S., Fang, Y., Wang, Y., Liu, J.: From fidelity to perceptual quality: a semi-supervised approach for low-light image enhancement. In: CVPR (2020)
65. Yang, W., Wang, W., Huang, H., Wang, S., Liu, J.: Sparse gradient regularized deep Retinex network for robust low-light image enhancement. IEEE Trans. Image Process. **30**, 2072–2086 (2021)
66. Zagoruyko, S., Komodakis, N.: Wide residual networks. arXiv preprint arXiv:1605.07146 (2016)
67. Zamir, S.W., et al.: Learning enriched features for real image restoration and enhancement. In: Vedaldi, A., Bischof, H., Brox, T., Frahm, J.-M. (eds.) ECCV 2020. LNCS, vol. 12370, pp. 492–511. Springer, Cham (2020). https://doi.org/10.1007/978-3-030-58595-2_30
68. Zhang, Y., Guo, X., Ma, J., Liu, W., Zhang, J.: Beyond brightening low-light images. Int. J. Comput. Vision **129**(4), 1013–1037 (2021)
69. Zhang, Y., Zhang, J., Guo, X.: Kindling the darkness: a practical low-light image enhancer. In: ACMMM (2019)
70. Zhang, Y., Di, X., Zhang, B., Wang, C.: Self-supervised image enhancement network: training with low light images only. arXiv preprint arXiv:2002.11300 (2020)
71. Zhang, Z., Zheng, H., Hong, R., Xu, M., Yan, S., Wang, M.: Deep color consistent network for low-light image enhancement. In: CVPR (2022)
72. Zhang, Z., Jiang, Y., Jiang, J., Wang, X., Luo, P., Gu, J.: STAR: a structure-aware lightweight transformer for real-time image enhancement. In: CVPR (2021)
73. Zhang, Z., Zhao, Z., Yu, J., Tian, Q.: ShiftDDPMs: exploring conditional diffusion models by shifting diffusion trajectories. arXiv preprint arXiv:2302.02373 (2023)

CoalUMLP: Slice and Dice! A Fast, MLP-Like 3D Medical Image Segmentation Network

Ruoyu Wu, Zifan Wu, Xue Hu, and Lei Zhang[✉]

China University of Mining and Technology-Beijing, Beijing 100083, China
zhanglei@cumtb.edu.cn

Abstract. 3D medical image segmentation tasks play a crucial role in clinical diagnosis. However, Handling vast data and intricate structures in Point-of-Care (POC) devices is challenging. While current methods use CNNs and Transformer models, their high computational demands and limited real-time capabilities limit their POC application. Recent studies have explored the application of Multilayer Perceptrons (MLP) to medical image segmentation tasks. However, these studies overlook the significance of local and global image features and multi-scale contextual information. To overcome these limitations, we propose CoalUMLP, an efficient vision MLP architecture designed specifically for 3D medical image segmentation tasks. CoalUMLP combines the strengths of CNN, Transformer, and MLP, incorporating three key components: the Multi-Scale Axial Permute Encoder (MSAP), Masked Axial Permute Decoder (MAP), and Semantic Bridging Connection (SBC). We reframe the medical image segmentation problem as a sequence-to-sequence prediction problem and evaluate the performance of our approach on the Medical Segmentation Decathlon (MSD) dataset. CoalUMLP showcases a state-of-the-art performance by significantly reducing the parameter count by 32.8% and computational complexity by 48.5%, all while maintaining a compact structure. Our results highlight the potential of CoalUMLP as a promising backbone for real-time medical image applications. It achieves a superior trade-off between accuracy and efficiency compared to previous Transformer and CNN-based models.

Keywords: 3D Medical Image Segmentation · MLP-like Model · Efficiency and Accuracy Trade-off · Point-of-Care (POC) Devices

1 Introduction

Medical image segmentation [6,17,30,32] is crucial in the medical field, as it aims to divide images into distinct tissue, organ, or lesion regions. It finds extensive applications in radiology and pathology to assist doctors in locating problem areas, diagnosing diseases, and formulating treatment plans. However, noise and complex structures in medical image data pose challenges for segmentation tasks, necessitating high-accuracy algorithms to handle fuzzy boundaries.

F. Liu et al. (Eds.): PRICAI 2023, LNAI 14327, pp. 81–92, 2024.
https://doi.org/10.1007/978-981-99-7025-4_7

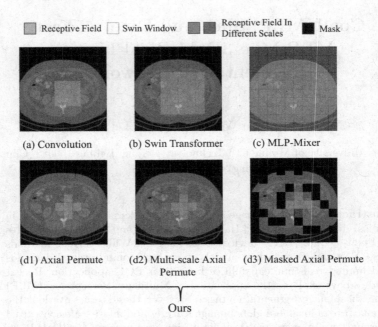

Fig. 1. This figure illustrates the differences in receptive fields among various backbone networks. (a) Convolution employs a 3 × 3 kernel. (b) Swin Transformer uses a window size of 4. (c) MLP-Mixer with global receptive field characteristics. (d1) Basic Axial Permute operation with a ShiftSize of 3 and dilation rate of 1. (d2) Core operations of MSAP, where different colors represent Axial Permute operations with varying shift sizes. (d3) Operations of MAP, where the image is randomly occluded by 30% using a binary mask before applying the Axial Permute operation.

Medical image segmentation methods can be broadly classified into three categories: CNN-based architecture [7,16,22], Transformer-based architecture [5, 26,28], and MLP-based architecture [9,17,23]. Convolutional Neural Networks (CNNs) [12,19,24,27] have played a pivotal role in computer vision, with classical networks like VGG [29] and ResNet [12] providing a solid foundation for tasks such as semantic segmentation. FCN [19] introduced the concept of replacing the last fully connected layer with convolutional layers, enabling segmentation on images of any size. UNet [22], based on an encoder-decoder convolutional network with skip connections, achieved significant success in medical image segmentation. Recent extensions like 3D UNet [7] and ResUNet++ [14] have improved performance in specific scenarios. However, one disadvantage of CNN is limited global perception and difficulty capturing long-range dependencies. Transformers [3,5,25,26] initially proposed for NLP tasks have been adapted for computer vision. TransUNet [5] combines the U-Net architecture with Transformers to enhance finer details. Other methods like Swin-Unet [3], HRViT [8], and SETR [26] have also demonstrated strong performance in medical image segmentation. However, one disadvantage of Transformers is their higher computational complexity compared to convolutional neural networks, which can limit their applicability in resource-constrained environments. MLP-based architecture [9,17,23] presents a concise framework using matrix transformations and MLP for information exchange between spatial features. For example, AS-MLP [17] incorporates axial shift to focus on local feature interaction. Hire-MLP [9] implements a hierarchical reordering operation for feature fusion. However, one disadvantage of MLP is its limited ability to model spatial relationships and capture local structures, which may restrict its performance in tasks requiring spatial awareness. In Fig. 1, we show the difference between the receptive fields of different feature fusion operations.

UNeXt [31] applies the MLP architecture to medical image segmentation, achieving excellent performance with fewer parameters, faster inference speed, and lower computational complexity. As computing power and datasets improve, researchers have found that simple MLPs can achieve comparable performance to Transformers and CNNs in computer vision tasks while reducing computation. UNeXt cleverly combines convolution with MLP, with convolution responsible for extracting local features and MLP integrating and abstracting these features. Challenges remain in optimizing the MLP architecture, extending it to 3D medical image segmentation, and enhancing local detail and global dependency modeling. Addressing these challenges will improve the efficiency, accuracy, and applicability of the MLP model in medical image segmentation tasks.

We propose CoalUMLP, a fusion strategy combining CNN, Transformer, and MLP for 3D medical image segmentation. By incorporating the U-shaped UNet structure, CoalUMLP captures multi-level image features for end-to-end training. Key components include the Multi-scale Axial Permute Encoder (MSAP) for spatial feature fusion, the Masked Axial Permute Decoder (MAP) for compact representations, and Semantic Bridging Connections (SBC) for multi-scale feature integration. CoalUMLP achieves superior performance on the Medical Segmentation Decathlon dataset, reducing parameters by 32.8% and computational complexity by 48.5% compared to UNETR, making it suitable for real-time medical imaging applications. In summary, the main contributions of this article are as follows:

(1) CoalUMLP effectively combines the strengths of CNN, Transformer, and MLP models for 3D medical image segmentation, leveraging the U-shaped structure of UNet. This integration enhances feature representations and enables end-to-end training.
(2) We introduce MSAP, which aggregates features from different spatial positions and applies multi-scale feature fusion. It focuses on spatial feature fusion, addressing the depth-related intricacies and ensuring consistent feature integration across varying image scales in 3D datasets.
(3) MAP is designed for compact representations, catering to the often denser and overlapping structures in 3D images. With the innovative idea of incorporating binary masks during training, the MAP aids in reducing the rank of the input matrix, promoting the model's generalization and adaptability to the intricate structures of unknown 3D data.

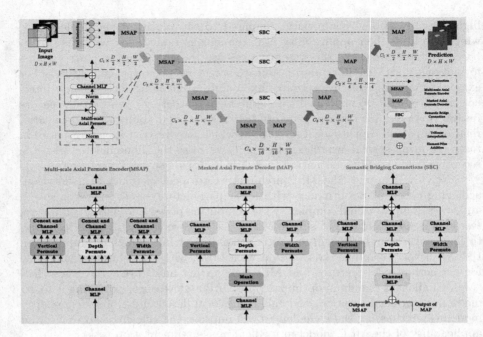

Fig. 2. Overview of CoalUMLP architecture. The overall architecture of CoalUMLP is described at the top of the figure; the structure of the MSAP module is described at the bottom left; the structure of the MAP module is described in the middle at the bottom; the structure of the SBC is described at the bottom right.

(4) Drawing inspiration from Transformer skip connections, SBC concatenates the output of MSAP and MAP. This innovative fusion ensures a cohesive interplay between multi-scale features, crucial for addressing the overlapping and adjacent structures commonly found in 3D medical images.

2   Method

2.1   Overview

As shown in Fig. 2, CoalUMLP follows the traditional U-shaped encoder-decoder architecture while improving its skip connections, encoders, and decoders. Unlike UNeXt and Mixed-Net [18], CoalUMLP completely abandons convolution blocks. After the image input, it first goes through the patch embedding layer, which divides the input image into patches (tokens) and performs linear embedding and layer normalization for each sub-block. The patches are input into the first stage Multi-scale Axial Permute Encoder (MSAP). Next, patch merging is performed for downsampling. In CoalUMLP, the encoder and decoder each contain four stages, with the number of MSAPs in each stage being 3, 3, 8, and 3, respectively. As the network depth increases, each patch's D, H, and W dimensions are reduced by half while the output channel number doubles. In the decoder, we replace the convolution layers in UNet with a Masked Axial Permute Decoder (MAP). The number of MAPs in each stage is the same as the number of MSAPs in the same stage, and upsampling is performed through cubic interpolation. The original skip connections are replaced by Semantic Bridging Connections (SBC). SBC receives the output of the current stage MSAP and MAP and connects them as input. It is then input into an Axial Permute (AP) module, and the result is passed to the next decoder stage, MAP. The Axial Permute operation can be described by the following equations Eqs.(1)–(2):

$$X_{Shift}^{Dim} = \text{MLP}(\text{Narrow}(\text{Roll}(\text{Chunk}(\text{Pad}(\text{MLP}(X^{Dim}))), d), d)). \tag{1}$$

$$X_{AP} = \text{MLP}(X_{Shift}^{D} + X_{Shift}^{H} + X_{Shift}^{W}). \tag{2}$$

In the above formulas, Pad is a padding operation used to add extra values (usually zeros) around the input data; Chunk is a chunking operation that splits the input data into multiple chunks; Narrow is a narrowing operation used to reduce the size of a particular dimension of the input data; X is the input image, X_{Shift}^{Dim} represents the input image X after Shift operation in the specific dimension Dim, X_{AP} represents the output after performing the AP operation, Dim represents the dimension of X, and d represents the shift size.

2.2 Multi-scale Axial Permute Encoder

The Multi-scale Axial Permute (MSAP) is the core operation of the Multi-scale Axial Permute Encoder. For an input feature $X \in R^{C \times D \times H \times W}$ that has undergone patch embedding, we perform Axial Permute operations on Y with different shift sizes along each dimension and concatenate them to obtain three new feature maps: Y^{D}, Y^{H}, and Y^{W}. We apply channel MLP operations to the three feature maps separately and then element-wise add their results. Next, we perform another channel MLP operation on the sum to obtain the final result, denoted as Y_{MSAP}. This process can be represented in Eqs.(3)–(4), where the $\left\{ X_{\text{Shift}}^{Dim}[i] \right\}_{i=1}^{n}$ represents a set of elements. Each element in this set is a version of the input image X transformed by the Shift operation in the Dim dimension. The index i ranges from 1 to n, indicating that there are n such transformed versions of X. Each i corresponds to a different shift size value from an array of shift sizes. Therefore, this set represents the collection of all transformed versions of X for each shift size value in the shift sizes array.

$$Y^{Dim} = Concat \left\{ X_{\text{Shift}}^{Dim}[i] \right\}_{i=1}^{n}. \tag{3}$$

$$Y_{MSAP} = MLP(MLP(Y^{D}) + MLP(Y^{H}) + MLP(Y^{W})). \tag{4}$$

2.3 Masked Axial Permute Decoder

The Axial Permute operation in the Masked Axial Permute Decoder (MAP) bears a resemblance to the Multi-scale Axial Permute Encoder (MSAP), with a key distinction being the elimination of the multi-scale feature fusion and the incorporation of a binary mask for noise introduction during training. This noise serves as a regularization form. The MAE [11] (Masked Autoencoder for Distribution Estimation) inspires using binary masks. In MAE, binary masks are added to the input data during training, setting some input data elements to zero. This forces the model to learn a robust, low-dimensional representation, enhancing the model's generalization ability.

X is the input image, and M is a binary mask matrix. The mask matrix M is the same shape as X, with elements being 0 or 1. The operations performed in MAP can be represented by Eq.(5):

$$Z_{MAP} = (X \odot M)_{AP}. \tag{5}$$

Here, $\odot$ denotes element-wise multiplication, and Z_{MAP} represents the output after applying the MAP operation. Some elements of X become zero due to this operation. The decoder's task is to recover the original data from $X \odot M$. The rank of $X \odot M$ may be lower than X after applying the mask, leading to a low-dimensional representation. It is an implicit regularization, constraining the decoder's representation space, thus enhancing generalization ability.

2.4 Semantic Bridging Connections

In traditional skip connections, a semantic gap can hinder the effective transfer of low-level features and high-level semantic information, impacting model performance. Our introduced Semantic Bridging Connections (SBC) address this by enhancing the transfer between encoder and decoder, overcoming the limitations of traditional connections that often use simple tensor operations. SBC provides a potent semantic link, ensuring adequate information transfer in complex scenarios. As depicted in Fig. 2, we draw on the Transformers' idea to facilitate an element-wise addition operation between the encoder and decoder outputs. This technique efficiently fuses local and high-level semantic features, boosting information transfer. The sum passes through the Axial Permute module, gets upsampled using trilinear interpolation three times, and is fed into the subsequent stage decoder. The operations performed in SBC can be represented by Eq.(6):

$$O_{ZBC} = (Y_{MSAP} \oplus Z_{MAP})_{AP}. \tag{6}$$

Here, $\oplus$ represents element-wise addition, and O_{ZBC} denotes the output after applying the SBC operation.

Table 1. Quantitative Comparisons of the segmentation performance in spleen & brain tumor segmentation

Networks	Spleen Segmentation (CT)		Brain tumor Segmentation (MRI)								#Params(M)↓	Flops(g)↓
	Spleen		WT		ET		CT		All			
Model	Dice↑	HD95↓	Dice↑	HD95↓	Dice↑	HD95↓	Dice↑	HD95↓	Dice↑	HD95↓		
UNet[22]	0.953	4.087	0.766	9.205	0.561	11.122	0.665	10.243	0.664	10.190	19.070	412.650
CoTr[15]	0.954	3.860	0.746	9.918	0.557	9.447	0.748	10.445	0.683	9.697	46.510	399.210
TransUNet[5]	0.950	4.031	0.706	14.027	0.542	10.421	0.684	14.501	0.644	12.983	96.070	48.340
SETR[26]	0.950	4.091	0.698	15.503	0.554	10.237	0.665	14.716	0.639	13.485	86.030	43.490
UNETR[10]	0.964	**1.333**	0.789	**8.266**	0.585	9.354	0.761	8.845	0.711	**8.822**	92.580	41.190
CoalUMLP(Ours)	**0.967**	3.161	**0.906**	19.711	**0.626**	**7.732**	**0.876**	**7.683**	**0.802**	11.708	**62.230**	**21.230**

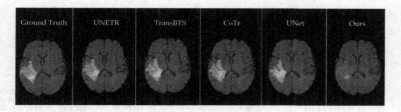

Fig. 3. CoalUMLP precisely captures intricate details in the segmentation results. The entire tumor, labeled as Whole Tumor (WT), encompasses a combination of red, blue, and green regions. The central portion of the tumor, known as the Tumor Core (TC), merges the red and blue regions. The green region signifies the Enhancing Tumor core (ET). (Color figure online)

3 Experiment

3.1 Dataset

We use the Medical Segmentation Decathlon (MSD) [1] dataset to assess our algorithm. This dataset encompasses ten tasks, each focusing on different organs and image modalities. We specifically chose two tasks for evaluation:

– Task09_Spleen: Aimed at precise spleen segmentation, this task employs abdominal CT images sourced from multiple hospitals. We partitioned the dataset into a training set of 41 images and a testing set of 20 images.
– Task01_BrainTumour: Dedicated to detailed brain tumor segmentation, it uses CT images from various medical centers. For this task, our dataset was divided into a training set with 484 images and a testing set comprising 266 images.

3.2 Implement Details

Evaluation Metrics: In the experiments, we use the Dice score [2] and the 95% Hausdorff distance (HD) [13] to evaluate the accuracy of the segmentation.

Settings: In this study, we use Pytorch [21] and the open-source library MONAI [4] (Medical Open Network for AI) for medical image processing to implement the model. Data augmentation techniques include Spacing Resampling, Scale Intensity Range, Crop Foreground, Random Crop by Positive and Negative Label, Random Flip, Random Rotate 90 Degrees, Random Scale Intensity, and Random Shift Intensity. The AdamW [20] optimizer is used for training for 500 epochs, with weight decay set to 1e-5 and momentum set to 0.99. The learning rate scheduling strategy uses Linear Warmup [12] and Cosine Annealing. The experiments are conducted on 4 NVIDIA RTX 3090 GPUs.

Table 2. Ablation study on different block number in each layer

Block number in each layer	Spleen Segmentation (CT)		Brain tumor Segmentation (MRI)							
	Spleen		WT		ET		TC		All	
	Dice↑	HD95↓	Dice↑	HD95↓	Dice↑	HD95↓	Dice↑	HD95↓	Dice↑	HD95↓
(3,3,3)	0.962	4.012	0.871	22.981	0.454	9.150	0.811	10.157	0.712	14.430
(3,3,3,3)	0.964	4.120	0.801	23.309	0.443	10.134	0.670	9.132	0.605	15.192
(3,3,8,3)	0.967	**3.161**	0.906	19.711	0.626	**7.732**	0.876	**7.683**	0.802	11.708
(3,3,12,3)	**0.970**	3.740	**0.913**	**19.005**	**0.639**	7.910	**0.884**	7.383	**0.812**	**11.432**

Table 3. Ablation study on different permuted dimension

Permute Dimension	Spleen Segmentation (CT)		Brain tumor Segmentation (MRI)							
	Spleen		WT		ET		TC		All	
	Dice↑	HD95↓	Dice↑	HD95↓	Dice↑	HD95↓	Dice↑	HD95↓	Dice↑	HD95↓
(D,H,W)	0.967	**3.161**	**0.906**	**19.711**	**0.626**	**7.732**	**0.876**	**7.683**	**0.802**	**11.708**
(D,W)	**0.970**	3.740	0.871	22.547	0.530	9.130	0.812	8.70	0.737	13.459
(D,H)	0.960	5.242	0.810	24.846	0.562	8.950	0.795	7.85	0.722	13.882
(H,W)	0.954	6.046	0.790	23.948	0.434	10.683	0.781	8.14	0.669	14.257

3.3   Comparison with SOTA

CoalUMLP performs superior in spleen and brain tumor segmentation tasks. The specific results are in Table 1 and Fig. 3. For spleen segmentation, CoalUMLP obtained a Dice score of 0.967, a 0.3% increase compared to the highest-scoring benchmark method, i.e., UNETR.

In terms of brain tumor segmentation, our model achieved Dice scores of 0.906, 0.626, and 0.876 in Whole Tumor (WT), Edema Tumor (ET), and Core Tumor (CT) segmentation, respectively. These scores correspond to improvements of 14.8%, 7.0%, and 15.1% over the highest-performing benchmark models in WT, ET, and CT segments, respectively.

CoalUMLP performed well on most metrics but struggled with the HD95 metric for Whole Tumor (WT). This challenge might arise from the model's limited global perception. The model must have strong global perceptual skills because WT morphology and location can differ among patients. However, the current structure of CoalUMLP may not be adept at capturing this global information, leading to occasional lapses in the precise delineation of the WT boundaries.

When considering computational efficiency, CoalUMLP outperforms all models in the benchmark by reducing the required parameters and FLOPs by 32.8% and 48.5%, respectively. The relationship between computational efficiency and model performance of different models is shown in Fig. 4. Without sacrificing performance, CoalUMLP's enhanced efficiency makes it a top model for these tasks.

Table 4. Ablation study on model component

ComponentModel	Spleen Segmentation (CT)		Brain tumor Segmentation (MRI)							
	Spleen		WT		ET		TC		All	
	Dice↑	HD95↓	Dice↑	HD95↓	Dice↑	HD95↓	Dice↑	HD95↓	Dice↑	HD95↓
CoalUMLP w/o Everything	0.958	5.120	0.754	27.064	0.454	12.564	0.669	14.635	0.625	18.087
CoalUMLP w/o MSAP	0.962	5.240	0.789	22.087	0.459	11.206	0.761	9.807	0.669	14.367
CoalUMLP w/o MAP	**0.965**	5.751	0.804	**19.451**	**0.589**	10.894	**0.850**	**8.471**	0.748	**12.939**
CoalUMLP w/o SBC	0.964	**5.082**	**0.871**	20.594	0.561	**10.064**	0.830	9.481	**0.754**	13.379

3.4 Ablation Study

We conducted a series of ablation experiments on all the datasets used to select the optimal model architecture settings and validate the effectiveness of each component in the CoalUMLP framework:

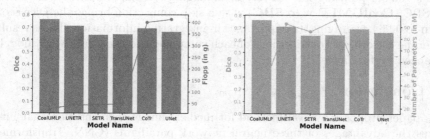

Fig. 4. Comparison Charts of Different Models. The y-axis represents the Dice score (higher is better), while the x-axis shows GFLOPs and parameter count (lower is better). CoalUMLP outperforms other networks in efficiency.

Different scales of CoalUMLP: Our study on the impact of different CoalUMLP model configurations, represented by the tuples (a, b, c, d), denotes the number of CoalUMLP blocks at each layer, as shown in Table 2, we found that performance enhancements start to plateau beyond a certain model depth.

The $(3, 3, 8, 3)$ configuration delivered a strong performance, with a Dice score of 0.967 and HD95 scores of 3.161 in spleen segmentation, outperforming the $(3, 3, 3)$ and $(3, 3, 3, 3)$ configurations. It also achieved superior Dice scores for WT, ET, and TC and HD95 scores for TC in brain tumor segmentation.

Adding more blocks, like in the $(3, 3, 12, 3)$ setup, had minimal impact on performance. Spleen segmentation saw a slight Dice score rise to 0.970 and a worse HD95 of 3.740. Brain tumor scores were comparable or slightly better than the $(3, 3, 8, 3)$ setup, showing limited benefits from added model complexity.

The difference between executing Axial Permutation in different dimensions: We assessed different Axial Permutation dimensions for performance and training speed. Table 3 shows the full (D, H, W) setup excelled in 3D medical image segmentation, with notable scores for Spleen and Brain tumor segmentation. The (D, W) configuration had a higher Dice score for Spleen but was overall less effective, indicating the H dimension's limited impact. Configurations omitting width or depth $((D, H)$ and $(H, W))$ performed worse, emphasizing the need for both depth and width. The height dimension seems less vital, especially for simpler tasks.

Component Analysis: This study highlights the significance of each component in the CoalUMLP model. Without these elements, the performance drops noticeably. For instance, when all components are removed (**CoalUMLP w/o Everything**), the model's Dice score falls to 0.958 and the HD95 to 5.10 for Spleen Segmentation, in contrast to our full model that achieves a Dice score of 0.967 and HD95 of 3.161.

As shown in Table. 4, removing the MSAP block (**CoalUMLP w/o MSAP**) results in a Dice score of 0.962, illustrating its role in capturing multi-scale features. Without the MAP block (**CoalUMLP w/o MAP**), the Dice score dips to 0.965, pointing out its role in managing spatial complexity. Replacing the SBC (**CoalUMLP w/o SBC**) with a skip connection brings the Dice score down to 0.964, signifying its importance in integrating information. These results underline the critical contributions of each component to the CoalUMLP model's enhanced performance.

4   Conclusion

This paper proposes a novel method for medical image segmentation that integrates the advantages of three neural network paradigms (CNN, Transformer, and MLP). The resulting architecture, CoalUMLP, effectively reduces the semantic gap between local context information and global semantic associations. Extensive experimental validation demonstrates that our approach surpasses existing techniques on two widely-recognized benchmark datasets. In future research, we plan to further explore how CoalUMLP can be applied to a broader spectrum of medical image analysis domains.

Acknowledgments.. This work is being supported by the National Natural Science Foundation of China under the Grant No. 52074299.

References

1. Antonelli, M., et al.: The medical segmentation decathlon. Nature Commun. **13**(1), 4128 (2022)
2. Bertels, J., et al.: Optimizing the Dice Score and Jaccard Index for medical image segmentation: theory and practice. In: Shen, D., et al. (eds.) Medical Image Computing and Computer Assisted Intervention – MICCAI 2019: 22nd International Conference, Shenzhen, China, October 13–17, 2019, Proceedings, Part II, pp. 92–100. Springer, Cham (2019). https://doi.org/10.1007/978-3-030-32245-8_11
3. Cao, H., et al.: Swin-Unet: Unet-like pure transformer for medical image segmentation. In: Karlinsky, L., Michaeli, T., Nishino, K. (eds.) Computer Vision – ECCV 2022 Workshops: Tel Aviv, Israel, October 23–27, 2022, Proceedings, Part III, pp. 205–218. Springer, Cham (2023). https://doi.org/10.1007/978-3-031-25066-8_9
4. Cardoso, M.J., et al.: Monai: An open-source framework for deep learning in healthcare. arXiv preprint arXiv:2211.02701 (2022)
5. Chen, J., et al.: Transunet: Transformers make strong encoders for medical image segmentation. arXiv preprint arXiv:2102.04306 (2021)
6. Chen, S., Xie, E., Ge, C., Chen, R., Liang, D., Luo, P.: Cyclemlp: A MLP-like architecture for dense prediction. arXiv preprint arXiv:2107.10224 (2021)
7. Çiçek, Ö., Abdulkadir, A., Lienkamp, S.S., Brox, T., Ronneberger, O.: 3D U-Net: learning dense volumetric segmentation from sparse annotation. In: Ourselin, S., Joskowicz, L., Sabuncu, M.R., Unal, G., Wells, W. (eds.) Medical Image Computing and Computer-Assisted Intervention – MICCAI 2016: 19th International Conference, Athens, Greece, October 17-21, 2016, Proceedings, Part II, pp. 424–432. Springer, Cham (2016). https://doi.org/10.1007/978-3-319-46723-8_49
8. Gu, J., et al.: Multi-scale high-resolution vision transformer for semantic segmentation. In: Proceedings of the IEEE/CVF Conference on Computer Vision and Pattern Recognition, pp. 12094–12103 (2022)
9. Guo, J., et al.: Hire-MLP: Vision MLP via hierarchical rearrangement. In: Proceedings of the IEEE/CVF Conference on Computer Vision and Pattern Recognition, pp. 826–836 (2022)
10. Hatamizadeh, A., et al.: UNETR: Transformers for 3D medical image segmentation. In: Proceedings of the IEEE/CVF Winter Conference On Applications of Computer Vision, pp. 574–584 (2022)
11. He, K., Chen, X., Xie, S., Li, Y., Dollár, P., Girshick, R.: Masked autoencoders are scalable vision learners. In: Proceedings of the IEEE/CVF Conference on Computer Vision and Pattern Recognition, pp. 16000–16009 (2022)
12. He, K., Zhang, X., Ren, S., Sun, J.: Deep residual learning for image recognition. In: Proceedings of the IEEE Conference on Computer Vision and Pattern Recognition, pp. 770–778 (2016)
13. Huttenlocher, D.P., Klanderman, G.A., Rucklidge, W.J.: Comparing images using the Hausdorff distance. IEEE Trans. Pattern Anal. Mach. Intell. **15**(9), 850–863 (1993)
14. Jha, D., et al.: Resunet++: An advanced architecture for medical image segmentation. In: 2019 IEEE International Symposium on Multimedia (ISM), pp. 225–2255. IEEE (2019)
15. Jiang, W., Trulls, E., Hosang, J., Tagliasacchi, A., Yi, K.M.: Cotr: Correspondence transformer for matching across images. In: Proceedings of the IEEE/CVF International Conference on Computer Vision, pp. 6207–6217 (2021)

16. Li, M., Wei, M., He, X., Shen, F.: Enhancing part features via contrastive attention module for vehicle re-identification. In: Conference on International Conference on Image Processing. IEEE (2022)
17. Lian, D., Yu, Z., Sun, X., Gao, S.: As-MLP: An axial shifted MLP architecture for vision. arXiv preprint arXiv:2107.08391 (2021)
18. Liu, Y., Qin, G., Lyu, K., Huang, Y.: Mixed-net: A mixed architecture for medical image segmentation. In: 2022 IEEE International Conference on Bioinformatics and Biomedicine (BIBM), pp. 2095–2102. IEEE (2022)
19. Long, J., Shelhamer, E., Darrell, T.: Fully convolutional networks for semantic segmentation. In: Proceedings of the IEEE Conference on Computer Vision and Pattern Recognition, pp. 3431–3440 (2015)
20. Loshchilov, I., Hutter, F.: Decoupled weight decay regularization. arXiv preprint arXiv:1711.05101 (2017)
21. Paszke, A., et al.: Pytorch: An imperative style, high-performance deep learning library. In: Advances in Neural Information Processing Systems 32 (2019)
22. Ronneberger, O., Fischer, P., Brox, T.: U-Net: convolutional networks for biomedical image segmentation. In: Navab, N., Hornegger, J., Wells, W.M., Frangi, A.F. (eds.) Medical Image Computing and Computer-Assisted Intervention – MICCAI 2015: 18th International Conference, Munich, Germany, October 5-9, 2015, Proceedings, Part III, pp. 234–241. Springer, Cham (2015). https://doi.org/10.1007/978-3-319-24574-4_28
23. Shen, F., Du, X., Zhang, L., Tang, J.: Triplet contrastive learning for unsupervised vehicle re-identification. arXiv preprint arXiv:2301.09498 (2023)
24. Shen, F., Peng, X., Wang, L., Zhang, X., Shu, M., Wang, Y.: Hsgm: A hierarchical similarity graph module for object re-identification. In: 2022 IEEE International Conference on Multimedia and Expo (ICME), pp. 1–6. IEEE (2022)
25. Shen, F., Xiangbo, S., Du, X., Tang, J.: Pedestrian-specific bipartite-aware similarity learning for text-based person retrieval. In: Proceedings of the 31th ACM International Conference on Multimedia (2023)
26. Shen, F., Xie, Y., Zhu, J., Zhu, X., Zeng, H.: Git: Graph interactive transformer for vehicle re-identification. IEEE Trans. Image Process. **32**, 1039–1051 (2023)
27. Shen, F., Zhu, J., Zhu, X., Huang, J., Zeng, H., Lei, Z., Cai, C.: An efficient multi-resolution network for vehicle re-identification. IEEE Internet of Things Journal (2021)
28. Shen, F., Zhu, J., Zhu, X., Xie, Y., Huang, J.: Exploring spatial significance via hybrid pyramidal graph network for vehicle re-identification. IEEE Trans. Intell. Transport. Syst. **23**(7), 8793–8804 (2021)
29. Simonyan, K., Zisserman, A.: Very deep convolutional networks for large-scale image recognition. arXiv preprint arXiv:1409.1556 (2014)
30. Tolstikhin, I.O., et al.: MLP-mixer: An all-MLP architecture for vision. Adv. Neural. Inf. Process. Syst. **34**, 24261–24272 (2021)
31. Valanarasu, J.M.J., Patel, V.M.: Unext: MLP-based rapid medical image segmentation network. In: Medical Image Computing and Computer Assisted Intervention-MICCAI 2022: 25th International Conference, Singapore, September 18–22, 2022, Proceedings, Part V, pp. 23–33. Springer (2022). https://doi.org/10.1007/978-3-031-16443-9_3
32. Yu, T., Li, X., Cai, Y., Sun, M., Li, P.: S2-MLP: Spatial-shift MLP architecture for vision. In: Proceedings of the IEEE/CVF Winter Conference on Applications of Computer Vision, pp. 297–306 (2022)

Enhancing Interpretability in CT Reconstruction Using Tomographic Domain Transform with Self-supervision

Baiyin Huang, Boheng Tan, Xiaoqin Tang, and Guoqiang Xiao[✉]

College of Computer and Information Science, Southwest University,
Chongqing, China
gqxiao@swu.edu.cn

Abstract. Computed tomography (CT) reconstruction faces difficulties in dealing with artifacts caused by imperfect imaging processes. Deep learning-based CT reconstruction models have been proposed to address these challenges, but they often lack interpretability since they use end-to-end neural networks to directly transform signals from sinograms to CT sections. Additionally, supervised methods are commonly used to guide network training, yet obtaining supervision information can be challenging in biomedical imaging systems. To overcome these limitations, we propose a new domain transform CT reconstruction framework that includes self-supervision. Our approach interprets sinogram signals as tomographic information in the CT section domain, which is then used to formulate pixel intensities with a simple mean operation. A refinement network is utilized to improve the quality of the CT images, which are further processed using the Radon transform to achieve simulated sinograms without requiring additional supervision. Our experimental results demonstrate the effectiveness of the proposed framework in both anatomical structure reconstruction and artifact reduction.

Keywords: CT reconstruction · Domain transform · Self-supervision

1 Introduction

In the medical field, X-ray based Computed Tomography(CT) imaging is essential for the clinical diagnosis and treatment. Analytical reconstruction methods such as Filtered Back Projection (FBP) [13], face intrinsic challenges in addressing artifacts or noises caused by imperfections in the imaging process or equipment, such as sparse-view projection, limited-angle imaging, low-dose imaging, etc. To improve the quality of CT reconstruction images, many influential works have been proposed, categorized as Direct image reconstruction, Iterative image reconstruction, and Deep image reconstruction [27]. Among these works, the

This work is partially supported by the National Natural Science Foundation of China Youth Found under Grant 62202391.

iterative reconstruction algorithms including SART [1] and POCS [5], as well as the regularization terms such as TV [10,29], have a reputable advantage in suppressing artifacts and improving image quality. However, these methods require high computational complexity due to iterative projections and back-projections [34]; even so, artifacts-free reconstruction is still unlikely to obtain complete guarantee.

In recent years, Deep image reconstruction (deep learning based) is raising its popularity for noise removal and image refinement. Some of these works focus on the sinogram domain, optimizing the signals to provide complete and substantial semantic information for the mathematical reconstruction process [15], or using network learning to optimize back-projection algorithm [24,25] and coordinate representation of signals position in the sinogram domain [31]. On the other way around, improving the quantity in image domain [6,7,33] has also been a way for many works to optimize the reconstruction. The typical solutions for image-domain optimization is to leverage a convolutional neural network to learn the mapping function between the inferior and prior superior images. There are some works that put their efforts in optimizing the sinograms and images simultaneously [8,9,17], aiming to interactively optimize the dual-domain information for refined reconstruction. Despite achieving promising performances in artifact suppression and quality refinement through supervised end-to-end networks, most of these works have limited capabilities for complex high-precision reconstruction. Because they rely on convolutional neural networks to directly learn the blackbox mapping between the sinograms and the reconstructed images for a faster domain transformation [28]. Moreover, acquiring supervision information can be practically challenging, especially for biomedical imaging systems. Certain works have integrated neural networks into iterative reconstruction frameworks to achieve greater interpretability and ultimately enhance the overall image quality [22,26,32]. However, Due to the iterative schema involved, these works often entail unavoidable computational complexity and significant time consumption. Additionally, the use of supervision is typically necessary to achieve optimal results in this framework.

With the aim of improving the interpretability for complex high-precision reconstruction and avoiding expensive or unattainable prior knowledge via supervised learning, we present a novel self-supervised CT reconstruction framework that utilizes tomographic domain transform module to convert sinogram signals into CT sections. This module could well bridge the information gap in the conversion between sinogram domain and CT image domain. It also explains how the signals in sinogram evolve and formulate the pixels in image. The output of the module is an initial reconstruction with a coarse anatomic structure that guides a refinement neural network to achieve elegant convergence for fine reconstruction. The reconstructed results are further projected by the Radon transform [4] to achieve a predicted sinogram for self-supervision. Different from the previous reconstruction methods that require either complex mathematical algorithms for better interpretability or supervision information for higher image quality, our approach enhances the reconstruction interpretability through the domain transform module just with simple mathematical operations and relies only on the observed sinogram without additional supervision required. Our experimental results on multiple datasets indicate that the proposed approach not only performs well in dealing with sufficient projection angles, but also achieves impressive reconstruction results on sparse-view sinograms.

2 Methodology

2.1 Radon Transform in CT Imaging

The primary objective of CT imaging is to assess the condition of tissues by measuring the extent of X-ray energy attenuation as it passes through the human body [4,12]. By rotating the X-ray at different angles θ around the object, one can acquire energy variations in different directions. The resulting sinogram represents the detected energy loss during the CT scanning process. It is a two-dimensional graph that displays signal intensity, with the vertical axis indicating the distance s between the source and detector, and the horizontal axis representing the measurement angle θ. In the context of CT imaging, different geometric structures are utilized for the process of forward projection. For the purpose of illustration, we specifically concentrate on the parallel beam geometry, considering the inherent correlations that exist among various geometries, including fan beam geometry. The projection process of parallel beams in CT imaging is visually depicted in Fig. 1.

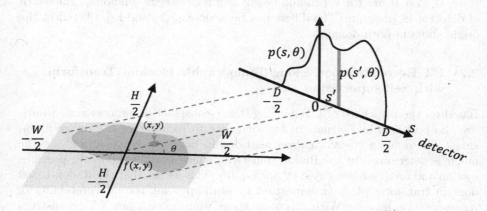

Fig. 1. Parallel X-Ray Beam Geometry.

The Radon transform, which is the main approach for obtaining simulated sinograms, is a mapping from the Cartesian rectangular coordinates (x, y) to a distance and an angel (s, θ), also known as polar coordinates. Applying the transform to an image with the density variation $f(x, y)$ for a given angle θ, its distance s in the sinogram domain is able to written mathematically as:

$$s = x\cos\theta + y\sin\theta \qquad (1)$$

The detector records the constantly changing angle θ and distance s, as well as the signal intensity $p(\theta, s)$ integrated on the corresponding ray path that goes through the object in the image domain, The signals in sinogram are formulated as:

$$p(\theta,s) = \int_{-\infty}^{\infty} \int_{-\infty}^{\infty} f(x,y)\delta(x\cos\theta + y\sin\theta - s)\,dx\,dy \qquad (2)$$

where $\delta(\cdot)$ is the Dirac delta function [13].

Note that the Eq. (1) and Eq. (2) separately describes the correlation of coordinates and signals transformed from sinogram to image domain, i.e. the projection process in CT imaging systems. While in the scenario of back projection (or reconstruction), given the coordinate (x, y) of a pixel in image domain, the projected (or detected) distance s in each projection angle θ is achievable via Eq. (1). The calculated N pairs of (s, θ) compose the coordinates for retrieving tomographic information in a sinogram, which actually formulates the image intensity of the pixel in image domain. N indicates the number of projection angles. This is the basic idea of our reconstruction method.

Since Eq. (1) describes a general correlation between the coordinates of two domains, practically there is an offset of origins in both sinogram and image domain. For this reason, the coordinate correlation is adapted as follows:

$$s(x, y, \theta) = (x - \frac{W}{2})\cos\theta + (y - \frac{H}{2})\sin\theta + \frac{D}{2} \qquad (3)$$

Here, W and H are the width and height of image size. D symbolizes the width of detector in sinogram. The differences between Eq. (1) and Eq. (3) reflect the origin shifts in both domains.

2.2 CT Reconstruction Using Tomographic Domain Transform with Self-supervision

Based on the principles of CT imaging, the reconstruction process aims to utilize the positions and signals in the sinogram to reconstruct the image intensities. The domain transformation relationship between the sinogram and the image is determined by the Radon transform, which was derived in the previous section and further represented by our Eq. (3). This means that the Radon-based domain transform plays an important role in improving the interpretability of reconstruction process. With this inspiration, we propose a new CT reconstruction approach that consists of tomographic domain transform, image formulation and reconstruction refinement. As show in Fig. 2, the tomographic domain transform module (in blue) acquires the tomographic information for a given pixel in image domain, and arrange them to a 3D matrix M. The size of the matrix is $H * W * N$, with H and W indicating the image size. The tomographic information is represented in the third dimension of M, which will be used for image formulation to obtain an initial reconstruction. To further improve the quality particularly for complex high-precision image, a refinement network is employed to suppress artifacts and identify prominent information.

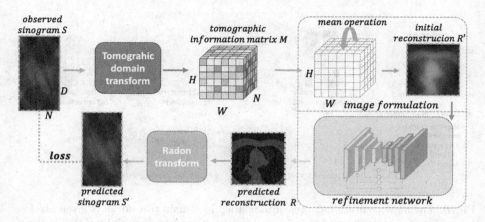

Fig. 2. The pipeline of proposed reconstruction network via self-supervision. The tomographic domain transform module acquires tomographic information for individual pixels, and the image formulation average them as initial intensities. Sequentially, a refinement network is employed for accurate reconstruction, followed by Radon transform to obtain the predicted sinogram for loss calculation.

Tomographic Domain Transform Module. It is used to bridge the transform mapping between sinogram signals and image intensities via a tomographic information matrix M. To acquire this 3D matrix, we explain the implementation details in Fig. 3. Given the observed sinograms and the coordinates (x, y) of image to be reconstructed, we first transform (x, y) to sinogram coordinates (s, θ) with Eq. (3). As a results, a pixel I in image corresponds to a sin curve in sinogram. In Fig. 3, there are three examples with each coordinate pair shown in a different color, i.e. blue, yellow or pink. This sin curve describes how the detection distance s varies as the projection angle θ changes. According to the principle of tomographic parallel CT imaging, the sinogram signals that contribute to the intensity formulation of pixel I are on this curve. To acquire these signals as tomographic information, we map the curve to the sinogram and represent it in a vector. The vectorized tomographic information for each pixel is represented in the third dimension of matrix M at location (x, y).

Image Formulation and Refinement Module. According to the principle of tomographic imaging, the intensity of a given pixel in image is formulated by an integral transform of tomographic signals. Therefore, the N-dimensional information at each position of matrix M corresponds to a reconstructed coordinate. In Fig. 2, this means that a simple sum or mean operation on the tomographic information (i.e. the third dimension of matrix M) is able to approximately reconstruct the intensity of pixel I with an initial result R'. Applying the mean operation directly in this way ensures that information from each dimension of matrix M is utilized during the process of dimensional reduction, and guarantees that the initial results obtain clear contour information without introducing

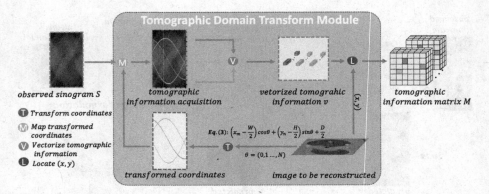

Fig. 3. The implementation details of tomogragphic domain transform. A given pixel in image domain is transformed to a sin curve in sinogram domain with Eq. (3). There are three examples shown in blue, yellow and pink. By mapping the curve to the observed sinogram, the tomographic information that corresponds to the formulation of pixel intensity is acquired, which is further vectorized and represented in the third dimension of matrix M at the location of (x, y). (Color figure online)

additional network parameters. Practically due to inevitable noises and undecomposable integrals in sinogram, the initial reconstruction may suffer from contour blur or a lack of details, especially for complex high-precision images. To address this issue, we proposed a refinement network to optimize the initial coarse results and enrich the semantic information. Due to the exceptional coarse-to-fine feature extraction capability inherited from the Encoder-Decoder architecture, as well as its performance in the field of medical imaging, the U-Net [3, 20] has been chosen as the backbone network for the refinement network. This step involves acquiring high-dimensional information from the initial result R', which might have been attenuated during preceding steps. By reemphasizing these high-dimensional features, it facilitates the recovery of detailed information. The integration of the inherent skip connections in the U-Net structure ensures that, during this process, the complete contour information from the initial reconstruction is fully utilized while also restoring the fine details within the image. Thus, the refinement network is capable of representing low- and high-level features with sufficient semantic information, which allows it to enhance details and suppress noise.

Loss Function via Self-supervision. Through self-supervision, deep image reconstruction trains models based solely on the observed sinograms, without any prior knowledge of the reconstruction. This is because that the predicted reconstruction can be projected to the sinogram domain for loss calculation via the Radon transform. To guide the training process of the refinement network in our reconstruction framework, we apply the differentiable Radon transform [19] to project the predicted reconstruction from U-Net to achieve the predicted sinogram for loss calculation. The projection angle and sparsity level of the projection process are the same as those of the observed sinograms, ensuring the effectiveness of the self-supervised process. The loss function is defined in Eq. (4) [30]:

$$\mathcal{L} = \sqrt{\parallel S' - S \parallel^2 + \epsilon^2} \tag{4}$$

where S represents the observed sinogram, S' indicates the predicted sinogram via Radon transform and constant ϵ is set to 10^{-3} to ensure that the $\mathcal{L}$ is differentiable.

3 Experimental Results

3.1 Datasets and Experimental Settings

Datasets. To evaluate the performance of the proposed reconstruction Network, we conduct the training and test on both simulated and real CT scans. The DL sparse-view CT challenge dataset, as described in [21], is a simulated dataset comprising 4000 clear breast phantom simulation images. These images exhibit a complex random structure and contain microcalcification-like objects. The LoDoPaB dataset [16] selected from LIDC/IDRI [2] (a real CT scan image set acquired from around 800 patients) contains 5000 real CT scans of human lung. Both the simulated and real images are randomly spit into training, validation and test set with a ratio of 6:2:2. The observed sinograms are generated by a parallel beam geometry, and the projection strategies are set as $\theta = (1°, 180°)$ with a variant number of angles $N = (30, 60, 180)$ to explore the performances on sparse-view reconstruction.

Experimental Settings and Evaluation Metric. To train the refinement network, we adopt the Adam optimizer [14] with $(\beta1, \beta2) = (0.9, 0.999)$ thanks to it elegant performance on convergence. The learning rate is initially set as 2×10^{-4} and steadily decreased to 1×10^{-6} using the cosine annealing strategy [18, 30]. The batch size is set as 4 on the Nvidia 3090 GPU, with a setting of 100 and 300 epochs on the simulated and real datasets, we apply the torch-radon package [19] for Radon transform. For evaluation, both visual and quantitative results are exhibited. As for quantitative evaluation, we choose peak signal to noise ratio (PSNR) and mean structural similarity index (SSIM) [11], to mainly measure the ability of noise suppression and structure reconstruction.

3.2 Comparison Experiments

We compare the proposed method with four classic reconstruction methods including FBP, SART-TV, N2 Learned [24] and Fourier MLP [23] on both the simulated and real datasets. While FBP and SART-TV are model-based with established reputation in Direct and Iterative image reconstruction, N2 Learned is self-supervised with a framework that combines FBP and neural networks.

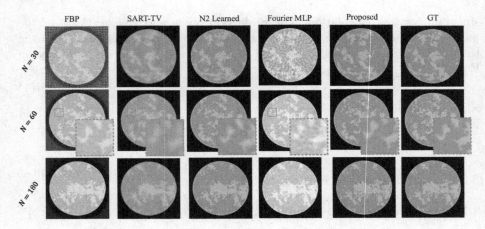

Fig. 4. The visualization performances of the different reconstruction methods on the simulated dataset with a variant number of projections in the range of for sparsity study.

The Fourier MLP is a new reconstruction framework that learns the mapping between locations and intensities with MLP network without additional supervision. The differences are visually and quantitatively exhibited.

Table 1. Quantitative results on the test set of the simulated DL sparse-view CT datasets.

DL Sparse-view CT	N=30		N=60		N=180	
	PSNR	SSIM	PSNR	SSIM	PSNR	SSIM
FBP	22.028	0.560	23.713	0.728	24.131	0.813
SART-TV	30.115	0.835	30.982	0.862	30.974	0.860
N2 Learned	35.331	0.919	38.399	0.964	42.240	0.986
Fourier MLP	29.177	0.664	34.154	0.831	35.871	0.908
Proposed	**38.173**	**0.945**	**42.662**	**0.983**	**44.257**	**0.992**

Visual Performance. The visual performances of the different reconstruction methods are shown in Fig. 4 on the simulated dataset, and Fig. 5 on the real dataset. We selected the most representative case with ($N = 60$) for magnification processing (shown in yellow bounding boxes) to clearly distinguish the performance of each comparative algorithm. It is observed that most algorithms perform well with sufficient angles ($N = 180$). However, when the number of projections decreases, the FBP algorithm suffers from ring artifacts due to the need for larger singoram information to fill the surrounding pixels. This problem also occurs in N2 Learned which uses FBP as a means of back-projection. SART-TV

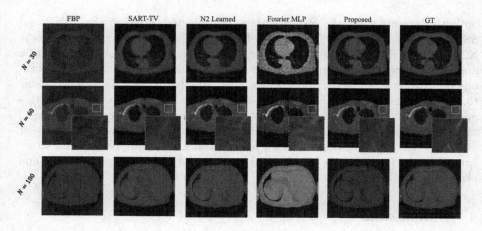

Fig. 5. The visualization performances of the different reconstruction methods on the LoDoPaB dataset with a variant number of projections in the range of for sparsity study.

sacrifices image quality for artifact removal, while Fourier MLP exhibits poor performance in removing artifacts. In contrast to the existing works, the proposed method is able to simultaneously suppress artifacts and preserve details. This is consistent with the visual results on the real dataset in Fig. 4.

Table 2. Quantitative results on the test set of the real LoDoPaB datasets.

LoDoPaB	N=30		N=60		N=180	
	PSNR	SSIM	PSNR	SSIM	PSNR	SSIM
FBP	20.490	0.519	20.623	0.568	22.238	0.717
SART-TV	25.393	0.694	28.295	0.756	30.711	0.794
N2 Learned	23.711	0.684	23.685	0.709	24.016	0.767
Fourier MLP	29.174	0.545	31.369	0.639	31.876	0.675
Proposed	**30.647**	**0.770**	**33.326**	**0.831**	**34.740**	**0.887**

Quantitative Comparison. The quantitative results of the different reconstruction methods are reported in Table 1 and Table 2 separately for the simulated and real dataset. The highest values of PSNR and SSIM for each projection strategy are highlighted in bold. The results on both datasets indicate that FBP has the worst performance across projection angles and evaluation metrics. The SART-TV on two datasets demonstrated its good performance in preserving image structure, and the method showed a stable performance on simulated data when the projection angles became sparse. However, its performance rapidly declined on real data. The Fourier MLP has good performances on both datasets when the object is densely projected, however the PSNR and SSIM drops sharply when N decreases to 30. Compared to the above methods, N2 Learned exhibits stable performance in noise suppression as the projection angles decrease, and this approach has significant advantages over other methods on synthetic datasets. Nonetheless, when applied to real data, it is unable to maintain its original advantages in quantitative values, indicating that this approach is highly sensitive to data distribution. As a comparison, the proposed method achieved advantages in various evaluation metrics compared to other methods, which proves that our work in addressing noise suppression and structure preservation achieves an observable outperformance across datasets and projection strategies.

4   Conclusion

In this paper, we proposed a self-supervised enhancing interpretability CT reconstruction method. The key step is to bridge the transform between the sinogram and image domains via a 3D matrix that collects tomographic information for a given image pixel. With this matrix, we are exempt from complex model-based algorithms such as FBP and obtain sufficient information for initial reconstruction in the absence of supervision. Meanwhile, a simple and efficient encoder-decoder refinement network ensures the reliability of the output results. The visual and quantitative experiments compare the proposed method with four reputable ones, and the outperforming results demonstrate the promise of our work in both noise suppression and structure maintenance regardless of variant projection sparsity. Furthermore, we have also observed that our method exhibits inconsistent performance on two types of data. This encourages us to focus on exploring different paradigms in our future work to mitigate the result disparities caused by variations in data distribution, thereby enhancing the robustness of the model.

References

1. Andersen, A.H., Kak, A.C.: Simultaneous algebraic reconstruction technique (sart): a superior implementation of the art algorithm. Ultrason. Imaging **6**(1), 81–94 (1984)
2. Armato, S.G., III., et al.: The lung image database consortium (LIDC) and image database resource initiative (IDRI): a completed reference database of lung nodules on CT scans. Med. Phys. **38**(2), 915–931 (2011)
3. Badrinarayanan, V., Kendall, A., Cipolla, R.: Segnet: A deep convolutional encoder-decoder architecture for image segmentation. IEEE Trans. Pattern Anal. Mach. Intell. **39**(12), 2481–2495 (2017)
4. Beatty, J.: The radon transform and the mathematics of medical imaging (2012)
5. Candes, E.J., Romberg, J.K.: Signal recovery from random projections. In: Computational Imaging III. vol. 5674, pp. 76–86. SPIE (2005)
6. Chen, H., et al.: Low-dose CT with a residual encoder-decoder convolutional neural network. IEEE Trans. Med. Imaging **36**(12), 2524–2535 (2017)

7. Chen, H., et al.: Low-dose CT denoising with convolutional neural network. In: 2017 IEEE 14th International Symposium on Biomedical Imaging (ISBI 2017), pp. 143–146. IEEE (2017)

8. Ernst, P., Chatterjee, S., Rose, G., Speck, O., Nürnberger, A.: Sinogram upsampling using primal-dual UNet for undersampled CT and radial MRI reconstruction. arXiv preprint arXiv:2112.13443 (2021)

9. Ge, R., et al.: DDPNet: a novel dual-domain parallel network for low-dose CT reconstruction. In: Wang, L., Dou, Q., Fletcher, P.T., Speidel, S., Li, S. (eds.) Medical Image Computing and Computer Assisted Intervention – MICCAI 2022: 25th International Conference, Singapore, September 18–22, 2022, Proceedings, Part VI, pp. 748–757. Springer, Cham (2022). https://doi.org/10.1007/978-3-031-16446-0_71

10. Getreuer, P.: Rudin-Osher-Fatemi total variation denoising using split Bregman. Image Process. Line **2**, 74–95 (2012)

11. Hore, A., Ziou, D.: Image quality metrics: PSNR vs. SSIM. In: 2010 20th International Conference on Pattern Recognition, pp. 2366–2369. IEEE (2010)

12. Jun, K.: Virtual multi-alignment theory of parallel-beam CT image reconstruction for rigid objects. Sci. Rep. **9**(1), 13518 (2019)

13. Kak, A.C., Slaney, M.: Principles of computerized tomographic imaging. In: SIAM (2001)

14. Kingma, D.P., Ba, J.: Adam: A method for stochastic optimization. arXiv preprint arXiv:1412.6980 (2014)

15. Lee, H., Lee, J., Kim, H., Cho, B., Cho, S.: Deep-neural-network-based Sinogram synthesis for sparse-view cCTimage reconstruction. IEEE Trans. Radiation Plasma Med. Sci. **3**(2), 109–119 (2018)

16. Leuschner, J., Schmidt, M., Baguer, D.O., Maaß, P.: The lodopab-ct dataset: A benchmark dataset for low-dose ct reconstruction methods. arXiv preprint arXiv:1910.01113 (2019)

17. Li, Z., et al.: Promising generative adversarial network based Sinogram inpainting method for ultra-limited-angle computed tomography imaging. Sensors **19**(18), 3941 (2019)

18. Loshchilov, I., Hutter, F.S.: Stochastic gradient descent with warm restarts (2016)

19. Ronchetti, M.: Torchradon: Fast differentiable routines for computed tomography. arXiv preprint arXiv:2009.14788 (2020)

20. Ronneberger, O., Fischer, P., Brox, T.: U-Net: convolutional networks for biomedical image segmentation. In: Navab, N., Hornegger, J., Wells, W.M., Frangi, A.F. (eds.) Medical Image Computing and Computer-Assisted Intervention – MICCAI 2015: 18th International Conference, Munich, Germany, October 5-9, 2015, Proceedings, Part III, pp. 234–241. Springer, Cham (2015). https://doi.org/10.1007/978-3-319-24574-4_28

21. Sidky, E.Y., Pan, X.: Report on the AAPM deep-learning sparse-view CT grand challenge. Med. Phys. **49**(8), 4935–4943 (2022)

22. Song, Y., Shen, L., Xing, L., Ermon, S.: Solving inverse problems in medical imaging with score-based generative models. arXiv preprint arXiv:2111.08005 (2021)

23. Trancik, M., et al.: Fourier features let networks learn high frequency functions in low dimensional domains. Adv. Neural. Inf. Process. Syst. **33**, 7537–7547 (2020)

24. Unal, M.O., Ertas, M., Yildirim, I.: Self-supervised training for low-dose CT reconstruction. In: 2021 IEEE 18th International Symposium on Biomedical Imaging (ISBI), pp. 69–72. IEEE (2021)

25. Unal, M.O., Ertas, M., Yildirim, I.: An unsupervised reconstruction method for low-dose CT using deep generative regularization prior. Biomed. Signal Process. Control **75**, 103598 (2022)
26. Wang, C., et al.: Improving generalizability in limited-angle CT reconstruction with Sinogram extrapolation. In: de Bruijne, M., et al. (eds.) Medical Image Computing and Computer Assisted Intervention – MICCAI 2021: 24th International Conference, Strasbourg, France, September 27–October 1, 2021, Proceedings, Part VI, pp. 86–96. Springer, Cham (2021). https://doi.org/10.1007/978-3-030-87231-1_9
27. Wang, G., Ye, J.C., De Man, B.: Deep learning for tomographic image reconstruction. Nature Mach. Intell. **2**(12), 737–748 (2020)
28. Wang, H., et al.: InDuDoNet: an interpretable dual domain network for CT metal artifact reduction. In: de Bruijne, M., et al. (eds.) Medical Image Computing and Computer Assisted Intervention – MICCAI 2021: 24th International Conference, Strasbourg, France, September 27–October 1, 2021, Proceedings, Part VI, pp. 107–118. Springer, Cham (2021). https://doi.org/10.1007/978-3-030-87231-1_11
29. Yu, H., Wang, G.: Compressed sensing based interior tomography. Phys. Med. Biol. **54**(9), 2791 (2009)
30. Zamir, S.W., et al.: Multi-stage progressive image restoration. In: Proceedings of the IEEE/CVF Conference on Computer Vision and Pattern Recognition, pp. 14821–14831 (2021)
31. Zang, G., Idoughi, R., Li, R., Wonka, P., Heidrich, W.: Intratomo: self-supervised learning-based tomography via sinogram synthesis and prediction. In: Proceedings of the IEEE/CVF International Conference on Computer Vision, pp. 1960–1970 (2021)
32. Zhang, H., Liu, B., Yu, H., Dong, B.: Metainv-net: meta inversion network for sparse view CT image reconstruction. IEEE Trans. Med. Imaging **40**(2), 621–634 (2020)
33. Zhang, H., et al.: Image prediction for limited-angle tomography via deep learning with convolutional neural network. arXiv preprint arXiv:1607.08707 (2016)
34. Zhao, J., Chen, Z., Zhang, L., Jin, X.: Unsupervised learnable sinogram inpainting network (sin) for limited angle CT reconstruction. arXiv preprint arXiv:1811.03911 (2018)

Feature Aggregation Network for Building Extraction from High-Resolution Remote Sensing Images

Xuan Zhou[✉] and Xuefeng Wei[✉]

Institut Polytechnique de Paris, Rte de Saclay, 91120 Palaiseau, France
{xuan.zhou,xuefeng.wei}@ip-paris.fr

Abstract. The rapid advancement in high-resolution satellite remote sensing data acquisition, particularly those achieving sub-meter precision, has uncovered the potential for detailed extraction of surface architectural features. However, the diversity and complexity of surface distributions frequently lead to current methods focusing exclusively on localized information of surface features. This often results in significant intra-class variability in boundary recognition and between buildings. Therefore, the task of fine-grained extraction of surface features from high-resolution satellite imagery has emerged as a critical challenge in remote sensing image processing. In this work, we propose the Feature Aggregation Network (FANet), concentrating on extracting both global and local features, thereby enabling the refined extraction of landmark buildings from high-resolution satellite remote sensing imagery. The Pyramid Vision Transformer captures these global features, which are subsequently refined by the Feature Aggregation Module and merged into a cohesive representation by the Difference Elimination Module. In addition, to ensure a comprehensive feature map, we have incorporated the Receptive Field Block and Dual Attention Module, expanding the receptive field and intensifying attention across spatial and channel dimensions. Extensive experiments on multiple datasets have validated the outstanding capability of FANet in extracting features from high-resolution satellite images. This signifies a major breakthrough in the field of remote sensing image processing. We will release our code soon.

Keywords: Building extraction · Remote sensing image processing · Deep learning

1 Introduction

Modern remote sensing technology, with its sub-meter high-resolution satellite data, provides a deeper understanding of the surface of the earth. Especially

---

X. Zhou and X. Wei—Equal contribution

F. Liu et al. (Eds.): PRICAI 2023, LNAI 14327, pp. 105–116, 2024.
https://doi.org/10.1007/978-981-99-7025-4_9

the extraction of buildings, a core task of remote sensing image feature extraction, provides critical information for urban planning, population estimation and disaster assessment [1]. However, as the resolution increases, the differences in shape, size, and style between buildings become more apparent. This intensifies intra-class differences and makes it difficult for the model to correctly distinguish between the land object background and the main body of the building. Moreover, factors such as trees and shadows can also reduce segmentation accuracy. Faced with the diversity and complexity of surface distribution, manual classification of land objects is time-consuming and expensive [2]. Therefore, how to extract detailed surface features from high-resolution remote sensing images [3, 4] has become a major challenge in the field of remote sensing image processing.

Most of the existing work concentrates on building extraction methods from high-resolution remote sensing images using machine learning, and while substantial progress has been made, these methods are heavily reliant on manual feature design. With the evolution of deep learning, particularly the Fully Convolutional Networks (FCNs) [5,6], they have demonstrated remarkable progress in enhancing the accuracy and efficiency of building extraction from high-resolution remote sensing images through end-to-end network structures. However, when dealing with high-resolution, complex structures and patterns of remote sensing images, they still face challenges of insufficient global context information. Recently, many researchers have started to use methods based on Transformer, using its powerful global context information acquisition ability to effectively extract complex and diverse land object features. However, its fully connected self-attention mechanism can lead to the neglect of spatial structure information. This results in redundant attention in image processing tasks, leading to a decline in performance in fine spatial information tasks such as building boundary extraction.

We propose a novel Feature Aggregation Network (FANet), which uses a Pyramid Vision Transformer (PVT) [7] in the encoder part of its new design. It effectively addresses attention map redundancy in conventional Transformer-based methods through multi-scale structural design. This revolutionary enhancement notably bolsters the accuracy and efficiency of our model in building extraction tasks. Specifically, the Aggregation Module strengthens the local information in the global features already extracted by the Transformer through spatial and channel information filtering. More precisely, its focus lies in optimizing and supplementing the Transformer's global features from a local perspective. The Difference Elimination Module enhances image comprehension by fusing features at different levels, thereby facilitating interpretation from both global and local perspectives. This effectively compensates for the Transformer's limitations in understanding spatial relationships. Concurrently, the Receptive Field Block and Dual Attention Module augment the model's perception of global and local features by expanding the receptive field and intensifying attention across both spatial and channel dimensions. The Fusion Decoder is responsible for effectively fusing features at high and low layers to output detailed land object extraction results. Extensive experiments on several datasets demonstrate the efficiency of our proposed FANet model in extracting detailed features from high-resolution remote sensing images. The multi-module cooperative design of the model marks a substantial advance in the field of remote sensing image processing. The main contributions of this research are:

1. We propose a FANet framework that enhances the accuracy of landmark building segmentation in high-resolution satellite remote sensing images.
2. The feature aggregation and dual attention modules, designed to filter information and enhance spatial and channel data, boost the model's accuracy and efficiency in extracting buildings from remote sensing images.
3. Experimental results show that FANet outperforms most state-of-the-art models on challenging datasets, demonstrating the effectiveness and robustness of our method in handling complex remote sensing image data.

2 Related Work

Building extraction has made significant strides in research and has played an important role in various fields, such as human activities and socio-economics among others. Earlier studies primarily relied on manually designed features, such as shape, context and shadow indices to identify buildings [8–10]. Subsequent research [11] began to introduce endmembers and associated filters to separate buildings from the background. With the advent of deep learning technologies, techniques such as Fully Convolutional Neural Networks (CNNs) [12] have been introduced into building extraction, significantly improving the execution of this task [13]. For instance, methods such as deep neural networks based on autoencoders [14] and CNNs based on a single path [15] have shown excellent performance in this regard. Despite these methods have proven the effectiveness of using deep neural networks for building extraction, they tend to overlook the impact of building layout changes.

To solve the aforementioned problem, researchers have proposed several methods for multi-scale feature extraction, such as parallel networks [17], and pyramid-based methods [16]. These methods can extract building features from different perspectives and scales, but may overlook the interaction between information at different scales. Meanwhile, to enhance the feature recognition capabilities of CNNs, some research began to introduce attention mechanisms [18,19], while others have achieved higher classification accuracy by integrating the advantages of different network structures or modules [20,21]. However, due to a lack of attention to edge details, the building contours extracted by these methods are often irregular. Recent research has begun to seek methods that reduce the amount of annotation work without sacrificing accuracy. For example, some of the latest methods [22] attempt to model the features of building edges and interiors more accurately through a coarse-to-fine hierarchical training strategy. These methods have been able to model the overall layout and detailed information of buildings effectively, capturing the detailed information inside buildings while ensuring edge accuracy.

However, we note that when dealing with high-resolution satellite remote sensing images, the accuracy of the aforementioned methods in dealing with the edge details of buildings is not ideal, often extracting irregular building contours.

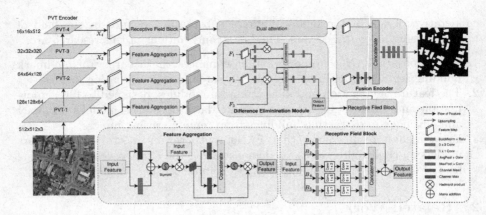

Fig. 1. The proposed Feature Aggregation Network (FANet) workflow. Starting with the Pyramid Vision Transformer for multi-scale feature extraction, the process seamlessly progresses through feature enrichment, integration, receptive field expansion, and dimension amplification, concluding with the Fusion Decoder outputting the final building segmentation.

To address this, we propose a Feature Aggregation Network (FANet) with a Pyramid Vision Transformer (PVT) [7] as the encoder. PVT is a network that employs vision transformers, capable of effectively combining global and local information to improve feature extraction and classification performance. With PVT, our FANet can effectively capture the detailed information inside buildings while ensuring edge accuracy, providing an effective solution for high-precision building extraction.

3   Methodology

We propose the Feature Aggregation Network (FANet), an innovative approach to the fine-grained extraction of buildings from high-definition remote sensing imagery. As illustrated in Fig. 1, FANet is designed around the concept of feature enrichment and integration. It starts with the extraction of multi-scale, long-range dependencies using the Pyramid Vision Transformer encoder. To these initial features, the Feature Aggregation Module provides further enrichment and the Difference Elimination Module integrates low-level details. By expanding the receptive field through the Receptive Field Block and intensifying the spatial and channel dimensions with the Dual Attention Module, FANet achieves a holistic understanding of the image data. The final building segmentation is realized by the Fusion Decoder. The subsequent sections provide a comprehensive exploration of these components and their intricate interplay.

3.1 Transformer Encoder

Given the extensive spatial coverage of remote sensing images, a Pyramid Vision Transformer (PVT) is employed to effectively extract features. The transformer-based backbone [23] processes an input image $I \in \mathbb{R}^{H \times W \times 3}$, generating pyramid features $X_i \in \mathbb{R}^{\frac{H}{2^{i+1}} \times \frac{W}{2^{i+1}} \times C_i}$, where $C_i \in 64, 128, 320, 512$ and $i \in 1, 2, 3, 4$. The channels of the low-layer features X_1, X_2, and X_3 are then acquired via convolutional units and passed to the Feature Aggregation Module (FAM).

This PVT model employs patches of different scales which are fed into Transformers at multiple levels, thereby forming a pyramid-like structure. This approach aids in capturing multi-scale image features, enhancing the model's performance while reducing the computational burden associated with high-resolution images. Specifically, we adopt PVTv2 [23], an improved version of PVT, which possesses a stronger feature extraction capability. Adapting PVTv2 to the task of image segmentation, we discard the last classification layer and design a segmentation head based on the multi-scale feature maps X_1, X_2, X_3, and X_4. These feature maps provide both lower-layer appearance information of building images and high-layer features.

3.2 Feature Aggregation Module

The Feature Aggregation Module (FAM) is employed to refine and enrich the low-layer features (X_1, X_2, X_3) in both spatial and channel dimensions. By applying Global Adaptive Average Pooling (GAvgPool) and Global Adaptive Max Pooling (GMaxPool), we generate channel response maps. The aggregation of these maps, after passing through a Sigmoid function, generates a probability map, R'. Subsequently, channel-level fusion is achieved by the element-wise multiplication of the input F and R', resulting in the feature map F_{channel}. The process can be mathematically expressed as:

$$F_{\text{channel}} = \text{Sigmoid}(\text{GAvgPool}(F) + \text{GMaxPool}(F)) \cdot F, \tag{1}$$

where $F_{\text{channel}} \in \mathbb{R}^{B \times C \times H \times W}$. This method ensures a balanced representation of global and salient features, leading to a comprehensive channel-wise feature profile.

Next, to perform spatial-level feature aggregation, we use the derived feature map F_{channel}. We compute mean and max responses across all channels, concatenate them, and pass through a convolution and a Sigmoid function. The resulting probability map, T', is used for spatial-level fusion, yielding F_{spatial} as follows:

$$F_{\text{spatial}} = \text{Sigmoid}(\text{concat}(\text{Mean}(F_{\text{channel}}), \text{Max}(F_{\text{channel}}))) \cdot F_{\text{channel}}, \tag{2}$$

where $F_{\text{spatial}} \in \mathbb{R}^{B \times C \times H \times W}$. This procedure enables the model to capture average representation and distinctive spatial characteristics, thus providing a more enriched spatial feature description.

3.3 Feature Refinement via Difference Elimination Module and Receptive Field Block

In our method, the Difference Elimination Module (DEM) and the Receptive Field Block (RFB) play critical roles in refining the initial low-level features and crafting a diverse, unified feature representation as shown in Fig. 1. Upon processing by the Feature Aggregation Module (FAM), initial low-level features are transformed into enhanced features (F_1, F_2, F_3). To reconcile differences between adjacent features, these undergo upsampling, convolution, and element-wise multiplication with higher layer maps, resulting in a composite feature representation. These maps are then funneled through the RFB, comprising five branches with adaptable kernel sizes and dilation rates in branches $k > 2$, capturing multi-scale information. The outputs from the last four branches are concatenated and element-wise added to the first branch's output, fostering rich feature interactions. The DEM and RFB synergistically address layer discrepancy issues and enhance the overall feature representation's diversity. The ensuing section will delve into the application of the Dual Attention Module that further refines these composite features, leading to more effective model performance.

3.4 Dual Attention Module for Enhanced Feature Interactions

The Dual Attention Module (DAM) refines high-layer features by capturing interactions across spatial and channel dimensions. It is designed to harness the dependencies inherent in the features along these dimensions, thus augmenting feature representation and enhancing the model's overall interpretive capacity.

The DAM takes an input feature map $A \in \mathbb{R}^{B \times C \times H \times W}$ and generates two new feature maps, B and C. These are utilized to compute a spatial attention map $S \in \mathbb{R}^{N \times N}$. Concurrently, a separate convolution operation on A interacts with S to produce the spatially refined feature map E. This is mathematically encapsulated as follows:

$$E_j = \gamma \sum_{i=1}^{N} \left(\frac{exp(B_i \cdot C_j)}{\sum_{i=1}^{N} exp(B_i \cdot C_j)} D_i \right) + A_j, \tag{3}$$

where γ is a learnable weight parameter that controls the trade-off between the original and the spatially-attended features, initialized as 0. This allows the model to progressively learn the optimal balance as training progresses.

In parallel, the module exploits channel-wise interdependencies by generating a channel attention map $X \in \mathbb{R}^{C \times C}$ directly from A. This map interacts with A to yield the channel-refined feature map M:

$$M_j = \beta \sum_{i=1}^{C} \left(\frac{exp(A_i \cdot A_j^T)}{\sum_{i=1}^{C} exp(A_i \cdot A_j^T)} A_i \right) + A_j, \tag{4}$$

where β is another learnable weight parameter, also initialized as 0. Similar to γ, it controls the mix between the original and the channel-attended features, letting the model learn the optimal balance during training.

The module concludes by combining the spatially and channel-wise refined feature maps, E and M, using an element-wise addition. A 1×1 convolution operation follows, reducing dimensions to complete the fusion enhancement of features. Consequently, the DAM effectively enhances the model's overall capability to understand complex scenes by promoting richer feature interdependencies.

3.5   Fusion Decoder and Loss Function

Our Fusion Decoder, shown in Fig. 1, integrates high-level global contexts with detailed local features, optimizing segmentation. High-level features, providing holistic target understanding, are resized to match low-level features, ensuring a comprehensive fusion. After merging, these features undergo convolutional refinement. A 1×1 convolution yields a predicted segmentation map, resized to the input image dimensions for the final result. The decoder maintains high-level contexts and leverages low-level details, enhancing segmentation. We use the Binary Cross Entropy (BCE) loss to measure consistency between predictions and ground truth.

4   Experiments

4.1   Datasets

To assess the efficiency of our method, we experimented with three public datasets, namely, the WHU Building dataset [17], the Massachusetts Building dataset [31], and the Inria Aerial Building Dataset [32]. The WHU Building dataset contains approximately 220,000 buildings from aerial images. We partitioned the 8189 images of 512×512 pixels into a training set (4736 images), a validation set (1036 images), and a test set (2416 images). The Massachusetts Building dataset, which includes 151 aerial images from the Boston area, was divided post non-overlapping cropping into 512×512 pixels, resulting in 3076 training images, 100 validation images, and 250 test images. Finally, the Inria Aerial Image Labeling Dataset, covering an area of $810 \, \text{km}^2$ across five cities, was split into 8271 training images and 1600 test images after removing training images without buildings. These three datasets, with their diverse geographical contexts, provide a rigorous testing environment for our proposed method.

4.2   Implementation Details

In our model, input image data and label data were cropped to a size of 512×512 pixels. The cropped images underwent data augmentation techniques, including random horizontal flipping and random Gaussian blurring, to generate the preprocessed dataset. Subsequently, all models were trained using the same parameter settings and environment. Our model was developed under the framework of Pytorch 1.8.1 and cuda 11.1, with the hardware of a single GeForce RTX 3090 with 24 GB of computation memory. The initial learning rate was set to

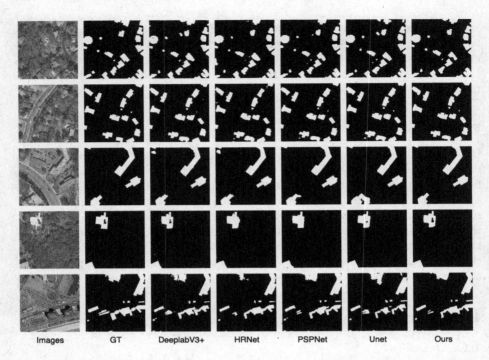

Fig. 2. Visual comparison between our results and those of state-of-the-art methods. The first and second columns represent the building images and the corresponding ground truth, respectively. Columns 3 to 7 display the results generated by UNet [24], PSPNet [25], Deeplabv3+ [26], HRNet [27], and Ours, respectively.

1×10^{-4}, and the Adam optimizer was employed. The learning rate was decayed by a factor of 10 every 50 epochs, and the training process lasted for a total of 100 epochs. To quantitatively evaluate the performance of the proposed method, this study employs four metrics, namely Precision, Recall, F1-score, and Intersection over Union (IoU).

4.3   Comparison with Other State-of-the-Art Methods

To evaluate the effectiveness of the proposed method, we compared our approach with other state-of-the-art methods, including UNet [24], PSPNet [25], Deeplabv3+ [26], HRNet [27], BOMSNet [28], LCS [29], and MSNet [30]. These comparisons were conducted when applied to the WHU Building dataset, the Massachusetts Building dataset, and the Inria Aerial Building Dataset. We performed a visual qualitative evaluation of the experimental results, as shown in Fig. 2. As can be observed from the results, compared to other state-of-the-art methods, our approach yielded superior results in building extraction. Quantitative evaluation results are shown in Table 1.

Table 1. Experimental Results for Various Datasets, The bolded data shown in the table indicates the best data on the corresponding metric and the data with underline indicates the second best one on the corresponding metric.

Dataset	Methods	IoU	F1	Pre	Recall
Massachusetts Building Dataset	UNet	67.61	80.68	79.13	82.29
	PSPNet	66.52	79.87	78.53	81.26
	Deeplabv3+	69.23	81.82	84.73	79.10
	HRNet	69.58	82.01	85.06	79.17
	MSNet	70.21	79.33	78.54	80.14
	Ours	**73.35**	**84.63**	**86.45**	**82.87**
Inria Aerial Building Dataset	UNet	74.40	85.83	86.39	84.28
	PSPNet	76.8	86.88	87.35	86.4
	Deeplabv3+	78.18	87.75	87.93	87.58
	HRNet	79.67	88.68	89.82	87.58
	BOMSNet	78.18	87.75	87.93	87.58
	LCS	78.82	88.15	89.58	86.77
	Ours	**81.05**	**89.53**	**90.49**	**88.60**
WHU Building Dataset	UNet	85.51	92.19	91.86	92.52
	PSPNet	86.68	92.55	92.25	92.86
	Deeplabv3+	85.78	92.35	93.45	91.27
	HRNet	87.85	93.21	94.22	92.23
	MSNet	89.07	93.96	**94.83**	93.12
	Ours	**90.01**	**94.74**	94.50	**94.98**

The rows represent different tested methods, and the columns represent different evaluation metrics. It can be observed that the method we proposed achieved the best performance across all three datasets. On the Massachusetts Building dataset, our proposed method surpassed the second-best method (i.e., MSNet) by approximately 4.47% in IoU, and surpassed the second-best method (i.e., HPNet) by approximately 3.19% and 1.63% in terms of F1-score and Precision, respectively. On the Inria Aerial Building Dataset, compared to HPNet, the IoU and Recall metrics of our proposed method increased by approximately 1.73% and 1.16%, respectively. On the WHU Building dataset, compared to MSNet, the Recall of our proposed method improved by approximately 2%. Experimental comparison with different methods indicates that our proposed method outperformed others on all three datasets.

4.4 Ablation Study

In our investigation, an exhaustive ablation study validates the efficacy of pivotal components within the FANet architecture, namely, the Feature Aggregation Module (FAM), Receptive Field Block (RFB), Dual Attention Module (DAM), and Difference Elimination Module (DEM). These experiments were carried out on the Massachusetts Building Dataset, employing standard benchmarks such as IoU, F1-score, Precision, and Recall.

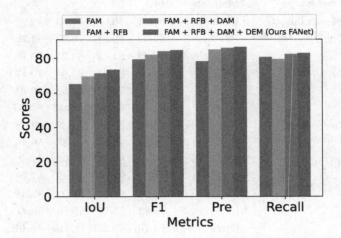

Fig. 3. The results of ablation experiment on Massachusetts Building Dataset.

As demonstrated in Fig. 3, FANet excels across all evaluation metrics. Preliminary experiments with solely FAM displayed a notable enhancement over the baseline model, thereby attesting FAM's effectiveness in information filtering. Upon integrating the RFB with FAM, the model's performance underwent further improvement, underlining the RFB's indispensable role in receptive field expansion. Models lacking the DEM performed sub-optimally in comparison to FANet, indicating that feature fusion amplifies the model's performance. Moreover, FANet surpassed the FAM+RFB+DAM configuration by approximately 2.8% in terms of IoU, accentuating the importance of feature fusion. In summary, the ablation study effectively highlighted the potency of each module within FANet. The stepwise integration of each module led to significant performance enhancements, underscoring their integral role within the network.

5   Conclusion

In this work, we propose a novel Feature Aggregation Network (FANet) for the fine-grained extraction of buildings in high-resolution satellite remote sensing images. This is to address the challenges posed by the variance in shape, size, and style among buildings, and the complex ground conditions that make it difficult to distinguish the main body of buildings. Experimental results on three open-source datasets have validated the effectiveness of the proposed network. FANet can accurately extract the boundaries of buildings in complex environments such as shadows and tree occlusions and achieve the complete extraction of buildings of different scales. For future research in building extraction, designing a robust model trained with less data presents a promising direction.

References

1. Nichol, J.E., Shaker, A., Wong, M.S.: Application of high-resolution stereo satellite images to detailed landslide hazard assessment. Geomorphology **76**, 68–75 (2006)
2. Shao, Z., Tang, P., Wang, Z., Saleem, N., Yam, S., Sommai, C.: BRRNet: a fully convolutional neural network for automatic building extraction from high-resolution remote sensing images. Remote Sens. **12**, 1050 (2020)
3. Hearst, M.A., Dumais, S.T., Osuna, E., Platt, J., Scholkopf, B.: Support Vector Machines. IEEE Intell. Syst. Appl. **13**(4), 18–28 (1998)
4. Biau, G., Scornet, E.: A random forest guided tour. TEST **25**, 197–227 (2016)
5. Chen, L., Papandreou, G., Kokkinos, I., Murphy, K., Yuille, A.L.: Deeplab: Semantic image segmentation with deep convolutional nets, atrous convolution, and fully connected CRFs. IEEE T. Pattern Anal. **40**(4), 834–848 (2017)
6. Chen, L., Zhu, Y., Papandreou, G., Schroff, F., Adam, H.: Encoder-decoder with atrous separable convolution for semantic image segmentation. In: ECCV, pp. 801–818 (2018)
7. Wang, W., et al.: Pyramid vision transformer: A versatile backbone for dense prediction without convolutions. In: ICCV (2021)
8. Sun, Z., Fang, H., Deng, M., Chen, A., Yue, P., Di, L.: Regular shape similarity index: a novel index for accurate extraction of regular objects from remote sensing images. IEEE Trans. Geosci. Remote Sens. **53**(7), 3737–3748 (2015)
9. Huang, X., Zhang, L.: A multidirectional and multiscale morphological index for automatic building extraction from multispectral GeoEye-1 imagery. Photogram. Eng. Remote Sens. **77**(7), 721–732 (2021)
10. Huang, X., Zhang, L.: Morphological building/shadow index for building extraction from high-resolution imagery over urban areas. IEEE J. Sel. Top. Appl. Earth Observ. Remote Sens. **5**(1), 161–172 (2012)
11. Plaza, A., Martinez, P., Perez, R., Plaza, J.: Spatial/spectral endmember extraction by multidimensional morphological operations. IEEE Trans. Geosci. Remote Sens. **40**(9), 2025–2041 (2002)
12. Long, J., Shelhamer, E., Darrell, T.: Fully convolutional networks for semantic segmentation. In CVPR, pp. 3431–3440, (2015)
13. Liu, W., Wang, Z., Liu, X., Zeng, N., Liu, Y., Alsaadi, F.E.: A survey of deep neural network architectures and their applications. Neurocomputing **234**, 11–26 (2017)
14. Protopapadakis, E., et al.: Stacked autoencoders driven by semisupervised learning for building extraction from near infrared remote sensing imagery. Remote Sens. **13**(3), 371 (2021)
15. Alshehhi, R., Marpu, P.R., Woon, W.L., Mura, M.D.: Simultaneous extraction of roads and buildings in remote sensing imagery with convolutional neural networks. ISPRS J. Photogramm. Remote Sens. **130**, 139–149 (2017)
16. Liu, Y., Chen, D., Ma, A., Zhong, Y., Fang, F., Xu, K.: Multiscale U-shaped CNN building instance extraction framework with edge constraint for high-spatial-resolution remote sensing imagery. IEEE Trans. Geosci. Remote Sens. **59**(7), 6106–6120 (2021)

17. Ji, S., Wei, S., Lu, M.: Fully convolutional networks for multisource building extraction from an open aerial and satellite imagery data set. IEEE Trans. Geosci. Remote Sens. **57**(1), 574–586 (2019)
18. Deng, W., Shi, Q., Li, J.: Attention-gate-based encoder-decodernetwork for automatical building extraction. IEEE J.-STARS. **14** 2611–2620 (2021)
19. Tian, Q., Zhao, Y., Li, J., Chen, J., Chen, X., Qin, K.: MultiscaleBuilding extraction with refined attention pyramid networks. IEEEGeosci. Remote S. **19**, 1–5 (2022)
20. Chatterjee, B., Poullis, C.: Semantic segmentation from remote sensordata and the exploitation of latent learning for classification of auxiliarytasks. Comput. Vis. Image Und. **210**, 103251 (2021)
21. Chen, M., et al.: DR-Net: An Improved Network for Building Extractionfrom High Resolution Remote Sensing Image. Remote Sens.-Basel **13**(2), 294 (2021)
22. Zhang, H., Liao, Y., Yang, H., Yang, G., Zhang, L.: A local-global dual-stream network for building extraction from very-high-resolution remote sensing images. IEEE Trans. Neural Netw. Learn. Syst. **33**(3), 1269–1283 (2022)
23. Wang, W., Xie, E., Li, X., et al.: Pvt v2: improved baselines with pyramid vision transformer. Comput. Visual Media **8**(3), 415–424 (2022)
24. Ronneberger, O., Fischer, P., Brox, T.: U-Net: convolutional networks for biomedical image segmentation. In: Navab, N., Hornegger, J., Wells, W.M., Frangi, A.F. (eds.) MICCAI 2015. LNCS, vol. 9351, pp. 234–241. Springer, Cham (2015). https://doi.org/10.1007/978-3-319-24574-4_28
25. Zhao, H., Shi, J., Qi, X., Wang, X., Jia, J.: Pyramid scene parsing network. In: Proceedings of the IEEE Conference on Computer Vision and Pattern Recognition, pp. 2881–2890 (2017)
26. Chen, L.-C., Zhu, Y., Papandreou, G., Schroff, F., Adam, H.: Encoder-decoder with atrous separable convolution for semantic image segmentation, arXiv:1802.02611 (2018)
27. Wang, J., Sun, K., Cheng, T., et al.: Deep high-resolution representation learning for visual recognition. IEEE Trans. Pattern Anal. Mach. Intell. **43**(10), 3349–3364 (2020)
28. Zhou, Y., et al.: BOMSC-Net: boundary optimization and multi-scale context awareness based building extraction from high-resolution remote sensing imagery. IEEE Trans. Geosci. Remote Sens. **60**, 1–17 (2022)
29. Liu, Z., Shi, Q., Ou, J.: LCS: A collaborative optimization framework of vector extraction and semantic segmentation for building extraction. IEEE Trans. Geosci. Remote Sens. **60**, 1–15 (2022)
30. Zhu, X., Liang, J., Hauptmann, A.: Msnet: A multilevel instance segmentation network for natural disaster damage assessment in aerial videos. In: Proceedings of the IEEE/CVF Winter Conference on Applications of Computer Vision, pp. 2023–2032 (2021)
31. Mnih, V.: Machine learning for aerial image labeling. In: University of Toronto (Canada) (2013)
32. Maggiori, E., Tarabalka, Y., Charpiat, G., et al.: Can semantic labeling methods generalize to any city? the inria aerial image labeling benchmark. In: 2017 IEEE International Geoscience and Remote Sensing Symposium (IGARSS). IEEE, pp. 3226–3229 (2017)

Image Quality Assessment Method Based on Cross-Modal

Teng Long[1,2], Li Chen[1,2(✉)], and Yubo Wang[1,2]

[1] School of Computer Science and Technology, Wuhan University of Science and Technology, Wuhan 430065, Hubei, China
[2] Hubei Province Key Laboratory of Intelligent Information Processing and Real-time Industrial System, Wuhan University of Science and Technology, Wuhan 430065, Hubei, China
chenli@wust.edu.cn

Abstract. Deep learning methods have achieved remarkable results in the direction of image quality assessment tasks. However, most of the related studies focus only on image unimodal, ignoring the potential advantages that come with the development of cross-modal techniques. Cross-modal models have implied a wealth of information, which provides new research directions and possibilities in the field of image quality assessment. In this paper, the feasibility of cross-modal models in image quality assessment is first explored for the image quality binary classification task. Subsequently, the optimization prompting method is combined with the tuning of the image encoder in the cross-modal model so that the cross-modal model can be used for image quality assessment scoring. To verify the feasibility of the cross-modal model on the image quality assessment task, an empirical analysis was conducted on the binary image quality dataset PQD, and it was found that the F1 score improved by 18% over the baseline model. Further, we propose an adaptive cross-modal image quality assessment method AC-IQA. On the image quality scoring dataset, compared with the previous optimal methods, AC-IQA improves the PLCC and SROCC metrics on the TID2013 dataset by 5.5% and 9.5%, respectively, and on the KADID dataset by 6.2% and 5.2%.

Keywords: Cross-modal · Image Quality Assessment · Prompt Optimization

1 Introduction

With the increasing number of images on the Internet, people have higher and higher requirements for the quality of images. Automatic assessment of image quality has become a critical task in the domain of computer vision. It is important to design methods that can accomplish this objective. In the past, image

This work was supported by National Natural Science Foundation of China (62271359).

F. Liu et al. (Eds.): PRICAI 2023, LNAI 14327, pp. 117–128, 2024.
https://doi.org/10.1007/978-981-99-7025-4_10

quality assessment methods mainly adopted manually designed feature extraction. Although these methods perform well on specific images or simulated data, the poor generalization of hand-designed features to real-life datasets makes them inconvenient for practical applications. Due to the advancement of deep learning techniques, many studies of image quality assessment have used cnn-based methods. The performance of deep learning methods has surpassed that of traditional methods, but the training process often uses only information from a single module of the image and ignores the role of other modal information for image quality assessment.

With the continuous progress of technology, cross-modal techniques have gradually matured in recent years with deep learning models capable of handling multiple data types, such as text, image, audio, and video. These models can capture the inter-relationship between different modalities to achieve more powerful and general representation learning. CLIP [17] is a pre-training model proposed by OpenAI to learn both image and text representations, which can train models to predict similarities between image and text to achieve zero-shot learning for various visual-language tasks. Furthermore, Stable Diffusion [18] is credited as the leading open source image generation model, which uses the CLIP model as the text encoder, and when performing a "text-to-image" task using a Stable Diffusion model, we often want to generate high quality images, add prompt such as "high quality" and "high precision" is effective. This indicates that the large cross-modal model of text-image has already implied the representation information for image quality assessment. This cross-modal technique provides new possibilities for image quality assessment.

To fill the gap of under-utilization of cross-modal information in image quality assessment tasks, we propose a cross-modal based approach for image quality assessment. First, the cross-modal model is introduced in the binary classification task, and the feasibility of using the cross-modal model for image quality assessment is demonstrated by a fine-tuning method. Second, the optimization prompting method is combined with the tuning of the image encoder in the cross-modal model so that the cross-modal model can be used for image quality assessment scoring. Finally, leading assessment metrics are achieved on multiple image quality assessment datasets.

2   Related Work

2.1   Deep Learning-Based Image Quality Assessment

Deep learning-based IQA (Image Quality Assessment) mainly focuses on convolutional neural network (CNN), whose convolutional structure brings it powerful feature extraction and feature mapping capabilities. Recent research on IQA methods has predominantly focused on constructing convolutional neural network models [8] and conducting joint research on multi-tasking using neural networks [22,25]. RankIQA [12] uses distorted images as a training set, and then uses transfer learning techniques to train deeper networks. Meta-IQA [31] explores the meta-knowledge shared by humans when assessing distorted images. CAE-IQA [2] focuses on spatial features in images and uses convolutional autoencoder to generate distortion maps for better results in training.NIMA [20] proposes the method to predict human subjective and perceptual distribution opinion scores.DBCNN [28] uses a deep bilinear model structure for adaptive determination and assessment of synthetic and real distortion in image quality. Even these deep learning based methods have improved results over traditional methods, they use only image single modality information and ignore image quality information in other modalities.

2.2   Cross-Modal Techniques

Cross-modal techniques are maturing, with deep learning models that can handle multiple data types, such as text, image, audio, and video. These models can capture the inter-relationship between different modalities to enable more powerful and general representation learning. CLIP is a pre-trained model proposed by OpenAI to learn both image and text representations. It trains the model by learning to predict matches between text and images, thus enabling zero-sample learning for multiple visual-language tasks. ViLBERT [13] is a BERT-based cross-modal model for visual-language tasks. The model comprises two distinct BERT structures that separately process image and text features. These features are then fused to perform cross-modal tasks. LXMERT [21] is a cross-modal pre-training model that simultaneously learns visual-language representations. It employs a self-attention mechanism to process image and text inputs and facilitates information exchange through a cross-modal self-attention layer.

Based on these cross-modal models, various downstream tasks have been explored. CLIPAdapter [3] uses Stochastic Gradient Descent (SGD) training to introduce a Multilayer Perceptron (MLP) into a pre-trained CLIP model. CoOp [30] and CoCoOp [29] introduce a co-optimization approach to jointly optimize prompts and model parameters. Tip Adapter [27] uses a caching model that corresponds to the labels in the database in order to store the features of the image during training. But it still employs handcraft prompts and cannot fully leverage the vast knowledge of CLIP model text encoders for tasks such as image quality assessment. It is difficult to design prompts manually and requires prompt optimization. Visual Prompt Tuning (VPT) [7] improves the performance of cross-modal models by customizing the prompts based on image inputs.

Most of these cross-modal models and techniques for downstream tasks have been developed, but they generally combine visual-language modal for image classification, segmentation, or detection, with little efforts in image quality assessment. The design of prompts for text encoder that the image quality information is implicit inside the visual cross-modal model, which provides a new direction for assessing the quality of images.

3   Methods

3.1   Exploring the Feasibility of Cross-Modal Models

Binary classification is a basic classical task for image quality assessment, such as high quality and low quality. When using a unimodal approach, only the image information is classified (Let 0 for high quality image labels and 1 for low quality image label). As shown in Fig. 1, this is a unimodal task with only image information.

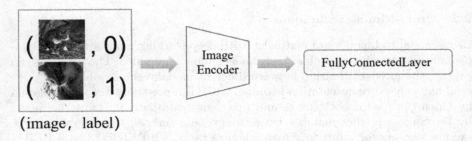

Fig. 1. Methods for unimodal image quality classification.

Image-text cross-modal models can be generally used in image classification, detection and segmentation. We find that the information on image quality is already implicit in the large cross-modal model of image-text. As shown in Fig. 2.

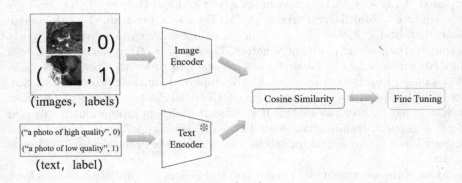

Fig. 2. Methods for cross-modal image quality classification.

In the text encoder of the cross-modal model CLIP, two different prompts of high and low quality are taken as input, and two text encoding feature$\{w_i\}_{i=\{0,1\}}$ are obtained. The cosine similarity is calculated with the image encoding feature x. The probability $p(y \mid x)$ of each image for the text prompts y is obtained as shown in Eq. 1, where sim indicates the calculation of the cosine similarity. We classify the images by selecting the prompt with the highest calculated value of cosine similarity to the image.

$$p(y|x) = sim(x, w_y) \qquad (1)$$

We found that in CLIP zero-shot inference, high and low quality images can be initially classified, while better results can be achieved using few-shot for learning after adding a fully connected layer for fine-tuning after calculating the cosine similarity.

3.2   Image Quality Score Assessment Based on Cross-Modality

In the area of image quality assessment, the majority of studies are focused on scoring tasks, which requires that the final result should be regressed to a score. After calculating the cosine similarity of the image and text, the results are normalized to fit the subsequent loss calculation, and the normalization function is in Eq. 2, and S is the final score.

$$S = \frac{exp\left(sim\left(x, w_0\right)\right)}{exp\left(sim\left(x, w_0\right)\right) + exp\left(sim\left(x, w_1\right)\right)} \qquad (2)$$

Image quality scoring is more complex than image quality classification. The text input with prompt can be adaptively optimized to enhance the coupling between images and prompt. In this work, this approach is called AC-IQA (Adaptable CLIP Image Quality Assessment), as shown in Fig. 3.

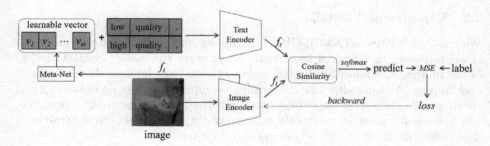

Fig. 3. AC-IQA method structure.

We put "low quality" and "high quality" as fixed prompts with a learnable vector prefix to tune the text encoder input. Text features f_t and image features f_i are obtained from two different modal encoders of CLIP respectively. The meta network uses two linear layers, with ReLU as the activation function in the middle, which incorporates the features of the image f_i into the learnable vector to adapt the text features f_t to the image. After normalizing the cosine similarity, in order to improve the sensitivity of the model to minute scoring errors, we backpropagate the prediction loss by using the mean square error (MSE) as a loss function.

4 Experiments

4.1 Datasets

This work conducted experiments on various image quality assessment tasks. The following datasets are used in this paper: the PQD [14] dataset explores the feasibility of cross-modal large models in image quality assessment; the TID2013 [16], KADID-10K [11] and CSIQ [10] datasets validates the advancement of our method in image quality scoring tasks.

PDQ comes from a total of 29690 photographic images in real scenes, and through manual classification, these images were categorized into 19,166 and 10,524 as low and high quality images respectively, of which 8,000 images are taken and split into the training set, validation set, and test set in a ratio of 7:1:2. This dataset is used to verify the applicability of the image-text cross-modal model in image quality assessment.

The TID2013, KADID-10K and CSIQ datasets were labeled with mean subjective opinion scores (MOS) of 3,000, 1,0125 and 866 images, respectively. In this paper, 80% and 20% of these datasets are used as training and test sets according to the commonly used methods in image quality assessment [4, 19]. To ensure statistical robustness, the training and test sets are randomly sampled 10 times, and the median of the 10 results is taken as the final result during the experiment.

4.2 Experimental Details

We use an NVIDIA RTX3070 GPU for training and testing, and our program is written using the Pytorch framework. To preserve the quality characteristics of the images, we simply apply data augmentation techniques such as cropping and flipping. Additionally, adaptive scaling is employed to handle datasets with varying scale sizes when inputting them into the model. The Adam optimizer and cosine annealing learning rate tuning strategy were used during training. The batch size is set to 16 for training and 4 for testing.

4.3 Evaluation Metrics

The proposed method was evaluated in different experiments using various metrics to assess its effectiveness. For binary classification, the F1 score was used to measure the effectiveness. In the image quality scoring task, we used two evaluation metrics, the Pearson linear correlation coefficient (PLCC) is defined by in Eq. 3:

$$PLCC = \frac{\sum_{i=1}^{N} (s_i - \bar{s})(p_i - \bar{p})}{\sqrt{\sum_{i=1}^{N} (s_i - \bar{s})^2 \sum_{i=1}^{N} (p_i - \bar{p})^2}} \tag{3}$$

where s_i and p_i represent the subjective and objective quality score of the i-th image, respectively. N denotes sample size, and $\bar{s}$ and $\bar{p}$ are the average subjective and objective quality scores, respectively. The Spearman rank-order correlation coefficient (SROCC) is defined by Eq. 4:

$$SROCC = 1 - \frac{6\sum_{i=1}^{N} d_i^2}{N(N^2 - 1)} \tag{4}$$

where N denotes sample size. For the i-th image, d_i is defined as the difference between its subjective and objective quality score rankings for i-th image.

4.4   Feasibility Research

The feasibility of the cross-modal approach in image quality assessment is explored using the PQD binary classification dataset, and the CLIP cross-modal model is introduced, with "low quality" and "high quality" as binary prompts words, and add a fully connected layer after the image encoder for fine-tuning. A simple image unimodal classification network based on ResNet50 [6] is constructed as a benchmark, and its parameters are initialized using KaiMing [5]. Correspondingly, the image encoder in CLIP also uses the ResNet50 architecture. The results of the experiment can be shown in the Table 1.

Table 1. Experiments of CLIP method and unimodal method for image quality classification.

Method	Epoch	Train samples	Accuracy↑	F1 score↑	Train time/s↓
unimodal(ResNet50)	30	2800	0.802	0.778	1913.78
CLIP(ResNet50)	0	0	0.642	0.684	0
CLIP(ResNet50)	6	32	0.804	0.818	110.88
CLIP(ResNet50)	6	64	0.863	0.872	112.43
CLIP(ResNet50)	6	1024	0.917	0.919	124.03
CLIP(ResNet50)	6	2800	0.890	0.891	153.63

In Table 1, it can be verified that the pre-trained model using CLIP exhibits a certain degree of image quality assessment capability even under zero sample conditions. After subsequent fine-tuning of the training, the performance has surpassed the results of the unimodal model with 2800 training samples after 30 rounds of training, using only 32 training samples for 6 rounds of training. In addition, in the scenario where the CLIP method is applied with 1024 training samples, its accuracy is improved by 14% and F1 score is improved by 18% compared to the unimodal model. The multimodal model has advantages over the unimodal model for the image quality binary classification task, as shown in Fig. 4.

The performance of CLIP decreases when it reaches 2800 train samples. We believe that this is due to overfitting on the training set, which leads to a degradation of the model's performance on the test set, which precisely illustrates the versatility of the CLIP pre-trained model for image quality assessment, and that too much training rather affects this advantage. Compared with the unimodal approach, the cross-modal approach requires the use of multiple encoders, which undoubtedly increases the consumption during inference. However, the advantages of the cross-modal approach in training are obvious, as can be seen from the data in Table 1, CLIP requires cross-modal feature extraction for both text and images when adapting to image quality classification training, but saves a lot of training time because fewer weights are updated, so that the cross-modal approach can quickly train the image quality assessment model.

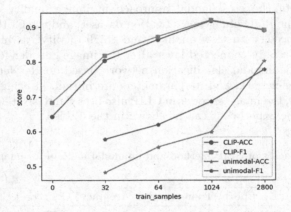

Fig. 4. Comparison of CLIP and unimodal methods in image quality classification.

Through this section of experiments, it can be demonstrated that the CLIP cross-modal model, although not explicitly labeled with quality information during pre-training, can be seen in the subsequent downstream tasks to have implicitly rich features of image quality. It provides feasibility for its role in image quality assessment.

4.5   Comparison Experiments

We compare several image quality assessment methods on several scoring label-based datasets TID2013, KADID-10K and CSIQ. Some of their labeling and prediction results are shown in Fig. 5.

The results of PLCC and SROCC are shown in Table 2. In the CSIQ dataset the SROCC of this paper method can reach the suboptimal result, while in both TID2013 and KADID datasets, this paper method reaches the optimal metric, compared to the suboptimal result the PLCC improves by 5.5% and 6.2%, respectively, and the SROCC improves by 9.5% and 5.2%, respectively.

predict:1.46
label:1.4

predict:2.52
label:2.67

predict:3.63
label:3.73

predict:4.53
label:4.63

Fig. 5. Test results on the KADID dataset

Table 2. Comparison experiments between AC-IQA and other methods on the TID2013 , KADID-10K and CSIQ datasets, where underlining represents sub-optimal results and the bolded font represents the best results.

Method	TID2013		KADID		CSIQ	
	PLCC↑	SROCC↑	PLCC↑	SROCC↑	PLCC↑	SROCC↑
PQR [24]	0.864	0.849	–	–	0.901	0.873
BRISQUE [15]	0.571	0.626	0.567	0.528	0.748	0.812
ILNIQE [26]	0.648	0.521	0.558	0.534	0.865	0.822
BIECON [9]	0.762	0.717	0.648	0.623	0.823	0.815
WaDIQaM [1]	0.855	0.835	0.752	0.739	0.844	0.852
DBCNN [28]	0.865	0.816	0.856	0.851	**0.959**	**0.946**
TIQA [23]	0.858	0.846	0.855	0.850	0.838	0.825
MetaIQA [31]	0.868	0.856	0.775	0.762	0.908	0.899
HyperIQA [19]	0.858	0.840	0.845	0.852	<u>0.942</u>	0.923
TReS [4]	<u>0.883</u>	<u>0.863</u>	<u>0.858</u>	<u>0.859</u>	<u>0.942</u>	0.922
AC-IQA(ours)	**0.932**	**0.945**	**0.924**	**0.920**	0.922	<u>0.932</u>

Among the compared methods, such as HyperIQA, which also use ResNet50 as an image feature extraction module like the method in this paper. However, compared to these unimodal methods, this work incorporates cross-modal information from text and achieves significant improvements in the metrics of the image quality scoring task. This is sufficient to demonstrate the rich information of image quality representation in the cross-modal model and the superiority of applying it to image quality assessment.

Table 3. Ablation experiments with or without using Prompt Optimization.

Method	TID2013		KADID	
	PLCC	SROCC	PLCC	SROCC
AC-IQA(w/o)	0.924	0.916	0.901	0.903
AC-IQA(w/)	**0.932**	**0.945**	**0.924**	**0.920**

4.6 Ablation Experiments

In order to verify the role of prompts optimization in cross-modal methods in image quality assessment, experiments were conducted with (w/) and without (w/o) the use of the Prompt Optimization method, respectively, as shown in Table 3.

The ablation experiments identified that after using the prompt optimization method, the PLCC and SROCC metrics improved by 0.8% and 3.1% on the TID2012 dataset, and by 2.6% and 0.9% on the KADID dataset. All the metrics improved, which indicates that the initial prompts designed manually, when the cross-modal model is applied to image quality assessment, not fully competent for the image quality assessment task. Optimization and adjusting prompts can lead to better performance in cross-modal model image quality assessment tasks.

5 Conclusion

This paper presents a novel approach for evaluating image quality by adapting and optimizing a cross-modal model. By adapting the vision-language models for image quality assessment, our method achieved superior results. Our approach innovatively leverages the rich perceptual information in cross-modal models to improve image quality assessment, opening up new avenues for further development in this field.

6 Outlook

In recent years, cross-modal techniques have made remarkable developments. This study only provides a preliminary discussion on the application of the vision-language cross-modal model CLIP in the field of image quality assessment. Looking ahead, we can try to combine other modalities such as audio and video with images to further enrich the image quality assessment methods. In addition, the cross-modal text model is closely related to the field of natural language processing, and we can achieve a more accurate description of image quality with the help of more advanced prompt optimization techniques. We firmly believe that with the continuous development of cross-modal technology, its application in the field of image quality assessment will become more and more efficient and in-depth.

References

1. Bosse, S., Maniry, D., Müller, K.R., Wiegand, T., Samek, W.: Deep neural networks for no-reference and full-reference image quality assessment. IEEE Trans. Image Process. **27**(1), 206–219 (2017)
2. Dendi, S.V.R., Dev, C., Kothari, N., Channappayya, S.S.: Generating image distortion maps using convolutional autoencoders with application to no reference image quality assessment. IEEE Signal Process. Lett. **26**(1), 89–93 (2018)
3. Gao, P., et al.: CLIP-Adapter: better vision-language models with feature adapters. arXiv preprint arXiv:2110.04544 (2021)
4. Golestaneh, S.A., Dadsetan, S., Kitani, K.M.: No-reference image quality assessment via transformers, relative ranking, and self-consistency. In: Proceedings of the IEEE/CVF Winter Conference on Applications of Computer Vision, pp. 1220–1230 (2022)
5. He, K., Zhang, X., Ren, S., Sun, J.: Delving deep into rectifiers: surpassing human-level performance on imagenet classification. In: Proceedings of the IEEE International Conference on Computer Vision, pp. 1026–1034 (2015)
6. He, K., Zhang, X., Ren, S., Sun, J.: Deep residual learning for image recognition. In: Proceedings of the IEEE Conference on Computer Vision and Pattern Recognition, pp. 770–778 (2016)
7. Jia, M., et al.: Visual prompt tuning. In: Avidan, S., Brostow, G., Cissé, M., Farinella, G.M., Hassner, T. (eds.) Computer Vision-ECCV 2022: 17th European Conference, Tel Aviv, Israel, October 23–27, 2022, Proceedings, Part XXXIII, vol. 13693, pp. 709–727. Springer, Cham (2022). https://doi.org/10.1007/978-3-031-19827-4_41
8. Jin, X., et al.: ILGNet: inception modules with connected local and global features for efficient image aesthetic quality classification using domain adaptation. IET Comput. Vision **13**(2), 206–212 (2019)
9. Kim, J., Lee, S.: Fully deep blind image quality predictor. IEEE J. Sel. Top. Sign. Proces. **11**(1), 206–220 (2017)
10. Larson, E.C., Chandler, D.M.: Most apparent distortion: full-reference image quality assessment and the role of strategy. J. Electron. Imaging **19**(1), 011006 (2010)
11. Lin, H., Hosu, V., Saupe, D.: KADID-10k: a large-scale artificially distorted IQA database. In: 2019 Eleventh International Conference on Quality of Multimedia Experience (QoMEX), pp. 1–3. IEEE (2019)
12. Liu, X., Van De Weijer, J., Bagdanov, A.D.: RankIQA: learning from rankings for no-reference image quality assessment. In: Proceedings of the IEEE International Conference on Computer Vision, pp. 1040–1049 (2017)
13. Lu, J., Batra, D., Parikh, D., Lee, S.: ViLBERT: pretraining task-agnostic visiolinguistic representations for vision-and-language tasks. In: Advances in Neural Information Processing Systems 32 (2019)
14. Luo, W., Wang, X., Tang, X.: Content-based photo quality assessment. In: 2011 International Conference on Computer Vision, pp. 2206–2213. IEEE (2011)
15. Mittal, A., Moorthy, A.K., Bovik, A.C.: No-reference image quality assessment in the spatial domain. IEEE Trans. Image Process. **21**(12), 4695–4708 (2012)
16. Ponomarenko, N., et al.: Image database TID2013: peculiarities, results and perspectives. Sign. process. Image Commun. **30**, 57–77 (2015)
17. Radford, A., et al.: Learning transferable visual models from natural language supervision. In: International Conference on Machine Learning, pp. 8748–8763. PMLR (2021)

18. Rombach, R., Blattmann, A., Lorenz, D., Esser, P., Ommer, B.: High-resolution image synthesis with latent diffusion models. In: Proceedings of the IEEE/CVF Conference on Computer Vision and Pattern Recognition, pp. 10684–10695 (2022)
19. Su, S., et al.: Blindly assess image quality in the wild guided by a self-adaptive hyper network. In: Proceedings of the IEEE/CVF Conference on Computer Vision and Pattern Recognition, pp. 3667–3676 (2020)
20. Talebi, H., Milanfar, P.: NIMA: neural image assessment. IEEE Trans. Image Process. **27**(8), 3998–4011 (2018)
21. Tan, H., Bansal, M.: LXMERT: learning cross-modality encoder representations from transformers. arXiv preprint arXiv:1908.07490 (2019)
22. Yan, W., Li, Y., Yang, H., Huang, B., Pan, Z.: Semantic-aware multi-task learning for image aesthetic quality assessment. Connect. Sci. **34**(1), 2689–2713 (2022)
23. You, J., Korhonen, J.: Transformer for image quality assessment. In: 2021 IEEE International Conference on Image Processing (ICIP), pp. 1389–1393. IEEE (2021)
24. Zeng, H., Zhang, L., Bovik, A.C.: A probabilistic quality representation approach to deep blind image quality prediction. arXiv preprint arXiv:1708.08190 (2017)
25. Zhang, H., Luo, Y., Zhang, L., Wu, Y., Wang, M., Shen, Z.: Considering three elements of aesthetics: multi-task self-supervised feature learning for image style classification. Neurocomputing **520**, 262–273 (2023)
26. Zhang, L., Zhang, L., Bovik, A.C.: A feature-enriched completely blind image quality evaluator. IEEE Trans. Image Process. **24**(8), 2579–2591 (2015)
27. Zhang, R., et al.: Tip-Adapter: training-free adaption of clip for few-shot classification. In: Avidan, S., Brostow, G., Ciss, M., Farinella, G.M., Hassner, T. (eds.) Computer Vision-ECCV 2022: 17th European Conference, Tel Aviv, Israel, October 23–27, 2022, Proceedings, Part XXXV, vol. 13695, pp. 493–510. Springer, Cham (2022). https://doi.org/10.1007/978-3-031-19833-5_29
28. Zhang, W., Ma, K., Yan, J., Deng, D., Wang, Z.: Blind image quality assessment using a deep bilinear convolutional neural network. IEEE Trans. Circuits Syst. Video Technol. **30**(1), 36–47 (2018)
29. Zhou, K., Yang, J., Loy, C.C., Liu, Z.: Conditional prompt learning for vision-language models. In: Proceedings of the IEEE/CVF Conference on Computer Vision and Pattern Recognition, pp. 16816–16825 (2022)
30. Zhou, K., Yang, J., Loy, C.C., Liu, Z.: Learning to prompt for vision-language models. Int. J. Comput. Vision **130**(9), 2337–2348 (2022)
31. Zhu, H., Li, L., Wu, J., Dong, W., Shi, G.: MetaIQA: deep meta-learning for no-reference image quality assessment. In: Proceedings of the IEEE/CVF Conference on Computer Vision and Pattern Recognition, pp. 14143–14152 (2020)

KDED: A Knowledge Distillation Based Edge Detector

Yachuan Li[1]([⊠])(iD), Xavier Soria P.[2](iD), Yun Bai[1](iD), Qian Xiao[1](iD), Chaozhi Yang[1](iD), Guanlin Li[1](iD), and Zongmin Li[1]([⊠])(iD)

[1] China University of Petroleum (East China), Qingdao 266500, Shandong, China
{liyachuan,baiyun,xiaoqian,liguanlin}@s.upc.edu.cn,lizongmin@upc.edu.cn
[2] National University of Chimborazo, 060110 Riobamba, Chimborazo, Ecuador
xavier.soria@unach.edu.ec

Abstract. Deep learning-based edge detectors are successful due to the large amount of supervisory information provided by manual labeling. However, there are inevitably errors in the manually labeled supervisory information (MLSI), which greatly mislead the learning of the models and become the bottleneck of deep learning-based edge detectors. To solve the drawbacks of MLSI, we propose a novel Knowledge Distillation based Edge Detector (KDED). By means of knowledge distillation, MLSI is transformed into edge probability map to supervise the learning of the models, which can effectively correct the errors in MLSI and represents disputed edges by probability. Adapting to the new training strategy and solving the sample imbalance problem, the Sample Balance Loss is proposed, which ensures the stability of the model and improve the accuracy. The experimental results indicate that KDED remarkably improves the accuracy without increasing the parameters and the computational cost. KDED achieves an ODS F-measure of 0.832 with 14.8 M parameters on BSDS500 dataset, which is significantly super to the results of previous methods. The source code is available at this link.

Keywords: Edge detection · Knowledge distillation · Sample balance loss

1 Introduction

Edge detection is a fundamental task used to obtain boundaries and visually remarkable edges of objects in images. Thus, it has been widely applied to other downstream tasks of computer vision, such as image segmentation [13], depth map prediction [29], and salient detection [28].

Edge detection is a typical binary classification task that divides the pixels of images into edges and non-edges. Earlier manual feature-based methods [3,17] rely on low-level cues to classify pixels. Since edges are semantically meaningful, using low-level cues to represent edges is a herculean work. From the past

F. Liu et al. (Eds.): PRICAI 2023, LNAI 14327, pp. 129–140, 2024.
https://doi.org/10.1007/978-981-99-7025-4_11

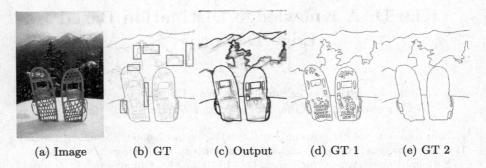

(a) Image   (b) GT   (c) Output   (d) GT 1   (e) GT 2

Fig. 1. (a) An image randomly selected from BSDS500 dataset. (b) GT is the abbreviation of ground truth, which refers to the collection of manually labeled supervisory information corresponding to the image. And red boxes are used to highlight contradictions between different labels (c) The prediction of the teacher network in our experiment. (d) and (e) are manually labeled supervisory information labeled by different people, which are part of ground truth in (b). (Color figure online)

few years, edge detection has achieved great success with the help of the excellent semantic information aggregation ability of Convolutional Neural Networks (CNN). HED [24], the pioneer of contemporary edge detector, firstly introduces multi-scale predictions and deep supervision into deep learning-based edge detection. Inspired by HED, many excellent methods [4,6,12] are produced, making deep learning-based methods known as the mainstream of edge detection. Deep learning-based methods are data-driven, in which the learning of the models is guided by manually labeled supervisory information (MLSI). MLSI has emerged as a crucial factor contributing to the deep learning-based edge detectors, as it helps models better understand semantic edges.

However, MLSI has huge drawbacks. Firstly, the annotation information is not accurate, which will mislead the learning of the models. As highlighted in the red boxes of Fig. 1(b), for the same edge, there are significant errors in the manual labels of different people. Second, different people have different definitions of edge when labeling edges, which seriously confuses the model, as shown in Fig. 1(d) and (e). Furthermore, single-pixel wide edge conflicts with the locally relevant of the convolution operation and increases the difficulty of model learning.

To address those drawbacks of MLSI, we develop a Knowledge Distillation based Edge Detector (KDED), in which a new label optimization strategy is proposed to eliminate the adverse effects of MLSI. Specifically, MLSI is transformed into edge probability map by knowledge distillation [7] to train our model. Therefore, the prior knowledge in the teacher network is exploited to eliminate the divergence in the definition of the edge and correct the error caused by the annotation. It can avoid the misdirection of the annotation error and effectively improve the accuracy of the results. In order to adapt to the new supervisory information, we proposed a new Sample Balance Loss (SBL) to further distribute the sample weights in the images, which can ensure the stable training of the student network and further improve the performance of the student network. The basic model of KDED is a compact twice fusion network based on VGG-16 [19]. The label optimization strategy and new loss function do not increase the number of parameters and computation cost of the network, either in training or inference.

The contributions of the paper are as follows: (1) To our knowledge, we systematically analyze and summarize the problems of MLSI in edge detection for the first time. (2) We propose a Knowledge Distillation based Edge Detector (KDED), in which a new label optimization strategy and the corresponding loss function are utilized to solve the problems existing in MLSI. (3) We verify the validity of KDED through extensive experiments. The accuracy of KDED is the second best result after EDTER [16], while the model size of KDED is **only 1/30 of EDTER**.

2   Related Work

2.1   Label Problems in Edge Detection

The problems existing in manually labeled supervisory information (MLSI) have been identified by previous researchers and corresponding solutions have been discussed. In view of labeling errors in MLSI, a new weighted cross entropy loss is proposed in RCF [12] to ignore controversial pixels through voting mechanism which prevents the network from being misled by false labels. This method is effective as long as the dataset contains multiple groups of annotation information. While it fails when an image has only one corresponding label in a dataset, which limits the scope of application of this method.

Unify the standard of edge in MLSI is a hard work, since everyone has a different idea of what an edge is. Different standards greatly weaken the generalization of the model. A noteworthy work is DexiNed [15], in which all visible lines are considered as edges. It is not flexible enough. We have developed a new standard for edges that does not crudely include all textures into edges but define edges through a trained network.

2.2   Knowledge Distillation

A large model is used as a teacher network to summarize the data, and then the prior knowledge can be taught to a smaller student network. The classic strategy of knowledge distillation is a common means of model compression. knowledge distillation can be categorized into online distillation [23] and offline distillation [10] according to whether the teacher network is learnable concurrently. Compared to offline methods, online methods increases training time for distillation learning, especially when the network of teachers is large. The high-capacity teacher in online settings is usually can not be addressed well.

We find that in addition to acceleration and model compression, knowledge distillation can also solve the problems in the MLSI mentioned above. Considering the flexibility and efficiency of the strategy, we adopts offline Response-Based Knowledge Distillation.

3 Method

Our proposal is divided into three parts: a compact edge detector, a knowledge distillation-based label correction strategy, and sample balance loss. In this section, these contributions will be presented specifically.

3.1 Compact Twice Fusion Network for Edge Detection

In recent years, the new edge detection methods obtain higher accuracy with considerably more parameters, although most of them [6,8,26] claim to employ the same backbone. To ensure the balance between accuracy and model size, we employ a Compact Twice Fusion Network (CTFN) [11], in which the redundant operations are removed and only necessary structures are preserved to keep the model lightweight. The structure of CTFN is displayed in Fig. 2.

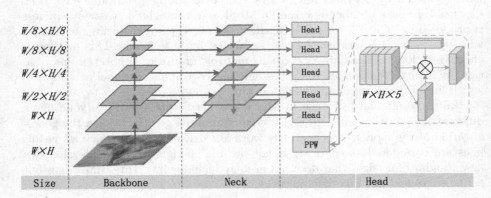

Fig. 2. The Architecture of CTFN.

Feature Extraction. To be fair, the features of CTFN is extracted by the same backbone as the existing methods [12,24], which is based on the feature extraction module of VGG16 [19]. The dilation rate of convolution layers in the last block is enlarged to 2 and the last pooling layer is removed. This can make the receptive field larger while retaining higher resolution features.

The backbone with the most parameters of CTFN is utilized to generate the multi-scale features.

The First Feature Fusion. In edge detection, edges and textures looks similar in appearance and can only be distinguished by high-level semantic information. One of the most effective ways is to enlarge the receptive field of the features. A larger receptive field is crucial for fine-scale branches, since their natural receptive fields are smaller. In the Neck of CTFN, we introduce a FPN-based feature fusion module, in which the fine-scale branch features get larger receptive field by being enhanced by the coarse branch features. It is remarkable that lightweight convolution layers and Group Normalization layers are indispensable before feature fusion to stabilize the propagation of the gradient.

The Second Feature Fusion. As displayed in Fig. 2, with the help of Head layers, multi-scale edges are generated by multi-scale features. These head layers, which only contain one 1×1 convolution, generate multi-scale edges by compressing the multi-scale features.

In the earlier studies [12,24], the weighted sum of multi-scale edges are directly applied to generate the final single-channel edge map. While it looks unreasonable that pixels in the same channel own equal significance during fusion. The following works [9,26] find the issue and try to assign various weight to each pixel regardless of whether they are in the same channel or not. However, additional operations lead to the increasing parameters and computation cost.

In the paper, a light-weight Pseudo Pixel-level Weighting (PPW) module is introduced, in which we decompose the weights of pixels into spatial weights and channel weights. By calculating the product of space weights and channel weights, we can assign a pseudo-weight to each pixel, and avoid a significant increase in the complexity of the model. To further compress the module, we employ a single 1×1 convolution to contral the channel weight and fuse them with multi-scale edges directly.

The prediction of PPW can be formalized as

$$P_{ij} = PPW(X_{ijk}) = \sum_{i=1}^{L} (X_{ijk} \times W_{ijk})$$
$$= \sum_{i=1}^{L} (X_{ijk} \times Wc_i \times Ws_{jk}) \tag{1}$$

where X and P represent the input and the output of PPW. Wc and Ws are used to represent the channel weight and the spatial weight. L is the number of edge generated by multi-scale features.

Although, PPW looks similar to CBAM [22], the biggest difference is that the purpose of CBAM is to enhance features, while The objective of PPW is to allocate weights to pixels in order to produce a single-channel edge map.

3.2 Knowledge Distillation Based on Label Correction

In the label correction strategy, CTFN training is performed in two steps. The training of the teacher network is supervised by MLSI in the first step.

EDTER [16] is utilized as the teacher network and the training process is completely consistent with the earlier works [12,24]. In the second step, MLSI is abandoned and the output of EDTER is directly used to supervise the training of CTFN. In this step, EDTER is only used to generate supervisory information and is no longer updated.

EDTER leverages Transformer's feature extraction capabilities to achieve the surprising result, but super-large-scale model size becomes a burden during training and inference. To ensure the efficiency of training, we directly load the official EDTER pre-training model, thus avoiding the training of teacher model EDTER. That's why we use an offline distillation. The edge probability maps generated by EDTER is utilized to train CTFN. In this way, EDTER only needs to inference once, which avoids that every epoch of training should contain EDTER's time-consuming inference.

Through these improvements, the training time of KDED is same as that of the original CTFN.

3.3   Sample Balance Loss

Edges and non-edges of images are extremely imbalanced, as a result, Weighted Cross-Entropy loss (WCE) becomes the most popular loss function in edge detection, the formula of which can be expressed as

$$WCE\,(p_i, y_i) = \begin{cases} -\alpha \log\,(p_i) & if \ y_i = 1 \\ -\beta \log\,(1 - p_i) & if \ y_i = 0 \\ 0 & otherwise \end{cases} \tag{2}$$

where p represents the edge map predicted by the model and y denotes the ground truth. $\alpha = |Y_+|/|Y|$ and $\beta = \lambda \cdot |Y_-|/|Y|$. $|Y_+|$ and $|Y_-|$ represent the number of edges and non-edges, separately. the hype-parameter λ is used to control the weight of edges over non-edges. $|Y| = |Y_+| + |Y_-|$. Since the annotation between different annotators may be controversial, the threshold γ is useful. Pixel i will be considered as an edge and define $y_i = 1$ when the ground truth y_i is larger than γ. While if $y_i = 0$, pixel i will be considered as a non-edge.

WCE requires binarized supervisory information as weights to balance edges and non-edges, while in the distillation learning of KDED, the supervisory information is the prediction of the teacher network, which is a probability map. Therefore, the weighting method of WCE cannot be applied directly. In addition, Kullback Leibler divergence loss (KL) [7], which is commonly used in distillation learning cannot solve the problem of sample imbalance, so it is not suitable for the training of KDED.

To meet the requirements of sample imbalance distillation learning of KDED, we propose a new loss function named Sample Balance Loss (SBL). The formula of SBL is expressed as

$$SBL\,(p_i, y_i) = \omega((1 - y_i)\log(p_i) + y_i \log(1 - p_i)) \tag{3}$$

where
$$\omega = \mu^{y_i} \|y_i - p_i\|^\delta \qquad (4)$$

p denotes the predicted edge map and y is for the supervisory information generated by EDTER. μ and δ are hyper-parameters to balance the samples. $\|\cdot\|$ represents Manhattan distance.

The supervisory information of KDED is the probability map, in which the boundary between positive and negative samples has been blurred, so it is not applicable to take the ratio of edges to non-edges as the basis of weighting. But inspired by WCE, we balance edges and non-edges according to the supervisory information p_i, too. The weight is expressed by μ^{y_i}. The hyper-parameter μ set by experiment is utilized to further adjust the weight. On the other hand, larger p_i means a higher probability that the pixel is an edge, so it is more reliable. Therefore, we should pay more attention to the information contained therein. A hyper-parameter δ is employed to increase the importance to the hard samples, which are those prone to misclassification.

SBL is applied to solve the problem of sample imbalance when using probability map as supervisory information. Combining the advantages of WCE and KL at the same time, SBL is the first loss function for distillation learning task of edge detection.

4   Experiments

4.1   Datasets and Implementation

KDED is tested on two benchmark datasets, BSDS500 [1] and NYUDv2 [18]. **BSDS500** is one of the most common edge detection datasets, including 500 images. The ratio of images used for training, validation, and testing is 2:1:2. Each image corresponds to 4–9 labels labeled by different people. We combine training set and validation sets to train models, and test set is used to evaluate. **NYUDv2** is a classical indoor scene dataset for semantic segmentation, the ground truth of edge is generated from segmentation. There are 1449 pairs of depth images and RGB images in NYUDv2, and there only one label for each image. We choose 795 images for training and the rest are for test. Due to the equipment limitation, we load the official pre-training parameters of teacher network to avoid the energy-intensive training. In NYUDv2, only the pre-training parameters of RGB mode are available, so we only test RGB images. For a fair comparison, we keep a same data augmentation method as previous works [9, 12]. Multi-scale test is consistent with EDTER [16] and The other settings are the same as for RCF [12]. During evaluation, Optimal Dataset Scale (ODS) F-measure and Optimal Image Scale (OIS) F-measure are used for all experiments.

4.2   Comparison with the State-of-the-Art Methods

To show the performance of KDED, a larger scale comparison is listed in Table 1. When training on the train-val set of BSDS500, KDED can get the

Table 1. Comparison on BSDS500. The highlighted in red and blue results are the best two results, respectively, and the same rules apply to the other tables. MS is short for the multi-scale test, + indicates training with extra PASCAL-Context data and ++ indicates training with extra PASCAL-Context data and using multi-scale during test. P indicate the number of model parameters (Million) and F means FLOPs.

Method	Pub.'year'			MS		+		++		P↓	F↓
		ODS	OIS	ODS	OIS	ODS	OIS	ODS	OIS		
Canny [3]	PAMI'86	0.611	0.676	–	–	–	–	–	–	–	–
Pb [14]	PAMI'04	0.672	0.695	–	–	–	–	–	–	–	–
SE [5]	PAMI'14	0.746	0.767	–	–	–	–	–	–	–	–
DeepEdge [2]	CVPR'15	0.753	0.772	–	–	–	–	–	–	–	–
CEDN [27]	CVPR'16	0.788	0.804	–	–	–	–	–	–	–	–
HED [24]	IJCV'17	0.788	0.807	–	–	–	–	–	–	–	–
CED [21]	TIP'18	0.803	0.820	–	–	0.815	0.833	–	–	–	–
LPCB [4]	ECCV'18	0.800	0.816	–	–	–	–	0.815	0.834	–	–
RCF [12]	PAMI'19	0.798	0.815	–	–	0.806	0.823	0.811	0.830	14.8	75.3
BAN [6]	IJCAI'21	0.810	0.827	0.816	0.834	–	–	–	–	15.6	142.2
BDCN [8]	PAMI'22	0.806	0.826	–	–	0.820	0.838	0.828	0.844	16.3	103.4
FCL [26]	NN'22	0.807	0.822	0.816	0.833	0.815	0.834	0.826	0.845	16.5	134.4
EDTER [16]	CVPR'22	0.824	0.841	–	–	0.832	0.847	0.848	0.865	468.8	802.3
KDED	–	0.811	0.825	0.826	0.842	0.821	0.837	0.832	0.849	14.8	75.9

ODS of 0.811 with single-scale test and obtains 0.826 with multi-scale test, which already outperforms most of the existing edge detectors. KDED can achieve 0.832 (ODS) and 0.849 (OIS) with the extra PASCAL-Context data and multi-scale test, which is second only to EDTER and far beyond other methods.

Although EDTER has obvious advantages in accuracy, it has great disadvantages in efficiency. We further compared the model size and computation cost of these edge detection methods with high accuracy. EDTER's advantage in accuracy is achieved regardless of efficiency. The parameters of EDTER reaches 468.8M, far exceeding the average value of existing methods, and more than 30 times that of KDED. Meanwhile, EDTER's FLOPs are more than 10 times the FLOPs of KDED. It is worth mentioning that even without multi-scale test, the inference speed of EDTER is still less than 5 fps, which is much slower than KDED with multi-scale test (around 10 fps). While the accuracy of the two is similar at this time. Compared with the methods other than EDTER, the efficiency of KDED is quite competitive. In Table 1, only the model size and computation cost of RCF can be compared with that of KDED, but the accuracy of KDED is much more than that of RCF.

In Fig. 3, some visible results are presented. It's easy to observe that KDED preserves more detail and is more effective in complex scenes.

Performance on NYUDv2. KDED is evaluated on RGB images and compared with other state-of-the-art methods. All results are generated by single-scale input. And The quantitative results are presented in Table 2. KDED

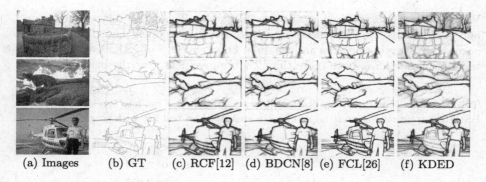

(a) Images   (b) GT   (c) RCF[12]   (d) BDCN[8]   (e) FCL[26]   (f) KDED

Fig. 3. Qualitative comparisons on the test set of BSDS500. GT is short for the ground truth.

achieves scores of 0.754 (ODS) and 0.77 (OIS), respectively. The experimental results are consistent with those of BSDS500 dataset, indicating that KDED achieves better performance. It performs second best, just behind EDTER, and significantly outperforms other methods.

Table 2. Comparison on NYUDv2. All results are generated with single-scale test.

Method	Pub.'year'	ODS	OIS
HED [24]	IJCV'17	0.720	0.734
RCF [12]	PAMI'19	0.729	0.742
AMH-Net [25]	NeurIPS'17	0.744	0.758
LPCB [4]	ECCV'18	0.739	0.754
BDCN [8]	PAMI'22	0.748	0.763
PiDiNet [20]	ICCV'21	0.733	0.747
EDTER [16]	CVPR'22	0.774	0.789
KDED (Ours)	–	0.754	0.770

The model size has nothing to do with datasets and the model computation overhead is positively correlated with the size of the images. So the model size and computation cost on NYUDv2 are not shown. The results in Table 1 can be utilized as a reference if desired.

4.3 Ablation Study

To verify each component of KDED and study the impact of hype-parameters, we perform ablation study.

Firstly, we show the impact of each component in Table 3, where the *Baseline* is RCF [12], *Neck* stands for FPN-based Neck, *PPW* is the Pseudo Pixel-level

Weighting module, *KD* is short for Knowledge distillation based label correction, and *SBL* means the Sample Balance Loss. Each component contributes to the accuracy to varying degrees and the final ODS and OIS of KDED are improved to 81.1% and 82.5%, both more than 2% improvement over the baseline.

Table 3. The numerical results for ablation study. The models are all trained on BSDS500 train-val set and the results are evaluated on test set with single-scale test.

Model	Neck	PPW	KD	SBL	ODS	OIS
Baseline					0.790	0.804
–	✓				0.798	0.815
CTFN	✓	✓			0.801	0.816
–	✓	✓	✓		0.810	0.823
KDED	✓	✓	✓	✓	0.811	0.825

Then, we verify the impact of the hyper-parameters in Sample Balance Loss (SBL), the results are listed in Table 4. SBL is critical that it solves the problem· that distillation learning does not work under the premise of sample imbalance. μ is used to adjust the weight between edges and non-edges and δ is for the simple and hard samples. When $\mu < 10$ or $\mu > 500$, the model can not converge. And when $10 \leq \mu \leq 500$, the selection of μ has little influence on the accuracy of the method. Compared with μ, the effect of δ on the accuracy of KDED is more regular. With the increase of δ, the accuracy of KDED increases firstly and then decreases, and the optimal result is obtained when $\delta = 2$.

Table 4. The effect of hyper-parameters in Sample Balance Loss. The models are trained with BSDS500 train-val set and evaluated on BSDS500 test set with multi-scale test.

μ	10	20	50	100	200	500	50	50	50	50
δ	2	2	2	2	2	2	0	1	2	3
ODS	0.821	0.820	0.821	0.820	0.820	0.819	0.819	0.820	0.821	0.820
OIS	0.836	0.837	0.837	0.836	0.834	0.835	0.834	0.836	0.837	0.837

5   Conclusion

We summarize the problems existing in manual labeling and propose a novel method KDED, which includes a compact twice fusion network, a knowledge distillation based label correction strategy and a corresponding sample balance loss. The accuracy of edge detection can be significantly improved without increasing the time of training and inference. More importantly, with the development of the edge detection, the accuracy of KDED can be further improved by using more advanced teacher networks.

Acknowledgements. This work was supported in part by National key r&d program under Grant 2019YFF0301800, in part by National Natural Science Foundation of China under Grant 61379106, in part by the Shandong Provincial Natural Science Foundation under Grant ZR2013FM036, and ZR2015FM011.

References

1. Arbelaez, P., Maire, M., Fowlkes, C., Malik, J.: Contour detection and hierarchical image segmentation. IEEE Trans. Pattern Anal. Mach. Intell. **33**(5), 898–916 (2010)
2. Bertasius, G., Shi, J., Torresani, L.: Deepedge: a multi-scale bifurcated deep network for top-down contour detection. In: Proceedings of the IEEE Conference on Computer Vision and Pattern Recognition, pp. 4380–4389 (2015)
3. Canny, J.: A computational approach to edge detection. In: Fischler, M.A., Firschein, O. (eds.) Readings in Computer Vision, pp. 184–203. Morgan Kaufmann, San Francisco (1987)
4. Deng, R., Shen, C., Liu, S., Wang, H., Liu, X.: Learning to predict crisp boundaries. In: Proceedings of the European Conference on Computer Vision (ECCV), pp. 562–578 (2018)
5. Dollár, P., Zitnick, C.L.: Fast edge detection using structured forests. IEEE Trans. Pattern Anal. Mach. Intell. **37**(8), 1558–1570 (2014)
6. Gao, L., Zhou, Z., Shen, H.T., Song, J.: Bottom-up and top-down: bidirectional additive net for edge detection. In: Proceedings of the Twenty-Ninth International Conference on International Joint Conferences on Artificial Intelligence, pp. 594–600 (2021)
7. Gou, J., Yu, B., Maybank, S.J., Tao, D.: Knowledge distillation: a survey. Int. J. Comput. Vision **129**, 1789–1819 (2021)
8. He, J., Zhang, S., Yang, M., Shan, Y., Huang, T.: Bdcn: bi-directional cascade network for perceptual edge detection. IEEE Trans. Pattern Anal. Mach. Intell. **44**(1), 100–113 (2022)
9. Huan, L., Xue, N., Zheng, X., He, W., Gong, J., Xia, G.S.: Unmixing convolutional features for crisp edge detection. IEEE Trans. Pattern Anal. Mach. Intell. **44**(10-Part-1), 6602–6609 (2022)
10. Li, T., Li, J., Liu, Z., Zhang, C.: Few sample knowledge distillation for efficient network compression. In: Proceedings of the IEEE/CVF Conference on Computer Vision and Pattern Recognition, pp. 14639–14647 (2020)
11. Li, Y., et al.: Compact twice fusion network for edge detection. arXiv preprint arXiv:2307.04952 (2023)
12. Liu, Y., et al.: Richer convolutional features for edge detection. IEEE Trans. Pattern Anal. Mach. Intell. **41**(08), 1939–1946 (2019)
13. Liu, Z., Liew, J.H., Chen, X., Feng, J.: Dance: a deep attentive contour model for efficient instance segmentation. In: Proceedings of the IEEE/CVF Winter Conference on Applications of Computer Vision, pp. 345–354 (2021)
14. Martin, D.R., Fowlkes, C.C., Malik, J.: Learning to detect natural image boundaries using local brightness, color, and texture cues. IEEE Trans. Pattern Anal. Mach. Intell. **26**(5), 530–549 (2004)

15. Poma, X.S., Riba, E., Sappa, A.: Dense extreme inception network: towards a robust cnn model for edge detection. In: Proceedings of the IEEE/CVF Winter Conference on Applications of Computer Vision, pp. 1923–1932 (2020)
16. Pu, M., Huang, Y., Liu, Y., Guan, Q., Ling, H.: Edter: edge detection with transformer. In: Proceedings of the IEEE/CVF Conference on Computer Vision and Pattern Recognition, pp. 1402–1412 (2022)
17. Shen, W., Wang, X., Wang, Y., Bai, X., Zhang, Z.: Deepcontour: a deep convolutional feature learned by positive-sharing loss for contour detection. In: Proceedings of the IEEE Conference on Computer Vision and Pattern Recognition, pp. 3982–3991 (2015)
18. Silberman, N., Hoiem, D., Kohli, P., Fergus, R.: Indoor segmentation and support inference from RGBD images. In: Fitzgibbon, A., Lazebnik, S., Perona, P., Sato, Y., Schmid, C. (eds.) ECCV 2012. LNCS, vol. 7576, pp. 746–760. Springer, Heidelberg (2012). https://doi.org/10.1007/978-3-642-33715-4_54
19. Simonyan, K., Zisserman, A.: Very deep convolutional networks for large-scale image recognition. arXiv preprint arXiv:1409.1556 (2014)
20. Su, Z., et al.: Pixel difference networks for efficient edge detection. In: Proceedings of the IEEE/CVF International Conference on Computer Vision, pp. 5117–5127 (2021)
21. Wang, Y., Zhao, X., Li, Y., Huang, K.: Deep crisp boundaries: from boundaries to higher-level tasks. IEEE Trans. Image Process. **28**(3), 1285–1298 (2018)
22. Woo, S., Park, J., Lee, J.Y., Kweon, I.S.: Cbam: convolutional block attention module. In: Proceedings of the European Conference on Computer Vision (ECCV), pp. 3–19 (2018)
23. Wu, G., Gong, S.: Peer collaborative learning for online knowledge distillation. In: Proceedings of the AAAI Conference on Artificial Intelligence, vol. 35, pp. 10302–10310 (2021)
24. Xie, S., Tu, Z.: Holistically-nested edge detection. Int. J. Comput. Vision **125**(1), 3–18 (2017)
25. Xu, D., Ouyang, W., Alameda-Pineda, X., Ricci, E., Wang, X., Sebe, N.: Learning deep structured multi-scale features using attention-gated crfs for contour prediction. Adv. Neural Inf. Process. Syst. **30** (2017)
26. Xuan, W., Huang, S., Liu, J., Du, B.: Fcl-net: towards accurate edge detection via fine-scale corrective learning. Neural Netw. **145**, 248–259 (2022)
27. Yang, J., Price, B., Cohen, S., Lee, H., Yang, M.H.: Object contour detection with a fully convolutional encoder-decoder network. In: Proceedings of the IEEE Conference on Computer Vision and Pattern Recognition, pp. 193–202 (2016)
28. Zhao, J.X., et al.: Egnet: edge guidance network for salient object detection. In: Proceedings of the IEEE/CVF International Conference on Computer Vision, pp. 8779–8788 (2019)
29. Zhu, S., Brazil, G., Liu, X.: The edge of depth: explicit constraints between segmentation and depth. In: Proceedings of the IEEE/CVF Conference on Computer Vision and Pattern Recognition, pp. 13116–13125 (2020)

Multiple Attention Network for Facial Expression Recognition

Wenyu Feng[1], Zixiang Fei[2(✉)], Wenju Zhou[1], and Minrui Fei[1]

[1] School of Mechatronic Engineering and Automation, Shanghai University, Shanghai 200444,
China
{fengwenyu,zhouwenju}@shu.edu.cn, mrfei@staff.shu.edu.cn
[2] School of Computer Engineering and Science, Shanghai University, Shanghai 200444, China
zxfei@shu.edu.cn

Abstract. Facial expression recognition (FER) has become increasingly important in the field of human-computer interaction. This paper proposes an improved
method with attention mechanism to improve FER performance. Our approach is
grounded in two crucial observations. Firstly, as multiple categories share similar underlying facial characteristics, distinguishing between them may be subtle.
Secondly, recognizing facial expressions demands a comprehensive approach by
encoding high-order interactions among localized features from multiple facial
regions simultaneously. To address these challenges, we introduce our MAN
model consisting of three key components: Multi-branch stack Residual Network
(MRN), Transitional Attention Network (TAN), and Appropriate Cascade Structure (ACS). The TAN learns objectives to maximize class separability, while the
MRN deploys attention heads to focus on various facial regions and generate attention maps. Additionally, the ACS module provides a more reasonable construction
method for the model. Comprehensive experiments on three publicly available
datasets (AffectNet, RAF-DB, and CK+) consistently achieves better expression
recognition performance. Compared to the ResNet network, our approach yielded
an improved accuracy of 3.3%, 3.2%, 4.1% and 1.8% on the Affectnet7 dataset,
Affectnet8 dataset, RAF-DB dataset, and CK+ dataset, respectively.

Keywords: Multi-branch Stack Residual Network · Transitional Attention
Network · Appropriate Cascade Structure · Facial Expression Recognition

1 Introduction

Facial expression recognition (FER) is a critical field in computer vision that aims
to enable computers to automatically detect and interpret emotions conveyed through
human facial expressions. These expressions play a fundamental role in human communication, conveying a wide spectrum of emotions and intentions. From the subtle
nuances of a raised eyebrow to the broad smiles of happiness, facial expressions are a
rich source of non-verbal cues that underlie our interactions and relationships.

Facial expressions have intrigued scholars, artists, and psychologists alike. They
serve as a powerful medium for the portrayal of emotions and thoughts in art and literature

© The Author(s), under exclusive license to Springer Nature Singapore Pte Ltd. 2024
F. Liu et al. (Eds.): PRICAI 2023, LNAI 14327, pp. 141–152, 2024.
https://doi.org/10.1007/978-981-99-7025-4_12

[1, 3]. In everyday life, they facilitate non-verbal communication, allowing individuals to convey feelings and intentions effectively [2, 4]. Moreover, professionals in fields such as behavioral analysis rely on facial expressions to discern hidden emotions and assess psychological states [5].

The significance of facial expressions extends to various practical applications. For instance, in the realm of healthcare, counseling psychologists can assess a patient's emotional state by continuously monitoring their facial expressions, aiding in the development of tailored treatment plans. Furthermore, research has shown that the facial expressions of elderly individuals with conditions like Alzheimer's disease differ from those of healthy individuals [6]. A robust facial expression classification method can be a valuable tool for early diagnosis and intervention in such cases.

Several large-scale datasets exist for FER. Initial research postulated six typical emotions, often referred to as basic emotions. The newest dataset includes neutrality or contempt, expanding the number of facial expression categories to 7–8. The latest research is more willing to test on multi-category datasets.

Despite significant progress in FER, several challenges persist. One notable challenge is discerning subtle differences between various facial expressions, especially in time-series data [7]. In time-series scenarios, multiple expressions may share similar underlying facial features, making precise recognition a complex task.

To address this challenge, various studies have employed attention mechanisms to focus on local details within facial expressions. However, achieving a balance between capturing subtle local changes and maintaining overall performance remains a significant obstacle.

While existing research in FER has made commendable strides, there is a gap in effectively addressing multi-region feature extraction in the analysis of facial micro-expressions. Current approaches often face challenges related to computational complexity [9] and the management of numerous hyperparameters [10]. Additionally, they sometimes struggle to effectively focus attention on all relevant regions of the face [8].

This paper aims to bridge this gap by proposing a novel approach: the Multi-Head Cross-Attention Network for Facial Expression Recognition. This innovative approach allows for attention to be distributed across multiple facial regions during feature extraction while efficiently managing computational resources. Prior studies have demonstrated the effectiveness of attention mechanisms [12] in focusing on local details, but a single attention mechanism may not suffice for comprehensive coverage of all relevant facial features [11]. We draw inspiration from such work [13] and propose a multi-head cross-attention network that fuses attention information from multiple locations, ultimately enhancing the recognition of subtle facial expressions.

The primary contributions of our research can be summarized as follows:

- Efficient Gradient Information Extraction: We introduce innovative methods for stacking multiple residual networks. This approach not only enhances the extraction of gradient information but also reduces computation time, improving the overall efficiency of facial expression recognition.
- Enhanced Feature Extraction and Differentiation: We proposed a multi-scale feature extraction method and attention mechanism in TAN, which enhances the backbone network's performance and maximizes the difference between categories.

- Innovative Cascade Structure: We adopted a more reasonable cascade structure called ACS, which is inspired by the YOLOv7 paper, to improve accuracy when applying the proposed structure to feature extraction architectures such as Resnet.
- Exceptional Performance: To validate our approach, we conducted rigorous evaluations on established Facial Expression Recognition datasets. The results speak for themselves, with remarkable accuracies of 63.2%, 58.6%, 85.6%, and 96.5% achieved on AffectNet7, AffectNet8, RAF-DB, and CK+ datasets, respectively. These outcomes underscore the effectiveness of our approach in the realm of facial expression recognition.

The subsequent parts of the paper are dedicated to providing a detailed exposition of our research. In Sect. 2, we conduct a review of literature related to the recognition of facial expressions with a particular focus on real-time classification networks and attention mechanisms. A explanation of our approach follows in Sect. 3. In Sect. 4, we present the results of our experimental evaluation. Our findings are then summarized in Sect. 5.

2 Related Work

2.1 Real-Time Classification Networks

Currently, state-of-the-art real-time classification networks are mainly based on Darknet [14], ResNet [15], MobileNet [16] and Transformer [17], which are efficient. However, these networks still have limitations in terms of network architecture, feature integration method, detection accuracy, and training efficiency. More specifically, (1) a faster and stronger network architecture is needed to improve processing speed and model performance; (2) a more effective feature integration method is required to capture more diverse and informative features; (3) a more accurate detection method is necessary to reduce false positives and negatives; (4) a more efficient training method is needed to speed up the training process and improve model convergence. We aim to address these limitations by proposing a new method that focuses on improving the issues associated with (1), (2), (3), and (4) mentioned above.

2.2 Attention Mechanism

The objective of the attention mechanism is to guide the network's focus to where it is most needed, playing a crucial role in visual perception [18]. When we employ convolutional neural networks (CNNs) to process images, it's desirable for the network to direct its attention to the relevant regions rather than considering everything indiscriminately. Manually specifying these attention areas is impractical. In recent years, researchers have introduced attention mechanisms into deep CNNs.

For instance, SENet [19] focuses on channel-wise attention for the input feature layer. It optimizes the network's attention to specific channels, thereby enhancing its performance. CBAM [20], on the other hand, combines both channel attention and spatial attention mechanisms, yielding superior results compared to SENet. CBAM processes the input feature layer and the attention mechanisms separately.

ECANet [21] also employs the channel attention mechanism and can be viewed as an improved iteration of SENet.

In recent years, several scholars have integrated the local attention mechanism into the backbone networks for facial expression classification. For instance, Zheng [22] introduced the Distraction Attention Network, a novel approach in facial expression recognition. This network extracts robust features by employing a large-margin learning objective to maximize class separability.

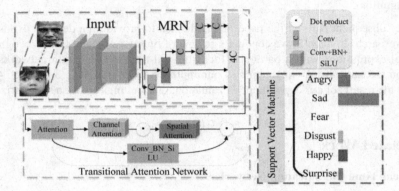

Fig. 1. Overview of our proposed MAN

3   Methodology

To enhance the quality of attention features, we propose a methodology composed of three main components: the Multi-branch stack Residual Network (MRN), the Transitional Attention Network (TAN), and the Appropriate Cascade Structure (ACS).

The MRN is responsible for extracting fundamental features from batches of facial images while preserving gradient information and emphasizing class differentiation. Subsequently, the TAN captures facial expression regions at various scales and explicitly trains attention maps to selectively focus on different areas. Finally, these attention maps are fused and employed to predict the expression category of the input image.

Our methodology incorporates a series of lightweight yet effective attention heads, each consisting of a spatial attention unit and a channel attention unit, stacked sequentially. The spatial attention unit utilizes convolution kernels of varying sizes, while the channel attention unit enhances feature extraction, emulating a coder-decoder structure. Both units seamlessly integrate into the input features. The overall framework of our proposed approach is depicted in Fig. 1.

Formally, let $x_i \in X$ be the input vector in the input feature space X, and Y be the corresponding label in the label space Y. For simplicity, the output features of our backbone can be expressed as:

$$x_i' = F(\omega_r, x_i) \tag{1}$$

where w_r are the network parameters.

The learning objective is framed as a two-class classification problem. For each sample x_i, we employ the cross-entropy loss.

$$L_i^{\text{det}} = -(y_i^{\text{det}} \log(p_i) + (1 - y_i^{\text{det}})(1 - \log(p_i))) \tag{2}$$

Here, p_i represents the probability produced by the network, indicating the likelihood of sample x_i being a face, while $y_i^{\text{det}} \in \{0, 1\}$ Denotes the corresponding ground-truth label.

3.1 Multi-branch Stack Residual Network

In the literature on designing efficient architectures, the primary focus is on the number of parameters and computations required. Memory access costs are also taken into account. Ma et al. [23] analyzed various aspects of model scaling in convolutional neural networks, including the ratio of input/output channels, the number of architecture branches, and the influence of different elements and operations on inference speed. Dollar et al. [24] considered activations in their model scaling methodology, emphasizing the significance of the quantity of elements in the output tensor of the convolutional layer. The CSPVoVNet [25] in Fig. 2(b) is an innovation of VoVNet [26]. CSPVoVNet's architecture not only takes basic design issues into account, but also analyses the gradient paths to make different weights learn more distinct features. The gradient examination method makes inference more precise. The ELAN in Fig. 2(c) found that mastery of the shortest and longest gradient paths yields improved learning and convergence in deeper networks. In RepVgg's training architecture, the author uses 3×3 and 1×1 Convolution obtains different gradient paths and multi-scale information, which are also used in the proposed architecture. Referring to the above structure, in this paper, we propose an ELAN-based variant whose main architecture is shown in Fig. 2(c).

The combined feature layer L includes $l_{1f} \sim l_{4f}$ from each gradient path. Where C is the Concat operation for L.

$$L = C(l_{1f}, l_{2f}, l_{3f}, l_{4f}) \tag{3}$$

3.2 Transitional Attention Network

The Proposed Attention Framework consists of two main components: the Spatial Attention Unit and the Channel Attention Unit. Firstly, the Spatial Attention Unit extracts spatial features from the input features, which are obtained through multi-scale feature fusion. Next, the Channel Attention Unit generates channel features from the spatial features. Finally, the attention features from both dimensions are integrated within the Attention Framework. Figure 3 illustrates the operations of the Channel Attention and Spatial Attention Units. The Channel Attention Unit employs global max and average pooling, followed by a dense block, ReLU activation, another full connection, and the sigmoid activation function. On the other hand, the Spatial Attention Unit conducts max and mean pooling on the channel, concatenates the results, applies a 7×7 convolution, and concludes with the sigmoid activation function.

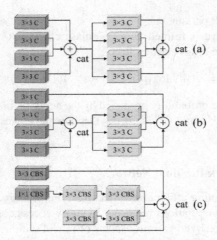

Fig. 2. Extended efficient layer aggregation networks

Formally, let C represent the channel attention heads, and M be the final attention maps of TAN. The result of the cross-attention can be expressed as:

$$M_i = x \times C_i(w_c, x), i \in \{1, k\} \tag{4}$$

where w_c represents the network parameters.

Similarly, consider S as the spatial attention head and A as the output spatial attention map, where N is the number of cross-attention heads. The resulting spatial attention A can be expressed as:

$$A_i = c_i \times S_i(w_s, c_i), i \in \{1, N\} \tag{5}$$

where w_s are the network parameters of C_i.

3.3 Appropriate Cascade Structure

Planned re-parameterized convolution is proposed in YOLOv7 [27]. When part of the structure is directly applied to a feature extraction architecture, such as ResNet, a significant reduction in accuracy is observed. This can be attributed to the fact that RepConv utilizes a combination of 3×3 convolution, 1×1 convolution, and identity connection. While this approach offers greater gradient diversity for various feature maps, it also undermines the residual structure of ResNet. To address this issue, we propose three feasible connection structures based on experimental results, as depicted in Fig. 4.

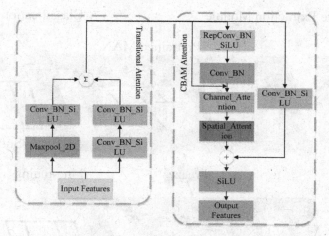

Fig. 3. Structure of proposed Transitional Attention Network

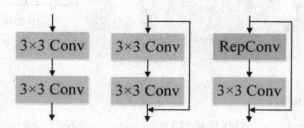

Fig. 4. Three correct connection structures

4 Experiments

4.1 Implementation Details

We conducted training and validation of our classification network approach using the RAF-DB dataset, starting with training the model from scratch. Subsequently, we employed the trained model as a pre-training model for the Affectnet and CK+ datasets. For this transfer learning process, we utilized the RAF-DB training set for model training and the RAF-DB test set for validation and hyperparameter selection.

Our experimental code was implemented in PyTorch and executed on a workstation equipped with an RTX 3090 24G GPU. The model underwent 200 training epochs, with the multi-branch stack residual structure in TAN set to a default value of 3. To optimize learning, we employed the learning rate reduction method known as cosine annealing. Specifically, we froze the model's parameters during the first 100 epochs of transfer learning and then unfroze them for the last 100 epochs (Fig. 5).

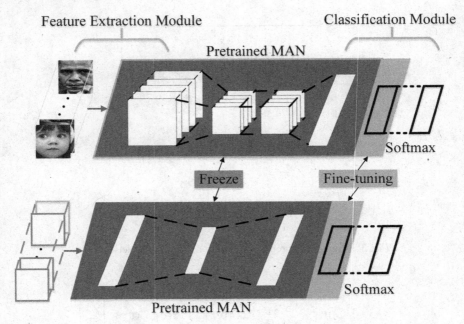

Fig. 5. Training stage

4.2 Ablation Studies

We evaluate the influence of MRN and TAN separately in Table 1. Our proposed method significantly enhances the performance of the original structure.

Table 1. Ablation studies in MAN

MRN	TAN	ACS	Accuracy
			81.5%
√		√	82.3%
	√	√	85.1%
√	√		85.2%
√	√	√	85.6%

4.3 Comparision with Previous Results

Based on the results presented in Table 2, it is evident that the method proposed in this paper achieves a favorable balance between speed and accuracy.

Our method achieves results with accuracy of 85.60% on the RAF-DB dataset and outperforms existing methods with an accuracy of 63.2% on AffectNet7. Furthermore,

Table 2. Performance comparison of different methods

Methods	Model_size	Affectnet7	Affectnet8	RAF-DB	CK+	FPS
Cbam_Resnet18	40.84M	62.6%	56.7%	85.1%	95.6%	65.69
MobilenetV2 [20]	8.8M	61.4%	55.6%	84.6%	95.9%	70.68
Resnet18 [19]	44.7M	59.9%	55.4%	81.5%	94.7%	66.64
MAN	28.7M	63.2%	58.6%	85.6%	96.5%	63.14
Improvement(compared with Resnet18)	↓35.8%	↑3.3%	↑3.2%	↑4.1%	↑1.8%	↑5.3%

the CK+ dataset demonstrates comparable accuracy of 96.5%. These results demonstrate the effectiveness of our method's components and their competitiveness across datasets.

Figure 6 presents the recognition confusion matrix of various algorithms in the RAF-DB dataset. It is evident that compared to other algorithms, our proposed algorithm achieves a higher recognition rate in a single performance. The expression with the lowest recognition rate is Fear, but it still reaches 0.73, with Happy achieving the highest recognition rate of 0.99.

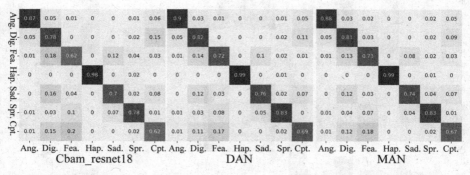

Fig. 6. The recognition confusion matrix of various algorithms under the RAF-DB dataset

The proposed method in this paper was tested using the RAF-DB dataset. Figure 7 presents a comparison between the Resnet18 algorithm and the proposed algorithm. It can be observed that the conventional Resnet18 algorithm has more error messages when capturing motion information, and it even fails to capture emotions in some static areas. In contrast, the proposed algorithm based on MAN has demonstrated a better performance in distinguishing dynamic and static regions, leading to improved accuracy in detecting emotions.

As can be seen from Fig. 8, by comparing the recognition results, we can clearly see that the proposed improvement method in this article can provide greater confidence to distinguish different types of emotions, especially when distinguishing difficult emotional expressions such as sadness. In contrast, traditional Resnet has a high possibility of false detection.

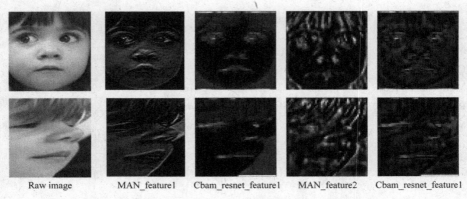

Fig. 7. The extraction effect of 2 algorithms in RAF-DB dataset

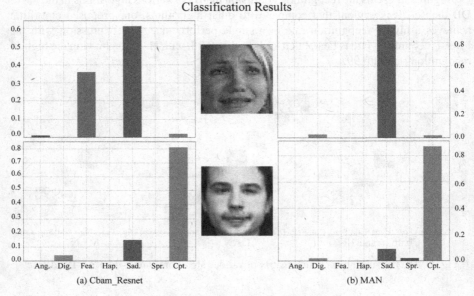

Fig. 8. MAN recognition display

5 Conclusion

This paper introduces an enhanced method for facial expression recognition, incorporating structures: the Multi-branch stack Residual Network (MRN), the Transitional Attention Network (TAN), and the Appropriate Cascade Structure (ACS). Specifically, MRN utilizes diverse gradients to capture distinctive facial features, and its streamlined architecture ensures efficient performance. TAN introduces an attention mechanism that prioritizes multiple local regions, thereby enhancing expression recognition accuracy.

In contrast, ACS optimizes the cascade structure, leading to a more efficient classification process. Notably, experiments conducted on three different datasets demonstrate the superior performance of our proposed approach. We believe that the method presented in this paper can provide valuable insights for future research on facial expression recognition.

Acknowledgement. This study is supported by the Shanghai Pujiang Program (No. 22PJ1403800) and the Natural Science Foundation of China (NSFC) under Grant 62203290.

References

1. Szajnberg, N.: What the face reveals: basic and applied studies of spontaneous expression using the facial action coding system. J. Am. Psychoanal. Assoc. **70**(3), 591–595 (2022)
2. Wang, X., Zhou, Z.: Facial age estimation by total ordering Preserving Projection. In: Proceedings of PRICAI 2016: Trends in Artificial Intelligence, pp. 603–615 (2016)
3. Wang, S., Yan, W., Li, X.: Micro-expression recognition using color spaces. IEEE Trans. Image Process. **24**(12), 6034–6047 (2015)
4. Fasel, B.: Automatic facial expression analysis: a survey. Pattern Recogn. **36**(1), 259–275 (2003)
5. Mai, G., Guo, Z., She, Y., Wang, H., Liang, Y.: Video-based emotion recognition in the wild for online education systems. In: Khanna, S., Cao, J., Bai, Q., Guandong, X. (eds.) PRICAI 2022: Trends in Artificial Intelligence: 19th Pacific Rim International Conference on Artificial Intelligence, PRICAI 2022, Shanghai, China, November 10–13, 2022, Proceedings, Part III, pp. 516–529. Springer, Cham (2022). https://doi.org/10.1007/978-3-031-20868-3_38
6. Fei, Z., Yang, E., Yu, L.: A novel deep neural network-based emotion analysis system for automatic detection of mild cognitive impairment in the elderly. Neurocomputing **468**, 306–316 (2022)
7. Jingyi, W., Qiu, B., Shang, L.: A calibration method for sentiment time series by deep clustering. In: Pham, D.N., Theeramunkong, T., Governatori, G., Liu, F. (eds.) PRICAI 2021: Trends in Artificial Intelligence: 18th Pacific Rim International Conference on Artificial Intelligence, PRICAI 2021, Hanoi, Vietnam, November 8–12, 2021, Proceedings, Part II, pp. 3–16. Springer, Cham (2021). https://doi.org/10.1007/978-3-030-89363-7_1
8. Cai, J., Meng, Z., Khan, A., et al.: Island loss for learning discriminative features in facial expression recognition. In: Proceedings of 13th IEEE International Conference on Automatic Face & Gesture Recognition (FG), pp. 302–309 (2018)
9. Farzaneh, A., Qi, X., Facial expression recognition in the wild via deep attentive center loss. In: Proceedings of IEEE Winter Conference on Applications of Computer Vision (WACV), pp. 2401–2410 (2021)
10. Li, Z., Wu, S., Xiao, G., et al.: Facial expression recognition by multi-scale cnn with regularized center Loss. In: Proceedings of 24th International Conference on Pattern Recognition (ICPR), pp. 3384–3389 (2018)
11. Wang, K., Peng, X., Yang, J.: Region attention networks for pose and occlusion robust facial expression recognition. IEEE Trans. Image Process. **29**, 4057–4069 (2020)
12. Shao, Z., Liu, Z., Cai, J., et al.: Facial action unit detection using attention and relation learning. IEEE Trans. Affect. Comput. **13**(3), 1274–1289 (2022)
13. Zhang, J., Liu, F., Zhou, A.: Off-tanet: a lightweight neural micro-expression recognizer with optical flow features and integrated attention mechanism. In: Pham, D.N., Theeramunkong, T., Governatori, G., Liu, F. (eds.) PRICAI 2021: Trends in Artificial Intelligence: 18th Pacific Rim

International Conference on Artificial Intelligence, PRICAI 2021, Hanoi, Vietnam, November 8–12, 2021, Proceedings, Part I, pp. 266–279. Springer International Publishing, Cham (2021). https://doi.org/10.1007/978-3-030-89188-6_20

14. Tian, Z., Shen, C., Chen, H., et al.: Fcos: a simple and strong anchor-free object detector. IEEE Trans. Pattern Anal. Mach. Intell. **44**(4), 1922–1933 (2022)

15. He, K., Zhang, X., Ren, S., et al.: Deep residual learning for image recognition. In: Proceedings of 2016 IEEE Conference on Computer Vision and Pattern Recognition (CVPR), pp. 770–778 (2016)

16. Howard, A., Sandler, M., Chu, G., et al.: Searching for mobilenetV3. In: Proceedings of IEEE/CVF International Conference on Computer Vision (ICCV), pp. 1314–24 (2019)

17. Vaswani, A., Shazeer, N., Parmar, N., et al.: Attention is all you need. In: Proceedings of 31st Annual Conference on Neural Information Processing Systems (NIPS), pp. 2401–2410 (2017)

18. Guo, M., Xu, T., Liu, J.: Attention mechanisms in computer vision: a survey. Comput. Visual Media **8**(3), 331–368 (2022)

19. Hu, J., Shen, L., Albanie, S.: Squeeze-and-excitation networks. IEEE Trans. Pattern Anal. Mach. Intell. **42**(8), 2011–2023 (2020)

20. Woo, S., Park, J., Lee, J.: Cbam: convolutional block attention module. In: Proceedings of 15th European Conference on Computer Vision (ECCV), pp. 3–19 (2018)

21. Wang, Q., Wu, B., Zhu, P.: Eca-net: efficient channel attention for deep convolutional neural networks. In: Proceedings of 2020 IEEE/CVF Conference on Computer Vision and Pattern Recognition (CVPR) (2020)

22. Wen, Z., Lin, W., Wang, T.: Distract your attention: multi-head cross attention network for facial expression recognition. arXiv preprint arXiv:2109.07270 (2021)

23. Ma, N., Zhang, X., Zheng, H.: ShuffleNet V2: practical guidelines for efficient cnn architecture design. In: Proceedings of 15th European Conference on Computer Vision (ECCV), pp. 122–138 (2018)

24. Dollar, P., Singh, M., Girshick, R..: Fast and accurate model scaling. In: Proceedings of IEEE/CVF Conference on Computer Vision and Pattern Recognition (CVPR), pp. 924–932 (2021)

25. Wang, C., Bochkovskiy, A., Liao, H.: Scaled-YOLOv4: scaling cross stage partial network. In: Proceedings of IEEE/CVF Conference on Computer Vision and Pattern Recognition (CVPR), pp. 13024–13033 (2021)

26. Lee, Y., Hwang, J., Lee, S.: An energy and gpu-computation efficient backbone network for real-time object detection. In: Proceedings of 32nd IEEE/CVF Conference on Computer Vision and Pattern Recognition (CVPR), pp. 752–760 (2019)

27. Wang, C., Bochkovskiy, A., Liao, H.: YOLOv7: Trainable bag-of-freebies sets new state-of-the-art for real-time object detectors. arXiv preprint arXiv:2207.02696 (2022)

PMT-IQA: Progressive Multi-task Learning for Blind Image Quality Assessment

Qingyi Pan[1,2], Ning Guo[1], Letu Qingge[3], Jingyi Zhang[2], and Pei Yang[1(✉)]

[1] Department of Computer Technology and Application, Qinghai University,
Xining, China
`yangpeinmgdx@sina.com`
[2] Center for Statistical Science and Department of Industrial Engineering,
Tsinghua University, Beijing, China
[3] Department of Computer Science, North Carolina A and T State University,
Greensboro, USA

Abstract. Blind image quality assessment (BIQA) remains challenging due to the diverse types of distortion and variable image content, which complicates the distortion patterns crossing different scales and aggravates the difficulty of the regression problem for BIQA. However, existing BIQA methods often fail to consider multi-scale distortion patterns and image content, and there has limited research on improving the performance of quality regression models through specific learning strategies. In this paper, we propose a simple yet effective Progressive Multi-Task Image Quality Assessment (PMT-IQA) model, which contains a multi-scale feature extraction module (MS) and a progressive multi-task learning module (PMT), to help the model learn complex distortion patterns and better optimize the regression issue to align with the law of human learning process from easy to hard. To verify the effectiveness of the proposed PMT-IQA model, we conduct experiments on four widely used public datasets, and the experimental results indicate that the performance of PMT-IQA is superior to the comparison approaches, and both MS and PMT modules improve the model's performance. The source code for this study is available at https://github.com/pqy000/PMT-IQA.

Keywords: Blind image quality assessment · easy-to-hard effect · multi-scale feature · progressive multi-task learning

1 Introduction

With the popularity of smartphones and other camera devices in recent years, a vast amount of images have been produced and play an increasingly important role in people's information interaction. However, these images could be distorted (i.e. quality degradation caused by noise, lossy compression, etc.) by various factors, including the professional level of the photographer, equipment

F. Liu et al. (Eds.): PRICAI 2023, LNAI 14327, pp. 153–164, 2024.
https://doi.org/10.1007/978-981-99-7025-4_13

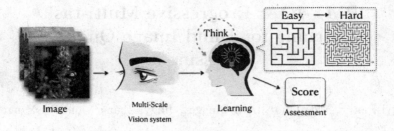

Fig. 1. Motivation diagram of the proposed PMT-IQA. We divide image quality assessment into two parts, which are multi-scale vision system and human learning law based image quality assessment.

performance, transmission and device storage, etc. Therefore, it is of great need to assess the quality of images. Although people can subjectively evaluate the image quality accurately and reliably, it is very limited in practical applications due to time-consuming and laborious [28]. Consequently, objective image quality assessment (IQA) [9], which aims to explore models for automatically evaluating the image quality in line with the human vision system (HVS), has attracted much attention in the past few years [28] [25]. Among all the objective IQA methods, blind IQA (BIQA), also called no-reference IQA (NR-IQA), approaches are the most challenging. "Blind" in this context refers to the fact that no pristine images (i.e. undistorted reference images) are required during the process of image quality evaluation. Yet much progress has been made on this topic, it is still an open and challenging issue, and in this study, we are committed to exploring the BIQA problem.

The diversity of distortion and variability in image content are the main reasons why BIQA is full of challenges. On the one hand, they complicate the distortion patterns, covering multiple scales, from local to global. On the other hand, the complex input space aggravates the difficulty of the regression problem for BIQA. However, existing works often fail to consider multi-scale distortion patterns and image content. Some attempts have been made to design end-to-end architectures for IQA. For example, Li *et al.* [15] extract features using a pre-trained deep convolutional neural network (DCNN). It is evident that DCNN learns global features due to the gradual expansion of the receptive field in the convolutional layers as the network becomes deeper. However, most real-world image data distortion patterns exist in local areas. Therefore, the global features are not enough to capture the complex distortions. In addition, the human learning process follows the law from easy to hard, which is known as the easy-to-hard effect proposed by Pavlov [19] in 1927. However, existing BIQA methods tend to solve the complex regression problem directly.

In this paper, we proposed a simple yet effective image quality assessment architecture inspired by the multi-scale characteristics of HVS and the from easy to hard law of human learning shown in Fig. 1. We name the proposed network as Progressive Multi-Task Image Quality Assessment (PMT-IQA), since it is designed to capture distortion-related patterns using a task transfer strategy simulating the from easy to hard human learning law. The idea behind the proposed model is as below. Firstly, we extract global-to-local distortion-aware features by designing a multi-scale semantic feature extraction module. Secondly, inspired by the from easy to hard learning law, we build a progressive multi-task learning scheme, which can gradually shift from an easy task (i.e. quality level classification) to a hard one (quality score regression). At last, we evaluate the performance of the proposed PMT-IQA on several widely used public IQA datasets, and the experimental results validate the effectiveness of the PMT-IQA model.

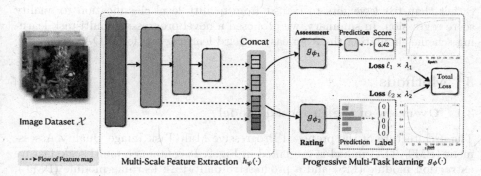

Fig. 2. Progressive Multi-Task learning Image Quality Assessment architecture. It divides the task of IQA into two steps: Multi-Scale Semantic Feature Extraction and Progressive Multi-Task learning.

2   Related Works

The development of deep neural network technology has greatly prompted the research of BIQA problem in the past few years. Zhang et al. [30] proposed a dual-branch network that adapts to both authentic and synthetic distortions. Su et al. [22] introduced a self-adaptive hyper network for real-world distorted images to address the challenges of diverse distortion types and various contents in real-world images. To overcome the issue of weak cross-scenario capability of BIQA models, Zhang et al. [31] presented a unified uncertainty-aware BIQA model that cover both laboratory and wild scenarios. In addition, some latest deep learning technologies, including contrastive learning [17], graph convolutional neural network [23], and transformers [5], have also been used for BIQA research. While these models have achieved impressive performance, they mainly focus on network architecture design, but rarely study how to make the models learn better. Furthermore, these existing models also rarely used multi-scale for feature extraction.

Inspired by the easy-to-hard effect [19], we proposed a new learning scheme that imitates the law of from easy to hard learning for BIQA. In fact, curriculum learning [2], which has received a lot of attention in the past decade [24], is a realization of this idea. It should be noted that curriculum learning simulates the from easy to hard learning law in terms of training data, which is to train a machine learning model from easier samples to hard ones. However, as the easy-to-hard effect indicates *"Early experience with an easy version of a discrimination task facilitates subsequent learning of a more difficult task"* [19], our idea is to simulate the from easy to hard learning law through progressive learning of related tasks with different difficulty levels. We utilize the multi-task architecture in our implementation. Different from existing multi-task based BIQA models [7,16], which simultaneously predict distortion type and image quality score, the two tasks (i.e. quality level prediction and quality score prediction) in our model are progressive. On the other hand, we employ dynamic task weights rather than fixed weights to transit from quality level classification to quality score regression. In summary, we proposed a novel progressive multi-task learning scheme simulating the from easy to hard learning law for BIQA.

3   Methods

3.1   Overview of the Proposed Model

The architecture of the proposed Progressive Mult-Task Image Quality Assessment (PMT-IQA) model is presented in Fig. 2. It contains a multi-scale feature extraction module (MS) and a progressive multi-task learning module (PMT). The MS module is designed to extract image features with stronger representation ability by utilizing multi-scale information, and the PMT module is used to simulate the from easy to hard learning law through a dynamically weighted two-head multi-task structure. The proposed PMT-IQA model can be mathematically represented as Eq. (1).

$$f_\theta(\cdot) = g_\phi \circ h_\psi(\cdot) \tag{1}$$

where $f_\theta(\cdot)$ represents the complete model with paramters θ, h_ψ is the MS module, which obtains local-to-global distortions, and PMT module g_ϕ learns complex regression problems. The operator $\circ$ in Eq. (1) represents the composition of modules g_ϕ and h_ψ, where the output of h_ψ serves as the input of g_ϕ. The definition of the parameters $\theta = \{\phi, \psi\}$ will be declared in the next section.

3.2   Multi-scale Semantic Feature Extraction

To characterize various distortions, we utilize convolutions to extract multi-scale features (from local to global), each of which corresponds to a feature map s_i. Assuming we have features on n scales, then we concatenate all features, as shown in Eq. (2).

$$h_\psi(x_i) = \text{concat}(s_1, \cdots s_j, \cdots, s_n) \tag{2}$$

More specifically, we use a pre-trained ResNet50 [6] as the backbone architecture in PMT-IQA and collect feature maps from four stages of ResNet50. Then we use 1×1 convolution and global average pooling for dimension alignment. The output of MS module $h(\cdot)$ is fed into the PMT module for prediction.

3.3 Progressive Multi-Task Image Quality Assessment

As introduced in Sect. 1, the diversity of distortion and variability of image content make the input space of quality scalar score regression issue complicated and increase the difficulty of model learning. To address this challenge, we propose a progressive multi-task learning scheme to mimic the from easy to hard human learning process. Specifically, in addition to the quality score prediction task, we introduce a relative simple quality-level classification task related to quality regression. During the model training process, we dynamically adjust the weights of the quality score prediction task and the quality-level classification task in the learning objective function, aiming to progressively shift the model's attention from the quality-level classification task to the quality score prediction task.

For the quality-level classification task, we divide the range of scalar quality scores into discrete sub-intervals, and let each sub-interval be a quality category, which represents a specific quality level, for the quality classification task. Let w be the interval length, $[y^{min}, y^{max}]$ be the range of quality score, then we can obtain K categories as:

$$K = \lfloor \frac{|y^{max} - y^{min}|}{w} \rfloor \tag{3}$$

For sample x_i with scalar quality score y_i, we can get the corresponding quality category label $y_i^c \in Y = \{1, \cdots, K\}$ by mapping y_i into the corresponding discrete quality interval.

As shown in Fig. 2, the PMT g_ϕ contains two parts: *scalar image quality score assessment* module $g_{\phi_1} : \mathbb{R}^h \to \mathbb{R}$ and *image quality level classification* module $g_{\phi_2} : \mathbb{R}^h \to [0,1]^K$. Both g_{ϕ_1} and g_{ϕ_2} are implemented using a simple Multilayer Perception (MLP), where g_{ϕ_1} is composed of four fully connected layers and g_{ϕ_2} contains three fully connected layers and one softmax layer. ReLU() is utilized as the activation function of the first 3 and 2 fully connected layers of g_{ϕ_1} and g_{ϕ_2}, respectively. Suppose $\phi_1 = \{W_1^{(\phi_1)}, W_2^{(\phi_1)}, W_3^{(\phi_1)}, W_4^{(\phi_1)}\}$ and $\phi_2 = \{W_1^{(\phi_2)}, W_2^{(\phi_2)}, W_3^{(\phi_2)}\}$, where $W_i^{(\phi_1)}$ and $W_i^{(\phi_2)}$ are the parameters of the i-th layer of g_{ϕ_1} and g_{ϕ_2} respectively, then for an input X (note that X is actually $[\hat{X}; 1]$ corresponding to real input $\hat{X}$ as $W_i^{\phi_j}$ represents weight and bias), g_{ϕ_1} and g_{ϕ_2} are defined as follows:

$$g_{\phi_1}(X) = W_4^{(\phi_1)}(\text{ReLU}(W_3^{(\phi_1)}(\text{ReLU}(W_2^{(\phi_1)}(\text{ReLU}(W_1^{(\phi_1)}X)))))) \tag{4}$$

$$g_{\phi_2}(X) = (\frac{\exp(o_1)}{\sum_{i=1}^{K} \exp(o_i)}, \cdots, \frac{\exp(o_K)}{\sum_{i=1}^{K} \exp(o_i)}) \tag{5}$$

where o_i is the i-th component of the output of the last fully connected layer of g_{ϕ_2}, which is defined as:

$$(o_1, \cdots, o_K) = W_3^{(\phi_2)}(\text{ReLU}(W_2^{(\phi_2)}(\text{ReLU}(W_1^{(\phi_2)}X)))) \tag{6}$$

Given the definition of g_{ϕ_1} and g_{ϕ_2}, the objective loss function in PMT-IQA can be defined in Eq. (7).

$$\lambda_1 \mathcal{L}_r(x, y) + \lambda_2 \mathcal{L}_c(x, y) \tag{7}$$

where $\mathcal{L}_r$ and $\mathcal{L}_c$ are the loss terms for the image quality score regression task and image quality level classification task, respectively. Parameters $\lambda_1, \lambda_2 > 0$ are dynamic hyper-parameters in the training procedure. In our implementation, we use ℓ_1 loss (defined as Eq. (8)) for $\mathcal{L}_r$ and cross-entropy loss (defined as Eq. (9)) for $\mathcal{L}_c$, respectively.

$$\mathcal{L}_r(x,y) = \frac{1}{n}\sum_{i=1}^{n} |y_i - g_{\phi_1}(h(x_i))| \tag{8}$$

$$\mathcal{L}_c(x,y) = -\frac{1}{n}\sum_{i=1}^{n}\sum_{c=1}^{K} (y_i)_c \log((g_{\phi_2}(h(x_i)))_c) \tag{9}$$

where $(\cdot)_c$ in Eq. (9) denotes the c-th component of $(\cdot)$.

To simulate the from easy to hard learning law [19], we make the model focusing on learning the classification task in the early stage of training, and gradually concentrates on scalar quality score assessment with the progress of training by dynamically adjusting the weights of the classification and regression tasks as:

$$\begin{aligned}\lambda_1(t) &= \frac{t}{T+1}\xi \\ \lambda_2(t) &= 1 - \lambda_1(t)\end{aligned} \tag{10}$$

where t represents the t-th epoch, T denotes the maximum epochs. ξ is a trade-off to balance the two losses' scale difference. We adopt the Adam optimizer [10] to optimize the PMT-IQA parameters ϕ and ψ jointly.

4   Experiment

4.1   Experimental Setup

Datasets. We use four publicly available IQA datasets, including LIVE Challenge (LIVE-C) [4], BID [3], LIVE [20], and CSIQ [13], to evaluate each IQA method. In these four datasets, BID and LIVE-C are authentic distortion datasets, where BID contains 586 figures with realistic blurry distortions, and LIVE-C includes 1162 real-world images collected by various cameras. In addition to authentic distortion datasets, we also evaluate PMT-IQA on two synthetic image datasets LIVE and CSIQ, which contain 779 and 866 images with 5 and 6 individual distortions, respectively.

Evaluation Metrics. We select two commonly-used evaluation metrics, Spearman's rank-order correlation coefficient (SRCC) [14] and Pearson's linear correlation coefficient (PLCC) [14], to evaluate the performances of IQA algorithms.

The definition of SRCC and PLCC are presented in Eq. 11 and Eq. 12, respectively. Both SRCC and PLCC range from -1 to 1, and a larger value indicates a better performance.

$$\text{SRCC} = 1 - \frac{6 \sum_i d_i^2}{n\left(n^2 - 1\right)} \tag{11}$$

$$\text{PLCC} = \frac{\sum_i \left(q_i - q_m\right)\left(\hat{q}_i - \hat{q}_m\right)}{\sqrt{\sum_i \left(q_i - q_m\right)^2 \sum_i \left(\hat{q}_i - \hat{q}_m\right)^2}} \tag{12}$$

where d_i denotes the rank difference between MOS and the predicted score of the i-th image, n is the number of images. q_i and $\hat{q}_i$ are MOS (DMOS) and the predicted score of the i-th image respectively, and q_m and $\hat{q}_m$ are average MOS (DMOS) value and average predicted score for all images.

Implementation Details. We follow the experimental protocol and settings in HyperIQA [22] for a fair comparison. Each dataset is divided into train and test set according to 4:1. The quality scores are scaled into [0,1] to improve stability, as shown in Fig. 3. During training, we augment each training image by randomly cropping and horizontally flipping ten times for LIVE-C and five times for the other three datasets according to HyoerIQA [22]. A recently proposed hyperparameter searching framework optuna [1] is employed to optimize hyperparameters and the values of hyperparameters of PMT-IQA on four datasets are reported in Table 1. In addition, dropout [21] and weight-decay [12] strategies are used to avoid over-fitting.

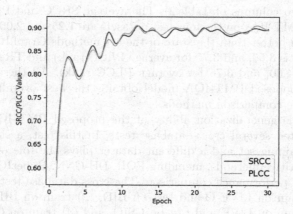

Fig. 3. SRCC and PLCC values of PMT-IQA on BID dataset in the training procedure.

Table 1. The hyperparameters obtained by Optuna on the four test datasets.

Dataset	LR	Batch	ξ	Optimizer
BID	1.09e-4	12	0.9419	Adam
LIVE-C	4.72e-4	12	0.9841	Adam
LIVE	3.23e-4	12	0.9941	Adam
CSIQ	4.72e-4	12	0.8931	Adam

4.2   Performance Evaluation

We select fourteen representative BIQA methods as strong baselines, including BRISQUE [18], ILNIQUE [29], AlexNet [11], ResNet50 [6], HOSA [26], BIECON [8], SFA [15], PQR [27], DB-CNN [30], HyperIQA [22], UNIQUE [31], CONTRIQUE [17], GraphIQA [23], and TRes [5], to evaluate the performance of our proposed PMT-IQA model.

The SRCC and PLCC values of each method on the four test datasets are listed in Table 2. From Table 2, we can find that the PMT-IQA approach outperforms all the comparison methods on BID and LIVE-C for both SRCC and PLCC evaluation. Our PMT-IQA model achieves the second-best results on LIVE dataset, only weaker than GraphIQA. For the other synthetic distortion dataset CSIQ, PMT-IQA also obtains the best SRCC value (0.949) and competitive PLCC value (0.951). In order to compare the performance of each method more intuitively, we also provide the ranks of all methods (i.e. the numbers in parentheses in Table 2) and the average ranks of SRCC and PLCC of each method (i.e. the last two columns of Table 2). The average SRCC and PLCC ranks of the proposed PMT-IQA on the four test datasets are 1.25 and 2.00, respectively, which are much better than the state-of-the-art methods GraphIQA [23] (average SRCC rank is 3.50, and 3.75 for average PLCC rank) and TReS [5] (average SRCC rank is 4.00, and 3.75 for average PLCC rank). All these results indicate tha our proposed PMT-IQA model obtains the best overall performance compared to the comparison methods.

To verify the generalization ability of the proposed PMT-IQA model, we further conducted several cross-database tests. In this test, a specific dataset is used as a training set and a different dataset plays the role of test set. We use four competitive methods, including PQR, DB-CNN, HyperIQA and TReS, as baselines for performance comparison. The cross-database tests include four settings: (1) train on LIVE-C and test on BID, (2) train on BID and test on LIVE-C, (3) train on LIVE and test on CSIQ, and (4) train on CSIQ and test on LIVE. The first two settings are for authentic distortion, while the last two are for synthetic distortion. Table 3 presents the SRCC values of the comparison methods and our proposed PMT-IQA model. We can see from the results that the proposed PMT-IQA model significantly outperforms the compared methods on all four cross-database tests.

Table 2. The SRCC and PLCC values of various methods on BID, LIVE-C, LIVE and CSIQ datasets and the average rank of SRCC and PLCC for each method. Best performance in boldface and numbers in parentheses indicate corresponding ranks. We report the median SRCC and PLCC in ten runs.

Methods	BID		LIVE-C		LIVE		CSIQ		Average Rank of	
	SRCC	PLCC	SRCC	PLCC	SRCC	PLCC	SRCC	PLCC	SRCC	PLCC
BRISQUE [18]	0.562(11)	0.593(11)	0.608(9)	0.629(13)	0.939(12)	0.935(11)	0.746(14)	0.829(10)	11.50(13)	11.25(12)
AlexNet [11]	–	–	0.766(10)	0.807(11)	0.932(13)	0.841(15)	0.766(13)	0.811(13)	12.00(14)	13.00(14)
ResNet50 [6]	0.583(10)	0.599(10)	0.824(9)	0.868(7)	0.947(10)	0.913(12)	0.823(9)	0.876(9)	9.50(9)	9.50(9)
ILNIQE [29]	0.516(13)	0.554(13)	0.432(11)	0.508(15)	0.903(14)	0.865(14)	0.806(11)	0.808(14)	12.25(15)	14.00(15)
HOSA [26]	0.721(9)	0.736(9)	0.640(8)	0.678(12)	0.946(11)	0.947(10)	0.741(15)	0.823(11)	10.75(11)	10.50(10)
BIECON [8]	0.539(12)	0.576(12)	0.595(10)	0.613(14)	0.961(8)	0.962(7)	0.815(10)	0.803(15)	10.00(10)	12.00(13)
SFA [15]	0.826(7)	0.840(7)	0.812(10)	0.833(10)	0.883(15)	0.895(13)	0.796(12)	0.818(12)	11.00(12)	10.50(10)
PQR [27]	0.775(8)	0.794(8)	0.857(3)	0.872(5)	0.965(6)	0.951(9)	0.873(8)	0.901(8)	6.25(7)	7.50(8)
DB-CNN [30]	0.845(6)	0.859(6)	0.851(5)	0.869(6)	0.968(5)	0.971(2)	0.946(3)	**0.959(1)**	4.75(6)	3.75(2)
HyperIQA [22]	0.869(3)	0.878(3)	0.859(2)	0.882(3)	0.962(7)	0.966(6)	0.923(5)	0.942(5)	4.25(4)	4.25(5)
UNIQUE [31]	0.858(5)	0.873(4)	0.854(4)	0.890(2)	0.969(2)	0.968(4)	0.902(7)	0.927(7)	4.50(5)	4.25(5)
CONTRIQUE [17]	–	–	0.845(7)	0.857(9)	0.960(9)	0.961(8)	0.942(5)	0.955(3)	7.00(8)	6.67(7)
GraphIQA [23]	0.860(4)	0.870(5)	0.845(7)	0.862(8)	**0.979(1)**	**0.980(1)**	0.947(2)	**0.959(1)**	3.50(2)	3.75(2)
TReS [5]	0.872(2)	0.879(2)	0.846(6)	0.877(4)	0.969(2)	0.968(4)	0.922(6)	0.942(5)	4.00(3)	3.75(2)
PMT-IQA (Proposed)	**0.874(1)**	**0.894(1)**	**0.866(1)**	**0.893(1)**	0.969(2)	0.971(2)	**0.949(1)**	0.951(4)	**1.25(1)**	**2.00(1)**

Table 3. SRCC comparison on cross-database tests. Best results in boldface.

Train on	Test on	PQR [27]	DB-CNN [30]	Hyper-IQA [22]	TReS [5]	PMT-IQA (Proposed)
LIVE-C	BID	0.714	0.762	0.756	0.870	**0.897**
BID	LIVE-C	0.680	0.725	0.770	0.765	**0.782**
LIVE	CSIQ	0.719	0.758	0.744	0.738	**0.766**
CSIQ	LIVE	0.922	0.877	0.926	0.932	**0.934**

4.3 Ablation Study

We conduct several subtle ablation studies on the four test datasets to further verify the effectiveness of MS and PMT modules. The variants are as follows:

(1) **ResNet**: Pre-trained ResNet50 architecture on ImageNet, adding fully connected layers for prediction (i.e., without MS and PMT).
(2) **Type1**: The entire architecture in Fig. 2 with only MS (i.e., without PMT).
(3) **Type2**: The entire architecture in Fig. 2 with MS and PMT using fixed λ_1 and λ_2, and we use $\lambda_1 = \lambda_2 = 0.5$ in our implementation based on test experiments.
(4) **PMT-IQA**: The entire architecture PMT-IQA in Fig. 2 with MS and PMT using dynamic task weights as Eq. 10.

We tune the hidden dimension to ensure variants have similar numbers of parameters to the completed PMT-IQA by removing the performance gain induced by model complexity for fairness. As shown in Fig. 4, we can see that PMT-IQA achieves the best performance compared with the other three variants on all four test datasets. In addition, both MS and PMT modules can bring performance improvement to the model. Compared with MS, PMT improves the

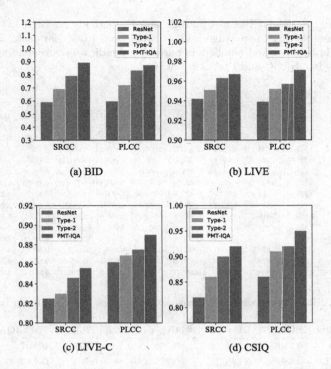

Fig. 4. The ablation study on the BID, LIVE, LIVE-C and CSIQ datasets.

overall performance more significantly for PLCC evaluation on LIVE, LIVE-C and CSIQ. Moreover, the comparison between the results of Type2 and PMT-IQA shows that the strategy of dynamically adjusting the task weights to make the network learn from an easy task to a complex task is effective. The novel progressive shift of tasks in PMT-IQA is essential in the training stage. Therefore, the ablation study results again verify the effectiveness of the proposed PMT-IQA.

5   Conclusion

In this paper, we propose a simple yet effective progressive multi-task learning model for blind image quality assessment. Our model contains a multi-scale feature extraction module and a progressive multi-task learning module to help the model learn complex distortion patterns by simulating the from easy to hard human learning law. Extensive experimental results show that despite the relatively simple architecture of the proposed PMT-IQA method, it can still achieve superior or competitive performance compared to various baselines on all the datasets.

Acknowledgments.. This work is supported by the National Natural Science Foundation of China under Grant 61866031.

References

1. Akiba, T., Sano, S., Yanase, T., Ohta, T., Koyama, M.: Optuna: a next-generation hyperparameter optimization framework. In: Proceedings of the 25th ACM SIGKDD International Conference on Knowledge Discovery Data Mining, pp. 2623–2631 (2019)
2. Bengio, Y., Louradour, J., Collobert, R., Weston, J.: Curriculum learning. In: Proceedings of the 26th Annual International Conference on Machine Learning, pp. 41–48 (2009)
3. Ciancio, A., da Silva, E.A., Said, A., Samadani, R., Obrador, P., et al.: No-reference blur assessment of digital pictures based on multifeature classifiers. IEEE Trans. Image Process. **20**(1), 64–75 (2010)
4. Ghadiyaram, D., Bovik, A.C.: Massive online crowdsourced study of subjective and objective picture quality. IEEE Trans. Image Process. **25**(1), 372–387 (2015)
5. Golestaneh, S.A., Dadsetan, S., Kitani, K.M.: No-reference image quality assessment via transformers, relative ranking and self-consistency. In: Proceedings of the IEEE/CVF Winter Conference on Applications of Computer Vision, pp. 1220–1230 (2022)
6. He, K., Zhang, X., Ren, S., Sun, J.: Deep residual learning for image recognition. In: Proceedings of the IEEE Conference on Computer Vision and Pattern Recognition, pp. 770–778 (2016)
7. Kang, L., Ye, P., Li, Y., Doermann, D.: Simultaneous estimation of image quality and distortion via multi-task convolutional neural networks. In: 2015 IEEE International Conference on Image Processing (ICIP), pp. 2791–2795. IEEE (2015)
8. Kim, J., Lee, S.: Fully deep blind image quality predictor. IEEE J. Sel. Top. Signal Process. **11**(1), 206–220 (2016)
9. Kim, J., Zeng, H., Ghadiyaram, D., Lee, S., Zhang, L., Bovik, A.C.: Deep convolutional neural models for picture-quality prediction: challenges and solutions to data-driven image quality assessment. IEEE Signal Process. Mag. **34**(6), 130–141 (2017)
10. Kingma, D.P., Ba, J.: Adam: a method for stochastic optimization. arXiv preprint arXiv:1412.6980 (2014)
11. Krizhevsky, A., Sutskever, I., Hinton, G.E.: Imagenet classification with deep convolutional neural networks. Adv. Neural Inf. Process. Syst. **25** (2012)
12. Krogh, A., Hertz, J.: A simple weight decay can improve generalization. Adv. Neural Inf. Process. Syst. **4** (1991)
13. Larson, E.C., Chandler, D.M.: Most apparent distortion: full-reference image quality assessment and the role of strategy. J. Electron. Imaging **19**(1), 011006 (2010)
14. Lehman, A.: JMP for basic univariate and multivariate statistics: a step-by-step guide. SAS Institute (2005)
15. Li, D., Jiang, T., Lin, W., Jiang, M.: Which has better visual quality: the clear blue sky or a blurry animal? IEEE Trans. Multimedia **21**(5), 1221–1234 (2018)
16. Ma, K., Liu, W., Zhang, K., Duanmu, Z., Wang, Z., Zuo, W.: End-to-end blind image quality assessment using deep neural networks. IEEE Trans. Image Process. **27**(3), 1202–1213 (2018)

17. Madhusudana, P.C., Birkbeck, N., Wang, Y., Adsumilli, B., Bovik, A.C.: Image quality assessment using contrastive learning. IEEE Trans. Image Process. **31**, 4149–4161 (2022)
18. Mittal, A., Moorthy, A.K., Bovik, A.C.: No-reference image quality assessment in the spatial domain. IEEE Trans. Image Process. **21**(12), 4695–4708 (2012)
19. Pavlov, I.: Conditioned reflexes. Les Etudes Philosophiques **17**(4) (1927)
20. Sheikh, H.R., Sabir, M.F., Bovik, A.C.: A statistical evaluation of recent full reference image quality assessment algorithms. IEEE Trans. Image Process. **15**(11), 3440–3451 (2006)
21. Srivastava, N., Hinton, G., Krizhevsky, A., Sutskever, I., Salakhutdinov, R.: Dropout: a simple way to prevent neural networks from overfitting. J. Mach. Learn. Res. **15**(1), 1929–1958 (2014)
22. Su, S., et al.: Blindly assess image quality in the wild guided by a self-adaptive hyper network. In: Proceedings of the IEEE/CVF Conference on Computer Vision and Pattern Recognition, pp. 3667–3676 (2020)
23. Sun, S., Yu, T., Xu, J., Zhou, W., Chen, Z.: Graphiqa: learning distortion graph representations for blind image quality assessment. IEEE Trans. Multimedia (2022)
24. Wang, X., Chen, Y., Zhu, W.: A survey on curriculum learning. IEEE Trans. Pattern Anal. Mach. Intell. **44**(9), 4555–4576 (2021)
25. Wang, Z., Bovik, A.C., Sheikh, H.R., Simoncelli, E.P.: Image quality assessment: from error visibility to structural similarity. IEEE Trans. Image Process. **13**(4), 600–612 (2004)
26. Xu, J., Ye, P., Li, Q., Du, H., Liu, Y., Doermann, D.: Blind image quality assessment based on high order statistics aggregation. IEEE Trans. Image Process. **25**(9), 4444–4457 (2016)
27. Zeng, H., Zhang, L., Bovik, A.C.: Blind image quality assessment with a probabilistic quality representation. In: 2018 25th IEEE International Conference on Image Processing (ICIP), pp. 609–613. IEEE (2018)
28. Zhai, G., Min, X.: Perceptual image quality assessment: a survey. Sci. China Inf. Sci. **63**(11), 1–52 (2020)
29. Zhang, L., Zhang, L., Bovik, A.C.: A feature-enriched completely blind image quality evaluator. IEEE Trans. Image Process. **24**(8), 2579–2591 (2015)
30. Zhang, W., Ma, K., Yan, J., Deng, D., Wang, Z.: Blind image quality assessment using a deep bilinear convolutional neural network. IEEE Trans. Circ. Syst. Video Technol. **30**(1), 36–47 (2018)
31. Zhang, W., Ma, K., Zhai, G., Yang, X.: Uncertainty-aware blind image quality assessment in the laboratory and wild. IEEE Trans. Image Process. **30**, 3474–3486 (2021)

Reduced-Resolution Head for Object Detection

Jiayuan Zhuang[1], Zheng Qin[2], Hao Yu[2,3], and Xucan Chen[1](✉)

[1] Intelligent Game and Decision Lab (IGDL), Beijing, China
zhuangjy12@alumni.nudt.edu.cn, xcchen18@139.com
[2] National University of Defense Technology, Changsha, China
qinzheng12@nudt.edu.cn, hao.yu@tum.de
[3] Technical University of Munich, Munich, Germany

Abstract. Utilizing a multi-scale strategy to address the challenge of significant variations in object sizes is a common approach in object detection. However, this strategy often results in significant computational overhead on high-resolution feature maps, leading to increased model complexity. This paper proposes a novel Reduced-resolution Head for Object Detection (RHOD). It can be seamlessly incorporated into most existing popular detectors, operating in a *plug-and-play* way. By replacing high-resolution feature maps with lower-resolution ones for regression and classification, our RHOD effectively eliminates the computational costs on high-resolution feature maps. Combined with the proposed Feature Fusion (FF), the final detection accuracy of the model can approach the accuracy of the original detector. Experimental results demonstrate that RHOD reduces the computational cost of the detector by approximately 15%–40% without sacrificing accuracy. This reduction in computational cost leads to a significant improvement in inference speed, with an increase of 1.2–5.0 frames per second (FPS). The code and models will be available at https://github.com/alpc128/RHOD.

Keywords: Computer vision · Deep learing · Object Detection

1 Introduction

The scale of objects on 2D images varies tremendously not only owing to their natural properties, but also due to the perspective projection when we observe them in the wild 3D world. As pointed out by [21], the smallest and largest 10% of 2D objects on the COCO dataset [16] occupy 0.024 and 0.472 of the images, respectively. Therefore, effectively addressing the significant scale variation of 2D objects is a fundamental challenge in object detection.

Existing approaches commonly employ a multi-scale pyramid strategy to address the significant scale variations [23] of objects to be detected, such as the Feature Pyramid Network (FPN) [14], which has become a standard architecture in recent works [15,24]. Compared with works [2] that rely solely on a single feature map to detect objects across various scales, FPN not only efficiently utilizes the hierarchical structure of Covolutional Neural Networks (CNN) but also

F. Liu et al. (Eds.): PRICAI 2023, LNAI 14327, pp. 165–176, 2024.
https://doi.org/10.1007/978-981-99-7025-4_14

assigns the tasks of object localization and classification to corresponding levels of feature maps based on the object's proportion in the image [2]. While this multi-scale pyramid strategy demonstrates promising capabilities in dealing with scale variation, it involves a trade-off between detection accuracy and inference speed. Detectors utilizing the multi-scale pyramid strategy often incur additional computational cost, which limits their applicability in scenarios such as embedded devices and mobile phones.

Currently, there have been some lightweight methods [9,18] that focus on researching smaller and lighter backbones. However, research specifically targeting the reduction of computational cost in the detection head remains limited. While reducing the computational cost incurred by the backbone network is important, addressing the computational cost introduced by the detection head is equally significant. Our work aims to bridge the research gap by proposing a detection head that effectively reduces computational cost without compromising detection accuracy.

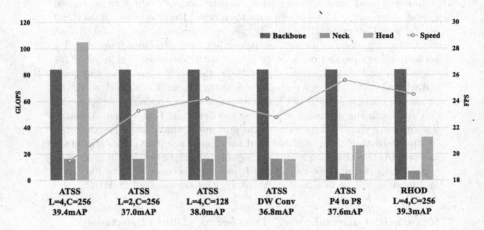

Fig. 1. Performance comparison of different cropping methods to reduce the computational cost of detection head occupation. Compared with methods such as reducing stacked network layers, reducing convolution channel, and using Depthwise Separate convolution, our RHOD not only greatly reduces the computational cost and improves the inference speed, but also maintains the accuracy of the detector.

To investigate how to prune this additional computational cost, this paper conducts experimental analysis and compares the efficiency of various pruning methods. It is found that commonly used pruning methods often lead to a decrease in detection accuracy, see Fig. 1. Through further analysis of the distribution of model computational costs, we find that the detection head's computation cost accounts for a significant proportion on high-resolution feature maps, more details see Fig. 2. Based on these observations as well as experiments, we propose a novel Reduced-resolution Head for Object Detection (RHOD). Its core idea is to use small-resolution feature maps with rich semantic information to predict objects that were traditionally assigned to high-resolution feature maps, thereby avoiding the extensive convolution operations performed on high-resolution feature maps. However, this approach may introduce a certain semantic gap between the feature map used to generate prediction results and the target objects. To bridge this semantic gap, we propose a Feature Fusion (FF) technique that combines high-resolution and low-resolution feature maps. The combination of these two techniques enables our RHOD to reduce the model's computational costs by approximately 15%–40%, while maintaining and even slightly enhancing the detection performance of the detector.

Our main contributions are summarized as follows:

- We compared various pruning methods and analyzed the unreasonable distribution of computational costs in the detect head of current mainstream detectors.
- We proposed RHOD (Reduced-Resolution Head for Object Detection), which significantly reduces the computational costs of detection models by using low-resolution feature maps for prediction.
- Extensive experiments on MS-COCO [16] dataset demonstrated that RHOD is a plug-and-play solution that effectively improves the inference speed of various detectors.

2   Related Works

CNN-Based Detector. Object detection based on CNN is generally divided into the family of two-stage detectors [7,20] or the family of one-stage detectors [17,19]. Firstly, anchor boxes [15] or anchor points [10,24] are densely placed on the image, and the location of each anchor or anchor point indicates the specific region which it focuses on [20]. Subsequently, based on these anchor boxes, the detector encodes and decodes the image features through one or multiple convolutional layers, ultimately achieving object category inference and bounding box localization. To enhance the model's robustness to object scale variations, CNN detectors commonly utilize FPN [14] to fuse the features from both shallow and deep, thereby constructing a feature pyramid that contains rich semantic information. After that, several works [6,22] have made improvements based on FPN and have achieved promising results. FPN has gradually become an essential component of most CNN-based detectors and takes a dominant role in the development of modern detectors. However, detectors using FPN typically incur larger computational cost, as this divide-and-conquer solution sacrifices the inference speed of the detector. In other words, there is a trade-off between inference speed and detection accuracy.

Lightweight Detector. In order to enable object detection models to run on low-power and computationally limited platforms, a common practice in the industry is to scale down the models [5,22] by reducing the number of network layers, decreasing network width, and pruning model parameters and computations. These practices represent the optimal trade-off between detection accuracy and speed. MobileNets [9] introduced depthwise separable convolutions, which replace standard convolutions with grouped convolutions and pointwise convolutions to reduce model computational cost. ShuffleNetV2 [18] proposed a series of practical methods to guide the design of more efficient detectors. Additionally, while there have been many optimization studies [3,11] targeting the backbone network of detectors, research specifically focused on designing the detection head to reduce model computations and improve inference speed is relatively limited. Light-Head R-CNN [13] effectively improves model inference speed by pruning the second stage of the two-stage detector. Different from these works, this paper proposes a novel detection head. Our experimental results demonstrate that there is still room for optimization in terms of computations for commonly used detection heads.

3   Method

3.1   Motivation and Analysis

FCOS [24] is a popular object detection with the classic "backbone-neck-head" architecture. The backbone network takes input images and extracts various features present in the images, while the neck usually incorporates FPN to fuse features and generate feature maps at different resolutions. The head consists of two branches with separate parameters but the same structure, handling object bounding box regression and class prediction tasks. Each branch typically consists of 4 stacked convolutional layers and 256 channels.

Heavy Head. We have conducted a statistical analysis and found that the computational cost of FCOS is primarily concentrated in the backbone and head. When employing ResNet-50 [8] backbone and setting the input size to 1280×800, the computation distribution is depicted in Fig. 1, indicates that the computational cost on the head even surpasses that of the backbone. This disproportionate ratio led us to believe that there is room for optimization in the computation of the head.

Table 1. Results on COCO *minival* by using ResNet-50 backbone. FLOPS is counted on the input size of 1280×800. FPS values are evaluated on a machine with a single NVIDIA 2080 Ti and using a batch size of 1.

Method	Layers	Channel	mAP	AP_{50}	AP_{75}	AP_S	AP_M	AP_L	#params	GFLOPS/FPS
ATSS [26]	4	256	39.4	57.6	42.8	23.6	42.9	50.3	32.1	205.3/19.5
	2	256	37.0	55.9	40.0	22.6	40.7	46.7	29.7	154.9/23.3
	4	128	38.0	56.1	41.2	22.4	41.7	48.5	28.7	133.9/24.2
	DW Conv		36.8	54.8	39.7	21.5	40.6	45.6	27.9	116.3/22.8
	P4 to P8		37.6	55.3	40.5	20.5	43.1	50.0	31.9	115.1/25.6

As shown in Table 1, we conduct several experiments to reduce the computational cost of detection heads and compare their accuracy and speed. The first row is the performance of FCOS with ATSS label assignment and its overall computational cost. In the second row, we reduced stacked network layers in the head from 4 to 2, which resulted in a decrease in computational cost (-50.4 GFLOPS) and an improvement in inference speed ($+3.8$ FPS), but it also led to a decrease in detection accuracy (-2.4 mAP). In the third row, we reduced the convolution channel in stacked network layers of the head from 256 to 128, significantly reducing the computational cost (-71.4 GFLOPS), improving the inference speed ($+4.7$ FPS), and also decreasing the accuracy (-1.4 mAP). In the fourth row, we replaced the regular convolutions in the detection head with depth-wise separable convolutions, while keeping the last convolutional layer in each branch unchanged. This method maximized the reduction in computational cost (-89 GFLOPS), slightly improved the inference speed ($+3.3$ FPS, since larger MAC [18]), but resulted in a significant drop in model accuracy (-2.6 mAP).

Although these methods can crop the computational cost of the detection head and increase FPS, they inevitably compromise the model's representational capacity. Whether it is reducing the stacked network layers, decreasing the convolution channel, or using depth-wise separable convolutions, the ability of detectors to capture complex patterns and features will be compromised. In other words, these methods still involve a *trade-off* between computational complexity and detection accuracy.

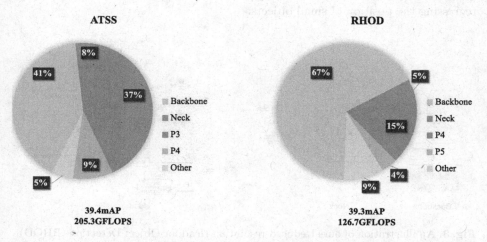

Fig. 2. Computational cost distribution of ATSS (left) and RHOD (right). The ATSS detection head accounts for over 50% of the total, with the highest computational cost observed on P_3, contributing to approximately 37% of the entire model's computation. In comparison, our RHOD reduces the computation cost by 78.6 GFLOPS.

Computational Cost Distribution. Actually, the detection head incurs the highest computational cost mainly on high-resolution feature maps, particularly

P_3. Denoting the output feature maps from the neck as $\mathcal{P} = \{P_i \in \mathbb{R}^{H \times W \times C}\}$, i indicates the pyramid level, typically ranging from 3 to 7. The downsampling rate of the feature maps is 2^i, meaning that the height (H) and width (W) of the feature map at level i are reduced by a factor of $\frac{1}{2^i}$ compared to the input image. Thus, P_3 has the largest spatial size. On the other hand, all the feature maps are processed equally through stacked convolutional network layers. It can be seen from Fig. 2, P_3 incurs the highest computational cost, accounting for approximately 72% of the computation in the detection head.

The simplest way to eliminate this computational cost is to exclude the use of P_3 for detection and instead start the detection head from P_4. The last row in Table 1 represents the case where P_4 to P_8 are sent into the head and generates the final prediction output. This results in a significant reduction in computational cost (-90.2 GFLOPS) and the highest increase in inference speed ($+6.1$ FPS). Unlike the previous methods discussed for reducing computational cost, this approach leads to a decrease in accuracy (-1.8 mAP), primarily due to the performance drop of the model detecting small objects. Specifically, the representative metric AP_s, which measures the detection performance on small objects, decreases, while the performance of the model for large and medium objects remains the same. We believe that this phenomenon is caused by two factors: First, insufficient *anchors/anchor points* for predicting small objects, leading to oscillation of the same predicted box between two or more ground truth objects, ultimately resulting in poor detection performance. Second, the absence of details reserved feature maps prevents the detector from accurately regressing the position of small objects.

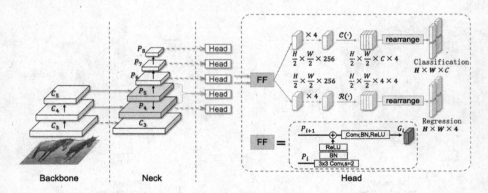

Fig. 3. An illustration of ours Reduced-resolution Head for Object Detection (RHOD). The feature map of pyramid level i and $i+1$ is fused through feature fusion to generate G_i, which has the same resolution as that of level $i + 1$. This fused feature map is responsible for detecting objects at pyramid level i.

3.2   Reduced-Resolution Head for Object Detection

We propose a novel detection head that can be seamlessly incorporated into existing detectors in a *plug-and-play* way. From experimental results, our detection head achieves comparable performance to existing detectors with significantly lower computational requirements. The whole structure is illustrated in Fig. 3. It is important to note that our method is also effective for two-stage detectors. For simplicity, we present an example using a one-stage detector.

We first allocate ground truth objects to feature maps from P_3 to P_7 according to the label assignment strategy of ATSS [26]. Then, we use feature maps from P_4 to P_8 for prediction. Unlike previous methods where each feature point predicts a single object, we enable each feature point to predict four objects corresponding to the feature map of previous layer. The final layer of regression branch predicts a $16D$ vector that represents four bounding boxes. The output of the regression is denoted as $\hat{B}$, its size is $\frac{H}{2} \times \frac{W}{2} \times 16$, we then rearrange this output to restore the resolution. Specifically, the feature point at position (x, y) corresponds to the four points in the feature map of previous layer at positions $(2x, 2y)$, $(2x, 2y+1)$, $(2x+1, 2y)$, and $(2x+1, 2y+1)$. By rearranging the predictions, we obtain a new output B, its size is $H \times W \times 4$. In summary, the process can be described as follows:

$$B[2x + i, 2y + j, t] = \hat{B}[x, y, (2i + j)t], \forall i,j \in \{0,1\}, x \in [0, \frac{H}{2}), y \in [0, \frac{W}{2}). \quad (1)$$

The output of the classification branch is processed as follows:

$$C[2x + i, 2y + j, c] = \hat{C}[x, y, (2i + j)c], \forall i,j \in \{0,1\}, x \in [0, \frac{H}{2}), y \in [0, \frac{W}{2}). \quad (2)$$

In the end, we obtain the output with the same size as the original detector, so there is no need to change the loss function. If the detector has additional auxiliary branches such as centerness [24] or IoU prediction [25], similar processing needs to be applied to those branches as well.

To address the issue of insufficient localization ability for small objects in the aforementioned method, we utilize the P_i and P_{i+1} feature maps to generate G_i, which has the same spatial size as P_{i+1}. This new feature map contains information from the lower-level feature map and provides more fine-grained features as well as clearer boundary and positional information for both the classification and regression branches. Experimental results demonstrate that using G_i improves the detection accuracy of the detector. Additionally, we have also discovered that in our method, the fusion of the P_3 in the neck module is not necessary. Instead, we can directly use the C_3 to predict, which saves approximately 9.4 GFLOPS of computational cost for the model.

4 Experiments

Dataset and Evaluation. All experimental results were generated on the COCO 2017 [16] detection dataset. Following common practices [4, 24], we used the *trainval35k* subset to train the models and *minival* subset to evaluate the performance. Performance measurement follows the COCO Average Precision (AP) metric.

Implementation and Trainning. Our RHOD is implemented in the MMDe-tection framework [1]. Unless otherwise specified, ResNet-50 [8] is chosen as the default backbone, and the input images are resized with the short side set to 800 pixels, while ensuring that the long side remains below 1333 pixels. The training was conducted using 8 NVIDIA V100 GPUs, with setting the batch size to 16 (2 images per GPU). Following [4, 12, 26], we used Stochastic Gradient Descent (SGD) as the optimizer and the initial learning rate is 0.01, which was reduced by a factor of 10 at the 8th and 11th epochs.

4.1   Ablation Study

We selected ATSS [26] as the baseline model for conducting ablation experiments. Detectors were trained using the ResNet-50 [8] backbone with single-scale training in $1\times$ schedule (12 epochs). The detector's performance was evaluated on the COCO *minival* dataset. When calculating GFLOPS, we set the input size to 1280×800. The FPS were obtained using the mmdetection framework and the testing was conducted on the same machine using a single NVIDIA 2080 Ti, with setting the batch size to 1.

Table 2. Ablation studies on COCO *minival*. **FF**: Feature Fusion.

Method	FF	C_3/P_3	mAP	AP_{50}	AP_{75}	AP_S	AP_M	AP_L	#params	GFLOPS/FPS
ATSS	–	–	39.4	57.6	42.8	23.6	42.9	50.3	32.1	205.3/19.5
ATSS*	–	–	37.6	55.3	40.5	20.5	43.1	50.0	31.9	115.1/25.6
RHOD			38.3	56.8	41.6	22.6	42.1	48.7	32.5	118.3/25.0
RHOD	Avg	P_3	38.8	57.3	42.1	22.5	42.7	49.6	33.9	133.1/24.2
RHOD	Max	P_3	38.7	57.0	42.2	22.5	42.5	50.0	33.9	133.1/24.2
RHOD	Conv	P_3	39.3	57.5	42.4	23.5	42.8	50.2	34.4	136.1/23.9
RHOD	Conv	C_3	39.3	57.8	42.5	23.4	42.9	50.1	33.8	126.7/24.5

More Prediction Boxes. We first attempted to restore the model's dense box predictions to the same level as ATSS. As shown in Tab. 2, the first row represents the performance of the original ATSS [26] model. For comparison with subsequent experiments, we listed the results of predicting corresponding objects using P_4 to P_8 in the second row. The follow row of the table represents our use of P_4 to P_8 feature maps to predict ground truth assigned to P_3 to P_7 using the ATSS label assignment scheme. This helps to avoid training oscillation and inference failures caused by a single anchor covering multiple ground truth objects. From the results, we observed that the model's performance improved by 0.7 mAP compared to predicting objects using P_4 to P_8, especially in terms of detecting small objects. The inference speed slightly decreased, as the increased number of predictions impacted the overall FPS performance.

Feature Fusion. In addition to increasing the number of predicted anchor boxes, we also studied different ways to reduce the resolution. Predicting objects using the P_i feature map to handle the responses of objects assigned to the P_{i-1} feature map can result in a semantic gap between the predicted objects and the ground truth. Therefore, we need to incorporate the P_{i-1} pyramid level feature map during prediction in the detection head. Experimental results show that downsampling the P_{i-1} feature map using max-pooling or avg-pooling for feature fusion leads to suboptimal detector accuracy, which aligns with the findings of [27]. We also compared the results of directly using the C_3 feature map and using the P_3 generated by FPN. We found that these two approaches have almost no difference in accuracy, but directly using C_3 can save computational cost and increase the FPS of the detector.

Table 3. Results on COCO *test-dev* using longer training schedules and different backbones. 'R': ResNet.

Method	Backbone	Epoch	mAP	AP_{50}	AP_{75}	AP_S	AP_M	AP_L	#params	GFLOPS/FPS
ATSS	R-50	24	42.4	60.6	46.3	25.5	46.5	52.8	32.1	205.3/19.5
RHOD	R-50	24	42.5	60.7	46.4	25.4	46.6	52.9	33.8	126.7/24.5
ATSS	R-101	24	43.6	62.1	47.4	26.1	47.0	53.6	51.1	281.4/15.1
RHOD	R-101	24	43.5	62.0	47.4	26.2	47.1	53.5	52.8	202.8/17.6

Longer Schedule and Different Backbone. To provide a more accurate and detailed comparison with the baseline, we also trained models using different backbones for 24 epochs, with learning rate reductions at 16 and 22 epochs. Following previous works [24,26], a multi-scale strategy was employed during training where a random value between 640 and 800 was selected as the length of the short side for image resizing. By uploading the models to the evaluation server, we obtained the results on the COCO *test-dev* dataset, as shown in Tab. 3. In the longer training schedule, our model achieved comparable accuracy to the original ATSS model, but with faster inference speed.

4.2   Applied to Other Detectors

RPN of Two Stage Detectors. We attempted to apply RHOD to the Region Proposal Network (RPN) of the two-stage detectors. Our experiments were conducted on Faster R-CNN [20]. The model utilized feature maps from P_2 to P_6, and ignores the computation cost of the ROI, the entire model consumed a high computation cost of 192.6 GFLOPS. Specifically, the high-resolution feature maps with a downsampling rate of 4 contributed to a computation cost of 75.5 GFLOPS in the neck and RPN. The first stage of the two-stage detector involves preliminary screening of candidate regions and rough estimation of object positions. Precise object location and category information are obtained in the second stage using features generated by Region of Interset (RoI). Here, the use of feature fusion doesn't significantly enhance model performance, and it may even sacrifice some speed. Therefore, feature fusion is not necessary in this context. We directly used feature maps from P_3 to P_8 for prediction in the RPN. The specific approach involves assigning each feature point in the RPN network to generate candidate region predictions corresponding to the four feature points produced by the next layer's feature map.

Table 4. Comparing typical two-stage detectors with and without RHOD on COCO *minival* by using ResNet-50 backbone.

Method	mAP	AP_{50}	AP_{75}	AP_S	AP_M	AP_L	#params	GFLOPS/FPS
Faster R-CNN	37.6	58.2	41.0	21.5	41.1	48.9	41.5	207.1/20.2
Faster R-CNN + RHOD	38.1	58.3	41.2	21.9	41.6	49.3	41.6	169.3/21.9
Mask R-CNN	38.2	58.8	41.4	21.9	40.9	49.5	44.1	260.1/17.1
Mask R-CNN + RHOD	38.4	59.0	41.9	21.8	41.5	50.1	44.2	222.4/18.3

As shown in Table 4 Our approach was able to save approximately 37.8 GFLOPS of computation cost, resulting in a 1.7 FPS improvement in the inference speed of Faster R-CNN. Furthermore, our method improved the accuracy of Faster R-CNN by 0.5 mAP. This improvement may be attributed to the higher-level feature maps containing better semantic information. Similar results were observed in Mask R-CNN [7]. However, it is worth noting that the computation cost of generating the P_2 feature map from the neck is still required in the ROI stage and cannot be replaced by C_2, which limits the computational cost savings. We will try to solve this problem in future work.

Table 5. Results on COCO *minival* by using ResNet-50 backbone.

Method	mAP	AP_{50}	AP_{75}	AP_S	AP_M	AP_L	#params	GFLOPS/FPS	Reference
OTA	40.7	58.4	44.3	23.2	45.0	53.6	32.2	199.8/19.5	CVPR21
OTA*	40.7	58.5	44.2	23.0	44.9	53.8	32.2	199.8/19.5	
OTA + RHOD	40.5	58.1	44.0	22.9	44.7	53.3	33.9	121.2/24.6	
DW	41.5	59.8	44.8	23.4	44.9	54.8	32.1	205.3/19.8	CVPR22
DW*	41.3	59.7	44.6	22.8	44.6	55.0	32.1	205.3/19.8	
DW + RHOD	41.2	59.5	44.5	22.5	44.5	55.2	33.8	126.7/24.8	

Newer and Stronger Detectors. We also tested our RHOD on the newer and stronger detectors [4,12]. OTA [4] optimizes the label assignment problem in object detection by using optimal transport, while DW [12] introduces a novel dual-weighted label assignment scheme to guide the training of the detector. These more powerful detectors, however, mainly focus on improving detection accuracy and lack consideration for the computational cost of the detectors. Our RHOD is also effective on them.

The first row in Table 5 represents the performance of these methods as reported in the original research papers or code repositories, while the second row shows the performance obtained by retraining these models in our environment. The experimental results show that when applying RHOD during the $1\times$ training schedule, it can approximate the accuracy of the original detector with significantly lower computational cost and faster inference speed.

5   Conclusion

In this paper, we conducted an in-depth analysis of the computational costs of current mainstream CNN detectors. We compared different methods for reducing the computational costs of the detection head and identified an unreasonable distribution of computational costs within the detection head. To address these issues, we proposed a new plug-and-play detection head called RHOD. Experimental results demonstrate that our RHOD significantly reduces the computational costs of the model and improves inference speed while maintaining accuracy. However, there are limitations to RHOD. It may not uniformly reduce computation costs across different detectors and the usage of RHOD could lead to a slight increase parameters compared to the original detector. We plan to address these issues in our future work.

References

1. Chen, K., et al.: Mmdetection: open mmlab detection toolbox and benchmark. arXiv preprint arXiv:1906.07155 (2019)
2. Chen, Q., Wang, Y., Yang, T., Zhang, X., Cheng, J., Sun, J.: You only look one-level feature. In: Proceedings of the IEEE/CVF Conference on Computer Vision and Pattern Recognition, pp. 13039–13048 (2021)
3. Ding, X., Zhang, X., Ma, N., Han, J., Ding, G., Sun, J.: Repvgg: making vgg-style convnets great again. In: Proceedings of the IEEE/CVF Conference on Computer Vision and Pattern Recognition, pp. 13733–13742 (2021)
4. Ge, Z., Liu, S., Li, Z., Yoshie, O., Sun, J.: Ota: optimal transport assignment for object detection. In: Proceedings of the IEEE/CVF Conference on Computer Vision and Pattern Recognition, pp. 303–312 (2021)
5. Ge, Z., Liu, S., Wang, F., Li, Z., Sun, J.: Yolox: exceeding yolo series in 2021. arXiv preprint arXiv:2107.08430 (2021)
6. Ghiasi, G., Lin, T.Y., Le, Q.V.: Nas-fpn: learning scalable feature pyramid architecture for object detection. In: Proceedings of the IEEE/CVF Conference on Computer Vision and Pattern Recognition, pp. 7036–7045 (2019)
7. He, K., Gkioxari, G., Dollár, P., Girshick, R.: Mask r-cnn: In: Proceedings of the IEEE International Conference on Computer Vision, pp. 2961–2969 (2017)
8. He, K., Zhang, X., Ren, S., Sun, J.: Deep residual learning for image recognition. In: Proceedings of the IEEE Conference on Computer Vision and Pattern Recognition, pp. 770–778 (2016)
9. Howard, A.G., et al.: Mobilenets: efficient convolutional neural networks for mobile vision applications. arXiv preprint arXiv:1704.04861 (2017)

10. Kong, T., Sun, F., Liu, H., Jiang, Y., Li, L., Shi, J.: Foveabox: beyound anchor-based object detection. IEEE Trans. Image Process. **29**, 7389–7398 (2020)
11. Lee, Y., Hwang, J.W., Lee, S., Bae, Y., Park, J.: An energy and gpu-computation efficient backbone network for real-time object detection. In: Proceedings of the IEEE/CVF Conference on Computer Vision and Pattern Recognition Workshops (2019)
12. Li, S., He, C., Li, R., Zhang, L.: A dual weighting label assignment scheme for object detection. In: Proceedings of the IEEE/CVF Conference on Computer Vision and Pattern Recognition, pp. 9387–9396 (2022)
13. Li, Z., Peng, C., Yu, G., Zhang, X., Deng, Y., Sun, J.: Light-head r-cnn: in defense of two-stage object detector. arXiv preprint arXiv:1711.07264 (2017)
14. Lin, T.Y., Dollár, P., Girshick, R., He, K., Hariharan, B., Belongie, S.: Feature pyramid networks for object detection. In: Proceedings of the IEEE Conference on Computer Vision and Pattern Recognition, pp. 2117–2125 (2017)
15. Lin, T.Y., Goyal, P., Girshick, R., He, K., Dollár, P.: Focal loss for dense object detection. In: Proceedings of the IEEE International Conference on Computer Vision, pp. 2980–2988 (2017)
16. Lin, T.-Y., et al.: Microsoft COCO: common objects in context. In: Fleet, D., Pajdla, T., Schiele, B., Tuytelaars, T. (eds.) ECCV 2014. LNCS, vol. 8693, pp. 740–755. Springer, Cham (2014). https://doi.org/10.1007/978-3-319-10602-1_48
17. Liu, W., et al.: SSD: single shot multibox detector. In: Leibe, B., Matas, J., Sebe, N., Welling, M. (eds.) ECCV 2016. LNCS, vol. 9905, pp. 21–37. Springer, Cham (2016). https://doi.org/10.1007/978-3-319-46448-0_2
18. Ma, N., Zhang, X., Zheng, H.T., Sun, J.: Shufflenet v2: practical guidelines for efficient cnn architecture design. In: Proceedings of the European Conference on Computer Vision (ECCV), pp. 116–131 (2018)
19. Redmon, J., Divvala, S., Girshick, R., Farhadi, A.: You only look once: unified, real-time object detection. In: Proceedings of the IEEE Conference on Computer Vision and Pattern Recognition, pp. 779–788 (2016)
20. Ren, S., He, K., Girshick, R., Sun, J.: Faster r-cnn: towards real-time object detection with region proposal networks. Adv. Neural Inf. Process. Syst. **28** (2015)
21. Singh, B., Davis, L.S.: An analysis of scale invariance in object detection snip. In: Proceedings of the IEEE Conference on Computer Vision and Pattern Recognition, pp. 3578–3587 (2018)
22. Tan, M., Pang, R., Le, Q.V.: Efficientdet: scalable and efficient object detection. In: Proceedings of the IEEE/CVF Conference on Computer Vision and Pattern Recognition, pp. 10781–10790 (2020)
23. Tan, Z., Wang, J., Sun, X., Lin, M., Li, H., et al.: Giraffedet: a heavy-neck paradigm for object detection. In: International Conference on Learning Representations (2021)
24. Tian, Z., Shen, C., Chen, H., He, T.: Fcos: fully convolutional one-stage object detection. In: Proceedings of the IEEE/CVF International Conference on Computer Vision, pp. 9627–9636 (2019)
25. Wu, S., Li, X., Wang, X.: Iou-aware single-stage object detector for accurate localization. Image Vis. Comput. **97**, 103911 (2020)
26. Zhang, S., Chi, C., Yao, Y., Lei, Z., Li, S.Z.: Bridging the gap between anchor-based and anchor-free detection via adaptive training sample selection. In: Proceedings of the IEEE/CVF Conference on Computer Vision and Pattern Recognition, pp. 9759–9768 (2020)
27. Zhuang, J., Qin, Z., Yu, H., Chen, X.: Task-specific context decoupling for object detection. arXiv preprint arXiv:2303.01047 (2023)

Research of Highway Vehicle Inspection Based on Improved YOLOv5

Fangyu Wu [ID] and Chengming Zou[✉]

School of Computer and Artificial Intelligence, Wuhan University of Technology,
Wuhan 430070, China
{wfy2390118575,zoucm}@whut.edu.cn

Abstract. Vehicle detection has become an important detection target for highways, but the traditional vehicle detection technology has poor real-time performance and large model parameters. The algorithm is based on YOLOv5, which introduces the improved network structure Ghostnet-C in the backbone layer to simplify the network structure and while increasing the detection speed of it. Subsequently, for further optimize the structure of the model, GSConv + Slim-neck structure is introduced in the neck layer. Finally, the CAS attention mechanism is used in the neck layer, which is developed in this paper, to change the focus of model predictions and get better results from the model. Compared with original YOLOv5, W-YOLO we propose in the paper reduces the amount of parameters by about 58.6%, the size of storage space by 58%, and the computation by 72.2%, while the accuracy can reach 75.6%. From the final results of experiments, we can discover that W-YOLO can significantly reduce the amount of parameters, model size and computation while guaranteeing accuracy, which can satisfy the requirements of highway vehicle detection more easily.

Keywords: vehicle detection · YOLOv5 · lightweight · attention mechanism

1 Introduction

Recently, As science continues to evolve, driverless and assisted driving technologies [1] are also making breakthroughs, and more and more vehicles are appearing in daily life, which also leads to congestion and traffic accidents on highways. Nowadays, video surveillance to understand the real-time traffic situation of highways and the size of the traffic flow is one of the effective ways to relieve highway congestion and reduce traffic accidents [2]. With the gradual complication of road conditions, effective and rapid detection of vehicle targets in video surveillance to deduce the traffic flow in real time is an important part of intelligent transportation research today [3].

At present, the emergence of deep learning-based vehicle target detection can better realize highway vehicle detection, which have higher accuracy and efficiency than traditional ways. Algorithms is subdivided into two categories based

© The Author(s), under exclusive license to Springer Nature Singapore Pte Ltd. 2024
F. Liu et al. (Eds.): PRICAI 2023, LNAI 14327, pp. 177–188, 2024.
https://doi.org/10.1007/978-981-99-7025-4_15

on whether or not initial screening is performed, one or two stage. Two-stage target detection usually uses region proposal(RP), and the common algorithms are R-CNN [4], Fast R-CNN [5], Faster R-CNN [6], R-FCN [7], etc. These algorithms will generally have higher accuracy, but will consume more time, which affects the efficiency of target detection. One-stage target detection algorithm uses the thought of regression to directly generate results after a single detection, with common algorithms such as Retina-Net [8], SSD [9], YOLO series [10], etc. These algorithms are more effective in real-time detection scenarios. The accuracy is slightly reduced compared to two-stage target detection algorithms, but the rate of prediction is greatly improved [11].

In vehicle detection, Tao et al. [12] proposed RCNN based on stereo prior for vehicle detection, combined RPN with Mask-branch mechanism and used RGB images to improve the accuracy. However, due to using of RPN, which is a two-stage target detection algorithm, it cannot meet our demand for fast detection. Based on YOLOv3, WANG et al. [13] proposed SVD-YOLO, which is incorporated a Ghostnet network structure, thus improving the scene segmentation of objects such as vehicles in real-time driving scenarios, but YOLOv3 is already a relatively backward YOLO series. Dong et al. [14] used the C3Ghost and Ghost modules and introduced the CBAM attention mechanism to reduce the floating point operations (FLOPs) based on YOLOv5. However, using only C3Ghost and Ghost modules does not better convey the relevant information of detected targets during feature fusion, so the accuracy improvement of the detected target is not high.

According to above researches, this paper designs an improved YOLO-based highway vehicle detection model called W-YOLO (Well-YOLO), and our contributions are summarized in three areas: (1) In the YOLOv5 backbone network, an improved GhostNet (GhostNet-C), which uses a small amount of parameters for feature extraction, is substituted into the model to improve the detection speed. (2) In the YOLOv5 neck layer, the structure of GSConv+Slim-neck is substituted into the model to minimize model complexity. (3) In the feature fusion, the improved CA attention (CAS) is designed and used in feature fusion for improving the accuracy.

2   Related Work

2.1   YOLOv5 Model

YOLOv5 is derived from the YOLO series and it is the fifth generation algorithm, which is improved from the YOLOv3 model. Among the YOLO series, YOLOv5 has a high detection accuracy while being more lightweight, and is the more widely used model in the YOLO series [15]. There are four different obtainable versions of YOLOv5, which can be categorized as YOLOv5x, YOLOv5l, YOLOv5m and YOLOv5s depending on the depth and width of the network. The size of the model is reduced for each of the four versions in turn. However, all four models above have the same structure, with following four major components: **Input**, **Backbone**, **Neck** and **Output**, and their structures are displayed in the Fig. 1.

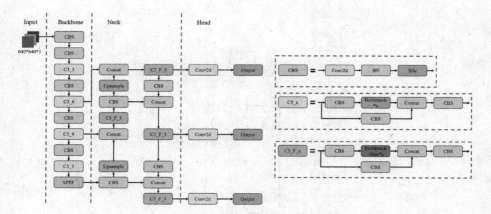

Fig. 1. YOLOv5 network structure. By using an approach named Mosaic data enhancement, YOLOv5 enrich the dataset and well enhance the ability and robustness of the network in the input layer. In the backbone layer, YOLOv5 mainly uses the CBS module as well as the C3 module for feature extraction and finally the SPPF module for feature fusion, which enhances the feature map feature expression. The neck layer uses a feature pyramid structure consisting of FPN+PAN [16], which enhances the network feature fusion. The main part of the output layer is three Detect detectors, which enable YOLOv5 to detect better.

2.2   The Improvement of YOLOv5

In the highway scenario, in order to achieve better vehicle detection, it is necessary for the model to have good real-time performance. Therefore, based on YOLOv5, this paper proposes a lightweight vehicle detection model called W-YOLO. Figure 2 explains the diagram of W-YOLO structure.

As shown in Fig. 2, to lighten the model more, W-YOLO introduces a modified GhostNet in the backbone layer and uses GSConv+Slim-neck to reduce model complexity in the neck layer. For the purpose of improving the loss of accuracy in the lightweight model, W-YOLO uses CAS attention mechanism for improvement of precision in the neck layer.

3   Method

3.1   Ghostnet-C

In order to lightweight the YOLOv5 model, W-YOLO improves the Ghostnet network and replaces the original YOLOv5 **Backbone**. Ghostnet is a lightweight

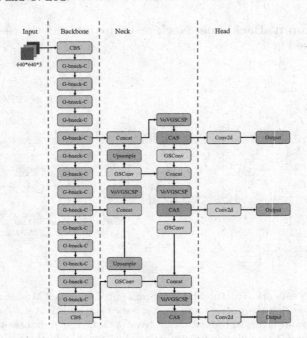

Fig. 2. Improved YOLOv5 network structure

network structure proposed by Han et al. [17]. Some of the formed feature maps have high similarity, so Han believe that more similar feature maps can be generated by performing linear operations on one of them to achieve the purpose of generating more feature maps with only a small number of parameters. Figure 3 shows the principle of Ghost module in Ghostnet network.

From Fig. 3, we are able to calculate that the normal convolution we usually use in YOLOv5 is approximately s times more computationally intensive than the Ghost convolution, so the Ghostnet network designed by Ghost-based module can greatly model the computation cost. However, the original Ghostnet network structure invokes the SE attention mechanism [18], which ignores the attention problem on the feature graph space, while the CBAM attention mechanism [19] considers the attention on the space and can achieve better results compared with the SE attention mechanism. Therefore, W-YOLO improves the original Ghostnet structure, and the improved GhostBottleneck structure is shown in Fig. 4.

3.2   GSConv+Slim-Neck

In order to speed up the computation of prediction and better achieve real-time vehicle detection, W-YOLO introduces the GSConv module and Slim-neck module [20] in **Neck**. Since the GSConv module preserves as much as possible the connectivity during the semantic information transfer of feature maps, the com-

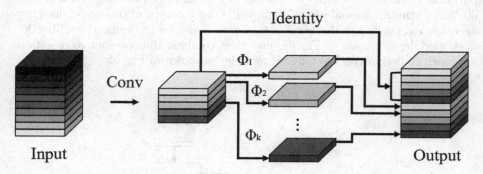

Fig. 3. The Ghost module. Supposing that the input size is $h \cdot w \cdot c$, and the output one is $h' \cdot w' \cdot c$, the edge length of the convolution kernel is k. In this case, FLOPs of conventional convolution are computed as $n \cdot h' \cdot w' \cdot c \cdot k \cdot k$, while FLOPs of the deeply separable convolutional Ghost module through Ghostnet are computed as $\frac{n}{s} \cdot h' \cdot w' \cdot c \cdot k \cdot k + \frac{n}{s} \cdot h' \cdot w' \cdot d \cdot d$, where d denotes the edge length of the convolution kernel within Ghost module, s denotes how many new feature maps are generated per convolved feature map. The ratio of boosted FLOPs can theoretically be calculated as $r_s = \frac{n \cdot h' \cdot w' \cdot c \cdot k \cdot k}{\frac{n}{s} \cdot h' \cdot w' \cdot c \cdot k \cdot k + \frac{n}{s} \cdot h' \cdot w' \cdot d \cdot d} = \frac{c \cdot k \cdot k}{\frac{1}{s} \cdot c \cdot k \cdot k + \frac{s-1}{s} \cdot d \cdot d} \approx \frac{s \cdot c}{s+c-1} \approx s$.

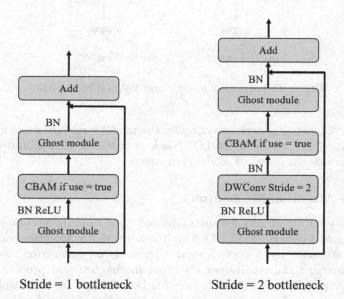

Fig. 4. Improved GhostBottleneck network structure. When use = true, the improved structure invokes the CBAM attention, and it is experimentally proven to achieve better results compared to the original SE attention.

putational cost of using GSConv instead of normal convolution in **Neck** is only 60–70% of that of normal convolution, while the accuracy of the model does not decrease too much. On the basis of GSConv, it can be to design the GSbottleneck module, as shown in Fig. 5a, and then combine the one-shot aggregation approach to design the VoVGSCSP module, as shown in Fig. 5b.

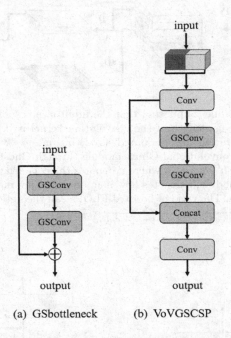

(a) GSbottleneck   (b) VoVGSCSP

Fig. 5. GSbottleneck module and VoVGSCSP module

Since GSConv+Slim-neck can simplify the model structure while guaranteeing a certain accuracy, in W-YOLO, **Neck** is replaced with Slim-neck, which greatly increases the speed of model operations.

3.3   CAS Attention Mechanism

To access key information of feature maps and improving the accuracy of image information processing, W-YOLO introduces the CAS attention mechanism. Currently, attention mechanism is used extensively on optimizing models. Hou et al. summarized the traditional attention mechanism and proposed a more efficient CA attention [21], which encodes both lateral and vertical location information into spatial attention, localization and target identification. Figure 6 illustrates the difference between the traditional SE attention mechanism and the CA attention mechanism.

However, the effect of channel C on attention is included in the CA attention mechanism. When the effect of spatial attention is not as clear as that of channel

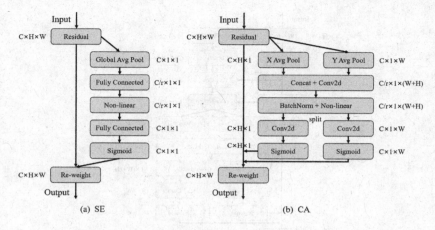

Fig. 6. Comparison of SE attention and CA attention

attention, channel attention may have an effect on both co-attendance obtained in the end. Therefore, as shown in Fig. 7, W-YOLO improves the CA attention mechanism into the CAS attention mechanism.

From Fig. 7, the new CAS attention mechanism first performs a channel attention on the feature map, followed by pooling the obtained features out into a $1 \cdot h \cdot w$ feature map, and finally a cooperative attention operation. In this way, the CAS attention mechanism separates the channel attention while preserving the original spatial co-attention part, thus reducing the influence of channel attention on spatial co-attention.

CAS attention first performs a channel attention, fusing the weights of channel attention into the feature map first, thus not affecting the weights of horizontal attention and vertical attention, as expressed by follows:

$$x'_c(i,j) = x_c(i,j) \cdot g_c \tag{1}$$

After that, CAS attention is squeezed and feature maps are pooled by channel dimension. Through this approach, we obtain a feature map of 1*h*w and then encoded horizontally and vertically respectively. The equation is expressed as:

$$X(i,j) = \frac{1}{C} \sum_{k=0}^{C-1} x'_c(i,j) \tag{2}$$

$$z_h(h) = \frac{1}{W} \sum_{i=0}^{W-1} X(h,i) \tag{3}$$

$$z_w(w) = \frac{1}{H} \sum_{j=0}^{H-1} X(j,w) \tag{4}$$

Finally, CAS attention activates the codes, joins the two sets of codes along the channel dimension, performs a $3 \cdot 3$ convolutional transformation, and then

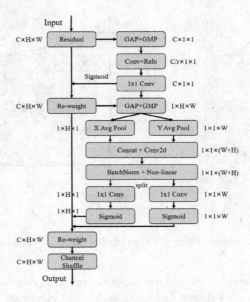

Fig. 7. The structure of CAS attention

separates the two sets of codes after the transformation and performs a $1 \cdot 1$ convolution as well as a sigmoid transformation. Finally, we multiply the obtained result with the feature map that has been transformed by channel attention. The equation is expressed as:

$$f = \delta(F_1([z_h, z_w])) \tag{5}$$

$$g_h = \sigma(F_h(f_h)) \tag{6}$$

$$g_w = \sigma(F_w(f_w)) \tag{7}$$

$$y_c(i, j) = x'_c(i, j) \cdot g_h(i) \cdot g_w(j) \tag{8}$$

In addition, W-YOLO also tested whether to use the feature maps after the channel attention transformation when performing collaborative attention extraction. The experimental comparison shows that using the channel-attention transformed feature maps for co-attentive extraction gives better results.

4   Experiment and Metrics

4.1   Experimental Environment and Data Set

We uses a Linux system with 1T of memory, Intel Xeon Gold 5117 CPU, NVIDIA Tesla P100 GPU, 32G graphics card, CUDA version 11.6, and PyTorch for model training as the experimental environment. The experiment uses vehicle datasets captured from different locations and divides the datasets using a ratio of approximately 8:2, with 4134 training sets and 1140 test sets. Some of data under training are shown in Fig. 8.

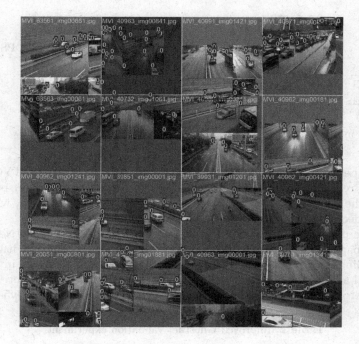

Fig. 8. Schematic diagram of train datasets

4.2 Metrics

To measure the effect, we use performance metrics such as mean Average Precision (mAP), the number of model parameters, the size of the storage space occupied by the model, the number of Giga Floating-point Operations Per Second (GFLOPS) and the number of frames per second (FPS) to judge the performance of the model.

4.3 Experiment and Experimental Analysis

For the purpose of verifying the performance of W-YOLO, we use ablation experiments to analyze. The same hyperparameters were used for the ablation experiments, and final data obtained is all shown in Table 1. Among them, YOLOv5-G represents the improved backbone network using the improved Ghostnet based on YOLOv5, YOLOv5-GS represents the improved neck layer using GSConv+Slim-neck based on YOLOv5-G, and W-YOLO is based on YOLOv5-GS with the added improved CAS attention mechanism.

Table 1. Ablation experiment results

model	mAP/%	Number of participants	Storage Space/MB	GFLOPS	FPS
YOLOv5	**77.4**	46108278	92.7	107.6	74.07
YOLOv5-G	75.4	21820940	44.2	41.6	84.03
YOLOv5-GS	72.9	**18924940**	**38.5**	**29.7**	**86.95**
*W-YOLO	75.6	19097050	38.9	29.9	85.47

* proposed method

The experimental data above indicates that compared with original YOLOv5, W-YOLO reduces the amount of parameters by 58.6%, the storage space size by 58%, the computation by 72.2%, and the FPS by 11.4 frames/s, while the accuracy decreases by only 1.8%.

For the purpose of validating the effectiveness of improved GhostNet structure, this paper uses the original YOLOv5 as a baseline and compares it with the model adding the Ghostnet structure and the improved one, as shown in Table 2. The model adding the Ghostnet structure is called YOLOv5-Ghostnet, and the model after adding the improved Ghostnet structure is called YOLOv5-G.

Table 2. Improved Ghostnet validation experiment

model	mAP/%	Number of participants	Storage Space/MB	GFLOPS	FPS
YOLOv5	**77.4**	46108278	92.7	107.6	74.07
YOLOv5-Ghostnet	72.5	21824934	**44.2**	**40.5**	**84.75**
YOLOv5-G	75.4	**21820940**	**44.2**	41.6	84.03

From the Table 2, we can see that YOLOv5-Ghostnet has significantly reduced the model size and increased the speed of prediction, although the accuracy has been reduced. While using YOLOv5-G on this basis, the detection speed do not change much, but the detection accuracy has increased, so lightweight of the model can be better achieved by using improved Ghostnet structure.

Furthermore, for the purpose of validating the effectiveness of the improved CA, CAS attention is now introduced based on the model YOLOv5-GS after the above two improvement methods, and the common SE and CA attention mechanisms are improved into the model respectively for comparison experiments, as shown in Table 3.

From Table 3, all three attention mechanisms bring some loss in detection speed, but all of them can significantly improve the model accuracy. These three experiments improve the model accuracy by 0.5%, 0.7%, and 2.7% respectively, with the improved CAS attention mechanism showing a greater improvement compared to the other two. In addition, the results for whether or not to use the feature maps after the channel attention transformation when performing collaborative attention extraction are also responded in Table 3, where W-YOLOn represents the model that does not use the feature maps after the channel attention

Table 3. Improved CA attention mechanism validation experiment

model	mAP/%	Number of participants	Storage Space/MB	GFLOPS	FPS
YOLOv5-GS	72.9	**18924940**	38.5	29.7	**86.95**
YOLOv5-GS-SE	73.4	18928524	38.5	29.7	**86.95**
YOLOv5-GS-CA	73.6	19057716	38.8	**29.9**	84.75
W-YOLO	**75.6**	19097050	**38.9**	**29.9**	85.47
W-YOLOn	73.6	19097050	**38.9**	**29.9**	85.47

transformation when performing collaborative attention extraction. By comparison we can discover that the CAS attention mechanism performs co-attentive extraction preferentially using the channel attention transformation better.

5   Conclusion

Aiming at the characteristics of traditional target detection methods under highway traffic environment such as insufficient detection accuracy and poor detection real-time, this paper, by introducing the improved Ghostnet, GSConv+Slimneck for lightweight, and then using the proposed CAS attention mechanism to enhance the accuracy of image processing, carries out an improvement on YOLOv5. The experimental data shows that W-YOLO reduces the size from 92.7 MB to 38.9 MB, reduces the parameters by about 27.01 million, and increases the FPS by 11.4 frames/s compared with the YOLOv5 model, which effectively improves the vehicle detection speed in the highway scenario, while the average accuracy decreases less. However, W-YOLO still has the problem of missed detection for some small target vehicles. If we can improve the detection rate of small target vehicle detection in future research, the model can achieve better results.

References

1. Hussain, M.M., Beg, M.S.: Using vehicles as fog infrastructures for transportation cyber-physical systems (T-CPS): fog computing for vehicular networks. Int. J. Softw. Sci. Comput. Intell. (IJSSCI) **11**(1), 47–69 (2019)
2. Arora, N., Kumar, Y., Karkra, R., Kumar, M.: Automatic vehicle detection system in different environment conditions using fast R-CNN. Multimedia Tools Appl. **81**(13), 18715–18735 (2022)
3. Doan, T.N., Truong, M.T.: Real-time vehicle detection and counting based on YOLO and DeepSORT. In: 2020 12th International Conference on Knowledge and Systems Engineering (KSE), pp. 67–72. IEEE (2020)
4. Girshick, R., Donahue, J., Darrell, T., Malik, J.: Rich feature hierarchies for accurate object detection and semantic segmentation. In: Proceedings of the IEEE Conference on Computer Vision and Pattern Recognition, pp. 580–587 (2014)
5. Girshick, R.: Fast R-CNN. In: Proceedings of the IEEE International Conference on Computer Vision, pp. 1440–1448 (2015)

6. Ren, S., He, K., Girshick, R., Sun, J.: Faster R-CNN: towards real-time object detection with region proposal networks. In: Advances in Neural Information Processing Systems, vol. 28 (2015)
7. Dai, J., Li, Y., He, K., Sun, J.: R-FCN: object detection via region-based fully convolutional networks. In: Advances in Neural Information Processing Systems, vol. 29 (2016)
8. Jaeger, P.F., et al.: Retina U-Net: embarrassingly simple exploitation of segmentation supervision for medical object detection. In: Machine Learning for Health Workshop, pp. 171–183. PMLR (2020)
9. Cui, L., et al.: MDSSD: multi-scale deconvolutional single shot detector for small objects. arXiv preprint arXiv:1805.07009 (2018)
10. Jiang, P., Ergu, D., Liu, F., Cai, Y., Ma, B.: A review of YOLO algorithm developments. Procedia Comput. Sci. **199**, 1066–1073 (2022)
11. Yao, J., Qi, J., Zhang, J., Shao, H., Yang, J., Li, X.: A real-time detection algorithm for kiwifruit defects based on YOLOv5. Electronics **10**(14), 1711 (2021)
12. Tao, C., He, H., Xu, F., Cao, J.: Stereo priori RCNN based car detection on point level for autonomous driving. Knowl. Based Syst. **229**, 107346 (2021)
13. Wang, H., et al.: SYGNet: a SVD-YOLO based GhostNet for real-time driving scene parsing. In: 2022 IEEE International Conference on Image Processing (ICIP), pp. 2701–2705. IEEE (2022)
14. Dong, X., Yan, S., Duan, C.: A lightweight vehicles detection network model based on YOLOv5. Eng. Appl. Artif. Intell. **113**, 104914 (2022)
15. Bochkovskiy, A., Wang, C.Y., Liao, H.Y.M.: YOLOv4: optimal speed and accuracy of object detection. arXiv preprint arXiv:2004.10934 (2020)
16. Kasper-Eulaers, M., Hahn, N., Berger, S., Sebulonsen, T., Myrland, Ø., Kummervold, P.E.: Detecting heavy goods vehicles in rest areas in winter conditions using YOLOv5. Algorithms **14**(4), 114 (2021)
17. Han, K., Wang, Y., Tian, Q., Guo, J., Xu, C., Xu, C.: GhostNet: more features from cheap operations. In: Proceedings of the IEEE/CVF Conference on Computer Vision and Pattern Recognition, pp. 1580–1589 (2020)
18. Hu, J., Shen, L., Sun, G.: Squeeze-and-excitation networks. In: Proceedings of the IEEE Conference on Computer Vision and Pattern Recognition, pp. 7132–7141 (2018)
19. Woo, S., Park, J., Lee, J.-Y., Kweon, I.S.: CBAM: convolutional block attention module. In: Ferrari, V., Hebert, M., Sminchisescu, C., Weiss, Y. (eds.) ECCV 2018. LNCS, vol. 11211, pp. 3–19. Springer, Cham (2018). https://doi.org/10.1007/978-3-030-01234-2_1
20. Li, H., Li, J., Wei, H., Liu, Z., Zhan, Z., Ren, Q.: Slim-neck by GSConv: a better design paradigm of detector architectures for autonomous vehicles. arXiv preprint arXiv:2206.02424 (2022)
21. Hou, Q., Zhou, D., Feng, J.: Coordinate attention for efficient mobile network design. In: Proceedings of the IEEE/CVF Conference on Computer Vision and Pattern Recognition, pp. 13713–13722 (2021)

STN-BA: Weakly-Supervised Few-Shot Temporal Action Localization

Na Ye[1($\boxtimes$)], Zhijie Zhang[1], Xiang Zhang[1], Baoshan Li[1], and Xiaoshu Wang[2]

[1] School of Information and Control Engineering, Xi'an University of Architecture and Technology, Xi'an 710000, China
yenanaye2003@126.com
[2] School of Environmental and Chemical Engineering,
Shenyang University of Technology, Shenyang 110000, China

Abstract. Existing Weakly-supervised Few-Shot Temporal Action Localization (WFTAL) methods often process feature snippets with limited information, resulting in prediction errors and poor localization performance. A novel model called Spatial-Temporal Attention Network with Boundary-check Algorithm (STN-BA) for WFTAL is proposed to address this issue. STN-BA enhances the discriminability of snippet features and has a particular fault tolerance mechanism. The proposed approach focuses on two main aspects: (1) a spatial-temporal attention module that establishes spatial-temporal relationships of action movement to enrich the feature information of each video snippet and (2) the implementation of a boundary-check algorithm to correct potential localization boundary errors. The network is trained to estimate Temporal Class Similarity Vectors (TCSVs) that measure the similarity between each snippet of untrimmed videos and reference samples. These TCSVs are then normalized and employed as a temporal attention mask to extract the video-level representation from untrimmed videos, enabling accurate action localization during testing. Experimental evaluations of the widely used THUMOS14 and ActivityNet1.2 datasets demonstrate that the proposed method outperforms state-of-the-art fully-supervised and weakly-supervised few-shot learning methods.

Keywords: Temporal Action Localization · Few-shot learning · Weakly supervised · spatial-temporal attention · boundary-check algorithm

1 Introduction

Temporal Action Localization (TAL) [2,7–10,15,20,25,27] is a crucial aspect of video comprehension that seeks to anticipate the initiation time, culmination time, and category of actions within an untrimmed video. Traditional TAL models depend on having extensive sets of annotated training samples for each individual class. However, collecting and making these annotated samples are not only very expensive but also unfeasible due to the existence of

F. Liu et al. (Eds.): PRICAI 2023, LNAI 14327, pp. 189–201, 2024.
https://doi.org/10.1007/978-981-99-7025-4_16

an infinite number of potential action classes. To address these challenges, recent research has focused on Weakly-supervised Temporal Action Localization (WTAL) [4,14], Few-shot Temporal Action Localization (FTAL) [11,22,23], and Weakly-supervised Few-shot Temporal Action Localization (WFTAL) [18,26] methods. WTAL only requires the classification label for the action during training, while FTAL only necessitates a few fully supervised examples for each action category. WFTAL combines the benefits of both approaches.

Weakly-supervised few-shot learning has been successfully applied to temporal action localization, with recent approaches such as [18] and [26]. Zhang et al. [26] introduced a multi-scale feature pyramid approach aimed at directly generating variable-scale temporal features. Xie et al. [18] proposed a network that focuses on learning to estimate similarity matrices. These matrices are harnessed in the creation of Temporal Class Activation Maps (TCAMs). However, it is important to note that these networks may encounter challenges when processing snippets that contain limited feature information. This can result in prediction errors for the snippets and subsequently lead to decreased performance in terms of localization accuracy.

We propose a novel model called Spatial-Temporal Attention Network with Boundary-check Algorithm (STN-BA) for WFTAL to address this issue. Similar to previous work [18] and [26], our model utilizes one/a few trimmed examples of novel class actions at test time and a large number of base class videos with only category labels during training, ensuring no overlap between the base and novel classes. Our method initially utilizes a spatial-temporal attention network to establish the motion relationship among snippets within the entire video. This process enriches the feature information of each snippet, ultimately enhancing the discriminability of snippet features. Furthermore, we introduce a boundary-check algorithm to mitigate any potential decrease in localization performance caused by prediction errors in particular snippets. This algorithm examines the accuracy of predicted boundary snippets by evaluating their error rates. Subsequently, it corrects frequently mispredicted snippets by setting an error tolerance threshold. The goal is to prevent the negative impact of prediction errors and improve overall localization accuracy.

Contributions:

- We propose a new model incorporating a spatial-temporal attention network to tackle the problem of limited information within video snippets.
- We introduce a boundary-check algorithm. This algorithm assesses the correctness of boundary snippets, identifying and correcting any boundary snippets' potentially erroneous predictions.
- We achieve state-of-the-art performance on the weakly-supervised and fully-supervised few-shot benchmarks for THUMOS14 [5], and ActivityNet1.2 [3].

2   Related Work

Temporal Action Localization (TAL). TAL is the task of predicting the temporal boundaries and class labels of action instances within untrimmed videos.

Early approaches to action localization utilized deep networks in the localization framework to accurately localize temporal boundaries, resulting in enhanced performance. Some studies have focused on designing effective temporal proposal schemes [2, 8, 10, 15, 20, 27], while others have explored improvements in temporal search methods [50, 51] or proposed better classifiers [7, 9, 25]. These methods predominantly rely on fully supervised approaches, necessitating a large amount of data labeled with action boundaries. However, collecting such data is challenging, expensive, and often subject to ambiguity when determining the boundaries of certain actions. Consequently, Few-Shot learning approaches have gained increasing attention in this domain.

Few-Shot Temporal Action Localization (FTAL). Fully-supervised few-shot learning has been applied to TAL [11, 22, 23]. Yang et al. The pioneering work of Yang et al. [23] marked the inception of integrating few-shot learning into the domain of temporal action localization. Their approach involved using a meta-learning strategy with several positively labeled and negatively labeled videos to guide the localization process. Similarly, Xu et al. [22] employed regional proposal networks to generate proposals with flexible boundaries, enabling more accurate localization. Nag et al. [11] adopted a different localization method. Their network first learned a similarity function, which was then used to classify each snippet in the untrimmed video. Although these FTAL methods integrate few-shot learning, they still rely on many videos with annotated temporal action boundaries during the training process.

Weakly-Supervised Few-Shot Temporal Action Localization (WFTAL). Recent research has focused on WFTAL [18, 26]. This approach streamlines the training process by relying solely on video-level annotations, reducing the need for annotated temporal action boundaries. Zhang et al. [26] pioneered a groundbreaking strategy centered around the direct construction of a multi-scale feature pyramid. This pyramid serves as a mechanism for generating variable-scale temporal features, effectively enabling the model to capture pertinent action-centric information across diverse temporal resolutions. Similarly, Xie et al. [18] introduced a network that harnesses the power of similarity matrices. Leveraging these TSMs, the network facilitates the creation of temporal attention masks, which in turn facilitate the extraction of comprehensive video-level representations from extensive untrimmed video datasets.

3   Method

In this paper, the problem of weakly-supervised few-shot temporal action localization in untrimmed videos is further addressed. Our framework involves two sets of input data: a sample set and a query set. The sample set comprises videos that serve as examples for a few classes. Each class in the sample set contains K-trimmed action instances, called the sample set S. The query set $Q = \{x_i\}_i^{N_q} = 1$ consists of untrimmed videos x_i with video-level annotations, where N_q is the number of untrimmed videos. Our objective is to localize the

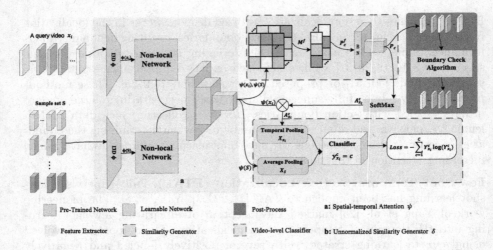

Fig. 1. Overview of the proposed method: Given a query video x_i and a sample set S, we first extract their feature representations using the I3D network ϕ and spatial-temporal attention network ψ. Then we gain the TSMs M^f by calculating pair-wise snippet feature similarity scores. Then the TCSVs $\tilde{P}_c$ is obtained by the unnormalized similarity generator δ. These TCSVs are then normalized and employed as a temporal attention mask $A_{x_i}^c$ to extract the video-level representation X_{x_i}. The sample video-level feature representation, denoted as X_S, is derived by employing a temporal average pooling operation on $\psi(S)$. The classifier predicts video-level categories. Finally, a threshold is set to determine the type of each snippet, and a bounds-checking algorithm is used to correct possible errors in the segment.

classes' actions in the sample set within these untrimmed videos. Following the protocol established in previous works such as [16,18,23], the method adopts a C-way K-shot episode training/testing setup. In each episode, from the training set, we perform a random selection of C classes. For each of the chosen classes, we sample K-trimmed action instances. These sampled instances are then combined to constitute the sample set denoted as S. Within the query set Q, the untrimmed videos are ensured to encompass at least one action instance. The proposed method consists of four main parts: the feature extractor, the similarity generator, the video-level classifier, and the post-processing module. Figure 1 visually depicts the comprehensive architecture of the model. Next, we will delve into the specifics of each component of the approach.

3.1 Feature Extractor

The feature extractor is mainly composed of two network modules, the I3D [1] network and the spatial-temporal attention network, where the I3D network ϕ is employed as a pre-trained network for the extraction of fundamental video features, similar to [12,13]. I3D extracts the RGB and TV-L1 optical flow [24] information in the video snippet by using the two-stream network. We use every

16 frames as a snippet and the outputs of the two-stream network are merged to generate the fundamental video features. It has been shown in previous work [2, 19] that this strategy benefits video action localization. The spatial-temporal attention network utilizes two non-local networks [17] with distinct weights to establish the motion relationship between snippets in the query set and the sample set videos. This approach is adopted due to the presence of substantial background information in the query set videos, whereas the sample set videos primarily contain action-related content. The non-local module consists of three weighted matrices W_Q, W_K, and W_V and calculating formula (1).

$$\psi(x_i) = \phi(x_i) + SoftMax \left(\frac{W_Q \cdot W_K{}^T}{\sqrt{d}} \cdot W_V \right) \cdot \sigma \tag{1}$$

where $W_Q = W_1 \cdot \phi(x_i)$, $W_K = W_2 \cdot \phi(x_i)$, $W_V = W_3 \cdot \phi(x_i)$, W_1 W_2 and W_3 were three weighting matrix, σ denotes a learnable parameter, initialized to 0, and d is the video feature dimension.

Given a query video x_i, we divide the video into N snippets according to a snippet of 16 frames. Each snippet by the I3D network ϕ encoding first, to generate the initial encode vector $\phi(x_i) = \{\phi(x_{i,n})\}_{n=1}^{N}$. Given the sample set with action examples and their labels, it is denoted by $S = \{(x_i, y_i)\}_{i=1}^{c*k}$, where "c" denotes the number of classes, and "k" signifies the number of samples per class. Similarly, we split each video in the sample set S into snippets. Then each snippet is encoded by the I3D network to generate the initial encoding vector of the sample set $\phi(S) = \{\phi(x_i, y_i)\}_{i=1}^{c*k}$. Then, a spatial-temporal attention network ψ is used to enrich the feature information of each snippet. Subsequently, the query video features $\psi(x_i)$ and sample set video features $\psi(S)$ are generated through two fully connected layers (FC). These FC layers have output sizes of 1024 and 128, respectively. Each layer is activated using the ReLU activation function. Furthermore, to mitigate overfitting, a dropout layer is introduced following the first FC layer.

3.2   Similarity Generator

The similarity generator consists primarily of the similarity calculation and the unnormalized similarity generator δ. Given the query video feature $\psi(x_i)$ and the sample set videos feature $\psi(S)$, we calculate the TSMs (Temporal Similarity Matrixes) $M^f = \{m_i^f\}_{i=1}^{c*k}$, where m_i^f is the similarity scores between all snippets of the query video and all snippets of the i-th sample set videos, and f is the similarity metric. By performing a max-pooling operation along the rows of M^f, we obtain the similarity vector P_{c*k}^f for each snippet of the query video for the sample video. By averaging the k-shot instances, we obtain the one-shot representation $\bar{P}_c^f$. We employ four different similarity vectors by utilizing various similarity metrics for both spatial (RGB) and temporal (optical flow) dimensions, which have been verified in [18] to be better than a single type of similarity metric feature. The four similarity vectors are subsequently combined and fed as inputs to the unnormalized similarity generator δ (similar to the unnormalized similarity generator by [18] contains batch normalization and FC layers). The output Temporal Class Similarity Vectors (TCSVs) is given by formula (2).

$$\tilde{P}_c = \delta(\bar{P}_c^{ip,RGB}, \bar{P}_c^{ip,OF}, \bar{P}_c^{cos,RGB}, \bar{P}_c^{cos,OF}) \tag{2}$$

Where "ip" and "cos" denote dot product and cosine similarity calculation, respectively, "RGB" refers to the spatial dimension, and "OF" refers to the time dimension.

3.3   Video-Level Classifier

Classification. After obtaining the TCSVs $\tilde{P}_c$, the application of the softmax operator results in the acquisition of Temporal Class Attention Masks (TCAMs), which are denoted as $A_{x_i}^c \in R^{N \times c}$. Next, the TCAM for each class is integrated into the query video feature $\psi(x_i)$ to obtain the attention features $\tilde{A}_{x_i}^c$ for each action category in the query video. With the weighted temporal average pooling [12] operation for each class on $\tilde{A}_{x_i}^c$, we obtain a video-level feature representation $X_{x_i} in R^{c \times d}$ of the query video x_i for each class. Simultaneously, we apply average temporal pooling to the sample set videos' feature $\psi(S)$ to obtain the feature representation $X_S \in R^{c*k \times d}$ of the sample set videos. We further average the k instances for computational convenience to obtain $X_S \in R^{c \times d}$. The final classification score of the query x_i is given by formula (3)

$$\hat{Y}_{x_i}^c = \frac{exp(- \parallel X_{x_i}(c,:) - X_S(c,:) \parallel^2)}{\sum_{i=1}^C exp(- \parallel X_{x_i}(i,:) - X_S(i,:) \parallel^2)} \tag{3}$$

Where X_{x_i} is the video-level representation of the query video for each class, $\bar{X}_S$ is the video-level representation for each class, and C is the number of categories.

Loss. Because we are working in a weakly-supervised context, our training is restricted to utilizing classification labels at the video level. After the video classifier obtains $\hat{Y}_{x_i}^c$, we use $Y_{x_i}^c$ to represent the ground truth label of the query video level. The classification loss is computed using the formula (4) to optimize the network and improve the differentiation of video-level categories.

Localization. After the video classifier obtains the classification result of the query video x_i, we can transform the TCSVs $\tilde{P}_c$ into the similarity score $\tilde{P}$ of the target category. A threshold is applied to the similarity scores in order to decide whether each snippet should be classified as part of the foreground or the background. The continuous foreground snippets are then combined to form the localization result. However, to address the potential errors in predicted boundaries arising from localization, we employ a boundary-check algorithm to correct any potential errors in the predicted boundaries. Following the standard practice in action localization, the proposed method predicts a set of action instances denoted as (s, e, p), where s represents the predicted start time, e represents the predicted end time, and p represents the predicted score of the action instance. The prediction score is computed by taking the average of the similarity scores of all snippets within the start and end segments.

$$Loss = -\sum_{c=1}^{C} Y_{x_i}^c \log\left(\hat{Y}_{x_i}^c\right) \tag{4}$$

3.4   Localization and Boundary-Check Algorithm

Algorithm 1. Boundary error rate check algorithm

Input: $start, end, scores[N_q], error\_rate$
Output: $start, end$

1: Given have predicted action instances: $start and end$, scores of query video snippets: $scores[N_q]$, and an $error rate$ to check whether the boundary is correct.
2: **while** $left\_flag \leftarrow True$ **do**
3:     $score \leftarrow scores[start - 1]$
4:     $Threshold = \frac{score}{average(scores(start,end))}$
5:     **if** $Threshold > Error_rate$ **then**
6:         start = start - 1
7:     **else**
8:         $left\_flag \leftarrow False$
9:     **end if**
10: **end while**
11: **while** $right\_flag \leftarrow True$ **do**
12:     $score \leftarrow scores[end + 1]$
13:     $Threshold = \frac{score}{average(scores(start,end))}$
14:     **if** $Threshold > Error\_rate$ **then**
15:         end = end + 1
16:     **else**
17:         $right\_flag \leftarrow False$
18:     **end if**
19: **end while**
20: **return** $start, end$

Boundary-Check Algorithm. The boundary-check algorithm consists of two components: the boundary error rate check algorithm and the fault tolerance algorithm. The boundary error rate check algorithm is responsible for reassessing the accuracy of the category (foreground or background) assigned to the boundary snippets of the predicted action instances. It calculates the boundary segment's error rate to estimate the misclassification probability. The step-by-step procedure is detailed in Algorithm 1.

The fault tolerance algorithm is crafted to rectify possible errors within snippets situated between two action instances in an untrimmed video. By setting a fault tolerance value, which represents the maximum allowable number of snippets between two action instances, the algorithm analyzes the number of snippets between each pair of consecutive action instances and corrects snippets that may be incorrect.

4 Experiment

4.1 Experiment Setup

Dataset. We assess the effectiveness of our approach using two widely employed datasets: THUMOS14 [5] and ActivityNet1.2 [3]. The THUMOS14 dataset encompasses 200 validation and 213 testing videos, featuring temporal annotations for 20 distinct classes. Among its action instances, the short ones are fractions of a second, and the long ones are several seconds. ActivityNet1.2 dataset comprises 4819 training videos and 2383 validation videos, encompassing annotations for 100 activity classes.

Setup. Few-shot learning requires that classes cannot be repeated during training and testing. Therefore, according to the setting of previous work [11,18,22,23], in THUMOS14, We employ a subset of the validation set containing six classes as the base classes for training the network model. Subsequently, the remaining 14 classes are considered novel classes for evaluating our weakly-supervised few-shot temporal action localization network. For ActivityNet 1.2, we split the 100 classes into 80/20 parts. The class division method we use is sequential division.

Metric. We adopt the standard metric [11,18,21–23], mean Average Precision (mAP) at different IoU thresholds (mAP@IoU) to evaluate our network. Specifically, on the THUMOS14 dataset, the mAP was evaluated at an IoU threshold of 0.5. In contrast, on ActivityNet1.2, the final mAP was computed as the average of mAP assessed across ten evenly spaced IoU thresholds ranging from 0.5 to 0.95. Additionally, the prediction accuracy for the untrimmed video-level categories: top-1 and top-3, is also reported in our experiment.

Implementation Details. Our network is optimized using Adam [6] with an initial learning rate of 10^{-4} and a 2x reduction in learning rate after 1000 episodes, a weight decay coefficient of $5 \cdot 10^{(-4)}$, an error rate is set to 0.75, the error tolerance rate is set to 2 and a dropout rate of 0.5. We train 5000 episodes. We utilized an RTX 3090 graphics card for our experiments. In the case of one-shot learning, the model's training time was approximately 15 min, whereas, for five-shot learning, the training time was extended to about 40 min.

4.2 Main Experimental Results

We conducted evaluations of our approach on both the THUMOS14 and ActivityNet1.2 datasets. Table 1 displays a comparison between our approach and other state-of-the-art methods, clearly indicating that our method outperforms all existing few-shot temporal action localization methods, spanning both fully and weakly supervised paradigms. To elaborate further, on the THUMOS14 dataset, our performance in terms of mAP@0.5 exceeds the current best performance [18] by 4.68%. For the ActivityNet1.2 dataset, our performance in mAP@0.5 surpasses the current best performance [18] by around 10%, and there is an improvement of approximately 8% in the mAP (avg) performance (average mAP between mAP@0.5 and mAP@0.95).

Table 2 illustrates that, despite a minor increase in computational cost compared to WOKB [18], our method delivers superior performance.

Table 1. Comparison of the proposed method with the state-of-the-art few-shot temporal action localization method on THUMOS14 and on the ActivityNet1.2, Where @1 denotes one-shot and @5 denotes five-shot

Supervision	Method	THUMOS14	ActivityNet1.2	
		mAP@0.5	mAP@0.5	mAP@0.5:0.95
Full	CDC@1 [15]	6.4	8.2	2.4
Full	CDC@5 [15]	6.5	8.6	2.5
Full	Sl. Window@1 [23]	13.6	22.3	9.8
Full	Sl. Window@5 [23]	14	23.1	10
Full	QAT@1 [11]	9.1	44.9	25.9
Full	QAT@5 [11]	13.8	51.8	30.2
Weak	WOKB@1 [18]	13.93	45.76	31.4
Weak	WOKB@5 [18]	14.2	52.59	35.3
Weak	SPN@1 [26]	14.3	41.9	26.5
Weak	SPN@5 [26]	16	45.0	28.8
Weak	**Ours@1**	**16.02**	**55.54**	**38.83**
Weak	**Ours@5**	**18.92**	**57.92**	**40.17**

4.3   Ablation Experiment

We conducted ablation experiments on our model to illustrate the effectiveness of the two core components of our method: the spatial-temporal attention module and the Boundary-check algorithm. For this section, we opted for the 5-way 1-shot evaluation setup on the ActivityNet1.2 dataset. This decision was driven by the better alignment of our method with the localization task characteristic of the ActivityNet1.2 dataset.

Table 2. Comparison of the computational cost FLOPs (G) and Parameters (M) of the different methods and their performance on ActivityNet1.2.

Method	FLOPs	Param	mAP@0.5:0.95
WOKB [18]	2.07G	2.46M	31.4
Our	2.23G	2.85M	38.83

Table 3. Ablation experiments of the spatial and temporal attention network, the 1-shot test is performed on the ActivityNet1.2.

Spatial Attention	Temporal Attention	mAP@0.5	mAP@0.5:0.95	Top-1	Top-2
×	×	49.3	33.59	75.6	93.8
×	√	53.23	36.86	79.6	95.1
√	×	50.1	33.96	77.6	94.5
√	√	**55.84**	**39.22**	**80.8**	**97.7**

The Impact of the Spatial-Temporal Attention Module on the Model.
Table 3 shows the performance disparities of our method when utilizing different attention models. Notably, the integration of both temporal and spatial attention into the model leads to a significant performance improvement. This outcome unequivocally underscores the efficacy of the spatial-temporal attention model in our approach.

Table 4. Ablation experiments of the boundary-check algorithm, the 1-shot test is performed on the ActivityNet1.2.

error rate	fault tolerate	mAP@0.5	mAP@0.5:0.95
×	0	49.3	33.59
0.95	2	53.53	37.95
0.85	2	55.83	38.64
0.75	**2**	**56.75**	**38.91**
0.65	2	53.15	36.45
0.75	0	52.86	37.01
0.75	1	54.28	37.34
0.75	3	52.75	38.18
0.75	4	52.55	36.54

The Impact of the Boundary-Check Algorithm. We evaluated our method under different error rates and fault tolerances values in Table 4. It is evident that the localization performance mAP@0.5 and mAP (avg) is the best when values of error rates and fault tolerances are 0.75 and 2. More specifically, when the model uses the boundary-check algorithm and sets the befitting values of error rates and fault tolerances, the model performs significantly better than without the boundary-check algorithm. The fault tolerance is set at 0 express not using the fault tolerance algorithm.

Table 5. Training in one dataset testing in another dataset, showing the temporal action localization performance mAP (%) under different tIoU thresholds, THUMOS14 → ActivityNet1.2 means training on THUMOS14, on ActivityNet1.2 carry out testing

tIoU	mAP@0.5	Top-1	Top-3
THUMOS14 → ActivityNet1.2@1	30.85	57.95	90.4
THUMOS14 → ActivityNet1.2@5	**43.3**	**73.6**	**96.76**
ActivityNet1.2 → THUMOS14@1	11.8	65.8	95
ActivityNet1.2 → THUMOS14@5	**21.1**	**82.56**	**98.06**

4.4 Generalization Test

In our generalization testing, we employ the THUMOS14 dataset for training and the ActivityNet1.2 dataset for testing. The THUMOS14 dataset predominantly comprises athletic actions such as shot put and pole vault, while the ActivityNet1.2 dataset primarily consists of common daily activities like handwashing and mopping. Given the substantial disparities in action categories between these two datasets, training on one and testing on the other allows us to substantiate our model's generalization performance.

Table 5 demonstrates our test results, indicating that even when we employ different datasets for model training, a satisfactory level of performance can still be achieved. Therefore, our model exhibits robust generalization capabilities.

5 Conclusion

This paper proposes a novel WFTAL method in video understanding. The method focuses on constructing the spatial-temporal relationship of actions in the video to ensure good generalization performance. The boundary-check algorithm is employed to correct prediction errors and improve localization performance. The experimental outcomes obtained from the THUMOS14 and ActivityNet1.2 datasets showcase the efficacy of our proposed method. These outcomes underscore the potential of our approach in the domain of video comprehension and action localization.

References

1. Carreira, J., Zisserman, A.: Quo Vadis, action recognition? A new model and the kinetics dataset. In: Proceedings of the IEEE Conference on Computer Vision and Pattern Recognition, pp. 6299–6308 (2017)
2. Chao, Y.W., Vijayanarasimhan, S., Seybold, B., Ross, D.A., Deng, J., Sukthankar, R.: Rethinking the faster R-CNN architecture for temporal action localization. In: Proceedings of the IEEE Conference on Computer Vision and Pattern Recognition, pp. 1130–1139 (2018)

3. Heilbron, F.C., Escorcia, V., Ghanem, B., Niebles, J.C.: ActivityNet: a large-scale video benchmark for human activity understanding. In: Proceedings of the IEEE Conference on Computer Vision and Pattern Recognition, pp. 961–970 (2015)
4. Hong, F.T., Feng, J.C., Xu, D., Shan, Y., Zheng, W.S.: Cross-modal consensus network for weakly supervised temporal action localization. In: Proceedings of the 29th ACM International Conference on Multimedia, pp. 1591–1599 (2021)
5. Jiang, Y.G., et al.: THUMOS challenge: action recognition with a large number of classes (2014). https://www.crcv.ucf.edu/THUMOS14/
6. Kingma, D.P., Ba, J.: Adam: a method for stochastic optimization. arXiv preprint arXiv:1412.6980 (2014)
7. Lin, T., Liu, X., Li, X., Ding, E., Wen, S.: BMN: boundary-matching network for temporal action proposal generation. In: Proceedings of the IEEE/CVF International Conference on Computer Vision, pp. 3889–3898 (2019)
8. Lin, T., Zhao, X., Shou, Z.: Single shot temporal action detection. In: Proceedings of the 25th ACM International Conference on Multimedia, pp. 988–996 (2017)
9. Lin, T., Zhao, X., Su, H., Wang, C., Yang, M.: BSN: boundary sensitive network for temporal action proposal generation. In: Ferrari, V., Hebert, M., Sminchisescu, C., Weiss, Y. (eds.) ECCV 2018. LNCS, vol. 11208, pp. 3–21. Springer, Cham (2018). https://doi.org/10.1007/978-3-030-01225-0_1
10. Long, F., Yao, T., Qiu, Z., Tian, X., Luo, J., Mei, T.: Gaussian temporal awareness networks for action localization. In: Proceedings of the IEEE/CVF Conference on Computer Vision and Pattern Recognition, pp. 344–353 (2019)
11. Nag, S., Zhu, X., Xiang, T.: Few-shot temporal action localization with query adaptive transformer. arXiv preprint arXiv:2110.10552 (2021)
12. Nguyen, P., Liu, T., Prasad, G., Han, B.: Weakly supervised action localization by sparse temporal pooling network. In: Proceedings of the IEEE Conference on Computer Vision and Pattern Recognition, pp. 6752–6761 (2018)
13. Paul, S., Roy, S., Roy-Chowdhury, A.K.: W-TALC: weakly-supervised temporal activity localization and classification. In: Ferrari, V., Hebert, M., Sminchisescu, C., Weiss, Y. (eds.) ECCV 2018. LNCS, vol. 11208, pp. 588–607. Springer, Cham (2018). https://doi.org/10.1007/978-3-030-01225-0_35
14. Shi, B., Dai, Q., Mu, Y., Wang, J.: Weakly-supervised action localization by generative attention modeling. In: Proceedings of the IEEE/CVF Conference on Computer Vision and Pattern Recognition, pp. 1009–1019 (2020)
15. Shou, Z., Chan, J., Zareian, A., Miyazawa, K., Chang, S.F.: CDC: convolutional-de-convolutional networks for precise temporal action localization in untrimmed videos. In: Proceedings of the IEEE Conference on Computer Vision and Pattern Recognition, pp. 5734–5743 (2017)
16. Sung, F., Yang, Y., Zhang, L., Xiang, T., Torr, P.H., Hospedales, T.M.: Learning to compare: relation network for few-shot learning. In: Proceedings of the IEEE Conference on Computer Vision and Pattern Recognition, pp. 1199–1208 (2018)
17. Wang, X., Girshick, R., Gupta, A., He, K.: Non-local neural networks. In: Proceedings of the IEEE Conference on Computer Vision and Pattern Recognition, pp. 7794–7803 (2018)
18. Xie, T.T., Tzelepis, C., Fu, F., Patras, I.: Few-shot action localization without knowing boundaries. In: Proceedings of the 2021 International Conference on Multimedia Retrieval, pp. 339–348 (2021)
19. Xie, T., Yang, X., Zhang, T., Xu, C., Patras, I.: Exploring feature representation and training strategies in temporal action localization. In: 2019 IEEE International Conference on Image Processing (ICIP), pp. 1605–1609. IEEE (2019)

20. Xu, H., Das, A., Saenko, K.: R-C3D: region convolutional 3D network for temporal activity detection. In: Proceedings of the IEEE International Conference on Computer Vision, pp. 5783–5792 (2017)
21. Xu, H., Kang, B., Sun, X., Feng, J., Saenko, K., Darrell, T.: Similarity R-C3D for few-shot temporal activity detection. arXiv preprint arXiv:1812.10000 (2018)
22. Xu, H., Sun, X., Tzeng, E., Das, A., Saenko, K., Darrell, T.: Revisiting few-shot activity detection with class similarity control. arXiv preprint arXiv:2004.00137 (2020)
23. Yang, H., He, X., Porikli, F.: One-shot action localization by learning sequence matching network. In: Proceedings of the IEEE Conference on Computer Vision and Pattern Recognition, pp. 1450–1459 (2018)
24. Yang, P., Hu, V.T., Mettes, P., Snoek, C.G.M.: Localizing the common action among a few videos. In: Vedaldi, A., Bischof, H., Brox, T., Frahm, J.-M. (eds.) ECCV 2020. LNCS, vol. 12352, pp. 505–521. Springer, Cham (2020). https://doi.org/10.1007/978-3-030-58571-6_30
25. Zhang, CL., Wu, J., Li, Y.: ActionFormer: localizing moments of actions with transformers. In: Avidan, S., Brostow, G., Cissé, M., Farinella, G.M., Hassner, T. (eds.) Computer Vision, ECCV 2022. LNCS, vol. 13664, pp. 492–510. Springer, Cham (2022). https://doi.org/10.1007/978-3-031-19772-7_29
26. Zhang, D., Dai, X., Wang, Y.F.: METAL: minimum effort temporal activity localization in untrimmed videos. In: Proceedings of the IEEE/CVF Conference on Computer Vision and Pattern Recognition, pp. 3882–3892 (2020)
27. Zhao, Y., Xiong, Y., Wang, L., Wu, Z., Tang, X., Lin, D.: Temporal action detection with structured segment networks. In: Proceedings of the IEEE International Conference on Computer Vision, pp. 2914–2923 (2017)

SVFNeXt: Sparse Voxel Fusion for LiDAR-Based 3D Object Detection

Deze Zhao[1], Shengjie Zhao[1,2(✉)], and Shuang Liang[2(✉)]

[1] College of Electronic and Information Engineering, Tongji University, Shanghai, China
deze@tongji.edu.cn
[2] School of Software Engineering, Tongji University, Shanghai, China
{shengjiezhao,shuangliang}@tongji.edu.cn

Abstract. Voxel-based 3D object detection methods have gained more popularity in autonomous driving. However, due to the sparse nature of LiDAR point clouds, voxels from conventional cubic partition lead to incomplete representation of objects in farther range. This poses significant challenges to 3D object perception. In this paper, we propose a novel 3D object detector dubbed **SVFNeXt**, a **S**parse **V**oxel **F**usion **Net**work that performs cross-representation (**X**) feature learning. It is because cylindrical voxel representation considers the rotational or radial scanning of LiDAR that we can better explore the inherent 3D geometric structure of point clouds. To further enchance cubic voxel features, we innovatively integrates the features of cylindrical voxels into cubic voxels, incorporating both local and global features. We particularly attend to informative voxels by two additional losses, striking a good speed-accuracy tradeoff. Extensive experiments on the WOD and KITTI datasets demonstrate consistent improvements over baselines. Our SVFNeXt achieves competitive results compared to state-of-the-art methods, especially for small objects(e.g., cyclist, pedestrian).

Keywords: 3D object detection · Autonomous driving · Voxel fusion

1 Introduction

3D object detection is an indispensable component in AD perception system and robotic domain. LiDAR-based 3D object detection has drawn the focus of researchers due to the rich depth and geometry provided by LiDAR point clouds. However, most methods primarily excel in large or densely sampled objects(e.g., car) while they often struggle to achieve satisfactory detection performance on small and distant hard cases(e.g., cyclist, pedestrian).

Previous voxel-based methods [2–8] voxelize point clouds and perform 3D sparse convolution on the voxels to extract features. However, due to the inherent sparsity and varying density of LiDAR point clouds, detectors utilizing ordinary cubic voxelization suffer from an increased number of empty voxels. This results in an incomplete representation of objects in the point clouds, missing object-level information. Additionally, the imbalanced points distribution in cubic voxels inevitably introduces significant computational overhead.

Building upon the limitations of cubic voxelization, [9] introduces a cylindrical voxelization approach. It partitions the point cloud in a manner that aligns with the rotational or radial scanning pattern of LiDAR. Naturally, voxels should be larger in regions where the point cloud becomes sparser. This voxel representation preserves the spatial structure of objects, resulting in more compact voxel features. It has been proven to exhibit superior performance in outdoor point cloud semantic segmentation task. Prior to it, there have been explorations of LiDAR-based multi-view fusion methods [10,11] applied to object detection. These methods concatenate voxel/pillar features from bird's-eye view and spherical/cylindrical view, and then propagate the features to points through voxel-point mapping to obtain point-level semantics.

From the above methods, they have the following drawbacks: 1) Traditional LiDAR-based detectors that solely use cubic voxels suffer from information loss due to inherent voxelization limitations, resulting in poor detection performance on small objects. 2) Methods [10,11] that fuse multiple representations of LiDAR point clouds employ a heavy voxel feature encoder (e.g., stacked PointNet) before the 3D backbone, which increases time and memory consumption. Although point-level features can provide fine-grained semantic information, they unavoidably introduce detrimental background noise from different views.

To address the aforementioned issues, we present a simple yet efficient 3D object detector, termed SVFNeXt, that effectively utilizes the complementary information from LiDAR cross-representation learning through sparse voxel fusion. Our method comprises three parts: Dynamic Distance-aware Cylindrical Voxelization (DDCV), Foreground Centroid-Voxel Selection-Query-Fusion (FCVSQF) and Object-aware Center-Voxel Transformer (OCVT).

Specifically, In the *DDCV* module, we adapt the cylindrical voxelization in [9] with non-uniform distance intervals along the ρ-axis. Consequently, much larger voxels are generated for distant regions. Furthermore, dynamic voxelization [11] avoids hard-coding the number of points within each voxel, maximizing points utilization without dropping any points, hence minimizing information loss. The *FCVSQF* module employs the centroid of points within each voxel as the query source and target instead of the voxel center, thus preserving the original 3D geometry and accurately representing voxel features. In order to save memory and prevent incurring background voxel noise, we focus on a few important foreground cubic centroid-voxels for local features query and fusion in cylindrical voxels. Additionally, we design a loss function to ensure the sampling of foreground centroid-voxels. The *OCVT* module further enhances the refined cubic voxel features by capturing long-range object-level global information via transformer [12]. It specially attends to voxels surrounding the object center.

The three modules unite to develop the final enhanced cubic voxels for compact and accurate detection. Extensive experiments on public benchmarks demonstrate that SVFNeXt significantly boosts the detection performance due to sparse voxel fusion, especially on small and distant objects. Meanwhile, we also show comparable results with the state-of-the-art methods on large objects (e.g., car, vehicle).

2   Related Work

2.1   Voxel-Based 3D Detectors

Mainstream voxel-based methods [2–4,7,8,22] typically partition the point cloud into cubic voxels and extract features using sparse convolutions. [2] utilizes more efficient 3D sparse convolutions to accelerate VoxelNet [6]. [7] collapses voxels into pillars along the z-axis and employs 2D convolutions to speed up. [3] refines proposals with RoI-grid pooling in a second stage. [4,8] aggregate voxel features using key points for box refinement. [22] addresses uneven point cloud density by considering point density within voxels. Although the regular grid structure of cubic voxelization enables efficient feature extraction with CNN, the receptive field is limited by the convolutional kernel. In contrast, our method enlarges the receptive field indirectly through cross-representation query.

2.2   Fusion-Based 3D Detectors

Fusion-based methods can be broadly categorized into multi-modal and multi-representation fusion. The former absorbs data from different sensors (e.g., LiDAR and camera), and has been supported by numerous methods [13,15,16]. Some [13,15] encode features from different modalities separately and fuse at the proposal-level or in the BEV feature map, while [16] employs attention mechanisms for feature fusion and alignment. However, feature misalignment and the additional branch may impact efficiency and real-time performance. The latter usually fuses data from the same source (e.g., LiDAR). [10,11] attempt point-level fusion of different views, but they may introduce noise and have limited impact on the receptive field. Nevertheless, our approach selectively enhances foreground centroid-voxels, with another alternative LiDAR representation to expand the receptive field and leverage complementary information.

2.3   Transformer-Based 3D Detectors

Transformer [12] has recently demonstrated its superiority in 2D vision tasks. Exploiting the permutation invariance of point clouds, applying transformer to 3D vision is a favorable choice. In pioneer works [17–21], attention mechanisms are employed at different stages of the 3D detection pipeline (e.g., 3D backbone [17–19], dense head [20], RoI head [21,22]) to learn contextual information. However, directly applying vanilla transformer to massive point clouds is infeasible in terms of time and space. Therefore, we focus specifically on voxels near the object center to capture long-range dependencies.

3   SVFNeXt for 3D Object Detection

We propose a sparse cross-representation voxel feature fusion and refinement method called SVFNeXt, integrating voxel-level features during the sparse features extraction. Our objective is to make minimal modifications and provide a simple and efficient plugin that can be easily incorporated into generic detection pipeline, as illustrated in Fig. 1. SVFNeXt consists primarily of three modules: Dynamic Distance-aware Cylindrical Voxelization (Sect. 3.1), Foreground Centroid-Voxel Selection-Query-Fusion (Sect. 3.2), and Object-aware Center-Voxel Transformer (Sect. 3.3).

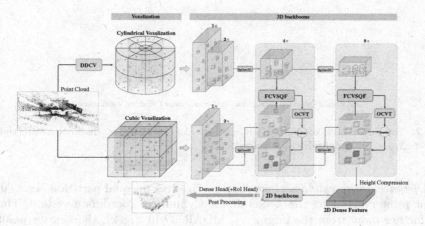

Fig. 1. A schematic overview of SVFNeXt.

3.1   Dynamic Distance-Aware Cylindrical Voxelization

To maintain the 3D geometric structure of objects in point clouds, adapt to the rotational scanning manner of LiDAR and varying sparsity of point clouds, we introduce dynamic distance-aware cylindrical voxelization, as shown in Fig. 2. This technique converts points from Cartesian coordinate to Cylindrical coordinate and partitions voxels unevenly along the ρ-axis without dropping any points, unlike [9].

Given a point cloud $P_{\text{cart}} = \{(x_i, y_i, z_i)\}_{i=1}^{N_{\text{p}}}$ defined in Cartesian coordinate system, its Cylindrical coordinate representation is calculated as $P_{\text{cyl}} = \{(\rho_i, \varphi_i, z_i)\}_{i=1}^{N_{\text{p}}}$, where

$$\rho_i = \sqrt{x_i^2 + y_i^2} \qquad \varphi_i = \arctan(\frac{y_i}{x_i}) \qquad z_i = z_i \tag{1}$$

where N_{p} is the number of points in the point cloud.

Dynamic voxelization [11] means points are assigned to the volume space of the grid dynamicly based on their spatial coordinates. As for cylindrical points set P_{cyl} and voxels set V_{cyl}, voxelization can be described as a bidirectional mapping between points and voxels, formally,

$$V_{\text{cyl}} = \{v_j \mid \mathcal{M}_v(p_i) = v_j, p_i \in P_{\text{cyl}}, \forall i\}_{j=1}^{M} \tag{2}$$

$$\mathcal{M}_p(v_j) = \{p_i \mid \forall p_i \in v_j, v_j \in V_{\text{cyl}}\} \tag{3}$$

where M is the number of non-empty voxels, $\mathcal{M}_v(\cdot)$ denotes mapping from point to voxel, $\mathcal{M}_p(\cdot)$ denotes mapping from voxel to point.

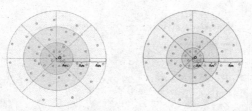

(a) Regular Cylindrical Voxelization   (b) Distance-aware Cylindrical Voxelization

Fig. 2. Top-down view of regular(left, $\Delta\rho_1 = \Delta\rho_2 = \Delta\rho_3$) vs. distance-aware(right, $\Delta\rho_1 < \Delta\rho_2 < \Delta\rho_3$) cylindrical voxelization.

Distance-aware cylindrical voxelization involves unequal partition across different ρ intervals along the ρ-axis in the Cylindrical coordinate system. Thus, the farther away from the origin(i.e., LiDAR, O in Fig. 2), the sparser points, the larger voxels, allowing more points to reside in, as shown in Fig. 2(b). Define voxel size as $V_s = (\Delta\rho, \Delta\varphi, \Delta z)$, discussed by cases,

$$V_s = \begin{cases} (\Delta\rho_1, \Delta\varphi, \Delta z), & 0 \leqslant \rho < \rho_1 \\ (\Delta\rho_2, \Delta\varphi, \Delta z), & \rho_1 \leqslant \rho < \rho_2 \\ (\Delta\rho_3, \Delta\varphi, \Delta z), & \rho \geqslant \rho_2 \end{cases} \tag{4}$$

where $\Delta\rho_1 < \Delta\rho_2 < \Delta\rho_3$, we can also term $[0, \rho_1)$ as close, $[\rho_1, \rho_2)$ as medium and $[\rho_2, +\infty)$ as far.

3.2 Foreground Centroid-Voxel Selection-Query-Fusion

Various approaches [3,4,8,21] have been explored to determine the voxel center as a representation of voxel feature position. However, they tend to treat voxels with different point distributions equally, inevitably misleading model and overlooking important geometric details. Observed by [22], we adopt voxel centroid as a position representative to achieve accurate feature querying. Besides, centroid aligns well with our DDCV module, which captures the distribution pattern of points within each voxel. Hence, we should first locate the centroid of each voxel after initial cubic and cylindrical voxelization.

Let's assume cylindrical voxels set $V_{\text{cyl}} = \{v_j = \{I_{\text{cyl}}^{v_j}, F_{\text{cyl}}^{v_j}\}\}_{j=1}^{M}$, cubic voxels set $V_{\text{cub}} = \{u_i = \{I_{\text{cub}}^{u_i}, F_{\text{cub}}^{u_i}\}\}_{i=1}^{N}$, for each representation, $I \in \mathbb{R}^3$ is the index of voxel and $F \in \mathbb{R}^{3+c}$ is the corresponding voxel feature, c is the number of channels of extra features(e.g., intensity, elongation). To illustrate, taking V_{cyl} as an example, voxel centroid can be computed by taking the average spatial coordinates of the points within the voxel. Specifically, for $v_j \in V_{\text{cyl}}$, centroid

$$\mathcal{C}_{\text{cyl}}^j = \frac{1}{\mathcal{N}(v_j)} \sum_{p_j \in v_j} p_j \tag{5}$$

where $p_j = (\rho_j, \varphi_j, z_j)$, $\mathcal{N}(v_j)$ is the number of points within the voxel v_j. Thus, for cubic voxels set V_{cub}, we can also compute voxel centroid $\mathcal{C}_{\text{cub}}^i$ the same way as Eq. 5.

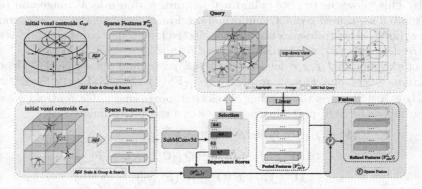

Fig. 3. The FCVSQF module. Initially, we locate the centroids and retrieve centroid-voxel features of both representations at scale s. We then selectively fuse foreground cubic centroid-voxels with cylindrical centroid-voxels by ball-query, resulting in $\mathbf{F}_{\text{cyl}}^{\mathcal{C}_s})_p$. Finally, we fuse the pooled features with the selected foreground cubic centroid-voxel features $(\mathbf{F}_{\text{cub}}^{\mathcal{C}_s})_f$, to generate refined cubic voxel features $(\mathbf{F}_{\text{cub}}^{\mathcal{C}_s})_f^r$.

Centroid-Voxel Features Retrieval. After obtaining the voxel centroids from two different voxel representations, we perform *Scale* and *Group* operations to get centroids $\mathcal{C}_*^s \in \mathbb{R}^{n_* \times 3}$ and corresponding voxel(i.e., centroid-voxel) indices $\mathbf{I}_*^{\mathcal{C}_s} \in \mathbb{R}^{n_* \times 3}$ from feature map $\mathbf{F}_*^s \in \mathbb{R}^{N_* \times c_s}$ from 3D sparse CNN at scale s. Then, *Search* the whole sparse feature map $\mathbf{F}_*^s$ for centroid-voxels based on indices and retrieve the associated voxel features $\mathbf{F}_*^{\mathcal{C}_s} \in \mathbb{R}^{n_* \times c_s}$, Here, $* = \{\text{cub}, \text{cyl}\}$, $n_* < N_*$, c_s is the channels of voxel features. Formally, given the initial voxel indices $\mathbf{I}_*$, voxel centroids $\mathcal{C}_*$ and downsample factors $D = \{1, 2, 4, 8\}$ of feature map $\mathbf{F}_*$ at each scale,

$$\mathbf{F}_*^{\mathcal{C}_s} = \mathcal{S}_2\left(\mathcal{G}\left(\mathcal{S}_1(\mathbf{I}_*, D_s), \mathcal{C}_*\right), \mathbf{F}_*^s\right) \tag{6}$$

where $s \in \{1, 2, 3, 4\}$, $\mathcal{S}_1$ denotes *Scale*, $\mathcal{G}$ denotes *Group*, $\mathcal{S}_2$ denotes *Search*.

Centroid-Voxels Selection-Query-Fusion. To obtain refined cubic centroid-voxel features, it is crucial to select the foreground centroid-voxels for feature aggregation. We focus on those that are important rather than all. Thus avoiding background noise from cylindrical centroid-voxels, which offers no benefit to detection. Unlike [17], which uniformly aggregates features from all non-empty voxels. Moreover, our method ensures expanded effective receptive field while maintaining high efficiency.

We follow the three steps: foreground cubic centroid-voxels *selection*, cross-representation *query*, and *fusion*. Referring to Fig. 3, with centroid-voxels from both representations involved, we focus more on the cubic one following the common practice, and the other as an auxiliary. Firstly, we select the top-k centroid-voxels as the query source according to foreground scores. Then, perform MSG ball-query [1] within the cylindrical centroid-voxels based on the related centroids. This allows us to pool cylindrical features within a local range and provide more fine-grained geometric information. Finally, we fuse the *pooled features* from cylindrical centroid-voxels with the selected foreground cubic centroid-voxel features. As a result, we obtain the *refined features*.

Let's assume that f, p, r denote *foreground, pooled* and *refined*, $\mathcal{S}, \mathcal{Q}, \mathcal{F}$ denote *Selection, Query* and *Fusion*, respectively, $\{(\mathbf{F}_{\mathrm{cub}}^{\mathcal{C}_s})_f, (\mathbf{F}_{\mathrm{cyl}}^{\mathcal{C}_s})_p, (\mathbf{F}_{\mathrm{cub}}^{\mathcal{C}_s})_f^r\} \in \mathbb{R}^{n_f \times c_s}$, $(\mathcal{C}_{\mathrm{cub}}^s)_f \in \mathbb{R}^{n_f \times 3}$, n_f is the number of selected foreground cubic centroid-voxels. Accordingly, the SQF part illustrated by Fig. 3 can be formulated as

$$[(\mathbf{F}_{\mathrm{cub}}^{\mathcal{C}_s})_f, (\mathcal{C}_{\mathrm{cub}}^s)_f] = \mathcal{S}\left(\mathrm{SubM3d}(\mathbf{F}_{\mathrm{cub}}^{\mathcal{C}_s}), \mathcal{C}_{\mathrm{cub}}^s\right) \tag{7}$$

$$(\mathbf{F}_{\mathrm{cyl}}^{\mathcal{C}_s})_p = \mathrm{Linear}\left(\mathcal{Q}\left((\mathcal{C}_{\mathrm{cub}}^s)_f, \mathcal{C}_{\mathrm{cyl}}^s, \mathbf{F}_{\mathrm{cyl}}^{\mathcal{C}_s}\right)\right) \tag{8}$$

$$(\mathbf{F}_{\mathrm{cub}}^{\mathcal{C}_s})_f^r = \mathcal{F}\left((\mathbf{F}_{\mathrm{cub}}^{\mathcal{C}_s})_f, (\mathbf{F}_{\mathrm{cyl}}^{\mathcal{C}_s})_p\right) \tag{9}$$

3.3   Object-Aware Center-Voxel Transformer

Previously, we obtain refined foreground cubic centroid-voxel features marked as features of interest to attend. They include fine-grained features from another more informative cylindrical representation, partially compensating for the loss of object information represented by cubic voxels. However, they may potentially lack interaction due to independent feature aggregation. Furthermore, it is essential to incorporate global information into the feature for detecting small and distant objects. Therefore, we propose OCVT, guided by the object center, to effectively capture long-range context at object level, as shown in Fig. 4.

3D Sparse Heatmap Generation. Leveraging the selected foreground centroids $(\mathcal{C}_{\mathrm{cub}}^s)_f$ from FCVSQF module, given each annotated bounding box B_k centered at (x_k, y_k, z_k), we calculate the distance between center of B_k and centroid $(\hat{x}_i^k, \hat{y}_i^k, \hat{z}_i^k)$ situated at B_k in $(\mathcal{C}_{\mathrm{cub}}^s)_f$. Then, a 3D Gaussian kernel is applied to confine the heatmap response within the range of [0,1]. Formally,

$$\hat{H}_i = \exp\left(-\frac{(x_k - \hat{x}_i^k)^2 + (y_k - \hat{y}_i^k)^2 + (z_k - \hat{z}_i^k)^2}{2\sigma_k^2}\right) \in [0, 1] \tag{10}$$

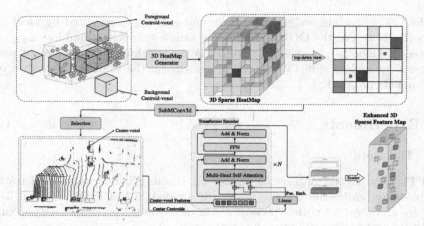

Fig. 4. The OCVT module. We first generate a 3D sparse heatmap based on *Foreground Centroid-voxels*, then sample *Center-voxels* around object center according to heatmap values, to perceive long-range object-level context with transformer encoder.

where σ_k is an object size-adaptive standard deviation [24], $\hat{H}_i$ is the heatmap value generated at centroid i. Taking all centroids, we obtain the final target *3D Sparse Heatmap* $\hat{\mathbf{H}}$, calculating a loss with the predicted heatmap $\mathbf{H}$. We thereby can carefully choose centroid-voxels closely aligned with the object center.

Center-Voxel Transformer. We focus solely on a subset of centroid-voxels closest to the object center to build object-level contextual dependencies, thereby improving efficiency. Similar to the *Selection* part in Fig. 3, the location of top K voxels based on the predicted heatmap scores will be taken out as the *center-voxels*. We denote center-voxel features as $(\mathbf{F}_{\text{cub}}^{\mathcal{C}_s})_{ctr}$, center centroids as $(\mathcal{C}_{\text{cub}}^{s})_{ctr}$, they are then fed into Transformer encoder block:

$$(\mathbf{F}_{\text{cub}}^{s})_{ctr} = \mathcal{T}(\mathbf{Q}, \mathbf{K}, \mathbf{V}) \tag{11}$$

$$\mathbf{Q} = \mathbf{W}_q(\mathbf{F}_{\text{cub}}^{\mathcal{C}_s})_{ctr} + \mathbf{E}_{pos}, \mathbf{K} = \mathbf{W}_k(\mathbf{F}_{\text{cub}}^{\mathcal{C}_s})_{ctr} + \mathbf{E}_{pos}, \mathbf{V} = \mathbf{W}_v(\mathbf{F}_{\text{cub}}^{\mathcal{C}_s})_{ctr} \tag{12}$$

where $\mathcal{T}$ denotes Transformer, $\mathbf{Q}$, $\mathbf{K}$, $\mathbf{V}$ are query, key, value features, $\mathbf{E}_{pos}$ is positional embedding transformed by a linear layer applied to $(\mathcal{C}_{\text{cub}}^{s})_{ctr}$.

Eventually, we scatter $(\mathbf{F}_{\text{cub}}^{s})_{ctr}$ back to the 3D sparse feature map at scale s, resulting in the enhanced cubic voxel features. The final enchanced features are equipped with both rich local features from cylindrical voxels, and long-range global contextual dependencies from object centers.

3.4 Loss Functions

The overall loss function comprises four components: foreground loss and heatmap loss from the 3D backbone, RPN loss and RCNN loss (for 2-stage models). We adhere to [3,4] for RPN loss $\mathcal{L}_{\text{rpn}}$ and RCNN loss $\mathcal{L}_{\text{rcnn}}$. Regarding the FCVSQF module, we employ foreground loss $\mathcal{L}_{fore}$ computed by focal loss [26] with BCE. For the OCVT module, we utilize sparse heatmap loss $\mathcal{L}_{hm}$ calculated by smooth-L1 loss. The final loss is the weighted sum of the four parts above: $\mathcal{L} = w_1\mathcal{L}_{fore} + w_2\mathcal{L}_{hm} + w_3\mathcal{L}_{rpn} + w_4\mathcal{L}_{rcnn}$, the weights we used in our experiments are $[1, 1, 1, 1]$, respectively.

4   Experiments

4.1   Datasets

KITTI. The KITTI dataset contains 7481 training samples and 7518 testing samples. Typically, the training data are divided into a *train* set with 3712 samples and a *val* set with 3769 samples. It uses average precision (AP) on easy, moderate and hard levels as evaluation metric.

Waymo Open Dataset. The WOD dataset consists of 798 sequences for training and 202 sequences for validation. The evaluation metrics include average precision (AP) and average precision weighted by heading (APH). We report the results on both LEVEL 1 (L1) and LEVEL 2 (L2) difficulty levels.

4.2   Implementation Details

For the cubic voxelization, we follow PV-RCNN [4] settings (i.e., voxel size and point cloud range) on both datasets. For the cylindrical voxelization, the ranges are $[0, 80]$ m, $[-\pi/2, \pi/2]$ **rad**, and $[-3, 1]$ m along the ρ, φ and z axis, respectively, with voxel size of $(0.05$ m, $\pi/180$ rad, 0.1 m) on **KITTI**. While on **WOD**, the ranges are $[0, 107.84]$ m, $[-\pi, \pi]$ rad and $[-2, 4]$ m along the ρ, φ and z axis. The voxel size is $(\Delta\rho, \pi/360$ rad, 0.15 m), $\Delta\rho$ varies as the DDCV module illustrated: the ranges across distance are $[0, 30.24)$ m, $[30.24, 50.24)$ m, $[50.24, 107.84]$ m, where the $\Delta\rho$ is set as 0.09 m, 0.10 m and 0.15 m accordingly.

4.3   Main Results

KITTI. With [2–5] as our baselines, the experimental results on *val* and *test* set are presented in Table 1 and Table 2, respectively. Our model exhibits notable improvements in both 3D and BEV mAP(e.g., 1.17%, 1.67%, and 3.02% 3D AP on Mod. level). Notably, our approach significantly enhances performance for *Ped.* and *Cyc.* categories at the moderate difficulty while maintaining strong capability for *Car* class. A visual comparison shown in Fig. 5 explains our method can better detect, align and orient objects. Moreover, our method shows competitive results on the *test* set and further verifys the effectiveness of our method.

Table 1. Performance comparison of 3D/BEV detection with AP R40 on KITTI *val* set. †: re-implemented by [27]. ‡: reported by [27]. SVF: Sparse Voxel Fusion.

Methods	3D Detection AP										BEV Detection AP										
	Car@0.7			Pedestrian@0.5			Cyclist@0.5			mAP	Car@0.7			Pedestrian@0.5			Cyclist@0.5			mAP
	Easy	Mod.	Hard	Easy	Mod.	Hard	Easy	Mod.	Hard	Mod.	Easy	Mod.	Hard	Easy	Mod.	Hard	Easy	Mod.	Hard	Mod.
SECOND‡	90.53	81.59	78.58	55.94	51.14	46.21	82.96	66.74	62.78	66.49	92.42	88.56	87.65	60.73	56.57	52.14	88.05	71.16	66.89	72.10
SECOND+SVF	90.61	81.39	78.00	59.01	54.40	49.16	80.80	67.19	63.17	67.66	94.43	90.53	87.64	63.98	59.32	55.12	85.02	73.53	69.57	74.47
improvement	0.08	-0.20	-0.58	3.07	3.26	2.95	-2.16	0.45	0.39	1.17	2.01	1.97	-0.01	3.25	2.75	2.98	-3.03	2.37	2.68	2.37
CenterPoint†	86.18	78.13	76.68	58.34	54.48	50.11	82.89	65.50	62.35	66.04	91.65	87.82	86.72	62.23	58.93	54.71	86.26	68.48	65.04	71.75
CenterPoint+SVF	86.90	77.61	76.45	62.48	57.55	52.81	82.79	67.98	64.12	67.71	92.41	89.07	87.11	67.48	62.08	57.75	87.40	72.49	68.48	74.54
improvement	0.72	-0.52	-0.23	4.14	3.07	2.70	-0.10	2.48	1.77	1.67	0.76	1.25	0.39	5.25	3.15	3.04	1.14	4.01	3.44	2.79
Voxel-RCNN‡	92.24	85.05	82.50	-	-	-	-	-	-	-	93.54	91.17	88.90	-	-	-	-	-	-	-
Voxel-RCNN+SVF	92.14	85.03	82.73	-	-	-	-	-	-	-	95.81	91.54	89.26	-	-	-	-	-	-	-
improvement	-0.10	-0.02	0.23	-	-	-	-	-	-	-	2.27	0.37	0.36	-	-	-	-	-	-	-
PV-RCNN‡	92.10	84.39	82.49	62.73	54.51	49.86	89.09	70.41	66.01	69.77	93.02	90.32	88.53	65.94	58.49	54.13	93.47	74.54	70.10	74.45
PV-RCNN+SVF	91.83	84.61	82.32	68.23	61.43	56.67	91.67	72.33	67.90	72.79	95.26	90.78	88.57	71.04	64.51	59.83	93.04	75.10	70.50	76.80
improvement	-0.27	0.22	-0.17	5.5	6.92	6.81	2.58	1.92	1.89	3.02	2.24	0.46	0.04	5.10	6.02	5.70	-0.43	0.56	0.40	2.35

Table 2. Performance comparison with different models on the KITTI *test* set for *Car* and *Cyclist*. The top-2 best performances are highlighted in **bold**.

Models	Car 3D (IoU = 0.7)			Cyclist 3D (IoU = 0.5)		
	Easy	Mod.	Hard	Easy	Mod.	Hard
SECOND [2]	83.34	72.55	65.82	71.33	52.08	45.83
PointPillars [7]	82.58	74.31	68.99	77.10	58.65	51.92
PointRCNN [14]	86.96	75.64	70.70	74.96	58.82	52.53
3DSSD [25]	88.36	79.57	74.55	82.48	64.10	56.90
PV-RCNN [4]	90.25	81.43	76.82	78.60	63.71	57.65
Voxel-RCNN [3]	**90.90**	81.62	77.06	-	-	-
PDV [22]	**90.43**	**81.86**	**77.36**	83.04	**67.81**	**60.46**
CT3D [21]	87.83	**81.77**	**77.16**	-	-	-
SVFNeXt(Ours)	88.40	81.69	77.09	**83.49**	66.45	59.60

Table 3. Performance comparison of 3D detection on WOD *val* set, training with 20% *train* set. ‡: reported by [27]. SVF: Sparse Voxel Fusion.

Methods	Vehicle		Pedestrian		Cyclist		ALL	
	L1(AP/APH)	L2(AP/APH)	L1(AP/APH)	L2(AP/APH)	L1(AP/APH)	L2(AP/APH)	L1(mAP/mAPH)	L2(mAP/mAPH)
SECOND‡	70.96/70.34	62.58/62.02	65.23/54.24	57.22/47.49	57.13/55.62	54.97/53.53	64.44/60.07	58.26/54.35
SECOND+SVF	73.69/73.14	65.52/65.01	68.25/57.25	60.41/50.55	61.84/60.38	59.53/58.12	67.93/63.59	61.82/57.89
Improvement	2.73/2.80	2.94/2.99	3.02/3.01	3.19/3.06	4.71/4.76	4.56/4.59	3.49/3.52	3.56/3.55
CenterPoint‡	71.33/70.76	63.16/62.65	72.09/65.49	64.27/58.23	68.68/67.39	66.11/64.87	70.70/67.88	64.51/61.92
CenterPoint+SVF	73.43/72.84	65.39/64.85	73.76/67.51	65.96/60.21	70.87/69.73	68.25/67.15	72.69/70.03	66.53/64.07
Improvement	2.10/2.08	2.23/2.20	1.67/2.02	1.69/1.98	2.19/2.34	2.14/2.28	1.99/2.15	2.02/2.15
Voxel-RCNN‡	76.13/75.66	68.18/67.74	78.20/71.98	69.29/63.59	70.75/69.68	68.25/67.21	75.03/72.44	68.57/66.18
Voxel-RCNN+SVF	76.93/76.46	68.56/68.14	80.07/74.36	71.66/66.32	72.47/71.37	69.83/68.76	76.49/74.06	70.02/67.74
Improvement	0.80/0.80	0.38/0.40	1.87/2.38	2.37/2.73	1.72/1.69	1.58/1.55	1.46/1.62	1.44/1.56
PV-RCNN‡	75.41/74.74	67.44/66.80	71.98/61.24	63.70/53.95	65.88/64.25	63.39/61.82	71.09/66.74	64.84/60.86
PV-RCNN+SVF	76.69/76.12	68.22/67.70	75.35/65.56	66.54/57.67	69.03/67.61	66.47/65.10	73.69/69.76	67.08/63.49
Improvement	1.28/1.38	0.78/0.90	3.37/4.32	2.84/3.72	3.15/3.36	3.08/3.28	2.60/3.02	2.23/2.63

WOD. We conduct experiments on the large-scale WOD and report the results in Table 3 and Table 4 on the *val* set. As shown in Table 3, our method consis-

Table 4. The detection results on WOD *val* set, training with <u>full</u> *train* set. †: re-implemented by [27] with kernel size as 3 in 3D backbone.

Models	Vehicle		Pedestrian		Cyclist		ALL
	L1(AP/APH)	L2(AP/APH)	L1(AP/APH)	L2(AP/APH)	L1(AP/APH)	L2(AP/APH)	L2(mAP/mAPH)
SECOND [2]	72.3/71.7	63.9/63.3	68.7/58.2	60.7/51.3	60.6/59.3	58.3/57.0	61.0/57.2
PointPillars [7]	72.1/71.5	63.6/63.1	70.6/56.7	62.8/50.3	64.4/62.3	61.9/59.9	62.8/57.8
Pillar-OD [11]	69.8/-	-/-	72.5/-	-/-	-/-	-/-	-/-
VoxSeT [18]	76.0/-	68.2/-	-/-	-/-	-/-	-/-	-/-
PDV [22]	76.9/76.3	69.3/68.8	74.2/66.0	65.9/58.3	68.7/67.6	66.5/65.4	67.2/64.2
CenterPoint-Voxel(SS) [5]	74.2/73.6	66.2/65.7	76.6/70.5	68.8/63.2	72.3/71.1	69.7/68.5	8.2/65.8
CenterPoint-Voxel(TS) [5]	76.6/76.0	68.9/68.4	79.0/73.4	71.0/65.8	72.1/71.0	69.5/68.5	69.8/67.6
PV-RCNN(anchor) [4]	77.5/76.9	69.0/68.4	75.0/65.6	66.0/57.6	67.8/66.4	65.4/64.0	66.8/63.3
PV-RCNN++(center) [8]	**79.3/78.8**	**70.6/70.2**	**81.3/76.3**	**73.2**/68.0	73.7/72.7	71.2/70.2	71.7/69.5
CenterFormer [20]	75.0/74.4	69.9/69.4	78.0/72.4	73.1/67.7	73.8/72.7	71.3/70.2	1.4/69.1
SWFormer [19]	77.8/77.3	69.2/68.8	80.9/72.7	72.5/64.9	-/-	-/-	-/-
VoxelNeXt† [23]	77.7/77.3	69.5/69.0	80.9/75.9	72.9/68.1	75.3/74.2	72.6/71.5	71.6/69.5
SVFNeXt(Ours)	78.1/77.6	69.8/69.4	81.2/76.2	**73.2/68.5**	**75.8/74.6**	**73.0/71.9**	**72.0/69.9**

Table 5. Effect of each component on WOD *val* set with [2] as baseline (blue), training with <u>20%</u> *train* set. DRCV: Regular voxelization in Fig. 2.

Exp.	DRCV	DDCV	FCVSQF	OCVT	Veh. APH(L2)		Ped. APH(L2)		Cyc. APH(L2)		ALL mAPH(L2)	
					overall	50m-inf	overall	50m-inf	overall	50m-inf	overall	50m-inf
1					62.0	33.4	47.5	31.5	53.5	35.0	54.3	33.3
2	✓				63.0	34.4	48.7	32.1	55.1	35.9	55.5	34.1
3		✓			63.5	34.8	49.0	32.5	55.6	36.3	56.2	34.5
4		✓	✓		64.5	36.6	50.0	33.3	57.2	38.2	57.2	36.0
5	✓		✓	✓	64.6	37.2	50.2	33.6	58.0	38.6	57.3	36.5
6		✓	✓	✓	**65.0**	**37.7**	**50.6**	**33.9**	**58.1**	**39.1**	**57.9**	**36.9**
Improvement					3.0	4.3	3.1	2.4	4.6	4.1	3.6	3.6

tently improves performance across all categories, similar to what we observe in KITTI. Notably, our method significantly outperforms baselines on mAPH (L2), with margins of 3.55%, 2.15%, 1.56%, and 2.63%, particularly for small objects. Furthermore, we summarize the comparison between our approach and state-of-the-art methods in Table 4.

4.4 Ablation Study

We conduct ablation studies on each proposed module shown in Table 5. The unified effect of the three modules results in a significant gain of 3.6% mAPH (L2) on both overall and far range (i.e., 50 m–inf).

DDCV. We observe that distance-aware voxelization (DDCV) outperforms regular voxelization (DRCV). The former shows improvements of 1.5%, 1.5% and 2.1% overall APH (L2) for *Veh.*, *Ped.*, and *Cyc.*, respectively. This confirms the capability of cylindrical voxels to provide richer information and refine object representation.

FCVSQF. It utilizes foreground centroids for feature fusion, preserving original geometric shape information. This optimization helps refine foreground voxel features and expands the receptive field through local query, particularly bene-fiting sparse, small and distant objects. Notably, it brings a performance gain of 1.5% mAPH (L2) on far range.

OCVT. Guided by object center, it models long-range contextual dependencies at object level with center-voxels, further refining the sparse voxel features. This brings a slight performance gain of 0.7% and 0.9% mAPH (L2) on overall and far range, respectively.

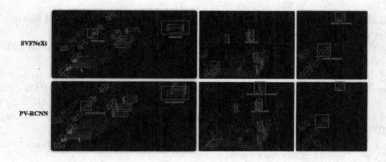

Fig. 5. A visual comparison of SVFNeXt vs. PV-RCNN on KITTI *val* set. Blue means ground truth, and green means detection box.

5   Conclusion

In this paper, we propose SVFNeXt, a plug-and-play fusion-based 3D backbone that can be applied to most voxel-based 3D detectors. As a rarely explored approach, we address the limitations of conventional cubic voxels by leveraging cylindrical voxels with more uniform points distribution, providing richer infor-mation for accurate detection. Our centroid-based cross-voxel query and local features fusion partially alleviate the issue of incomplete object representation in cubic voxels, incorporating fine-grained features and enlarging receptive field. What's more, the object-level global information learning further refines feature representations, benefiting the subsequent detection. Extensive experiments on the public benchmarks serve as a compelling evidence of our model efficacy.

Note that our approach falls slightly short of the state-of-the-art methods on larger objects in some case. Our subsequent endeavor involves delving into model generalization to narrow this gap and enhance its performance.

Acknowledgements. This work is supported in part by the National Key Research and Development Project under Grant 2019YFB2102300, in part by the National Natural Science Foundation of China under Grant 61936014, 62076183, 61976159, in part by the Shanghai Municipal Science and Technology Major Project under Grant 2021SHZDZX0100, in part by the Shanghai Science and Technology Innovation Action Plan Project No. 22511105300 and 20511100700, in part by the Natural Science Foundation of Shanghai under Grant 20ZR147350, in part by the Fundamental Research Funds for the Central Universities.

References

1. Qi, C.R., Yi, L., Su, H., Guibas, L.J.: PointNet++: deep hierarchical feature learning on point sets in a metric space. In: NIPS, pp. 5105–5114 (2017)
2. Yan, Y., Mao, Y., Li, B.: SECOND: sparsely embedded convolutional detection. Sensors **18**(10), 3337 (2018)
3. Deng, J., Shi, S., Li, P., Zhou, W., Zhang, Y., Li, H.: Voxel R-CNN: towards high performance voxel-based 3D object detection. In: AAAI, pp. 1201–1209 (2021)
4. Shi, S., Guo, C., Jiang, L., Wang, Z., Shi, J., Wang, X., Li, H.: PV-RCNN: point-voxel feature set abstraction for 3D object detection. In: CVPR, pp. 10529–10538 (2020)
5. Yin, T., Zhou, X., Krahenbuhl, P.: Center-based 3D object detection and tracking. In: CVPR, pp. 11784–11793 (2021)
6. Zhou, Y., Tuzel, O.: VoxelNet: end-to-end learning for point cloud based 3D object detection. In: CVPR, pp. 4490–4499 (2018)
7. Lang, A.H., Vora, S., Caesar, H., Zhou, L., Yang, J., Beijbom, O.: PointPillars: fast encoders for object detection from point clouds. In: CVPR, pp. 12697–12705 (2019)
8. Shi, S., et al.: PV-RCNN++: point-voxel feature set abstraction with local vector representation for 3D object detection. Int. J. Comput. Vision **131**(2), 531–551 (2023). https://doi.org/10.1007/s11263-022-01710-9
9. Zhu, X., et al.: Cylindrical and asymmetrical 3D convolution networks for lidar segmentation. In: CVPR, pp. 9939–9948 (2021)
10. Zhou, Y., et al.: End-to-end multi-view fusion for 3D object detection in lidar point clouds. In: CoRL, pp. 923–932 (2020)
11. Wang, Y.: Pillar-based object detection for autonomous driving. In: Vedaldi, A., Bischof, H., Brox, T., Frahm, J.-M. (eds.) ECCV 2020. LNCS, vol. 12367, pp. 18–34. Springer, Cham (2020). https://doi.org/10.1007/978-3-030-58542-6_2
12. Vaswani, A., et al.: Attention is all you need. In: NIPS, pp. 5998–6008 (2017)
13. Chen, X., Ma, H., Wan, J., Li, B., Xia, T.: Multi-view 3D object detection network for autonomous driving. In: CVPR, pp. 1907–1915 (2017)
14. Shi, S., Wang, X., Li, H.: PointRCNN: 3D object proposal generation and detection from point cloud. In: CVPR, pp. 770–779 (2019)
15. Liang, T., et al.: BEVFusion: a simple and robust lidar-camera fusion framework. In: NeurIPS, pp. 10421–10434 (2022)
16. Li, Y., et al.: DeepFusion: lidar-camera deep fusion for multi-modal 3D object detection. In: CVPR, pp. 17182–17191 (2022)
17. Mao, J., et al.: Voxel transformer for 3D object detection. In: CVPR, pp. 3164–3173 (2021)
18. He, C., Li, R., Li, S., Zhang, L.: Voxel set transformer: a set-to-set approach to 3D object detection from point clouds. In: CVPR, pp. 8417–8427 (2022)

19. Sun, P., et al.: SWFormer: sparse window transformer for 3D object detection in point clouds. In: Avidan, S., Brostow, G., Cissé, M., Farinella, G.M., Hassner, T. (eds.) Computer Vision – ECCV 2022: 17th European Conference, Tel Aviv, Israel, October 23–27, 2022, Proceedings, Part X, pp. 426–442. Springer, Cham (2022). https://doi.org/10.1007/978-3-031-20080-9_25

20. Zhou, Z., Zhao, X., Wang, Yu., Wang, P., Foroosh, H.: CenterFormer: center-based transformer for 3D object detection. In: Avidan, S., Brostow, G., Cissé, M., Farinella, G.M., Hassner, T. (eds.) Computer Vision – ECCV 2022: 17th European Conference, Tel Aviv, Israel, October 23–27, 2022, Proceedings, Part XXXVIII, pp. 496–513. Springer, Cham (2022). https://doi.org/10.1007/978-3-031-19839-7_29

21. Sheng, H., et al.: Improving 3D object detection with channel-wise transformer. In: ICCV, pp. 2743–2752 (2021)

22. Hu, J.S., Kuai, T., Waslander, S.L.: Point density-aware voxels for lidar 3D object detection. In: CVPR, pp. 8469–8478 (2022)

23. Chen, Y., Liu, J., Zhang, X., Qi, X., Jia, J.: VoxelNeXt: fully sparse voxelnet for 3D Object detection and tracking. In: CVPR, pp. 21674–21683 (2023)

24. Law, H., Deng, J.: CornerNet: detecting objects as paired keypoints. In: Ferrari, V., Hebert, M., Sminchisescu, C., Weiss, Y. (eds.) Computer Vision – ECCV 2018. LNCS, vol. 11218, pp. 765–781. Springer, Cham (2018). https://doi.org/10.1007/978-3-030-01264-9_45

25. Yang, Z., Sun, Y., Liu, S., Jia, J.: 3DSSD: point-based 3D single stage object detector. In: CVPR, pp. 11040–11048 (2020)

26. Lin, T.Y., Goyal, P., Girshick, R., He, K., Dollár, P.: Focal loss for dense object detection. In: ICCV, pp. 2980–2988 (2017)

27. Team O.D.: OpenPCDet: an open-source toolbox for 3D object detection from point clouds (2020). https://github.com/open-mmlab/OpenPCDet

Traffic Sign Recognition Model Based on Small Object Detection

Fei Gao[✉], Wanjun Huang, Xiuqi Chen, and Libo Weng

College of Computer, Zhejiang University of Technology, Hangzhou 310023, China
gfei_jack@163.com

Abstract. Traffic sign recognition is a popular task in the field of computer vision, but it faces challenges such as small object size, complex scenes, and real-time requirements. In this paper, a model framework is proposed to comprehensively improves the detection and recognition of traffic signs. To address small objects, FlexCut data augmentation is introduced, which generates non-repetitive sub-images through the strategy of maximizing sample region cropping. This approach enhances the detection ability of small objects. Additionally, PIoU loss function based on keypoints is also investigated, which accurately guides the position and shape of the bounding boxes by considering factors such as overlap area, distance, aspect ratio, and geometric size. Furthermore, the YOLOv5s network is enhanced by integrating the TransformerBlock module, SimAM attention mechanism, and Decoupled detection head to enhance the receptive field and feature extraction capability. In the experiments conducted on the TT100K dataset,, the proposed YOLOv5T achieves significant performance with an mAP@0.5 of 87.5% and an mAP@0.5:0.95 of 66.1%. These results validate the effectiveness of the proposed approach in addressing traffic sign recognition problems.

Keywords: Small object · Traffic sign recognition · Data augmentation · Loss function

1 Introduction

Traffic signs are crucial for guiding and warning vehicles on roads. Various methods have been developed for traffic sign detection, which can be broadly classified into four categories: traditional handcrafted features, machine learning, LIDAR-based approaches, and deep learning methods. However, traditional approaches have limitations in terms of accuracy, generalization, and robustness, making them unsuitable for real-time applications. Although machine learning methods can assist in fast detection, they often require manual feature engineering and lag behind deep learning methods in terms of accuracy and real-time performance. Recently, there has been growing interest in object detection algorithms based on mobile laser scanning technology. However, these methods face challenges in data collection, calibration, and standardization, which can result in higher costs and pose as obstacles to their widespread adoption.

F. Liu et al. (Eds.): PRICAI 2023, LNAI 14327, pp. 216–227, 2024.
https://doi.org/10.1007/978-981-99-7025-4_18

To comprehensively improve the effectiveness of traffic sign recognition, an innovative framework for traffic sign detection and recognition is proposed. Firstly, FlexCut data augmentation method is introduced to specifically tackle small object sizes. By maximizing the sample region cropping strategy and extreme geometric shapes, non-repetitive sub-images containing all samples are generated, the method generates non-repetitive sub-images that encompass all the samples. This significantly improves the model's detection capability for small objects. Secondly, a keypoint-based PIoU loss function is proposed, which takes into account the overlap area, distance, aspect ratio and geometric dimensions between the object box and predicted box. This precise loss function accurately guides the model in learning the position and shape of the object box. Finally, the YOLOv5s network is enhanced by integrating the TransformerBlock module, SimAM attention mechanism, and Decoupled detection head. This integration aims to improve the model's receptive field and feature extraction capability, thereby effectively enhancing the accuracy of traffic sign detection and recognition. The effectiveness of the proposed YOLOv5T model in addressing key issues in traffic sign recognition is validated through experimental evaluation on the TT100K dataset. The results demonstrate excellent performance and accuracy at different IoU thresholds. The main contributes are as follows:

- FlexCut data augmentation method is introduced to enhance the detection capability for small objects.
- PIoU loss function based on key points is proposed to accurately guide the model in learning the position and shape of the object box.
- A model named YOLOv5T is designed by integrating the TransformerBlock module, SimAM attention mechanism and Decoupled detection head to improve the accuracy of traffic sign detection and recognition.

2   Related Work

2.1   Data Augmentation

The robustness of a model can be enhanced by effective data augmentation through simulating realistic data scenarios, generating diverse equivalent data from limited samples and increasing dataset diversity. Operations like rotation, flipping, and aspect ratio adjustment introduces variations to single images. Another approach involves combining contextual information from different images, including Mixup [22], Cutout [4], CutMix [21], and Mosaic [2]. Mixup blends two randomly selected images with weighted labels. Cutout removes regions from an image to simulate object occlusion. CutMix replaces the cutout region with a corresponding region from another image, and labels are allocated based on the filled region's proportion. YOLOv5's Mosaic technique randomly selects four images, applies scaling, crops, and combines them to create new training samples.

2.2   Loss Function

Early regression loss functions often used L1 norm, L2 norm, and other proxies. UnitBox [19] proposed a cross-linked IoU loss function, which uses the overlap area between predicted and object boxes as a regression constraint. For non-overlapping cases, Hamid Rezatofighi et al. introduced the generalized IoU (GIoU) [10], which constrains the relative distance between the boxes. To address the issue when the object box fully contains the predicted box, Zhaohui Zheng et al. [23] introduced the distance-based IoU (DIoU), as GIoU fails to reflect the actual situation in such cases. They further developed the complete IoU (CIoU) [24], which incorporates overlap area, normalized center point distance, and aspect ratio as constraints, resulting in improved accuracy and convergence speed of bounding box regression. CIoU is an improvement over DIoU and reduces to DIoU when the aspect ratios of the predicted and object boxes are consistent. In current object detection tasks, IoU-based loss functions, including the popular variant alpha-IoU [5], are extensively used for bounding box prediction.

2.3   Deep Learning For Small Object Detection

Li et al. [7] pioneered the use of GANs in small object detection, improving traffic sign detection by generating high-resolution representations to bridge the gap between small and large objects. Yang et al. [18] proposed a coarse-to-fine approach to mitigate the loss of small details caused by downsampling in traffic sign detection. Liu et al. [9] introduced IPGnet (Image Pyramid Guidance Network) to incorporate rich spatial and semantic information at each layer. Leng et al. [6] developed IENet (Internal-External Network) for robust detection using both appearance and context. Yan et al. [15] proposed LocalNet, which focuses on detailed information modeling to enhance small object representation. Lim et al. [8] leveraged multi-scale features and additional contextual information. Singh et al. [13] introduced SNIP (Scale Normalization for Image Pyramids) for selective gradient backpropagation and scale normalization in multi-scale training. Chen et al. [3] presented a feedback-driven data augmentation model for small object detection. Yang et al. [17] proposed an end-to-end deep network with a two-stage strategy for traffic sign recognition. Reveiro et al. [11] utilized laser scanning for reverse calibration-based traffic sign detection.

3   Method

3.1   FlexCut Data Augmentation

The core idea of FlexCut data augmentation is to randomly group all sample images within a batch (with 4 images per group), and then recombine the images in each group using a strategy that maximizes cropping. This process is repeated multiple times to generate diverse recombined image data. Figure 1 illustrates the overall workflow of FlexCut data augmentation.

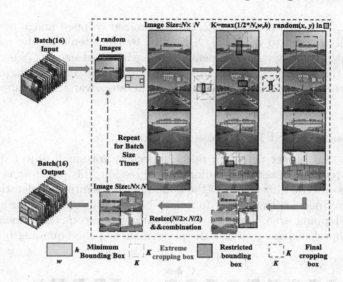

Fig. 1. FlexCut Data Augmentation Flowchart

For each group of sample images with a size of $N \times N$, denoted as $P_t = \{P_1, P_2, P_3, P_4\}$, the minimum bounding box $B_t = \{X_t, Y_t, W_t, H_t\}$ that can encompass the labels is defined, where (X_t, Y_t) represents the center point coordinates of the bounding box, and (W_t, H_t) represent its width and height. Our objective is to extract, for each image within the group, a maximized sample image of size $N/2 \times N/2$ that contains all the labels while preserving their spatial relationships.

While ensuring the inclusion of all labels, the size of the cropping box can be determined using the following formula (Eq. 1):

$$K_{\text{temp}} = \max\left(N/2, W, H\right) \tag{1}$$

Once the size of the cropping box is determined, it is necessary to establish the central coordinates of the cropping box. At this point, the most extreme cropping positions involve placing the cropping box at the bottom-right, bottom-left, top-right, and top-left corners of the sample image. This leads to the constrained range of cropping box center coordinates, as depicted in Eq. (2):

$$\begin{cases} X_{\max} = \min\left(X - W/2 + K_{\text{temp}}/2, N - K_{\text{temp}}/2\right) \\ X_{\min} = \max\left(X + W/2 - K_{\text{temp}}/2, K_{\text{temp}}/2\right) \\ Y_{\max} = \min\left(Y - H/2 + K_{\text{temp}}/2, N - K_{\text{temp}}/2\right) \\ Y_{\min} = \max\left(Y + H/2 - K_{\text{temp}}/2, K_{\text{temp}}/2\right) \end{cases} \tag{2}$$

By randomly selecting values for $X' \in [X_{\min}, X_{\max}]$ and $Y' \in [Y_{\min}, Y_{\max}]$, the maximized cropping box $B' = \{X', Y', K_{\text{temp}}, K_{\text{temp}}\}$ can be obtained. Cropping of size $K_{\text{temp}}/2 \times K_{\text{temp}}/2$ can then be performed at the position with center coordinates (X', Y'), resulting in a maximized cropped image containing all labels. If K_{temp} is greater than $N/2$, the maximized cropped image needs to be proportionally resized to $N/2 \times N/2$. Finally, by concatenating the resulting 4 maximized sample images, an augmented sample image of size $N \times N$ is obtained. To enhance the diversity of the sample images, the FlexCut data augmentation process can be repeated multiple times to generate a variety of sample image data.

3.2   Keypoint-Based PIoU Loss Function

Considering that object detection tasks, especially for small object detection, have higher requirements for bounding box regression, this paper aims to incorporate the geometric dimensions of the bounding boxes into consideration of the loss function. Specifically, the loss function should fully consider four geometric factors: overlapping area, distance, aspect ratio, and geometric dimensions, in order to comprehensively evaluate the performance of the bounding boxes.

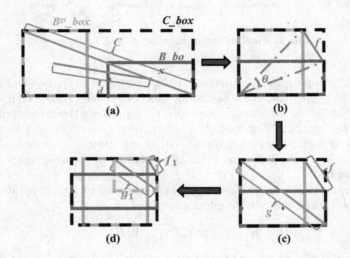

Fig. 2. Normalized distance, aspect ratio, and geometric dimensions

The Point-based Intersection over Union (PIoU) loss function can be defined as Eq. (3):

$$L_{PIoU} = \lambda + \alpha + \beta \qquad (3)$$

In Eq. (3), the three terms, λ, α, and β, represent the overlapping area, distance, and geometric dimensions/aspect ratio, respectively. β is a special term that combines the geometric dimensions and aspect ratio with unified constraints. The formulas for all the constraint terms are shown in Eq. (4):

$$\begin{cases} \lambda = 1 - IoU \\ \alpha = \dfrac{\rho^2(b, b^{gt})}{c^2} \\ \beta = \dfrac{f^2}{g^2} \end{cases} \qquad (4)$$

In the equation, λ represents the constraint on the overlapping area, which is the Intersection over Union (IoU) loss function. α represents the constraint on the distance between the predicted box and the ground truth box. The variables $b = (x, y)$ and $b^{gt} = (x^{gt}, y^{gt})$ denote the center points of the predicted box B and the ground truth box B^{gt}, respectively. In Fig. 2(a) of the diagram, c represents the diagonal length of the box C, which is the minimum bounding box that encloses both the predicted box B and the ground truth box B^{gt}. ρ denotes the Euclidean distance.

If we consider aligning the starting points of the predicted box B and the ground truth box B^{gt}, as shown in Fig. 2(b) and 2(c) of the diagram, f can represent the distance between the two boxes in terms of geometric shape differences, and g is the diagonal length of the minimum bounding box. From this, we can see that the key to the unified constraint on geometric dimensions and aspect ratio lies in the constraint on f. If we further expand β, we can obtain Eq. (5):

$$\begin{cases} f^2 = 4f_1^2 = \left(w^{gt} - w\right)^2 + \left(h^{gt} - h\right)^2 \\ g^2 = 4g_1^2 = \max\left(w^{gt}, w\right)^2 + \max\left(h^{gt}, h\right)^2 \\ \beta = \frac{\left(w^{gt} - w\right)^2 + \left(h^{gt} - h\right)^2}{\max(w^{gt}, w)^2 + \max(h^{gt}, h)^2} \end{cases} \tag{5}$$

In the equation, w, h, w_g^{gt}, and h_g^{gt} represent the width and height of the predicted box B and the ground truth box B^{gt}, respectively. If we align the center points of the predicted box B and the ground truth box B^{gt}, as shown in Fig. 2(d) of the diagram, eliminating the influence of the normalized distance represented by the α term, we can observe that the β term remains unaffected. As one of the loss terms, β ensures that the PIoU loss function does not degrade like GIoU or DIoU under certain conditions.

3.3   The Proposed YOLOv5T

By implementing optimizations in three aspects of the YOLOv5 network architecture, we have designed an enhanced YOLOv5 model named YOLOv5T. In the Backbone section, it integrates the TransformerBlock [1] module as the input layer of SPPF to enhance the feature extraction capability. In the Neck section, it introduces the SimAM [16] attention mechanism to improve feature representation and generalization. In the Head section, it replaces the original three independent detection heads with the Anchor-free Decoupled Head [16], which comprehensively enhances the detector's performance and its ability to perceive object scales. The overall network structure of YOLOv5T is depicted in Fig. 3, where the red box represents modules that are either optimized or newly added based on the original YOLOv5 network structure.

Integrating the TransformerBlock into the BackBone structure strengthens the capturing of relationships between input feature maps, thus extracting richer contextual information and enhancing feature representation. The core of the C3TR module is the TransformerBlock, which is primarily applied to the feature

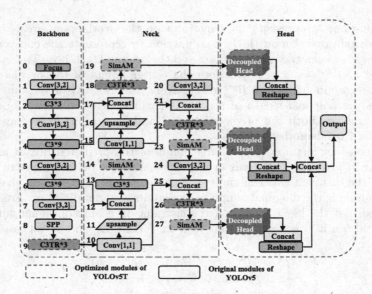

Fig. 3. YOLOv5T architecture

extraction part of the backbone network, replacing the previous C3 input module of SPPF. The Transformer layer in the TransformerBlock relies on the self-attention mechanism. The self-attention mechanism can capture global dependencies within a sequence. In the self-attention mechanism, each element in the input sequence can interact with other elements to determine its importance within the entire sequence. It can then reweight the inputs based on these importance scores.

By applying the SimAM attention mechanism after each aggregation operation in the Neck section, it serves two main purposes. Firstly, it adaptively calculates the similarity between features, weights, and fuses features with high similarity to enhance the feature representation and generalization capabilities. Secondly, the SimAM module itself does not introduce any additional parameters, thereby improving the training and inference performance of the model without significantly increasing computational complexity or the number of parameters.

For traffic sign detection, which belongs to the small object detection task, it requires the detector to have high sensitivity to object sizes. The decoupled detection head, compared to the original YOLOv5 detection head, achieves the following two advantages: Firstly, by decoupling the classification and regression tasks, it speeds up the model training process. Secondly, based on the anchor-free approach, it better adapts to different sizes of object detection tasks, thus improving the detection accuracy.

4   Experiments

4.1   Dataset

We conducted comprehensive experiments on the TT100K dataset. This dataset offers nearly 100,000 street view images, encompassing 30,000 instances of traffic signs. These street view images capture a diverse range of lighting intensities and weather conditions, while the capture angles closely resemble a driver's perspective. Within the TT100K dataset, the traffic signs correspond to 45 distinct categories. Each traffic sign instance is meticulously annotated with category labels, bounding boxes, and pixel masks. The images boast a resolution of 2048 × 2048 pixels. Notably, approximately 42% of the traffic signs in the TT100K dataset fall into the category of small objects, with a pixel area smaller than 32 × 32. Consequently, performing tasks such as traffic sign detection and recognition on the TT100K dataset presents a challenging endeavor.

4.2   Experimental Analysis

To validate the effectiveness of our designed YOLOv5T network, we conducted ablation experiments on the TT100K dataset using the YOLOv5T network. The objects of dismantling mainly included the combination of PIoU loss function and FlexCut data augmentation, the Transformer module, the SimAM attention mechanism, and the anchor-free-based Decoupled detection head. The basic network for comparison included the original YOLOv5s-org network and the

Fig. 4. Example Detection Results of YOLOv5s and YOLOv5T-Ours Models

YOLOv5s-Base network, which includes the PIoU-based baseline loss and Flex-Cut data augmentation method. The image input size for the dismantling experiments was mainly 640 × 640, with some experiments conducted on images of size 1280 × 1280 to assess the overall performance of the model.

The results of the dismantling experiments on the YOLOv5T network are shown in Table 1. From the table, it can be observed that under the 640x640 image input condition, the combination of PIoU loss function and FlexCut data augmentation achieved a 1.5% improvement in mAP@0.5 and a 0.7% improvement in mAP@0.5:0.95. The network structure optimization based on the Transformer module, SimAM attention mechanism, and Decoupled detection head achieved a combined improvement of 2.4% in mAP@0.5 and 0.9% in mAP@0.5:0.95. The overall YOLOv5T model, when combined with the PIoU loss function and FlexCut augmentation technique, achieved a 3.8% improvement in mAP@0.5 and a 1.9% improvement in mAP@0.5:0.95 compared to the original YOLOv5s model.

Table 1. Optimization ablation experiments of YOLOv5T on the TT100K dataset

Model	Parameters (M)	F1	mAP@0.5 (%)	mAP@0.5: 0.95(%)	Resolution
YOLOv5s-org	7.17	80.9	83.7	64.2	640 × 640
(CIoU+Mosaic)	7.18	91.1	93.8	73.9	1280 × 1280
YOLOv5s-org	7.17	81.9	84.9	64.5	640 × 640
(PIoU+Mosaic)	7.18	91.6	93.9	74.0	1280 × 1280
YOLOv5s-org	7.17	80.9	84.2	64.1	640 × 640
(CIoU+FlexCut)	7.18	91.2	93.9	74.0	1280 × 1280
YOLOv5s-Base	7.17	82.1	85.2	64.9	640 × 640
(PIoU+FlexCut)	7.18	91.7	94.3	74.6	1280 × 1280
Base+TransformerBlock	7.14	82.8	86.2	65.2	640 × 640
Base+SimAM	7.17	82.7	85.7	65.0	640 × 640
Base+Anchor free	8.90	83.1	85.9	65.3	640 × 640
YOLOv5T Ours(Base+all) improv.±	**8.93**	**85.5**	**87.5 + 3.8**	**66.1 + 1.9**	640 × 640
	8.94	**92.3**	**94.9 + 1.1**	**75.2 + 0.6**	1280 × 1280

To evaluate the overall optimization effect of YOLOv5T, it was compared with other models based on YOLOv5s, including YOLOv5s-A2 [20], SC-YOLO [12], and CDFF-s [14]. The comparison results are displayed in Table 2, where the experimental data for YOLOv5s-A2, SC-YOLO, and CDFF-s are sourced from the original works. From the table, it can be observed that although YOLOv5T model has some detection optimization advantages for traffic sign recognition tasks, it suffers from the issue of having a larger number of network parameters, which requires further optimization. However, it should be noted that the comparison was conducted under GPU limitations, which may affect the performance comparison.

The YOLOv5s and YOLOv5T models were tested on the validation set, and some detection results are shown in the figure. From the examples in the detection results, it can be observed that the YOLOv5T model has better capabilities in detecting small objects compared to the YOLOv5s model. This can be seen in

Table 2. Experimental Results for Traffic Sign Detection and Recognition Task

Model	Parameters (M)	mAP@0.5 (%)	F1	FPS (f/s)	Resolution	GPU
YOLOv5s-org	7.17	83.7	80.9	76.9	640 × 640	RTX 2070S
YOLOv5s-A2 [20]	7.9	87.3	–	**87.7**	640 × 640	RTX 3060
SC-YOLO [12]	7.2	**90.4**	87.2	33.7	640 × 640	RTX3080
CDFF-s [14]	–	90.13	–	62.5	608 × 608	Titan V
YOLOv5T – Ours	8.93	87.5	**85.5**	47.6	640 × 640	RTX 2070S

the specific comparison between Fig. 4(a-1) and Fig. 4(b-1). Additionally, there is a slight improvement in the confidence level of traffic sign recognition. Please refer to the comparisons between Fig. 4(a-2) and Fig. 4(b-2) for more detailed information.

5   Conclusion

This research paper focuses on the field of traffic sign detection and recognition. Firstly, a FlexCut data augmentation strategy is proposed to maximize the preservation of positive samples and image semantics. Secondly, a keypoint-based PIoU (Position-sensitive Intersection over Union) loss function is introduced to further accurately guide the position and shape of predicted bounding boxes. Lastly, a traffic sign detection and recognition model named YOLOv5T is designed based on the YOLOv5s network, which comprehensively optimizes the performance of traffic sign detection and recognition. Experimental results on the TT100K dataset demonstrate that YOLOv5T is a fast, lightweight, and high-precision model. Based on the current experimental results, noticeable progress has been achieved through a series of improvements. However, there are still certain limitations, as the experiments have been conducted solely on the TT100K dataset. Subsequent research will involve conducting similar experiments on a broader range of traffic sign datasets.

Acknowledgements. This work is being supported by the National Key Research and Development Project of China under Grant No. 2020AAA0104001, the Zhejiang Lab. under Grant No. 2019KD0AD011005, the Zhejiang Provincial Science and Technology Planning Key Project of China under Grant No. 2021C03129, and the Zhejiang Provincial Natural Science Foundation of China under Grant No.LQ22F020008.

References

1. Ashish, V.: Attention is all you need. In: Advances Neural Information Processing system **30**, I (2017)
2. Bochkovskiy, A., Wang, C.Y., Liao, H.Y.M.: Yolov4: optimal speed and accuracy of object detection. arXiv Preprint. arXiv:2004.10934 (2020)
3. Chen, C., et al.: RRNet: a hybrid detector for object detection in drone-captured images. In: Proceedings of the IEEE/CVF International Conference on Computer Vision Workshops (2019)

4. DeVries, T., Taylor, G.W.: Improved regularization of convolutional neural networks with cutout. arXiv preprint arXiv:1708.04552 (2017)
5. He, J., Erfani, S., Ma, X., Bailey, J., Chi, Y., Hua, X.S.: Alpha-IoU: a family of power intersection over union losses for bounding box regression. In: Advanced in Neural Information Processing Systems, vol. 34, pp. 20230–20242 (2021)
6. Leng, J., Ren, Y., Jiang, W., Sun, X., Wang, Y.: Realize your surroundings: exploiting context information for small object detection. Neurocomputing **433**, 287–299 (2021)
7. Li, J., Liang, X., Wei, Y., Xu, T., Feng, J., Yan, S.: Perceptual generative adversarial networks for small object detection. In: Proceedings of the IEEE Conference on Computer Vision and Pattern Recognition, pp. 1222–1230 (2017)
8. Lim, J.S., Astrid, M., Yoon, H.J., Lee, S.I.: Small object detection using context and attention. In: 2021 International Conference on Artificial Intelligence in Information and Communication (ICAIIC), pp. 181–186. IEEE (2021)
9. Liu, Z., Gao, G., Sun, L., Fang, L.: IPG-Net: image pyramid guidance network for small object detection. In: Proceedings of the IEEE/CVF Conference on Computer Vision and Pattern Recognition Workshops, pp. 1026–1027 (2020)
10. Rezatofighi, H., Tsoi, N., Gwak, J., Sadeghian, A., Reid, I., Savarese, S.: Generalized intersection over union: a metric and a loss for bounding box regression. In: Proceedings of the IEEE/CVF Conference on Computer Vision and Pattern Recognition, pp. 658–666 (2019)
11. Riveiro, B., Díaz-Vilariño, L., Conde-Carnero, B., Soilán, M., Arias, P.: Automatic segmentation and shape-based classification of retro-reflective traffic signs from mobile lidar data. IEEE J. Sel. Top. Appl. Earth Obs. Remote Sens. **9**(1), 295–303 (2015)
12. Shi, Y., Li, X., Chen, M.: SC-YOLO: a object detection model for small traffic signs. IEEE Access **11**, 11500–11510 (2023)
13. Singh, B., Davis, L.S.: An analysis of scale invariance in object detection snip. In: Proceedings of the IEEE Conference on Computer Vision and pattern Recognition, pp. 3578–3587 (2018)
14. Wang, L., Wang, L., Zhu, Y., Chu, A., Wang, G.: CDFF: a fast and highly accurate method for recognizing traffic signs. Neural Comput. Appl. **35**(1), 643–662 (2023)
15. Yan, Z., Zheng, H., Li, Y., Chen, L.: Detection-oriented backbone trained from near scratch and local feature refinement for small object detection. Neural Process. Lett. **53**, 1921–1943 (2021)
16. Yang, L., Zhang, R.Y., Li, L., Xie, X.: SimAM: a simple, parameter-free attention module for convolutional neural networks. In: International Conference on Machine Learning, pp. 11863–11874. PMLR (2021)
17. Yang, T., Long, X., Sangaiah, A.K., Zheng, Z., Tong, C.: Deep detection network for real-life traffic sign in vehicular networks. Comput. Netw. **136**, 95–104 (2018)
18. Yang, Z., et al.: Prior knowledge guided small object detection on high-resolution images. In: 2019 IEEE International Conference on Image Processing (ICIP), pp. 86–90. IEEE (2019)
19. Yu, J., Jiang, Y., Wang, Z., Cao, Z., Huang, T.: UnitBox: an advanced object detection network. In: Proceedings of the 24th ACM International Conference on Multimedia, pp. 516–520 (2016)
20. Yuan, X., Kuerban, A., Chen, Y., Lin, W.: Faster light detection algorithm of traffic signs based on yolov5s-a2. IEEE Access, 19395–19404 (2022)
21. Yun, S., Han, D., Oh, S.J., Chun, S., Choe, J., Yoo, Y.: CutMix: regularization strategy to train strong classifiers with localizable features. In: Proceedings of the IEEE/CVF International Conference on Computer Vision, pp. 6023–6032 (2019)

22. Zhang, H., Cisse, M., Dauphin, Y., Lopez-Paz, D.: Mixup: beyond empirical risk management. In: 6th International Conference Learning Representations (ICLR), pp. 1–13 (2018)
23. Zheng, Z., Wang, P., Liu, W., Li, J., Ye, R., Ren, D.: Distance-IoU loss: faster and better learning for bounding box regression. In: Proceedings of the AAAI Conference on Artificial Intelligence, vol. 34, pp. 12993–13000 (2020)
24. Zheng, Z., et al.: Enhancing geometric factors in model learning and inference for object detection and instance segmentation. IEEE Trans. Cybern. **52**(8), 8574–8586 (2021)

A Multi-scale Multi-modal Multi-dimension Joint Transformer for Two-Stream Action Classification

Lin Wang, Ammar Hawbani$^{(\boxtimes)}$, and Yan Xiong

University of Science and Technology of China, Hefei 230026, Anhui, China
xiaquhet@mail.ustc.edu.cn, {anmande,yxiong}@ustc.edu.cn

Abstract. Multi-modal, multi-scale, and multi-dimensional (spatiotemporal) video representation learning have *each* been studied adequately in its own form, respectively, but rather in an *isolated* way from each other, not yet *jointly*. It is well known in statistical machine learning that *joint* data distributions provide new information that cannot be achieved by its individual components. Therefore we propose M^3T: a Multi-scale Multi-modal Multi-dimension (M^3) joint Transformer model for two-stream video representation learning, which is built upon a two-stream multi-scale vision transformer backbone. M^3T is densely augmented with three attention modules, which are mutually orthogonal against each other, at each down-sampling layer of the backbone. Experiments conducted on the Kinetics 400 data set demonstrate the effectiveness of the proposed method. The qualitative performance also demonstrates that our model can learn more informative complementary representation.

Keywords: Multi-modal representation learning · Vision transformer · Video classification · Self-supervision · Optical flow regression

1 Introduction

It is well known in existing video representation learning research, respectively, that:

- Multi-modal joint distribution provides new information that each individual composing modalities *cannot* achieve;
- Multi-scale joint distribution provides new information that each individual composing sampling resolutions *cannot* achieve;
- Multi-dimension (spatiotemporal) joint distribution provides new information that each individual composing dimensions, *cannot* achieve, *neither* spatially, *nor* temporally;

However, a *further* performance-driven potential from multiple distributions is ignored in existing works, which is: the multi-modal + multi-scale + multi-dimension joint distribution also yields, secondarily, new information that each individual forms of its composing sub-multiple distributions *cannot* achieve (Fig. 1).

To address the above absence in the current work, we propose M^3T, which augments the hierarchical down-sampling backbones of the deep neural network with horizontal and vertical cross-attentions, so as to facilitate the triple cross-complementary representation learning of two-stream video data (Fig. 2 and 3).

F. Liu et al. (Eds.): PRICAI 2023, LNAI 14327, pp. 228–233, 2024.
https://doi.org/10.1007/978-981-99-7025-4_19

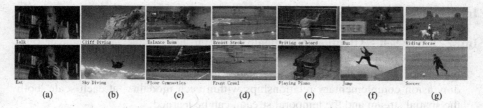

Fig. 1. The dominant characteristics of real world actions vary across both scales and modalities, both appearances and motions, both spatially and temporally, which naturally raise the need for multi-scale multi-modal multi-dimension 3-fold representation learning methods.

2   The Proposed Method

The proposed M³T is built upon a two-stream multi-scale vision transformer backbone, densely augmented with three attention modules, which are mutually orthogonal against each other, at each down-sampling layers of the backbone:

Intra - Layer Cross - Attention (HA) firstly, in the *horizontal* direction within the layer, focusing on the learning of cross - modal complementary relationships;

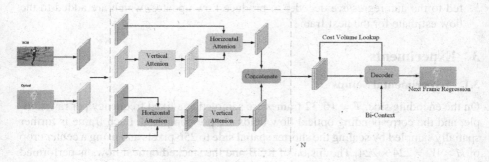

Fig. 2. The upper-level architecture of our proposed M³T, consists of two branches of MViT [2] with identical internal structures but different input modalities. The internal structure of the proposed layer-by-layer horizontal and vertical cross-attentions is only shown at the first layer (subsequent layers remain the same and are thus omitted).

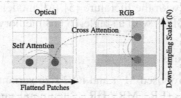

Fig. 3. How to decouple self- and cross-attention during the 3-fold (triple) joint distribute pre-training of the two-stream data.

Inter - Layer Soft - Attention (VA) secondly, in the *vertical* direction across stacked layers, focusing on the learning of cross - scale complementary relationships;

Intra - Layer Self - Attention (SA) finally, with the help of the layer-by-layer self-attention, which has already been self-contained by the standard vision transformer backbone, without the need of any newly introduced modifications, the cross - dimension complementary relationships within each modality, at each scale, both the spatial stream and the temporal stream, can be learned;

2.1   Training Schemes

During pre-training, optical flow regression is used as a proxy task:

1. Firstly, extract 8 times down-sampling features for RGB and optical flow frames, normalized by the color scale mapping of [0, 255], and then use the method we proposed to construct two cost volumes.
2. At each iteration, generate supervisory signals by looking-up the difference between the current flow estimate and the index within a pre-computed ground truth cost volume: If the current flow estimate is $flow = (f_x, f_y)$, then the lookup center for pixel location (h, w) becomes $(h + f_y, w + f_x)$. Since there is no optical flow field info provided in the original data set, the ground truth cost volume is approximately extracted by a teacher model [7].
3. The flow estimated for the current frame, together with its contextual features, are fed to the autoregressive decoder to produce flow updates, which are added to the flow estimate for the next frame .

3   Experiments

3.1   Experimental Setups

On the encoding side, $T = 16, 32$ frames are sampled at a fixed frequency per raw sample, and the corresponding optical flow fields are pre-computed. Each frame is further spatially sampled by scaling the shorter spatial side to 256 pixels and using a center crop of $H \times W = 224 \times 224$. The fusion of RGB and the stacked optical flows is performed by non-maximum suppression (NMS) [8]. On the decoding side, the scores of the T frames from the last layer are averaged as the final prediction for that sample. Both pre-training and fine-tuning are trained with ADAM optimizer, with an initial learning rate of 10^{-3}, which decreases to 10^{-4} after entering the saturation. Training schedule stops after $n_{max} = 80$ epochs and 2 augmentation repetitions. More detailed optimization settings are consistent with the literature [5]. All models are trained on 8 Google Cloud Nvidia Tesla V100 GPUs with a single 16 GB memory.

3.2   Results and Discussions

As shown in Table 1, the proposed M^3T and its 2 size variants(Base / Large), 3 spatial sampling resolution variants (LR / MR / HR), 2 temporal sampling resolution variants ($T = 16 / 32$) achieve competitive overall classification accuracies, on the test split of Kinetics-400 [4], under the conventional fine-tuning strategies, where all parameters except the output layer are frozen upon the convergence of the pre-training.

Table 1. The average classification accuracy (%) of the proposed M³T, with three different spatial sampling resolutions ($LR = 224 \times 224/MR = 256 \times 256/HR = 384 \times 384$), two different temporal sampling resolutions ($T = 16 \times 4/32 \times 2$), and MViT backbone variants of two different parameter capacities, across all categories on the Kinetics-400 Val, compared with the S.o.t.a. methods (best values highlighted in bold).

Model	Backbone	Pre-train	Resolution ($H \times W$)	#Frames/Clip† (T)	GFLOPs × Views‡	Params	Accuracy-1(%)	Accuracy-5(%)
TSM [6]	ResNet50	ImageNet	256×256	8	33×10	24.3M	74.1	91.2
X3D-M[3]	X2D	None	256×256	16	6.2×30	3.8M	76.0	92.3
X3D-L[3]	X2D	None	356×356	16	24.8×30	6.1M	77.5	92.9
X3D-XL[3]	X2D	None	356×356	16	48.4×30	11M	79.1	93.9
X3D-XXL[3]	X2D	None	356×356	16	194.1×30	20.3M	**80.4**	**94.6**
ViT [1]	Base-16	ImageNet-21k	224×224	8	179.6 × 30	87.2 M	76.02	92.52
M³T (LR)	MViT-Base 16×4 ($T \times \tau$)	ImageNet-21k	224×224	16	159.2 × 30	75.9 M	79.40	92.91
M³T (MR)		ImageNet-21k	256×256	16	184.3 × 30	75.9 M	79.68	93.55
M³T (HR)		ImageNet-21k	384×384	16	413.7 ×30	75.9 M	80.14	93.91
M³T -32(HR)		ImageNet-21k	384 × 384	32	620.0 × 30	75.9 M	81.18	94.78
M³T -Large(HR)	MViT-Large 16×4	ImageNet-21k	384×384	16	1466.2 × 30	259.9 M	80.40	95.39
M³T -Large-32(HR)		ImageNet-21k	384×384	32	2197.6 × 30	259.9 M	**81.2**	**95.45**

3.3   Visualizations

The layer-by-layer attention visualizations of M³T and its three ablated variants on some representative frame samples on Kinetics 400 Val are shown in Fig. 4. It can be observed that under the effect of cross-dimension, cross-scale, and cross-modality triple orthogonal attention, the M³T shows a consistent improvement in terms of abstract semantic understanding compared to the ablated groups on video content with different characteristics:

- On video samples dominated by global shots from a far perspective, as selected in the first example, "Wind Surfing", "Riding Horse", "Busking", "Cliff Diving", "Sky Diving", "Present Weather Forecast", etc., M³T shows a tendency to shift the gravity center of the vertical attention parameters to the upper layers of the backbone, and the self-attention distribution of the bottom layer tends to be more even, compared with its ablation counterparts;
- On video samples dominated by close-up shots, as selected in the second example, "Eat Dough Nut", "Changing Wheel", "Petting Cat", "Flipping Pancake", "Grind Meat", "Cut Watermelon", "Brush Hair", "Dog Grooming", "Frying Vegetable", "Write", etc., M³T shows a tendency to shift the parameter center of gravity towards the bottom layer of the backbone, and the self-attention distribution tends to show a higher local contrast and a larger variance, compared with its ablation counterparts;
- On video samples dominated by static appearance or dynamic movement patterns, as selected in the third example, "Triple Jump", "Ski Jump", "Drive", "Hitting Baseball", "Golf Chipping", "High Jump", etc., M³T shows a tendency to shift the gravity center of the horizontal attention parameters to one side of the backbone, compared with its

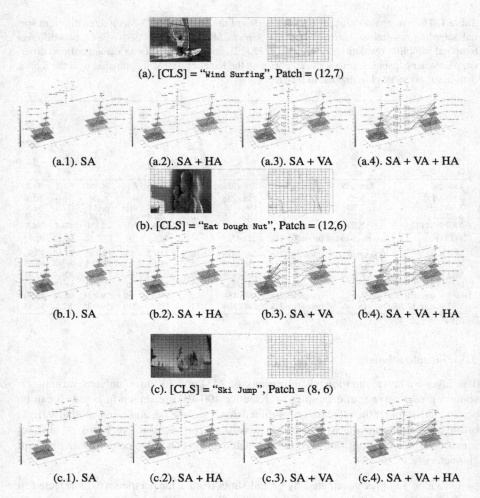

Fig. 4. Attention visualizations of the proposed M^3T (SA + VA + HA) and its three variants, on Kinetics 400, which are: the two-stream MViT [2] backbone (SA), + Cross Modal Attention (SA + HA), + Cross Scale Attention (SA + VA). The color grid indicates the self-attention distribution of the patch position relative to the class label [CLS], and the line thickness denotes the strength of the cross-attention distribution connected to the corresponding patch location.

ablation counterparts, and the self-attention distribution of both sides tends to be more distinct, to better capture the complementary information between two-stream modalities that cannot be shared within each other.

4   Conclusions

With the aim at the exploration of the triple joint cross-complementing capability of multiple scales, dimensions, and modalities, we propose M^3T, whose effectiveness of learning complementary representations from the joint data distribution is verified on Kinetics 400 [4], and qualitative analysis also shows that, the three attention modules promote each other: with the assistance of horizontal and vertical attention, the highly activated self-attentions tend to converge to visual/optical flow regions with more accurate semantic associations, and vice versa. A main disadvantages of this work, for the moment, is that the verification of the effectiveness of the proposed method is mainly based on an empirical standpoint. We hope that interested researchers with a stronger background in statistical machine learning and information geometry can offer a more in-depth insight and push this work to a higher theoretical level. Further exploitations may also include more diverse forms of joint distributions and more diverse scenarios of down stream applications, which we leave for future efforts.

Acknowledgements. This paper is supported by the Innovation Team and Talents Cultivation Program of the National Administration (No. ZYYCXTD-D-202208)

References

1. Dosovitskiy, A., et al.: An image is worth 16x16 words: transformers for image recognition at scale. In: International Conference on Learning Representations (2021). https://openreview.net/forum?id=YicbFdNTTy
2. Fan, H., Xiong, B., Mangalam, K., Li, Y., Yan, Z., Malik, J., Feichtenhofer, C.: Multiscale vision transformers (2021)
3. Feichtenhofer, C.: X3d: expanding architectures for efficient video recognition. In: 2020 IEEE/CVF Conference on Computer Vision and Pattern Recognition (CVPR), pp. 200–210 (2020). DOI: https://doi.org/10.1109/CVPR42600.2020.00028
4. Kay, W., et al.: The kinetics human action video dataset (2017)
5. Kingma, D.P., Ba, J.: Adam: a method for stochastic optimization. In: ICLR (Poster) (2015). https://arxiv.org/abs/1412.6980
6. Lin, J., Gan, C., Han, S.: Tsm: temporal shift module for efficient video understanding. In: 2019 IEEE/CVF International Conference on Computer Vision (ICCV), pp. 7082–7092. IEEE Computer Society, Los Alamitos, CA, USA (nov 2019). https://doi.org/10.1109/ICCV.2019.00718,https://doi.ieeecomputersociety.org/10.1109/ICCV.2019.00718
7. Pérez, J.S., Meinhardt-Llopis, E., Facciolo, G.: Tv-l1 optical flow estimation. Image Process. On Line **2013**, 137–150 (2013)
8. Zhao, J., Snoek, C.G.M.: Dance with flow: Two-in-one stream action detection. In: Computer Vision and Pattern Recognition, pp. 9935–9944 (2019)

Adv-Triplet Loss for Sparse Attack on Facial Expression Recognition

Weitao Li[1,2]([✉]), Shijun Li[1,2], and Lin Shang[1,2]

[1] State Key Laboratory for Novel Software Technology, Nanjing University,
Nanjing 210023, China
{liweitao,211300078}@smail.nju.edu.cn, shanglin@nju.edu.cn
[2] Department of Computer Science and Technology, Nanjing University,
Nanjing 210023, China

Abstract. The susceptibility of current Deep Neural Networks (DNNs) to adversarial examples has been a significant concern in deep learning methods. In particular, sparse adversarial examples represent a specific category of adversarial examples that can deceive the target model by perturbing only a few pixels in images. While existing sparse adversarial attack methods have shown achievements, the current results of sparsity and efficiency are inadequate and require significant improvements. This paper introduces an adv-triplet loss and proposes a search attack method to attack the Face Expression Recognition (FER) system with minimal pixel perturbations. Specifically, we propose an adv-triplet loss function and utilize its gradient information to generate pixels for adversarial examples. Extensive experiments conducted on the CK+ and Oulu-CASIA datasets demonstrate the superiority of our proposed method over several state-of-the-art sparse attack methods.

Keywords: Adversarial examples · Facial expression recognition · Adv-triplet loss

1 Introduction

Deep Neural Networks (DNNs) have significantly succeeded in computer vision tasks, including Facial Expression Recognition (FER), which is a challenging task of automatic expression analysis. With the development of DNNs, FER has been applied in various significant areas such as human-computer interaction [2], surveillance [4] and self-driving cars [5].

Despite the success of current DNNs, they are shown to be vulnerable to adversarial examples [1,3], which are carefully crafted images designed to fool the targeted model by adding imperceptible perturbations to the original clean images. Adversarial attacks are developing rapidly and have achieved remarkable success in fooling DNN-based systems.

In this paper, we propose an adv-triplet loss search attack algorithm to attack and examine the insecurity of current FER systems. We propose a new adv-triplet loss function to perturb the output of FER models. A new adv-triplet

F. Liu et al. (Eds.): PRICAI 2023, LNAI 14327, pp. 234–239, 2024.
https://doi.org/10.1007/978-981-99-7025-4_20

loss function is designed as a guide to search pixels requiring perturbed to generate adversarial examples. The triplet loss function [7] is suitable for nearest neighbour classification, which can be employed for the FER system. The triplet loss minimizes the distance between an anchor and a positive, both of which have the same identity, and maximizes the distance between the anchor and a negative of a different identity. On the contrary, in order to generate adversarial examples that make the targeted model wrong, we aim to maximize the distance between an anchor and the positive and to minimize the distance between the anchor and the negative. Then, we select the optimal pixels to perturb based on the gradient information of the adversarial triplet loss until a successful attack is achieved. We conduct extensive experiments on two databases, including CK+ [6] and Oulu-CASIA [8], to verify the performance of our method.

2   Method

2.1   Problem Definition

We denote $\mathbf{x}$ as the source image and y as its corresponding ground-truth label. A clean input $\mathbf{x}$ is classified as $\arg\max f_c(x) = y$, where $f_c(x)$ is the output logit value for class c. An adversarial example $\mathbf{x}^{adv} = \mathbf{x} + \mathbf{r}$ is generated by adding perturbations to the source image and makes the source image $\mathbf{x}$ misclassified.

To get better sparsity, the sparse attack takes ℓ_0-norm as adversarial perturbation distance calculation formula, which means finding the smallest number of pixels needed to perturb. In this paper, we consider an untargeted attack. So the objective of the untargeted attack and the perturbation under the ℓ_0-norm constraint can be formulated as:

$$\min_{\mathbf{r}} |\mathbf{r}|_0 \text{ subject to } \arg\max f_c(x^{adv}) \neq y. \tag{1}$$

Since Eq.(1) is an NP-hard problem, it can not be solved in polynomial time to get an analytical solution. Then, we resort to finding an approximate optimal solution through an iterative search algorithm. Figure 1 gives an overview of the proposed Adv-Triplet loss Search Attack (ATSA) method.

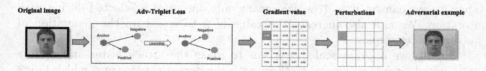

Fig. 1. Overview of the proposed ATSA method.

2.2   Adv-Triplet Loss Function

To generate adversarial examples, we simultaneously aim to maximize the feature distance between images of the same category and minimize the distance between images of different categories.

We have:

$$\mathcal{L}_{adv-tri} = \max(\max_{\substack{j \neq a \\ j = 1, \ldots, K}} \parallel f(x_c^a) - f(x_c^j) \parallel_2^2$$

$$- \parallel f(x_c^a) - f(x_c^i) \parallel_2^2 + \Delta, \ 0)$$

(2)

where x_c^a is the original image that we want to generate an adversarial example, x_c^j and x_c^i are the images from different expression categories and the same expression category of the same identity x_c respectively, $f(x)$ is the output logit value after regularization of the targeted classification model and that means $\parallel f(x) \parallel_2^2 = 1$, K is the number of the total facial expression categories, $\parallel \cdot \parallel_2^2$ is the square of L_2 norm used as the distance metric, and Δ is a margin threshold. Equation (2) attacks in the form of triplet loss, where the distance of the easiest distinguished pairs of images is encouraged to be small. In contrast, the distance of the hardest distinguished pairs of images is encouraged to be large.

2.3   Adv-Triplet Loss Search Attack

We use a binary mask $\mathbf{m}$ to denote whether a pixel is selected and initialize $\mathbf{m}$ with all zeros. In each iteration, we run a forward-backwards pass with the latest modified image $\mathbf{x}_t^{adv}$ to calculate the gradient of the adv-triplet loss function to $\mathbf{x}_t^{adv}$. Moreover, the pixels with more significant gradient values are regarded as contributing more adversaries.

$$\mathbf{g}_t = \nabla_{\mathbf{x}_t^{adv}} \mathcal{L} \left(f \left(\mathbf{x}_t^{adv} \right), f \left(\mathbf{x}^j \right), f \left(\mathbf{x}^i \right) \right)$$

(3)

Overall, we use the gradient information of the loss function as guiding information to generate adversarial examples heuristically. As the value of the loss function decreases, the probability of success in generating adversarial examples also increases.

In each iteration process, we add the first k unselected pixels into the targeted perturbation pixels set, which contain the biggest $\mathbf{g}_t$ values and change corresponding values of binary mask $\mathbf{m}$ into 1. These selected pixels will not be selected in the next iteration, which means we update all the selected pixels in each iteration. In addition, k is a hyperparameter. If we want to get the best sparsity, we can set it to 1, which means only one pixel is selected during each iteration. We can also increase the value of k to speed up the generation of adversarial examples.

Finally, we apply a scaled gradient to make the attack faster and update $\mathbf{x}_t^{adv}$ based on $\hat{\mathbf{g}}_t$ and binary mask $\mathbf{m}$ with the perturb step size ϵ, which limits the maximum deviation of the perturbation. The entire process of the ATSA method is outlined in Algorithm 1.

3   Experiments and Results

Datasets. We test our attack algorithm on deep convolutional neural network architectures with the CK+ and Oulu-CASIA datasets. We use VGG19

Algorithm 1. ATSA: Adv-Triplet Loss Search Attack

Input: Source image $\mathbf{x}_0$, targeted model f, maximum iterative steps N_{max}, perturbations threshold ϵ, select number k, binary mask $\mathbf{m}$

Output: adversarial example $\mathbf{x}^{adv}$

Initialize: $\mathbf{m} \leftarrow 0$, $n \leftarrow 0$, $\mathbf{x}^{adv} \leftarrow \mathbf{x}_0$

1: search pixels until find an adversarial example
2: **while** $n < N_{max}$ and $\mathbf{x}^{adv}$ is not adversarial **do**
3:      $\mathbf{g}_t \leftarrow \nabla_{\mathbf{x}_t^{adv}} \mathcal{L}\left(f\left(\mathbf{x}_t^{adv}\right), f\left(\mathbf{x}^j\right), f\left(\mathbf{x}^i\right)\right)$ ▷ Eq. (3)
4:      $\mathbf{g}_t' \leftarrow \mathbf{g}_t \cdot (1 - \mathbf{m})$
5:      $d_1, d_2, \ldots d_k = \operatorname{argmax}_k(|\mathbf{g}_t'|)$
6:      $\mathbf{m}_{d_1, d_2, \ldots d_k} = 1$
7:      $\hat{\mathbf{g}}_t \leftarrow \frac{\mathbf{g}_t \cdot \mathbf{m}}{|\mathbf{g}_t \cdot \mathbf{m}|}$
8:      $\mathbf{x}_{t+1}^{adv} = \operatorname{Clip}_{\mathbf{x}}\left(\mathbf{x}_t^{adv} - \epsilon \cdot \hat{\mathbf{g}}_t\right)$
9:      $n \leftarrow n + 1$
10: **end while**
11: **return** $\mathbf{x}^{adv}$

---

and ResNet18 as facial expression classification models and use 10-fold cross-validation evaluation methods for training on the datasets. The input size of both datasets is $44 \times 44 \times 3$.

Evaluation Metrics. To evaluate our algorithm and compare it with related works, we report the attack success rate (ASR), the average ℓ_p-norm (p = 0, 1, 2, ∞) of perturbations, and the average execution time.

3.1 Sparsity Evaluation

Results on CK+. The average ℓ_p-norm and the ASR of the generated perturbation on the CK+ dataset of two different classification models are presented in Table 1. The table shows that our algorithm can achieve a 100% attack success rate on both the VGG19 and ResNet18 classification models. For σ-PGD$_0$, under the pre-defined sparsity number 300, it fails to attack with a 100% attack success rate. In detail, the attack success rate of σ-PGD$_0$ on the VGG19 and ResNet18 models are 51.57% and 48.35%, respectively, which are much lower than our algorithm. In the meantime, our algorithm can achieve a 100% attack success rate while only needing to perturb 65.31 pixels on the VGG19 model and 72.48 pixels on the ResNet18 model. Since σ-PGD$_0$ compute the standard deviation of each color channel with two immediate neighbouring pixels and the original pixel, the allowable perturbation values range of pixels is limited, so σ-PGD$_0$ achieves lower ℓ_2-norm and ℓ_∞-norm than our algorithm. Compared to other sparse adversarial attack algorithms, our algorithm achieves the best ℓ_0-norm and ℓ_1-norm on both models. This demonstrates the effectiveness of the proposed method. The Sparse-Fool and our algorithm all achieve a 100% attack success rate. However, since our algorithm adopts an iterative search method, our algorithm significantly outperforms the SparseFool with the lowest ℓ_0-norm, ℓ_1-norm, ℓ_2-norm and ℓ_∞-norm. This also illustrates the superiority of our algorithm.

Table 1. Statistics of attack success rate (ASR) and average ℓ_p-norms ($p = 0, 1, 2, \infty$) of nontargeted attack on CK+ and Oulu-CASIA datasets.

Dataset	Method	VGG19					ResNet18				
		ASR	ℓ_0	ℓ_1	ℓ_2	ℓ_∞	ASR	ℓ_0	ℓ_1	ℓ_2	ℓ_∞
CK+	σ-PGD$_0$	51.57	300.00	35.65	**2.21**	**0.248**	48.35	300.00	34.31	**2.12**	**0.228**
	PGD$_0$	94.79	100.00	69.64	7.29	0.978	88.24	100.00	67.67	7.94	0.980
	SparseFool	100	70.86	38.47	4.08	0.866	100	84.99	33.03	4.31	0.877
	ATSA(Ours)	100	**65.31**	**23.54**	2.54	0.667	100	**72.48**	**27.29**	3.10	0.742
Oulu-CASIA	σ-PGD$_0$	79.34	300.00	**17.12**	**1.13**	**0.185**	77.41	300.00	**20.38**	**1.29**	**0.186**
	PGD$_0$	100	100.00	46.25	5.45	0.908	98.24	100.00	53.14	6.13	0.967
	SparseFool	100	124.96	62.17	4.92	0.648	100	108.62	48.22	3.94	0.761
	ATSA(Ours)	100	**81.97**	26.67	3.92	0.678	100	**80.37**	28.86	3.09	0.743

Results on Oulu-CASIA. Experimental results of different sparse adversarial attack algorithms on the Oulu-CASIA dataset are listed in Table 1. Seen from it, our algorithm achieves a 100% attack success rate on both models. The σ-PGD$_0$ also fails to attack with a 100% attack success rate on the Oulu-CASIA dataset with a pre-defined sparsity number, larger than our algorithm. The PGD$_0$ achieves 100% and 98.24% attack success rates on the VGG19 model and ResNet18 model, respectively. However, our method achieves the same 100% attack success rate with the least number of perturbed pixels. And the ℓ_1-norm, ℓ_2-norm and ℓ_∞-norm of PGD$_0$ are significant higher than our algorithm on both models.

3.2 Invisibility Evaluation

For adversarial examples, invisibility is a crucial evaluation. In Fig. 2, we show some adversarial examples. The adversarial examples are generated under the perturbations $\epsilon = 10$ and the selected number $k = 1$. Compared with the original images, these adversarial examples are almost identical and indistinguishable from the human perception's perspective. Furthermore, these examples of high adversarial quality also show that our method has promising performance in sparsity and invisibility.

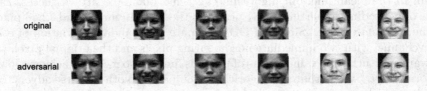

Fig. 2. Adversarial examples for the CK+ dataset, as generated by our method on the VGG19 model. The first row is the original images, and the second row is the corresponding adversarial examples.

Also, as can be seen in Fig. 2, from the second and the last adversarial sample in the second row, the perturbations are concentrated around the critical area: the corners of the mouth and the corners of the eye, which are the essential parts in the FER. This demonstrates that our adv-triplet loss function has minimized the distance of images from different categories, and it pays attention to the expressive features used for facial expression classification.

4   Conclusion

In this paper, we address the vulnerability of current Facial Expression Recognition(FER) systems by introducing an adv-triplet loss search attack method to perturb the output of targeted models. By leveraging gradient information from the adv-triplet loss, our method intelligently selects the most appropriate pixels to perturb until a successful attack achieves significantly better sparsity compared to existing state-of-the-art sparse adversarial attack methods. Furthermore, we highlight the importance of future studies focusing on dynamic image sequences within the FER systems.

Acknowledgement. This work is supported by the National Natural Science Foundation of China (No.51975294).

References

1. Athalye, A., Engstrom, L., Ilyas, A., Kwok, K.: Synthesizing robust adversarial examples. In: Proceedings of the 35th International Conference on Machine Learning, ICML 2018, Stockholmsmässan, Stockholm, Sweden, 10–15 July 2018. Proceedings of Machine Learning Research, vol. 80, pp. 284–293 (2018)
2. Bartlett, M.S., Littlewort, G., Fasel, I., Movellan, J.R.: Real time face detection and facial expression recognition: development and applications to human computer interaction. In: IEEE Conference on Computer Vision and Pattern Recognition, CVPR Workshops 2003, Madison, Wisconsin, USA, 16–22 June 2003, p. 53 (2003)
3. Goodfellow, I.J., Shlens, J., Szegedy, C.: Explaining and harnessing adversarial examples. In: 3rd International Conference on Learning Representations, ICLR 2015, San Diego, CA, USA, 7–9 May 2015, Conference Track Proceedings (2015)
4. Kamgar-Parsi, B., Lawson, W., Kamgar-Parsi, B.: Toward development of a face recognition system for watchlist surveillance. IEEE Trans. Pattern Anal. Mach. Intell. **33**(10), 1925–1937 (2011)
5. Lisetti, C.L., Nasoz, F.: Affective intelligent car interfaces with emotion recognition. In: Proceedings of 11th International Conference on Human Computer Interaction, Las Vegas, NV, USA (2005)
6. Lucey, P., Cohn, J.F., Kanade, T., Saragih, J., Ambadar, Z., Matthews, I.: The extended cohn-kanade dataset (ck+): A complete dataset for action unit and emotion-specified expression. In: 2010 IEEE Computer Society Conference on Computer Vision and Pattern Recognition-workshops, pp. 94–101 (2010)
7. Schroff, F., Kalenichenko, D., Philbin, J.: Facenet: a unified embedding for face recognition and clustering. In: IEEE Conference on Computer Vision and Pattern Recognition, CVPR 2015, Boston, MA, USA, 7–12 June 2015, pp. 815–823 (2015)
8. Zhao, G., Huang, X., Taini, M., Li, S.Z., Pietikälnen, M.: Facial expression recognition from near-infrared videos. Image Vis. Comput. **29**(9), 607–619 (2011)

Credible Dual-X Modality Learning for Visible and Infrared Person Re-Identification

Wen Zhang, Zili Zhang$^{(\boxtimes)}$, Lu Gong, Jiali Zhang, and Mingkang Li

College of Computer and Information Science, Southwest University,
Chongqing 400715, China
maggie2021@email.swu.edu.cn, zhangzl@swu.edu.cn

Abstract. Visible-Infrared person Re-Identification (VI-ReID) is essential for public security. However, it poses a significant challenge due to the distinct reflection frequencies of visible and infrared modalities, leading to a substantial semantic gap between them. A novel modality-transform-based Dual-X method is proposed to narrow the gap between modalities. The modality generators in Dual-X will generate corresponding auxiliary modalities for both visible and infrared modalities, which is achieved through a lightweight channel-level transformation. The newly generated modality images complement the original modal information and are concatenated into the network to facilitate modality-shared and capture modality-specific features. In addition, as softmax is often overconfident on most multi-modal data, an uncertainty estimation algorithm is introduced to quantify the credibility of the model output while providing classification probabilities. By providing reliable uncertainty estimations and reducing uncertainty loss during training, the model's predictions can be more credible. Extensive experiments were conducted, and the results demonstrated that the proposed approach outperforms state-of-the-art methods by more than 3.7% accuracy on both SYSU-MM01 and RegDB datasets, demonstrating the effectiveness of our approach.

Keywords: Visible-Infrared person Re-Identification · Pedestrian Retrieval · Cross-modal Learning

1 Introduction

Person Re-Identification(ReID) is crucial for current intelligent surveillance systems and aims to identify specific queries from a vast gallery of camera acquisitions. Most current ReID works focus only on visible cameras. But in practical applications, visible-infrared cameras are more frequently used for more precise imaging. This modal transition between infrared and visible leads to a large amount of cross-modal data, resulting in a new person Re-Identification task called Visible-Infrared Person Re-identification (VI-ReID).

Unlike single-modality ReID, VI-ReID aims to match person images of the same identity from different modalities. A modality-transform-based learning

© The Author(s), under exclusive license to Springer Nature Singapore Pte Ltd. 2024
F. Liu et al. (Eds.): PRICAI 2023, LNAI 14327, pp. 240–246, 2024.
https://doi.org/10.1007/978-981-99-7025-4_21

approach named Generative Adversarial Network (GAN) [1,10] is often used, which can restore the missing color information by transforming infrared images into visible ones. However, the high number of parameters in GAN and the lack of corresponding cross-modal supervision can lead to unreliable generation quality. Inspired by Transitive Transfer Learning [9] in the field of transfer learning and X-modal [5] in person Re-Identification, a cross-modal modality generator called Dual-X is proposed to reduce the semantic gap between different modalities. The design of the Dual-X modality reformulates the original Infrared-Visible task as an Infrared-X_{rgb}-X_{ir}-Visible task, and the lightweight structure configuration ensures that it does not impose a significant computational burden on the network. As shown in Fig. 1 (a), the physical properties of the two modalities lead to a notable intermodal gap within the same category. By generating the intermediate auxiliary modalities X_{rgb} and X_{ir}, as shown in Fig. 1 (b), the gap is effectively bridged, resulting in precise cross-modal matching.

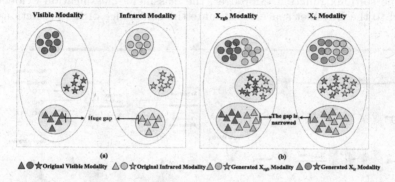

Fig. 1. Illustration of Dual-X. Different shapes represent different categories; different colors represent different modalities.

In traditional deep learning models, softmax is usually used as the output of the network's last layer. However, when facing multi-modal data with distribution shift, using the same softmax for embedding a shared space leads to unreliable results due to different data distributions in the two modalities. Some methods use distributions instead of deterministic weight parameters through Bayesian Neural Networks (BNNs) to give uncertainty to deep models. However, in cross-modal data, high computational costs for BNNs and incomplete prior knowledge can lead to inaccurate model predictions. Therefore, we proposed an uncertainty estimation algorithm based on Evidence Deep Learning (EDL) [7] to provide classification evidence while outputting prediction results.

The main contributions are summarized as follows:

- Generating an auxiliary Dual-X modality to reduce the semantic gap between visible and infrared modality images;

- Introducing an uncertainty estimation algorithm to reduce the classification uncertainty caused by softmax and ensure the output of our model is credible;
- Our framework surpasses the state-of-the-art by more than 3.7% accuracy on both the SYSU-MM01 and RegDB datasets.

2   Methodology

2.1   Overview

As shown in Fig. 2, a pair of visible and infrared images, denoted as V and I, with their labels are fed into the modality generator of the Dual-X module, generating two auxiliary modalities, namely X_{rgb} and X_{ir}. Next, the two original and their respective generated auxiliary modalities are combined and passed through the ResNet-50 feature extractor to learn modality-shared features. For obtaining more fine-grained local features, the shared features are divided into four parts, as proposed by Sun et al. [8], to extract the local features for identity prediction using the softmax function. Moreover, the classifier's classification evidence is mapped to the Dirichlet space to estimate the confidence of the predictions.

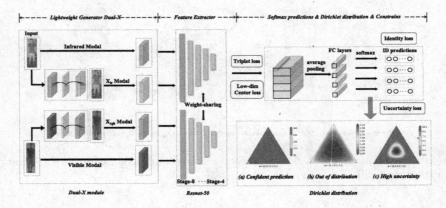

Fig. 2. Framework of the proposed Credible Dual-X Modality Learning method.

2.2   Dual-X Module

To address this challenge without imposing an excessive computational burden on the network, we propose a progressive convolution approach, which involves the generation of two auxiliary intermediate modalities, namely Dual-X. The generator G in Dual-X comprises two 1×1 convolutional layers and a ReLU activation layer and can produce auxiliary modalities for both visible and infrared images. These generated modalities provide supplementary information for improving model learning with the original modalities. The transformation can be mathematically represented as follows:

$$X_{rgb} = G_{rgb}(V), \tag{1}$$

$$X_{ir} = G_{ir}(I), \tag{2}$$

2.3   Uncertainty Estimation Algorithm

To alleviate the issue of unreliable softmax output, an evidence-based uncertainty estimation approach called Subjective Logic (SL) [2] is employed. This approach maps the classification evidence to Dirichlet space to obtain the classification uncertainty. For a K-classification problem, SL assigns a classification probability b_k and an evidence-based uncertainty u_k to each category, where k in $(1, ...K)$ represents the k-th category, and K denotes the total number of categories. The equations for b_k and u_k are as follows:

$$b_k = \frac{e_k}{S_v} = \frac{a_k - 1}{S}, \tag{3}$$

$$u_k = 1 - \sum_{k=1}^{K} b_k = \frac{K}{S}. \tag{4}$$

Through SL, evidence $e_k =< e_1, ... ,e_K >$ and the Dirichlet distribution parameter $a_k =< a_1,...a_K >$ are connected, where a_k is calculated as $a_k = e_k + 1$. The Dirichlet strength S is calculated as $S = \sum_{i=1}^{K}(e_i + 1) = \sum_{i=1}^{K} a_i$.

3   Experiment and Analysis

3.1   Experimental Settings

Datasets. Two publicly available datasets are adopted in our experiments. The SYSU-MM01 dataset comprises 491 identity-labeled images, consisting of visible and infrared images. The model in SYSU-MM01 is tested under *all-search* mode and *indoor-search* mode. On the other hand, the RegDB dataset includes images of 412 pedestrian identities, with ten visible and ten infrared images for each identity. And the evaluation in RegDB employs two query modes, namely *visible-to-infrared* and *infrared-to-visible*.

Evaluation Metrics. In our experiments, three mainstream metrics are adopted: the Cumulative Matching Characteristics (CMC) curve, the mean Average Precision (mAP), and the mean Inverse Negative Penalty (mINP).

Implementation Details. The proposed method is implemented using the PyTorch on a single TITAN Xp GPU. We adopt the ResNet-50 as our backbone and augment it with a modified Part-based Convolutional Baseline (PCB) [8] to extract local features as our baseline. SGD is adopted as our optimizer. The input image is resized to 384×192, and each modality has a batch size of 4.

3.2   Ablation Study

This section presents a separate evaluation of the proposed components on both SYSU-MM01 and RegDB datasets. The results are presented in Table 1.

Table 1. Ablation experiments on SYSU-MM01 and RegDB datasets.

Settings	SYSU-MM01(all)		RegDB(V-I)	
	Rank-1	mAP	Rank-1	mAP
Baseline	63.19	60.61	89.42	81.39
Baseline+Un	66.92	63.33	90.24	82.47
Baseline+Dual-X	69.17	64.80	91.60	84.79
Baseline+Dual-X+Un	**70.04**	**65.38**	**93.05**	**89.23**

3.3 Comparison with State-of-the-Art Methods

As presented in Table 2 and Table 3, our proposed method is benchmarked against state-of-the-art techniques published in top-tier conferences such as CVPR, ICCV, AAAI, and others, within the domain of VI-ReID in the last four years.

Comparisons on SYSU-MM01. The results of the comparison on SYSU-MM01 are shown in Table 2. Our proposed model exhibits significantly superior performance than other methods.

Table 2. Comparisons with the state-of-the-art methods on SYSU-MM01.

Settings		All search					Indoor search				
Method	Venue	Rank-1	Rank-10	Rank-20	mAP	mINP	Rank-1	Rank-10	Rank-20	mAP	mINP
cmGAN [1]	IJCAI2018	26.97	67.51	80.56	27.80	–	31.63	77.23	89.18	42.19	–
D^2RL [11]	CVPR2019	28.90	70.60	82.40	29.20	–	–	–	–	–	–
AlignGAN [10]	ICCV2019	42.40	85.00	93.70	40.70	–	45.90	97.60	94.40	54.30	–
X-Modal [5]	AAAI2020	49.92	89.79	95.96	50.73	–	–	–	–	–	–
DDAG [13]	ECCV2020	54.75	90.39	95.81	53.02	39.62	61.02	94.06	98.40	67.98	62.61
cm-SSFT [6]	CVPR2020	61.60	89.20	93.90	63.20	–	70.50	94.90	97.70	72.60	–
AGW [14]	TPAMI2021	47.50	84.39	62.14	47.65	35.30	54.17	91.14	85.98	62.97	59.23
MCLNet [3]	ICCV2021	65.40	93.33	97.14	61.98	47.39	72.56	96.98	99.20	76.58	72.20
MID [4]	AAAI2022	60.27	92.90	–	59.40	–	64.86	96.12	–	70.12	–
FMCNet [15]	CVPR2022	66.34	–	–	62.51	–	68.15	–	–	63.82	–
Ours	–	70.04	95.78	98.58	65.38	50.11	75.82	97.81	99.42	79.58	75.71

Comparisons on RegDB. The comparison results on RegDB are illustrated in Table 3. Our method demonstrates strong performance in both visible-to-infrared and infrared-to-visible settings.

Table 3. Comparisons with the state-of-the-art methods on RegDB.

Settings		Visible to Infrared					Infrared to Visible				
Method	Venue	Rank-1	Rank-10	Rank-20	mAP	mINP	Rank-1	Rank-10	Rank-20	mAP	mINP
HCML [12]	AAAI2018	24.44	47.53	56.78	20.08	–	21.70	45.02	55.58	22.24	–
D^2RL [11]	CVPR2019	43.40	66.10	76.30	44.10	–	–	–	–	–	–
AlignGAN [10]	ICCV2019	57.90	–	–	53.60	–	56.30	–	–	53.40	–
X-Modal [5]	AAAI2020	62.21	83.13	91.72	60.18	–	–	–	–	–	–
DDAG [13]	ECCV2020	69.34	86.19	91.49	63.46	–	68.06	85.15	90.31	61.80	–
cm-SSFT [6]	CVPR2020	72.30	–	–	72.90	–	71.00	–	–	71.70	–
AGW [14]	TPAMI2021	70.05	86.21	91.55	66.37	50.19	70.04	87.12	91.84	65.90	51.24
MCLNet [3]	ICCV2021	80.31	92.70	96.03	73.07	57.39	75.93	90.93	94.59	69.49	52.63
MID [4]	AAAI2022	87.45	95.74	–	84.85	–	84.29	93.44	–	81.41	–
FMCNet [15]	CVPR2022	89.12	–	–	84.43	–	88.38	–	–	83.36	–
Ours	–	**93.05**	**97.70**	**98.99**	**89.23**	**80.80**	**90.63**	**97.91**	**99.08**	**83.45**	**68.96**

4   Conclusion

This paper focused on the task of Visible-Infrared person Re-Identification (VI-ReID). In order to tackle the challenge of cross-modal matching and reduce the semantic gap between cross-modal images, a lightweight Dual-X module is proposed that expands two-mode images into four-mode features with minimal additional cost. Additionally, to mitigate the issue of unreliable softmax results in multi-modal data, an evidence-based uncertainty estimation algorithm is introduced, which maps the classification evidence to the Dirichlet space to obtain the classification uncertainty. Moreover, by proposing an appropriate uncertainty loss function, more classification evidence can be obtained to enhance the reliability of predictions. The proposed method is extensively evaluated on both SYSU-MM01 and RegDB datasets, demonstrating its outstanding performance.

References

1. Dai, P., Ji, R., Wang, H., Wu, Q., Huang, Y.: Cross-modality person re-identification with generative adversarial training. In: IJCAI, p. 6 (2018)
2. Han, Z., Zhang, C., Fu, H., Zhou, J.T.: Trusted multi-view classification. arXiv preprint arXiv:2102.02051 (2021)
3. Hao, X., Zhao, S., Ye, M., Shen, J.: Cross-modality person re-identification via modality confusion and center aggregation. In: Proceedings of the IEEE/CVF International Conference on Computer Vision, pp. 16403–16412 (2021)
4. Huang, Z., Liu, J., Li, L., Zheng, K., Zha, Z.J.: Modality-adaptive mixup and invariant decomposition for rgb-infrared person re-identification. arXiv preprint arXiv:2203.01735 (2022)
5. Li, D., Wei, X., Hong, X., Gong, Y.: Infrared-visible cross-modal person re-identification with an x modality. In: Proceedings of the AAAI Conference on Artificial Intelligence, pp. 4610–4617 (2020)
6. Lu, Y., et al.: Cross-modality person re-identification with shared-specific feature transfer. In: Proceedings of the IEEE/CVF Conference on Computer Vision and Pattern Recognition, pp. 13379–13389 (2020)

7. Sensoy, M., Kaplan, L., Kandemir, M.: Evidential deep learning to quantify classification uncertainty. In: Advances in Neural Information Processing Systems, pp. 3183–3193 (2018)
8. Sun, Y., Zheng, L., Yang, Y., Tian, Q., Wang, S.: Beyond part models: person retrieval with refined part pooling (and a strong convolutional baseline). In: Ferrari, V., Hebert, M., Sminchisescu, C., Weiss, Y. (eds.) ECCV 2018. LNCS, vol. 11208, pp. 501–518. Springer, Cham (2018). https://doi.org/10.1007/978-3-030-01225-0_30
9. Tan, B., Song, Y., Zhong, E., Yang, Q.: Transitive transfer learning. In: Proceedings of the 21th ACM SIGKDD International Conference on Knowledge Discovery and Data Mining, pp. 1155–1164 (2015)
10. Wang, G., Zhang, T., Cheng, J., Liu, S., Yang, Y., Hou, Z.: Rgb-infrared cross-modality person re-identification via joint pixel and feature alignment. In: Proceedings of the IEEE/CVF International Conference on Computer Vision, pp. 3623–3632 (2019)
11. Wang, Z., Wang, Z., Zheng, Y., Chuang, Y.Y., Satoh, S.: Learning to reduce dual-level discrepancy for infrared-visible person re-identification. In: Proceedings of the IEEE/CVF Conference on Computer Vision and Pattern Recognition, pp. 618–626 (2019)
12. Ye, M., Lan, X., Li, J., Yuen, P.: Hierarchical discriminative learning for visible thermal person re-identification. In: Proceedings of the AAAI Conference on Artificial Intelligence, pp. 7501–7508 (2018)
13. Ye, M., Shen, J., J Crandall, D., Shao, L., Luo, J.: Dynamic dual-attentive aggregation learning for visible-infrared person re-identification. In: Vedaldi, A., Bischof, H., Brox, T., Frahm, J.-M. (eds.) ECCV 2020. LNCS, vol. 12362, pp. 229–247. Springer, Cham (2020). https://doi.org/10.1007/978-3-030-58520-4_14
14. Ye, M., Shen, J., Lin, G., Xiang, T., Shao, L., Hoi, S.C.: Deep learning for person re-identification: a survey and outlook. IEEE Trans. Pattern Anal. Mach. Intell. **44**(6), 2872–2893 (2021)
15. Zhang, Q., Lai, C., Liu, J., Huang, N., Han, J.: Fmcnet: feature-level modality compensation for visible-infrared person re-identification. In: Proceedings of the IEEE/CVF Conference on Computer Vision and Pattern Recognition, pp. 7349–7358 (2022)

Facial Expression Recognition in Online Course Using Light-Weight Vision Transformer via Knowledge Distillation

Jinfeng Wang[✉] and Zicong Zhang[✉]

College of Mathematics and Informatics, South China Agricultural University,
Guangzhou, China
wangjinfeng@scau.edu.cn, zzc199788@126.com

Abstract. It is essential for teachers to master students' current learning status in online courses so that they can adjust teaching mode and rhythm. To accurately describe students' emotion changing during studying online course, we propose a framework that combines a light-weight facial expression recognition(FER) classification model-MobileViT, which has been improved by modifying the fusion block and enhanced by introducing knowledge distillation(KD), with an online course platform. First of all, the face detecting, tracking and clustering are applied to extract face sequence of each student. Then, an improved MobileViT is used to extract emotional features in each frame of online course for classification and prediction. Students' facial images are collected via the camera of their devices, analyzed using MobileViT, and classified into 7 basic emotions. Our improved MobileViT is efficient because it can be processed in real time on each student's mobile device which does not require to send their facial videos to teacher's PC or remote server. Finally, the proposed improved MobileViT is tested on public face datasets RAFD, RAF-DB and FER2013 comparing with some mainstream models. Experimental results indicate that our model has competitive results and better efficiency than others.

Keywords: Facial expression recognition · Online education · Vision transformer · Knowledge distillation

1 Introduction

Many schools and universities are adopting online education as one of the main teaching methods [10]. However, online courses have been widely questioned as they lack timely and effective communication or feedback between students and teachers. Emotions are a fundamental part of humans, which are the most powerful and universal signals used to convey emotional states and intentions [1]. Accurately recognizing facial expressions is of great research significance in education. Most current facial expression recognition tasks typically use large-scale deep convolutional neural networks and multimodal features of audio, faces and

F. Liu et al. (Eds.): PRICAI 2023, LNAI 14327, pp. 247–253, 2024.
https://doi.org/10.1007/978-981-99-7025-4_22

body pose. To protect students' privacy, the best solution is to process facial videos directly on their own devices and only upload processed data rather than raw videos of the learning process [9]. Therefore, an improved light-weight network MobileViT is proposed for facial expression classification, which modifies the fusion module and introduces the pre-trained deep neural network for knowledge distillation.

2   Related Work

Facial expression is one of the most important ways for humans to express their emotions. Researcher divided typical facial expressions into six categories: anger, disgust, fear, happiness, sadness and surprise. Later, Matsumoto [7] provided enough proofs for another universal facial expression. Commonly used public facial expression datasets add neutral to these 6 typical facial expressions to form 7 basic emotional labels, such as FER2013 [3] and RAF-DB [6] and RAFD [5]. Transformers was originally proposed by Vaswani [13] for machine translation. Vision Transformer(ViT) [2] applied transformers to computer vision tasks for the first time. Later, Touvron [12] proposed a Data-efficient image Transformer(DeiT) by introducing teacher-student distillation strategy. At the same time, a hybrid architecture of vision transformers appeared. For example, VOLO [15] proposes an outlook attention. Later, a light-weight hybrid architecture is adaptive to mobile devices, MobileViT [8], was proposed. Knowledge distillation is a technique to transfer knowledge from a complex model to a simpler one. One of the earliest works was proposed by Geoffrey Hinton [4] in 2015. Due to the nature of label softening, distillation can also be considered as a regularization strategy. The teacher's supervision sometimes causes a misalignment between the real label and the image [14,16]. So knowledge distillation can transfer inductive biases in a student model by using a teacher model.

3   Method

A framework is proposed to analyze students' emotions in online courses, which is mainly composed of two parts: student side and teacher side, as shown in Fig. 1. It is separated into two device platforms for individual processing, aiming to ensure that students do not need record and upload personal learning videos on their devices, which can prevent privacy leaks. Students can contribute to the evaluation of the course only by providing their facial features. Besides, online course or conference software cannot completely display the clear facial image of all students in one frame, so students who agree to contribute their faces to help the course evaluation in the learning state can be shown in online course meeting. The improved MobileViT is focus on the fusion module. The local representation in stead of the input features will be concatenated with global representation as shown in Fig. 2. Output of the local representation can learn the low level features of original input image, which can reduce the redundant information carried by the original data. Theoretically, it can provide better image feature

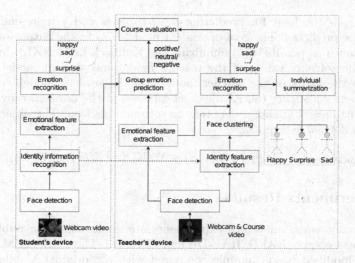

Fig. 1. Online course framework

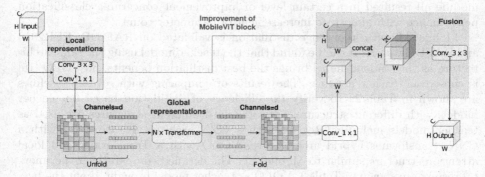

Fig. 2. Improved MobileViT block

information for subsequent concatenating with global representation. Knowledge distillation(KD) is introduced into MobileViT to obtain better performance without changing the model size and parameter amount. Soft targets [11] can be estimated by a softmax function as shown in Eq. (1). A temperature factor τ is introduced to control the importance of each soft target.

$$p\left(z_i, \tau\right) = \frac{\exp\left(z_i/\tau\right)}{\sum_j \exp\left(z_j/\tau\right)} \tag{1}$$

where z_i is the logit for predicting the i-th class and j represents all the classes to be predicted. The goal of student model is to fit the output of teacher model as much as possible by minimizing the Kullback-Leibler(KL) divergence between the softmax values of the teacher model and student model. Let Z_t and Z_s be the logits of the teacher model and the student model. λ denotes the coefficient balancing the KL divergence loss and the cross-entropy(CE) on ground truth labels y, and ψ denotes the softmax function. The objective loss function is defined as Eq. (2).

$$\mathcal{L}_{\text{Total}} = (1 - \lambda)\mathcal{L}_{\text{CE}}\left(\psi\left(Z_s\right), y\right) + \lambda\tau^2 \text{KL}\left(\psi\left(Z_s/\tau\right), \psi\left(Z_t/\tau\right)\right) \tag{2}$$

4   Experiments Results

In this section, some analytical experiments are implemented on public facial emotion datasets, i.e. RAFD, RAF-DB and FER2013. The results of MobileViT using the modified fusion module compared with the original MobileViT are shown in Table 1. Regardless of the size of the model, modifying the fusion module all resulted in a certain level of improvement concerning classification performance with almost no increasement of parameter count.

MobileViT with knowledge distillation is validated on RAF-DB, FER2013 and RAFD datasets. It can be found that the teacher model using the same architecture as the student model brings the best distillation benefits. So VOLO [15] is chosen as teacher network. The results of comparing with several baselines are shown in Table 2. To verify the efficiency of distillation based on teacher models with different structure, networks with different structures are used as teacher models including RegNet with a CNN architecture, CoAtNet with a CNN, transformer hybrid architecture, VOLO with a Transformer and local attention structure similar to MobileViT. The detailed comparative experimental results are shown in Table 3. VOLO as teacher model brought about the best distillation benefits using the same architecture as the student model, although the hybrid architecture of CoAtNet shows the highest prediction accuracy. So, the structure of teacher model should be similar to the student model as possible. Moreover, transformer with local attention structure is a more effective mechanism for image feature extraction, which considers the local representation of the image and inherits the inductive bias of CNNs.

Table 1. Comparing Original MobileViT with modified the fusion architecture.

Model	Params	Dataset		
		RAF-DB	FER2013	RAFD
		Top-1 Accuracy		
MobileViT-XXS	1.268M	73.89%	57.51%	95.45%
MobileViT-XXS(Local)	**1.296M**	**74.51%**	**57.94%**	**95.86%**
MobileViT-XS	2.309M	75.36%	58.71%	97.10%
MobileViT-XS(Local)	**2.398M**	**75.72%**	**58.92%**	**97.72%**
MobileViT-S	5.566M	77.05%	60.30%	97.93%
MobileViT-S(Local)	**5.797M**	**77.61%**	**60.41%**	**98.55%**

Table 2. Comparing MobileViT via knowledge distillation with several models.

Model	Params	FLOPS	Memory	Model size	Dataset		
					RAF-DB	FER2013	RAFD
					Top-1 Accuracy		
EfficientNet-B0	5.247M	0.386G	77.99MB	20.17MB	74.28%	57.37%	95.45%
MobileNet v3-Large 1.0	5.459M	0.438G	55.03MB	20.92MB	72.62%	57.57%	93.79%
Deit-T	5.679M	1.079G	49.34MB	21.67MB	71.68%		
ShuffleNet v2 2x	7.394M	0.598G	39.51MB	28.21MB	75.13%	58.30%	96.07%
EfficientNet-B1	7.732M	0.570G	109.23MB	29.73MB	73.47%	57.23%	94.20%
MobileViT-XXS&VOLO-D2	**1.268M**	**0.257G**	**53.65MB**	**4.85MB**	77.64%	60.50%	95.65%
MobileViT-XXS(Local)&VOLO-D2	**1.296M**	**0.265G**	**53.65MB**	**4.96MB**	**78.75%**	**63.20%**	**96.69%**
ResNet-18	11.690M	1.824G	34.27MB	44.59MB	79.40%	61.19%	98.14%
ResNet-50	25.557M	4.134G	132.76MB	97.49MB	**80.15%**	61.35%	97.72%
VOLO-D1	25.792M	6.442G	179.49MB	98.39MB	79.20%	60.62%	95.45%
Swin-T	28.265M	4.372G	106.00MB	107.82MB	77.18%		97.10%
ConvNeXt-T	28.566M	4.456G	145.73MB	109.03MB	73.63%	56.95%	94.00%
EfficientNet-B5	30.217M	2.357G	274.87MB	115.93MB	75.07%	58.90%	94.82%
EfficientNet-B6	42.816M	3.360G	351.93MB	164.19MB	75.29%	60.54%	95.24%
ResNet-101	44.549M	7.866G	197.84MB	169.94MB	79.60%	61.88%	97.93%
MobileViT-XS&VOLO-D2	**2.309M**	**0.706G**	**135.32MB**	**8.84MB**	78.75%	61.28%	97.72%
MobileViT-XS(Local)&VOLO-D2	**2.398M**	**0.728G**	**135.32MB**	**9.18MB**	79.79%	**63.91%**	**98.34%**
ConvNeXt-S	50.180M	8.684G	233.58MB	191.54MB	74.97%	58.74%	92.75%
VOLO-D2	57.559M	13.508G	300.40MB	219.57MB	79.40%	60.04%	97.72%
ResNet-152	60.193M	11.604G	278.23MB	229.62MB	79.63%	61.91%	97.93%
CoAtNet-2	73.394M	15.866G	589.92MB	280.23MB	**82.89%**	64.76%	98.96%
RegNetY-16GF	83.467M	15.912G	322.94MB	318.87MB	79.24%	62.68%	97.52%
MobileViT-S&VOLO-D2	**5.566M**	**1.421G**	**162.18MB**	**21.28MB**	81.03%	63.50%	98.96%
MobileViT-S(Local)&VOLO-D2	**5.797M**	**1.473G**	**162.18MB**	**22.16MB**	81.42%	**65.19%**	**99.17%**

Table 3. MobileViT performance based on different architectures.

Teacher Model	Dataset			Teacher Model	Dataset		
	RAF-DB	FER2013	RAFD		RAF-DB	FER2013	RAFD
	Top-1 Accuracy				Top-1 Accuracy		
RegNetY-16GF	79.24%	62.68%	97.52%	RegNetY-16GF	79.24%	62.68%	97.52%
CoAtNet-2	**82.89%**	**64.76%**	**98.96%**	CoAtNet-2	**82.89%**	**64.76%**	**98.96%**
VOLO-D2	79.40%	62.13%	97.72%	VOLO-D2	79.40%	62.13%	97.72%
MobileViT(MViT)&KD				MobileViT(MViT)(Local)&KD			
MViT-XXS&RegNetY-16GF	76.17%	58.94%	**96.89%**	MViT-XXS(Local)&RegNetY-16GF	76.14%	59.51%	**97.52%**
MViT-XXS&CoAtNet-2	77.05%	**61.47%**	96.07%	MViT-XXS(Local)&CoAtNet-2	77.31%	61.49%	97.10%
MViT-XXS&VOLO-D2	**77.64%**	60.50%	95.65%	MViT-XXS(Local)&VOLO-D2	**78.75%**	63.20%	96.69%
MViT-XS&RegNetY-16GF	77.41%	60.60%	97.31%	MViT-XS(Local)&RegNetY-16GF	78.23%	60.71%	97.93%
MViT-XS&CoAtNet-2	78.36%	**62.59%**	97.52%	MViT-XS(Local)&CoAtNet-2	79.50%	62.70%	**98.34%**
MViT-XS&VOLO-D2	**78.75%**	61.28%	**97.72%**	MViT-XS(Local)&VOLO-D2	**79.79%**	63.91%	98.34%
MViT-S&RegNetY-16GF	78.78%	62.13%	98.14%	MViT-S(Local)&RegNetY-16GF	79.89%	62.15%	98.76%
MViT-S&CoAtNet-2	79.34%	**63.90%**	98.14%	MViT-S(Local)&CoAtNet-2	80.64%	64.08%	98.55%
MViT-S&VOLO-D2	**81.03%**	63.50%	**98.96%**	MViT-S(Local)&VOLO-D2	**81.42%**	**65.19%**	**99.17%**

5   Conclusion

By modifying the fusion module and adding knowledge distillation, the performance of the proposed MobileViT was improved. A good application embedding this model into online courses is proposed, i.e., a framework of emotion analysis for online course. This framework can be integrated into many existing online learning tools to quickly and accurately evaluate students' emotions during courses. Experiment results showed that teachers can find out whether students are in negative emotions or confused in courses to improve their own curriculum teaching programs and quality of online courses. Finally, the memory usage and parameters of the improved MobileViT are relatively low by comparing with baselines.

References

1. AlZu'bi, S., et al.: A novel deep learning technique for detecting emotional impact in online education. Electronics **11**(18), 2964 (2022)
2. Dosovitskiy, A., et al.: An image is worth 16x16 words: transformers for image recognition at scale. arXiv preprint arXiv:2010.11929 (2020)
3. Goodfellow, I.J., et al.: Challenges in representation learning: a report on three machine learning contests. In: Lee, M., Hirose, A., Hou, Z.-G., Kil, R.M. (eds.) ICONIP 2013. LNCS, vol. 8228, pp. 117–124. Springer, Heidelberg (2013). https://doi.org/10.1007/978-3-642-42051-1_16
4. Hinton, G., Vinyals, O., Dean, J.: Distilling the knowledge in a neural network. arXiv preprint arXiv:1503.02531 (2015)
5. Langner, O., Dotsch, R., Bijlstra, G., Wigboldus, D.H., Hawk, S.T., Van Knippenberg, A.: Presentation and validation of the radboud faces database. Cogn. Emot. **24**(8), 1377–1388 (2010)
6. Li, S., Deng, W., Du, J.: Reliable crowdsourcing and deep locality-preserving learning for expression recognition in the wild. In: Proceedings of the IEEE Conference on Computer Vision and Pattern Recognition, pp. 2852–2861 (2017)

7. Matsumoto, D.: More evidence for the universality of a contempt expression. Motiv. Emot. **16**(4), 363–368 (1992)
8. Mehta, S., Rastegari, M.: Mobilevit: light-weight, general-purpose, and mobile-friendly vision transformer. arXiv preprint arXiv:2110.02178 (2021)
9. Savchenko, A.V., Savchenko, L.V., Makarov, I.: Classifying emotions and engagement in online learning based on a single facial expression recognition neural network. IEEE Trans. Affect. Comput. **13**(4), 2132–2143 (2022)
10. Shen, J., Yang, H., Li, J., Cheng, Z.: Assessing learning engagement based on facial expression recognition in mooc's scenario. Multimedia Syst., 1–10 (2022)
11. Tang, Z., Wang, D., Zhang, Z.: Recurrent neural network training with dark knowledge transfer. In: 2016 IEEE International Conference on Acoustics, Speech and Signal Processing (ICASSP), pp. 5900–5904. IEEE (2016)
12. Touvron, H., Cord, M., Douze, M., Massa, F., Sablayrolles, A., Jégou, H.: Training data-efficient image transformers & distillation through attention. In: Proceeding of International Conference on Machine Learning, pp. 10347–10357. PMLR (2021)
13. Vaswani, A., et al.: Attention is all you need. In: Advances in Neural Information Processing Systems 30 (2017)
14. Wei, L., Xiao, A., Xie, L., Zhang, X., Chen, X., Tian, Q.: Circumventing outliers of autoaugment with knowledge distillation. In: Vedaldi, A., Bischof, H., Brox, T., Frahm, J.-M. (eds.) ECCV 2020. LNCS, vol. 12348, pp. 608–625. Springer, Cham (2020). https://doi.org/10.1007/978-3-030-58580-8_36
15. Yuan, L., Hou, Q., Jiang, Z., Feng, J., Yan, S.: Volo: vision outlooker for visual recognition. IEEE Trans. Pattern Anal. Mach. Intell. (2022)
16. Yuan, L., Tay, F.E., Li, G., Wang, T., Feng, J.: Revisiting knowledge distillation via label smoothing regularization. In: Proceedings of the IEEE/CVF Conference on Computer Vision and Pattern Recognition, pp. 3903–3911 (2020)

AI Impact

A Deep Reinforcement Learning Based Facilitation Agent for Consensus Building Among Multi-Round Discussions

Shiyao Ding$^{(\boxtimes)}$ and Takayuki Ito

Kyoto University, Kyoto-shi, Kyoto 606-8501, Japan
{ding,ito}@i.kyoto-u.ac.jp

Abstract. Achieving consensus among diverse opinions through multi-round discussions can be a complex process. The advent of large language models (LLMs) offers promising avenues for resolving this challenge, given their prowess in understanding and analyzing human sentiments. However, existing approaches typically focus on single-round discussion, limiting their effectiveness in real-world discussion scenarios. In response to this, we proposes a two-layer facilitation agent modeled a multi-round discussion as a Markov decision process (MDP) to foster efficient agreement. The model comprises a high-level reinforcement learning-based agent, deciding the optimal facilitation action such as facilitation time and facilitation prompt. In the low-level, a large language model that generates the facilitation message based on the facilitation action. Our agent dynamically chooses facilitation moments, generates novel content, and directs the discussion towards consensus. Our methodology was validated across several different topic-based discussions, demonstrating excellent performance in achieving agreement swiftly across all.

Keywords: Facilitation agent · Reinforcement learning · Large language models

1 Introduction

Consensus building is pivotal for successful human collaboration and finds applications in domains like large-scale decision-making [5], multi-stakeholder public policy formulation [11], and inter-laboratory comparisons [3], where it becomes particularly crucial when ethical values clash [8]. Although attaining consensus among varied opinions is challenging, advancements in artificial intelligence (AI) have bolstered the consensus-building process. Facilitation agents exemplify this, enhancing the process by condensing discussions, offering guidance, and promoting efficient communication. Chatbots, for instance, facilitate multi-stakeholder discussions, gathering ideas to address conflicting needs and encouraging stakeholders to understand diverse perspectives [13].

Emerging large language models (LLMs) like the GPT-3 [2] present innovative solutions, leveraging their profound ability to discern and assess human

F. Liu et al. (Eds.): PRICAI 2023, LNAI 14327, pp. 257–268, 2024.
https://doi.org/10.1007/978-981-99-7025-4_23

sentiments. Bakker et al. [1] exemplify this by fine-tuning a 70-billion-parameter LLM to craft statements garnering widespread approval. Similarly, Ding and Ito [6] introduced a self-agreement framework, enabling LLMs to independently generate agreements, bypassing the need for human oversight.

However, these models typically consider a single-round case where the process concludes once an agreement is generated. In real-world scenarios, achieving consensus often transpires through multiple rounds of discussions, escalating the complexity of the task. In this paper, we consider to develop a facilitation agent in multi-round discussions which faces two key challenges: 1) determining the dynamic optimal facilitation action relative to different phases of discussions and 2) devising an optimal policy to expedite users' consensus. To tackle these issues, this paper formulates multi-round discussion as a Markov Decision Process (MDP) and introduces a novel two-layer facilitation agent. By formulating the MDP, the paper leverages the principles of reward and punishment in decision-making, enabling dynamic facilitation at any given discussion moment.

The high-level layer consists of a reinforcement learning (RL)-based agent that intelligently determines the optimal facilitation timing. The second layer features a large language model capable of generating agreements based on the current state of the discussion. This two-layer structure aims to supersede the limitations of existing facilitation agents and offer a more dynamic, efficient, and effective facilitation process. The agent is trained to identify the most opportune moments for facilitation, thus ensuring more impactful interventions.

Contrary to traditional facilitation agents, the LLM component of our agent is not confined to the current content. It has the potential to generate new content, offering innovative perspectives or solutions to augment the discussion. Furthermore, it can steer the discussion towards a final agreement, a crucial function missing in many existing facilitation agents. This capability to shepherd a discussion towards consensus while injecting new, relevant content renders our facilitation agent a powerful instrument for productive discussions. We evaluate our model's performance on several different topic-based discussions. For each topic, the proposed method demonstrates impressive efficacy. The results affirm that our facilitation agent can expedite the consensus process among all participants.

Our contribution are summarized as follows.

- We model a multi-user, multi-round discussion process as a dynamic decision-making problem. The objective is to ascertain an optimal policy that enables all users to reach an agreement with fewer discussion rounds.
- We propose a two-layer facilitation agent where the high-level module determines the type of facilitation required; subsequently, a lower-level LLM-based module generates facilitation content in response to the high-level facilitation command.
- We also furnish a standard Gym environment, readily compatible with various RL frameworks. Also, we evaluate our model's performance across various topics, showing the proposed method's commendable efficiency in each case.

2   Related Work

The concept of applying facilitation agent for discussions has been explored and demonstrated to be a promising avenue for enhancing online discussions. For instance, Yang et al., [16] proposed method that utilizes a Case-Based Reasoning (CBR) application to foster crowd-scale deliberation. The CBR approach mitigates the risk of flaming in online discussions by offering a structured and objective methodology for analyzing and discussing cases.

In recent years, the development of the transformer model, unveiled in 2017, has marked a significant milestone in the field of natural language processing (NLP) [14]. Pretrained large language models predicated on this transformer model can be broadly divided into three categories: autoregressive models, masked language models, and encoder-decoder models [9]. Autoregressive models such as GPT [12], make predictions for subsequent tokens based on the preceding sequence. In contrast, masked models like BERT [4] employ a strategy where a portion of the input text is obscured and the model is trained to predict the masked tokens based on the context. Encoder-decoder models, suitable for tasks such as translation, encode the entire input sequence and decode it to produce the output [7].

These Large Language Models (LLMs) have demonstrated significant potential in tasks requiring the reconciliation of diverse opinions. For instance, Bakker et al. [1] explored a multi-user scenario, fine-tuning a 70B LLM to reach an agreement among varying viewpoints. They focused on single-round discussions that conclude once an agreement is generated. Similarly, Ding and Ito [6] introduced a framework called "Self-Agreement" for fine-tuning LLMs to achieve consensus among divergent opinions, independent of human-annotated data. In this framework, the fine-tuning dataset, comprising diverse opinions and agreement sets, is generated by GPT-3.

Traditional facilitation agents, which often produce predefined content or seldom generate new material, may restrict participants in identifying potential agreement candidates. While LLM-based models can produce novel facilitation messages, they typically focus on single-round conversations, limiting their practicality in real-world discussions. To address these challenges, we have designed an LLM-based facilitation agent tailored for multi-user, multi-round discussions that aims to harmonize varied preferences.

3   Problem Formulation

3.1   Problem Description

The multi-round discussion problem initiates with a given topic and each user is assigned a fundamental viewpoint related to it. Consequently, each user formulates a statement grounded in their foundational standpoint. As illustrated in Fig. 1, the topic is "what do you want to eat for dinner", and a fundamental viewpoint is assigned to each user. For instance, Tom's assigned perspective is his dislike for fish, while David's viewpoint reflects his preference for salads.

Firstly, the user Tom initiates the discussion by sharing an opinion related to the given topic. Following this, each user expresses their viewpoint, taking into account the previously shared opinions.

A round is deemed complete when all users have expressed their opinions, paving the way for the subsequent round. Beginning from the second round, we commence the evaluation of each opinion in relation to the inputs (the viewpoints of other users). This process allows us to compute a score vector $[sc_t^1, sc_t^2, ..., sc_t^n]$ for round t, which quantifies the degree of alignment between each opinion and the rest. With this score vector, we can define criteria to ascertain whether the discussion should conclude. For instance, consensus might be considered achieved when all scores exceed a predefined threshold δ, i.e., $\forall i \quad sc_t^i \geq \delta$. This condition implies that all participants' opinions are sufficiently harmonized, indicating that an agreement has been reached. The goal of multi-round discussions is to attain a consensus among various opinions within the fewest possible number of rounds.

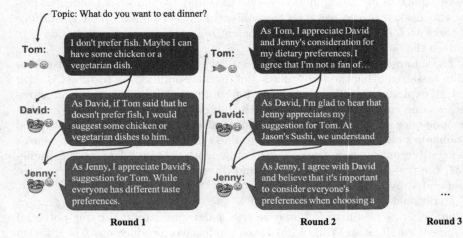

Fig. 1. A example of multi-round discussion process.

3.2   Formulation of Multi-round Discussion as a MDP

We formulate the multi-round discussion as an MDP as shown below.

State A round is defined as an event where all users express their individual opinions. Each user utilizes their fundamental viewpoint, the opinions of other users, and a potential facilitation message as inputs. Once all users have voiced their opinions, the discussion transitions to the next round. At each round, $\mathbf{op} = [op^1, op^2, ..., op^n]$ is the opinion vector recording the current viewpoints of all users. The agreement score function is $f_{as} : FM \times OP \rightarrow [0, 1]$ where $fm \in FM$ can be a facilitation message or a set of other users' current opinions. From this, we can compute an agreement score $sc^i = f_{as}(fm, op^i)$ based on each user's opinion op^i. This score reflects the user's satisfaction with the current stage of discussion. In this paper, we employ gpt-3.5-turbo-0613 to evaluate an agreement score. The prompt for evaluating agreement score includes two parts: The first part is about system role: "I want you return a score between 0 and 1 to evaluate how agreement A match opinion OP. 0 means agreement A does not reflect opinion OP and 1 means agreement A totally reflects opinion OP. At each time I enter the agreement A: and user opinion OP:, then I want you return the score in the format "score=()" ". The second part is the specific content of agreement A and user opinion OP. Through the experiment we found that gpt-3.5 not only return the score but also return the reason of the score.

Therefore, we define the state of round t as:

$$s_t = [sc_t^1, sc_t^2, ..., sc_t^n] \tag{1}$$

This state comprises the opinions op of all users. We define an absorb state s_{abs} where an agreement is considered reached if

$$\forall i \in n, \qquad sc_i \geq \delta \tag{2}$$

Here, $\delta \in [0, 1]$ denotes the agreement score threshold. Determining the value of δ presents a trade-off. If δ is set high, achieving consensus may become challenging, often requiring numerous steps to reach an agreement. Conversely, with a lower δ, it might be simpler to achieve consensus compared to a higher δ value. However, this could lead to participants being less satisfied with the final agreement.

Action. The facilitation agent must decide whether to perform a facilitation action. The action set is defined as $A = \{0, 1, 2\}$ where $a = 0$ means no facilitation action is taken, and each user simply uses the other users' opinions as input, $a = 1$ signifies that the agent generates a facilitation message to all users, and $a = 2$ prompts users for additional opinions. Selecting the optimal actions can be challenging as it dynamically changes with the phase of the discussion.

Reward. The discussion's objective is to reach the absorb state (agreement) as quickly as possible. Hence, we define a reward function as

$$r(s, a, s') = \begin{cases} r_{agreement} & \text{if} \quad s' \quad \text{is} \quad s_{abs} \\ -unit_r & \text{otherwise} \end{cases} \tag{3}$$

where $r_{agreement}$ is a positive value which is much bigger than the value of $unit_r$.

Objective Function. We consider a policy $\pi : S \times A \to [0, 1]$ which is utilized to select a facilitation action based on the current discussion state. That means, given the current state s, the facilitation action a is determined according to policy π. Subsequently, influenced by the chosen facilitation action, the discussion transitions to the next state following the transition function T. This process continues until an agreement state (absorb) s_{abs} is reached.

Consequently, we obtain a trajectory $h = [s_1, a_1, s_2, ..., s_T, a_T, s_{T+1}]$ that encapsulates the dynamic discussion process. Correspondingly, we calculate the discounted sum return $R(h) = \sum_t \gamma^{t-1} r(s[t], a[t], s[t+1])$ of immediate rewards along this trajectory. The objective of reaching an agreement as soon as possible is transferred to optimizing the policy π that maximizes the expected discounted sum return, defined as:

$$\pi^* = \arg\max_\pi E_\pi[R(h)] \tag{4}$$

Here, E_π represents the expectation under policy π and γ denotes the discount factor.

4   Algorithm

We have modeled the dynamic discussion process as a MDP. In this section, we introduce a two-layer facilitation agent designed to learn an optimal facilitation policy for multi-round discussions.

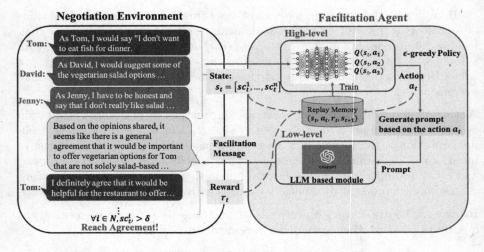

Fig. 2. The framework of the two-layer facilitation agent model.

Model Architecture. Our facilitation agent employs a two-layer architecture, shown in Fig. 2. The high-level layer observes the current state of discussion and instructs the lower-level facilitation agent accordingly. This high-level layer harnesses a Deep Q-Network (DQN), a form of reinforcement learning, to efficiently steer the multi-round discussion process towards an agreement. By defining the problem in terms of states, actions, and rewards, as detailed in the previous section, we enable the DQN to learn the optimal policy regarding the timing and necessity of the facilitation agent's interjections.

Specifically, a DQN-based agent is used, which outputs the Q-values for each action. The Q-value function $Q : \mathcal{S} \times \mathcal{A} \rightarrow \mathbb{R}$, often used to learn the optimal policy for agents, assesses the quality resulting from taking particular actions in given states [10,15]. This DQN accepts as input the opinion vector s_t at each round, containing the scores reflecting user satisfaction with the current phase of discussion. The Q-value function is defined as follows:

$$Q^*(s,a) = \mathbb{E}_\pi \big[R(h) \mid s[1] = s, a[1] = a \big].$$

$Q(s,a)$ represents the expected cumulative rewards, discounted over time, after taking action a in state s. Consequently, an optimal strategy can be derived by selecting the action that maximizes the Q-value.

The action to be performed by the facilitation agent is chosen based on an ϵ-greedy strategy to maintain a balance between exploration and exploitation. The agent will either generate and send a facilitation message or permit users to take others' opinions as input without facilitation. Over time, the agent learns to select actions that lead to an overall higher reward, i.e., reaching the absorb state faster. The DQN continues to guide the discussion process until the absorb state s_{abs} is reached, indicating that a consensus has been achieved among all users. This state is defined by all scores surpassing a threshold δ, indicating the alignment of all participants' opinions. The discussion episode spanning multiple rounds concludes either upon reaching the consensus state or after a predetermined maximum number of discussion rounds.

Based on the decisions made by the high-level layer, the low-level module, powered by a LLM, produces relevant prompts. We have established a fixed correlation between facilitation actions and the ensuing prompts. For example, when $a = 1$, the system produces a prompt steering the conversation towards consensus, such as "Given the diverse viewpoints discussed, it appears we have some common ground. Shall we delve into the areas of agreement and craft a solution that encompasses these shared views?". Although this mapping can also be learned adaptively, it is not the main of this paper.

5   Evaluation

5.1   Evaluation Setting

Discussion Topics and Participants. This study thoroughly investigates four distinct topics, each involving three discussants. For every topic, we designate a unique character role for each participant, ensuring these roles reflect varied perspectives related to the discussion theme. Example: For the topic "What do you want for dinner?", one of the discussants is role-playing as Tom. The character description for Tom is as follows: "Tom dislikes fish." More comprehensive information about the topics and the roles assigned to the discussants is provided in Table 1.

Opinion Generation. Each discussant's opinion, which serves as their initial standpoint in the discussions, is generated using the gpt-3.5-turbo-0613 model. We achieve this by inputting the designated character description and the statements made by the other participants into the model. This approach ensures

Table 1. The topic and viewpoint used in the evaluation.

Topic	Name	Viewpoint
Topic 1: What do you want to eat dinner?	Tom	Tom does not like fish
	David	David is a restauranteur at the Jason's Suchi restaurant on Bruswick Street Fitzroy. He is always looking for ways to make the process fo runing his business easier for his custormers; David Bourne likes salad
	Jenny	Jenny does not like salad
Topic 2: The pros and cons of anonymity on the Internet	Tom	Tom believes that anonymity is important and necessary to protect privacy. He is concerned that the absence of anonymity may potentially suppress individual opinions and actions
	David	David thinks that anonymity poses risks and requires regulation. For example, it can lead to harassment, defamation, fraudulent activities, and cybercrime
	Jenny	Jenny believes that a balance is required between anonymity and real identities. Both have their advantages and disadvantages, and appropriate differentiation is necessary
Topic 3: The proliferation of AI-driven autonomous vehicles and the risk of traffic accidents	Tom	Tom is optimistic about AI-driven autonomous vehicles, believing they can greatly reduce traffic accidents through advanced sensors and algorithms
	David	David is skeptical about AI-driven autonomous vehicles, expressing concerns about technical glitches, hacking vulnerabilities, and potential legal and ethical challenges
	Jenny	Jenny sees the potential of AI-driven autonomous vehicles to improve road safety, but emphasizes the need for robust regulations, comprehensive testing, and public acceptance to address potential risks and ensure responsible deployment
Topic 4: The issues of privacy and data protection in social media	Tom	Tom strongly advocates for privacy and data protection in social media, emphasizing the need for robust regulations and user control to prevent misuse of personal information
	David	David expresses concerns about privacy in social media, but believes that users should take personal responsibility by being cautious with the information they share and using privacy settings effectively
	Jenny	Jenny recognizes the importance of privacy and data protection in social media, calling for a collective effort involving both users and social media platforms to ensure transparency, informed consent, and secure data practices

that the generated opinions are aligned with the character roles while also being influenced by the discussion's dynamics.

Evaluation Metrics: The primary objective is to gauge the performance of our two-layer facilitation algorithm. We do this by juxtaposing its efficacy against a baseline - a random policy. In this random policy approach, the high-level agent makes an arbitrary choice for the facilitation action $a \in A$. Subsequently, the low-level agent utilizes this randomly determined action to generate the facilitation prompt. The hyperparameters of the DQN are set as follows: learning rate = 0.01 and discount factor = 0.9.

5.2   Evaluation Results

For each experimental setup, we conducted simulations over 500 episodes, with a maximum step limit of 10 per episode. If an agreement is not reached within these steps, the episode is terminated. We gauge the performance of our model by analyzing agreement scores for each setup, which demonstrate how these scores evolve during the learning process. Figure 3 (a)-(d) presents the agreement scores at the final round of each episode, displaying how scores generally increase as the number of learning episodes progress. To illustrate, let's consider topic 2 on "The pros and cons of anonymity on the Internet." For this topic, Tom, David, and Jenny have the following beliefs:

- Tom believes in the necessity and importance of anonymity for privacy protection, and he fears that without it, individual opinions and actions might be suppressed.
- David perceives anonymity as risky and needing regulation, as it could lead to harassment, defamation, fraudulent activities, and cybercrime.
- Jenny asserts the need for a balance between anonymity and real identities. She acknowledges the merits and demerits of both, and advocates for suitable differentiation.

For the issue of anonymity on the internet, which is inherently divisive, the contrasting perspectives of Tom, David, and Jenny signify the complexities of real-world debates. Initially, the model faced challenges in fostering consensus. However, by the end of the simulations, the agent adeptly navigated the nuances, facilitating an agreement score beyond 0.9. This underscores the model's capacity to understand and handle multifaceted dialogues. While Topic 3 recorded an average agreement score of 0.8, its performance exhibited some inconsistencies. This variability could be attributed to the intricacies of the topic and the initial exploration strategies of the agent. Yet, post the 15-epoch mark, the model displayed heightened stability, emphasizing its capability to adjust to challenges and uncertainties.

Figure 3 (e)–(h) provides a clear contrast between our proposed method and a random policy. The initial performance overlap is anticipated, as the agent is in its early exploration phase. However, the subsequent divergence, where our

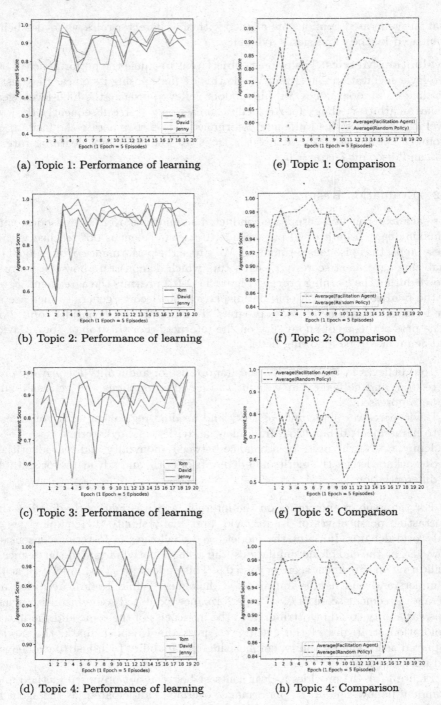

(a) Topic 1: Performance of learning

(e) Topic 1: Comparison

(b) Topic 2: Performance of learning

(f) Topic 2: Comparison

(c) Topic 3: Performance of learning

(g) Topic 3: Comparison

(d) Topic 4: Performance of learning

(h) Topic 4: Comparison

Fig. 3. (a)-(d) The performance of agreement scores of three discussants in four topics. (e)-(h) Comparison of the average agreement score between our proposed method and random policy.

facilitation agent markedly outperforms the random policy, is a testament to its ability to learn and refine its strategies effectively.

The figures emphasize a pivotal observation: the agent not only improves its agreement scores over time but also becomes increasingly consistent in achieving high scores. This consistency is indicative of the model's robustness and its potential applicability in real-world scenarios.

These results highlight the effectiveness of our facilitation algorithm, which progressively learns to steer discussions towards agreement within the given round limit. Moreover, it demonstrates an enhanced stability and consistency in performance over time.

6   Conclusion

We introduced a two-layer facilitation agent designed to help discussions reach consensus. This agent uses deep reinforcement learning to guide interventions and incorporates large language models to produce fitting prompts. Our tests found that the agent consistently leads discussions towards agreement and outperforms random strategies. While there are other single-agent RL algorithms available, our paper focuses on a broader framework for deep reinforcement learning aimed at consensus building.

This facilitation agent has diverse applications: enhancing team discussions in businesses, assisting conflict resolution, guiding online dialogues, and facilitating group learning in education. As we employ AI in discussions, addressing biases and ethical issues is crucial. Our agent, built on pre-trained LLMs, is aware of these challenges. Moving forward, we plan to refine our model to ensure more inclusive and balanced discussions, keeping in line with the principles of ethical AI use.

Acknowledgement. This work was supported by a CREST Grant (JPMJCR20D1) from Japan Science and Technology Agency (JST) and a Grant-in-Aid for Scientific Research (C) (23K11230) from the Japan Society for the Promotion of Science (JSPS).

References

1. Bakker, M., et al.: Fine-tuning language models to find agreement among humans with diverse preferences. Adv. Neural. Inf. Process. Syst. **35**, 38176–38189 (2022)
2. Brown, T., et al.: Language models are few-shot learners. Adv. Neural. Inf. Process. Syst. **33**, 1877–1901 (2020)
3. Coulon, R., Judge, S.: An evolutionary algorithm for consensus building in inter-laboratory comparisons. Metrologia **58**(6), 065007 (2021)
4. Devlin, J., Chang, M.W., Lee, K., Toutanova, K.: Bert: pre-training of deep bidirectional transformers for language understanding. arXiv preprint arXiv:1810.04805 (2018)
5. Ding, R.X., et al.: Large-scale decision-making: Characterization, taxonomy, challenges and future directions from an artificial intelligence and applications perspective. Inform. Fusion **59**, 84–102 (2020)

6. Ding, S., Ito, T.: Self-agreement: a framework for fine-tuning language models to find agreement among diverse opinions. arXiv preprint arXiv:2305.11460 (2023)

7. Du, Y., et al.: Guiding pretraining in reinforcement learning with large language models. arXiv preprint arXiv:2302.06692 (2023)

8. Leslie, D.: Tackling covid-19 through responsible ai innovation: five steps in the right direction. Harvard Data Sci. Rev. **10** (2020)

9. Min, B., et al.: Recent advances in natural language processing via large pre-trained language models: A survey. arXiv preprint arXiv:2111.01243 (2021)

10. Mnih, V., et al.: Human-level control through deep reinforcement learning. Nature **518**(7540), 529–533 (2015)

11. Raab, J., Susskind, L.: New approaches to consensus building and speeding up large-scale energy infrastructure projects (2022)

12. Radford, A., Narasimhan, K., Salimans, T., Sutskever, I., et al.: Improving language understanding by generative pre-training (2018)

13. Shin, J., Hedderich, M.A., Lucero, A., Oulasvirta, A.: Chatbots facilitating consensus-building in asynchronous co-design. In: Proceedings of the 35th Annual ACM Symposium on User Interface Software and Technology, pp. 1–13 (2022)

14. Vaswani, A., et al.: Attention is all you need. In: Advances in neural information processing systems 30 (2017)

15. Watkins, C.J., Dayan, P.: Q-learning. Mach. Learn. **8**(3–4), 279–292 (1992)

16. Yang, C., Gu, W., Ito, T.: Toward case-based reasoning facilitation for online discussion in deliberation. In: 2019 IEEE 23rd International Conference on Computer Supported Cooperative Work in Design (CSCWD), pp. 517–523. IEEE (2019)

A Heuristic Framework for Personalized Route Recommendation Based on Convolutional Neural Networks

Ruining Zhang, Chanjuan Liu[✉], Qiang Zhang, and Xiaopeng Wei

School of Computer Science and Technology, Dalian University of Technology, Dalian 116024,
China
dgjxzrn@mail.dlut.edu.cn, chanjuan.pkucs@gmail.com

Abstract. Personalization of travel routes significantly impacts people's quality of life and production efficiency. The personalized route recommendation (PRR) problem has personalized requirements and the goal of providing users with personalized route suggestions. Most of the existing work focuses on improving either the personalization or the availability of recommended routes, rather than both. In response to the above problems, a Personalized-Neural-Network-Heuristic framework (PNNH) is proposed, which can improve the personalization degree of the recommended routes and ensure their availability simultaneously. The PNNH framework consists of two stages: preference modeling and route recommendation. In the preference modeling stage, a prediction component with Graph Convolutional Network (GCN) as the core is constructed to learn the potential preference characteristics in the user's historical travel information, and then a heuristic algorithm is constructed by using the evaluation value output by the prediction component reflecting the transition probability, thus introducing the user preference characteristics into its cost evaluation function. In the route recommendation stage, an improved heuristic algorithm is used for route planning, and the route planning results are recommended to users. A strategy of narrowing the search scope for the heuristic algorithm is proposed, which can ensure that the route reaches its destination. Based on the PNNH framework, a set of algorithms can be constructed. The NeuroMLR-Dijkstra-A* algorithm (NDA*) is constructed and used in the experiment to evaluate the performance of the PNNH framework. Experimental results demonstrate the superiority of the PNNH framework.

Keywords: Personalized recommendation · Route recommendation · A*
algorithm · Lipschitz embedding · Graph convolutional networks (GCN)

1 Introduction

Transportation is an essential part of people's daily lives, and route choice is directly related to life and production. The current route recommendation service is not perfect, which limits the development of life and production to some extent. Personalized Route Recommendation (PRR) aims to generate user-specific route recommendations in response to the user's route request [1].

F. Liu et al. (Eds.): PRICAI 2023, LNAI 14327, pp. 269–280, 2024.
https://doi.org/10.1007/978-981-99-7025-4_24

Route recommendation services are broadly classified into two types: route recommendation based on digital maps and route recommendation based on trajectory data. The route recommendation service based on digital maps is the traditional navigation service and can only provide users with route suggestions without discrimination. When compared with the route recommendation service based on digital maps, the route recommendation service based on trajectory data considers the users' preference characteristics and focuses more on the quality of the recommended routes. PRR is a type of one based on trajectory data.

The related work on PRR focuses on extracting users' personalized characteristics and recommending routes based on personalized characteristics. In some studies, machine learning is used to extract users' personalized characteristics [2–4]. Many studies also use RNN to extract characteristics [5, 6]. Other studies used methods other than machine learning, such as the Mixed Gaussian Model [7]. For another work focus, various methods for generating routes have been proposed in related work [8–10]. Most of the above methods focus on considering more influencing factors in the evaluation process of user preferences, which can achieve a high success rate of route recommendation, but most of them ignore the improvement of the personalized degree of the recommended route.

In recent years, embedding users' personalized characteristics into the route recommendation process by improving heuristic algorithms has become a research hotspot of PRR. Related research has provided a variety of implementation methods [11–13]. Some of these studies use neural networks, such as MP neural cell model [14]. Most of the above methods are devoted to improving the personalization degree of the recommended route, but most of them ignore the routes' availability, which represents whether the route can reach the destination and be adopted by users.

At present, NeuroMLR (The Neural Approach to the Most Likely Route Problem) neural network [15] outperforms comparable methods and comes closest to the idea of this work. Jain et al. measured the prediction accuracy of the recommended route using precision and recall, which resulted in an improvement in prediction accuracy and the success rate of the recommended route to reach the destination. However, after combining the NeuroMLR neural network with the classical graph search algorithm, there is still room for improvement in the personalized degree of the recommended routes. Some recommended routes have not yet arrived at their destination, and there is still room for improvement in their availability.

In summary, the current PRR methods have the limitation of not simultaneously improving the personalization degree of the recommended route and ensuring its availability. To this end, this paper presents three contributions: (1) We propose a Personalized-NN-Heuristic (PNNH) framework for individualized route recommendation by embedding graph convolutional networks (GCNs) into heuristic algorithms. PNNH provides a general method for constructing the evaluation function of heuristic algorithms using the evaluation values output by neural networks. Preference modeling and route recommendation are completed via GCN and heuristic algorithms, respectively. (2) A PRR algorithm based on the PNNH framework is proposed, namely the NDA* (NeuroMLR-Dijkstra-A*) algorithm. The effect of the NeuroMLR neural network is incorporated into the cost evaluation of the A* algorithm via evaluation metrics, making the routes superior. The A* algorithm's iterative process is improved, ensuring route availability. (3) A strategy of narrowing the search scope is proposed to improve the success rate of route recommendation. The NDA* algorithm makes A* algorithm only search for key nodes when it fails to directly recommend the route, thus ensuring its availability.

2 Basic Concepts of PRR

Concept 1 (Road Network). The road network is abstracted as a directed graph, with road intersections abstracted as nodes and sections between intersections abstracted as edges. G represents the road network. V represents the set of nodes.

Concept 2 (Route). There are two ways to represent routes: nodes and edges. The edge-based route expression is $R(s, d) = \{e_1, \cdots, e_{k-1}\}$ where $e_i = (v_i, v_{i+1})$ represents the ith edge on the route.

Based on the method of representing routes by edges and the first-order Markov hypothesis, the expression of the route obtained by solving is given in Eq. (1). Among them, $Pr(e_i|v_i, d, t)$ represents the probability of edge e_i on R, $s \in V$ represents the starting node, $d \in V$ represents the ending node.

$$R^*(s, d) = \arg \max_{\forall R \in G} \prod_{i=1}^{|R|} \Pr(e_i|v_i, d, t) = \arg \min_{\forall R \in G} \sum_{i=1}^{|R|} -\log(Pr(e_i|v_i, d, t)) \quad (1)$$

3 PNNH Framework

3.1 Design of PNNH Framework

PNNH framework divides the process of solving PRR into two stages: preference modeling and route recommendation (Fig. 1).

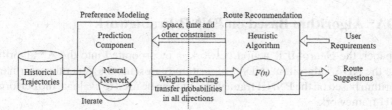

Fig. 1. The structure of the PNNH framework.

Concept 3 (Preference Modeling). The conditional distribution of the conditional transition probability of the user's trip in the road network G is extracted from the user's historical trajectory dataset D.

Concept 4 (Route Recommendation). Given the distribution of conditional transition probability, a route R which maximizes the evaluation metrics is determined.

Design of Preference Modeling Stage. In the preference modeling stage, PNNH framework uses an appropriate neural network model to learn the potential preference characteristics in the user's historical trajectory data and models the user's preference characteristics. PNNH framework uses the user's preference model to construct the prediction component of the algorithm. The output data of the prediction component can reflect the transfer probability of the user in all transferable directions at the next moment. In the preference modeling stage, PNNH framework personalizes route recommendation service.

Design of Route Recommendation Stage. In the route recommendation stage, PNNH framework adopts appropriate heuristic algorithm, uses user's preference characteristics to plan routes, and recommends the output results to users as route suggestions. PNNH framework embeds the prediction component into the heuristic function of heuristic algorithm. The heuristic algorithm utilizes the output data of the prediction component to calculate the heuristic function, which introduces the user's preference characteristics into route planning. In the route recommendation stage, PNNH framework improves the personalization degree of the recommended route.

3.2   Evaluation of PNNH Framework

The performance of PNNH framework cannot be directly evaluated, so an algorithm instance is constructed based on PNNH framework, and the evaluation of PNNH framework is achieved by evaluating the performance of the algorithm. In our work, NeuroMLR neural network [15], which has excellent performance in similar methods and is the closest to the idea of this paper, and A* algorithm in heuristic algorithms are selected to construct NDA* algorithm. By comparing the results of route recommendation using NDA* algorithm and using each component of NDA* algorithm alone, it is proved that the route recommended by NDA* algorithm has a higher degree of personalization and its availability is ensured, and thus demonstrates the superiority of PNNH framework.

4   NDA* Algorithm Based on PNNH Framework

In this paper, the NeuroMLR neural network is incorporated into the A* algorithm to generate the NDA* algorithm. NDA* algorithm represents the general performance of the algorithm based on the PNNH framework and can be used to evaluate the performance of PNNH framework.

4.1   Preference Modeling Based on NeuroMLR Neural Network

In the PRR problem, the probability that the user selects the next road segment to pass when transferring, viz., the distribution of the transfer probability, reflects the user's preference characteristics. The algorithm models the preference characteristics of users by estimating the distribution of transition probability, and then realizes the personalization of recommendation results.

According to Eq. (1), the conditional transition probability $Pr(e|curr, d, t)$ needs to be modeled, where $e = (curr, v)$, $curr \in V$ represents the current node. Due to the unknown real distribution of transition probability in G, this paper estimates the real distribution of transition probability by accessing D, where D is the sample extracted from the real distribution. In this paper, NeuroMLR neural network is used to model the transition probability [15].

NeuroMLR neural network is composed of graph convolutional networks (GCNs) and Lipschitz embedded, which can learn node attributes. GCN transmits information learned during the training process to less accessed or not accessed nodes via the message-passing mechanism, allowing the algorithm to generalize. Principal component analysis (PCA) is used to express the traffic situation in the road network at time t in a low dimension, and multilayer perceptron (MLP) is used to estimate the transfer probability. The neural network adopts the end-to-end training method, and integrates v, $curr$, d and the characteristics of traffic conditions at t time.

4.2 Route Heuristic Algorithm

The optimal route is the one with the maximum value of evaluation metrics from the starting node to the ending node. The route planning component composed of NeuroMLR neural network provides alternative routes for the algorithm to provide alternative routes for the algorithm to filter out the $curr$ for the next iteration.

In this paper, different evaluation metrics are used to construct the heuristic function. The expression of the heuristic function is shown in Eq. (2). Among them, *Precision* represents precision, *Recall* represents recall, w_1 represents the weight of *Precision*, w_2 represents the weight of *Recall*, w_1 and w_2 satisfy the relationship $w_1 + w_2 = 1$.

$$H(n) = w_1 * Precision + w_2 * Recall \tag{2}$$

In terms of improving the success rate of path recommendation, if the recommended route fails to reach the ending node d when the A* algorithm is terminated, NDA* algorithm will ensure that the generated route can reach the destination by narrowing the search range of A* algorithm. The main steps are shown in Table 1.

5 Experimental Validation and Result Analysis

This paper designs experiments to compare the NDA* algorithm with the algorithm using the NeuroMLR neural network algorithm, the classical graph search algorithm, and the algorithm composed of the combination of the classical graph search algorithm and the A* algorithm. NDA* algorithm performs the best in terms of *Precision*, *Recall*, and success rate. The superior performance of NDA* algorithm can prove the superiority of the PNNH framework.

5.1 Experimental Setup

Datasets. This paper uses four real datasets and road network information extracted from OpenStreetMap [16]. The dataset includes taxi trajectory datasets from Beijing

Table 1. The main steps of recommending after narrowing the search scope.

Algorithm 1: recommending after narrowing the search scope

1:
R_{ND}^* ←route planned by NeuroMLR–Dijkstra algorithm
R_D^* ←route planned by Dijkstra algorithm
R_{NB}^* ←route planned by NeuroMLR-Bellman-ford algorithm
R_B^* ←route planned by Bellman–ford algorithm

Initialize(trip):

2:
    for $i \leftarrow 0$ **to** length of *trip* **do**
        add i to the open list and $F(i) \leftarrow 0$
    end for

Initialize(R_{ND}^*) and *Initialize(R_D^*)* and *Initialize(R_{NB}^*)* and *Initialize(R_B^*)*

3:
$curr \leftarrow s$

4:
for $i \leftarrow 0$ **to** length of open list **do**
    $R_{ci}^* \leftarrow$ route from *curr* to i planned by NeuroMLR − Dijkstra
    $R_{id}^* \leftarrow$ route from i to d planned by NeuroMLR − Dijkstra
    $G(i) \leftarrow G(curr) + w_1 * (Precision\ of\ R_{ci}^*) + w_2 * (Recall\ of\ R_{ci}^*)$
    $H(i) \leftarrow w_1 * (Precision\ of\ R_{id}^*) + w_2 * (Recall\ of\ R_{id}^*)$
    $F(i) \leftarrow G(i) + H(i)$
end if

5:
for $i \leftarrow 0$ **to** length of open list **do**
if $F(i)$ is the largest one **then**
    $curr \leftarrow i$
end if
end for

6:
if $curr = d$ **or** open list is empty **then**
    return R^*
else
    continue

7:
for $i \leftarrow 0$ **to** length of open list **do**
if $i = curr$ **then**
    remove i from the open list and add i to the close list
end if
end for

8:
if $curr = d$ **or** open list is empty **then**
    return to step 4
else
    return to step 5

(BJG) [17], Chengdu (CHG) [18], Harbin (HRB) [19], and Porto (PT) [20]. The value of the function $\tau_t(e)$ of the average time taken to pass through road segment e at time t is defined as the average time taken by all vehicles passing through road segment e in the hour preceding time t. After data preprocessing, the statistics of the dataset are shown in Table 2.

Table 2. Datasets and processed datasets.

Dataset	Number of nodes	Number of edges	Number of trajectories	Average trajectory length/km	Average number of edges in the trajectory
Beijing (BJG)	31,199	72,156	1,382,948	7.39	36.08
Chengdu (CHG)	3,973	9,255	3,600,503	4.54	22.93
Harbin (HRB)	6,598	16,292	1,133,548	10.92	56.81
Porto (PT)	5,330	11,491	1,426,312	5.27	51.07

Evaluation Metrics. In the experiment, *Precision*, *Recall* and success rate are selected as evaluation metrics. The route generated by the algorithm is R^*.

On the one hand, in order to evaluate the personalization degree of the route recommended by the algorithm, the experiment uses *Precision* and *Recall* as the evaluation metrics and takes the real route R extracted from the testing set as the standard to calculate the evaluation value of route R^* on the above two evaluation metrics. The formulas for calculating *Precision* and *Recall* are given in Eq. (3) and Eq. (4). Among them, $\delta(e)$ represents the length of edge e.

$$Precision = \frac{\sum_{e \in (R \cap R^*)} \delta(e)}{\sum_{e \in R^*} \delta(e)} \tag{3}$$

$$Recall = \frac{\sum_{e \in (R \cap R^*)} \delta(e)}{\sum_{e \in R} \delta(e)} \tag{4}$$

Precision is the evaluation metric for the recommended result R^*, which reflects how many segments of the recommended route will be selected by users when they actually travel; *Recall* is the evaluation metric for the route R actually selected by the user, which reflects how many road segments are recommended in the route actually selected by the user. The larger the values of *Precision* and *Recall*, the closer the recommended route R^* is to the actual route R selected by users, that is, the higher the degree of personalization of the route.

On the other hand, to evaluate the availability of the route, the experiment takes success rate as the evaluation metric and calculates the proportion of routes that can reach the destination in the recommended routes of the algorithm to all routes. The formula for calculating the success rate is given in Eq. (5).

$$\text{success rate} = 100\% \times$$
$$\frac{\text{the number of routes recommended by the algorithm to reach the destination}}{\text{the total number of routes recommended by the algorithm}} \quad (5)$$

The success rate is an evaluation metric for a specific dataset, which reflects the ability of any route recommended by the algorithm to meet the basic navigation needs of users in terms of the dataset. The higher the success rate, the less the recommended route cannot meet the basic navigation needs of users due to the failure of recommended route. That is, the stronger the availability of the route.

To complete the difference analysis, we use independent samples T-test with p-value to determine whether there is a significant difference in the evaluation metrics between baseline algorithms and NDA* algorithm. The smaller the p-value, the more significant the difference.

Parameters. The parameters of the NeuroMLR-Dijkstra component and the NeuroMLR-Dijkstra algorithm are selected by following the way of [15].

5.2 Baselines

The NDA* algorithm is tested and its performance is compared with that of NeuroMLR-Dijkstra algorithm, NeuroMLR-Bellman-ford algorithm, Dijkstra algorithm, Bellman-ford algorithm, A* algorithm, Dijkstra-A* algorithm, and Bellman-ford A* algorithm.

The NeuroMLR-Dijkstra algorithm and the NeuroMLR-Bellman-ford algorithm can represent the general performance of the algorithm composed of the combination of NeuroMLR neural network and classical graph search algorithm. According to Jain et al. [15], the NeuroMLR-Dijkstra algorithm can represent the most advanced level of PRR algorithms. Dijkstra algorithm, Bellman-ford algorithm and A* algorithm can represent the general performance of classical graph search algorithms. Dijkstra-A* algorithm and Bellman-ford-A* algorithm are constructed in the same way as NDA* algorithm. The above two algorithms can represent the general performance of the algorithm composed of classical graph search algorithm and A* algorithm.

5.3 Experimental Results and Analysis

Evaluation of Overall Effect. Table 3 shows the evaluation values of NDA* algorithm and baselines on evaluation metrics *Precision* and *Recall* when taking 2000 samples from the test set. The bolded data represent the highest values in each set of samples. Each benchmark algorithm is T-tested against the NDA* algorithm, and the p-value is indicated in parentheses. Due to space limitations, values less than 0.05 are omitted and not shown. Most of the Table 3's p-values are less than 0.05. When the p-value is less than the significance level of 0.05, a substantial difference exists, which means the performance of NDA* algorithm has been greatly improved in comparison with baseline algorithms.

Table 3. Evaluation results of eight algorithms on four datasets.

Algorithms	Precision/%				Recall/%			
	BJG	CHG	HRB	PT	BJG	CHG	HRB	PT
NDA*	77.03	**90.96**	**69.87**	75.28	**82.68**	**91.65**	**56.30**	77.20
NeuroMLR-Dijkstra	75.58 (**0.150**)	87.35	65.77	**78.17**	74.23	84.75	48.20	70.53
NeuroMLR-Bellman-ford	75.58 (**0.127**)	87.35	65.77	**78.17**	74.23	84.75	48.20	70.53
Dijkstra	63.57	74.93	63.40	60.18	64.50	74.21	47.08	57.33
Bellman-ford	63.57	74.93	63.40	60.18	64.50	74.21	47.08	57.33
Dijkstra-A*	65.63	79.26	53.37	65.30	79.63	87.69	50.62	75.98 (**0.202**)
Bellman-ford-A*	**79.63**	80.98	54.81	67.52	81.44 (**0.148**)	89.07	51.54	**77.21** (**0.995**)
A*	0.00	0.00	0.00	0.00	0.00	0.00	0.00	0.00

By comparing the evaluation values in Table 3, it can be seen that the NDA* algorithm produces the majority of the highest values. When using the same set of samples, the *Precision* and *Recall* of the NDA* algorithm are basically greater than those of the baseline algorithms.

The test results for other sample sizes are shown in Fig. 2. In Fig. 2, the abscissa represents the number of samples and the ordinate represents *Precision* or *Recall*. Each line represents an algorithm's *Precision* or *Recall* for a certain number of samples. The higher the line, the better the algorithm's performance. The red line represents the NDA* algorithm. Taking (a) as an example, the numerical value represents *Precision* and the highest points are 80.42, 78.11, 73.40, 75.61 and 79.63, four of which are obtained by NDA* algorithm. Most of the highest points in each column are red. As a whole, the red line is at the top. The same is true for the other figures. The above results show that the NDA* algorithm has the highest *Precision* and *Recall*, indicating the highest degree of personalization.

The reachability of NeuroMLR-G, CssRNN, and DeepSt is calculated by the experiment in reference [15]. The concept of reachability is related to the success rate in this paper. Table 4 shows the success rate of the above algorithms and the NDA* algorithm. The bold data shows the highest success rate attained on each dataset.

Using BJG as an example, the success rates of NeuroMLR-G, CssRNN, and DeepSt are 99.1%, 91.7%, and 8.7%, respectively, which are lower than the NDA* algorithm's success rate of 100%. The same is true for HRB. The above experimental results show that the strategy of narrowing the search scope improves the success rate, thus ensuring the availability of the routes recommended by the algorithm.

Effectiveness of Heuristic Algorithm. In Table 3, the *Precision* and *Recall* of NDA* algorithm are basically greater than those of NeuroMLR-Dijkstra algorithm, NeuroMLR-Bellman-ford algorithm, Dijkstra algorithm and Bellman-ford algorithm

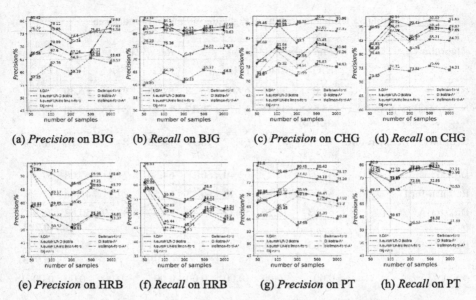

(a) *Precision* on BJG   (b) *Recall* on BJG   (c) *Precision* on CHG   (d) *Recall* on CHG

(e) *Precision* on HRB   (f) *Recall* on HRB   (g) *Precision* on PT   (h) *Recall* on PT

Fig. 2. Curve of the variation of evaluation results with the number of test samples.

Table 4. Success rate of four algorithms on two datasets.

Datasets	Success rate/%			
	NDA*	NeuroMLR-G	CssRNN	DeepSt
BJG	100.0	99.1	91.7	8.7
HRB	100.0	99.1	95.3	8.1

under the same set of samples. The above experimental results indicate that compared to the algorithm composed of NeuroMLR neural network and classical graph search algorithm, and the classical graph search algorithm, the recommended route of NDA* algorithm is closer to the route actually selected by the user and has a higher degree of personalization.

Effectiveness of Neural Networks. In Table 3, the *Precision* and *Recall* of NDA* algorithm are basically greater than those of Dijkstra-A* algorithm and Bellman-ford-A* algorithm under the same set of samples. The above experimental results show that compared with the algorithm composed of the classical graph search algorithm and A* algorithm alone, using NeuroMLR neural network to model preferences effectively improves the personalization degree of recommended routes.

Universality of PNNH Framework. In Table 3, when using the same set of samples, the routes recommended by the Dijkstra-A * algorithm and Bellman-ford-A* algorithm outperform the routes recommended by the Dijkstra and Bellman-ford algorithms. The above experimental results show that compared with the classical graph search algorithm, the route recommended by the algorithm formed by the combination of the classical graph search algorithm and the A* algorithm has a relatively higher degree of personalization. This conclusion further proves that the performance of the algorithm constructed by PNNH framework is superior to that of the participating algorithms used alone, and the PNNH framework is universal.

6   Conclusion

At present, the PRR method needs to be improved in many aspects, such as not improving the personalization degree of recommended routes and ensuring their availability at the same time. In response to the main problems in current PRR methods, this paper proposes a PNNH framework.

In the fields of AI applications such as intelligent driving and robot route planning, the PNNH framework can use neural networks and heuristic algorithms pertinently to constitute corresponding algorithms. In practice, users' choice of routes is influenced by multiple factors, and their preferences and demands may vary depending on the scenarios. In future work, this paper will focus on the corresponding relationship between user behavior and its influencing factors, and realize the dynamic adjustment of decision-making factors for route recommendation, so as to improve the flexibility and personalization degree of the recommended route.

Acknowledgements. This study was supported by the National Natural Science Foundation of China (Grant Nos. 62172072).

References

1. Wang, J., Wu, N., Zhao, W., et al.: Empowering A* search algorithms with neural networks for personalized route recommendation. In: Proceedings of the 25th ACM SIGKDD International Conference on Knowledge Discovery & Data Mining, pp. 539–547 (2019)
2. Ji, S., Wang, Z., Li, T., Zheng, Y.: Spatio-temporal feature fusion for dynamic taxi route recommendation via deep reinforcement learning. Knowl.-Based Syst. 205(Oct.12), 106302.1–106302.12 (2020)
3. Nawaz, A., Huang, Z., Wang, S.: SSMDL: semi-supervised multi-task deep learning for transportation mode classification and path prediction with GPS trajectories. In: Proceedings of Asia-Pacific Web (APWeb) and Web-Age Information Management (WAIM) Joint International Conference on Web and Big Data, pp. 391–405, Tianjin, China (2020)
4. Yang, Y., Pan, X., Yao, X., Wang, S., Han, L.: PHR: a personalized hidden route recommendation system based on hidden Markov model. In: Proceedings of Asia-Pacific Web (APWeb) and Web-Age Information Management (WAIM) Joint International Conference on Web and Big Data, pp. 535–539, Tianjin, China (2020)
5. Mou, N., Jiang, Q., Zhang, L., et al.: Personalized tourist route recommendation model with a trajectory understanding via neural networks. Int. J. Digit. Earth 15(1), 1738–1759 (2022)
6. Chen, X., Zhang, H., Xiao, F., et al.: Route planning by merging local edges into domains with LSTM. In: 25th International Conference on Intelligent Transportation Systems (ITSC). IEEE, Macau (2022)

7. Zhao, J., Kan, Y., et al.: Research on personalized route recommendation algorithm based on historical trajectory. Comput. Digit. Eng. **49**(11), 2254–2259 (2021)
8. Sanchez, P., Bellogin, A.: Applying reranking strategies to route recommendation using sequence-aware evaluation. User Model. User-Adap. Inter. **30**(4), 659–725 (2020)
9. Ge, Y., Li, H., Tuzhilin, A.: Route recommendations for intelligent transportation services. IEEE Trans. Knowl. Data Eng. **33**(3), 1169–1182 (2021)
10. Chen, D., Bu, X., Huang, H., Du, Y., Gao, G., Sun, Y.: Idle taxi route recommendation algorithm based on waiting point planning. Comput. Eng. **48**(2), 297–305 (2022)
11. Sun, Z., Luo, Y., Zheng, X., Zhang, H.: Intelligent travel route recommendation method integrating user emotion and similarity. Comput. Sci. **48**(z1), 226–230 (2021)
12. Kanimozhi, U., Sannasi, G., et al.: A user preference tree based personalized route recommendation system for constraint tourism and travel. Soft. Comput. **26**(3), 1499 (2022)
13. Liang, F., Chen, H., Lin, K., et al.: Route recommendation based on temporal-spatial metric. Comput. Electr. Eng. **97**, 107549 (2022)
14. Zhou, X., Su, M., Feng, G., Zhou, X.: Intelligent tourism recommendation algorithm based on text mining and MP nerve cell model of multivariate transportation modes. IEEE Access **9**, 98121–98157 (2021)
15. Jain, J., Bagadia, V., Manchanda, S., Ranu, S.: NeuroMLR: robust & reliable route recommendation on road networks. In: 35th Conference on Neural Information Processing Systems (NeurIPS 2021) (2021)
16. Planet. https://planet.osm.org. https://www.openstreetmap.org. Accessed 2017
17. Lian, J., Zhang, L.: One-month Beijing taxi GPS trajectory dataset with taxi IDs and vehicle status. In: Proceedings of 1st International Workshop on Data-Acquisition to Analysis (DATA), pp. 3–4, New York, USA (2018)
18. DiDi driving behavior open dataset. https://gaia.didichuxing.com/. Accessed 2020
19. Li, X., Cong, G., Sun, A., Cheng, Y.: Learning travel time distributions with deep generative model. In: Proceedings of World Wide Web Conference (WWW), pp. 1017–1027, San Francisco, CA, USA (2019)
20. Moreira-Matias, L., Gama, J., Ferreira, M., Mendes-Moreira, J., Damas, L.: Predicting taxi–passenger demand using streaming data. IEEE Trans. Intell. Transp. Syst. **14**(3), 1393–1402 (2013)

Approximate Supplement-Based Neighborhood Rough Set Model in Incomplete Hybrid Information Systems

Xiong Meng[1,2], Jilin Yang[1,2(✉)], Die Wu[1,2], and Tang Liu[1,2]

[1] Department of Computer Science, Sichuan Normal University, Chengdu, China
jilinyang@sicnu.edu.cn
[2] Visual Computing and Virtual Reality Key Laboratory of Sichuan Province,
Sichuan Normal University, Chengdu, China

Abstract. Incomplete hybrid information systems (IHISs) contain hybrid data (e.g., categorical data, numerical data) and incomplete data. With the development of big data, IHISs widely exist in various practical applications. Due to the heterogeneity of hybrid data and the complex semantics of incomplete data, effectively processing the IHIS has become a significant challenge. The established indiscernibility relations of the existing studies for dealing with IHIS over-amplify the uncertainty of missing values, which may achieve unsatisfactory results. In this paper, we propose an approximate supplement-based neighborhood rough set model (AS-NRSM) to deal with the data of IHISs. Specifically, we propose a method to approximate supplement missing values with known values or constructed interval values, and the original IHIS is becoming the constructed IHIS*. Then, we formulate a novel similarity function to construct the improved neighborhood tolerance relation and the corresponding neighborhood tolerance classes. Finally, we design two experiments on 5 UCI data sets by introducing three performance metrics. Experimental results illustrate that the proposed AS-NRSM has higher classification performance than the two representative models.

Keywords: Incomplete data · Hybrid data · Neighborhood rough sets · Incomplete hybrid information systems

1 Introduction

With the fast development of the information era, more and more data in the real world show heterogeneous and incomplete. For example, the medical records contain categorical data, e.g., blood type (O, A, B, AB), gender (Male, Female) and marital status (Married, Unmarried), and numerical data, e.g., blood lipid (mmol/L), body temperature ($^\circ C$) and height (cm). In addition, due to some unpredictable factors like human omission or equipment failure, missing data

F. Liu et al. (Eds.): PRICAI 2023, LNAI 14327, pp. 281–293, 2024.
https://doi.org/10.1007/978-981-99-7025-4_25

will occur occasionally. At present, in the fields of data mining and knowledge discovery, methods of efficiently processing these heterogeneous and incomplete data have become a research hotspot.

Rough set theory is an effective tool for addressing vague and uncertain issues, and has been used successfully in many realms [6, 8, 12, 19–21]. The classical rough set model can only deal with complete and categorical data in information systems (ISs) based on equivalence relation. ISs with incomplete and hybrid data are called incomplete hybrid information systems (IHISs), which exist widely in practical applications. Thus, many investigations have extended the rough set model to process the information systems with hybrid data [1, 3, 11, 14, 18] and incomplete data [9, 10, 13, 15] separately.

Recently, there has been an increasing interest in simultaneously considering hybrid data and incomplete data [2, 5, 16, 22, 23]. Huang et al. [5] given two pseudo-distance functions according to two semantics of missing value (i.e., "lost value" and "do not care") in IHISs. For only one semantic of missing value, namely, "lost value", Ge et al. [2] proposed an improved neighborhood rough set model (NRSM) in an IHIS to process the missing data. Zhang et al. [22] proposed an attribute reduction algorithm in IHIS by introducing the Dempster-Shafer evidence theory in the distance function. Wang et al. [16] proposed the decision-theoretic rough set model in IHIS with image and employed it in a medical diagnosis example. However, in these models, missing values are generally considered to be equal to all known values in the corresponding domain. Intuitively, the lost value should be similar to part of values in the corresponding domain, rather than be equal to all known values. Therefore, the existing models amplify the uncertainty of lost values, which may acquire unreasonable classification results. The specific analysis and statement of the problem are presented in Sect. 2.

To better describe the uncertainty of lost values and improve the classification performance in IHIS, we propose an Approximate Supplement-based Neighborhood Rough Set Model (AS-NRSM). Considering the heterogeneity of categorical and numerical data, we firstly approximately supplement lost values with known categorical or interval values, to avoid the uncertainty amplification caused by the above-mentioned models. Then the IHIS is becoming a constructed IHIS* with only one semantic (i.e., "do not care"). In the constructed IHIS*, we define the corresponding similarity function to simultaneously deal with three data types: categorical, numerical, and the replaced interval values. Then, we construct the AS-NRSM based on the similarity function. Finally, two experiments are designed and implemented to verify the effectiveness of the proposed AS-NRSM.

The main contributions are presented as follows. (1) To describe the uncertainty of missing values as accurately as possible, we propose a method of approximate supplement for the lost values in the original IHIS. (2) To address three types of data in the constructed IHIS*, we define a novel similarity function to measure the similarity between objects. (3) We design an algorithm of AS-NRSM and introduce three performance metrics into the AS-NRSM to verify the performance of the proposed model. This paper is organized as follows. In Sect. 2, some basic notions of IHIS are reviewed and a specific analysis of the existing models is given. In Sect. 3, we give a method of approximating supplements and discuss the similarity function in IHIS*. The AS-NRSM will be established eventually. In Sect. 4, several experiments are carried out on 5 UCI data sets to compare the performance of the proposed method and two existing methods. Finally, the conclusion of this paper and the possible future works are presented in Sect. 5.

2   Preliminaries

In this section, we briefly review some concepts about IHIS. Then, we shortly analyze the irrationality of two existing NRSMs when processing some cases in IHIS.

2.1   Incomplete Hybrid Information Systems (IHISs)

An IHIS can be denoted as $\Omega = (U, A, V, f, ?, *)$, where $A = A^C \cup A^N, A^C \cap A^N = \emptyset$, and A is a non-empty finite set of attribute, A^C and A^N are the categorical and numerical attribute sets, respectively. "?" and "*" denote two semantics of missing values, namely, "lost value" and "do not care".

Table 1. $\Omega = (U, A, V, f, ?, *)$

U	a_1	a_2	a_3	a_4	a_5
x_1	S	A	0.6	0.8	0.9
x_2	M	*	*	0.2	0.5
x_3	*	C	0.3	0.2	0.6
x_4	?	B	?	0.2	?
x_5	S	?	0.1	?	0.1
x_6	M	?	?	?	?
x_7	M	?	?	?	?
x_8	M	*	*	0.9	0.1

Example 1. We use Table 1 to illustrate an IHIS, where $U = \{x_1, \cdots, x_8\}$, $A = \{a_1, \cdots, a_5\}$. For categorical attribute set $A^C = \{a_1, a_2\}$, $V_{a_1} = \{S, M\}$ and $V_{a_2} = \{A, B, C\}$, we have some objects with missing values, e.g., $f(x_3, a_1) = *$, $f(x_4, a_1) = ?$. For numerical attribute set $A^N = \{a_3, a_4, a_5\}$, $V_{a_3}, V_{a_4}, V_{a_5} \in [0, 1]$, there are some missing values, e.g., $f(x_2, a_3) = *$, $f(x_4, a_3) = ?$.

To cope with the numerical data, the theory of neighborhood rough sets (NRSs) is introduced [1,4,17]. For numerical attribute A^N, through a neighborhood radius $\delta \in [0, 1]$. The neighborhood relation $N_{A^N}^\delta$ is defined by:

$$N_{A^N}^\delta = \{(x, y) \in U^2 \mid \forall a \in A^N, d_a(x, y) \leq \delta\}, \tag{1}$$

where $d_a(x, y)$ is the distance of x and y on the attribute $a \in A^N$. For any $x \in U$, the neighborhood class $N_{A^N}^\delta(x)$ is defined by:

$$N_{A^N}^\delta(x) = \{(x, y) \in U^2 \mid \forall a \in A^N, (x, y) \in N_{A^N}^\delta\}. \tag{2}$$

In IHIS, Huang et al. [5] proposed Three-Way Neighborhood Decision Model (TWNDM). Ge et al. [2] constructed an Improved Neighborhood Rough Set Model (INRSM). The lost value can be equivalent to any one of the known values in the corresponding domain in TWNDM and INRSM. The specific analysis of the two models are given in Example 2.

Example 2. Consider the IHIS in Example 1, we assume the neighborhood radius $\delta = 0.2$, the neighborhood classes $N_A^\delta(x)$ are respectively constructed based on TWNDM [5] and INRSM [2] as Table 2.

Table 2. Neighborhood classes

Method	TWNDM	INRSM
$N_A^\delta(x_1)$	$\{x_1\}$	$\{x_1, x_6, x_7\}$
$N_A^\delta(x_2)$	$\{x_2, x_3, x_5, x_6, x_7\}$	$\{x_2, x_3, x_5, x_6, x_7\}$
$N_A^\delta(x_3)$	$\{x_2, x_3, x_6, x_7\}$	$\{x_2, x_3, x_4, x_5, x_6, x_7\}$
$N_A^\delta(x_4)$	$\{x_2, \boldsymbol{x_4}, \boldsymbol{x_5}, x_6, x_7\}$	$\{x_2, x_3, \boldsymbol{x_4}, \boldsymbol{x_5}, x_6, x_7, x_8\}$
$N_A^\delta(x_5)$	$\{\boldsymbol{x_4}, \boldsymbol{x_5}\}$	$\{x_3, \boldsymbol{x_4}, \boldsymbol{x_5}, x_6, x_7, x_8\}$
$N_A^\delta(x_6)$	$\{x_2, x_3, x_5, \boldsymbol{x_6}, \boldsymbol{x_7}, x_8\}$	$\{x_1, x_2, x_3, x_4, x_5, \boldsymbol{x_6}, \boldsymbol{x_7}, x_8\}$
$N_A^\delta(x_7)$	$\{x_2, x_3, x_5, \boldsymbol{x_6}, \boldsymbol{x_7}, x_8\}$	$\{x_1, x_2, x_3, x_4, x_5, \boldsymbol{x_6}, \boldsymbol{x_7}, x_8\}$
$N_A^\delta(x_8)$	$\{x_6, x_7, x_8\}$	$\{x_3, x_4, x_6, x_7, x_8\}$

We note that TWNDM and INRSM are not very reasonable when dealing with the following two special cases.

(1) The lost values of two objects always alternate. As shown in Table 1, for $\forall a \in A$, objects x_4 and x_5 always satisfy two conditions: (1) if $f(x_4, a) \neq ?$ then $f(x_5, a) = ?$, (2) if $f(x_5, a) \neq ?$ then $f(x_4, a) = ?$. Intuitively, objects x_4 and x_5 are unlikely to be similar. Hence, it is unreasonable to classify x_4 and x_5 into the same neighborhood class. However, by TWNDM and INRSM, we have $x_4 \in N_A^\delta(x_5)$ and $x_5 \in N_A^\delta(x_4)$.
(2) If two objects have the same or similar known values under very few attributes, and the rest values are all lost. As shown in Table 1, objects x_6 and x_7 have only one known value in a_1, and the rest of their values are all lost values. The possibility that x_6 and x_7 to be similar is very low. Therefore, it's unreasonable to classify x_6 and x_7 into the same neighborhood class. Still, we have $x_6 \in N_A^\delta(x_7)$ and $x_7 \in N_A^\delta(x_6)$ by TWNDM and INRSM.

Herein, the lost value is assumed to be equivalent to all known values in the corresponding domain, which increase the uncertainty of the lost value, and further leads to unreasonable classification results. This problem has been explicated and shown in Example 1 and 2. In the following, we propose an approximate supplement method for solving this problem.

3 Approximate Supplement-Based NRSM

3.1 Approximate Supplement in IHIS

In this subsection, we propose the method of approximate supplement in IHIS. Let x be an object with the lost value "?" in IHIS. Then the lost value will be approximately supplemented by the known categorical value or a constructed interval value.

In an IHIS, $\forall a \in A^N$, let $V_a^\dagger = \{v_a^1, v_a^2, v_a^3, \cdots, v_a^n\}$ be a known value set of attribute a, and $n = |V_a^\dagger|$ be the number of known values in attribute a. For any $a \in A^N$, we have the standard deviation in attribute a:

$$Std_a = \sqrt{\frac{\sum_{i=1}^{n}(v_a^i - \text{AVG}_a)^2}{n}},\tag{3}$$

where AVG_a is the average value of $V_a^\dagger$, i.e., $\text{AVG}_a = \sum_{i=1}^{n} v_a^i / n$.

$$\delta_a = \frac{Std_a}{\lambda},\tag{4}$$

where λ is a parameter for the neighborhood radius.

Definition 1. *Suppose $\Omega = (U, A, V, f, *, ?)$ is an IHIS, $A = A^C \cup A^N$. For any $x, y \in U$, the distance function in the categorical attribute $a \in A^C$ is defined by*

$$d_a(x,y) = \begin{cases} 0, & x = y \vee f(x,a) = f(y,a); \\ 0, & f(x,a) = * \vee f(y,a) = *; \\ 0, & f(x,a) =? \vee f(y,a) =?; \\ 1, & otherwise. \end{cases}\tag{5}$$

And the distance function under the numerical attribute $a \in A^N$ is defined by

$$d_a(x,y) = \begin{cases} 0, & x = y \vee f(x,a) = * \vee f(y,a) = *; \\ \delta_a, & (f(x,a) =? \wedge f(y,a) \in V_a^\dagger) \\ & \vee (f(x,a) \in V_a^\dagger \wedge f(y,a) =?) \\ & \vee (f(x,a) =? \wedge f(y,a) =?); \\ \frac{|f(x,a)-f(y,a)|}{|max(a)-min(a)|}, & otherwise, \end{cases}\tag{6}$$

where $max(a)$ and $min(a)$ are the maximum and minimum values in attribute a.

In Eq. (6), when two objects have a lost value "?" or a do not care value "*", the distance between them is no longer considered to be 0, but is considered to be δ_a. Intuitively, two objects have a slim probability to be equal under the numerical attribute in these cases. Therefore, the neighborhood radius δ_a is introduced.

Definition 2. *Let* $\Omega = (U, A, V, f, *, ?)$ *be an IHIS. The distance function under the attribute set A is defined as follows:*

$$d_A(x, y) = \frac{\sum_{k=1}^{|A|} d_{a_k}(x, y)}{|A|}, \tag{7}$$

where $|\cdot|$ denotes the cardinality of a set.

Definition 3. *Let* $\Omega = (U, A, V, f, *, ?)$ *be an IHIS, for any $a \in A$, we have*

$$X_c(a) = \{x | x \in U, f(x, a) \neq * \wedge f(x, a) \neq ?\}, \tag{8}$$

where the complete class $X_c(a)$ denotes the set of all objects with known values in attribute a.

For any $x \in U$, we can easily find an object from $X_c(a)$ which is the most similar to x, i.e.,

$$sim(x) = \{y \in X_c(a) \mid min(d_A(x, y))\}, \tag{9}$$

where $min(d_A(\cdot))$ means the minimal distance under the attribute set A. When $f(x, a) = ?$ and $a \in A^C$, the known categorical value of the object which is the most similar to x can be used to supplement the "lost value", i.e.,

$$f^*(x, a) = f(sim(x), a). \tag{10}$$

When $f(x, a) = ?$ and $a \in A^N$, a constructed interval value is used to replace the "lost value", i.e.,

$$f^*(x, a) = [max(0, f(sim(x), a) - \delta_a), min(f(sim(x), a) + \delta_a, 1], \tag{11}$$

where $f^*(x, a) \in [0, 1]$ when $a \in A^N$. By approximately supplementing the lost value "?", we can maintain the uncertainty of the lost value "?" to some extent.

Example 3. We continue with the IHIS in Example 1 and assume $\lambda = 2$. For all of the "lost value" in IHIS, such as $f(x_4, a_1) = ?$ and $f(x_6, a_3) = ?$, we have $sim(x_4) = x_2$ and $sim(x_6) = x_3$, according to Eqs. (7), (8) and (9). Therefore, we can obtain $f^*(x_4, a_1) = f(x_2, a_1) = [M]$ and $f^*(x_6, a_3) = [f(x_3, a_3) - \delta_{a_3}, f(x_3, a_3) + \delta_{a_3}] = [0.197, 0.403]$ to instead of "?", respectively, according to Eqs. (10) and (11). Similarly, we can approximately supplement all of the "lost value" in IHIS to get a constructed IHIS* as shown in Table 3.

3.2   Construction of AS-NRSM in IHIS*

The constructed IHIS* contains four types of data: (1) the categorical attribute values; (2) the crisp value under the numerical attribute; (3) the "do not care" value, i.e., "*"; (4) the supplemented interval value under the numerical attribute. In this subsection, a novel similarity function is given for dealing

Table 3. A constructed IHIS*

U	a_1	a_2	a_3	a_4	a_5
x_1	S	A	0.6	0.8	0.9
x_2	M	*	*	0.2	0.5
x_3	*	C	0.3	0.2	0.6
x_4	[M]	B	[0, 0.203]	0.2	[0.346, 0.654]
x_5	S	[B]	0.1	[0.04, 0.36]	0.1
x_6	M	[B]	[0.197, 0.403]	[0.04, 0.36]	[0.346, 0.654]
x_7	M	[C]	[0.197, 0.403]	[0.74, 1]	[0, 0.254]
x_8	M	*	*	0.9	0.1

with three types of data in the constructed IHIS*, i.e., (1), (2) and (4). Moreover, considering (3) in IHIS*, we would discuss the neighborhood tolerance relation and neighborhood tolerance classes based on the defined similarity function. Consequently, we propose AS-NRSM in the constructed IHIS*.

Considering the supplemented values in categorical attributes are known categorical values, and in numerical attributes, they are interval values within a width of 2δ, we proposed the following similarity function.

Definition 4. *Let* $\Omega = (U, A, V, f, *)$ *be a constructed IHIS*, $x, y \in U$, the similarity function under attribute* $a \in A^C \cup A^N$ *is defined by*

$$
S_a^*(x, y) = \begin{cases}
1, & a \in A^C \land f(x, a) = f(y, a); \\
0, & a \in A^C \land f(x, a) \neq f(y, a); \\
1, & a \in A^N \land |f(x, a) - f(y, a)| \leq \delta_a; \\
\frac{2 \star min(|v_x^l - v_y^r|, |v_y^l - v_x^r|)}{(v_x^r - v_x^l) + (v_y^r - v_y^l)}, & a \in A^N \land (v_x^l \neq v_x^r \land v_y^l \neq v_y^r) \land \\
& |f(sim(x), a) - f(sim(y), a)| \leq 2\delta_a; \\
1 - \frac{|f(x, a) - (v_y^l + v_y^r)/2|}{(v_y^r - v_y^l)}, & a \in A^N \land (v_x^l = v_x^r \land v_y^l \neq v_y^r) \land \\
& (v_y^l \leq f(x, a) \leq v_y^r); \\
0, & otherwise,
\end{cases}
\tag{12}
$$

where $|\cdot|$ denotes the absolute value.

Herein, v_x^l and v_x^r are the left and right endpoints of the interval $f(x, a)$, respectively. When $v_x^l = v_x^r$, $f(x, a)$ is a crisp value in the original IHIS. When $v_x^l < v_x^r$, $f(x, a)$ is an interval value in the constructed IHIS*. To more intuitively understand the proposed functions for the similarity of interval values in Eq. (12), the possible overlapping interval between the two objects with two interval values is shown in Fig. 1-(a), one interval value and one crisp value is shown in Fig. 1-(b).

In the light of tolerance relation [7], we give the neighborhood tolerance relation based on the defined similarity function as follows.

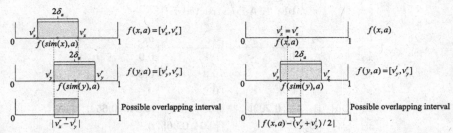

(a) Two objects with two interval values (b) Two objects with one interval value and
one crisp value

Fig. 1. The possible overlapping interval of two different cases.

Definition 5. *Let* $\Omega = (U, A, V, f, *)$ *be a constructed IHIS*,* δ_a *is a neighborhood radius. For* $\forall a \in A$, *neighborhood tolerance relation* NT_a^δ *is defined by*

$$NT_a^\delta = \{(x, y) \in U^2 \mid S_a^*(x, y) \geq \zeta \vee (f(x, a) = * \vee f(y, a) = *)\}, \qquad (13)$$

where $\zeta \in [0, 1]$ is a threshold for similarity and NT_a^δ satisfies symmetry and reflexivity.

Definition 6. *Let* $\Omega = (U, A, V, f, *)$ *be a constructed IHIS*, for* $\forall a \in A$, *the neighborhood tolerance class of any object* $x \in U$ *is defined by*

$$NT_a^\delta(x) = \{y \in U \mid (x, y) \in NT_a^\delta\}. \qquad (14)$$

The neighborhood tolerance class under the attribute set A is defined by

$$NT_A^\delta(x) = \{y \in U \mid \forall a \in A, (x, y) \in NT_a^\delta\} = \bigcap_{a \in A} NT_a^\delta(x). \qquad (15)$$

Example 4. We continue with Example 3 and suppose $\zeta = 0.2$. According to Eqs. (13), (14) and (15), we can build neighborhood classes of every object as follows:

As shown in Table 4, the neighborhood classes of TWNDM, INRSM are far looser than AS-NRSM:

(1) Objects x_4 and x_5 are in the same neighborhood class, i.e., $x_4 \in N_A^\delta(x_5), x_5 \in N_A^\delta(x_4)$ in TWNDM and INRSM, but by AS-NRSM they are irrelevant.
(2) Objects x_6 and x_7 are in the same neighborhood class, i.e., $x_6 \in N_A^\delta(x_7), x_7 \in N_A^\delta(x_6)$ in TWNDM and INRSM, but by AS-NRSM, they are irrelevant.

According to analysis in Example 2, the possibility that objects x_4 and x_5, x_6 and x_7 belong to the same neighborhood class is very low. By the method of AS-NRSM, these objects are classified into the appropriate neighborhood tolerance classes, namely, the classification based on AS-NRSM we proposed is more reasonable. The algorithm of AS-NRSM can be described as follows:

Table 4. Neighborhood classes of three methods

Method	TWNDM	INRSM	AS-NRSM
$N_A^\delta(x_1)$	$\{x_1\}$	$\{x_1, x_6, x_7\}$	$\{x_1\}$
$N_A^\delta(x_2)$	$\{x_2, x_3, x_5, x_6, x_7\}$	$\{x_2, x_3, x_5, x_6, x_7\}$	$\{x_2, x_3, x_4, x_6\}$
$N_A^\delta(x_3)$	$\{x_2, x_3, x_6, x_7\}$	$\{x_2, x_3, x_4, x_5, x_6, x_7\}$	$\{x_2, x_3\}$
$N_A^\delta(x_4)$	$\{x_2, \boldsymbol{x_4}, \boldsymbol{x_5}, x_6, x_7\}$	$\{x_2, x_3, \boldsymbol{x_4}, \boldsymbol{x_5}, x_6, x_7, x_8\}$	$\{x_2, \boldsymbol{x_4}\}$
$N_A^\delta(x_5)$	$\{\boldsymbol{x_4}, \boldsymbol{x_5}\}$	$\{x_3, \boldsymbol{x_4}, \boldsymbol{x_5}, x_6, x_7, x_8\}$	$\{\boldsymbol{x_5}\}$
$N_A^\delta(x_6)$	$\{x_2, x_3, x_5, \boldsymbol{x_6}, \boldsymbol{x_7}, x_8\}$	$\{x_1, x_2, x_3, x_4, x_5, \boldsymbol{x_6}, \boldsymbol{x_7}, x_8\}$	$\{x_2, \boldsymbol{x_6}\}$
$N_A^\delta(x_7)$	$\{x_2, x_3, x_5, \boldsymbol{x_6}, \boldsymbol{x_7}, x_8\}$	$\{x_1, x_2, x_3, x_4, x_5, \boldsymbol{x_6}, \boldsymbol{x_7}, x_8\}$	$\{\boldsymbol{x_7}, x_8\}$
$N_A^\delta(x_8)$	$\{x_6, x_7, x_8\}$	$\{x_3, x_4, x_6, x_7, x_8\}$	$\{x_7, x_8\}$

Algorithm 1. The Algorithm of AS-NRSM

Input: (1) An IHIS $\Omega = (U, A, V, f, *, ?)$, where $U = \{x_i, x_j \mid 1 \leq i, j \leq n\}$ and $A = \{a_k \mid 1 \leq k \leq m\}$; (2) The neighborhood radius parameter λ.
Output: Neighborhood tolerance classes $NT_A^\delta(x)$.
1: for $1 \leq k \leq m$ do
2:   for $1 \leq i \leq n$ do
3:     if $f(x_i, a_k) \neq$ "?" $\wedge f(x_i, a_k) \neq$ "*" then
4:       $f(x_i, a_k) \in V_{a_k}^\dagger$; // $V_{a_k}^\dagger$ is the known values set in attribute a_k;
5: Compute the neighborhood radius δ_{a_k};
6: for $1 \leq i \leq n$ do // Approximately replacing the lost values by Definition 3;
7:   for $1 \leq j \leq n$ do
8:     if $\forall a_k \in A, f(x_i, a_k) = ?$ then
9:       According to Equations (7), (8) and (9), compute $d_A(x_i, x_j)$, $X_c(a_k)$ and $sim(x_i)$;
10:       According to Equations (10) and (11), replace the lost value by $f^*(x_i, a_k)$;
11: for $1 \leq i \leq n$ do // calculating the distances by Definition 4;
12:   for $1 \leq j \leq n$ do
13:     for $1 \leq k \leq m$ do
14:       According to Equation (12), compute $d_{a_k}^*(x_i, x_j)$ in IHIS*;
15: According to Definition 5, compute NT_a^δ;
16: According to Definition 6, compute $NT_a^\delta(x)$ and $NT_A^\delta(x)$.

The time complexity of Algorithm 1 is $O(mn^2)$.

4 Experiments and Analysis

4.1 Performance Comparisons of Different Algorithms

To better reflect the performance of the proposed algorithm, we conducted simulation experiments. The 5 data sets are downloaded from the University of California at Irvine (UCI) data sets (http://archive.ics.uci.edu/ml/) and displayed in Table 5. The applicability and performance of TWNDM, INRSM and AS-NRSM were evaluated for different types of data.

Table 5. The description of data sets

No.	Datasets	Objects	Conditional attributes (A)			Decision attribute (d)
			Categorical(A^C)	Numerical(A^N)	Total($|A|$)	
1	Segment	2310	0	19	19	1
2	Heart	270	0	12	12	1
3	Annealing	798	9	6	15	1
4	MPG	398	4	5	9	1
5	Abalone	4177	1	8	9	1

We constructed three levels of missing values in the complete data set, that is, (1) Replacing 0%, 5%, and 10% known values as the low-missing level. (2) Replacing 15%, 20%, and 25% known values as the medium-missing level. (3) Replacing 30%, 35%, and 40% known values as the high-missing level. Especially, the missing values are composed of "lost value" and "do not care" values with a ratio of 4:1 when carrying out AS-NRSM and TWNDM algorithms. Besides, all of the missing values are "lost value" when performing INRSM algorithms because the semantic of "do not care" is not considered in INRSM.

Herein, we introduce three metrics for measuring the neighborhood class quality, namely, Precision (P), Recall (R) and F1-score $(F1)$. When the classification is too loose, it will get low P and $F1$ and high R. When classification is too strict, R and $F1$ will be low, and conversely, P will be high. We apply the three metrics to the 5 data sets of Table 5, the experimental results are shown in Table 6. We can get P of AS-NRSM is 0.95 ± 0.05 in the low-missing level of the Segment data set, where 0.95 is the average performance in 0%, 5%, and 10% missing values and 0.05 is the standard deviation. Similarly, we can obtain the average performance metrics of algorithms at the medium-missing level and high-missing level. Herein, the optimal metrics are highlighted in bold. It is observed that three metrics: P, R and $F1$ of three algorithms decrease with the level of missing values increase. However, as the level of missing values increases, the $F1$ of TWNDM and INRSM is lower than AS-NRSM in most data sets.

Table 6. Performance comparison by three algorithms in different data sets.

Data sets	Missing Level	AS-NRSM			TWNDM			INRSM		
		P	R	F1	P	R	F1	P	R	F1
Segment	Low	**0.95 ± 0.05**	**0.95 ± 0.05**	**0.95 ± 0.05**	0.88 ± 0.12	**0.96 ± 0.04**	0.91 ± 0.08	0.80 ± 0.06	0.95 ± 0.01	0.87 ± 0.03
	Medium	**0.82 ± 0.05**	0.82 ± 0.05	**0.82 ± 0.05**	0.60 ± 0.06	0.90 ± 0.01	0.73 ± 0.04	0.62 ± 0.05	**0.93 ± 0.00**	0.75 ± 0.02
	High	**0.70 ± 0.02**	0.68 ± 0.06	**0.69 ± 0.04**	0.35 ± 0.07	0.85 ± 0.01	0.50 ± 0.07	0.49 ± 0.06	**0.90 ± 0.01**	0.68 ± 0.03
Heart	Low	**1.00 ± 0.00**	0.99 ± 0.01	0.99 ± 0.01	0.93 ± 0.08	**1.00 ± 0.00**	0.96 ± 0.04	0.98 ± 0.02	0.91 ± 0.02	0.94 ± 0.02
	Medium	**0.98 ± 0.01**	0.97 ± 0.00	**0.97 ± 0.01**	0.49 ± 0.19	**0.99 ± 0.01**	0.65 ± 0.17	0.83 ± 0.08	0.88 ± 0.01	0.85 ± 0.05
	High	0.90 ± 0.02	0.96 ± 0.01	**0.93 ± 0.01**	0.15 ± 0.08	**0.98 ± 0.00**	0.25 ± 0.12	0.63 ± 0.04	0.86 ± 0.01	0.73 ± 0.02
Annealing	Low	**1.00 ± 0.00**	0.98 ± 0.02	**0.99 ± 0.01**	0.99 ± 0.01	0.98 ± 0.02	**0.99 ± 0.01**	0.96 ± 0.03	0.89 ± 0.02	0.93 ± 0.02
	Medium	**0.99 ± 0.00**	0.93 ± 0.01	**0.96 ± 0.01**	**0.99 ± 0.00**	0.92 ± 0.01	**0.96 ± 0.00**	0.89 ± 0.02	0.86 ± 0.01	0.87 ± 0.02
	High	0.98 ± 0.00	0.93 ± 0.01	**0.95 ± 0.00**	0.99 ± 0.01	0.92 ± 0.01	**0.95 ± 0.00**	0.82 ± 0.02	0.82 ± 0.01	0.82 ± 0.01
MPG	Low	0.96 ± 0.03	0.99 ± 0.01	**0.97 ± 0.02**	0.94 ± 0.06	0.96 ± 0.05	0.95 ± 0.05	0.87 ± 0.02	0.81 ± 0.02	0.83 ± 0.02
	Medium	0.85 ± 0.06	0.88 ± 0.02	**0.86 ± 0.04**	0.78 ± 0.04	**0.89 ± 0.01**	0.83 ± 0.02	0.85 ± 0.01	0.77 ± 0.01	0.80 ± 0.01
	High	0.74 ± 0.03	0.82 ± 0.03	**0.78 ± 0.03**	0.67 ± 0.03	**0.86 ± 0.02**	0.76 ± 0.03	0.77 ± 0.02	0.73 ± 0.01	0.75 ± 0.01
Abalone	Low	0.89 ± 0.10	0.94 ± 0.05	0.92 ± 0.08	**0.89 ± 0.10**	0.96 ± 0.06	**0.95 ± 0.05**	0.76 ± 0.04	**0.96 ± 0.00**	0.86 ± 0.02
	Medium	**0.82 ± 0.03**	0.86 ± 0.01	**0.84 ± 0.03**	0.75 ± 0.03	0.87 ± 0.03	0.80 ± 0.03	0.63 ± 0.03	**0.95 ± 0.00**	0.79 ± 0.02
	High	**0.72 ± 0.03**	0.85 ± 0.03	**0.78 ± 0.00**	0.64 ± 0.00	0.86 ± 0.02	0.74 ± 0.01	0.55 ± 0.02	**0.94 ± 0.01**	0.75 ± 0.01

Due to $F1$ being a more comprehensive metric than P and R to evaluate the performance of the algorithms, we choose $F1$ as the judging metric. To make a more intuitive comparison of different algorithms, we take 0% - 40% of missing values as x-axis to observe the metric $F1$ changes of three algorithms, as shown in Fig. 2. The performance $F1$ of the three algorithms decreases with the increase of missing ratio, while the proposed algorithm AS-NRSM can achieve optimal performance in most datasets.

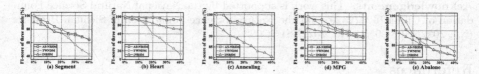

Fig. 2. F1-score of algorithms in different ratios of missing values

In order to explore the influence of different neighborhood parameters λ on the classification performance, we conduct a comparative experiment in a low missing level. Specifically, we move λ from 1 to 5 with a step of 0.5 to compare the $F1$ performance of three algorithms under different δ neighborhoods constructed by λ.

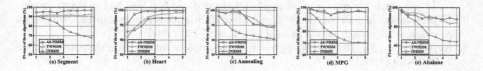

Fig. 3. $F1$ of algorithms in different neighborhood parameter λ

As shown in Fig. 3, the performance $F1$ of INRSM is sensitive to parameter λ, which decreases as the λ becomes larger in (a) Segment, (c) Annealing, (d) MPG and (e) Abalone, and increases as the parameters become larger in (b) Heart. In addition, the $F1$ of AS-NRSM and TWNDM in the 5 data sets are basically synchronous floating. Still, it's observed that AS-NRSM can achieve the optimal performance $F1$ in most data sets, and is more stable than the other two algorithms.

5 Conclusion and Future Work

Recently, a few studies have emerged to focus on dealing with incomplete hybrid data in IHISs. However, the indiscernibility relations of the existing studies are too loose, and may lead to unreasonable classification results. To describe the uncertainty of missing values as much as possible and enhance the performance of classification, we proposed the Approximate supplement-based Neighborhood

Rough Set Model (AS-NRSM). First, the lost values in IHIS have been approximately replaced by the known values or interval values. Then we obtained a constructed IHIS* with only one semantic from the original IHIS. Next, we defined a novel similarity function for the constructed IHIS* which contains three types of data. Then, the AS-NRSM is constructed for an IHIS*. Finally, comparative experiments are carried out to prove the performance of AS-NRSM. In the future, we will extend our work to a more comprehensive and realistic data environment to validate the effectiveness of the model.

Acknowledgements. This work is supported by the National Natural Science Foundation of China (62072320) and the Natural Science Foundation of Sichuan Province (No. 2022NSFSC0569, No. 2022NSFSC0929).

References

1. Chen, H.M., Li, T.R., Fan, X., Luo, C.: Feature selection for imbalanced data based on neighborhood rough sets. Inf. Sci. **483**, 1–20 (2019)
2. Ge, H., Yang, C., Xu, Y.: Incremental updating three-way regions with variations of objects and attributes in incomplete neighborhood systems. Inf. Sci. **584**, 479–502 (2021)
3. Hu, Q., Xie, Z., Yu, D.: Hybrid attribute reduction based on a novel fuzzy-rough model and information granulation. Pattern Recogn. **40**(12), 3509–3521 (2007)
4. Hu, Q., Yu, D., Liu, J., Wu, C.: Neighborhood rough set based heterogeneous feature subset selection. Inf. Sci. **178**, 3577–3594 (2008)
5. Huang, Q.Q., Li, T.R., Huang, Y.Y., Yang, X.: Incremental three-way neighborhood approach for dynamic incomplete hybrid data. Inf. Sci. **541**, 98–122 (2020)
6. Kryszkiewicz, M.: Properties of incomplete information systems in the framework of rough sets. Rough Sets Knowl. Disc. **1**, 422–450 (1998)
7. Kryszkiewicz, M.: Rough set approach to incomplete information systems. Inf. Sci. **112**, 39–49 (1998)
8. Kryszkiewicz, M.: Rules in incomplete information systems. Inf. Sci. **113**, 271–292 (1999)
9. Luo, C., Li, T.R., Yao, Y.Y.: Dynamic probabilistic rough sets with incomplete data. Inf. Sci. **417**, 39–54 (2017)
10. Luo, J.F., Fujita, H., Yao, Y.Y., Qin, K.Y.: On modeling similarity and three-way decision under incomplete information in rough set theory. Knowl. Based Syst. **191**, 105251 (2020)
11. Pan, X.H., He, S.F., Wang, Y.M.: Multi-granular hybrid information-based decision-making framework and its application to waste to energy technology selection. Inf. Sci. **587**, 450–472 (2022)
12. Pawlak, Z.: Rough sets. IJICS **11**, 341–356 (1982)
13. Stefanowski, J., Tsoukiás, A.: Incomplete information tables and rough classification. Comput. Intell. **17**, 545–566 (2001)
14. Sun, B., Ma, W., Chen, D.: Rough approximation of a fuzzy concept on a hybrid attribute information system and its uncertainty measure. Inf. Sci. **284**, 60–80 (2014)
15. Sun, L., Wang, L.Y., Ding, W.P., Qian, Y.H., Xu, J.C.: Neighborhood multigranulation rough sets-based attribute reduction using Lebasque and entropy measures in incomplete neighborhood decision systems. Knowl. Based Syst. **192**, 105373 (2019)

16. Wang, P., Zhang, P., Li, Z.: A three-way decision method based on gaussian kernel in a hybrid information system with images: An application in medical diagnosis. Appl. Soft Comput. **77**, 734–749 (2019)
17. Wang, Q., Qian, Y., Liang, X., Guo, Q., Liang, J.: Local neighborhood rough set. Knowl. Based Syst. **153**, 53–64 (2018)
18. Xu, J., Qu, K., Sun, Y., Yang, J.: Feature selection using self-information uncertainty measures in neighborhood information system. Appl. Intell. **53**, 4524–4540 (2022)
19. Yang, J.L., Yao, Y.Y.: Semantics of soft sets and three-way decision with soft sets. Knowl. Based Syst. **194**, 105538 (2020)
20. Yang, J.L., Yao, Y.Y.: A three-way decision-based construction of shadowed sets from Atanassov intuitionistic fuzzy sets. Inf. Sci. **577**, 1–21 (2021)
21. Yao, Y.Y.: Neighborhood systems and approximate retrieval. Inf. Sci. **176**, 3431–3452 (2006)
22. Zhang, Q., Qu, L., Li, Z.: Attribute reduction based on d-s evidence theory in a hybrid information system. Int. J. Approx. Reason. **148**, 202–234 (2022)
23. Zhang, X., Chen, X., Xu, W., Ding, W.: Dynamic information fusion in multi-source incomplete interval-valued information system with variation of information sources and attributes. Inf. Sci. **608**, 1–27 (2022)

Attention-Guided Self-supervised Framework for Facial Emotion Recognition

Saif Hassan[1,2(✉)], Mohib Ullah[1], Ali Shariq Imran[1], and Faouzi Alaya Cheikh[1]

[1] Norwegian University of Science and Technology, 2815 Gjøvik, Norway
saif.hassan@iba-suk.edu.pk
[2] Department of Computer Science, Sukkur IBA University, Sukkur, Pakistan

Abstract. Facial expression recognition is pivotal in computer vision and finds applications across various domains. In this paper, we proposed a self-supervised learning approach for precise facial expression recognition. Our approach leverages recent advancements in diffusion models, specifically the Classification and Regression Diffusion (CARD) model. To enhance the discriminative capability of our model, we integrate the Convolutional Block Attention Module (CBAM), an effective attention mechanism, to extract pertinent and discriminative feature maps. Furthermore, we capitalize on unlabelled data by using the simple contrastive learning framework of self-supervised learning (SSL) to extract meaningful features. To evaluate the performance, we conduct extensive experiments on the FER2013 dataset, comparing our results with existing benchmarks. The findings reveal significant performance improvements, achieving 66.6% accuracy on the FER2013 dataset. The quantitative results demonstrate the efficacy of our proposed SSL-based model in achieving accurate and robust facial expression recognition.

Keywords: Diffusion models · Convolutional block attention · Self-supervised learning · Facial expression recognition

1 Introduction

Facial expression detection from images is critical in comprehending human emotions and behaviour and finding applications in diverse fields such as human-computer interaction [1], affective computing, psychology, and social robots [2]. To create intelligent systems capable of real-time perception, understanding [3], and response to human emotions [4], precise and effective recognition and understanding of facial expressions are vital. Extensive research has been devoted to the advancement of robust and automated techniques for facial expression recognition. The progress in computer vision and deep learning has played a pivotal role in achieving significant breakthroughs in this area. The ability to identify crucial facial features and classify expressions from static photos has attracted considerable attention from both academia and industry. Recently, researchers have proposed various approaches [5–8] on the FER2013 dataset to improve the overall

F. Liu et al. (Eds.): PRICAI 2023, LNAI 14327, pp. 294–306, 2024.
https://doi.org/10.1007/978-981-99-7025-4_26

performance. Mao et al. [7] proposed to improve the performance of the FER2013 dataset by integrating focal loss [9] and CosFace loss [10] into the ResNet-18 model. The experimental results demonstrate that using CosFace loss improves the validation accuracy to 61.88% compared to 60.73% with traditional cross-entropy. Similarly, Luo et al. [5] focuses on designing a data augmentation method to improve the performance of the FER2013 dataset. The data augmentation approach implemented in the study leads to a significant improvement in performance. However, it is noted that the ResNet18 [11] model did not perform well, achieving only 58.6% accuracy on the FER2013 dataset. The work of Wu et al. et al. [6] introduces a novel Edge-AI-driven framework for FER. The proposed framework focuses on two key aspects: algorithmic improvements and system architecture. The study introduces two attention modules [12] for improving feature extraction and classification precision on the algorithmic front: Scalable Frequency Pooling (SFP) and Arbitrary-oriented Spatial Pooling (ASP). An edge-cloud joint inference architecture is suggested to achieve low-latency inference. This design includes an optional cloud offloading of attention modules and a lightweight backbone network on edge devices. Performance analyses show that the suggested method achieves a good trade-off between classification accuracy and inference latency, making it an attractive option for real-time FER applications. However, they have achieved 63.25% accuracy on the FER2013 dataset. In recent years, image diffusion models [13] have emerged as a class of algorithms that capture and propagate information across pixels in an image over time. These models are based on the concept of diffusion processes, treating images as dynamic systems where pixel-level interactions occur iteratively. The primary goal of image diffusion models is to capture and emphasize the spatiotemporal dynamics in the image data. Denoising diffusion-based conditional generative models [14] is a type of generative model that aim to generate high-quality and denoised samples while incorporating conditional information. These models combine the principles of diffusion models and conditional generative modelling to gradually remove noise from input data and generate samples that align with specific conditions. By iteratively updating the data elements based on their neighbours, the models reduce noise while preserving the underlying structure. In this work, we utilized a very recent diffusion-based model (CARD) [15] along with the CBAM attention module to improve the performance of the FER2013 dataset. Overall, our work on facial expression recognition makes the following contributions:

- Utilized the CARD model, a diffusion-based approach, for accurate facial expression recognition.
- Incorporated the attention module (CBAM) to extract relevant and discriminative feature maps, enhancing the performance of our model.
- A self-supervised pre-trained model employing SimCLR was utilized to learn feature representation.
- Demonstrated significant improvements in accuracy and performance over previous state-of-the-art methods, validating the effectiveness of our proposed approach for facial expression recognition.

The subsequent sections of the paper are structured as follows: In Sect. 2, we provide a comprehensive description of our proposed model, ResNet18 with CBAM, the self-learning strategy, along with detailed architecture specifications. Moving on to Sect. 3, we delve into the specifics of the dataset employed for our experiments, outline the performance metrics utilized, and provide implementation details. Section 4 presents the quantitative and qualitative results obtained from our evaluation and analysis. Finally, in Sect. 5, we offer final remarks to conclude the paper, summarizing the key insights and contributions of our research.

2 Methodology

Our proposed method consists of three main components, Classification and Regression Diffusion Models (CARD) Model [15], ResNet18 [16] as the backbone and Convolution Block Attention Module (CBAM) [17] and the self-supervised training strategy [18].

2.1 CARD Model

A novel conditional generative model named the CARD model [15] has been introduced, effectively addressing supervised learning problems in regression and classification tasks. By employing trainable diffusion processes, this model estimates the conditional distribution of the output variable given the input variable. Unlike traditional regression analysis or classification models, the CARD model not only provides predictions but also estimates the associated uncertainty, offering a more comprehensive understanding of the conditional distribution. In classification tasks, the CARD model incorporates model confidence at the instance level through the stochastic nature of its generative model's outputs. In contrast, regression tasks employ a re-parameterization technique to recover the noise term's distribution. The model demonstrates state-of-the-art performance on benchmark regression tasks and accurately simulates the conditional distribution with various density modes. Further, two diffusion processes are described with equations in the CARD model, diffusion noising and diffusion denoising.

Diffusion Noising Process. The diffusion noising process is also called forward conditional process distributions [15]. CARD model defines diffusion noising process with diffusion schedule $\{\beta_t\}_{t=1:T} \in (0,1)^T$ as:

$$q\left(\boldsymbol{y}_t \mid \boldsymbol{y}_0, f_\phi(\boldsymbol{x})\right) = \mathcal{N}\left(\boldsymbol{y}_t; \sqrt{\bar{\alpha}_t}\boldsymbol{y}_0 \\ + \left(1 - \sqrt{\bar{\alpha}_t}\right) f_\phi(\boldsymbol{x}), (1 - \bar{\alpha}_t)\boldsymbol{I}\right) \quad (1)$$

The Eq. 1 describes the conditional distribution $q\left(\boldsymbol{y}_t \mid \boldsymbol{y}_0, f_\phi(\boldsymbol{x})\right)$ in the diffusion model. It represents the noising process and is defined as a Gaussian distribution $\mathcal{N}$ with mean $\sqrt{\bar{\alpha}_t}\boldsymbol{y}_0 + (1 - \sqrt{\bar{\alpha}_t}) f\phi(\boldsymbol{x})$ and covariance $(1 - \bar{\alpha}_t)\boldsymbol{I}$. Here, $\boldsymbol{y}_t$ is the intermediate prediction, $\boldsymbol{y}_0$ is the observed response variable, and $f_\phi(\boldsymbol{x})$ is the prior knowledge of the relation between $\boldsymbol{x}$ and $\boldsymbol{y}_0$. The terms $\alpha_t := 1 - \beta_t$ and $\bar{\alpha}_t := \prod_t \alpha_t$ define the diffusion schedule.

Diffusion Desnoising Process. The diffusion denoising process, also known as the re- verse process is a tractable formulation that allows for the computation of the forward process posterior:

$$q\left(\boldsymbol{y}_{t-1} \mid \boldsymbol{y}_t, \boldsymbol{y}_0, \boldsymbol{x}\right) = q\left(\boldsymbol{y}_{t-1} \mid \boldsymbol{y}_t, \boldsymbol{y}_0, f_\phi(\boldsymbol{x})\right)$$
$$= \mathcal{N}\left(\boldsymbol{y}_{t-1}; \tilde{\boldsymbol{\mu}}\left(\boldsymbol{y}_t, \boldsymbol{y}_0, f_\phi(\boldsymbol{x})\right), \tilde{\beta}_t \boldsymbol{I}\right) \qquad (2)$$

$$where, \tilde{\boldsymbol{\mu}} := \underbrace{\frac{\beta_t \sqrt{\bar{\alpha}_{t-1}}}{1 - \bar{\alpha}_t}}_{\gamma_0} \boldsymbol{y}_0 + \underbrace{\frac{(1 - \bar{\alpha}_{t-1}) \sqrt{\alpha_t}}{1 - \bar{\alpha}_t}}_{\gamma_1} \boldsymbol{y}_t$$

$$+ \underbrace{\left(1 + \frac{(\sqrt{\bar{\alpha}_t} - 1)\left(\sqrt{\alpha_t} + \sqrt{\alpha_{t-1}}\right)}{1 - \bar{\alpha}_t}\right)}_{\gamma_2} f_\phi(\boldsymbol{x}),$$

$$\tilde{\beta}_t := \frac{1 - \bar{\alpha}_{t-1}}{1 - \bar{\alpha}_t} \beta_t.$$

The Eq. 2 represents this process, where the conditional distribution of $\boldsymbol{y}_{t-1}$ given $\boldsymbol{y}_t$, $\boldsymbol{y}_0$, and $\boldsymbol{x}$ is denoted as $q\left(\boldsymbol{y}_{t-1} \mid \boldsymbol{y}_t, \boldsymbol{y}0, f_\phi(\boldsymbol{x})\right)$. It can be approximated by a Gaussian distribution with mean $\tilde{\boldsymbol{\mu}}\left(\boldsymbol{y}_t, \boldsymbol{y}_0, f_\phi(\boldsymbol{x})\right)$ and covariance $\tilde{\beta}_t \boldsymbol{I}$. The mean term $\tilde{\boldsymbol{\mu}}$ is computed based on a combination of input variables, while $\tilde{\beta}_t$ is determined by the values of $\bar{\alpha}_{t-1}$, $\bar{\alpha}_t$, and β_t.

2.2 Convolutional Block Attention Modules (CBAM)

Convolutional Block Attention Modules (CBAMs) [17] are a particular class of attention mechanisms that can be incorporated into convolutional neural networks (CNNs) to focus attention on particular valuable regions in feature maps. According to Fig. 1, CBAM is made up of two parts: the Channel Attention Module (CAM) and the Spatial Attention Module (SAM). The CAM computes the importance of each feature channel by performing a global pooling operation (e.g., max pooling) followed by two fully connected layers. The CAM is described in Eq. 3 where $M_c(F)$ represents the channel attention vector obtained from the input feature map F. The equation consists of two branches: one involving average pooling F_{avg}^c and the other involving max pooling F_{max}^c. The feature maps

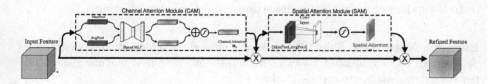

Fig. 1. Convolutional Block Attention Module

resulting from these poolings are passed through Multi-Layer Perceptron (MLP) layers with weight matrices W_0 and W_1. The outputs of the MLP branches are then summed and passed through a sigmoid activation function σ to obtain the final channel attention vector $M_c(F)$. The output of the CAM is a channel-wise attention map that scales the feature maps in a channel-wise manner.

$$M_c(F) = \sigma \left(W_1 \left(W_0 \left(F_{\text{avg}}^c \right) \right) + W_1 \left(W_0 \left(F_{\text{max}}^c \right) \right) \right) \tag{3}$$

The SAM, on the other hand, described in Eq. 8, computes the importance of each spatial location by performing two convolutional operations followed by a max pooling operation. The output of the SAM is a spatial attention map that scales the feature maps in a spatial-wise manner.

$$F_{\text{avg}}^s = \text{AvgPool}\left(F, \text{pool\_size}, \text{stride} \right) \tag{4}$$

$$F_{\text{max}}^s = \text{MaxPool}\left(F, \text{pool\_size}, \text{stride} \right) \tag{5}$$

$$\left[F_{\text{avg}}^s; F_{\text{max}}^s \right] = \text{Concat}\left(F_{\text{avg}}^s, F_{\text{max}}^s \right) \tag{6}$$

$$f^{7\times7} = \text{Conv}\left(\left[F_{\text{avg}}^s; F_{\text{max}}^s \right], \text{filter\_size} = 7, \text{stride} = 1 \right) \tag{7}$$

$$M_s(F) = \sigma(f^{7\times7}) \tag{8}$$

The channel-wise and spatial-wise attention maps are then multiplied to produce the final attention maps that can be used to weight the feature maps in a selective manner. The attention maps are normalized to sum to one so that the information is preserved. The CBAM module can be inserted into any CNN architecture, and it has been shown to improve the performance of various computer vision tasks, such as image classification and object detection.

2.3   Simple Contrastive Learning (SimCLR)

SimCLR (Simple Contrastive Learning) [18] is a popular self-supervised learning algorithm that aims to learn powerful visual representations from unlabeled data. It utilizes contrastive learning principles to encourage similar representations for augmented views of the same sample and dissimilar representations for augmented views of different samples. Following is a mathematical explanation of SimCLR's key components and steps.

Data Augmentation. SimCLR applies data augmentation to create two augmented views, denoted as x_i and x_j, for each input image x. These augmentations include random cropping, color distortions, and Gaussian blurring.

Encoder Networks. SimCLR employs a shared encoder network, denoted as f_θ, to map the augmented views of a sample into a shared feature space. The network parameters are represented as θ.

Similarity Function. SimCLR uses the cosine similarity function to measure the similarity between two feature embeddings. The cosine similarity between two vectors u and v is computed as:

$$\text{sim}(u, v) = \frac{u \cdot v}{\|u\| \cdot \|v\|}, \tag{9}$$

where $u \cdot v$ represents the dot product between u and v, and $\|u\|$ and $\|v\|$ represent the Euclidean norms of u and v, respectively.

Contrastive Loss. SimCLR formulates the contrastive loss to maximize agreement between positive pairs (augmented views of the same sample) and minimize agreement between negative pairs (augmented views of different samples). The contrastive loss is calculated as the negative log-likelihood of the similarity between positive pairs compared to the sum of similarities between positive and negative pairs, normalized by a temperature parameter τ:

$$L = -\log\left(\frac{\exp(\text{sim}(f_\theta(x_i), f_\theta(x_j))/\tau)}{\sum_k \exp(\text{sim}(f_\theta(x_i), f_\theta(x_k))/\tau)}\right), \tag{10}$$

where x_i and x_j represent the augmented views of the same sample, x_k represents the augmented view of a different sample, $f_\theta(.)$ represents the shared encoder network, $\text{sim}(.,.)$ denotes the cosine similarity function, and τ is the temperature parameter. Minimizing this contrastive loss encourages the encoder network to learn representations that capture meaningful and discriminative features for the given task. By training the encoder network θ using this contrastive loss, SimCLR learns powerful visual representations from unlabeled data, which can then be used for downstream tasks like facial expression recognition.

2.4   Architecture Details

The FER2013 dataset is classified using the CARD model architecture, which is depicted in Table 1. The flattened input image, with initial dimensions of $48*48*1$, is first given an encoder. The output dimension of the encoder, which has three fully connected layers, is 4096. The technique turns the input image into a 4096-dimensional representation. Next, the one-hot encoded label vector, denoted as y_t, is concatenated with the output $f_\phi(x)$ from the pre-trained Sim-CLR self-supervised model. The final step is to perform a fully connected (FC) layer to the output vector with 4096 dimensions. By performing a Hadamard product (element-wise multiplication) between the generated output vector and a timestep embedding, the response embedding is conditional on the timestep. As a result, a response embedding that considers the particular timestep is produced. The image embedding and the response embedding are integrated by performing another Hadamard product. This integration combines the information from both variables. The final step involves passing the integrated vector through two more FC layers with a total of 4096 output dimensions. A batch

Table 1. CARD ε_θ Network Architecture

Input	
	x: Input data
	y_t: One-hot encoded label vector
	$f_\phi(x)$: Pre-trained SimCLR model
	t: Timestep
Layers	
	$l_{1,x} = \sigma(\text{BN}(g_{1,x}(x)))$
	$l_{2,x} = \sigma(\text{BN}(g_{2,x}(x)))$
	$l_{3,x} = \text{BN}(g_{1,x}(x))$
	$l_{1,y} = \sigma(\text{BN}(g_{1,y}(y_t \oplus f_\varphi(x)) \odot g_{1,b}(t)))$
	$l_1 = l_{3,x} \odot l_{1,y}$
	$l_2 = \sigma(\text{BN}(g_{2,a}(l_1) \odot g_{2,b}(t)))$
	$l_3 = \sigma(\text{BN}(g_{3,a}(l_2) \odot g_{3,b}(t)))$
Output	
	$g_4(l_3)$: Final output of the network

normalizing layer and a Softplus non-linearity before the Hadamard product with the timestep embedding follow every one of these layers.

Pre-trained self-supervised model:

- The pre-trained self-supervised model is trained on the RAF-DB dataset [19].
- The SimCLR network is not fine-tuned during the training. It is only used for feature extraction.

Optimizer:

- In each experiment, $f_\phi(x)$ is trained using the Adam optimizer.

The output of the last fully-connected layer is a fully-connected layer with an output dimension of 1, which comes after the Hadamard product with the timestep embedding. For the classification challenge, this layer acts as the noise prediction layer. It is significant to observe that a batch normalizing layer and a Softplus non-linearity are present with each of the fully-connected layers, with the exception of the output layer. These additional operations help in improving the network's performance and the non-linearity of the model. Overall our proposed method works in a way that first, we pre-trained the model on unlabelled data using SimCLR self-supervised method to learn feature representations along with ResNet18 backbone as the feature extractor. Next, we added the CBAM (Convolutional Block Attention Module) module, which selectively emphasizes important features while suppressing irrelevant ones, improving model performance. We added the CBAM module after each ResNet block. In order to construct a conditional distribution of class probabilities given the input image, we finally swapped out the final fully connected layer of ResNet18 with the CARD model.

3   Experiments

3.1   FER2013 Dataset

The facial expression recognition dataset known as FER2013 [20] consists of 35,887 instances (images) sized at 48×48 pixels, which are further divided into a training set and a test set. The test set comprises 3,589 images, while the training set contains 28,709 images. These images are annotated with one of seven emotion categories, namely anger, disgust, fear, happiness, sadness, surprise, and neutral. In the training set, the happiness category has the highest frequency, with 8,094 images, followed by sadness with 5,591 images and surprise with 5,424 images. The least common category is disgust, with only 1,254 images. The fear category consists of 4,625 images, the angry category has 4,486 images, and the neutral category has 3,587 images. The distribution of images among the emotion categories in the test set mirrors that of the training set, where happiness remains the most frequent category with 895 images. In comparison, disgust remains the least frequent, with only 56 images. To gain insight into the representation of different emotions, the images in the dataset effectively portray distinct emotions. Overall, the FER2013 dataset is a valuable resource for researchers in facial expression recognition, with a diverse range of facial expressions and a balanced distribution of images across the emotion categories. However, the relatively small number of images in the disgust category may limit the ability of models trained on this dataset to accurately recognize this emotion.

3.2   Performance Evaluation Metrics

To measure the overall performance of our proposed model, we use accuracy, class-wise accuracy and Patch Accuracy vs Patch Uncertainty (PAvPU). Accuracy is a commonly used performance metric for classification models. It measures the percentage of correctly predicted instances among all instances in a dataset. Class-wise accuracy calculates the proportion of correctly classified samples in each class separately.

Similarly, Patch Accuracy vs Patch Uncertainty (PAvPU) is a performance evaluation metric that quantifies the percentage of predictions that are either accurate when the model is certain of them or inaccurate when the model is uncertain of them. The metric helps to determine how well the model can differentiate between confident and uncertain predictions. It is calculated as the total number of accurate predictions divided by the sum of the number of accurate predictions when the model is certain, the number of accurate but uncertain predictions, and the number of inaccurate but definite predictions. As shown in Eq. 11, the $n_{ac}, n_{au}, n_{ic}, n_{iu}$ indicates the proportion of correct predictions when the model is certain (confident) about them, accurate but uncertain, inaccurate but certain, as well as inaccurate and uncertain.

$$PAvPU = \frac{n_{ac} + n_{iu}}{n_{ac} + n_{au} + n_{ic} + n_{iu}} \tag{11}$$

In other words, PAvPU considers the model's predictions' accuracy and uncertainty. A higher PAvPU score means that the model is more likely to be accurate when it is confident and inaccurate when it is unsure. Therefore, a model with a higher PAvPU is preferred, as it shows the model is capable of making accurate predictions when it is confident and uncertain about its predictions when the model is likely to be wrong.

3.3   Implementation Details

In this study, we used PyTorch as the primary deep learning framework for conducting their experiments. We ran the experiments on a Ubuntu OS equipped with an NVIDIA GeForce RTX 2080 Ti graphics card. The network architecture of the CARD model [15] is simple for classification task which is described as: Let x be the input image to the diffusion model, with dimensions $48 * 48 * 1$ (for FER2013 dataset), and y_t be the target label for the classification task at time step t. Let $f_\phi(x)$ represent the encoder's output, which is a 4096-dimensional representation of x that was created by using three fully-connected layers. To create a vector of the same size, we concatenate y_t and $f_\phi(x)$ and run them through a fully connected layer with an output dimension of 4096. To produce a response embedding that is conditional on the timestep, we next execute a Hadamard product between this vector and a timestep embedding. The variables are then integrated using a second Hadamard product between the picture embedding $f_\phi(x)$ and the response embedding. Two more fully-connected layers with an output dimension of 4096 each are applied to the final vector. Following each of these fully-connected layers is a Hadamard product with a batch normalizing layer and a timestep embedding layer, followed by a Softplus nonlinearity. Finally, we feed the output of the previous fully connected layer via the noise prediction-representing first fully connected layer. A non-linearity does not follow the output layer. Along with CARD diffusion model, we performed two experiments: ResNet18 and used CBAM with combination of ResNet18. The objective of these experiments was to improve and compare the performance of the models on the FER2013 dataset. The Table 2 lists various parameters and their corresponding values for a both experiments. The parameters include the number of classes, the dimensions of the input data, the architecture of the model, the parameters for the diffusion, the training and testing batch sizes, the optimizer and its learning rate, and the number of epochs for training. The table is organized in a format, with the parameter names listed in the left column and the respective values in the right column. The values for some parameters are listed as multiple options separated by a vertical bar (|), indicating that these have been tested with different batch sizes during training.

The performance of each model was evaluated using the accuracy of the overall model, class-wise accuracy and PAvPU. These evaluation metrics are defined in Sect. 3.2. We compared the performance of models and discussed them in Sect. 4. Overall, the experiments provided valuable insights into the effectiveness of different models using CARD for facial expression recognition on the FER2013 dataset.

Table 2. Parameter values for the model.

Parameter	Value(s)
num_classes	7
data_dim	2304
feature_dim	4096
hidden_dim	4096
arch	resnet18
beta_schedule	linear
beta_start	0.0001
beta_end	0.02
timesteps	1000
batch_size (training)	32 | 64 | 128
n_epochs	1000
batch_size (testing)	64
optimizer	Adam
lr	0.001

4   Results

The three experiments are evaluated using accuracy and PAvPU score. Table 3 presents the accuracy and Patch Accuracy vs Patch Uncertainty (PAvPU) score for three different methods, CARD + ResNet18 and CARD + ResNet18 + CBAM, and with the self-supervised method for the FER2013 dataset. The Method column lists the two different methods used for the experiment, while the Accuracy column lists the overall *Accuracy* achieved by each method. The score for Patch Accuracy vs Patch Uncertainty, which evaluates a model's performance on a patch of the image while accounting for prediction uncertainty, is listed in the $PAvPU$ ($\alpha = 0.05$) column. From the table, we can see that our proposed SSL-based approach outperforms the existing benchmarks. Furthermore, we can see that the addition of the CBAM module has also improved both the accuracy and the PAvPU score of the CARD + ResNet18 method. The accuracy has increased from 61.3% to 64.8%, while the PAvPU score has increased from 65.0% to 66.5%. Using the SimCLR method, our model achieved the highest accuracy among all experiments. This indicates that the addition of SimCLR and CBAM has improved the ability of the model to make accurate predictions on specific patches of facial images while considering the uncertainty of the prediction. Overall, the results suggest that using the SSL-based method along with incorporating attention mechanisms such as CBAM can lead to improvements in the performance of deep learning vision models for vision-based tasks such as; facial expression recognition tasks.

Table 3. Accuracy and PAvPU score for FER2013 Dataset

Method	Accuracy (%)	PAvPU ($\alpha = 0.05$) (%)
Mao [7]	61.88	-
Luo et al. [5]	58.6 (ResNet18)	-
Wu et al. [6]	63.25	-
CARD + ResNet18	61.3	65.0
CARD + ResNet18 + CBAM	64.8	66.5
Proposed SSL	**66.6**	**66.9**

5   Conclusion

We proposed a model that improves facial expression recognition by using the diffusion model. Our model combined the SimCLR self-supervised method for feature extraction and integrated the Convolutional Block Attention Module (CBAM) into the model architecture. We trained and evaluated our model on the FER2013 dataset, and the model demonstrated significant performance improvements compared to previous approaches, confirming the effectiveness of our approach. Yet, the CARD model requires significant training time, a facet open for optimization. Future research offers ample prospects to advance facial expression recognition. Firstly, a promising avenue involves integrating multimodal information, wherein the fusion of facial expressions with speech or body gestures can potentially yield more holistic and precise recognition systems. Secondly, it would be beneficial to explore real-time and efficient implementations of the proposed model, allowing for its seamless deployment in resource-constrained environments. These directions hold significant potential for further advancements in facial expression recognition.

Acknowledgment. We're thankful to NORPART-CONNECT for their support and funding, enabling us to conduct this research. The European Union also supported the work through the Horizon 2020 Research and Innovation Programme within the ALAMEDA project (addressing brain disease diagnosis and treatment gaps) under grant agreement No GA 101017558.

References

1. Houssein, E.H., Hammad, A., Ali, A.A.: Human emotion recognition from EEG-based brain-computer interface using machine learning: a comprehensive review. Neural Comput. App. **34**(15), 12527–12557 (2022)
2. Ullah, H., Khan, S.D., Ullah, M., Cheikh, F.A.: Social modeling meets virtual reality: an immersive implication. In: Del Bimbo, A., et al. (eds.) ICPR 2021. LNCS, vol. 12664, pp. 131–140. Springer, Cham (2021). https://doi.org/10.1007/978-3-030-68799-1_10
3. Mao, W., Zhang, J., Yang, K., Stiefelhagen, R.: Panoptic lintention network: Towards efficient navigational perception for the visually impaired. In 2021 IEEE International Conference on Real-time Computing and Robotics (RCAR), pp. 857–862. IEEE (2021)
4. Ullah, M., Ullah, H., Khan, S.D., Cheikh, F.A.: Stacked LSTM network for human activity recognition using smartphone data. In: 2019 8th European Workshop on Visual Information Processing (EUVIP), pp. 175–180. IEEE (2019)
5. Luo, J., Xie, Z., Zhu, F., Zhu, X.: Facial expression recognition using machine learning models in fer2013. In: 2021 IEEE 3rd International Conference on Frontiers Technology of Information and Computer (ICFTIC), pp. 231–235. IEEE (2021)
6. Yirui, W., Zhang, L., Zonghua, G., Hu, L., Wan, S.: Edge-AI-driven framework with efficient mobile network design for facial expression recognition. ACM Trans. Embedded Comput. Syst. **22**(3), 1–17 (2023)
7. Mao, Y.: Optimization of facial expression recognition on ResNet-18 using focal loss and cosface loss. In: 2022 International Symposium on Advances in Informatics, Electronics and Education (ISAIEE), pp. 161–163. IEEE (2022)
8. Munsif, M., Ullah, M., Ahmad, B., Sajjad, M., Cheikh, F.A.: Monitoring neurological disorder patients via deep learning based facial expressions analysis. In: Maglogiannis, I., Iliadis, L., Macintyre, J., Cortez, P. (eds.) Artificial Intelligence Applications and Innovations. AIAI 2022 IFIP WG 12.5 International Workshops. AIAI 2022. IFIP Advances in Information and Communication Technology, vol. 652, pp. 412–423. Springer, Cham (2022). https://doi.org/10.1007/978-3-031-08341-9_33
9. Lin, T.-Y., Goyal, P., Girshick, R., He, K., Dollár, P.: Focal loss for dense object detection. In: Proceedings of the IEEE International Conference on Computer Vision, pp. 2980–2988 (2017)
10. Wang et al. Cosface: large margin cosine loss for deep face recognition. In: IEEE Conference on Computer Vision and Pattern Recognition, pp. 5265–5274 (2018)
11. Chen, X., Wang, Z., Cheikh, F.A., Ullah, M.: 3D-resnet fused attention for autism spectrum disorder classification. In: Peng, Y., Hu, S.-M., Gabbouj, M., Zhou, K., Elad, M., Xu, K. (eds.) ICIG 2021. LNCS, vol. 12889, pp. 607–617. Springer, Cham (2021). https://doi.org/10.1007/978-3-030-87358-5_49
12. Mamadou, K., Ullah, M., Nordbø, Ø., Cheikh, F.A.: Multi-encoder convolution block attention model for binary segmentation. In: 2022 International Conference on Frontiers of Information Technology (FIT), pp. 183–188. IEEE (2022)
13. Croitoru, F.-A., Hondru, V., Ionescu, R.T., Shah, M.: Diffusion models in vision: a survey. IEEE Trans. Pattern Anal. Mach. Intell. (2023)
14. Ho, J., Jain, A., Abbeel, P.: Denoising diffusion probabilistic models. Adv. Neural. Inf. Process. Syst. **33**, 6840–6851 (2020)
15. Han, X., Zheng, H., Zhou, M.: Card: Classification and regression diffusion models (2022). arXiv preprint arXiv:2206.07275

16. He, K., Zhang, X., Ren, S., Sun, J.: Deep residual learning for image recognition. In: Proceedings of the IEEE Conference on Computer Vision and Pattern Recognition, pp. 770–778 (2016)

17. Woo, S., Park, J., Lee, J.-Y., Kweon, I.S.: CBAM: convolutional block attention module. In: Ferrari, V., Hebert, M., Sminchisescu, C., Weiss, Y. (eds.) ECCV 2018. LNCS, vol. 11211, pp. 3–19. Springer, Cham (2018). https://doi.org/10.1007/978-3-030-01234-2_1

18. Chen, T., Kornblith, S., Norouzi, M., Hinton, G.: A simple framework for contrastive learning of visual representations. In: International Conference on Machine Learning, pp. 1597–1607. PMLR (2020)

19. Li, S., Deng, W., Du, J.P.: Reliable crowdsourcing and deep locality-preserving learning for expression recognition in the wild. In: Proceedings of the IEEE Conference on Computer Vision and Pattern Recognition, pp. 2852–2861 (2017)

20. Goodfellow, I.J., et al.: Challenges in representation learning: a report on three machine learning contests. In: Lee, M., Hirose, A., Hou, Z.-G., Kil, R.M. (eds.) ICONIP 2013. LNCS, vol. 8228, pp. 117–124. Springer, Heidelberg (2013). https://doi.org/10.1007/978-3-642-42051-1_16

BeECD: Belief-Aware Echo Chamber Detection over Twitter Stream

Guan Wang[1], Weihua Li[1(✉)], Shiqing Wu[3], Quan Bai[2],
and Edmund M.-K. Lai[1]

[1] Auckland University of Technology, Auckland, New Zealand
guan.wang@autuni.ac.nz, {weihua.li, edmund.lai}@aut.ac.nz
[2] University of Tasmania, Hobart, Australia
quan.bai@utas.edu.au
[3] University of Technology Sydney, Sydney, Australia
shiqing.wu@uts.edu.au

Abstract. The phenomenon known as the "echo chamber" has been widely acknowledged as a significant force affecting society. This has been particularly evident during the Covid-19 pandemic, wherein the echo chamber effect has significantly influenced public responses. Therefore, detecting echo chambers and mitigating their adverse impacts has become crucial to facilitate a more diverse exchange of ideas, fostering a more understanding and empathetic society. In response, we use deep learning methodologies to model each user's beliefs based on their historical message contents and behaviours. As such, we propose a novel, content-based framework built on the foundation of weighted beliefs. This framework is capable of detecting potential echo chambers by creating user belief graphs, utilizing their historical messages and behaviours. To demonstrate the practicality of this approach, we conducted experiments using the Twitter dataset on Covid-19. These experiments illustrate the potential for individuals to be isolated within echo chambers. Furthermore, our in-depth analysis of the results reveals patterns of echo chamber evolution and highlights the importance of weighted relations. Understanding these patterns can be instrumental in the development of tools and strategies to combat misinformation, encourage the sharing of diverse perspectives, and enhance the collective well-being and social good of our digital society.

Keywords: Echo Chamber · Covid-19 · Belief Graph · Ego Network

1 Introduction

Nowadays, online social platforms have become one of the key sources for people to perceive information. It also reshapes the way of searching, filtering and disseminating information [17]. Modelling and analysing the influence and dissemination of information on social networks, including information maximization, social sentiment analysis, concern detection, etc. [12,19], have become prominent

F. Liu et al. (Eds.): PRICAI 2023, LNAI 14327, pp. 307–319, 2024.
https://doi.org/10.1007/978-981-99-7025-4_27

subjects [11,14]. One of the main perspectives of social media is to expose users to like-minded peers, which may result in echo chambers that could reinforce users' pre-existing viewpoints and drive the communities to be more polarized [7]. Individuals in these communities are easily affected by their surroundings. Estimating the extent to which an individual is isolated in an echo chamber is helpful in breaking the isolation.

Jamieson et al. were the first to define the phenomenon occurring on social media platforms where information within a community is amplified and metaphorically term it as the "echo chamber" [10]. To determine whether an individual is isolated within an echo chamber, we focus on their surroundings and behaviours. Therefore, we define the echo chamber from an individual perspective. This phenomenon is characterized by an individual who:

- Resides in a community that echoes their opinion, wherein most neighbours share similar views.
- Inhabits this community, where the individual's perspectives are repeatedly reinforced by community members.
- Self-reinforces by engaging in communication that aligns with their viewpoint.

The prominence of the echo chamber phenomenon has been heightened by the outbreak of Covid-19. Recognised globally as a pandemic, Covid-19 has become a leading topic of discussion. Conversations around this subject vary widely, encompassing themes such as vaccine hesitancy and vaccination-related deaths. Under these conditions, social platforms provide a conducive environment for misinformation propagation due to the lack of editorial supervision. As a result, echo chambers have emerged among users, significantly influencing responses to the Covid-19 pandemic [2]. For example, if members of a community consistently engage with and promote content sceptical of Covid-19 vaccinations, the community can be highly identified as an echo chamber resistant to the prevailing medical advice on vaccines.

To address this challenging issue, we propose a novel approach to detect the echo chamber phenomenon and estimate the corresponding degree. In pursuing this aim, we explore the utility of knowledge graphs in identifying echo chambers from an individual perspective and propose a content-based framework that constructs belief graphs for each individual. During this construction process, we extract triplets from the individual's related Twitter content, including tweets, retweets, and replies. To assess the impact of individual behaviours, we incorporate them as distinct parameters to calculate weights for these triplets. Extensive experiments are conducted, and the results explicitly show that modelling an individual's belief graphs with weighted relations can effectively reveal an individual's trends on a specific topic and identify the echo chambers to which the individual belongs.

2   Related Work

2.1   Echo Chambers on Social Platforms

Social platforms have subtly altered the way people access information and formed echo chambers, isolating them in the process [7]. The detection of echo chambers has been a research focus across various fields [4,18], serving as the first step towards mitigating this phenomenon.

Social structures typically manifest in two distinct forms, i.e., global perspective and individual perspective. Most research has studied echo chambers from a global perspective or topological viewpoint, primarily focusing on user interactions while overlooking the source of these interactions [5,6]. Cinelli et al. analyze echo chambers by assessing whether the overall network is strongly polarized towards two sides of a controversy, emphasizing user interaction networks [7]. Cossard et al. explore echo chambers within vaccine communities using clustering techniques, demonstrating the existence of echo chambers within real social networks [8].

Analyzing extensive topological structure datasets from a global perspective necessitates high-performance computing resources. The ego network centred around a focal user offers a feasible way to model a community, enabling measurement of the echo chamber degree with a focus on that user. Thus, inspired by Li et al. and Valerio et al., we incorporate the concept of the ego network in our study [3,13]. Li et al. propose agent-based influence diffusion models, where the influence cascading process is modelled as an evolutionary pattern driven by individuals' actions. Valerio et al. analyze the micro-level structural properties of online social networks and demonstrate that ego networks play a significant role in social networks, impacting information diffusion within the network.

2.2   Content-Based Echo Chamber Detection

Content-based methods identify echo chambers by analyzing the information texts produced by individuals. Villa et al. propose both a topology-based and content-based approach, analyzing the topological structure of the social network and sentiment aspects related to the content [21]. Cinelli et al. conduct a comparative analysis on a large-scale dataset to identify echo chambers through social network homophily. They define "leaning" as the attitude expressed by a piece of content towards a specific topic about the content [7]. Abd-Alrazaq et al. propose a text-mining method on a large dataset, considering information texts but neglecting temporal information, which can provide contextual insights [1]. Lwin et al. and Xue et al. demonstrate that discourses on Twitter about Covid-19 continually evolve, develop, or change over time [15,22]. Inspired by these studies, we restructure the dataset into chronologically user-specific streams.

Most existing studies solely consider the content of information but overlook individual behaviours and content weights, which demonstrate the significance of content on individuals. For instance, reading a message doesn't explicitly reveal an individual's thoughts about the message. However, a subsequent 'like' or 'upvote' implies that the individual agrees with this message, thereby increasing the weight of information from this message in the corresponding belief graph. We argue that beliefs in individuals' minds carry different weights, and not all beliefs hold equal significance. As a result, behaviours offer valuable insights into people's perspectives on related messages.

Therefore, we propose a belief-aware echo chamber detection framework incorporating content and individual behaviours. Our framework constructs belief graphs for each individual in our dataset, considering their behaviours. To measure the degree of echo chambers, we calculate the similarities between the belief graphs of the focal user and their neighbours. With this framework, social platforms can detect communities where members are primarily exposed to reinforcing views, potentially limiting the diversity of thoughts and contributing to polarization.

3   Belief-Aware Echo Chamber Detection

In this section, we formally define related terms and explain the proposed belief-aware echo chamber detection framework.

3.1   Formal Definitions

Two types of graph structures are utilized in this work: one is the ego network, a directed graph $G =< U, E >$ that includes a focal user and its neighbours, and the other is the user belief graph $BG =< H, WR, T >$.

Definition 1. *An **ego network** consists of a focal user u_f and their neighbouring users, denoted as $U = \{u_0, ..., u_n\}$. Each user, represented by $u_i \in U$, corresponds to a node in this directed network. Each $edge(u_i, u_j)$ between nodes is directed as the flow of information, indicating that user u_i follows, replies to, or mentions user u_j. Each user in an ego network also has a unique belief graph, representing their personal network of beliefs, which is clarified in Definition 2.*

Definition 2. *A **belief graph** is a unique graph containing multiple triplets $BG = \{H, WR, T\}$, where H and T refer to nodes in belief graphs, and $WR = \{wr_i | 0 < i < m\}$ represents relations between nodes, defined as weighted relations. The belief graph is constructed by extracting triplets from users' historical messages and behaviours on corresponding messages across various topics.*

Definition 3. ***Similarity** $sim(v_i, v_j)$ refers to the distance between two vectors in a low-dimensional space. The similarity is a value between $[0, 1]$, where 0 implies completely contrary viewpoints, while 1 signifies identical viewpoints.*

Definition 4. ***Echo chamber degree** $p(u, k)$ is a measure that evaluates the likelihood of an echo chamber. A higher degree suggests a higher probability that an individual experiences an echo chamber related to a specific topic k.*

Definition 5. *Topic* k *refers to the label of each message, e.g., m_k. The topic set is denoted as $T = \{T_0, T_1, ..., T_n\}$. Messages with the same topics express similar discourse. One message is assigned only one topic. In our framework, topics are used for graph partitioning.*

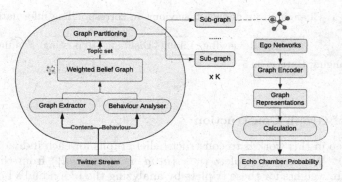

Fig. 1. The brief overall process of the framework.

As illustrated in Fig. 1, we determine the echo chamber degree in 5 phases:

- Construct a belief graph for each individual, considering both their Twitter stream and their user behaviours.
- Partition the corresponding part of an individual's belief graph into sub-graphs according to different topics.
- Select an individual and its neighbours to create an ego network based on their followee/follower relations and mentioning behaviour.
- Calculate the similarities of sub-graphs on a given topic between the focal user and its neighbours to assess the closeness of their beliefs.
- Quantify the echo chamber degree by evaluating their average similarity and information entropy.

A sub-graph is a graph partitioned from an individual's complete belief graph given a specific topic. Sub-graphs are used to compare users. Messages refer to texts that users receive and post, including tweets, retweets, and replies. User behaviours refer to user operations on a social platform, including:

- Viewing: Users view messages posted by their neighbours (followees) or recommended by the platform.
- Liking: Users like a message by clicking the blank heart symbol.
- Disliking: Users express dislike for a message by cancelling their liking behaviour, i.e., clicking the solid heart symbol.
- Reposting: Users repost viewed messages.
- Sending: Users post a message or reply to someone in their own words.

We presume each behaviour reflects a different perspective on corresponding messages and aids in modelling changes in user beliefs. For example, when a user likes a message, we increase the weight of triplets extracted from this message by assigning a changing rate to the weight. The changing rates are defined for different behaviours as shown in Table 1:

Table 1. Changing rate of each behaviour on corresponding information.

	Reviewing	Liking	Disliking	Reposting	Sending
Changing Rate(r)	0.5	2	−2	1	2

3.2 Belief Graph Construction

The first step in this work is to construct belief graphs for each individual in the ego network. We extract triplets (i.e., {*head, relation, tail*}) from the content and calculate weights for these triplets by analyzing the individual's behaviours. We then attach the weights to the relations, resulting in weighted relations. A belief graph that reflects an individual's belief consists of multiple triplets with weighted relations. We use Stanford OpenIE [1] to extract triplets from texts.

To calculate the weights, we employ a logarithmic function to prevent the weights from reaching extremely high or low. This logarithmic transformation helps maintain a balanced range of weights. The function is defined as follows:

$$w_i = ln(w_i^{'} + r_i) + 1, \tag{1}$$

where $w_i^{'}$ is the previous weight of the same triplet and r_i is the changing rate as shown in Table 1.

During extraction, the same triplets may be extracted multiple times. For each new triplet, the initial weight is defined as 0, and its current weight is calculated based on the changing rate of the corresponding behaviour. When we encounter the identical triplet, we add the change in weight according to the current behaviour to its previous weight (i.e., $w_i^{'}$ in Eq. 1).

3.3 Belief Graph Partitioning

A complete belief graph of an individual encompasses information from several topics. Comparing complete graphs may allow irrelevant information to affect performance on the given topic. Hence, we perform a graph partitioning step before transforming graphs into graph representations.

In this step, we utilize word embeddings from a word2vec model [16] to identify nodes within the belief graph that have similar words to the given topic

---

[1] https://nlp.stanford.edu/software/openie.html.

and keywords. The cosine similarity function, as shown below, is utilized to measure the similarity between word embeddings. Nodes and relations in both directions are subsequently used to form the sub-graph.

$$sim(v_i, v_j) = \frac{v_i \cdot v_j}{\parallel v_i \parallel\parallel v_j \parallel}, \tag{2}$$

where v_i and v_j denote word embeddings obtained from the word2vec model.

3.4   Echo Chamber Detection

To compare the similarities among belief graphs, we convert these topological structure graphs into vector representations. This is achieved through training Graph Attention Networks (GATs) on each individual's belief graph to generate graph representations. Different from the original GATs [20], we introduce the weighted relation features $R = \{r_{i,j} | 0 < i < n, 0 < j < n\}$ as the initial attention coefficient. The weighted relation features are used during the attention calculation as follows:

$$e_{i,j} = a(W\hat{h}_i, W\hat{h}_j, r_{i,j}) \tag{3}$$

Equation 3 represents the importance of node j's features to node i. W denotes a weight matrix used to parameterize a shared linear transformation, $\hat{h}_i$ represents the features of node i, and $r_{i,j}$ is the weighted relation from node i to node j. To collect all features of the whole graph, we add a global node to each graph. This global node is linked to every node in the graph, and its representation represents the entire graph.

We hypothesize that similar graphs express similar beliefs on relevant topics. To test this, we compute the similarity between individuals' belief graphs. We apply the graph representations generated by the trained GATs to a cosine similarity function to calculate these similarities:

$$sim(h_i^k, h_u^k) = \frac{h_i^k \cdot h_u^k}{\parallel h_i^k \parallel\parallel h_u^k \parallel}, \tag{4}$$

where h_i^k denotes the representation of user i's sub-belief graph on topic k, and $\parallel h_i^k \parallel$ represents the Euclidean norm of h_i^k. h_u^k refers to the representation of the focal user's sub-graph on topic k. The average similarities are then calculated as follows:

$$avg(h_u^k) = 1/n \sum_{i=1}^{n} sim(h_i^k, h_u^k), \tag{5}$$

where n describes the number of the focal user's neighbours.

In addition to similarity, inspired by [9], we also consider information entropy from information theory and statistical mechanics to calculate the probability of an individual being isolated in an echo chamber. The equation is as follows:

$$H(g_u^k) = - \sum_{k \subseteq K} p_k \cdot ln(p_k), \qquad (6)$$

where p_k is the percentage of a user's sub-graph on topic k, and g_u^k refers to the belief graph of the focal user of an ego network on topic k. Finally, we use both average similarity and information entropy to measure the echo chamber using the following equation:

$$p(u, k) = avg(h_u^k) \cdot H(g_u^k), \qquad (7)$$

where u represents a focal user. A higher $p(u, k)$ indicates a greater likelihood that u is isolated in an echo chamber. In such a case, the ego network centred around user u is a $p(u, k)$ possibility echo chamber on topic k.

4   Experiments and Analysis

This section provides details of two experiments conducted to validate the efficacy of the proposed Belief-based Echo Chamber Detection model. The first experiment evaluates the similarities in responses of echo chamber members to multiple related messages. The second experiment implements an ablation study to elucidate the progression of the Belief Graph module within the BeECD framework and to investigate the impact of weighted relations on belief graphs.

4.1   Data Collection and Organisation

The experiments utilize a dataset gathered from Twitter related to Covid-19. This dataset, part of the continually updated Covid-19 Twitter chatter dataset maintained by Georgia State University's Panacea Lab, spans a crucial six-month period from December 2020 to May 2021. This time frame is particularly significant as it encompasses a period when several candidate vaccines displayed safety and the ability to generate immune responses. The proposed BeECD can be applied to any dataset. In this paper, we leverage Covid-19 as the dataset to validate this approach.

Each individual's content and behaviours are organised into a chronological stream, including the user's tweets, tweets from the user's neighbours, retweets, replies, corresponding tweets, likes, and liked tweets. We limit our focus solely to English tweets, replies, and retweets, and uniquely, we include retweets in the streams of each individual, allowing us to process retweeting behaviour and corresponding content concurrently.

To facilitate computation, we extracted a sub-graph from the total dataset, comprising 285 users, 3,587 interconnections, and 42,478 posts, which include tweets, retweets, and replies.

4.2   Experiment 1: Response Analysis

In this experiment, we hypothesize that each user within an ego network can respond appropriately to one or multiple similar messages, anticipating that responses from like-minded users will exhibit greater similarity than those from dissimilar users. The implications of this phenomenon in real-world contexts are substantial. Consider, for instance, an ego network exhibiting an 80% echo chamber probability. If the average response probabilities within this network align closely with this percentage, it will signify that most users within the network are engaged in disseminating and consuming similar information. In a practical sense, this may translate to a reinforcement of a specific narrative or perspective. The resulting lack of engagement with diverse viewpoints could amplify polarization. This may create a self-reinforcing cycle in which users are confined to information confirming their pre-existing beliefs, thereby becoming increasingly resistant to alternative viewpoints or evidence contradicting their established convictions.

In addition to calculating the echo chamber probabilities, we subsequently train an encoder-decoder structured language model on the entire dataset, feeding 20 random messages from the test set into each ego network based on the same topic that the ego network inclines towards. The language model is used to assess the similarity of the users' responses. By comparing the echo chamber probabilities and response similarities, we assess the efficacy of the proposed framework. The results depicted in Fig. 2 corroborate our hypothesis.

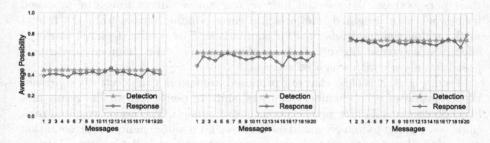

Fig. 2. The probabilities of detected echo chamber and user response similarities.

By presenting the outcomes from three distinct ego networks with varying degrees of echo chamber probabilities, it's clear that the average response probabilities align with the calculated echo chamber probabilities.

This experiment sheds light on the intricate relationship between online interactions and the formation of echo chambers. The observed alignment between the echo chamber probability and user response patterns underscores the role digital platforms play in shaping real-world perspectives, emphasizing the need for further research and interventions in this domain.

4.3   Experiment 2: Belief Graph Impact Analysis

The second experiment seeks to understand the influence of weighted relations on the evolution of echo chambers. We additionally train Graph Attention Networks (GATs) that do not account for the properties of relations during the training process. Belief graphs are initiated using data from the first two months of six, following which the remaining data is partitioned into 25 unique time intervals. From each interval of the users' Twitter streams, users' beliefs and behaviours are extracted and used to update their corresponding belief graphs.

By partitioning data into distinct time intervals, we highlight the significance of temporal evolution in shaping users' beliefs. This process shows the importance of identifying the beliefs and understanding how they transform and develop over time. Such an approach corresponds to real-world scenarios, where individuals often undergo phases or shifts in their perspectives. These changes may be influenced by various factors, such as past experiences, exposure to new information, or personal growth, reflecting the complexity and dynamism of human belief systems.

We anticipate that our framework, which incorporates weighted relations, is capable of detecting variations in user beliefs, including instances where these beliefs intensify before subsequently diminishing. This approach offers insight into the dynamic nature of belief changes. On the other hand, in the absence of such weighted relations, a user's beliefs appear to remain unaltered and static. This lack of dynamism obscures the potential to observe the evolutionary patterns of echo chambers, even in cases where users undergo significant shifts in their perspectives. We selected four representative curves from our proposed framework with weighted relations and corresponding curves from the framework lacking weighted relations for comparison. The results depicted in Fig. 3 effectively showcase different patterns of evolution of echo chambers in our proposed framework with weighted relations.

From Fig. 3, it is clear that our proposed framework can effectively represent the evolution of echo chambers or users' shifting perspectives. The result also highlights a crucial difference between the two models. The use of weighted relations, as opposed to non-weighted ones, allows for a more nuanced representation of the complexities inherent in human interactions and belief systems. In real-world terms, not all interactions influence our beliefs equally. Some might have a significant impact due to the trustworthiness of the source or the emotional resonance of the content, while others might be casually scrolled past without much thought. Thus, incorporating weighted relations can more accurately model how real people might be influenced by their digital interactions.

Understanding the evolution of echo chambers using advanced models like GATs with weighted relations is crucial in today's digital age. Such insights provide a clearer picture of how beliefs change over time on platforms like Twitter, emphasizing the need for digital platforms to prioritize diverse content exposure and critical thinking among their users.

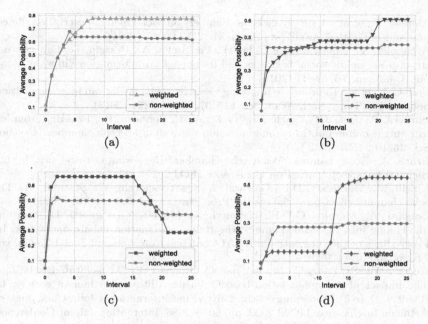

Fig. 3. The evolution of echo chambers.

5   Conclusion and Prospective Research Directions

In this study, we introduce a novel content-based methodology for echo chamber detection on social networks, coined as the belief-aware echo chamber detection approach shedding light on the intricate relationship between online interactions and the formation of echo chambers. We leverage Knowledge Graph technology to construct user belief graphs, taking into account both message content and user behaviour. Additionally, we train modified Graph Attention Networks, incorporating weighted relations into the computation process. Similarities between user belief graphs are then computed. The experimental results indicate promising effectiveness and demonstrate real-world implications of our approach in analyzing echo chambers on social platforms.

However, the detection of echo chambers represents a seminal work, and addressing the subsequent effects presents significant challenges. Future research endeavours will focus on strategies for mitigating the echo chambers, further advancing the understanding and management of social network dynamics.

References

1. Abd-Alrazaq, A., Alhuwail, D., Househ, M., Hamdi, M., Shah, Z., et al.: Top concerns of tweeters during the covid-19 pandemic: infoveillance study. J. Med. Internet Res. **22**(4), e19016 (2020)

2. Alatawi, F., et al.: A survey on echo chambers on social media: description, detection and mitigation. arXiv preprint arXiv:2112.05084 (2021)
3. Arnaboldi, V., Conti, M., La Gala, M., Passarella, A., Pezzoni, F.: Ego network structure in online social networks and its impact on information diffusion. Comput. Commun. **76**, 26–41 (2016)
4. Bail, C.A., et al.: Exposure to opposing views on social media can increase political polarization. Proc. Natl. Acad. Sci. **115**(37), 9216–9221 (2018)
5. Barberá, P., Jost, J.T., Nagler, J., Tucker, J.A., Bonneau, R.: Tweeting from left to right: is online political communication more than an echo chamber? Psychol. Sci. **26**(10), 1531–1542 (2015)
6. Bruns, A.: Echo chamber? What echo chamber? Reviewing the evidence. In: 6th Biennial Future of Journalism Conference (FOJ 2017) (2017)
7. Cinelli, M., Morales, G.D.F., Galeazzi, A., Quattrociocchi, W., Starnini, M.: The echo chamber effect on social media. Proc. Natl. Acad. Sci. **118**(9) (2021)
8. Cossard, A., Morales, G.D.F., Kalimeri, K., Mejova, Y., Paolotti, D., Starnini, M.: Falling into the echo chamber: the Italian vaccination debate on twitter. In: Proceedings of the International AAAI Conference on Web and Social Media, vol. 14, pp. 130–140 (2020)
9. Hu, Y., Wu, S., Jiang, C., Li, W., Bai, Q., Roehrer, E.: AI facilitated isolations? The impact of recommendation-based influence diffusion in human society. In: Raedt, L.D. (ed.) Proceedings of the Thirty-First International Joint Conference on Artificial Intelligence, IJCAI 2022, pp. 5080–5086. International Joint Conferences on Artificial Intelligence Organization (2022)
10. Jamieson, K.H., Cappella, J.N.: Echo Chamber: Rush Limbaugh and the Conservative Media Establishment. Oxford University Press, Oxford (2008)
11. Jiang, C., D'Arienzo, A., Li, W., Wu, S., Bai, Q.: An operator-based approach for modeling influence diffusion in complex social networks. J. Soc. Comput. **2**(2), 166–182 (2021)
12. Li, W., Bai, Q., Jiang, C., Zhang, M.: Stigmergy-based influence maximization in social networks. In: Booth, R., Zhang, M.-L. (eds.) PRICAI 2016. LNCS (LNAI), vol. 9810, pp. 750–762. Springer, Cham (2016). https://doi.org/10.1007/978-3-319-42911-3_63
13. Li, W., Bai, Q., Zhang, M.: Agent-based influence propagation in social networks. In: 2016 IEEE International Conference on Agents (ICA), pp. 51–56. IEEE (2016)
14. Li, W., Bai, Q., Zhang, M.: Siminer: a stigmergy-based model for mining influential nodes in dynamic social networks. IEEE Trans. Big Data **5**(2), 223–237 (2018)
15. Lwin, M.O., et al.: Global sentiments surrounding the covid-19 pandemic on twitter: analysis of twitter trends. JMIR Public Health Surveill. **6**(2), e19447 (2020)
16. Mikolov, T., Chen, K., Corrado, G., Dean, J.: Efficient estimation of word representations in vector space (2013)
17. Morini, V., Pollacci, L., Rossetti, G.: Toward a standard approach for echo chamber detection: reddit case study. Appl. Sci. **11**(12), 5390 (2021)
18. Romer, D., Jamieson, K.H.: Patterns of media use, strength of belief in covid-19 conspiracy theories, and the prevention of covid-19 from march to July 2020 in the united states: survey study. J. Med. Internet Res. **23**(4), e25215 (2021)
19. Shi, J., et al.: Automated concern exploration in pandemic situations - COVID-19 as a use case. In: Uehara, H., Yamaguchi, T., Bai, Q. (eds.) PKAW 2021. LNCS (LNAI), vol. 12280, pp. 178–185. Springer, Cham (2021). https://doi.org/10.1007/978-3-030-69886-7_15
20. Veličković, P., Casanova, A., Lió, P., Cucurull, G., Romero, A., Bengio, Y.: Graph attention networks (2018)

21. Villa, G., Pasi, G., Viviani, M.: Echo chamber detection and analysis. Soc. Netw. Anal. Min. **11**(1), 1–17 (2021)
22. Xue, J., Chen, J., Chen, C., Zheng, C., Li, S., Zhu, T.: Public discourse and sentiment during the covid 19 pandemic: using latent dirichlet allocation for topic modeling on twitter. PLoS ONE **15**(9), e0239441 (2020)

Building an Egyptian-Arabic Speech Corpus for Emotion Analysis Using Deep Learning

Sarah Safwat[1]([✉]), Mohammed A. -M. Salem[1], and Nada Sharaf[2]

[1] The German University in Cairo, New Cairo, Egypt
{sarah.khaled,mohammed.salem}@guc.edu.eg
[2] The German International University, Cairo, Egypt
nada.hamed@giu-uni.de

Abstract. Emotionally intelligent Virtual Assistants (VAs) are increasingly gaining popularity, especially with the digitization of different life aspects. The focus of our work is to build VAs that can understand the emotional state of users from their Egyptian-Arabic speech. This requires the availability of large emotional datasets to be able to train accurate models. Available corpora include different languages and dialects. However, the Egyptian-Arabic dialect, in particular, shows a significant gap. The main contribution of this paper is to fill this gap by gathering a semi-natural Egyptian-Arabic dataset. The dataset includes six emotions: happiness, sadness, anger, neutral, surprise, and fear. To the best of the authors' knowledge, it is considered as the first Egyptian-Arabic dataset to include surprise and fear emotions. Also, a Deep Learning (DL) model is introduced that is able to detect the first 4 emotions with average accuracies of 70.3% and 73% for an imbalanced dataset and a balanced dataset, respectively, and the first 5 emotions with average accuracies of 65% and 66% for an imbalanced dataset and a balanced dataset, respectively.

Keywords: Speech emotion recognition · Deep learning · Acoustic features

1 Introduction

Emotion-based Artificial Intelligence (AI) is a growing research area nowadays. Emotions play a crucial role in how humans interact with one another. Thus, developing VAs that could understand the emotional state of the humans and how they react would significantly improve their interaction. Emotionally intelligent VAs [28] may be useful in a variety of fields, including business and healthcare. They can be used to detect any change in pitch or tone in the customers' voices that signals their dissatisfaction during calls at call centers in order to achieve better business performance. Also, in health care, because of AI's capacity to identify signs of mental health conditions such as depression, bipolar disorder, post-traumatic stress disorder, and other anxiety disorders through voice

F. Liu et al. (Eds.): PRICAI 2023, LNAI 14327, pp. 320–332, 2024.
https://doi.org/10.1007/978-981-99-7025-4_28

analysis, VAs could allow psychiatrists to monitor patients' well-being between clinic appointments.

Emotions may be recognized through analyzing different aspects such as facial expressions and hand gestures in the case of video, tone of voice in the case of speech and punctuation in the case of written text [17]. The work presented in this paper is primarily concerned with speech emotion recognition, and more particularly, emotion recognition from the acoustic features of speech.

Non-verbal communication and the way in which the words are spoken carries a lot of essential information about the emotional state and the intention of the speaker. The same textual message would be conveyed with different semantics by incorporating appropriate emotions. In other words, the semantics of a spoken word cannot be comprehended solely by reading the text. Thus, in addition to the speech context, speech systems should be able to interpret non-linguistic information like emotions. [17].

The task of Speech Emotion Recognition (SER) requires huge amounts of labelled data in order to achieve high emotion classification accuracy [15]. Thus, collecting data for this particular task has been the focus of studies for many years. Emotional speech is also influenced by the spoken language, and particularly the origin and culture of the speaker [21]. The majority of emotional speech databases used take into account European languages. Asian languages have also seen a rise in the number of emotional speech databases recently. However, there is not much material about African emotional speech databases [23]. Particularly for Arabic, there are extremely few emotional speech databases in different dialects. Despite the fact that Egyptian-Arabic is one of the most popular dialects in Arabic, only one dataset existed. The available Egyptian-Arabic dataset is called (EYASE) [2]. It consists of 579 utterances and only four available emotional states. Consequently, the main goal for this paper was to collect a larger emotional speech dataset in Egyptian-Arabic dialect with a wider range of emotions.

This paper introduces an Egyptian-Arabic emotional speech dataset (EAED) that consists of 3,614 audio files recorded from multiple Egyptian TV series. The dataset includes five emotions which are: happiness, sadness, anger, surprise and fear alongside the neutral speech. To be a total of six different emotional states. The selection of emotions included was based on Paul Ekman's suggestion that there are six basic emotions: anger, disgust, fear, happiness, sadness and surprise [9]. Thus, the dataset included five of the six basic emotions. And, disgust emotion was discarded because after analysing the chosen TV series, it was found that it almost does not exist. For the same reason, the majority of semi-natural datasets lack this emotion. And, since it is uncommon, this means that they are of less need for a virtual assistant. Moreover, a DL model is then proposed for the task of emotion classification. Consequently, the main contributions of this paper could be summarized as follows:

1. Filling the resource gap in Egyptian-Arabic emotional speech through EAED, which consists of 3,614 utterances, with the following specifications:

- It is the first Egyptian-Arabic emotional speech dataset to include surprise and fear emotions.
- It involves huge number of speakers compared to the available Egyptian-Arabic corpus (72 speakers versus 6 speakers).
- It was collected from more than one TV series with different genres to ensure its ability to train more generalized models.
2. Investigating the effect of using a proposed DL model for the task of Egyptian-Arabic SER achieving comparable results with existing methods.

Section 2 includes the related work and benchmark emotional speech corpora with multiple languages and dialects. Section 3 includes the details of the data collection process. Section 4 contains the detailed description of our dataset. Section 5 includes the steps followed in order to validate the reliability of our data. Section 6 includes the proposed DL model. Last but not least, Sect. 7 states the results of the proposed model on EAED.

2   Related Work

Emotional speech datasets can be classified into four categories which are natural, semi-natural, acted and elicited datasets [2]. Natural emotional speech datasets are those recorded from call centers or TV shows [1]. They are considered as natural since the recorded speech reflects genuine emotions and natural reactions without any intended exaggerations or deliberate dramatisation. Semi- Natural datasets are those recorded from movies or TV series with professional actors speaking the dialogue [1]. However, real-life situations requiring the involvement of emotional expression, are presented to the performers. The main challenge in natural and semi-natural data sets is that, many human labelers must listen to the recorded audio files in order to choose the most accurate label for an audio file, which takes a lot of time. They also suffer from background noise. Acted datasets are a type of emotional speech dataset that is gathered by the help of professional actors and actresses, who are then asked to say a set of linguistically neutral sentences with various predefined emotions [17]. Elicited datasets is quite similar to acted datasets. However, elicited datasets are gathered by people with no acting experience, which makes them less efficient. Acted and elicited data sets are prone to over-fitting because they are captured in noise-free environments. However, the noise-free environments makes the task of feature extraction easier.

Regarding the common practices for gathering acted and elicited emotional corpora, EMODB [6], which is one of the most commonly used datasets in the field of SER, was recorded in an anechoic chamber with the help of 10 professional actors. The audio files were recorded at a 48-kHz sampling rate and then down-sampled to 16 kHz. Furthermore, RAVDESS [19], which is a multimodal database of emotional speech and song in North American accent, was generated by 24 professional actors vocalizing lexically-matched statements. Each expression is produced at two levels of emotional intensity, with an additional neutral expression. In addition, IITKGP-SEHSC [18] is an Indian acted database that is recorded using 10 professional actors. Fifteen Hindi text prompts were chosen for recording. All the sentences were emotionally neutral in meaning. Each artist must speak the 15 words in a single session using the eight fundamental emotions. All the audio files were recorded at a 16 kHz sampling rate. Last but not least, KSUEmotions [22], which is an elicited emotional speech database designed for Modern Standard Arabic (MSA), was generated with the help of fourteen speakers. The speakers were from three Arab countries: Yemen, Saudi Arabia and Syria. The recorded corpus was perceptually tested by nine listeners (six male and three female) and the audio files were recorded using 16 KHz sampling frequency.

Regarding the common practices for gathering natural and semi-natural emotional corpora, a Chinese natural emotional speech dataset was created using 20 different episodes from a Chinese talk-show. The number of speakers is 53 (16 males and 37 females). Speech signals were sampled at 16 KHz. Four different human testers have been assigned to listen to the audio files in order to test its reliability. Then, some of the audios were discarded and recollected [30]. Also, a Saudi semi-natural database was created from YouTube videos taken from the popular Saudi YouTube channel Telfaz11 [4]. The audio files were extracted from videos, which were divided into smaller chunks. The chunks were around 1 to 9 s in length. As a preprocessing step, the noise, background music, and silence were removed. The final dataset was composed of 113 utterances recorded by male actors and 62 utterances recorded by female actresses.

Table 1 shows more details for the available emotional speech corpora and emphasizes the gap in the Egyptian-Dialect compared to other languages, and how the proposed dataset contributes in filling this significant gap.

One of the most widely used classifiers for the task of SER is neural networks including both Convolutional Neural Networks (CNNs) and Long Short Term Memory networks (LSTMs) [5, 12, 24, 25].

3   Dataset Collection

In this paper, we have collected an Arabic emotional speech dataset with Egyptian dialect called EAED. The dataset is a semi-natural one as it was collected from a collection of well-known Egyptian TV series. A batch of undergraduate Engineering students in computer science department was recruited for the data collection task. The students were grouped into teams of four. Each group was asked to watch the episodes of one TV series carefully and then divide it into smaller chunks of audio files containing emotional tone of voices. Each audio file ranged in length from 1 to 8 s depending on the completion time of the given sentence. Our dataset contains six different emotions: happiness, sadness, anger, neutral, surprise, and fear. The inclusion of the surprise and fear emotions in the dataset is one of our primary contributions. As such, it is the first dataset of Egyptian-Arabic that include those two emotions. All audio files were recorded using the open source Audacity Software at sampling rate 44.1 KHz. Then, four different human labelers including the one who recorded the audio

Table 1. Emotional Speech Datasets

	Dataset Name	Language	Type	Files	Emotions
[6]	EmoDB	German	Acted	535	anger, boredom, disgust, fear, happiness, sadness and neutral (7)
[19]	Ravdess	North American	Acted	7,356	calm, happy, sad, angry, fearful, surprise, and disgust (7)
[11]	SAVEE	English	Acted	480	anger, disgust, fear, happiness, sadness, surprise and neutral (7)
[3]	TESS	English	Elicited	2,800	neutral, sad, surprise, calm, happiness, fear, disgust and anger (8)
[7]	IEMOCAP	English	Acted	10,039	happiness, anger, sadness, frustration and neutral (5)
[18]	IITKGP-SEHSC	Indian	Acted	12,000	anger, disgust, fear, happy, neutral, sad, sarcastic and surprise (8)
[30]	-	Chinese	Natural	800	anger, joy, sadness and neutral (4)
[4]	Telfaz11	Saudi-dialect	Semi-Natural	175	angry, happy, sad, and neutral (4)
[13]	ADED	Algerian-dialect	Semi-Natural	200	fear, anger, sadness and neutral(4)
[22]	KSUEmotions	MSA	Elicited	1,680	neutral, sadness, happiness, surprise, and anger (5)
[2]	EYASE	Egyptian-dialect	Semi-Natural	579	angry, happy, neutral and sad. (4)
-	Proposed EAED	Egyptian-dialect	Semi-Natural	3,614	angry, happy, neutral, sad, surprise and fearful (6)

file were assigned to hear the audio file in order to annotate it. All the pre-aggregated labels as well as some useful metadata for each audio file including speaker name, gender, age group and series name were saved in csv files. However, after reviewing the csv files, some ties in the annotations were detected. Consequently, a fifth labeler was assigned for the task of tie-breaking. Then, the label with the maximum voting was chosen for each file. The audio files for each series are grouped in a separate folder. Each folder consists of multiple folders, one for each actor/actress in the series. In each actor/actress folder, the audio files are named in the following convention: AA_BB _CC.wav

AA: Actor unique ID

BB: the emotion label

CC: a number to uniquely identify the file inside the folder

Example: NellyKarim_happy_01.wav is a file in a folder that belongs to an actress whose name is Nelly Karim and the emotion being conveyed is happy.

4 Dataset Description

Our dataset was constructed from five different well known Egyptian TV series.

Here are some statistical data for the five chosen series, including the number of speakers and the proportion of males and females involved:

- Leaalasear: 23 speakers were involved (8 males and 15 females).
- SahebELSaada: 21 speakers were involved (12 males and 9 females).
- SuitsArabic: 16 speakers were involved (8 males and 8 females).
- ElSayad: 7 speakers were involved (2 males and 5 females).
- AshamIblis: 12 speakers were involved (7 males and 5 females).

Table 2. Number of emotional utterances in each series

Series Name	Neutral	Sad	Happy	Angry	Surprise	Fearful	Total
Leaalasear	120	143	147	145	91	29	675
SahebELSaada	338	125	80	260	65	42	910
SuitsArabic	127	80	72	138	108	60	585
ElSayad	296	160	93	223	66	20	858
AshamIblis	123	113	36	143	117	54	586

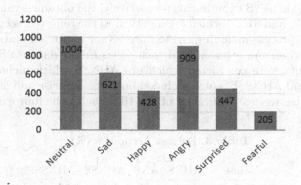

Fig. 1. Emotions Statistics in EAED.

Table 2, shows the number of audio files for each emotion separately in each series. Figure 1, shows the number of utterances of each emotion in the whole dataset. It is obvious that, the fear emotion has the least number of utterances due to the lack of this emotion in the selected series. The data is available for research purposes on the following link: http://ieee-dataport.org/11495.

326 S. Safwat et al.

5 Dataset Validation

EYASE dataset was taken as a baseline dataset for this work. A set of different acoustic features were extracted from EYASE based on the findings of [2].

- Prosodic features such as pitch, intensity, jitter, and shimmer were retrieved using parsel-mouth [14]. Then, statistical features such as mean, minimum, maximum, standard deviation and range were computed from both pitch and intensity.
- Spectral features were also extracted including the first three formants, the mean of the first twelve Mel-frequency Cepstral Coefficients (MFCCs) and long-term average spectrum (LTAS). For LTAS, mean, minimum, maximum, standard deviation, range and slope were computed.
- Wavelet features were also computed. Each audio signal were decomposed using four-level daubechies wavelet decomposition using Pywavelet Python library. Then, wavelet energies and entropies [8] for each approximation and detail sub-bands were computed.

Consequently, a total of 49 features were extracted. Then, Stratified K Fold cross validation [29] (K = 10) was used in order to make sure that the samples in each fold were balanced and not biased to a certain emotion class. Then, they were fed into a support vector machine (SVM) classifier. Also, Grid search was used to choose the best hyper parameters to be used for the SVM.

Two different independent speaker experiments were conducted: one including the four available emotions in the dataset: happy, sad, angry and neutral (AHNS) and the other excluding the happy emotion (ANS). For the AHNS experiment and the ANS experiment, respectively, the obtained validation accuracies were 66.8% and 81.2% which are identical to the reported accuracies in [2]. Then, the same process including the feature vector extracted and the classifier used was applied on the utterances of each series in our dataset. However, two more experiments were conducted which are AHNSS which included the surprise emotion and AHNSSF which included both the surprise and fear emotions. Table 3 shows the average accuracies of the 10 folds for the four experiments.

Table 3. Dataset Accuracies (%)

Series Name	AHNS	ANS	AHNSS	AHNSSF
EYASE	66.8	81.2	NA	NA
Leaalasear	69.5	80.3	62.6	60.2
SahebELSaada	73.8	80.3	68.4	65.6
SuitsArabic	70.5	82	65.1	58.7
ElSayad	68.4	76.5	63.4	61.3
AshamIblis	69.4	75.9	58.8	54.4

6   Deep Learning Model

The second aim of this paper, is to investigate the use of DL in the task of SER
from Egyptian-Arabic speech. The proposed DL model is built by connecting
three main blocks. Each block consists of a one dimensional convolutional layer
followed by a Batch Normalization (BN) layer. The convolution layer plays the
role of a local feature extractor. When the data is passed into the convolution
layer, the convolution kernel slides over the input. Then, dot product between
the entries of the kernel and the input is computed in order to produce a feature
map [31]. The BN transformation keeps the mean activation around 0 and the
activation standard deviation near 1. Normalizing the activations of the convolutional layer by the BN layer improves the performance of deep networks and
makes them more stable [31].

The first block is followed by a Leaky Rectified Linear Unit (ReLU) activation
function layer [20] with an alpha equals to 0.2. Leaky ReLU was found to be
better than using the normal ReLU. This is due to the fact that the extracted
feature vector has a lot of negative values, which lead to the dying ReLU problem
[20] where the negative values in the feature vector are assigned to 0, instead
of having a slope. The second and third blocks are followed by a Max pooling
layer. Max-pooling is the most commonly used non-linear function. It calculates
the maximum value for each sub-region in the feature map, and uses it to create
a down-sampled feature map [27].

Table 4. Proposed Deep Learning Architecture

Type	Output Shape	Kernel	stride
Convolution	(None,177,128)	5	1
Convolution	(None,177,128)	5	1
Max Pooling	(None,89,128)	2	2
Convolution	(None,89,64)	5	1
Max Pooling	(None,45,64)	2	2

All Max Pooling and Convolutional layers have the SAME padding. This
model is designed to learn 1D feature vector extracted from each audio clip. Thus,
all layers in the network are one dimensional. The first and second convolutional
layers consist of 128 kernels. The third layer consists of 64 kernels. Then, there is
a Flatten layer followed by a Dense fully connected layer with 128 units. Last but
not least, the output layer is a dense layer with either four or five units depending
on the number of emotions in each experiment and soft-max activation function.
Drop out layers with a rate of 0.25 are used after each block in order to avoid
over fitting [26]. Table 4 shows a summary of the layers included in the proposed
model.

Regarding the features extracted, the same 49-long feature vector used for
SVM was extracted in addition to, 128 Log-Mel Spectrograms with maximum

frequency equal to 8000 forming a total of 177 features. The input feature vector was then normalized using the standard scaler normalization technique. The data was then split in to 10 stratified K Folds. Regarding the training parameters, the batch size was set to 16 and the Stochastic Gradient Descent (SGD) optimizer [16] was used with learning rate equals to 0.001 and with momentum equals to 0.8. The loss function used was categorical cross entropy.

7 Independent-Speaker Multi-class Emotion Classification Results

For the purpose of training, the fear emotion was not included due to the limited number of fear emotion files which might lead to poor results. Then, two approaches were followed. The first approach was to construct a balanced dataset consisting of 2,140 audio files, in which all five emotion classes have equal number of utterances, from EAED dataset. The second one was to compose a combined dataset using EAED and EYASE [2] datasets. However, the results of the online surveys, that were used to validate EYASE in [10], indicated that the happy emotion in EYASE was not accurately labeled. Thus, all the happy audio files in EYASE dataset were removed. Two experiments were conducted in both approaches: AHNS, and AHNSS.

Regarding the imbalanced dataset, the average of the accuracies resulting from 10 folds after 150 epochs was equal to 70.3% (Max: 76%, Min: 67%) and 65% (Max: 68%, Min: 63%) for the AHNS and AHNSS experiments respectively. Figure 2, shows the confusion matrices from one of the folds in the AHNS (left) and AHNSS (right) experiments. Tables 5 and 6 show the recall, precision and f1-scores values for each emotion separately for one of the folds in both experiments. The happy emotion has the lowest values due to the limited number of happy audio files in our dataset compared to other emotions.

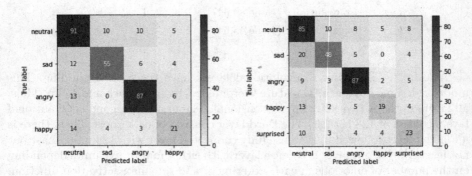

Fig. 2. Confusion Matrices for imbalanced dataset

Regarding the balanced dataset, the average of the accuracies resulting from 10 folds after 80 epochs was equal to 73% (Max: 81%, Min: 67%) and 66%

Table 5. Classification results for AHNS Experiment

	Precision(%)	Recall(%)	F1-score(%)
Neutral	70	78	74
Sad	80	71	75
Angry	82	82	82
Happy	58	50	54
Accuracy(%)			74

Table 6. Classification results for AHNSS Experiment

	Precision(%)	Recall(%)	F1-score(%)
Neutral	62	73	67
Sad	73	62	67
Angry	80	82	81
Happy	63	44	52
Surprised	52	52	52
Accuracy(%)			68

(Max: 71%, Min: 62%) for the AHNS and AHNSS experiments respectively. Figure 3, shows the confusion matrices from one of the folds in the AHNS (left) and AHNSS (right) experiments. Tables 7 and 8 show the recall, precision and f1-scores values for each emotion separately for one of the folds in both experiments.

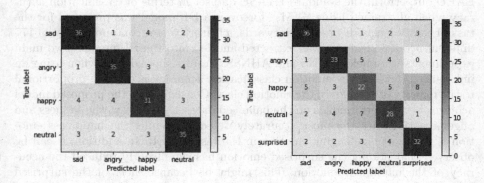

Fig. 3. Confusion Matrices for balanced dataset

Table 7. Classification results for AHNS Experiment for balanced dataset

	Precision(%)	Recall(%)	F1-score(%)
Neutral	80	81	80
Sad	82	84	83
Angry	83	81	82
Happy	76	74	75
Accuracy(%)			80

Table 8. Classification results for AHNSS Experiment for balanced dataset

	Precision(%)	Recall(%)	F1-score(%)
Neutral	65	67	66
Sad	78	84	81
Angry	77	77	77
Happy	58	51	54
Surprised	73	74	74
Accuracy(%)			71

8   Conclusion

To fill the gap in resources in the Egyptian-Arabic emotional speech corpora, a semi-natural emotional dataset was introduced in this paper. A total of 3,614 utterances were recorded in six basic emotional states. Most of the subsets of EAED outperform the standard EYASE dataset in terms of classification accuracy when all trained using SVM. Moreover, a DL model was proposed for the task of emotion classification. Afterwards, a feature vector containing a set of 177 different acoustic features was extracted and fed into the DL model. Two main experiments were held: AHNS and AHNSS. Results showed that when using an imbalanced dataset, the emotion classification accuracy is directly proportional to the number of samples in the emotion class. Consequently, the proposed model achieves better performance on the balanced dataset. Moreover, the sadness and anger emotions are the most accurately detected. While, the happiness emotion is the most challenging emotion in the task of SER. In addition, it can be observed that adding the surprised emotion has significantly reduced the accuracy of the happiness emotion. This might be because most of the surprised utterances included are surprisingly happy. In the future, further fine-tuning of the DL model should take place for better results. Data augmentation techniques could also be applied to increase the dataset size and improve performance.

References

1. Abbaschian, B.J., Sierra-Sosa, D., Elmaghraby, A.: Deep learning techniques for speech emotion recognition, from databases to models. Sensors **21**(4), 1249 (2021)

2. Abdel-Hamid, L.: Egyptian Arabic speech emotion recognition using prosodic, spectral and wavelet features. Speech Commun. **122**, 19–30 (2020)

3. Agarwal, G., Om, H.: Performance of deer hunting optimization based deep learning algorithm for speech emotion recognition. Multimedia Tools Appl. **80**(7), 9961–9992 (2021)

4. Aljuhani, R.H., Alshutayri, A., Alahdal, S.: Arabic speech emotion recognition from Saudi dialect corpus. IEEE Access **9**, 127081–127085 (2021)

5. Badshah, A.M., Ahmad, J., Rahim, N., Baik, S.W.: Speech emotion recognition from spectrograms with deep convolutional neural network. In: 2017 International Conference on Platform Technology and Service (PlatCon), pp. 1–5. IEEE (2017)

6. Burkhardt, F., Paeschke, A., Rolfes, M., Sendlmeier, W.F., Weiss, B., et al.: A database of German emotional speech. In: Interspeech, vol. 5, pp. 1517–1520 (2005)

7. Busso, C., et al.: Iemocap: interactive emotional dyadic motion capture database. Lang. Resour. Eval. **42**, 335–359 (2008)

8. Ekici, S., Yildirim, S., Poyraz, M.: Energy and entropy-based feature extraction for locating fault on transmission lines by using neural network and wavelet packet decomposition. Expert Syst. Appl. **34**(4), 2937–2944 (2008)

9. Ekman, P.: Basic emotions, chapter 3. Handbook of Cognition and Emotion. Wiley, Sussex (1999)

10. El Seknedy, M., Fawzi, S.: Speech emotion recognition system for Arabic speakers. In: 2022 4th Novel Intelligent and Leading Emerging Sciences Conference (NILES), pp. 86–89. IEEE (2022)

11. Fayek, H.M., Lech, M., Cavedon, L.: Towards real-time speech emotion recognition using deep neural networks. In: 2015 9th International Conference on Signal Processing and Communication Systems (ICSPCS), pp. 1–5. IEEE (2015)

12. Hifny, Y., Ali, A.: Efficient Arabic emotion recognition using deep neural networks. In: ICASSP 2019-2019 IEEE International Conference on Acoustics, Speech and Signal Processing (ICASSP), pp. 6710–6714. IEEE (2019)

13. Horkous, H., Guerti, M.: Recognition of emotions in the Algerian dialect speech. Int. J. Comput. Digit. Syst. **10**(1), 245–254 (2021)

14. Jadoul, Y., Thompson, B., De Boer, B.: Introducing parselmouth: A python interface to praat. J. Phon. **71**, 1–15 (2018)

15. Jahangir, R., Teh, Y.W., Hanif, F., Mujtaba, G.: Deep learning approaches for speech emotion recognition: state of the art and research challenges. Multimedia Tools Appl. 1–68 (2021)

16. Keskar, N.S., Socher, R.: Improving generalization performance by switching from Adam to SGD. arXiv preprint arXiv:1712.07628 (2017)

17. Koolagudi, S.G., Rao, K.S.: Emotion recognition from speech: a review. Int. J. Speech Technol. **15**(2), 99–117 (2012)

18. Koolagudi, S.G., Reddy, R., Yadav, J., Rao, K.S.: IITKGP-SEHSC: Hindi speech corpus for emotion analysis. In: 2011 International Conference on Devices and Communications (ICDeCom), pp. 1–5. IEEE (2011)

19. Livingstone, S.R., Russo, F.A.: The Ryerson audio-visual database of emotional speech and song (RAVDESS): a dynamic, multimodal set of facial and vocal expressions in north American English. PLoS ONE **13**(5), e0196391 (2018)

20. Mastromichalakis, S.: Alrelu: a different approach on leaky relu activation function to improve neural networks performance. arXiv preprint arXiv:2012.07564 (2020)

21. Meddeb, M., Karray, H., Alimi, A.M.: Building and analysing emotion corpus of the arabic speech. In: 2017 1st International Workshop on Arabic Script Analysis and Recognition (ASAR), pp. 134–139. IEEE (2017)

22. Meftah, A., Qamhan, M., Alotaibi, Y.A., Zakariah, M.: Arabic speech emotion recognition using KNN and KSUEmotions corpus. Int. J. Simul. Syst. Sci. Technol. (2020)

23. Mustafa, M.B., Yusoof, M.A., Don, Z.M., Malekzadeh, M.: Speech emotion recognition research: an analysis of research focus. Int. J. Speech Technol. **21**(1), 137–156 (2018)

24. Mustaqeem, Kwon, S.: A CNN-assisted enhanced audio signal processing for speech emotion recognition. Sensors **20**(1), 183 (2019)

25. Parry, J., et al.: Analysis of deep learning architectures for cross-corpus speech emotion recognition. In: Interspeech, pp. 1656–1660 (2019)

26. Şengür, D., Siuly, S.: Efficient approach for EEG-based emotion recognition. Electron. Lett. **56**(25), 1361–1364 (2020)

27. Singh, P., Verma, A., Chaudhari, N.S.: Deep convolutional neural network classifier for handwritten devanagari character recognition. In: Satapathy, S.C., Mandal, J.K., Udgata, S.K., Bhateja, V. (eds.) Information Systems Design and Intelligent Applications. AISC, vol. 434, pp. 551–561. Springer, New Delhi (2016). https://doi.org/10.1007/978-81-322-2752-6_54

28. Yang, Y., Ma, X., Fung, P.: Perceived emotional intelligence in virtual agents. In: Proceedings of the 2017 CHI Conference Extended Abstracts on Human Factors in Computing Systems, pp. 2255–2262 (2017)

29. Zeng, X., Martinez, T.R.: Distribution-balanced stratified cross-validation for accuracy estimation. J. Exp. Theor. Artif. Intell. **12**(1), 1–12 (2000)

30. Zhang, S.: Emotion recognition in Chinese natural speech by combining prosody and voice quality features. In: Sun, F., Zhang, J., Tan, Y., Cao, J., Yu, W. (eds.) ISNN 2008. LNCS, vol. 5264, pp. 457–464. Springer, Heidelberg (2008). https://doi.org/10.1007/978-3-540-87734-9_52

31. Zhao, J., Mao, X., Chen, L.: Speech emotion recognition using deep 1D & 2D CNN LSTM networks. Biomed. Signal Process. Control **47**, 312–323 (2019)

Finding the Determinants of Lower Limb Amputations Related to Diabetic Foot Ulcer - A Logistic Regression Classifier

Sabiha Khan[1] and Karuna Reddy[2(✉)]

[1] College of Medicine, Nursing and Health Sciences, Fiji National University, Suva, Fiji
sabiha.khan@fnu.ac.fj
[2] School of Information Technology, Engineering, Mathematics, and Physics, The University of the South Pacific, Laucala Campus, Suva, Fiji
karuna.reddy@usp.ac.fj

Abstract. Research is required for understanding the factors that contribute to Lower Extremity Amputation (LEA), especially in an area like Fiji that has a unique set of lifestyle factors and dietary habits. In such a developing country where T2DM-related amputations are one of the highest in the world, predicting the magnitude of the risk of LEA is vital for improving the care of Type 2 Diabetes Mellitus patients. Thus, this study developed a statistical model to predict quantifiable risk factors or predictors for LEA among T2DM patients from the three tertiary hospitals in Fiji. Such a model could possibly assist practitioners to understand the dynamics surrounding the problem and come up with possible solutions that may help reduce or prevent limb loss among diabetics. From the binary logistic regression classifier created via the 10-Fold Cross-Validation technique, we find that predictors such as length of stay (los), illness duration, the medical conditions of thrombocytosis and leukocytosis, gender, age category, hypertension, and low haemoglobin levels are key determinants of LEA. These predictors are statistically significant and have small to moderate effects on the outcome. The model has high sensitivity and performs very well, which indicates that it is correctly identifying a large portion of patients with amputations, thus minimizing the risk of false negatives.

Keywords: Binary Logistic Regression · Classification model · Machine Learning · Lower Extremity Amputation (LEA) · Diabetes Risk Factors

1 Introduction

Type 2 diabetes mellitus (T2DM) is a chronic and lifelong disease and a major health problem all over the world. The International Diabetes Federation (IDF) estimates the global prevalence of diabetes to be approximately 9.1% [1]. A report released by the World Health Organization (WHO) estimated that 422

F. Liu et al. (Eds.): PRICAI 2023, LNAI 14327, pp. 333–344, 2024.
https://doi.org/10.1007/978-981-99-7025-4_29

million adults worldwide were living with T2DM in 2014, among which 25% were unaware that they were diabetic. The report also projected that T2DM will be the seventh leading cause of death by the year 2030. The Western Pacific region has the highest diabetes burden in the world, and it is estimated that up to 1 in 3 adults in the Pacific Island population has T2DM. [2]. Fiji is no exception to this problem, T2DM is common in Fiji and it poses an enormous threat to the health of Fiji citizens, as it prominently contributes to Fiji's high mortality rates [24] The estimated prevalence of T2DM in Fiji was 16% in 2002, which is twice the global prevalence [17]. Almost one in every three Fijian is being diagnosed with diabetes [24].

Lower limb amputation (LEA) is a surgical procedure to remove a limb or a part of it on the lower extremity of a person due to diabetic complications. It is one of the most feared, devastating, and multifactorial complications experienced by people with T2DM. People with T2DM who have poorly controlled blood sugar levels are at an increased risk of developing peripheral neuropathy and peripheral vascular disease, which can lead to reduced blood and sensation in the lower limbs, which increases the risk of injury, infection, foot ulcer and then subsequent sepsis that can progress to a point where amputation become necessary [33]. A global review of LEA incidence reported that the incidence of LEA in diabetics ranges from 46.1 to 9600 per 100,000 [23]. Another study reported that the estimated age-adjusted incidence rates for LEAs with T2DM range from 2.1/1000 to 13.7/1000 person year worldwide [19].

Variation in incidence has been attributed to many factors such as the complex nature of foot infections, strategies for limb salvage, the clinical expertise of surgeons, patient preferences, accessibility and quality of health care, population, and study design used in various studies [31,32]. People with T2DM have 10–30 times increased risk of LEA compared with non-T2DM [4,26,33]. About 80% of all LEAs occur due to T2DM and 85% of these start with a foot ulcer [25]. Fifty percent of these people will become infected and half of the patients who have a foot ulcer die within 5 years [38]. Wounds that cannot heal can lead to re-amputation [9].

Treatment and care strategies vary on the level of amputation. Determination of the clinical characteristics and risk factors of each level of LEA is crucial to understanding the processes that may save limbs among T2DM patients. Data on diabetic-related amputation are lacking in Fiji. Statistics on risk factors are important for disease prevention and intervention. While there is some available information regarding LEAs, to a lesser extent, descriptives about their risk factors, no research has yet utilized the available information in Fiji to model the magnitude of the predictiveness of these risk factors for LEAs. This information is also hardly available though for the Fiji population, so that is an information gap that this research will fill. More importantly, such a model would be able to assist surgeons and other health care providers for T2DM patients, in making early decisions about when to be aggressive in treating certain risk factors among patients, when the model indicates that there is a high risk of possible LEA.

2   Literature Review

Pacific literature on factors associated with LEA due to T2DM is limited. A study published found that the main factors for LEA were delaying treatment, use of traditional treatments, and insufficient knowledge about foot care [34]. Furthermore, literature on specific factors associated with diabetic LEAs is also limited in Fiji. The occurrence of LEA due to T2DM differs by ethnicity, as it occurs more among indigenous Fijians [20]. It is estimated that there is a T2DM-associated LEA performed every 8 h in Fiji [Times F]. These statistics are quite worrying, as it translates to an immense future burden on the health sector in Fiji.

A wide range of risk factors for LEAs related to Diabetes Foot Ulcer (DFU) had been reported, which included longer duration of diabetes mellitus [7,41], previous diabetic ulcer histories and previous amputation histories [10], poor glycemic control [37], hypertension [27,41], coronary artery disease [41], hyperlipidaemia [27], severity of peripheral arterial disease (PAD) [7,22,27,40], diabetic neuropathy [28], osteomyelitis [7,22,41,42], Wagner grade [30,40], age [7,11,41], sex [40], smoking history [8], anemia [12], higher WBC count [18], presence of microvascular [13,42], and macrovascular complications [21,41], chronic kidney disease and ulcer size [22,40], high baseline inflammatory markers, including C-reactive protein (CRP) levels, low BMI [41].

The applications of AI are vast and varied in the area of medical sciences, where numerous data mining algorithms have been employed in the literature. Chemello et al. [14] provide a thorough review of these applications in diabetes-related data. An extensive systematic review is also presented by [15] on AI-based approaches that are suitable for predicting multiple diabetes-related complications. Below find further applications of data mining methods used in diabetes-related data.

A prospective study was conducted in Singapore using Stepwise Logistic Regression by Zameer et al. among 100 patients who were diagnosed or treated at the National University Hospital to identify the predictive factors of lower extremity amputations in diabetic foot infections [8]. The study revealed significant univariate predictive factors for limb loss including age above 60 years, gangrene, monomicrobial infections, high white blood cell (WBC) count, low hemoglobin, and creatinine. Another cross-sectional study was conducted in Saudi Arabia using multivariable logistic regression by Al-Rubeaan et al. among 62,681 patients aged 25 and more. The study revealed significant risk factors were Charcot joints, peripheral vascular disease, neuropathy, diabetes duration of more than 10 years, insulin use, retinopathy, nephropathy, over 45 years of years, cerebral vascular disease, poor glycemic control, coronary artery disease, male gender, smoking, and hypertension to be significant risk factors [30].

Recently, research by [32] conducted a retrospective study in Jordan using a Multivariate Logistic Regression model among 225 T2DM patients who were admitted to King Abdullah University Hospital, to identify the independent predictors of major lower extremity amputations (LEA) among type 2 diabetic patients. This study considered many risk factors such as foot characteristics (History of foot problems, Ulcer, Gangrene, Ischemia, Diabetic neuropathy, Clinical evidence of infections, Wagner's grade); Demographic (gender, age), and Health characteristics' (BMI, duration of diabetes, Antidiabetic treatments, glycemic control, ESR, smoking, Hypertension, Cardiac diseases, chronic renal diseases, stroke). Among them, poor glycemic control, longer duration of diabetes, renal impairment, gangrene, and insulin use were found as independent predictors of major amputation among Diabetic patients [8].

The literature review presented above identifies several gaps in determining independent predictors of LEAs among T2DM. There are several risk factors for LEA in diabetes that have been cited in the literature. However, there are inconsistencies among the studies. These inconsistencies in risk factors may have been attributed to factors such as genetic profiles and cultural features of the population studied. In addition, despite the adequacy and richness of existing data sources, the LEA in T2DM in Fiji remains poorly described. Furthermore, the factors associated with amputations in these patients are yet to be identified. Thus, this study is conducted to identify the factors associated with amputation among T2DM patients in the Fijian population. Rarely studies have reported any findings or published any diabetes-related data, which makes it very difficult for researchers to identify risk factors for diabetes-related LEA in Fiji. Through this research, will want to reduce that gap, by collecting data and identifying patients with risk factors associated with amputation. This could prompt increased patient education, monitoring, and rehabilitation efforts that may aid in the prevention of further amputation and its associated morbidity in the future.

3   Research Methodology

3.1   Data Collection

We performed a retrospective review of the records of 1792 diabetic inpatients who had undergone wound debridement or lower extremity amputation due to foot ulcer at all three tertiary care hospitals in Fiji from January 2016 to December 2019. We first identified 3587 patient records with a hospital discharge list diagnosis of Type 2 diabetes mellitus (E11) with foot ulcer due to multiple causes (E11.73) according to the International Classification of Disease (ICD-10 AM) from Patient Information System (PATIS). After removing duplicate records (n = 517), missing folders (n = 969), any surgical information missing (n = 8), patients who had refused surgery (n = 59), patients who had undergone any LEA before the study period (n = 26), any missing information in the patients' observation folder in the independent variables (n = 194), 1792 diabetic patients folders/medical histories were reviewed.

The collected data had information on demographic characteristics (sex, age, ethnicity, place of residence), hypertension, ischaemic heart disease, Wagner grades, hospital length stay, smoking history, lab investigations (random blood sugar, hemoglobin level, total white blood cell count), and the history of any renal problem (eGFR).

Hypertension was defined as systolic blood pressure ≥ 140 mmHg, diastolic blood pressure ≥ 90 mmHg, or the use of anti-hypertensive medications. The World Health Organization cut-off point for diagnosis of anemia is a hemoglobin level of 12.0 g/dl for females and 13.0 g/dl for males. Having an abnormally high number of white blood cells (≥ 12K) in the blood was classified as the 'leukocytosis' condition. Similarly, an abnormally high platelet count (≥ 450K) in the blood was classified as the 'thrombocytosis' condition. For the main outcome variable, patients were divided into two groups: non-LEA, and any LEA group. LEA group refers to the patients who had undergone any amputation during the study period and the non-LEA group considers patients who had wound debridement or incision & drainage during the study period.

3.2   Classification Model

The binary nature of the outcome variable (**amputation = 1 & non-amputation = 0**) requires the utilization of a data mining algorithm called **Binary Logistic Regression** (BLR), which is from the family of Generalized Linear Models (GLM). The BLR classifier predicts the probability of the occurrence of amputation and non-amputation based on a set of predictors, which we refer to as the determinants, by fitting data to a logistic curve. The model is then updated in such a way that important relationships between predictors and the outcome variable, significant or lack thereof, are chosen. During this process, some statistically significant predictors and some important predictors were retained due to the nature of their effects on the outcome variable. The mathematical representation of the BLR classifier can be written as the equation:

$$logit(y) = \beta_0 + \beta_1 x_1 + \beta_2 x_2 + \cdots + \beta_k x_k \tag{1}$$

where β_i, $i = 1, 2, ..., k$ are the beta weights or the coefficient estimates of the model, $x_1, x_2, \cdots, x_k$ are the predictors, and y is a response to predict amputation or non-amputation, and $logit(y) = ln(1/(1-y))$. The above equation can also be written as

$$y = \frac{1}{1 + e^{\beta_0 + \beta_1 x_1 + \beta_2 x_2 + \cdots + \beta_k x_k}} \tag{2}$$

The model was created using the machine learning workflow whereby the classifier is learned using 75% training data with 10-fold cross-validation and its model performance and evaluations was done on the 25% test data. This algorithm was carried out in **R** using the **tidymodels** framework.

4   Results and Discussion for the Binary Logistic Regression Classifier

Initially, the full model approach [22] was used for the model-building process, where all potential variables were included in the model. However, as we encountered complex relationships between predictors and the outcome, it became apparent that this approach was impractical to consider due to its limitations. Consequently, we opted for variable selection using univariate methods to address this issue, as proposed by [20]. Those variables that showed statistical significance ($p < 0.25$) in the univariate analysis were included in the multivariate model, which was then continuously updated systematically through trial and test. Finally, a reasonable combination of predictors was chosen, based on the clinical meaningfulness of the relationships that are scientifically plausible, to be part of the final model to predict amputation. Dealing with highly correlated predictors helped reduce the complexity of the model, which led to a more pragmatic prediction model.

Presented in Table 1 are the exponentiated model coefficients known as **Odds Ratio (OR)** which traditionally assess the effect of a predictor variable on the response variable, given that the other predictor variables are "held constant" (known as the ceteris-paribus assumption). The 95% confidence intervals (CI) of these ORs and their corresponding p-values at 5% level of significance are also given. For the continuous predictors, OR $\geq$ 1 indicates that the event is more likely to occur as the predictor increases, and OR $\leq$ 1 indicates that the event is less likely to occur as the predictor increases. For categorical predictors, the OR for a particular category is with respect to a reference category, which is stated for each predictor in the first column of Table 1. For all predictors, the reference categories below the name of the predictors are in the first column. For **gender**, it refers to the odds of having an amputation in Females versus Males, i.e., women are 0.64 times as likely to have an amputation compared to males, after adjusting for all other predictors in the model. This means that if we choose "female" as the reference category, the result will provide the odds of having an amputation in men as compared to women. Thus, men are likely to have about 1.6 times higher risk of amputation compared to women after adjusting for other

Table 1. The Binary Logistic Regression Model Results

Predictor	Category	OR	95% CI	p-value
gender (ref: Male)	Female	0.64	0.50, 0.83	<0.001
agecat(ref: <=40)	40–60	1.67	1.00, 2.76	0.047
	60+	1.94	1.15, 3.25	0.012
ethnicity (ref: i-Taukei)	FoID	0.79	0.60, 1.03	0.084
	Others	0.75	0.30, 2.05	0.6
length of stay		1.11	1.07, 1.15	<0.001
hypertension (ref: No)	Yes	1.34	1.04, 1.72	0.025
illness_duration(ref: <1 month)	>=1 month	2.39	1.60, 3.69	<0.001
Hb_low (ref: No)	Yes	1.37	1.04, 1.81	0.027
leucocytosis (ref: No)	Yes	1.48	1.14, 1.93	0.003
thrombocytosis (ref: No)	Yes	1.94	1.41, 2.70	<0.001

factors in the model or keeping other factors fixed or constant. Note that this effect is statistically significant (p-value < 0.001 at 5% level of significance).

For the predictor of age in categories, (**agecat**, which has categories of <=40, 40–60, and >=61), separate ORs are calculated for each of the other categories relative to a particular reference category (in this case it's <=40 years: thus, comparisons are made as such: <=40 vs 40–60, <=40 vs >=60). Thus, with the ORs given we say that 40–60 years old patients are about 1.7 times more likely to get an amputation compared to the reference category of <=40 years old patients. Similarly, patients who >= 61 years old have about twice the odds of getting an amputation compared to <= 40 years old patients, after keeping other factors fixed in the model. Both effects are statistically significant as shown on the p-value column.

For **ethnicity**, the i-Taukei patients are about $1/0.79 = 1.3$ times more likely (meaning about 30% greater chance) to get an amputation compared to FoID patients. This relationship is statistically significant with a p-value = 0.084 at 10% level of significance. Similarly, compared to the patients from the 'Other' ethnicity group, i-Taukei patients have about 1.33 times greater odds of getting an amputation, after keeping other factors fixed in the model.

For the continuous predictor of **length of stay** in hospital in days, for a one-unit increase in **length of stay** (a day more at the hospital), we expect to see about 11% higher odds of risking an amputation. So, if a patient stays about 7 more days at the hospital, the risk of an amputation more than doubles ($1.11^7 = 2.1$). This 11% per-day increase obviously does not depend on the value that other predictors are held at.

There are 1.34 times greater odds of getting an amputation for patients who are **hypertensive** compared to those that are not, while holding all other predictors constant. Similarly, there are 2.4 times higher odds of amputation if the duration of the illness has been >=1 month compared to < 1 month, keeping all other factors fixed. Similarly, we can interpret the effects of **Hb_low** (low haemoglobin), **leukocytosis** and **thrombocytosis** on patients, as having about 1.4, 1.5, and 2 times higher odds (respectively) of amputation compared to patients that do not have these conditions, while keeping other predictors constant. All of these predictors are statistically significant at 5% level of significance as shown in the last column of Table 1.

Figure 1 below presents the effects plot which visualizes the effects of each predictor. The variable importance plot of each of these key predictors is also given on the right.

The effects plot on the left illustrates the relationship between the predictors and the outcome variable of amputation and how it changes with respect to each predictor while holding other variables constant. The effects plot on the left provides a clear understanding of the direction and magnitude of the effects of each_predictor on amputation, allowing for easier visualization, interpretation and communication of the model's findings. Thus, it is seen that **illness duration, length of stay, thrombocytosis, lekcocytosis, age category,**

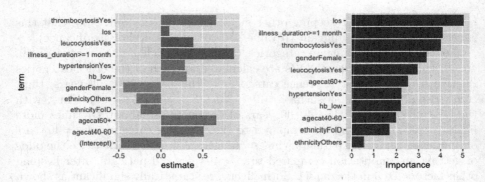

Fig. 1. LHS: Effects Plot; and RHS: Variable Importance Plot

gender, hypertension and even **ethnicity** have moderate to strong and statistically significant effects on the risk of amputation in diabetes patients.

The bars in the variable importance plot given on the right of Fig. 1 give the predictor's contribution to the model's performance. VIP is a measure of the importance of each predictor variable in the model in terms of its impact on the overall prediction accuracy. VIP plot ranks the variables based on their importance, allowing us to identify the most influential variables in the model. This information can be useful for feature selection, identifying key drivers, and prioritizing variables for further analysis or decision-making. Thus, as earlier seen in the effects plot and the subsequent discussion, the top five predictors, in order of importance, are: **length of stay, illness duration, thrombocytosis, gender, leukocytosis, age category, hypertension** and **low haemoglobin** help predict the risk of amputation due to T2DM in Fijian patients.

4.1   Model Evaluation

Model evaluation is carried out to assess its performance and accuracy in predicting amputation. Several evaluation metrics and techniques, such as accuracy, confusion matrix, precision and recall, and the receiver operating curve together with the area under the curve, are utilized to measure the effectiveness of the model. These are presented in Fig. 1.

The table on the left of Fig. 2 provides the **Confusion matrix**, a table showing the model's predictions versus the actual outcomes and has the true positives (TP), true negatives (TN), false positives (FP), and false negatives (FN). From the model and this confusion matrix, given on the right side of Fig. 2 are the evaluation measures such as accuracy, precision, recall, and F1 score. An accuracy of 0.772 signifies that overall, the moderately strong model makes about 77% correct predictions, however, this alone may not provide a comprehensive evaluation since the data is imbalanced in terms of the distribution of amputations and non-amputations.

The Receiver Operating Curve (ROC) (figure is omitted) and its Area Under the Curve (AUC) were found to be 0.69. The AUC is more descriptive than

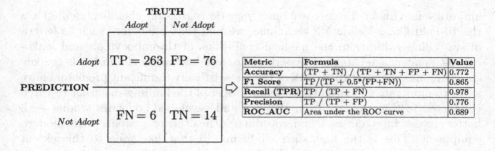

Fig. 2. The Confusion Matrix and its Measures

accuracy because it is a balance of accuracy and false positive rate. This indicates that the overall measure of the model's discriminatory power model performance is moderately strong. For interpretation, the higher the AUC, the better the model performs.

A **precision** of 0.776 identifies the model can correctly predict about 78% of the positive instances (i.e., amputation = 1) out of the total amputations. A recall (also known as sensitivity or true positive rate) value of 0.978 tells us that the proportion of **97.8%** of actual positive cases (amputation = 1 or 'yes') are correctly identified as amputations by the model. This value also indicates that the model has a lower rate of falsely labeling positive instances as negative. The **F1 score** of 0.865 is a single measure that combines precision and recall. This score is a balanced measure of this model's accuracy because it's able to identify amputation cases correctly (recall) and has the ability to avoid misclassifying the non-amputation cases (precision).

Sensitivity is the measure that we will heavily depend on in this research. In this application, we care about correctly classifying a positive amputation more than incorrectly classifying a negative. In this case, a high recall or sensitivity indicates that the model is correctly identifying a large portion of patients with amputations, minimizing the risk of false negatives (i.e., classifying a patient with amputation as a non-amputation patient). In medical or health-related areas, such as predicting if a patient has a mental illness, it is extremely important to have a low false positive rate because telling someone they have it when they do not can cause a lot of emotional stress. Thus, in this research, sensitivity is the important metric that can be used for evaluating the performance of the classification model, particularly when the focus is on minimizing false negatives or capturing as many positive cases of amputations as possible. A **97.8%** sensitivity means that the model is a very strong model in terms of predicting the positive instances of amputations in T2DM patients.

5 Conclusion

From this study of 1792 Type II Diabetes Mellitus patients in Fiji, we find that there are some key predictors that significantly influence lower extremity amputations (LEA). From the binary logistic regression classifier created via the 10-Fold Cross-Validation technique, we find that predictors such as length of stay, illness duration, the medical conditions of thrombocytosis and leukocytosis, gender, age category, hypertension, and low haemoglobin levels are key determinants of amputations. All of these statistically significant predictors have small to moderate effects on the outcome. Most of the findings in earlier research conducted in this area are from Western and developed countries studies with better access to structured and coordinated healthcare systems with modern equipment. This is the first such study in Fiji that has gone to this extent of data collection and validation in this area, thus enabling us to make more informed decisions to assist us in understanding the dynamics of amputations. The model has a high rate of sensitivity, which indicates that it is correctly identifying a large portion of patients with amputations, thus minimizing the risk of false negatives (i.e., classifying a patient with amputation as a non-amputation patient). The people of Fiji are quite different from individuals of western and developed countries and the predictors of amputation could be different as well. The model created would certainly be able to assist surgeons and other health practitioners for T2DM patients, in making targeted decisions about treating certain risk factors in patients that could potentially avoid loss of limbs through amputations.

References

1. IDF: IDF Diabetes Atlas, 8th Edition edn. Brussels, Belgium (2017)
2. Cook, J.J., Simonson, D.C.: Epidemiology and health care cost of diabetic foot problems. In: Veves, A., Giurini, J., LoGerfo, F. (eds.) The Diabetic Foot, pp. 17–32. Springer (2012). https://doi.org/10.1007/978-1-61779-791-0_2
3. Aziz, Z., Lin, W.K., Nather, A., Huak, C.Y.: Predictive factors for lower extremity amputations in diabetic foot infections. Diabet Foot Ankle **2**, 7463 (2011)
4. Agwu, E., Dafiewhare, E.O., Ekanem, P.E.: Possible diabetic-foot complications in sub-saharan Africa. In: Dinh, D.T. (ed.) Global Perspective on Diabetic Foot Ulcerations, pp. 3–14. IntechOpen (2011)
5. Alvarsson, A., Sandgren, B., Wendel, C., Alvarsson, M., Brismar, K.: A retrospective analysis of amputation rates in diabetic patients: can lower extremity amputations be further prevented? Cardiovasc. Diabetol. **11**(1), 18 (2012)
6. Acar, E., Kacıra, B.K.: Predictors of lower extremity amputation and reamputation associated with diabetic foot. J. Foot Ankle Surg. **56**, 1218–1222 (2017)
7. Peter-Riesch, B.: The diabetic foot: the never-ending challenge. Endocr. Dev. **31**, 108–134 (2016)
8. Aziz, Z., Wong, K.L., Nather, A., Chan, Y.: Predictive factors for lower extremity amputations in diabetic foot infections. Diabetic Foot & Ankle. **2**,(2011). https://doi.org/10.3402/dfa.v2i0.7463
9. Czerniecki, J.M., et al.: Predicting reamputation risk in patients under-going lower extremity amputation due to the complications of peripheral artery disease and/or diabetes. Br. J. Surg. **106**(8), 1026–1034 (2019)
10. Crawford, F., Cezard, G., Chappell, F.M., Murray, G.D., Price, J.F., Sheikh, A., et al.: A systematic review and individual patient data meta-analysis of prognostic

factors for foot ulceration in people with diabetes: the international research collaboration for the prediction of diabetic foot ulcerations (PODUS). Health Technol. Assess. **19**, 1–207 (2015)

11. Chu, Y.-J., Li, X.-W., Wang, P.-H., Xu, J., Sun, H.-J., Ding, M., et al.: Clinical outcomes of toe amputation in patients with type 2 diabetes in Tianjin. China. Int Wound J. **13**, 175–81 (2016)

12. Chuan, F., Zhang, M., Yao, Y., Tian, W., He, X., Zhou, B.: Anemia in patients with diabetic foot ulcer. Int. J. Low Extrem. Wounds **15**, 220–6 (2016)

13. Carlson, T., Reed, J.F., 3rd.: A case-control study of the risk factors for toe amputation in a diabetic population. Int. J. Low Extrem. Wounds **2**, 19–21 (2003)

14. Chemello, G., Salvatori, B., Morettini, M., Tura, A.: Artificial intelligence methodologies applied to technologies for screening, diagnosis and care of the diabetic foot: a narrative review. Biosensors **12**(11), 985 (2022)

15. Gosak, L., Martinović, K., Lorber, M., Stiglic, G.: Artificial intelligence based prediction models for individuals at risk of multiple diabetic complications: a systematic review of the literature. J. Nurs. Manag. **30**(8), 3765–3776 (2022)

16. Fleischer, A.E., Wrobel, J.S., Leonards, A., Berg, S., Evans, D.P., Baron, R.L., et al.: Post-treatment leukocytosis predicts an unfavorable clinical response in patients with moderate to severe diabetic foot infections. J. Foot Ankle Surg. **50**, 541–6 (2011)

17. Health FMo: Fiji Non-Communicable Diseases. In: STEPS Survey Suva, Fiji (2005)

18. Jeong, E.-G., et al.: Depth and combined infection is important predictor of lower extremity amputations in hospitalized diabetic foot ulcer patients. Korean J. Intern. Med. **33**(5), 952–960 (2017)

19. Krittiyawong, S., et al.: Thailand diabetes registry project: prevalence and risk factors associated with lower extremity amputation in Thai diabetics. J. Med. Assoc. Thai. **89**(Suppl 1), S43–S48 (2006)

20. Kumar, K., et al.: Descriptive analysis of diabetes-related amputations at the Colonial War Memorial Hospital, Fiji, 2010–2012. Public Health Action **4**(3), 155–158 (2014)

21. Laclé, A., Valero-Juan, L.F.: Diabetes-related lower-extremity amputation incidence and risk factors: a prospective seven-year study in Costa Rica. Rev. Panam. Salud Publica **32**(192–8), 23 (2012)

22. Lee, J.H., et al.: Risk factors affecting amputation in diabetic foot. Yeungnam Univ. J. Med. **37**(4), 314–320 (2020). https://doi.org/10.12701/yujm.2020.00129. eISSN 2384–0293

23. Moxey, P., et al.: Lower extremity amputations-a review of global variability in incidence. Diabet. Med. **28**(10), 1144–1153 (2011)

24. MOHMS: Fiji Ministry of Health and Medical Services Annual Report 2015 (2015)

25. Musa, R., et al.: Factors associated with amputation among patients with diabetic foot ulcers in a Saudi population. BMC. Res. Notes **11**(260), 1–5 (2018)

26. Pendsey, S.: Reducing diabetic foot problems and limb amputation: an Experience from India. In: Dinh, D.T. (ed.) Global Perspective on Diabetic Foot Ulcerations, pp. 15–24. INTECH Open Access Publisher (2011)

27. Pemayun, T.G.D., Naibaho, R.M., Novitasari, D., Amin, N., Minuljo, T.T.: Risk factors for lower extremity amputation in patients with diabetic foot ulcers: a hospital-based case-control study. Diabet Foot Ankle **6**, 29629 (2015)

28. Prompers, L., et al.: Prediction of outcome in individuals with diabetic foot ulcers: focus on the differences between individuals with and without peripheral arterial disease. The EURODIALE Study. Diabetologia **51**, 747–755 (2008)

29. Verrone Quilici, T.M., de Sá, F., Franzin Vieira, A.E., Toledo, M.I.: Risk factors for foot amputation in patients hospitalized for diabetic foot infection. J. Diabetes Res. **2016**, 8931508 (2016)

30. Sun, J.H., Tsai, J.S., Huang, C.H., Lin, C.H., Yang, H.M., Chan, Y.S., et al.: Risk factors for lower extremity amputation in diabetic foot disease categorized by Wagner classifcation. Diabetes Res. Clin. Pract. **95**, 358–63 (2012)

31. Schaper, N., Apelqvist, J., Bakker, K.: Reducing lower leg amputations in diabetes: a challenge for patients, healthcare providers and the healthcare system. Diabetologia **55**(7), 1869–1872 (2012)

32. Shatnawi, N.J., Al-Zoubi, N.A., Hawamdeh, H.M., Khader, Y.S., Garaibeh, K., Heis, H.A.: Predictors of major lower limb amputation in type 2 diabetic patients referred for hospital care with diabetic foot syndrome. Diabetes Metab. Syndr. Obes. **11**, 313–319 (2018)

33. Sadriwala, Q.S., Gedam, B.S., Akhtar, M.A.: Risk factors of amputation in diabetic foot infections. Int. Surg. J. **5**(4), 1399–1402 (2018)

34. Tin, S.T.W., Gadabu, E., Iro, G., Tasserei, J., Colagiuri, R.: Diabetes related amputations in Pacific Islands countries: a root cause analysis of precipitating events. Diabetes Res. Clin. Pract. **100**(2), 230–234 (2013)

35. Times, F.: Three Amputations a day in Fiji due to Diabetes. Fiji Times, In. (2018)

36. Uysal, S., et al.: Risk factors for amputation in patients with diabetic foot infection: a prospective study. Int. Wound J. **14**(6), 1219–1224 (2017)

37. Vella, L., Formosa, C.: Characteristics predicting the outcome in individuals with diabetic foot ulcerations. J. Am. Podiatr. Med. Assoc. **107**, 180–91 (2017)

38. Weledji, E.P., Fokam, P.: Treatment of the diabetic foot-to amputate or not? BMC Surg. **14**(83), 1–6 (2014)

39. West, M., Chuter, V., Munteanu, S., Hawke, F.: Defining the gap: a systematic review of the difference in rates of diabetes-related foot complications in Aboriginal and Torres Strait Islander Australians and non-Indigenous Australians. J. Foot Ankle Res. **10**, 48 (2017)

40. Wang, L., Li, Q., Chen, X., Wang, Z.: Clinical characteristics and risk factors of lower extremity amputation in patients with diabetic foot. Pak. J. Med. Sci. **38**(8), 2253–2258 (2022). https://doi.org/10.12669/pjms.38.8.5635

41. Yesil, S., et al.: Predictors of amputation in diabetics with foot ulcer: single center experience in a large Turkish cohort. Hormones **8**(4), 286–295 (2009)

42. Zubair, M., Malik, A., Ahmad, J.: Incidence, risk factors for amputation among patients with diabetic foot ulcer in a North Indian tertiary care hospital. Foot **22**, 24–30 (2012)

Frequency Domain Feature Learning with Wavelet Transform for Image Translation

Huan Zhao[✉], Yujiang Wang, Tingting Li, Song Wang, Lixuan Li, Xupeng Zha, and Zixing Zhang

College of Computer Science and Electronic Engineering, Hunan University, Changsha, China
hzhao@hnu.edu.cn

Abstract. Image-to-image translation serves as an essential field of research in computer vision. Existing models frequently cause accidental distortion over non-target attributes, leading to overfitting of the generated image to the reference domain and poor visual quality. To address this problem, we propose *Frequency Domain Feature Learning with Wavelet Transform*, namely FDFL-WT, which with better non-target attributes retention and more precise image capture of style. This method utilizes the wavelet transform to capture the image's approximation coefficients and diagonal coefficients, then we suggest wavelet reconstruction loss and wavelet translation loss. The former comprehensively records the context information of the source image to make the generated image realistic, whereas the latter improves the generator's capacity to decouple attributes by assisting the model in efficiently retaining image content attributes. Experimental results on CelebA-HQ dataset indicate that FDFL-WT achieves about a 7.03% performance improvement comparing with methods in the FID score of realism and disentanglement tests.

Keywords: Frequency domain · Image-to-image translation · Style transfer · Wavelet transform

1 Introduction

Image-to-image translation refers to the transformation of a image to another image, covering a wide range of fields: style transfer [23,29,31], super-resolution [18,20], image inpainting [16,25], etc. Recent advanced image-to-image translation models can be grouped into two main categories: (1) Uncontrollable

This work was supported by the National Key Research and Development Program of China under Grant 2020YFB1713400, the National Natural Science Foundation of China under Grant 62076092 and the Special Project of Foshan Science and Technology Innovation Team under Grant FS0AA-KJ919-4402-0069.

F. Liu et al. (Eds.): PRICAI 2023, LNAI 14327, pp. 345–357, 2024.
https://doi.org/10.1007/978-981-99-7025-4_30

attribute model that transfers the overall style features of reference image to source image. (2) Controllable attribute model that only transfers the style of the reference image to the target attribute. Generally, the controllable attribute model is more user-friendly than the uncontrollable attribute model.

In the controllable attribute model, a major challenge is that non-target attributes are frequently tampered with in the image translationprocess, resulting in the loss of the content features in the source images and subsequent generated images over-adapt to the reference domain. One reason of this challenge is that most existing models commonly use reconstruction loss [27,32] and cycle consistency loss [9,33], which only constrain the generator at the pixel-level. The preceding challenges raise the following essential question: how we can enhance the retention of non-target attributes while maintaining the integrity of style embedding.

To address this problem, we integrate frequency domain information into the image translation process to incorporate more of the source domain image attributes for preservation. The wavelet transform enables converting an image from the spatial domain to the frequency domain so as to retrieve the image's frequency domain features. It may extract approximation coefficients, vertical coefficients, horizontal coefficients, and diagonal coefficients from an image, in accordance with the theory of previous work [1,12]. Among them, the approximation coefficients maintains the original image to the greatest possible extent, whereas the diagonal coefficients captures the contour features and certain details of the original image in the horizontal and vertical directions. Based on the characteristics of these two coefficients, we introduce them to the task of image translation for frequency domain feature learning.

We propose a novel framework, called *Frequency Domain Feature Learning with Wavelet Transform* (FDFL-WT). We seek to set constraints in a different way from the Fourier transform [2,7] in the frequency domain perspective inspired by [3]. The specific approach is to utilize high-pass and low-pass filters to extract the approximation coefficients and diagonal coefficients of the image at first. The approximation coefficients of the image, dubbed LL, can be obtained after two low-pass filters of the image. And the diagonal coefficients, dubbed HH, can be obtained after two high-pass filters of the image (see Fig. 1(a)). Then, LL is used in the image reconstruction process; HH is utilized in the image translation process. These two different losses, called wavelet reconstruction loss and wavelet translation matching loss, are applied to tune the codec process of the generator. Experiments on CelebA-HQ dataset reveal that FDFL-WT has a very positive impact on authenticity and decoupling. Our contributions of FDFL-WT as follows:

- We design a wavelet reconstruction loss. The wavelet reconstruction loss enhances the authenticity of the generated image by employing the approximation coefficients of the image obtained through the wavelet transform in image translation tasks.
- We design a wavelet translation loss. The wavelet translation loss exploits the differential coefficients extracted by wavelet transform, and thus successfully

limits the tampering of non-target attributes when dealing with an image-to-image translation task and has more details reserved.
- Numerous experimental results on the CelebA-HQ dataset indicate that compared with the existing methods, FDFL-WT obtains competitive results in terms of realism and disentanglement.

2   Related Work

Uncontrollable Attribute Image Translation Model. The uncontrollable attribute image translation model aims to transform all attributes of the source domain image into another style. For the sake of making overall appearance of the generated image harmonious and organic, it is a specific type of style transfer. Pix2Pix [11] realizes the overall conversion of images from one domain to another by inputting pairs of images and passing them through the generator based on U-Net [22] structure and the discriminator based on PatchGAN. CycleGAN [33] designs cycle consistency loss to promote consistency between the content of the generated image and the source image, allowing unpaired images to be style migrated. PGGAN [13] employs the concept of "progressive development", and the resolution of the generated image increases with the progress of the epoch for producing high-qulity images.

Controllable Attribute Image Translation Model. The objective of controllable attribute image translation model is to alter a specific area of the source domain image while protecting non-target attributes and concentrating only on the transfer effect of the target attributes. StyleGAN [14] uses the mapping network to decouple the late code, and then applies affine transformation to obtain style features of different dimensions, which represent different attributes. After combining random Gaussian noise and layer-by-layer input into the synthesis network, the final style fusion image is obtained. StarGAN v2 [4] obtains the style code of the target style through the mapping network or the extractor network, then combine the style code and the source domain image by adaptive instance normalization (AdaIN) to generate the target domain image with high diversity and high controllability. By arranging the original labels into a hierarchical structure, HiSD [17] realizes the controllability of the target attributes and avoids unintentional manipulation of non-target attributes by attaching condition variables to the discriminator.

Spatial Frequency Domain. The space made up of image components is known as the spatial domain, and it is typically handled in pixel-space. The frequency domain is the domain that reflects the target frequency and peak amplitude, and the image is transformed from the spatial domain to the frequency domain by different digital filters [21,26,28]. Wavelet transform is a typical technique to convert spatial information into frequency domain information.

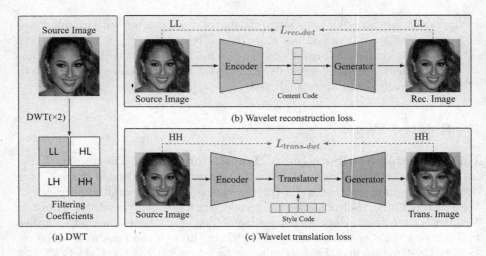

Fig. 1. Overview of the proposed FDFL-WT image-to-image translation framework that contains (a) the discrete wavelet transform (DWT) operation, (b) the wavelet reconstruction process, and (c) the wavelet translation process.

DW-GAN [5] used the approach of wavelet transform to disassemble and reconstruct the image layer by layer, simulating the process of encoding and decoding, and achieved high quality image generation results. Linfeng et al. [30] introduced the idea of the wavelet transform into knowledge distillation, distilling only high-frequency components so that the generator can better generate high-frequency components. Yue et al. [6] devised wavelet-based skip connections in order to transmit high-frequency signals to the decoder and generate images with high resolution. Mu et al. [3] provided a way to incorporate the Fourier transform into the style transfer model, which also allows effective control of the properties of the generated image from a frequency domain perspective to be preserved.

3   Methodology

Our method is based on Image-to-image Translation via Hierarchical Style Disentanglement (HiSD) [17] framework that employs an encoder-generator neural network architecture. The overall structure consists of an encoder E, a generator G, and a translator T. Our image source is the image space $\chi = \mathbb{R}^{H \times W \times 3}$. Given a source domain image $x \in \chi$, in the process of reconstruction, x is first fed through the encoder E to acquire $e = E(x)$, and then the generator G decodes e to produce reconstructed image $x_{rec} = G(e)$. In the process of translation, x also receives $e = E(x)$ through the encoder E first, and then the translator T fuses style encoding s_{trg} with $E(x)$ to get $e_{trg} = T(e, s_{trg})$, where s_{trg} can be derived from either latent code or reference images, and subsequent the generator decodes e_{trg} to get translated image $x_{trg} = G(e_{trg})$.

3.1   Wavelet Transform Based Image Processing

We adopt the wavelet transform to extract image characteristics for frequency domain image processing. In this paper, one low-pass filter and three high-pass filters are used to process the image's contents. The convolution procedure with a predetermined step size of 2 completes the filtering. Four different kinds of coefficients i.e., x_{LL}, x_{LH}, x_{HL}, and x_{HH} for the image can be obtained by filtering the image via four different filters. We use $f_{LL} = \left(\begin{smallmatrix} 1 & 1 \\ 1 & 1 \end{smallmatrix}\right)$, $f_{LH} = \left(\begin{smallmatrix} 1 & 1 \\ -1 & -1 \end{smallmatrix}\right)$, $f_{HL} = \left(\begin{smallmatrix} -1 & 1 \\ -1 & 1 \end{smallmatrix}\right)$, and $f_{HH} = \left(\begin{smallmatrix} -1 & 1 \\ 1 & -1 \end{smallmatrix}\right)$ as filters refers to [5]. Applying the low-pass filter f_{LL} to the original image x results in the approximation coefficients x_{LL}. The (p, q)-th value of x_{LL} is:

$$x_{LL}(p,q) = x(2p-1, 2q-1) + x(2p-1, 2q) + x(2p, 2q-1) + x(2p, 2q). \quad (1)$$

We denote this process as $x_{LL} = W_{LL}(x)$, and the reconstructed image x_{rec}'s approximation coefficients $x_{LL,rec}$ are expressed similarly to x_{LL}. Applying the high-pass filter f_{HH} to the original image x results in the diagonal coefficients x_{HH}. The (p, q)-th value of x_{HH} is:

$$x_{HH}(p,q) = x(2p-1, 2q-1) - x(2p-1, 2q) - x(2p, 2q-1) + x(2p, 2q). \quad (2)$$

We denote this process as $x_{HH} = W_{HH}(x)$, and the translated image x_{trg}'s diagonal coefficients $x_{HH,trg}$ are expressed similarly to x_{HH}.

3.2   Training Objectives

Wavelet Reconstruction Loss. During the image reconstruction process, the reconstructed image x_{rec} must be as consistent as possible with the source domain image x. The approximation coefficients can retain the main content of the source domain image and be combined with the pixel-level reconstruction loss in the spatial domain to simultaneously improve the capabilities of the encoder and generator. Therefore, this method calculates the difference between the source domain image x's approximation coefficients x_{LL} and the reconstructed image x_{rec}'s approximation coefficients $x_{LL,rec}$ and urges the generator to produce images similar to the source domain image. Designing the reconstruction loss at the frequency domain level as follow:

$$\begin{aligned} L_{rec\text{-}dwt} &= \mathbb{E}_{x \sim \chi}[\|W_{LL}(x) - W_{LL}(G(E(x)))\|_1] \\ &= \mathbb{E}_{x \sim \chi}[\|x_{LL} - x_{LL,rec}\|_1]. \end{aligned} \quad (3)$$

Wavelet Translation Loss. During the image translation process, we want the translated image x_{trg} to be as consistent as possible with the source domain image x in terms of overall contour and some details while correctly migrating the target style s_{trg}. The contour and details of the image can be effectively extracted using the diagonal coefficients. It can lessen the alteration of non-target properties while preserving more of the source domain image's details when combined with the cyclic consistency loss at the pixel-level. For the sake of preserving more of the non-target attributes from the source domain image, this method leverages the source image x's diagonal coefficients x_{HH} and the translated image x_{trg}'s diagonal coefficients $x_{HH,trg}$, then designs the translation loss at the frequency domain level as follow:

$$
\begin{aligned}
L_{trans-dwt} &= \mathbb{E}_{x \sim \chi}[\| W_{HH}(x) - W_{HH}(G(T(E(x), s_{trg}))) \|_1] \\
&= \mathbb{E}_{x \sim \chi}[\| x_{HH} - x_{HH,trg} \|_1].
\end{aligned}
\tag{4}
$$

Original Spatial-Domain Loss. HiSD has the original loss in the spatial domain. By combining the $L_{rec-dwt}$ with the $L_{trans-dwt}$, it can achieve complementary effects. HiSD uses three loss functions, including adversarial loss L_{adv}, reconstruction loss L_{rec}, and style loss L_{sty}. The style objective measures the deviation between the style code used to generate the image and the style code fed into the translator T to enhance the translator T's capacity for fusing different styles. We denote L_{org} as the combination of three loss functions:

$$
L_{org} = L_{adv} + \lambda_{rec} L_{rec} + \lambda_{sty} L_{sty},
\tag{5}
$$

where λ_{rec} and λ_{sty} are the weights of the reconstruction objective and the style objective, for simplicity of calculation, they are set to $\lambda_{rec} = \lambda_{sty} = 1$.

Overall Loss. Combining all the above loss functions, the final overall loss is formalized as:

$$
L_{FDFL-WT} = L_{org} + \lambda_{rd} L_{rec-dwt} + \lambda_{td} L_{trans-dwt},
\tag{6}
$$

where λ_{rd} and λ_{td} are the weights of $L_{rec-dwt}$ and $L_{trans-dwt}$. For simplicity of calculation, in this paper they are set to $\lambda_{rd} = \lambda_{td} = 1$.

4 Experiments

In this section, FDFL-WT is applied to HiSD [17], a face controllable attribute image translation model with controllable attributes, and the results demonstrate that FDFL-WT not only enhances the quality of the generated images but also better preserves the identity of the source domain images.

4.1 Baselines

We use HiSD [17], FDIT [3] and STIIE [10] as our baselines. HiSD intends to change just the attributes within the target when applying style transfer to an image, which is congruent with the purpose of our method. By injecting condition variables into the discriminator, HiSD enhances the model's decoupling capability and proposes the translator module for style fusion. HiSD evaluates both the realism and disentanglement of the generated images, which can visualize the image quality and the degree of retention of non-target attributes. As a result, in the relevant studies in this work, HiSD serves as one of the baselines.

FDIT creates loss functions on the pixel-level and in the frequency domain, employs a Gaussian kernel to filter the image, and applies frequency domain

Source   Reference   HiSD   FDIT   FDFL-WT

Fig. 2. Reference-based image translation test results on the CelebA-HQ dataset.

information to the style transfer task via the Fourier transform. Also in the frequency domain perspective to solve the image quality problem in image translation and the non-target attribute tampering problem, it is very appropriate to compare our work with FDIT. The experimental results of FDIT are also examined in the tests to compare the differences in efficacy between FDFL-WT and FDIT. The HiSD is expanded to include FDIT, and the same testing and training procedures are followed.

As the latest image translation model, STIIE combines Transformer [24] with StyleGAN for attribute editing and image inversion. Like HiSD, STIIE also has the function of editing bangs, so it is compared as one of the baselines in this paper. In addition, the gender and age attributes are used in the disentanglement test, in HiSD, these two attributes are trained as conditional variables during the training process. The age attribute is not included in all the attributes controlled by STIIE, so it is not meaningful to test the disentanglement. Therefore, Table 1 does not contain the STIIE's disentanglement test results.

4.2 Dataset and Evaluation Indicators

We evaluate FDFL-WT on the CelebA-HQ [13, 19] dataset. This dataset contains about 30,000 high-definition faces with labels. The first 3,000 images of the dataset are used as training set and the remaining about 27,000 images are used as test set with 'Hair color', 'Bangs', 'Glasses', and 'Bangs'(with attributes 'with'

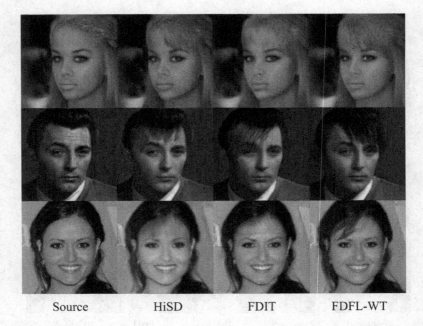

| Source | HiSD | FDIT | FDFL-WT |

Fig. 3. Latent-based image translation test results on the CelebA-HQ dataset.

and 'without') for testing the quality of style transfer, and 'Male' and 'Young' for testing the decoupling capability.

Frechét Inception Distance (FID) [8] is applied as an evaluation metric in the experiment. FID as a widely recognised evaluation metric for image generation, measures the distribution distance between real samples and generated images. A lower FID indicates that the closer the two distributions are, the better the image effect will be.

4.3   Implementation Details

We carried out the proposed model on two RTX 2080Ti, the deep learning framework used is PyTorch, and utilized images of the 1024×1024 size as input. Encoder E contains a convolution layer followed by two residual blocks, translator T contains one convolution layer followed by two residual blocks and an attention module, generator G contains two residual blocks followed by one convolution layer. For other settings, Adam [15] optimizer is employed, the batch size is 8, the empirical decay rates $(\beta_1, \beta_2) = (0, 0.99)$, and the learning rate is 0.0001.

4.4   Experimental Results

In this section, we evaluate our method on single-attribute style transfer of faces, the latent-guided task and the reference-guided task are both utilized to generate images. Specifically, the main objective is to convert the face images without

Table 1. Results comparison among FDFL-WT, HiSD, FDIT and STIIE.

Method	Realism (FID)			Disentanglement (FID)		
	Latent	Reference	Gap	Latent	Reference	Gap
HiSD	24.59	24.45	0.14	77.86	77.34	0.52
FDIT	24.20	23.99	0.21	77.73	76.83	0.90
STIIE	40.14	40.57	0.43	–	–	–
FDFL-WT	**22.86**	**22.83**	**0.03**	**74.51**	**74.18**	**0.33**

bangs into the face images with bangs, and 3000 training set images are selected at random 40,000 times to train the model. In order to more accurately assess the effectiveness of the methodology, the generated images are tested for realism and disentanglement. Figure 2 displays several test results.

Realism. We shall evaluate the discrepancy between the generated fake image and the source imageto verify the validity of generated images. For this purpose, all the images without bangs in the test set are transformed into images with bangs utilizing both the latent-guided task and the reference-guided task.

Latent code is taken from the random Gaussian noise of normal distribution and used to generate random style code, so that the generated images can possess bangs of various styles. Figure 3 shows some character images with bangs generated under the guidance of late code. FDFL-WT has more natural bangs, and the skin color and background color of the characters closer to the source image. The reference image is taken from all the character images with bangs in the CelebA-hq dataset, and the reference images of each generated image are randomly selected from them to guide the source image to generate an image with reference image style.

The CelebA-HQ dataset's images with bangs and all images created using the aforementioned two techniques are both employed to calculate FIDs. A lower FID represents a closer distribution between the two, indicating that the model is more realistic at transforming the target attributes. In order to test the stability of the model, we also introduce 'Gap', which is the difference between latent's value and reference's value. The narrower the gap, the more stable the model is for both image generation techniques. Additionally, it is necessary to process the images with bangs used for FID comparison so that their resolution matches that of the generated images. Table 1 displays the experimental results of the realism test.

Disentanglement. In the disentanglement test, all images with 'male', 'young' tags without bangs in the test set are transformed into images with bangs using both the latent-guided task and the reference-guided task, and the FID is calculated with all images with 'male', 'young' tags with bangs in the CelebA-HQ dataset. Like the realism test, the random Gaussian noise generation style is used in the latent-guided task, and a random image with bangs is used for guidance in each generation process of the reference-guided task, and the images

Table 2. The effect of using different frequency domain coefficients.

Method	Realism (FID)			Disentanglement (FID)		
	Latent	Reference	Gap	Latent	Reference	Gap
Rec3	23.88	23.51	0.37	76.56	76.95	0.39
HL	23.30	22.99	0.31	75.42	76.66	1.24
LH	24.00	24.02	**0.02**	77.56	77.50	**0.06**
Trans3	23.52	23.24	0.28	76.34	76.79	0.45
FDFL-WT	**22.86**	**22.83**	0.03	**74.51**	**74.18**	0.33

Table 3. Quantitative results of the ablation study.

Method	Realism (FID)			Disentanglement (FID)		
	Latent	Reference	Gap	Latent	Reference	Gap
-trans	23.61	22.85	0.76	76.06	75.68	0.38
-rec	23.61	23.60	**0.01**	74.98	75.56	0.58
FDFL-WT	**22.86**	**22.83**	0.03	**74.51**	**74.18**	**0.33**

used for comparison are processed to make the resolution consistent with the generated images. The experiment is designed in this manner to examine the model's capacity for holding onto irrelevant attributes, the disentangle test will yield a subpar result if the age or gender of any image is altered. In a similar vein, the model's capacity to decouple, or maintain the non-target attributes, is strengthened the lower the FID.

The Effect of Using Different Frequency Domain Feature. The wavelet transform extracts four different types of coefficients from the image, but our method does not employ the vertical and horizontal coefficients. We also experimented with their application. We first calculate of reconstruction loss using approximation coefficients, vertical coefficients, and horizontal coefficients, in this way, it is expected to extract the features of the reconstructed image to the maximum extent in the horizontal and vertical directions while using approximation coefficients. However, this method brings information redundancy and confusion, resulting in poor generation effect, this phenomenon can be seen in Rec3 throughout Table 2.

In the process of translation, the vertical coefficients or the horizontal coefficients only focus on the characteristics of one direction, which is obviously not comprehensive enough for calculating translation loss. The HL and LH experimental results in Table 2 also prove this view. In addition, we also use the combination of vertical, horizontal, and differential coefficients to calculate translation loss. Similarly, the combination of the three will lead to redundancy and confusion, as can be seen from the Trans3 in Table 2.

4.5   Ablation Study

In this section, we test the effect of adding a single loss function on the experimental effect by means of control variables. The loss of wavelet reconstruction is more obvious for the improvement of realism, and the loss of wavelet translation is more obvious for the improvement of disentanglement, these can be derived from Table 3. The ablation experiment demonstrates that the wavelet loss reconstruction tends to strengthen the image's authenticity, while the wavelet loss translation tends to prevent the modification of non-target attributes. The reason for this is because the frequency domain information utilized is distinct. Approximation Coefficients capture image color, lighting, and other characteristics, while diagonal coefficients correspond to sharp edges and significant object details. Comparing the experimental results of adding only wavelet reconstruction loss (-trans), only wavelet translation loss (-rec), or both (FDFL-WT), a positive effect is observed between the two loss functions. This further proves the necessity of introducing the wavelet transform and the validity of our proposed method.

5   Conclusion

In this paper, we propose a novel method *Frequency Domain Feature Learning with Wavelet Transform* (FDFL-WT) for the style transfer task. The key idea is to enhance the generator's ability to grab features by employing the approximation coefficients and the diagonal coefficients in the reconstruction as well as translation processes; both of these characteristics are extracted by the wavelet transform. Extensive experiments have been conducted to evaluate the FDFL-WT approach in terms of realism and disentanglement, and confirm that FDFL-WT yields better style transfer quality and a stronger ability to retain non-target attributes. Most of image-to-image translation model can be easily integrated with FDFL-WT. One of the limitations of FDFL-WT is that only the generated part is constrained, so the objective of the future work is to enhance the performance of the discriminator by incorporating the wavelet transform concept into the adversarial loss discriminator.

References

1. Bae, W., Yoo, J.J., Ye, J.C.: Beyond deep residual learning for image restoration: persistent homology-guided manifold simplification. In: CVPR Workshops, pp. 1141–1149 (2017)
2. Brigham, E.O.: The Fast Fourier Transform and Its Applications. Prentice-Hall, Inc. (1988)
3. Cai, M., Zhang, H., Huang, H., Geng, Q., Li, Y., Huang, G.: Frequency domain image translation: more photo-realistic, better identity-preserving. In: ICCV, pp. 13910–13920 (2021)
4. Choi, Y., Uh, Y., Yoo, J., Ha, J.: StarGAN v2: diverse image synthesis for multiple domains. In: CVPR, pp. 8185–8194 (2020)

5. Fu, M., Liu, H., Yu, Y., Chen, J., Wang, K.: DW-GAN: a discrete wavelet transform GAN for nonhomogeneous dehazing. In: CVPR Workshops, pp. 203–212 (2021)
6. Gao, Y., et al.: High-fidelity and arbitrary face editing. In: CVPR, pp. 16115–16124 (2021)
7. Heideman, M., Johnson, D., Burrus, C.: Gauss and the history of the fast Fourier transform. IEEE ASSP Mag. **4**(1), 14–21 (1984)
8. Heusel, M., Ramsauer, H., Unterthiner, T., Nessler, B., Hochreiter, S.: GANs trained by a two time-scale update rule converge to a local nash equilibrium. In: NeurIPS, pp. 6626–6637 (2017)
9. Hiasa, Y., et al.: Cross-modality image synthesis from unpaired data using Cycle-GAN - effects of gradient consistency loss and training data size. In: MICCAI, pp. 31–41 (2018)
10. Hu, X., et al.: Style transformer for image inversion and editing. In: CVPR, pp. 11327–11336 (2022)
11. Isola, P., Zhu, J., Zhou, T., Efros, A.A.: Image-to-image translation with conditional adversarial networks. In: CVPR, pp. 5967–5976 (2017)
12. Jiang, L., Dai, B., Wu, W., Loy, C.C.: Focal frequency loss for image reconstruction and synthesis. In: ICCV, pp. 13899–13909 (2021)
13. Karras, T., Aila, T., Laine, S., Lehtinen, J.: Progressive growing of GANs for improved quality, stability, and variation. In: ICLR (2018)
14. Karras, T., Laine, S., Aila, T.: A style-based generator architecture for generative adversarial networks. In: CVPR, pp. 4401–4410 (2019)
15. Kingma, D.P., Ba, J.: Adam: a method for stochastic optimization. In: ICLR (2015)
16. Li, X., Guo, Q., Lin, D., Li, P., Feng, W., Wang, S.: MISF: multi-level interactive Siamese filtering for high-fidelity image inpainting. In: CVPR, pp. 1859–1868 (2022)
17. Li, X., et al.: Image-to-image translation via hierarchical style disentanglement. In: CVPR, pp. 8639–8648 (2021)
18. Liang, J., Zeng, H., Zhang, L.: Details or artifacts: a locally discriminative learning approach to realistic image super-resolution. In: CVPR, pp. 5647–5656 (2022)
19. Liu, Z., Luo, P., Wang, X., Tang, X.: Deep learning face attributes in the wild. In: ICCV, pp. 3730–3738 (2015)
20. Ma, J., Liang, Z., Zhang, L.: A text attention network for spatial deformation robust scene text image super-resolution. In: CVPR, pp. 5901–5910 (2022)
21. Ramaswamy, K.R., Csurcsia, P.Z., Schoukens, J., den Hof, P.M.J.V.: A frequency domain approach for local module identification in dynamic networks. Autom. **142**, 110370 (2022)
22. Ronneberger, O., Fischer, P., Brox, T.: U-Net: convolutional networks for biomedical image segmentation. In: Navab, N., Hornegger, J., III, W.M.W., Frangi, A.F. (eds.) MICCAI, pp. 234–241 (2015)
23. Tao, T., Zhan, X., Chen, Z., van de Panne, M.: Style-ERD: responsive and coherent online motion style transfer. In: CVPR, pp. 6583–6593 (2022)
24. Vaswani, A., et al.: Attention is all you need. In: NIPS, pp. 5998–6008 (2017)
25. Wang, T., Zhang, Y., Fan, Y., Wang, J., Chen, Q.: High-fidelity GAN inversion for image attribute editing. In: CVPR 2022, pp. 11369–11378
26. Wang, Y., Xu, C., Xu, C., Tao, D.: Packing convolutional neural networks in the frequency domain. IEEE Trans. Pattern Anal. Mach. Intell. **41**(10), 2495–2510 (2019)
27. Xiao, S., Wang, S., Chang, L.: Image reconstruction based on fused features and perceptual loss encoder-decoder residual network for space optical remote sensing images compressive sensing. IEEE Access **9**, 50413–50425 (2021)

28. Xu, K., Qin, M., Sun, F., Wang, Y., Chen, Y., Ren, F.: Learning in the frequency domain. In: CVPR, pp. 1737–1746 (2020)
29. Yang, S., Jiang, L., Liu, Z., Loy, C.C.: Pastiche master: exemplar-based high-resolution portrait style transfer. In: CVPR, pp. 7683–7692 (2022)
30. Zhang, L., Chen, X., Tu, X., Wan, P., Xu, N., Ma, K.: Wavelet knowledge distillation: towards efficient image-to-image translation. In: CVPR, pp. 12454–12464 (2022)
31. Zhang, Y., Li, M., Li, R., Jia, K., Zhang, L.: Exact feature distribution matching for arbitrary style transfer and domain generalization. In: CVPR, pp. 8025–8035 (2022)
32. Zhao, H., Gallo, O., Frosio, I., Kautz, J.: Loss functions for image restoration with neural networks. IEEE Trans. Comput. Imaging **3**(1), 47–57 (2017)
33. Zhu, J., Park, T., Isola, P., Efros, A.A.: Unpaired image-to-image translation using cycle-consistent adversarial networks. In: ICCV, pp. 2242–2251 (2017)

Graph-Guided Latent Variable Target Inference for Mitigating Concept Drift in Time Series Forecasting

Fang Yu, Shijun Li[(✉)], and Wei Yu[(✉)]

School of Computer Science, Wuhan University, Wuhan 430072, Hubei, China
{shjli,yuwei}@whu.edu.cn

Abstract. With the proliferation of the Internet of Things (IoT), there is an abundance of data available to humans. However, the monitoring environments for data collection are becoming increasingly diverse, leading to the occurrence of concept drift in the collected data. Concept drift refers to the phenomenon where the distribution of data changes over time, making it challenging for prediction models trained on historical data to adapt to the changing distribution. Previous research has primarily focused on predicting or compensating for distributions with fixed durations in Euclidean space to mitigate non-stationarity. However, we have observed that concept drift often occurs at different time scales, and detecting them using fixed scales has inherent limitations. Based on this observation, we propose a Graph-Guided Latent Variable Target Inference network that maps current data and variable duration query targets onto a graph neural network in latent space. We apply self-attention transformations to the representations and correlations on the graph in the dimensions of time, features, and query targets. The model updates its parameters based on these non-Euclidean correlation patterns, enabling the graph to evolve towards the direction of the query targets and obtain an evolved latent distribution. Finally, the decoder generates a prediction data stream regarding the query targets based on the evolved latent distribution. The experiments were conducted on five datasets, where our proposed method was compared against the five most advanced baselines. The findings demonstrated a substantial advantage in prediction performance provided by our approach.

Keywords: Graph neural network · Time Series Concept drift · Variable Target Inference · Latent Space

1 Introduction

Time series prediction tasks are prevalent in various industries, such as server traffic forecasting [1], traffic flow prediction [2], and weather forecasting [3]. Deep learning based techniques have achieved impressive results in these fields and have become the state-of-the-art methods [4]. These methods typically assume that the data follows an independent and identically distributed (i.i.d.) pattern, meaning that the distribution of the data remains relatively stable over time. However, with the development of IoT

© The Author(s), under exclusive license to Springer Nature Singapore Pte Ltd. 2024
F. Liu et al. (Eds.): PRICAI 2023, LNAI 14327, pp. 358–369, 2024.
https://doi.org/10.1007/978-981-99-7025-4_31

technology, the sampling environments of sensors have become more complex, leading to temporal concept drift and making time series data tend to be non-stationary. This has become a critical factor hindering the prediction performance of deep learning models [5]. Concept drift refers to the phenomenon where the data distribution changes over time, manifesting as non-stationarity in the temporal dimension of the data stream. For example, the development of wearable devices has provided convenience for human health monitoring, but the subjectivity of human activities can result in the devices being used in non-standard scenarios [6], causing changes in the distribution of the collected data. Concept drift often leads to overfitting in deep neural networks and a decrease in generalization ability, impeding the training and prediction of models [7]. Therefore, it is crucial to model the frequently changing data distribution and devise corresponding strategies during the model training phase. Some studies aim to mitigate inefficient concept drift by detecting and adjusting for it [8]. Others use statistical analysis on time series to derive measures and reconstruct data distributions using empirical knowledge [9, 10]. However, these empirical methods may overlook detailed real data information.

We have observed that the aforementioned research tends to define concept drift as an absolute concept, namely, the degree of distribution shift exceeding a certain threshold within a fixed time scale [7]. However, in reality, changes in data distribution can occur at any time scale, and when the observation scale changes, time series often exhibit varying degrees of distribution changes. For example, when observing city electricity consumption on a daily time scale, hot weather may cause a short-term surge in electricity usage. But when observed on an annual time scale, a sharp decrease in city electricity consumption can be observed in the years following the COVID-19 pandemic [11]. Therefore, we consider concept drift as a relative concept that exhibits different drift characteristics at different time scales.

To incorporate the investigation of target time scales into the representation learning of time series, we propose Graph-Guided Latent Variable Target Inference (GLVTI) that starts with the conditional priors of time series and introduces variable-scale target query time. By constructing the log-likelihood of the conditional priors, we infer the architecture of this variable-scale neural network, providing an interface for multi-domain time series prediction. GLVTI constructs a graph neural network guided by the variable target time in the latent space, embedding attribute features, temporal features of the source domain, and target domain time features into a non-Euclidean space. This enables effective representation of the dynamic correlations of the latent distribution patterns of the data stream and inferring the latent representation graph after concept drift. The main contributions of this paper are as follows:

- We propose Graph-Guided Latent Variable Target Inference (GLVTI) that starts with the conditional priors of time series and introduces variable-scale target query time.
- We construct a graph neural network guided by variable target time in the latent space of GLVTI, which embeds attribute features, temporal features of the source domain, and target domain time features into a non-Euclidean space.
- In comparison with several mainstream baseline methods, GLVTI has achieved superior predictive performance.

2 Related Work

Concept drift in time series can be classified based on specific criteria [12], including sudden occurrence rate and periodicity. Regardless of the criteria used, the occurrence of concept drift requires reference to the data from both the source domain and the target domain (also referred to as context data) [13]. In reality, most monitored time series are influenced by periodic factors, and this drift pattern exhibits seasonality but still contains a small amount of abrupt or random distribution changes [14]. Adaptive techniques have been applied to time series forecasting tasks to address abrupt and periodic concept drift [15, 16]. They typically assume that more recent known data is closer in distribution to the data to be predicted, and thus tend to assign greater weights to the most recent data while gradually discarding earlier data. Some studies feed historical data to the model and train the model to minimize the difference between the model's output and future predicted values [17]. Other studies focus on designing time-sensitive neural networks to directly control the evolution direction of network parameters over time [18], or characterize the temporal invariance of data based on adversarial methods [19]. In addition to adaptive methods, there are also approaches that utilize static statistical principles or distance functions to represent and mitigate data distribution [20, 21]. These models have good interpretability but are limited by their shallow depth and limited data representation capacity. In recent years, neural network prediction models based on self-attention mechanisms have emerged [34, 35], which, due to their powerful data representation capabilities and long-range prediction abilities, allow the models to directly overcome the negative effects of data concept drift.

We propose GLVTI, a unique active concept drift adaptation method for distribution adaptation. Unlike previous methods, GLVTI equally values historical and recent data from the source domain, recognizing potential seasonal patterns across time and multi-dimensional attributes. By using graph representation, GLVTI captures these correlations, transforming distribution changes into graph topology alterations, actively mitigating concept drift effects on forecasting.

3 Graph-Guided Latent Variable Target Inference

A subsection sample we consider a multi-dimensional time series dataset, denoted as $X = \{(x_i, t_i)|i = 1, 2, ...N\}$, where $x_i \in \mathbb{R}^k$ represents the i-th sample containing attribute values from k different sensor categories. The sampling time, t_i, of each sample is not required to be equidistant, which is a unique characteristic of the Graph-Guided Latent Variable Target Inference (GLVTI) approach, allowing for variable time spans within the source domain. For the task of time series forecasting, it is necessary to establish a mapping relationship defined as:

$$G : X(t_{1:h}) \rightarrow X(t_{h+1:h+\lambda}) \tag{1}$$

where G represents the mapping for the time series forecasting task, mapping h time series values from t_1 to t_h on the interval to λ time series prediction values from t_{h+1} to $t_{h+\lambda}$ $(\lambda \in z^+)$. The definition of Eq. (1) differs from traditional fixed-scale predictions due to the time span variable λ, which defines a target span-variable forecasting task.

Furthermore, this definition has a specific implication: considering G as a neural network mapping and assuming $X(t_{h+1:h+\lambda})$ is known, $X(t_{h+1:h+\lambda})$ can serve as self-supervised signals to train the neural network G for $X(t_{1:h})$.

3.1 Variable Target Inference

The training objective of our proposed model is to generate predictions in the target domain that are close to the true values based on the source domain time series $X(t_{1:h})$ and target domain time $t_{h+1:h+\lambda}$, as follows:

$$\max \log P\big[X(t_{h+1:h+\lambda})|t_{1:h+\lambda}, X(t_{1:h})\big] \tag{2}$$

where P represents probability. Since the prior distribution of the data is unknown, directly solving for the maximum log-likelihood is not feasible. In indirect inference methods, variational inference is an effective deterministic approximation method. However, Eq. (2) involves a conditional prior with a variable target domain time, which differs from variational inference [22]. Nevertheless, it can still be derived based on the fundamental framework of Variational Bayesian Expectation Maximization [23]. By applying the Newton-Leibniz formula [24], we have:

$$\log p\big[X(t_{h+1:h+\lambda})|t_{1:h+\lambda}, X(t_{1:h})\big] = D_{KL}\big\{q\big[z|X(t_{1:h+\lambda}), t_{1:h+\lambda}\big]||p\big[z|X(t_{1:h+\lambda}), t_{1:h+\lambda}\big]\big\}$$
$$+ \int_z q\big[z|X(t_{1:h+\lambda}), t_{1:h+\lambda}\big] \log \frac{p\big[z, X(t_{h+1:h+\lambda})|t_{1:h+\lambda}, X(t_{1:h})\big]}{q\big[z|X(t_{1:h+\lambda}), t_{1:h+\lambda}\big]} dz$$
$$\tag{3}$$

where z represents a newly introduced latent variable. In Eq. (3), the KL-divergence term is greater than 0, thus we have:

$$\log p\big[X(t_{h+1:h+\lambda})|t_{1:h+\lambda}, X(t_{1:h})\big] \geq \mathbb{E}_{z \sim q[z|X(t_{1:h+\lambda}), t_{1:h+\lambda}]}\bigg\{\sum_{i=1}^{\lambda} \log p\big[X(t_{h+i})|t_{h+i}, z\big]\bigg\} -$$
$$D_{KL}\big\{q\big[z|X(t_{1:h+\lambda}), t_{1:h+\lambda}\big]||p\big[z|X(t_{1:h}), t_{1:h}\big]\big\}$$
$$\tag{4}$$

Equation (4) provides an approximate method to solve Eq. (2), where the expectation part can be approximated using a neural network. The conditional prior $p[z|X(t_{1:h}), t_{1:h}]$ in the KL-divergence term is uncertain, but it can be approximated by the posterior $q[z|X(t_{1:h}), t_{1:h}]$. The KL-divergence, assuming a Gaussian distribution, can be directly computed from a preset probability expression. Hence, the model's loss function is defined as:

$$L = D_{KL}\big\{q\big[z|X(t_{1:h+\lambda}), t_{1:h+\lambda}\big]||q\big[z|X(t_{1:h}), t_{1:h}\big]\big\}$$
$$- \mathbb{E}_{z \sim q[z|X(t_{1:h+\lambda}), t_{1:h+\lambda}]}\bigg\{\sum_{i=1}^{\lambda} \log p\big[X(t_{h+i})|t_{h+i}, z\big]\bigg\} \tag{5}$$

According to Eq. (5), it can be observed that minimizing the loss function is equivalent to maximizing the log-likelihood in Eq. (2). This process aims to maximize the expectation term as much as possible while minimizing the KL-divergence. It means that the neural network should strive to make the posterior of the expectation term approach the prior as closely as possible and achieve regularization by minimizing the KL-divergence. This helps prevent overfitting and improves the model's generalization ability.

3.2 General Architecture

We designed the overall architecture of the GLVTI network based on Eq. (5), as shown in Fig. 1. The input information consists of the source domain time series $X(t_{1:h})$, the time $t_{1:h}$, and the query time $t_{h+1:h+\lambda}$ as the target domain. Since λ is an arbitrary positive integer, the entire query target span is variable. The historical observed data is fed into the encoder Encoder-d. The specific structure of the encoder can be defined based on the specific prediction task.

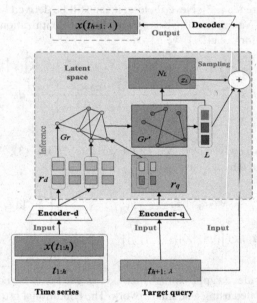

Fig. 1. The general architecture of GLVTI can be divided into three parts, working from bottom to top. The first part is the encoding stage of the information. The encoder, Encoder-d, encodes the data within the source domain into a latent representation $r_d \in \mathbb{R}^{m \times n_d}$, while the encoder, Encoder-r, encodes the variable target time within the target domain into $r_q \in \mathbb{R}^{m \times n_q}$. The second part is the graph-evolving neural network Gr, in the latent space. It evolves guided by the target time r_q. r_d and r_q serve as node embeddings within Gr. Through model training, Gr evolves into an approximate latent graph Gr', that captures the changes occurring due to concept drift. The third part is the decoder and the output stage of the entire neural network. The decoder is a set of fully connected neural networks. It integrates information from different semantic levels and produces a reconstructed output in the target domain, guided by the variable target.

3.3 The Evolution of Latent Graphs

The graph Gr in the latent space is updated through a self-attention mechanism, adjusting the weights of nodes and edges to evolve the non-Euclidean relational patterns from the input information towards the target domain query time, resulting in the updated graph Gr'. In the initial stage, Gr consists of time series nodes di ($i = 1,2,...,nd$) and target time nodes qi ($i = 1,2,...,nq$). The former represents the latent features of the i-th batch of time series, denoted as rd's i-th column, while the latter represents the latent feature components of the i-th target time sequence, denoted as rq's i-th column.

To facilitate formal expression and unify these two types of nodes within the same graph, we define them as:

$$V = \{v_i | v_i \in r_d \cup r_q\} \tag{6}$$

where V represents the node set of graph Gr, and v_i represents the i-th node after numbering the elements of the set in order. The edges between nodes represent their association weights.

In the initial stage, all nodes are connected by edges with weights set to 1. After the graph is updated, edges with weights below a threshold η will be pruned. We define the edge weights in Gr using the weight calculation method from GAT [25]. Then, we utilize our newly designed attention mechanism to update each node. For any two nodes vi and vj in Gr, the weight of the edge between them is

$$e(v_i, v_j) = \frac{\exp\left\{U\left[a_{ij}^T \cdot (W_i(v_i \oplus q_c) \oplus W_j v_j \oplus W_c q_c)\right]\right\}}{\sum\limits_{k=1}^{n_1+n_2} \exp\left\{U\left[a_{ij}^T \cdot (W_i(v_i \oplus q_c) \oplus W_j v_k)\right]\right\}} \tag{7}$$

where $e(v_i, v_j)$ represents the weight of the edge from vi to vj. The matrices $W_i \in \mathbb{R}^{l \times 2m}$ and $W_j \in \mathbb{R}^{l \times m}$ represent the linear transformation matrices for vi and vj, respectively, and these two learnable matrices reduce the dimensionality of the nodes to l. qc represents the target-guided node, which is the target time node connected by the edge with the highest weight to v_i. When v_i and q_c are the same node, the target-guided node of v_i is v_i itself. $a_{ij} \in \mathbb{R}^{3l \times 1}$ denotes the learnable attention coefficient between v_i and v_j. The role of the target-guided node is to inject the most important target time information into each node of the graph. When updating w_i, the weight of this target information is adjusted, allowing the graph neural network to establish a micro-level association with the target time information. The operator $\oplus$ denotes concatenation of vectors on the left and right sides. U represents the nonlinear function leakyReLU. If $e(v_i, v_j)$ is below the lower threshold value η of the edge weight, the graph neural network removes this edge and does not restore it in future updates.

For node v_i, the update is performed as follows:

$$v_i' = \text{sigmoid}\left[\sum_{k=1}^{n_1+n_2} e(v_i, v_k) W_{i,k} v_i\right] \tag{8}$$

where $W_{i,k}$ represents the linear transformation matrix for the edge between v_i and v_j. It can be observed that the update of v_i' incorporates its attention information with all other nodes, resulting in each node in the updated graph Gr' containing both global information and target time information. In Eq. (8), the target time information is embedded in each updated node, enabling the nodes to carry the semantics of the target time at a microscopic level.

3.4 Decoding and Forecasting

After the update of the graph in the latent space, the latent features of the time series are fused with the latent target time information. The model training process drives the evolution of the graph towards the target time, resulting in an evolved latent distribution. This process requires both the representation information of the entire graph and the information of the evolved distribution, both of which can be obtained from the updated graph Gr'.

First, let's define the latent representation of the graph:

$$L = \sum_{i=1}^{n_1+n_2} \text{sigmoid}\big[W_A\big(v_i' \oplus A_i\big) + b_i\big] \tag{9}$$

where L represents the overall latent representation of the graph, A_i represents the weighted adjacency matrix of v_i, W_A and b_i represent learnable linear transformation matrices and bias vectors, respectively. Furthermore, we apply a non-linear transformation to L, mapping it to the distribution parameters of the latent distribution:

$$\mu_L = a_u \cdot \tanh\big(W_\mu L + b_\mu\big) \tag{10}$$

$$\sigma_L = a_\sigma \cdot \text{sigmoid}(W_\sigma L + b_\sigma) \tag{11}$$

where μ_L represents the mean of the evolved latent Gaussian distribution, and σ_L represents the corresponding standard deviation. W_μ and b_μ denote the learnable linear transformation matrix and bias vector for generating the mean. Similarly, W_σ and b_σ denote the learnable linear transformation matrix and bias vector for generating the standard deviation. a_μ and a_σ represent scaling factors for the mean and standard deviation, respectively. Finally, GLVTI employs the reparameterization technique to sample from the evolved latent distribution, obtaining the sampled information z_L that follows the new latent distribution: $z_L \sim N\big(\mu_L, \sigma_L^2\big)$. Based on the conditional prior in the expectation term of Eq. (4), GLVTI integrates three types of information in its latent space and passes them to the decoder, as $R = z_L \oplus L \oplus t_{h+1:h+\lambda}$. The decoder employs fully connected neural networks to aggregate information from multiple pathways and output the final result.

4 Experiments

The experiment is divided into two parts: the first part examines the predictive performance of GLVTI, and the second part is a ablation study to assess the contribution of each component in GLVTI's predictive performance. The experimental data is derived from regions of time series where multi-scale concept drift occurs densely, as well as from typical weak stationary regions, including the Electricity (ELE) dataset [26], it encompasses the power usage of 321 clients spanning from 2012 to 2014, with electricity measurements in KWh taken at 15-min intervals. PSM [27] is a time series of 26 application server nodes recorded by eBay Inc. SMD [28] originates from a prominent tech corporation and maintains a record. The dataset encompasses 38 dimensions. MSL [29] consists of 55 dimensions sourced from NASA's Mars Science Laboratory rover. SWaT [30] comprises 51 sensors extracted from an incessantly operational water infrastructure system. The experiment compares GLVTI with five competitive baselines: ARF [31], Condor [32], ODE-RNN [33], Informer [34] and Autoformer [35]. The encoder portions of Informer and Autoformer both inherit the multi-head attention mechanism from BERT.

For GLVTI, the encoder serves as the interface for data feature extraction, and we adopt the Bert-based self-attention mechanism by default [36]. The optimizer used is ADAM, with a learning rate set between $1e-5$ and $1e-4$. During initialization, the edge weights of the graph neural network are set to 1. The time span variable λ is set as a random integer following a uniform distribution between 0 and 1 times the length of the source domain time series. The scaling coefficients a_μ and a_σ are set to 0 and 1, respectively. The edge weight lower threshold η is set to 0.015.

4.1 Evaluating Predictive Performance

In this section, we evaluate the predictive performance of GLVTI. For each dataset, the training set constitutes 80% of the data, while the remaining portion serves as the test set. GLVTI-FC refers to GLVTI with a fully connected neural network as the encoder. GLVTI-GRU indicates the use of GRU as the encoder. GLVTI-BERT represents the default configuration with BERT [36] as the encoder. The experimental results are presented in Table 1.

Table 1. Time series Forecasting Performance (MSE as %)

Methods	ELE	PSM	SMD	MSL	SWaT
ARF	132.93	106.70	105.82	195.72	123.90
Condor	188.17	156.34	195.52	188.20	136.49
ODE-RNN	194.65	131.56	146.21	171.69	156.65
Autoformer	102.45	94.51	98.39	96.19	105.25
Informer	89.77	83.36	87.40	92.30	97.27
GLVTI-FC	141.78	104.81	142.97	157.60	106.34
GLVTI-GRU	124.49	113.71	122.79	148.35	141.18
GLVTI-BERT	**86.34**	**82.05**	**82.47**	**86.37**	**91.70**

From the experimental results, it can be observed that the GLVTI method outperforms other baseline methods. Among the baseline methods, Autoformer and Informer, which are based on self-attention mechanisms, significantly outperform the other baselines, indicating the advantage of self-attention in mitigating concept drift. GLVTI-BERT, inheriting the advantages of global feature extraction from self-attention mechanisms, achieves even better predictive performance than all baseline methods. Both GLVTI-FC and GLVTI-GRU lack the self-attention mechanism in the encoder, resulting in a significant drop in predictive performance. However, they still outperform the Condor and ODE-RNN models alone. This indicates that the graph neural network in the latent space evolves on variable scales, enabling the model to adapt well to concept drift in the data, thereby outperforming the original structures of the respective encoders.

4.2 Ablation Experiments

In this section, we conduct experiments to evaluate the model's performance when the three key components of GLVTI are missing. This indirectly assesses the contributions of these components to the model's performance. The first group of experiments involves removing the graph neural network, and the encoder directly outputs distribution parameters according to VAE standards. The second group of experiments modifies the training method for variable-scale target domain time by using fixed distance samples of 5 time units as the supervised signal (average of the variable target time span). The third group of experiments removes the target time from being injected into the decoder alongside the raw data. The fourth experimental model involves retaining the original configuration with all components, which is our proposed GLVTI. The experimental results are presented in Table 2.

Table 2. Ablation results (MSE as %)

Strategy	ELE	PSM	SMD	MSL	SWaT
GNN-	117.41	101.75	108.15	92.60	154.82
Fixed λ	93.29	94.75	112.32	104.36	97.89
t-	89.01	89.64	95.71	90.94	119.78
GLVTI	86.34	82.05	82.47	86.37	91.70

In Table 2, a minus sign "−" indicates the removal of the corresponding component. "GNN-" represents the removal of the graph neural network's evolutionary mechanism in the latent space. "Fixed λ" denotes the modification of the variable-scale target domain time to a fixed time span. "t-" indicates that the target time is no longer included as an input to the model. "GE" represents the Graph Evolution Neural Network for removing latent space.

The experimental results show that removing the GNN component leads to the most significant degradation in model performance, indicating that concept drift indeed involves non-Euclidean transformations of multivariate time series, and our designed GNN structure is capable of effectively extracting such patterns. Fixing the target time span also greatly impacts the model's predictive performance. Removing the input of the target time has a negative effect on the model as well, although the extent of performance degradation is not as significant as the first two cases.

5 Conclusion

This research addresses the concept drift issue in time series prediction by introducing a novel method, Graph-Guided Latent Variable Target Inference (GLVTI). Unlike prior studies, we view concept drift as a relative notion with varying drift characteristics across different time scales. We propose a variable-scale target query time and infer a neural network architecture based on conditional priors. By creating a target-guided neural network in the latent space, we effectively capture dynamic time series correlation patterns and infer the latent representation graph post-concept drift. GLVTI outperforms other methods in multiple experiments, with ablation studies highlighting the importance of graph neural network embedding and variable-scale target time guidance in enhancing model performance. This work offers a fresh approach to multi-domain time series prediction, suggesting future research to extend GLVTI's application and further assess its performance and robustness.

References

1. Zhang, C., Cui, L., Yu, S., James, J.Q.: A communication-efficient federated learning scheme for iot-based traffic forecasting. IEEE Internet Things J. **9**(14), 11918–11931 (2021)
2. Shengdong, M., Zhengxian, X., Yixiang, T.: Intelligent traffic control system based on cloud computing and big data mining. IEEE Trans. Industr. Inf. **15**(12), 6583–6592 (2019)
3. Han, J., Liu, H., Zhu, H., Xiong, H., Dou, D.: Joint air quality and weather prediction based on multiadversarial spatiotemporal networks. In: Proceedings of the 35th AAAI Conference on Artificial Intelligence (2021)
4. Salinas, D., Flunkert, V., Gasthaus, J., Januschowski, T.: DeepAR: probabilistic forecasting with autoregressive recurrent networks. Int. J. Forecast. **36**(3), 1181–1191 (2020)
5. Agrahari, S., Singh, A.K.: Concept drift detection in data stream mining: a literature review. J. King Saud Univ.-Comput. Inf. Sci. **34**(10), 9523–9540 (2022)
6. Casado, F.E., Lema, D., Criado, M.F., Iglesias, R., Regueiro, C.V., Barro, S.: Concept drift detection and adaptation for federated and continual learning. Multimedia Tools Appl. 1–23 (2022)
7. Zenisek, J., Holzinger, F., Affenzeller, M.: Machine learning based concept drift detection for predictive maintenance. Comput. Ind. Eng. **137**, 106031 (2019)
8. Lu, J., Liu, A., Dong, F., Gu, F., Gama, J., Zhang, G.: Learning under concept drift: a review. IEEE Trans. Knowl. Data Eng. **31**(12), 2346–2363 (2018)
9. Passalis, N., Tefas, A., Kanniainen, J., Gabbouj, M., Iosifidis, A.: Deep adaptive input normalization for time series forecasting. IEEE Trans. Neural Networks Learn. Syst. **31**(9), 3760–3765 (2019)
10. Kim, T., Kim, J., Tae, Y., Park, C., Choi, J.H., Choo, J.: Reversible instance normalization for accurate time-series forecasting against distribution shift. In: International Conference on Learning Representations (2021)
11. Abu-Rayash, A., Dincer, I.: Analysis of the electricity demand trends amidst the COVID-19 coronavirus pandemic. Energy Res. Soc. Sci. **68**, 101682 (2020)

12. Ren, S., Liao, B., Zhu, W., Li, K.: Knowledgemaximized ensemble algorithm for different types of concept drift. Inf. Sci. **430**, 261–281 (2018)

13. Žliobaitė, I., Pechenizkiy, M., Gama, J.: An overview of concept drift applications. In: Japkowicz, N., Stefanowski, J. (eds.) Big Data Analysis: New Algorithms for a New Society. Studies in Big Data, vol. 16, pp. 91–114. Springer, Cham (2016). https://doi.org/10.1007/978-3-319-26989-4_4

14. Khamassi, I., Sayed-Mouchaweh, M., Hammami, M., Ghedira, K.: Discussion and review on evolving data streams and concept drift adapting. Evol. Syst. **9**(1), 1–23 (2018)

15. Ben-David, S., Blitzer, J., Crammer, K., Kulesza, A., Pereira, F., Wortman Vaughan, J.: A theory of learning from different domains. Mach. Learn. **79**(1), 151–175 (2010)

16. Ganin, Y., et al.: Domain-adversarial training of neural networks. J. Mach. Learn. Res. **17**(1), 2096–2030 (2016)

17. Hoffman, J., Darrell, T., Saenko, K.: Continuous manifold based adaptation for evolving visual domains. In: Proceedings of the IEEE Conference on Computer Vision and Pattern Recognition, pp. 867–874 (2014)

18. Mancini, M., Rota Bulo, S., Caputo, B., Ricci, E.: AdaGraph: unifying predictive and continuous domain adaptation through graphs. In: Proceedings of the IEEE/CVF Conference on Computer Vision and Pattern Recognition, pp. 6568–6577 (2019)

19. Wang, H., He, H., Katabi, D.: Continuously indexed domain adaptation. In: International Conference on Machine Learning, pp. 9898–9907 (2020)

20. Du, Y., et al.: AdaRNN: adaptive learning and forecasting of time series. In: Proceedings of the 30th ACM International Conference on Information & Knowledge Management, pp. 402–411 (2021)

21. Kim, T., Kim, J., Tae, Y., Park, C., Choi, J.-H., Choo, J.: Reversible instance normalization for accurate timeseries forecasting against distribution shift. In: International Conference on Learning Representations (2022)

22. Dhaka, A.K., Catalina, A., Welandawe, M., Andersen, M.R., Huggins, J., Vehtari, A.: Challenges and opportunities in high dimensional variational inference. Adv. Neural. Inf. Process. Syst. **34**, 7787–7798 (2021)

23. Chen, J., Zhu, J., Teh, Y.W., Zhang, T.: Stochastic expectation maximization with variance reduction. In: Advances in Neural Information Processing Systems, vol. 31 (2018)

24. Zorich, V.A., Paniagua, O.: Mathematical Analysis II, vol. 220. Springer, Heidelberg (2016)

25. Velickovic, P., Cucurull, G., Casanova, A., Romero, A., Lio, P., Bengio, Y.: Graph attention networks. stat **1050**(20), 10–48550 (2017)

26. Ertugrul, F.O.: Forecasting electricity load by a novel recurrent extreme learning machines approach. Int. J. Electr. Power Energy Syst. **78**, 429–435 (2016)

27. Abdulaal, A., Liu, Z., Lancewicki, T.: Practical approach to asynchronous multivariate time series anomaly detection and localization. In: Proceedings of the 27th ACM SIGKDD Conference on Knowledge Discovery & Data Mining, pp. 2485–2494 (2021)

28. Su, Y., Zhao, Y., Niu, C., Liu, R., Sun, W., Pei, D.: Robust anomaly detection for multivariate time series through stochastic recurrent neural network. In: Proceedings of the 25th ACM SIGKDD International Conference on Knowledge Discovery & Data Mining, pp. 2828–2837 (2019)

29. Hundman, K., Constantinou, V., Laporte, C., Colwell, I., Soderstrom, T.: Detecting spacecraft anomalies using LSTMs and nonparametric dynamic thresholding. In: Proceedings of the 24th ACM SIGKDD International Conference on Knowledge Discovery & Data Mining, pp. 387–395 (2018)

30. Shen, L., Li, Z., Kwok, J.: Timeseries anomaly detection using temporal hierarchical one-class network. Adv. Neural. Inf. Process. Syst. **33**, 13016–13026 (2020)

31. Sun, Y., Pfahringer, B., Gomes, H.M., Bifet, A.: SOKNL: a novel way of integrating K-nearest neighbours with adaptive random forest regression for data streams. Data Min. Knowl. Disc. **36**(5), 2006–2032 (2022)
32. Zhao, P., Cai, L.-W., Zhou, Z.-H.: Handling concept drift via model reuse. Mach. Learn. **109**(3), 533–568 (2020)
33. Rubanova, Y., Chen, R.T.Q., Duvenaud, D.K.: Latent ordinary differential equations for irregularly-sampled time series. In: Advances in Neural Information Processing Systems, vol. 32, pp. 5320–5330. Curran Associates, Inc. (2019)
34. Zhou, H., et al.: Informer: Beyond efficient transformer for long sequence time-series forecasting. In: Proceedings of the AAAI Conference on Artificial Intelligence, vol. 35(12), pp. 11106–11115 (2021)
35. Wu, H., Xu, J., Wang, J., Long, M.: AutoFormer: decomposition transformers with auto-correlation for long-term series forecasting. Adv. Neural. Inf. Process. Syst. **34**, 22419–22430 (2021)
36. Kenton, J.D.M.W.C., Toutanova, L.K.: BERT: pre-training of deep bidirectional transformers for language understanding. In: Proceedings of NAACL-HLT, vol. 1, p. 2 (2019)

Optimization of Takagi-Sugeno-Kang Fuzzy Model Based on Differential Evolution with Lévy Flight

Xiao Feng, Yongbin Yu[✉], Jingye Cai, Hao Wang, Xiangxiang Wang, Xinyi Han, and Jingya Wang

School of Information and Software Engineering, University of Electronic Science and Technology of China, Chengdu 610054, Sichuan, China
ybyu@uestc.edu.cn

Abstract. In this article, a novel evolutionary algorithm called differential evolution with Lévy flight (DEFL) algorithm was proposed to optimize the Takagi-Sugeno-Kang fuzzy model (TSK fuzzy model) by finding the optimal hyper-parameter combination. DEFL consists of the conventional differential evolution (DE) algorithm as the primary search method and Lévy flight which is adopted to improve the early convergence problem of DE by its more changeable step size. Moreover, an adaptive soft-switch factor is designed to achieve the balance between exploration and exploitation according to the fitness of parent individuals, which can enhance the searching ability of DEFL. To verify the high performance of our proposed DEFL, two simulations are conducted. First, the five test functions: Ackley, Rastrigin, Sphere, Dixon & Price, and Perm are performed to verify the searching ability of DEFL and other three evolutionary algorithms: genetic algorithm (GA), particle swarm optimization (PSO), and DE are adopted for comparison. Then, TSK fuzzy model optimized by DEFL is adopted on eight datasets for classification tasks which are compared with the other nine methods. The first simulation shows that DEFL has the best searching ability compared with other algorithms. The accuracy and ranks of the optimized TSK fuzzy model on eight tasks demonstrate the high performance of the model improved by DEFL.

Keywords: Differential evolution (DE) algorithm · Lévy flight · classification · Takagi-Sugeno-Kang fuzzy model (TSK fuzzy model)

1 Introduction

Takagi–Sugeno–Kang fuzzy model (TSK fuzzy model) as one of the most important methods adopted broadly in various applications is applied in different fields such as pattern recognition, control system design, and regression to achieve great success because of its strong interpretability and scalability [3, 13, 15, 16, 20]. Nevertheless, the classification task with a large size or dimensionality of the

F. Liu et al. (Eds.): PRICAI 2023, LNAI 14327, pp. 370–383, 2024.
https://doi.org/10.1007/978-981-99-7025-4_32

data forces the conventional TSK fuzzy model to desire more membership functions and fuzzy rules for fitting, which means that the parameters of the model increase exponentially so that the dimensionality curse is unavoidable and the interpretability of the model is also affected [5]. Furthermore, the outliers contained in the dataset may lead to performance degradation since the TSK model is sensitive to outliers [4]. Thus, many works focused on these problems. For example, Xia et al. innovated a transformation matrix to make the margins between classes more discriminative and deployed cross-rule and cross-view to reduce the complexity of the TSK fuzzy model in [18]. In [19], a novel adaptive operator was used as the approximator of the minimum T-norm to equip the conventional TSK fuzzy model to enhance the ability of the model in solving high-dimensional problems. Jiang et al. proposed a CNN-based born-again TSK fuzzy model for the classification task, in which a noniterative learning method called least learning machine with knowledge distillation was proposed to accelerate the training time and the CNN model was utilized to reduce the dimensionality by extracting the dark knowledge from the datasets [7].

According to the above works, deploying various optimization techniques can efficiently handle the dimensionality curse and simplify the structure of the TSK fuzzy model. However, the introduction of hyper-parameters in the optimizers owns a direct impact on the performance of the model, which demonstrates the importance of finding out the optimal hyper-parameter setting set for specific tasks [8]. Grid search, random search, evolutionary algorithms (EAs), and bayesian optimization are the most popular methods in the hyper-parameters tuning. Alibrahim and Ludwig [1] pointed out that the EA method perform the best performance on optimization since the fastest convergence on finding the best parameters. Besides, the complex and high-dimensional solution space constructed by the hyper-parameters is not smooth which has a low fitting with the Bayesian optimization, the enumeration-based grid search, and the randomness-based random search. Therefore, considering the nonlinear relationship between these hyper-parameters and the system performance, EAs with strong searching ability in multidimensional solution space are appropriate to realize efficiency parameter adjustment for the TSK fuzzy model. In addition, EAs are compatible with different optimization tasks because of their flexible architecture and data-driven characteristic. Therefore, the EA-based TSK fuzzy models are proposed in some research. In [12], the genetic algorithm (GA) was used to optimize the inverse TSK fuzzy model adopted to approximate the nonlinearities of the electrical generator and uncertainties of modeling to improve the control performance of an oscillating water column. Askari et al. utilized the TSK fuzzy model to forecast the high-frequency response of gas networks to nodal consumption in forthcoming days and deployed the particle swarm optimization (PSO) algorithm with least squares estimation for parameter identification of the TSK fuzzy model [2]. As for high-dimensional data, a GA-based genetic programming algorithm was proposed in [10] to explore the best architecture for the TSK fuzzy model to alleviate the detrimental effect of distance concentration hampering the effectiveness of standard TSK fuzzy models. However, the aforementioned methods adopt the conventional EAs for searching which have the weakness of slow or early convergence since their single searching behaviors, which causes the imbalance between the exploration (global search for traversing solution space) and exploitation (local search for extracting better solutions from candidate individuals) [6,9,14]. For example, the crossover and mutation operators of GA are carried out based on a random function, which causes strong exploration and weak exploitation. Conversely, the differential evolution (DE) algorithm and PSO own strong exploitation characteristics while lacking exploration since the information of parent individuals is adopted to participate in the generation of offspring. Consequently, balancing the exploration and exploitation of the EAs is one of the effective optimization methods to enhance their searching ability.

Based on the above works and challengings, the DE algorithm with Lévy flight (DEFL) is proposed in this paper. Various optimization techniques proposed in [5,17] are integrated into a conventional TSK fuzzy model. To improve the performance of the TSK fuzzy model on classification tasks and explore the optimal optimizer combination, a novel search algorithm called differential evolution with Lévy flight (DEFL) is proposed. DE algorithm as the main search method is adopted to provide the exploitation ability for DEFL, which accelerates the proposed DEFL convergence. Lévy flight, which has an impressive exploration characteristic since its more changeable step size, is deployed in the mutation operator of the DE algorithm to handle the early convergence of the DE. During the execution phase of the mutation operator, an adaptive soft-switch factor design on the basis of the differential vectors generated by the parent individuals is proposed to adjust the searching behavior of DEFL. The proposed DEFL is used to search the optimal hyper-parameters for the TSK fuzzy model to enhance the performance of the model on the classification tasks. Eight datasets are collected for the simulations to verify the high performance of the TSK fuzzy model optimized by our proposed algorithm. This paper has the following contributions.

1) Batch normalization, uniform regularization, and AdaBound are integrated into the conventional TSK fuzzy model.
2) A novel search algorithm called DEFL is proposed to search the best hyper-parameters of the TSK fuzzy model to obtain high performance on classification tasks, which deploys Lévy flight in the mutation operator of DE to overcome the early convergence weakness.
3) An adaptive soft-switch factor is designed to balance the exploitation and exploration of DEFL according to the fitness of selected parent individuals.

2   TSK Fuzzy Neural Network

2.1   Classical TSK Fuzzy Model

Defining the TSK fuzzy model has N fuzzy rules $\mathcal{R} = \{\mathcal{R}_1, \mathcal{R}_2, \cdots, \mathcal{R}_N\}$. In terms of arbitrary fuzzy rule $\mathcal{R}_n$ $(n = 1, 2, \cdots, N)$ for the input data $\boldsymbol{x} =$

$[x_1, x_2, \cdots, x_M]$ with M-dimensional feature vector, it can be presented as **IF-THEN** formulation by

$$\mathcal{R}_n : \textbf{IF } x_1 \text{ is } X_{r,1} \text{ and } \cdots \text{ and } x_M \text{ is } X_{n,M},$$

$$\textbf{THEN } y_n^1(\boldsymbol{x}) = \sum_{m=1}^{M} \omega_{n,m}^1 x_m + b_n^1 \text{ and } \cdots \text{and } y_n^C(\boldsymbol{x}) = \sum_{m=1}^{M} \omega_{n,m}^C x_m + b_n^C \quad (1)$$

where $X_{n,m}$ $(m = 1, 2, \cdots, M)$ denotes the fuzzy set for the n-th rule with the m-th dimensional feature vector of the input data, $y_n^c(\boldsymbol{x})$ $(c = 1, 2, \cdots, C)$ is the output of each rule for the c-th class in a classification problem, and $\omega_{n,m}^c$ and b_n^c are the consequent parameters similar to the weight and bias in the conventional neural network model, respectively.

Defining $y^c(\boldsymbol{x})$ is the prediction of the TSK fuzzy model, which can be obtained by $y_n^c(\boldsymbol{x})$ as

$$y^c(\boldsymbol{x}) = \sum_{n=1}^{N} \bar{f}_n(\boldsymbol{x}) y_n^c \boldsymbol{x} \quad (2)$$

where $\bar{f}_n(\boldsymbol{x})$ presents the normalized value of the firing level $f_n(\boldsymbol{x})$ for the corresponding $\mathcal{R}_n$ and is computed through

$$\bar{f}_n(\boldsymbol{x}) = \frac{f_n(\boldsymbol{x})}{\sum_{k=1}^{N} f_k(\boldsymbol{x})}. \quad (3)$$

The calculation of the firing level $f_n(\boldsymbol{x})$ can be described as

$$f_n(\boldsymbol{x}) = \prod_{m=1}^{M} \mu_{X_{n,m}}(x_m), \quad (4)$$

in which $\mu_{X_{n,m}}$ is the membership function (MF) and the membership grade $\mu_{X_{n,m}}(x_m)$ is calculated by

$$\mu_{X_{n,m}}(x_m) = \exp\left(-\frac{(x_m - \zeta_{n,m})^2}{2\sigma_{n,m}^2}\right) \quad (5)$$

where $\zeta_{n,m}$ and $\sigma_{n,m}$ are the mean and the standard deviation of the MF on the basis of the Gaussian. Thus, (4) can be further written as

$$f_n(\boldsymbol{x}) = \exp\left(-\sum_{m=1}^{M} \frac{(x_m - \zeta_{n,m})^2}{2\sigma_{n,m}^2}\right). \quad (6)$$

2.2 Optimization Techniques Implementation

In [5,17], some optimization techniques were adopted in the FNN model and successfully improved the performance of the model. Thus, these optimizers are utilized in our method and summarized in this part.

Batch Normalization. Batch normalization (BN) is an effective method to accelerate training processing by separating the normalized training data. Assuming that $BN_{\gamma,\beta}(\cdot)$ is the BN operator, the input data x_b $(b = 1, 2, \cdots, B)$ selected in the minibatch $\mathcal{B} = \{x_1, x_2, \cdots, x_B\}$ can be handled according to

$$BN_{\gamma,\beta}(x_b) = x_b^{BN} = \gamma\hat{x}_b + \beta \tag{7}$$

where γ and β are the learning parameters, and $\hat{x}_b$ is obtained by

$$\hat{x}_b = \frac{x_b - \zeta_{\mathcal{B}}}{\sqrt{\sigma_{\mathcal{B}}^2 + \epsilon}}, \tag{8}$$

in which $\zeta_{\mathcal{B}}$ and $\sigma_{\mathcal{B}}$ denote the mean and standard deviation for the elements in the minibatch, and ϵ is set to 1e-10 to prevent singularity.

Uniform Regularization. Considering the TSK fuzzy model may be under the influence of the "rich get richer" problem [11], uniform regularization (UR) is added to the loss function design. To prevent the model from overfitting, $\mathcal{L}_2$ regularization is also adopted. The loss function $\mathcal{L}$ is formed as following,

$$\mathcal{L}(x_b^{BN}) = \mathcal{L}_{CE}(x_b^{BN}) + \eta\mathcal{L}_2(x_b^{BN}) + \lambda\mathcal{L}_{UR}(x_b^{BN}), \tag{9}$$

where η and λ are the tradeoff parameter and the weight decay coefficient, disparately. $\mathcal{L}_{CE}$ is the cross-entropy loss, $\mathcal{L}_2$ denotes the L_2-regularized loss, and $\mathcal{L}_{UR}$ is defined as the UR loss computed by

$$\mathcal{L}_{UR} = \sum_{n=1}^{N} \left(\frac{1}{B} \sum_{b=1}^{B} \bar{f}_r(x_b^{BN} - \frac{1}{N}) \right) \tag{10}$$

AdaBound. Assuming that ϑ_ι is an arbitrary parameter vector in the TSK fuzzy model at the ι-th epoch $(\iota = 1, 2, \cdots, \iota_{\max})$, which can be updated by

$$\vartheta_\iota = \vartheta_{\iota-1} - \hat{\kappa} \odot \hat{s}_\iota \tag{11}$$

where $\hat{\kappa}$ is the learning rate obtained by

$$\hat{\kappa} = \max \left[l(\iota), \min \left(u(\iota), \frac{\kappa_0}{\sqrt{\hat{r}_\iota} + \epsilon} \right) \right] \tag{12}$$

in which κ_0 presents the initial learning rate, $\hat{s}_\iota$ and $\hat{r}_\iota$ are the corrected values yielded through

$$\hat{s}_\iota = \frac{s_\iota}{1 - \rho_1^\iota}, \hat{r}_\iota = \frac{r_\iota}{1 - \rho_2^\iota} \tag{13}$$

for the compensation on the first-order and second-order moment estimations s_ι and r_ι which can be calculated by

$$s_\iota = \rho_1 s_{\iota-1} + (1 - \rho_1)\nabla\mathcal{L}(\vartheta_\iota), r_\iota = \rho_2 r_{\iota-1} + (1 - \rho_2)\nabla^2\mathcal{L}(\vartheta_\iota) \tag{14}$$

with setting parameters $\rho_1 = 0.9$ and $\rho_2 = 0.999$, and $l(\iota)$ and $u(\iota)$ are the lower and upper bound functions derived by

$$l(\iota) = \alpha \left(1 - \frac{1}{(1-\rho_2)\iota + 1} \right), u(\iota) = \alpha \left(1 + \frac{1}{(1-\rho_2)\iota} \right) \qquad (15)$$

where $\alpha \in [0,1]$ is the scale factor.

3   DELF Algorithm Design

3.1   Optimization Task Formulation

According to the aforementioned contents, five hyper-parameters: number of fuzzy rule N, minibatch size B, tradeoff parameter η, weight decay coefficient λ, and scale factor α are selected to be the search objects for DELF algorithm. The pseudo-code is shown in **Algorithm** 1 and the system is shown in Fig. 1.

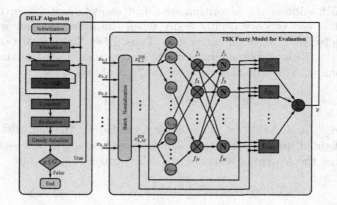

Fig. 1. Optimization based on the DEFL algorithm for the TSK fuzzy model.

Defining $\boldsymbol{M}_g = [\boldsymbol{M}_{1,g}, \boldsymbol{M}_{2,g}, \cdots, \boldsymbol{M}_{P,g}]^\mathrm{T}$ $(g = 1, 2, \cdots, G)$ is the g-th iteration containing P individuals and G is the max iteration for DELF algorithm. For an arbitrarily individual $\boldsymbol{M}_{p,g}$, let $\boldsymbol{M}_{p,g} = [N_{p,g}, B_{p,g}, \eta_{p,g}, \lambda_{p,g}, \alpha_{p,g}]$ $(p = 1, 2, \cdots, P)$. Thus, the goal of DELF algorithm is to explore the optimal combination of the five hyper-parameters for the TSK fuzzy model, which means the best individual $\boldsymbol{M}^*$.

3.2   Evaluation Function Design

To characterize the performance on the classification task of the TSK fuzzy model with every hyper-parameter combination (also called individual), the evaluation function is formed as

$$\mathcal{F}_{p,g} = \mathcal{C}_\mathrm{train}(\boldsymbol{M}_{p,g}) + \mathcal{C}_\mathrm{test}(\boldsymbol{M}_{p,g}) \qquad (16)$$

where $\mathcal{C}_{\mathrm{train}}(\mathcal{M}_{p,g})$ and $\mathcal{C}_{\mathrm{test}}(\mathcal{M}_{p,g})$ denote the accuracy for the TSK fuzzy model with $\mathcal{M}_{p,g}$ on the training and test sets, respectively. It is worth pointing out that only the training set is used to perform backpropagation for the learning and $\mathcal{C}_{\mathrm{test}}(\cdot)$ is adopted to evaluate the versatility for the TSK fuzzy model. Considering $\mathcal{C}_{\mathrm{test}}(\cdot)$ as one of the evaluation factors to guide the search performance of DELF during exploration even if it does not participate in the learning phase directly, which could be regarded as data leakage. Thus, we split each dataset to be three parts: 70% samples are selected randomly to be the training set, 20% as the test set, and the remaining 10% samples are used to be the validation set which is just adopted to get the accuracy $\mathcal{C}_{\mathrm{val}}(\mathcal{M}^*)$ of the optimal TSK fuzzy model found by DELF algorithm.

3.3   Mutation Operator with Lévy Flight

The conventional DE algorithm has a strong ability for exploration since the mutated offspring yielded on the basis of the differential vectors among the parents, which endows the algorithm with fast convergence. Nevertheless, the defect of early convergence occurs easily when the differences among parents become smaller with iteration increasing. Thus, Lévy flight with variable step size is added in the mutation operator of the conventional DE algorithm to avoid this shortcoming. The mutation member $\mathcal{M}_{p,g}^{\mathrm{m}}$ is obtained by

$$\mathcal{M}_{p,g+1}^{\mathrm{m}} = \mathcal{M}_{p,g}^{\mathrm{DE}} + \varphi_{p,g}\mathcal{M}_{p,g}^{\mathrm{LF}} \tag{17}$$

in which $\mathcal{M}_{p,g}^{\mathrm{DE}}$ and $\mathcal{M}_{p,g}^{\mathrm{LF}}$ are the offspring yielded by the mutation operator and Lévy flight disparately and φ is our proposed adaptive soft-switch factor used to adjust the searching behavior of DELF, which is formed as

$$\varphi_{p,g} = \frac{1}{5^{\sigma_{\mathcal{F}}}}. \tag{18}$$

$\sigma_{\mathcal{F}}$ denotes the standard deviation for the fitness vector $\mathcal{F}_{p,g}^{\mathrm{s}}$ containing three fitness corresponding to the randomly selected individuals.

Before the mutation operator conducts every time for the p-th $\mathcal{M}_{p,g}^{\mathrm{DE}}$ at g-th generation, three individuals are chosen and sorted as best one $\mathcal{M}_{\mathrm{best}}$, medium one $\mathcal{M}_{\mathrm{med}}$, and worst one $\mathcal{M}_{\mathrm{worst}}$ by fitness. Then, $\mathcal{M}_{p,g}^{\mathrm{DE}}$ can be yielded by

$$\mathcal{M}_{p,g}^{\mathrm{DE}} = \mathcal{M}_{\mathrm{best}} + F_{p,g}(\mathcal{M}_{\mathrm{med}} - \mathcal{M}_{\mathrm{worst}}) \tag{19}$$

in which the scaling factor $F_{p,g}$ is obtained by

$$F_{p,g} = F_{\mathrm{l}} + (F_{\mathrm{u}} - F_{\mathrm{l}})\frac{\mathcal{F}_{\mathrm{med}} - \mathcal{F}_{\mathrm{best}}}{\mathcal{F}_{\mathrm{worst}} - \mathcal{F}_{\mathrm{best}}}, \tag{20}$$

where $[\mathcal{F}_{\mathrm{best}}, \mathcal{F}_{\mathrm{med}}, \mathcal{F}_{\mathrm{worst}}] = \mathcal{F}^{\mathrm{s}}$, and set $F_{\mathrm{l}} = 0.1$ and $F_{\mathrm{u}} = 0.6$.

The each element $\mathcal{M}_{r,p,g}^{\mathrm{LF}} \in \mathcal{M}_{p,g}^{\mathrm{LF}}$ $(r = 1, 2, \cdots, 5)$ can be calculated through

$$\mathcal{M}_{r,p,g}^{\mathrm{LF}} = \mathcal{M}_{r,p,g} + \chi\mathcal{S}(v) \tag{21}$$

Algorithm 1: DELF for the Optimization of TSK Fuzzy Model

Input: Population: P; Max Generation: G; Lower: $\mathcal{M}_l$; Upper: $\mathcal{M}_u$

Output: Best parameter set $\mathcal{M}^* = [N^*, B^*, \eta^*, \lambda^*, \alpha^*]$

1   **for** $p = 1$ *to* P **do**
2 | $\mathcal{M}_{p,0} = \mathcal{M}_l + rand(0,1) \cdot (\mathcal{M}_u - \mathcal{M}_l)$;
3   **end**
4   $g = 1$;
5   **while** $g \leq G$ **do**
6 | ▶ (Mutation Operator)
7 | **for** $p = 1$ *to* P **do**
8 | | $\mathcal{M}_{p,g}^m = Mutation(\mathcal{M}_{g-1}, \mathcal{F}_{g-1})$;
9 | **end**
10 | ▶ (Crossover Operator)
11 | **for** $p = 1$ *to* P **do**
12 | | $\mathcal{M}_{p,g}^c = Crossover(\mathcal{M}_{g-1}, \mathcal{M}_g^m, \mathcal{F}_{g-1})$;
13 | **end**
14 | ▶ (Evaluation Operator)
15 | **for** $p = 1$ *to* P **do**
16 | | $\mathcal{F}_{p,g}^c = Evaluation(\mathcal{M}_{p,g})$;
17 | **end**
18 | ▶ (Greedy Selection)
19 | $\mathcal{M}_g, \mathcal{F}_g, \mathcal{M}^*, \mathcal{F}^* \leftarrow$ Obtain the final current population from $\{\mathcal{M}_g^c, \mathcal{M}_{g-1}\}$ according to $\{\mathcal{F}_g^c, \mathcal{F}_{g-1}\}$;
20 | $g \leftarrow g + 1$;
21   **end**
22 **return** Best parameter set: $\mathcal{M}^* = [N^*, B^*, \eta^*, \lambda^*, \alpha^*]$;

---

where χ is defined as step factor and set to $\chi = 0.01$ [6]. Lévy distribution is

$$\mathcal{S}(v) = \frac{1}{\pi} \int_0^\infty e^{-\varepsilon q^\psi} \cos(qv) dq, 0.3 \leq \psi \leq 1.99 \tag{22}$$

which can be approximated by

$$\mathcal{S}(v) = \frac{u}{|v|^{1/\psi}} \tag{23}$$

$$u \sim N(0, \sigma_u^2), v \sim N(0, \sigma_v^2) \tag{24}$$

$$\sigma_u = \left(\frac{\Gamma(1 + \psi) \sin(\pi\psi/2)}{\Gamma(\frac{1+\psi}{2}) \psi 2^{(\psi-1)/2}} \right), \sigma_v = 1 \tag{25}$$

in which $\psi = 3/2$ is a constant parameter.

3.4 Crossover Operator

After obtaining the mutation members, the crossover operator is performed to get selected individuals from the parents and offspring. For each element $\mathcal{M}_{r,p,g}^{c} \in \mathcal{M}_{p,g}^{c}$, the formulation can be written as

$$\mathcal{M}_{r,p,g}^{c} = \begin{cases} \mathcal{M}_{r,p,g}, & \text{if } \text{rand}(0,1) \leq \wp_{p,g} \\ \mathcal{M}_{r,p,g}^{m}, & \text{if } \text{rand}(0,1) > \wp_{p,g} \end{cases} \tag{26}$$

where an adaptive crossover rate $\wp$ is

$$\wp_{r,g} = \wp_{l} + (\wp_{u} - \wp_{l}) \frac{\max(\mathcal{F}_g) - \mathcal{F}_{p,g}}{\max(\mathcal{F}_g) - \min(\mathcal{F}_g)}, \tag{27}$$

in which $\wp_{l} = 0.1$ and $\wp_{u} = 0.9$ without loss of generality.

4 Simulation Result Analysis

4.1 Searching Ability Comparison

To demonstrate the improvement of our proposed method, the simulation of DEFL is conducted on five test functions. Moreover, DE, PSO, GA, and four variant DE-based methods are used as comparison methods to illustrate the searching ability of DEFL.

Each algorithm is conducted with 50 trials on each test function for obtaining the objective results. The iteration and the population for every algorithm are set the same as 1000 and 30, disparately. The mean final fitness of every algorithm on every test function is shown in Table 1. According to the results, the proposed DEFL obtained the smallest mean fitness on all the test functions, which verified the stability and strong searching ability of our proposed method. Figure 2 shows that GA and PSO performed fast convergence at the early phase, although both of them fell into the local optimal solutions. Besides, Lévy flight deployed in DEFL improved its searching behavior successfully since the mean search convergence became faster and the mean final fitness got smaller compared to the conventional DE and the four variants of the DE-based methods.

Table 1. Mean final fitness.

Function	DE	GA	PSO	DEFL (pro.)	DE (DE/rand/1)	DE (DE/best/1)	DE (DE/current-to-best/1)	DE (DE/rand/2)
Ackley	1.127	1.4994	4.5836	**0.0881**	0.9948	10.5706	3.3504	0.81641
Rastrigin	0.9763	2.3301	6.1632	**0.0546**	0.1087	5.344	0.3068	0.1216
Sphere	0.4932	0.8809	5.6036	**0.2305**	0.2362	7432.7022	3.6231	280.3486
Dixon & Price	3.0761	7.4926	38.0112	**2.4367**	21.7012	275.7157	36.5622	41.014
Perm	1.0074	1.7925	1.2662	**0.2251**	0.3482	2.3101	0.7345	0.5545

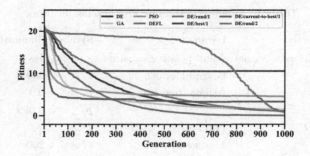

Fig. 2. The mean fitness convergence of the eight EAs on the Ackley test function.

4.2 TSK Fuzzy Model Optimization

8 classification datasets downloaded from the UCI Machine Learning Repository (https://archive.ics.uci.edu/ml/datasets) are adopted to validate the efficiency of our proposed method, which are listed in Table 2. 70% samples are selected randomly to be the training set, 20% samples as the test set for DELF exploration, and 10% are adopted to be the validation set to achieve a more fair and substantial comparison with other methods shown in [5]. The other simulation parameters of the proposed and comparison methods are summarized in Table 3.

Table 2. Dataset Information.

No.	Dataset	·No. of Samples	No. of Feartures	No. of Classes
1	Vehicle	846	18	4
2	Biodeg	1055	41	2
3	DRD	1151	19	2
4	Yeast	1484	8	10
5	Steel	1941	27	7
6	IS	2310	19	7
7	Waveform21	5000	21	3
8	Page-blocks	5473	10	5

For each dataset, five trials are performed to demonstrate the stability of our proposed search method and the results of these trials are summarized in Table 4. It can be found that DELF can explore the optimal solution at each trial on each dataset for the TSK fuzzy model to obtain high accuracy on training, test, and validation samples, which illustrates the stability of DELF.

For each dataset, the optimal solution with the highest fitness is selected from the five trials for the comparison with other nine methods and the information of the selected individual is listed in Table 5. It is worth noting that the

Table 3. Simulation Parameters for Classification.

Objective	Parameter	Symbol	Simulation
TSK Fuzzy Model	Small positive constant	ϵ	1e−10
	Learning epoch	ι	200
	Attenuation rate	ρ_1	0.9
		ρ_2	0.999
DELF	Population	P	20
	Max generation	G	200
	Search range	S_N	[1, 50]
		S_B	[16, 512]
		S_η	[0, 10]
		S_λ	[0, 50]
		S_α	[0, 1]

Table 4. Simulation results of DELF on the eight datasets

Dataset	Tri. 1			Tri. 2			Tri. 3			Tri. 4			Tri. 5			Avg.
	Train.	Test	Val.	Train.	Test	Val.	Train.	Test	Val.	Train.	Test	Val.	Train.	Test	Val.	Val.
Vehicle	0.9088	0.8639	0.8353	0.8801	0.8639	0.8000	0.9155	0.8284	0.8588	0.8750	0.8580	0.8588	**0.9020**	**0.8876**	0.8706	0.8447
Biodeg	0.9093	0.9289	0.9143	0.9229	0.9005	0.8762	0.9012	0.9242	0.9048	**0.9120**	**0.9289**	0.8476	0.8836	0.9005	0.9143	0.8914
DRD	0.7581	0.7913	0.7391	0.7854	0.7217	0.6870	0.7730	0.7609	0.7391	**0.7667**	**0.7957**	0.6783	0.7667	0.7087	0.7130	0.7113
Yeast	0.6343	0.6229	0.5608	**0.6275**	**0.6667**	0.6081	0.6112	0.6195	0.5946	0.6506	0.5791	0.5405	0.6304	0.6330	0.5676	0.5743
Steel	0.7719	0.7397	0.7113	**0.7638**	**0.7526**	0.7577	0.7631	0.7113	0.7577	0.7491	0.7139	0.7784	0.7469	0.7526	0.7268	0.7463
IS	**0.9586**	**0.9654**	0.9610	0.9555	0.9524	0.9740	0.9685	0.9534	0.9307	0.9586	0.9481	0.9394	0.9474	0.9502	0.9524	0.9515
Waveform21	0.8743	0.8700	0.8740	**0.8671**	**0.8920**	0.8820	0.8806	0.8620	0.8380	0.8743	0.8840	0.8720	0.8697	0.8720	0.8540	0.8640
page-blocks	0.9569	0.9580	0.9634	0.9601	0.9534	0.9744	**0.9590**	**0.9626**	0.9744	0.9517	0.9580	0.9671	0.9559	0.9644	0.9762	0.9711

best hyper-parameter settings searched by our proposed method for the model on different datasets are different, which demonstrates that the setting of the hyper-parameters is desired for various tasks. However, the hyper-parameter setting is counter-intuitive on some tasks, for example, the selection of the hyper-parameters for the TSK fuzzy model on the DRD and Waveform datasets is different even if they own a similar number of features and classes, which causes difficult design through empirical tuning and illustrate the necessity of DEFL. Moreover, according to the best setting plan obtained by DEFL, we can find that some optimizer is redundant (such as η for Vehicle or λ for Waveform21), which means that the implementation of the optimizer should be carefully validated based on the specific situation. In other words, blindly deploying the optimizer in the TSK fuzzy model may not achieve performance improvement.

Before the comparison among our proposed method and other methods, each best parameter set $\mathcal{M}^*$ selected from five trials for each dataset were deployed on the TSK fuzzy model and run 30 times with $\iota = 500$, and the mean of the accuracy was calculated to participate in the comparison. Table 6 summarized the results of the ten algorithms on the eight datasets, which shows that the optimized TSK fuzzy model performed the best performance on the half datasets and obtained the highest average accuracy. In addition, the performance of the TSK

Table 5. Information of the best individual for each search on eight datasets.

Dataset	Simulation	N^*	B^*	η^*	λ^*	α^*
Vehicle	Tri. 5	43	100	0	4.2036	0.0312
Biodeg	Tri. 4	50	121	5.0435	50	0.0959
DRD	Tri. 4	50	87	10	14.2328	0.0819
Yeast	Tri. 2	50	212	0	28.7210	0.0689
Steel	Tri. 2	49	59	0	24.1667	0.0911
IS	Tri. 1	50	98	0	50	0.1174
Waveform21	Tri. 2	26	87	0	0	0.1072
Page-blocks	Tri. 3	49	75	0	38.8136	0.1891

fuzzy model deploying the searched best parameter set was improved on all the datasets compared to the conventional TSK fuzzy models, which demonstrates the effectiveness of our proposed method. To further estimate the improvement generated from the proposed DEFL, the ranks were displayed in Table 7. Obviously, the mean rank of the model adopting the setting parameters searched by DEFL is the smallest, which also presents the strong searching ability of DEFL for optimization of the TSK fuzzy model and stability on various datasets.

Table 6. Accuracy of the ten algorithms on the eight datasets [1]

Dataset	CART	RF	JRip3	PART	TSK-FCM-LSM	TSK-MBGD	TSK-MBGD-BN	TSK-MBGD-UR	TSK-MBGD-UR-BN	DELF
Vehicle	0.6907	0.7407	0.6892	0.7110	0.7411	0.6970	0.7354	0.7089	0.7907	**0.8164**
Biodeg	0.8202	0.8572	0.8222	0.8362	0.8377	0.8523	0.8531	0.8539	0.8609	**0.8836**
DRD	0.6283	0.6589	0.6240	0.6364	0.6824	0.6623	0.6618	0.6713	0.6720	**0.6973**
Yeast	0.5564	**0.5963**	0.5731	0.5340	0.5851	0.5673	0.5770	0.5722	0.5725	0.5913
Steel	0.7017	0.7328	0.7135	0.7120	0.6527	0.5864	0.7110	0.7248	0.7350	**0.7392**
IS	0.9320	0.9529	0.9481	**0.9608**	0.9571	0.5762	0.7557	0.8559	0.9501	0.9518
Waveform21	0.7641	0.8369	0.7908	0.7843	**0.8647**	0.6779	0.8002	0.8363	0.8234	0.8582
Page-blocks	0.9651	**0.9688**	0.9681	0.9677	0.9499	0.9375	0.9419	0.9515	0.9580	0.9682
Average	0.7573	0.7931	0.7661	0.7678	0.7838	0.6946	0.7545	0.7719	0.7953	**0.8133**

1. The detail information about the comparison methods can be found in [5].

Table 7. Ranks of the ten algorithms on the eight datasets

Dataset	CART	RF	JRip3	PART	TSK-FCM-LSM	TSK-MBGD	TSK-MBGD-BN	TSK-MBGD-UR	TSK-MBGD-UR-BN	DELF
Vehicle	9	4	10	6	3	8	5	7	2	1
Biodeg	10	3	9	8	7	6	5	4	2	1
DRD	9	7	10	8	2	5	6	4	3	1
Yeast	9	1	5	10	3	8	4	7	6	2
Steel	8	3	5	6	9	10	7	4	2	1
IS	7	3	6	1	2	10	9	8	5	4
Waveform21	9	3	7	8	1	10	6	4	5	2
Page-blocks	5	1	2	4	8	10	9	7	6	3
Average	8.5	3.125	6.75	6.375	4.375	8.375	6.375	5.625	3.875	**1.875**

5   Conclusion

In this paper, we proposed the DELF algorithm to explore the optimal architecture of the TSK fuzzy model on the classification task. Five hyper-parameters contained in the three optimization techniques were adopted as search objects. To overcome the weakness of the conventional DE about the local optimal problem, Lévy flight with the more changeable step size was used in the mutation operator. Moreover, an adaptive soft-switch factor was designed to balance the search behavior according to the fitness of the selected members in the mutation operator. Nine algorithms were used for comparison with the TSK fuzzy model designed by our proposed method on eight datasets. The simulation results illustrated that the architecture of the model searched by our proposed method has high performance compared with other algorithms. Besides, the TSK fuzzy model optimized by DELF performed better on most classification tasks than the model designed through the empirical design. As for the optimization techniques, the TSK fuzzy model desiring different implementation plans of them on the different tasks is proofed, which is meaningful and illuminating.

References

1. Alibrahim, H., Ludwig, S.A.: Hyperparameter optimization: comparing genetic algorithm against grid search and Bayesian optimization. In: 2021 IEEE Congress on Evolutionary Computation (CEC), pp. 1551–1559. IEEE (2021)
2. Askari, S., Montazerin, N., Fazel Zarandi, M.: Modeling energy flow in natural gas networks using time series disaggregation and fuzzy systems tuned by particle swarm optimization. Appl. Soft Comput. **92**, 106332 (2020)
3. Cervantes, J., Yu, W., Salazar, S., Chairez, I.: Takagi-sugeno dynamic neuro-fuzzy controller of uncertain nonlinear systems. IEEE Trans. Fuzzy Syst. **25**(6), 1601–1615 (2017)
4. Chuang, C.C., Su, S.F., Chen, S.S.: Robust tsk fuzzy modeling for function approximation with outliers. IEEE Trans. Fuzzy Syst. **9**(6), 810–821 (2001)
5. Cui, Y., Wu, D., Huang, J.: Optimize tsk fuzzy systems for classification problems: minibatch gradient descent with uniform regularization and batch normalization. IEEE Trans. Fuzzy Syst. **28**(12), 3065–3075 (2020)
6. Feng, X., Muramatsu, H., Katsura, S.: Differential evolutionary algorithm with local search for the adaptive periodic-disturbance observer adjustment. IEEE Trans. Industr. Electron. **68**(12), 12504–12512 (2021)
7. Jiang, Y., Weng, J., Zhang, X., Yang, Z., Hu, W.: A CNN-based born-again tsk fuzzy classifier integrating soft label information and knowledge distillation. IEEE Trans. Fuzzy Syst. **31**(6), 1843–1854 (2023)
8. Kumar, N., Susan, S.: Particle swarm optimization of partitions and fuzzy order for fuzzy time series forecasting of COVID-19. Appl. Soft Comput. **110**, 107611 (2021)
9. Li, S., Gu, Q., Gong, W., Ning, B.: An enhanced adaptive differential evolution algorithm for parameter extraction of photovoltaic models. Energy Convers. Manage. **205**, 112443 (2020)
10. Safari Mamaghani, A., Pedrycz, W.: Genetic-programming-based architecture of fuzzy modeling: towards coping with high-dimensional data. IEEE Trans. Fuzzy Syst. **29**(9), 2774–2784 (2021)

11. Shen, T., Ott, M., Auli, M., Ranzato, M.: Mixture models for diverse machine translation: tricks of the trade. In: Chaudhuri, K., Salakhutdinov, R. (eds.) Proceedings of the 36th International Conference on Machine Learning. Proceedings of Machine Learning Research, vol. 97, pp. 5719–5728 (2019)
12. Silva, J.M., Vieira, S.M., Valério, D., Henriques, J.C.: Ga-optimized inverse fuzzy model control of OWC wave power plants. Renewable Energy **204**, 556–568 (2023)
13. Tao, X., Yi, J., Pu, Z., Xiong, T.: Robust adaptive tracking control for hypersonic vehicle based on interval type-2 fuzzy logic system and small-gain approach. IEEE Trans. Cybern. **51**(5), 2504–2517 (2021)
14. Tarkhaneh, O., Shen, H.: An adaptive differential evolution algorithm to optimal multi-level thresholding for MRI brain image segmentation. Expert Syst. Appl. **138**, 112820 (2019)
15. Wang, X., et al.: Dynamic pinning synchronization of fuzzy-dependent-switched coupled memristive neural networks with mismatched dimensions on time scales. IEEE Trans. Fuzzy Syst. **30**(3), 779–793 (2022)
16. Wang, X., et al.: Novel heterogeneous mode-dependent impulsive synchronization for piecewise t-s fuzzy probabilistic coupled delayed neural networks. IEEE Trans. Fuzzy Syst. **30**(7), 2142–2156 (2022)
17. Wu, D., Yuan, Y., Huang, J., Tan, Y.: Optimize tsk fuzzy systems for regression problems: minibatch gradient descent with regularization, droprule, and adabound (MBGD-RDA). IEEE Trans. Fuzzy Syst. **28**(5), 1003–1015 (2020)
18. Xia, K., et al.: Tsk fuzzy system for multi-view data discovery underlying label relaxation and cross-rule & cross-view sparsity regularizations. IEEE Trans. Industr. Inf. **17**(5), 3282–3291 (2021)
19. Xue, G., Wang, J., Yuan, B., Dai, C.: Dg-aletsk: a high-dimensional fuzzy approach with simultaneous feature selection and rule extraction. IEEE Trans. Fuzzy Syst. 1–15 (2023)
20. Yang, C., Deng, Z., Choi, K.S., Wang, S.: Takagi-sugeno-kang transfer learning fuzzy logic system for the adaptive recognition of epileptic electroencephalogram signals. IEEE Trans. Fuzzy Syst. **24**(5), 1079–1094 (2016)

RPL-SVM: Making SVM Robust Against Missing Values and Partial Labels

Sreenivasan Mohandas[✉] and Naresh Manwani[ID]

Machine Learning Lab, KCIS, IIIT Hyderabad, Hyderabad, India
`sreenivasanm6@gmail.com, naresh.manwani@iiit.ac.in`

Abstract. With increased data availability, data quality is the biggest
problem in using AI models. The data may suffer from missing values
and noisy values. Another major challenge is to get accurate labels for
feature vectors in the training data. In contrast, in many applications, we
can only get weak labels (for example, partial labels, positive-unlabeled
data, bandit feedback, etc.). In this paper, we consider uncertainty in
both features and labels. More specifically, we assume that feature vectors have missing attributes and are only given partial labels. We present
a novel second-order cone programming framework to learn robust classifiers that can tolerate uncertainty in the observations of partially labeled
multiclass classification problems. The proposed approach, RPL-SVM,
is based on a chance-constrained framework. Experimental results show
that RPL-SVM efficiently learns multiclass classifiers with missing values
in a partial label setting. This demonstrates the remarkable resilience of
RPL-SVM to real-world observational uncertainties.

Keywords: Multiclass classification · Missing values · Partial labels ·
Second order cone programming

1 Introduction

Most state-of-the-art classification algorithms assume the training data contains actual labels for each example. However, data labeling is costly and time-
consuming, which makes access to actual class labels challenging. An alternative
to an actual label is a set of candidate labels called partial labels [6,15]. Learning
can happen successfully if the partial label set contains the true label. Partially
labeled data is more accessible and offers a less expensive option for learning
with precise labels. Cour et al. [6] describe a general risk minimization approach
for learning with partial labels. This approach can adjust any common convex
loss function to work in the partial label environment. Since the ground-truth
label is not available for a specific instance, the loss is determined by comparing the average score of the candidate label set to the maximum score in the
complementary label set. The approach proposed in [17] updates latent label
distributions through iterative self-training techniques to learn classifiers using

© The Author(s), under exclusive license to Springer Nature Singapore Pte Ltd. 2024
F. Liu et al. (Eds.): PRICAI 2023, LNAI 14327, pp. 384–395, 2024.
https://doi.org/10.1007/978-981-99-7025-4_33

partial labels. On the other hand, leveraged weighted loss (LWS) [25] based app-roach strikes a balance between losses on candidate labels and unassigned ones in the risk function. To enhance the performance of partial label learning, PiCO [24] combines contrastive representation learning with a novel class prototype-based label disambiguation.

All the above algorithms for partial label learning assume that the feature vectors do not suffer from missing values and other noise processes. However, real-world data is often noisy, incomplete, or uncertain due to various factors such as measurement errors, data collection limitations, etc. Ignoring this ambi-guity can lead to biased or inaccurate models. Imputation methods for handling missing values are discussed in [8, 21]. Missing or noisy feature values can also be seen in AI applications where data privacy is of prime importance. Differential privacy [10] is a key approach to ensure data privacy. Most approaches to imple-menting differential privacy in the AI models rely on adding noise in the feature vectors [4]. This added feature noise can deteriorate the overall performance of the classifiers, even in partial label settings. There are other scenarios where noisy features co-occur with partial labels. When there are missing (or noisy) attributes in a feature vector, different annotators may assign various labels to it. Considering all these different labels for such noisy feature vector result in partial labels. One real-world application where this can be observed is online object annotation [18]. Much work has been done to develop robust methods to learn classifiers in the presence of missing values and feature noise [14, 22]. But these methods do not consider label ambiguity. Learning with missing or noisy features in a partial label setting is still a challenging problem.

This paper addresses the problem of learning a robust classifier with miss-ing attributes and partial labels. We propose a robust support vector machine (SVM) formulation to handle uncertainty in labels and features. We use a chance-constrained programming approach [16] [1]. This approach can learn classifiers for any distribution with finite mean and covariance. The robust formulation is a second-order cone program (SOCP). We call the proposed formulation RPL-SVM, which stands for **R**obust **P**artial label **S**upport **V**ector **M**achine. The key contributions of the paper are as follows.

1. This paper proposes an RPL-SVM framework that handles uncertainties in input feature vectors and output labels.
2. We provide both linear and nonlinear RPL-SVM formulations. Nonlinear RPL-SVM uses nonlinear kernels to learn robust classifiers.
3. Provides a comprehensive experimental evaluation of RPL-SVM's perfor-mance against state-of-the-art baselines on various benchmark datasets with different degrees of missing attributes and partial labels.

2   Multiclass Partial Label SVM (PL-SVM)

Let us consider the problem of multiclass classification given a partially labeled training set. Let $\mathcal{X} \subseteq \mathbb{R}^d$ be the feature space from which the instances are drawn and $\mathcal{Y} = \{1, \ldots, L\}$ be the label space. In the partial label setting, every instance $\mathbf{x} \in \mathcal{X}$ is associated with a candidate label set $Y \subseteq \mathcal{Y}$. The set of labels not present in the candidate label set is denoted by $\bar{Y}$. The ground-truth label associated with $\mathbf{x}$ is denoted by lowercase y. It is assumed that the actual label y lies within the set Y (i.e., $y \in Y$). Let $\{(\mathbf{x}_1, Y_1), \ldots, (\mathbf{x}_n, Y_n)\}$ be the training set. The objective is to learn a classifier $h : \mathcal{X} \to \mathcal{Y}$. Let $W \in \mathbb{R}^{d \times L}$ be the weight matrix of the classifier $h(\mathbf{x})$. The ith column vector $\mathbf{w}_i$ of W denotes the weight vector of the ith class. The maximum margin approach to learning a multiclass classifier using partial labels solves the following optimization problem [5,20,23].

$$
\min_{\mathbf{w}, \xi} \frac{1}{2} \sum_{j=1}^{L} \|\mathbf{w}_j\|^2 + C \sum_{i=1}^{n} \xi_i
$$

$$
\text{s.t.} \left[|Y_i|^{-1} \sum_{y \in Y_i} \mathbf{w}_y - \mathbf{w}_j \right]^\top \mathbf{x}_i \geq 1 - \xi_i; \ \forall j \in \bar{Y}_i \quad i = 1 \ldots n \tag{1}
$$

$$
\xi_i \geq 0; \quad i = 1 \ldots n
$$

where $\bar{Y}_i = \mathcal{Y} \setminus Y_i$. In the above formulation, C is used set a trade-off between sum of errors $\sum_{i-1}^{n} \xi_i$ and complexity term $\sum_{j=1}^{L} \|\mathbf{w}_j\|^2$. When the partial label set only contains the true class label, the SVM formulation in Eq. (1) becomes the same as the multiclass SVM formulation proposed in [7].

3   Imputing Missing Values

This paper uses the expectation-maximization (EM) based algorithm proposed in [8] to impute the missing values. We impute missing attributes in the partial label setting using the Dempster algorithm [8] as follows. Given a partial label set Y, let S_Y denote the examples of the partial label set Y. Let $m \subset \{1, 2, \ldots, d\}$ denote the set of missing features in S_Y. and $a = \{1, 2, \ldots, d\} \setminus a$ be the set of available features. Thus, any $\mathbf{x} \in S_Y$ is composed of $\mathbf{x}_m$ and $\mathbf{x}_a$ (i.e. $\mathbf{x} = (\mathbf{x}_a, \mathbf{x}_m)$). Let $\boldsymbol{\mu}_Y$ denote the mean of the samples in S_Y and Σ_Y as the corresponding covariance matrix. Thus, $\boldsymbol{\mu}_Y$ and Σ_Y are decomposed as $\boldsymbol{\mu}_Y = \begin{bmatrix} \boldsymbol{\mu}_{Y_a} \\ \boldsymbol{\mu}_{Y_m} \end{bmatrix}$ and $\Sigma_Y = \begin{bmatrix} \Sigma_{Y_{aa}} & \Sigma_{Y_{am}} \\ \Sigma_{Y_{ma}}^\top & \Sigma_{Y_{mm}} \end{bmatrix}$. Where $\boldsymbol{\mu}_{Y_a} = \frac{1}{|S_Y|} \sum_{\mathbf{x} \in S_Y} \mathbf{x}_a$ and $\Sigma_{Y_{aa}} = \frac{1}{|S_Y|} \sum_{\mathbf{x} \in S_Y} (\mathbf{x}_a - \boldsymbol{\mu}_{Y_a})(\mathbf{x}_a - \boldsymbol{\mu}_{Y_a})^\top$. $\boldsymbol{\mu}_{Y_m}$ and $\Sigma_{Y_{mm}}$ are the mean and covariance matrix of the missing features. $\Sigma_{Y_{ma}}$ is the covariance matrix between missing and available features. Let $S_{Y,comp}$ be the subset of S_Y with no missing attributes. Similarly, $S_{Y,miss}$ is the subset of S_Y with missing features. In this algorithm, we start with initial estimates of the mean and covariance from the available observations as $\boldsymbol{\mu}_{Y_m}^{(0)} = \frac{1}{|S_{Y,comp}|} \sum_{\mathbf{x} \in S_{Y,comp}} \mathbf{x}_m$, $\Sigma_{Y_{mm}}^{(0)} = \frac{1}{|S_{Y,comp}|} \sum_{\mathbf{x} \in S_{Y,comp}} (\mathbf{x}_m - \boldsymbol{\mu}_{Y_m}^{(0)})(\mathbf{x}_m - \boldsymbol{\mu}_{Y_m}^{(0)})^\top$, $\Sigma_{Y_{ma}}^{(0)} = \frac{1}{|S_{Y,comp}|} \sum_{\mathbf{x} \in S_{Y,comp}} (\mathbf{x}_m - \boldsymbol{\mu}_{Y_m}^{(0)})(\mathbf{x}_a - \boldsymbol{\mu}_{Y_a}^{(0)})^\top$ We then iterate over the following two steps of imputing the missing values and re-estimating the mean and covariance until convergence.

1. **Imputing the missing values:** For each $\mathbf{x} \in S_{Y,miss}$, impute as $\hat{\mathbf{x}}_m^{(k)} = \boldsymbol{\mu}_{Y_m}^{(k)} + \Sigma_{Y_{ma}}^{(k)} \Sigma_{Y_{aa}}^{-1} (\mathbf{x}_a - \boldsymbol{\mu}_{Y,a})$.

2. **Re-estimating mean and covariance matrix:** $\boldsymbol{\mu}_{Y_m}^{(k)} = \frac{1}{|S_Y|} \sum_{\mathbf{x} \in S_Y} \mathbf{x}_m$, $\Sigma_{Y_{mm}}^{(k)} = \frac{1}{|S_Y|} \sum_{\mathbf{x} \in S_Y} (\mathbf{x}_m - \boldsymbol{\mu}_{Y_m}^{(k)})(\mathbf{x}_m - \boldsymbol{\mu}_{Y_m}^{(k)})^\top$, $\Sigma_{Y_{ma}}^{(k)} = \frac{1}{|S_Y|} \sum_{\mathbf{x} \in S_Y} (\mathbf{x}_m - \boldsymbol{\mu}_{Y_m}^{(k)})(\mathbf{x}_a - \boldsymbol{\mu}_{Y_a}^{(k)})^\top$, $\Sigma_{Y_{mm}}^{(k)} = \Sigma_{Y_{mm}}^{(k-1)} - \Sigma_{Y_{ma}}^{(k)} \Sigma_{Y_{aa}}^{-1} (\Sigma_{Y_{ma}}^{(k)})^\top$.

4   RPL-SVM Linear: Robust Formulation for Linear Classifiers with Partial Labels and Missing Values

The partial label SVM described in Sect. 2 assumes that training data does not suffer from missing values and other noise processes. Here, we describe the formulation of our proposed approach RPL-SVM which can also handle missing values in the feature vectors. Let us assume that the training examples $\mathbf{x}_i$, $i = c+1 \ldots, n$ have missing feature values. We use the imputation method described in Sect. 3 to fill in missing values in these feature vectors. Let $\bar{\mathbf{x}}_i$ be the imputed feature vector of $\mathbf{x}_i$. The imputation method may add some feature noise in $\mathbf{x}_i$, which can cause separability constraints hard to satisfy. Thus, we replace the separability constraints involving $\mathbf{x}_i$ with the following probabilistic constraints.

$$p\left(\left[|Y_i|^{-1} \sum_{y \in Y_i} \mathbf{w}_y - \mathbf{w}_j\right]^\top \bar{\mathbf{x}}_i \geq 1 - \xi_i\right) \geq \kappa_i, \ \forall j \in \bar{Y}_i; \quad i = c+1 \ldots n.$$

Here, the probability is with respect to the distribution of $\bar{\mathbf{x}}_i$. Here, we require that $\bar{\mathbf{x}}_i$ be correctly classified with probability greater than κ_i. κ_i ranges in the interval $(0,1]$. A large value of κ_i will result in a good classifier with a low risk of making mistakes. Directly solving this probability constraint is challenging. We assume that the second moment of $\bar{\mathbf{x}}_i$ exists to solve this. Note that Y_i is the partial label set for $\bar{\mathbf{x}}_i$. To consider the first and second moment of $\bar{\mathbf{x}}_i$, we need to consider all the examples having Y_i as a partial label set. Let μ_{Y_i} and Σ_{Y_i} be the mean and covariance matrix corresponding to the partial label set Y_i. We want the above inequality to hold even for the worst-case distribution having mean μ_{Y_i} and covariance Σ_{Y_i}, leading to the following constraints.

$$\inf_{\bar{\mathbf{x}}_i \in (\mu_{Y_i}, \Sigma_{Y_i})} p\left(\left[|Y_i|^{-1} \sum_{y \in Y_i} \mathbf{w}_y - \mathbf{w}_j\right]^\top \bar{\mathbf{x}}_i \geq 1 - \xi_i\right) \geq \kappa_i, \ \forall j \in \bar{Y}_i.$$

We get the following conditions using multivariate Chebyshev inequality [3, 14, 19].

$$\sup_{\bar{\mathbf{x}}_i \in (\mu_{Y_i}, \Sigma_{Y_i})} p\left(\left[|Y_i|^{-1} \sum_{y \in Y_i} \mathbf{w}_{y_i} - \mathbf{w}_j\right]^\top \bar{\mathbf{x}}_i \leq 1 - \xi_i\right) = \frac{1}{1 + d^2} \leq 1 - \kappa_i; \quad (2)$$

$$\forall j \in \bar{Y}_i, \ i = c+1 \ldots n$$

where $d^2 = \inf\limits_{\left[\frac{1}{|Y_i|}\sum_{y\in Y_i}\mathbf{w}_y-\mathbf{w}_j\right]^\top \bar{\mathbf{x}}_i\leq 1-\xi_i} (\bar{\mathbf{x}}_i - \mu_{Y_i'})^\top \Sigma_{Y_i}^{-1}(\bar{\mathbf{x}}_i - \mu_{Y_i})$. This constraint always holds for a family of distributions with the same second-order moments. In the worst case, equality is reached. Next, we rewrite Eq. (2) which is discussed in following theorem.

Theorem 1. *Let where* $\gamma_i = \sqrt{\frac{\kappa_i}{1-\kappa_i}}$, *then constraint in Eq. (2) is rewritten as*

$$\left[|Y_i|^{-1}\sum_{y\in Y_i}\mathbf{w}_y - \mathbf{w}_j\right]^\top \mu_{Y_i} - (1-\xi_i) \geq \gamma_i\left\|\Sigma_{Y_i}^{1/2}\left(\frac{1}{|Y_i|}\sum_{y\in Y_i}\mathbf{w}_y - \mathbf{w}_j\right)\right\|.$$

Proof. We rewrite d^2 as follows.

$$d^2 = \inf_{\mathbf{C}^\top\mathbf{Z}\geq f}\mathbf{Z}^\top\mathbf{Z} \tag{3}$$

where $\mathbf{Z} = \Sigma_{Y_i}^{-\frac{1}{2}}(\bar{\mathbf{x}}_i - \mu_{Y_i})$, $\mathbf{C}^\top = \left[\frac{1}{|Y_i|}\sum_{y\in Y_i}\mathbf{w}_y - \mathbf{w}_j\right]^\top\Sigma_{Y_i}^{\frac{1}{2}}$ and $f = 1 - \xi_i - \left[\frac{1}{|Y_i|}\sum_{y\in Y_i}\mathbf{w}_y - \mathbf{w}_j\right]^\top\mu_{Y_i}$. The Lagrangian of the optimization problem in Eq. (3) is written as $L(\mathbf{Z},\lambda) = \mathbf{Z}^\top\mathbf{Z} + \lambda(f - \mathbf{C}^\top\mathbf{Z})$, where λ is the Lagrangian multiplier corresponding to the inequality constraint. KKT optimality conditions are: $2\mathbf{Z} = \lambda\mathbf{C}$; $f = \mathbf{C}^\top\mathbf{Z}$. Substituting $\mathbf{Z}$ in f, we get $f = \mathbf{C}^\top\mathbf{Z} = \frac{\lambda}{2}\mathbf{C}^\top\mathbf{C}$. Thus, $\lambda = \frac{2f}{\mathbf{C}^\top\mathbf{C}}$ and $\mathbf{Z} = \frac{f\mathbf{C}}{\mathbf{C}^\top\mathbf{C}}$. From Eq. (2), we know that $d^2 \geq \frac{\kappa_i}{1-\kappa_i}$. Substituting $\mathbf{Z}$ value in Eq. (3) yields, $d^2 = \mathbf{Z}^\top\mathbf{Z} = \frac{(f\mathbf{C})^\top(f\mathbf{C})}{(\mathbf{C}^\top\mathbf{C})^\top(\mathbf{C}^\top\mathbf{C})} = \frac{|f|^2}{(\mathbf{C}^\top\mathbf{C})}$. Thus, $d = \frac{|f|}{\|\mathbf{C}\|}$. Using $d \geq \left(\frac{\kappa_i}{1-\kappa_i}\right)^{1/2}$, we get following constraint by substituting f and $\mathbf{C}$ values.

$$\left[|Y_i|^{-1}\sum_{y\in Y_i}\mathbf{w}_y - \mathbf{w}_j\right]^\top \mu_{Y_i} - (1-\xi_i) \geq \sqrt{\frac{\kappa_i}{1-\kappa_i}}\left\|\Sigma_{Y_i}^{1/2}(|Y_i|^{-1}\sum_{y\in Y_i}\mathbf{w}_y - \mathbf{w}_j)\right\|$$

$\square$

Thus, using the above constraints for $i = c+1,\ldots,n$, the robust SVM formulation for partial label data with missing values is as follows.

$$\min_{\mathbf{w},\xi}\ \frac{1}{2}\sum_{j=1}^{L}\|\mathbf{w}_j\|^2 + C\sum_{i=1}^{n}\xi_i$$

$$\text{s.t.}\ \left[|Y_i|^{-1}\sum_{y\in Y_i}\mathbf{w}_y - \mathbf{w}_j\right]^\top \mu_{Y_i} \geq 1 - \xi_i + \gamma_i\left\|\Sigma_{Y_i}^{\frac{1}{2}}\left[|Y_i|^{-1}\sum_{y\in Y_i}\mathbf{w}_y - \mathbf{w}_j\right]\right\|;$$

$$\forall j \in \bar{Y}_i;\quad i = c+1\ldots n$$

$$\left[|Y_i|^{-1}\sum_{y\in Y_i}\mathbf{w}_y - \mathbf{w}_j\right]^\top \mathbf{x}_i \geq 1 - \xi_i;\quad \forall j \in \bar{Y}_i;\quad i = 1\ldots c$$

$$\xi_i \geq 0;\quad i = 1\ldots c$$

$$\tag{4}$$

Note that for $i = c + 1 \ldots n$, the separability constraints force the mean μ_{Y_i} of partial label set Y_i to achieve higher score with $\frac{1}{Y_i} \sum_{y_i \in Y_i} \mathbf{w}_{y_i}$ compared to any other $\mathbf{w}_y$ ($y \notin Y_i$). On the other hand, examples $i = 1, \ldots, c$ are not facing any missing attribute. Thus, for $i = 1, \ldots, c$, we require that the example $\mathbf{x}_i$ achieve higher score with $\frac{1}{Y_i} \sum_{y_i \in Y_i} \mathbf{w}_{y_i}$ compared to any other $\mathbf{w}_y$ ($y \notin Y_i$).

5 RPL-SVM Nonlinear: Robust Formulation for Nonlinear Classifiers with Partial Labels

This section extends the proposed RPL-SVM formulation for learning nonlinear classifiers. We first assume a feature map $\phi : \mathbb{R}^d \to \mathcal{H}$ corresponding to a Mercer's kernel $K : \mathbb{R}^d \times \mathbb{R}^d \to \mathbb{R}_+$. Where $\mathcal{H}$ is the reproducing kernel Hilbert space (RKHS) corresponding to the kernel K. We assume that each $\mathbf{w}_y$ ($y = 1 \ldots L$) is a linear combination of all the examples. Thus, $\mathbf{w}_y = \sum_{i=1}^{c} \alpha_i^y \phi(\mathbf{x}_i) + \sum_{i=c+1}^{n} \bar{\alpha}_i^y \phi(\bar{\mathbf{x}}_i)$, $y = 1 \ldots L$. Where $\bar{\mathbf{x}}_i$ is achieved by imputing missing values of $\mathbf{x}_i$. We reformulate the optimization problem in Eq. (1) as a SOCP by removing $\|\mathbf{w}\|^2$ from the objective and adding a constraint $\|\mathbf{w}\|^2 \leq \Lambda$ as follows.

$$
\min_{\xi} \sum_{i=1}^{n} \xi_i
$$

$$
\text{s.t.} \quad [|Y_i|^{-1} \sum_{y_i \in Y_i} \mathbf{w}_{y_i} - \mathbf{w}_y]^\top \phi(\mathbf{x}_i) \geq 1 - \xi_i; \quad \forall y \in \bar{Y}_i, \ i = 1 \ldots c
$$

$$
[|Y_i|^{-1} \sum_{y_i \in Y_i} \mathbf{w}_{y_i} - \mathbf{w}_y]^\top \phi(\bar{\mathbf{x}}_i) \geq 1 - \xi_i; \quad \forall y \in \bar{Y}_i, \ i = c + 1 \ldots n \tag{5}
$$

$$
\sum_{i=1}^{L} \|\mathbf{w}_i\|^2 \leq \Lambda; \quad \xi_i \geq 0; \quad \forall 1 \leq i \leq n
$$

The optimization problem in Eq. (5) can be shown equivalent to the optimization problem in Eq. (1) for appropriate choices of C and Λ. Substituting $\mathbf{w}_y = \sum_{i=1}^{c} \alpha_i^y \phi(\mathbf{x}_i) + \sum_{i=c+1}^{n} \bar{\alpha}_i^y \phi(\bar{\mathbf{x}}_i)$, $y = 1 \ldots L$ in the constraints of the optimization problem in Eq. (5) will be as follows.

$$
\left\langle \frac{1}{|Y_i|} \sum_{y \in Y_i} \left(\sum_{k=1}^{c} \alpha_k^y \phi(\mathbf{x}_k) + \sum_{k=c+1}^{n} \bar{\alpha}_k^y \phi(\bar{\mathbf{x}}_k) \right), \phi(\mathbf{x}_i) \right\rangle - \left\langle \sum_{k=1}^{c} \alpha_k^j \phi(\mathbf{x}_k), \phi(\mathbf{x}_i) \right\rangle
$$

$$
- \left\langle \sum_{k=c+1}^{n} \bar{\alpha}_k^j \phi(\bar{\mathbf{x}}_k), \phi(\mathbf{x}_i) \right\rangle \geq 1 - \xi_i; \ \forall j \in \bar{Y}_i, \ i = 1 \ldots c
$$

$$
\Rightarrow \frac{1}{|Y_i|} \sum_{y \in Y_i} \left(\sum_{k=1}^{c} \alpha_k^y K(\mathbf{x}_k, \mathbf{x}_i) + \sum_{k=c+1}^{n} \bar{\alpha}_k^y K(\bar{\mathbf{x}}_k, \mathbf{x}_i) \right) - \sum_{k=1}^{c} \alpha_k^j K(\mathbf{x}_k, \mathbf{x}_i)
$$

$$
- \sum_{k=c+1}^{n} \bar{\alpha}_k^j K(\bar{\mathbf{x}}_k, \mathbf{x}_i) \geq 1 - \xi_i, \ \forall j \in \bar{Y}_i, \ i = 1 \ldots c
$$

$$\Rightarrow \frac{1}{|Y_i|} \sum_{y \in Y_i} \langle \boldsymbol{\alpha}^y, \tilde{K}(\mathbf{x}_i) \rangle - \langle \boldsymbol{\alpha}^j, \tilde{K}(\mathbf{x}_i) \rangle \geq 1 - \xi_i; \forall j \in \bar{Y}_i, \ i = 1 \dots c$$

where

$$\tilde{K}(\mathbf{x}_i) = [K(\mathbf{x}_1, \mathbf{x}_i), \dots, K(\mathbf{x}_c, \mathbf{x}_i), K(\bar{\mathbf{x}}_{c+1}, \mathbf{x}_i), \dots, K(\bar{\mathbf{x}}_n, \mathbf{x}_i)]^\top$$
$$\boldsymbol{\alpha}^y = [\alpha_1^y, \dots, \alpha_c^y, \bar{\alpha}_{c+1}^y, \dots, \bar{\alpha}_n^y]^\top.$$

Similarly, constraints for $i = c + 1 \dots n$ will be

$$|Y_i|^{-1} \sum_{y \in Y_i} \langle \boldsymbol{\alpha}^y, \tilde{K}(\bar{\mathbf{x}}_i) \rangle - \langle \boldsymbol{\alpha}^j, \tilde{K}(\bar{\mathbf{x}}_i) \rangle \geq 1 - \xi_i; \forall j \in \bar{Y}_i, \ i = c + 1 \dots n$$

where $\tilde{K}(\bar{\mathbf{x}}_i) = [K(\mathbf{x}_1, \bar{\mathbf{x}}_i), \dots, K(\mathbf{x}_c, \bar{\mathbf{x}}_i), K(\bar{\mathbf{x}}_{c+1}, \bar{\mathbf{x}}_i), \dots, K(\bar{\mathbf{x}}_n, \bar{\mathbf{x}}_i)]^\top$. The non linear version of the RPL-SVM is obtained by considering the uncertainty in $\tilde{K}(\mathbf{x}_i)$. We assume that examples $\mathbf{x}_i$, $i = c + 1 \dots n$ have missing feature values. Probabilistic constraint takes the below form under noisy attributes in $\tilde{K}(\mathbf{x}_i)$.

$$p\left(\left[|Y_i|^{-1} \sum_{y \in Y_i} \boldsymbol{\alpha}^y - \boldsymbol{\alpha}^j \right]^\top \tilde{K}(\mathbf{x}_i) \geq 1 - \xi_i \right) \geq \kappa_i, \ \forall j \in \bar{Y}_i, \ i = c + 1 \dots n$$

We continue to regard $\tilde{K}(\mathbf{x}_i)$ as a random vector, just like in the original problem. Using a similar approach as in the linear case, we can show that these probabilistic constraints lead to the following equivalent constraints.

$$\left[|Y_i|^{-1} \sum_{y \in Y_i} \boldsymbol{\alpha}^y - \boldsymbol{\alpha}^j \right]^\top \tilde{K}(\mu_{Y_i}) \geq 1 - \xi_i + \gamma_i \left\| \Sigma_{Y_i}^{\frac{1}{2}} (|Y_i|^{-1} \sum_{y_i \in Y_i} \boldsymbol{\alpha}^y - \boldsymbol{\alpha}^j) \right\|$$
$$\forall j \in \bar{Y}_i, \ i = c + 1 \dots n$$

where $\tilde{K}(\mu_{Y_i}) = [K(\mathbf{x}_1, \mu_{Y_i}), \dots, K(\mathbf{x}_c, \mu_{Y_i}), K(\bar{\mathbf{x}}_{c+1}, \mu_{Y_i}), \dots, K(\bar{\mathbf{x}}_n, \mu_{Y_i})]^\top$. Σ_{Y_i} is the covariance of $\tilde{K}(\mathbf{x}_i)$ which is in $\tilde{K}$-space. Thus, the nonlinear formulation of RPL-SVM is as follows.

$$\min_{\xi} \sum_{i=1}^n \xi_i$$

s.t. $\left[|Y_i|^{-1} \sum_{y \in Y_i} \boldsymbol{\alpha}^y - \boldsymbol{\alpha}^j \right]^\top \tilde{K}(\mu_{Y_i}) \geq 1 - \xi_i + \gamma_i \left\| \Sigma_{Y_i}^{\frac{1}{2}} \left[\frac{1}{|Y_i|} \sum_{y \in Y_i} \boldsymbol{\alpha}^y - \boldsymbol{\alpha}^j \right] \right\|;$

$$\forall j \in \bar{Y}_i, \ i = c + 1 \dots n$$

$$\left[|Y_i|^{-1} \sum_{y \in Y_i} \boldsymbol{\alpha}^y - \boldsymbol{\alpha}^j \right]^\top \tilde{K}(\mathbf{x}_i) \geq 1 - \xi_i; \quad \forall y \in \bar{Y}_i, \ i = 1 \dots c$$

$$\sum_{j=1}^L \|\boldsymbol{\alpha}^j\|^2 \leq \Lambda; \quad \xi_i \geq 0; \quad \forall 1 \leq i \leq n;$$

(6)

where $\gamma_i = \sqrt{\frac{\kappa_i}{1 - \kappa_i}}$ and $\boldsymbol{\alpha}^y = [\alpha_1^y, \dots, \alpha_n^y]^\top$.

6   Experiments

In this section, we show the experimental results of the proposed approach. We perform experiments on Wine, Glass4, IRIS, Dermatology, Waveform, SatImage, Exasens, and Shuttle 5 datasets [2]. The details of the datasets used are provided in Table 1. Among these datasets, Exasens has actual missing attributes. In this dataset, 75% of samples have four missing attribute values. We divide each dataset into train and test data with a 67:33 ratio.

Table 1. Experiment datasets description

Dataset	Wine	Glass4	IRIS	Dermatology	Waveform	SatImage	Shuttle	Exasens
# Samples	119	131	150	366	5000	6435	58000	399
# attributes	13	9	4	33	21	36	9	7
# classes	3	4	3	6	3	6	5	4

For benchmarking, we use the following three state-of-the-art approaches.

1. Partial label multiclass SVM (PL-SVM) [6]: This is SVM based approach for multiclass classification using partial labels described in Sect. 3.
2. Partial label KNN (PL-KNN) [13]: This approach uses a generalization of KNN for learning with partial labels. We use $k = 5$ for our experiments.
3. PICO [24]: This is a deep learning approach for learning with partial labels, surpassing all other competing models [25] [17] [12] [11].

Introducing Missing Features. We ensure that 50% of training samples per class contain missing feature values. In a feature vector, some $R\%$ of feature values are deleted to create missing attribute data. We considered different values for the percentage of missing attributes (R) based on the datasets. We have tested with different percentages of missing attributes (25%, 50%, and 75%).

Creating Partial Labels. We create partial labels for training data as follows. Let k be the total number of classes. To create a partial label set of size c, first, we keep the original label in the set. The rest of the $c - 1$ labels from the remaining $k - 1$ labels are chosen randomly. We consider partial label sets of sizes 2 and 4 for Dermatology, SatImage, and Shuttle5 datasets. For the Glass4 dataset, we consider partial label sets of sizes 2 and 3. For IRIS, Wine, Exasens, and Waveform datasets, we consider partial label sets of size 2.

6.1   Experimental Setup

Once missing values are filled using the imputation algorithm described in Sect. 3, we learn classifiers using the proposed algorithm RPL-SVM and the baseline algorithms. We compare the test accuracy of RPL-SVM with PL-SVM, PL-KNN, and PICO. We calculated the average test data classification accuracy for each algorithm by repeating the experiments 50 times. For RPL-SVM, we have considered various κ values. We used cvxpy [9], an open-source Python-embedded modeling language for convex optimization with MOSEK solver for SOCP. The experiments are conducted on a 2.6 GHz 6-Core Intel Core i7 processor with 16 GB 2667 MHz DDR4 memory.

Table 2. Experiment results

Dataset	Partial Label Size	Missing Attributes	RPL-SVM	PL-SVM	PL-KNN	PICO
IRIS	2	25%	**0.04 ± 0.02**	0.05 ± 0.03	0.1 ± 0.04	0.04 ± 0.03
		50%	**0.05 ± 0.02**	0.06 ± 0.03	0.1	0.06
Wave-form	2	25%	**0.14 ± 0.01**	0.15 ± 0.04	0.27	0.14 ± 0.02
		50%	**0.14 ± 0.01**	0.15	0.26	0.14 ± 0.02
		75%	**0.14 ± 0.01**	0.15 ± 0.01	0.27	0.14 ± 0.02
Wine	2	25%	**0.05 ± 0.02**	0.08 ± 0.02	0.31	0.16 ± 0.01
		50%	**0.06 ± 0.03**	0.09 ± 0.03	0.34	0.18
		75%	**0.08 ± 0.03**	0.11 ± 0.04	0.36	0.17
Glass4	2	25%	**0.04 ± 0.03**	0.1 ± 0.12	0.05	0.08
		50%	**0.06 ± 0.04**	0.25 ± 0.12	0.06	0.08
	3	25%	**0.1 ± 0.07**	0.24 ± 0.11	0.11	0.27
		50%	**0.1 ± 0.07**	0.32 ± 0.12	0.13	0.37
Derma-tology	2	10%	**0.02**	0.03	0.04	0.02 ± 0.01
		25%	**0.02**	0.03	0.04	0.08
	4	10%	**0.03 ± 0.01**	0.04 ± 0.02	0.1	0.3 ± 0.04
		25%	**0.03 ± 0.01**	0.04	0.1	0.3 ± 0.05
Sat-Image	2	25%	0.14 ± 0.01	0.17 ± 0.09	0.15	**0.12 ± 0.01**
		50%	0.14 ± 0.01	0.17 ± 0.09	0.15	**0.12 ± 0.01**
		75%	0.14	0.17 ± 0.09	0.15	**0.11**
	4	25%	0.22	0.4	0.24	**0.15**
		50%	0.22 ± 0.02	0.4 ± 0.04	0.24	**0.15 ± 0.01**
		75%	0.22 ± 0.02	0.4 ± 0.04	0.24	**0.17**
Shuttle5	2	25%	**0.02 ± 0.02**	0.13 ± 0.03	0.03	0.05
		50%	**0.02 ± 0.12**	0.13 ± 0.03	0.03	0.08
		75%	**0.02 ± 0.02**	0.13 ± 0.03	0.04	0.05
	4	25%	0.35 ± 0.05	0.45 ± 0.07	0.47	**0.08**
		50%	0.35 ± 0.05	0.45 ± 0.07	0.48	**0.08**
		75%	0.35 ± 0.06	0.45 ± 0.08	0.48	**0.07**
Exasens	2	75%	**0.45 ± 0.09**	0.83 ± 0.06	0.54 ± 006	0.47 ± 0.09

6.2 Performance Comparison Results of RPL-SVM with Baselines

Table 2 provides average test error rates observed for different datasets with different configurations. We have considered kernel-based formulations in the proposed RPL-SVM and baseline PL-SVM approach. For RPL-SVM, we have

Table 3. Training times (in minutes) comparison of various algorithms across all partial label set sizes.

Dataset	Wine	Galss4	IRIS	Dermatology	Exasens	Waveform	SatImage	Shuttle 5
RPL-SVM	0.03	0.08	0.03	2.3	0.3	118	145	188
PL-SVM	0.02	0.07	0.02	2.1	0.25	112	138	174
PL-KNN	0.03	0.06	0.03	1.8	0.03	10	15	19
PICO	69	65	71	76	81	83	115	128

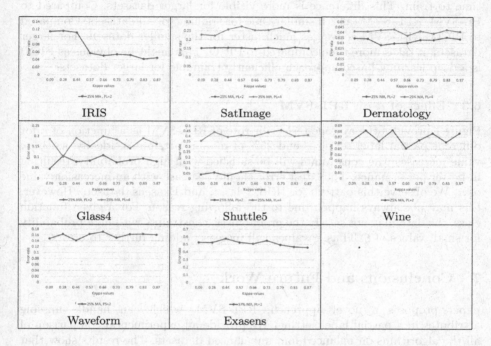

Fig. 1. Average error rates for different κ values using RPL-SVM algorithm. MA-Missing attributes, PL- Partial label set size

reported the results with the best κ value for comparison. For RPL-SVM and PL-SVM, we consider polynomial kernel with degree 2 and Gaussian kernel in our experiments. We report all algorithms' average test error rates and standard deviation values. We only represented standard deviation values up to two decimals and ignored the rest. We observe that the performance of RPL-SVM does not change much with increasing partial label set size and with the increase in the percentage of missing attributes. Thus, it shows the robustness of RPL-SVM against missing attributes and partial labels. RPL-SVM outperforms PL-SVM and PL-KNN for all configurations of missing attributes and partial label set sizes. Compared to PICO, RPL-SVM outperforms IRIS, Waveform, Wine, Glass4, and Dermatology datasets for all configurations of missing attributes and partial label set sizes. For the Shuttle5 dataset, RPL-SVM outperforms PICO for a partial label set of size two and all percentages of missing attributes. For the Exasens dataset, RPL-SVM outperforms all benchmark algorithms. Table 3 provides the training times for the algorithms considered. We see that Wine, Glass4, IRIS, Dermatology, and Exasens datasets are small datasets (i.e., fewer examples). For such datasets, RPL-SVM converges faster. On the other hand, RPL-SVM takes much more time to converge on Waveform, SatImage, and Shuttle5, which are larger datasets. Compared to Pl-KNN, RPL-SVM takes more time to train. This difference is more visible for larger datasets. Compared to PL-SVM, RPL-SVM takes a similar time for training for all datasets. Compared to PICO, RPL-SVM converges much faster for the smaller datasets. For larger datasets, it takes more time compared to PICO. This might be obvious as PICO is a deep learning-based approach efficiently trainable for larger datasets.

6.3   Effect of κ on RPL-SVM

Figure 1 provides the average test error rate of RPL-SVM as a function of κ for different partial label set sizes and 25% of missing attributes. Ideally, as the κ value increases, the constraints will be satisfied with high probability, resulting in better performance. Thus, test error should decrease with an increasing value of κ. We observe this pattern for IRIS, Glass4, and Exasens datasets. However, this may not always happen due to the following reason. For a given function class, the data may not satisfy the probabilistic constraints with high probability for small values of ξ. Thus, ξ values will increase, adding further to errors.

7   Conclusions and Future Work

paper proposes a novel approach, RPL-SVM, which can handle missing attributes in a partial label setting. We provide an experimental comparison of all the algorithms on balanced and unbalanced datasets. The results show that RPL-SVM outperforms benchmark algorithms. RPL-SVM's potential is evident, but addressing scalability for larger datasets and exploring multi-label classification applications is crucial. Further investigation into optimization techniques, robustness in uncertain scenarios, and broader applications could establish RPL-SVM as a robust tool for real-world uncertainty handling, advancing machine learning's impact across domains.

References

1. Ben-Tal, A., Nemirovski, A.: Lectures on modern convex optimization - analysis, algorithms, and engineering applications. In: MPS-SIAM Series on Optimization (2001)
2. Blake, C.: UCI repository of machine learning databases (1998)
3. Boyd, S.P., Vandenberghe, L.: Convex optimization. J. Am. Stat. Assoc. **100**, 1097–1097 (2005)

4. Chaudhuri, K., Monteleoni, C., Sarwate, A.D.: Differentially private empirical risk minimization. J. Mach. Learn. Res. JMLR **12**, 1069–1109 (2009)
5. Collins, M.: Discriminative training methods for hidden Markov models: theory and experiments with perceptron algorithms. In: Proceedings of EMNLP, pp. 1–8 (2002)
6. Cour, T., Sapp, B., Taskar, B.: Learning from partial labels. J. Mach. Learn. Res. **12**(42), 1501–1536 (2011)
7. Crammer, K., Singer, Y.: On the algorithmic implementation of multiclass kernel-based vector machines. J. Mach. Learn. Res. **2**, 265–292 (2002)
8. Dempster, A.P., Laird, N.M., Rubin, D.B.: Maximum likelihood from incomplete data via the EM - algorithm plus discussions on the paper (1977)
9. Diamond, S., Boyd, S.P.: CVXPY: a python-embedded modeling language for convex optimization. JMLR **17**, 2909–2913 (2016)
10. Dwork, C., Roth, A.: The algorithmic foundations of differential privacy. Found. Trends Theor. Comput. Sci. **9**, 211–407 (2014)
11. Feng, L., Kaneko, T., Han, B., Niu, G., An, B., Sugiyama, M.: Learning with multiple complementary labels. In: Proceedings of the 37th International Conference on Machine Learning, PMLR 119:3072–3081 (2020)
12. Feng, L., et al.: Provably consistent partial-label learning. arXiv:abs/2007.08929 (2020)
13. Hüllermeier, E., Beringer, J.: Learning from ambiguously labeled examples. Intell. Data Anal. **10**, 419–439 (2005)
14. Lanckriet, G.R.G., Ghaoui, L.E., Bhattacharyya, C., Jordan, M.I.: A robust minimax approach to classification. JMLR **3**, 555–582 (2003)
15. Liu, L.-P., Dietterich, T.G.: A conditional multinomial mixture model for superset label learning. In: NIPS (2012)
16. López, J., Maldonado, S.: Multi-class second-order cone programming support vector machines. Inf. Sci. **330**, 328–341 (2016)
17. Lv, J., Xu, M., Feng, L., Niu, G., Geng, X., Sugiyama, M.: Progressive identification of true labels for partial-label learning. In: ICML (2020)
18. Lyu, G., Feng, S., Wang, T., Lang, C., Li, Y.: GM-PLL: graph matching based partial label learning. IEEE Trans. Knowl. Data Eng. **33**, 521–535 (2019)
19. Marshall, A.W., Olkin, I.: Multivariate Chebyshev inequalities. Ann. Math. Stat. **31**, 1001–1014 (1960)
20. Rätsch, G., Smola, A.J., Mika, S.: Adapting codes and embeddings for polychotomies. In: Proceedings of NIPS, pp. 529–536 (2002)
21. Schober, P., Vetter, T.R.: Missing data and imputation methods. Anesth. Analg. **131**, 1419–1420 (2020)
22. Shivaswamy, P.K., Bhattacharyya, C., Smola, A.J.: Second order cone programming approaches for handling missing and uncertain data. J. Mach. Learn. Res. **7**(47), 1283–1314 (2006)
23. Taskar, B., Guestrin, C., Koller, D.: Max-margin Markov networks. In: Proceedings of the NIPS, pp. 25–32 (2003)
24. Wang, H., et al.: Pico: contrastive label disambiguation for partial label learning. arXiv:abs/2201.08984 (2022)
25. Wen, H., Cui, J., Hang, H., Liu, J., Wang, Y., Lin, Z.: Leveraged weighted loss for partial label learning. arXiv:abs/2106.05731 (2021)

Spatial Gene Expression Prediction Using Coarse and Fine Attention Network

Cui Chen, Zuping Zhang$^{(\boxtimes)}$, Abdelaziz Mounir, Xin Liu, and Bo Huang

School of Computer Science and Engineering, Central South University,
Changsha 410083, China
{214701013,zpzhang,Mouniraziz,194701016,bo.huang}@csu.edu.cn

Abstract. Spatial Transcriptomics (ST) quantitatively interprets human diseases by providing the gene expression of each fine-grained spot (*i.e.*, window) on a tissue slide. This paper focuses on predicting gene expression in specific windows on a tissue slide image. However, gene expression related to image features typically exhibits diverse spatial scales. To spatially model these features, we propose the Coarse and Fine Attention Network (CFANet). At the coarse level, we employ a coarse-to-fine strategy to acquire adaptable global features. Through coarse-gained areas (*i.e.*, area) guiding to realize sparse external window attention by filtering out the most irrelevant feature areas. At the fine level, using dynamical convolutions realizes internal window attention to obtain dynamic local features. By iterating our CFAN Block, we construct features for different gene types within the slide image windows to predict gene expression. Particularly, without any pre-training, on 10X Genomics breast cancer data, our CFANet achieves an impressive PCC@S of **81.6%** for gene expression prediction, surpassing the current SOTA model by **5.6%**. This demonstrates the potential of the model to be a useful network for gene prediction. Code is available (https://github.com/biyecc/CFANet).

Keywords: Spatial Transcriptomics · Gene Expression Prediction · Deep Learning · Transformer · Tissue Slide Image

1 Introduction

Based on the findings presented in Natural Methods [1], Spatial Transcriptomics (ST) has emerged as the future technique in disease research due to its capability to capture gene expression data with high-resolution spatial information. However, obtaining ST requires advanced technologies like the $10\times$ Genomics Visium system, which is extremely expensive. This poses a challenge to the widespread adoption of ST. Considering that tissue slide images are more accessible and affordable, the predictions of spatial gene expression data from tissue slide images hold the potential to generate virtual ST data. To effectively and efficiently predict gene expression within specific windows of slide images (Fig. 1), we propose a novel solution called Coarse and Fine Attention Network (CFANet).

© The Author(s), under exclusive license to Springer Nature Singapore Pte Ltd. 2024
F. Liu et al. (Eds.): PRICAI 2023, LNAI 14327, pp. 396–408, 2024.
https://doi.org/10.1007/978-981-99-7025-4_34

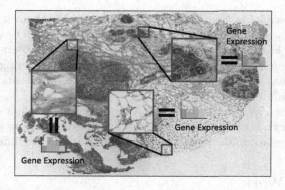

Fig. 1. Overview of fields. Each window of a tissue slide image is with distinct gene expression. Here is an example, we have a tissue slide image with three windows, and each of the windows corresponds with expression of four different gene types. Our goal is to predict the gene expression of each window.

Previous studies have explored the use of neural networks, specifically STNet [2] and NSL [3] for predicting gene expression. STNet utilizes transfer learning by fine-tuning a pretrained DenseNet model, while NSL relies on convolution operations to map the color intensity to gene expression. Although these approaches show promise for high throughput analysis, they have faced two significant limitations a lack of local feature aggregation and vulnerable assumption. To address these limitations, recent studies have proposed the Exemplar Guided Network (EGN) [4] and the Exemplar Guided Graph Network (EGGN) [5] were proposed. They combine exemplar learning with the vanilla Vision Transformer (ViT) [6] and Graph Convolutional Network (GCN), respectively. However, on the one hand, the vanilla ViT suffers from a quadratical complexity due to its quadratic relationship with the input image size, on the other hand, it is difficult for the exemplar extract needs to introduce additional information, such as prior knowledge of gene expression within windows of the exemplar.

Based on above discussion, we propose CFANet . It flexibly merges coarse-gained areas (*i.e.*, areas) and fine-grained spot (*i.e.*, window) features, for predicting gene expression prediction. Specifically, each CFAN Block consists of two levels: Sparse Adaptive Global area Attention (SAGA) as coarse level and Multi-scale Dynamic Local window Attention (MDLA) as fine level. SAGA considers that not all the key-value pairs are useful, so SAGA filters out the most irrelevant areas to realize sparse external window attention. On the other hand, MDLA introduces a fully convolutional neural network (CNN) inspired by the network designs of Transformer. This enables the dynamic aggregation of local features and facilitates internal window attention. Our contributions are summarised below:

- In this paper, we propose CFANet , a global and local attention network, to effectively and efficiently predict gene expression from the slide image window. Experiments conducted on two standard benchmark datasets show our superiority when compared with SOTA approaches.

- At the coarse level, we propose the SAGA module with a coarse-to-fine strategy to obtain adaptive global features. By effectively filtering out the most irrelevant areas and focusing on sparse external window attention, the routing area is successfully obtained.
- At the fine level, we develop the MDLA module with dynamical convolutions to effectively extract local features and realize internal window attention. This module enables accurate capturing of the spatial locality of different windows.

2   Related Work

Gene Expression Prediction. Measuring gene expression is a fundamental process in the advancement of new treatments [7] for diseases. There are two distinct approaches for predicting gene expression: based on DNA sequences and slide images. The gene expression within slide images plays a crucial role in determining the characteristics of the tissue, Deep Learning methods have been introduced to this process, the image-based approaches can be categorized into two branches. The first brunch focuses on bulk RNA-Seq and single-cell RNA, which measures gene expression within a large predefined area of up to $10^5 \times 10^5$ in corresponding slide images and the cellular level, respectively. However, both of these approaches result in the loss of rich spatial information about gene expression, which is crucial when studying tissue heterogeneity. The second brunch, known as Spatial Transcriptomics (ST), is a novel approach that employs DNA barcodes to different windows within the tissue and captures spatial information. He et al. designed the STNet [2], which is the first to consider integrating the slide image with ST. Dawood et al. [3] propose an NSL, which is 'color-aware'. Recently, Yang et al. have proposed two exemplar guided deep neural network, named EGN [4] and EGGN [5].

Vision Transformer. ViT [6] employs self-attention mechanism, splitting each image into patches and treating them as tokens. It exhibits noteworthy efficiency in various classification tasks but relies on full self-attention mechanism, which leads to quadratic growth in computational complexity as the image size increases. To tackle this dilemma, recent studies focus on sparse attention [8]. Ramachandran et al. have proposed the local window self-attention mechanism, as well as its shifted or haloed variants. These mechanisms facilitate interactions between different windows, offering a solution to the problem of computational complexity. Furthermore, Dong et al. [8] propose both horizontal and vertical stripes window self-attention.

Self Attention in CNN. Self-attention mechanisms have been widely adopted in the field of computer vision tasks. Several works [9,10] have proposed incorporating self-attention layers, either channel-based or position-based, to enhance convolutional networks. SENet establishes channel relationships within the convolutional network by employing global average pooling to squeeze the features.

Dual attention network [10] utilize both channel-based and position-based attention mechanisms individually. Then, the resulting features from both attention modules can be combined through either element-wise addition or concatenation. These combined features are integrated into the convolutional output following each stage. In contrast, GCNet [9] combines SENet and the non-local network to create a hybrid attention mechanism. This mechanism effectively combines information from both channel and spatial relationships within a single attention module.

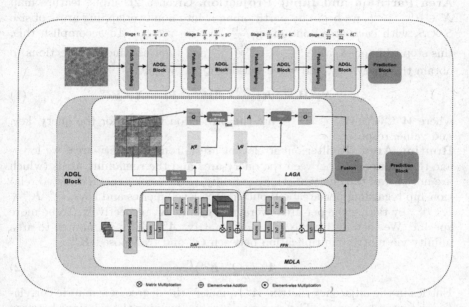

Fig. 2. Network architecture of the proposed CFANet. Each CFAN Block fuses LAGA and MDLA for global and local feature extraction. By gathering key-value pairs in the top k relevant areas, LAGA utilizes sparse external window attention. MDLA contains a fully CNN model DAF and the gated FFN to capture the local features of the windows. Finally, CFANet has a prediction block with the fusion feature representation, to achieve the gene expression prediction task.

3   Method

Sparse Adaptive Global area Attention (SAGA). Several works [8,11,12] have proposed various sparse attention mechanisms to address the time and space complexity challenges associated with vanilla Transformer. These mechanisms selectively apply applying all pairs. Existing approaches, however, either rely on handcrafted static patterns or share the same subset of key-value pairs among all queries.

To tackle the dilemma of handcrafted approaches, we design a SAGA module that facilitates adaptively sparse global attention through coarse-to-fine strategy.

The key idea of strategy is to automatically filter out irrelevant areas at a coarse level, resulting in a small subset of routed areas. Subsequently, this areas guided fine-grained window to effectively capture sparse external window attention (Note that, the routing areas are obtained by calculating the similarity between areas and belongs to the query-area level, in query-window level, all windows in the same area will attend to the same windows that belong to the routing areas). We give a detailed explanation of coarse-to-fine strategy as follows.

– **Area Partition and Input Projection.** Given a 2D input feature map $X \in \mathbb{R}^{C \times H \times M}$, we begin by partitioning it into non-overlapping areas of size $S \times S$, with each area containing $\frac{HW}{S^2}$ feature vectors. To accomplish this, this step reshape X as $X^a \in \mathbb{R}^{S^2 \times \frac{HW}{S^2} \times C}$ and then use linear projections to obtain the query, key, and value tensors, $Q, K, V \in \mathbb{R}^{S^2 \times \frac{HW}{S^2} \times C}$:

$$Q_i = X_i{}^a W^q, \quad K_i = X_i{}^a W^k, \quad V_i = X_i{}^a W^v, \tag{1}$$

where $W^q, W^k, W^v \in \mathbb{R}^{C \times C}$ are the projection weights for the query, key, and value, respectively.
– **Routing Area.** To filter out irrelevant areas from the query-area, we leverage the relationship between the query-area and the remaining areas (which are not part of the query-area). Specifically, we first construct a directed relationship regarding per-area and obtain area-level queries and keys, $Q^a, K^a \in \mathbb{R}^{S^2 \times C}$, by taking the per-area average of Q and K, respectively. To be more specific, We then derive the adjacency matrix, $A^a \in \mathbb{R}^{S^2 \times S^2}$, of area-to-area affinity via matrix multiplication between Q^a and transposed K^a:

$$A^a = Q^a (K^a)^T. \tag{2}$$

Entries in the adjacency matrix, A^a, quantify the degree of semantic correlation between two areas. The core step involves pruning the relations between areas, keeping only top$k$ connections. Specifically, we derive a routing index matrix, $I_a \in \mathbb{N}^{S^2 \times k}$, with the row-wise top$k$ operator:

$$I^a = \text{topkIndex}(A^a). \tag{3}$$

Hence, the ith row of I^a contains k indices of most relevant areas for the ith area.
– **external window attention.** With the area-to-area routing index matrix I^a, the application of external window attention becomes possible. For each query window within area j, it attend to all key-value pairs that are located in the union of k routed areas indexed with $I^a_{(j,1)}, I^a_{(j,2)}, ..., I^a_{(j,k)}$. To GPU friendly, We gather key and value first, *i.e.*,

$$K^g = \text{gather}(K, I^a), \quad V^g = \text{gather}(V, I^a), \tag{4}$$

where $K_i{}^g, V_i{}^g \in \mathbb{R}^{S^2 \times \frac{kHW}{S^2} \times C}$ are gathered key and value tensor. We can then apply attention mechanisms on the gathered key-value pairs as:

$$O_i = \text{Attention}(Q_i, K^g, V^g). \tag{5}$$

Note that we can parallelize the computation of the attention weights and the attended representations across all tokens in all regions, which makes our approach computationally efficient.

Multi-scale Dynamic Local window Attention (MDLA). Although the SAGA is able to extract features through sparse external attention by adaptively filtering areas. However, as mentioned above, SAGA considers coarse level similarity (*i.e.*, each window belonging to the same query-area shares the same routed area for external window attention. However, this arrangement is deemed insufficient. Considering the locality of different windows, we design a MDLA module to facilitate internal window attention.

Specifically, to investigate the local features dynamically, MDLA initially estimates spatial-variant filters with multi-scale convolution, which contains 3×3 kernel with dilation factors of 1, 3, and 5. Subsequently, filters are estimated and employed as dynamic local attention to enhance the aggregation of local features within the input. Lastly, following the approach employed by Transformer, which utilizes a feed-forward network to refine feature representation, we utilize a gated feed-forward network, as proposed in [13] to improve the performance of the aggregated features.

– **Depth-wise Aggregation Feature (DAF).** For a given feature $X_i \in \mathbb{R}^{H \times W \times C}$ obtained by a layer norm followed by 1×1 convolution, we propose a dynamic weight generation network inspired by the squeeze and excitation network (SENet). Unlike traditional SENet architectures, our network omits normalization layers and non-linear activations to ensure the generation of dynamic weights. To better capture local information, we incorporate two depth-wise convolutional layers within the SENet framework. The utilization of depth-wise convolutional operations allows efficient modeling of local attention.

The proposed dynamic weight generation is achieved by:

$$X = \text{DWConv}_{7 \times 7}(\text{DWConv}_{7 \times 7}(\text{Conv}_{1 \times 1}(X_i))), X \in \mathbb{R}^{H \times W \times \gamma C}$$
$$X_{out} = \text{Conv}_{1 \times 1}(X), X_{out} \in \mathbb{R}^{H \times W \times G \times K^2} \tag{6}$$
$$W(\text{x}) = \mathcal{R}(X_{out}), W(\text{x}) \in \mathbb{R}^{G \times K \times K}$$

where γ represents the squeezing factor; $\text{DWConv}_{7 \times 7}$ represents a depth-wise convolution operation with a filter size of 7×7 pixels, $\text{Conv}_{1 \times 1}$ represents a convolution operation with a filter size of 1×1 pixel. The function $\mathcal{R}$ denotes a reshaping operation, and x represents the pixel index. For each pixel, a correlated dynamic kernel of size $K \times K$ is utilized for dynamic convolution.

Using the generated pixel-wise weight W, we can obtain the aggregated feature as follows:

$$\hat{X}^l = W \circledast X_i, \tag{7}$$

where $\circledast$ represents the operation of dynamic convolution, which utilizes a weight-sharing mechanism for each channel.

The detailed architecture of the dynamic weight generation network is illustrated in Fig. 2. Similar to the multi-head self-attention [13], we divide the number of feature channels into G heads and learn separate dynamic weights in parallel.

- **Feed-Forward Network (FFN).** Additionally, to enhance the capability of feature representation, we incorporate an improved feed-forward network, as proposed in [13], for processing the aggregated feature $\hat{X}$:

$$L_i = FFN(\hat{X}^l), \tag{8}$$

$FFN(\cdot)$ denotes a feed-forward network.

- **Fusion.** We fuse the external window attention O_i with the internal window attention L_i, we have:

$$Y_i = \text{Fusion}(O_i, L_i) \tag{9}$$

where MLP_f is a single-layer perception. In addition, there are many Fusion methods for O_i and L_i. This paper selects the most straightforward method: directly adding them. In our extensive experimentation, we discovered that other complex fusion methods have a negligible influence on the results of gene expression prediction.

Prediction Block. We apply the fusion feature map for prediction. We have:

$$y_i = \text{MLP}_f(Y_i) \tag{10}$$

Objective. CFANet is optimized using the mean squared loss $\mathcal{L}_2$ and batch-wise PCC $\mathcal{L}_{\text{PCC}}$. The overall objective is achieved by:

$$\mathcal{L}_E = \mathcal{L}_2 + \mathcal{L}_{\text{PCC}}. \tag{11}$$

4   Experiments

4.1   Datasets

We conducted experimental studies using two available datasets, namely the STNet dataset [2] and the 10x Genomics datasets[1]. The STNet dataset contains approximately 30,612 pairs of windows and gene expression data. These data were obtained from 68 slide images, which were collected from 23 patients. Following study [2], our objective is to predict the expression levels of 250 gene types exhibiting the highest mean values across the dataset. As for the 10xProteomic dataset, it comprises 32,032 slide image windows and gene expression data obtained from 6 slide images. To ensure consistency and comparability, the setting is similar to the STNet dataset.

---

[1] https://www.10xgenomics.com/resources/datasets.

4.2   Experimental Set-Up

Evaluation Metrics. Following [4,5], here we also employ three metrics to compare: Pearson correlation coefficient (PCC), mean squared error (MSE), and mean absolute error(MAE). All the experimental results are presented 1×10^1. Specifically, to assess performance, we employ the PCC at three different quantiles: PCC@F, PCC@S, and PCC@M, which correspond to the first quantile, median, and mean of PCC, respectively. PCC@F reflects the PCC for the least performing model predictions, while PCC@S and PCC@M measure the median and mean of correlations for each gene type. Given the predictions and ground truths (GTs) for all of the slide image windows. Higher values for PCC@F, PCC@S, and PCC@M indicate better performance. Furthermore, MSE and MAE quantify the deviation between predictions and GTs on a per-sample basis for each gene type within each slide image window, lower MSE and MAE value signifies better performance.

Implementation Details. The setting of CFANet following before study setting. During training, CFANet is trained from scratch for 100 epochs, with a batch size of 32. We set the learning rate to 5×10^{-4} with a cosine annealing scheduler. To control overfitting, we apply a weight decay of 1×10^{-4}. SAGA is sparse transformer blue with a patch size of 32, the embedding dimension is 1024, the feedforward dimension is 4096, the model consists of 16 attention heads and have a depth of 8. All experiments were conducted using 2 NVIDIA A10 GPUs, allowing for efficient processing and training of the model.

4.3   Experimental Results

We have conducted quantitative gene expression prediction comparisons between our CFANet and SOTA methods using the STNet dataset and the 10x Genomics datasets (Table 1). All the experimental results are presented 1×10^1. We highlight the best results and use '-' to indicate unavailable results. Models are evaluated using four-fold cross-validation and three-fold cross-validation on the datasets mentioned above. We evaluate the effectiveness of our CFANet experimentally on a series of prior SOTA works, which include models in gene expression prediction [2–5] and, as well as models in ImageNet classification ViT [6], MPViT [14], CycleMLP [15]. Our CFANet outperforms the SOTA methods in these PCC-related metrics(Note that, PCC-related evaluation metrics are of utmost importance in our task.).

(i) Our CFANet exhibits a significant superiority over the baseline methods when considering the PCC-related evaluations. It is crucial to highlight that a significant proportion of gene types within this first quantile exhibit skewed expression distributions, which represents the most challenging aspect of the prediction task. Our method surpasses the second-best approach by nearly **10%** in terms of PCC@S, indicating a significant improvement in capturing correlations for these particularly challenging gene types. This evaluates the performance of the median of correlations for all types of genes. As mentioned above, PCC-related evaluation metrics are the most important in our task. Our CFANet utilizes both the Coarse and Fine Attention outperforms marginally in terms of in PCC-related evaluation metrics, However, it achieves similar MSE and MAE as the EGGN model, are currently the SOTA model in gene expression prediction within tissue slide images.

(ii) CycleMLP and MPViT are the SOTA methods in the ImageNet classification task, our CFANet are better than them on every each metric.

(iii) The FlOPs and Time were compared with the most advanced gene prediction model, and the results showed that CFANet was effective and efficient. Under the same backbone, the FLOPs of EGN are five times that of CFANet, and the running time is the processing time of a dataset plus inference time. Due to the trouble of EGN and EGGN pre-processing, the running time is very large.

Table 1. Comparison to prior works.

Methods	FLOPs (m)	Time (s)	STNet Dataset					10x Genomics Dataset				
			MAE	MSE	PCC@F	PCC@S	PCC@M	MAE	MSE	PCC@F	PCC@S	PCC@M
STNet [2]	-	-	0.45	1.70	0.05	0.92	0.93	1.24	2.64	1.25	2.26	2.15
NSL [3]	-	-	-	-	−0.71	0.25	0.11	-	-	−3.73	1.84	0.25
ViT [6]	-	-	0.42	1.67	0.97	1.86	1.82	0.75	2.27	4.64	5.11	4.90
CycleMLP [15]	-	-	0.44	1.68	1.11	1.95	1.91	0.47	1.55	5.88	6.60	6.32
MPViT [14]	-	-	0.45	1.70	0.91	1.54	1.69	0.55	1.56	6.40	7.15	6.84
EGN [4]	5031.08	2663.25	0.41	1.61	1.51	2.25	2.02	0.54	1.55	6.78	7.21	7.07
EGGN [5]	-	2319.32	**0.39**	**1.61**	2.12	3.05	2.92	**0.35**	**1.31**	7.06	7.60	7.44
CFANet	1026.35	406.3	0.63	1.66	**2.12**	**3.06**	**3.00**	0.40	1.49	**8.00**	**8.16**	**8.02**

Quantitative Evaluation. The visualization of the latent space (Fig. 3), achieved by considering the SOTA models in gene expression prediction. STNet dataset have two additional labels, namely tumor and normal, we utilized these labels for annotations. In visualization, We randomly selected 256 representations of the slide image window for each label. The visualized results also show the advantages of CFANet.

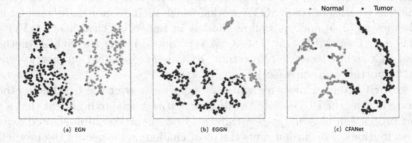

(a) EGN   (b) EGGN   (c) CFANet

Fig. 3. Quantitative evaluation of the SOTA models. We use t-SNE to reduce the dimension of the model potential space. We annotated with additional labels (*i.e.*, tumor and normal) from the STNet dataset.

4.4   Ablation Study

The capability of each component by conducting a detailed ablation study in the 10x Genomics datasets.

Effectiveness of the CFANet Architectures. As one of the key components in our CFANet , Fusion block merges the SAGA with MDLA to enhance feature aggregation. We compare the proposed method with two baselines, one involving the 'SAGA only' module, and the other involving the 'MDLA only'. The results are presented in Table 2. It is evident that the model achieves the best gene expression prediction results when these two modules are fused. We have employed the simplest method of combining them. However, through our extensive experiments, we have found that more complex fusion way have little influence on the results of gene expression prediction.

Table 2. Ablation study on CFANet architectures.

Methods	'SAGA only'	'MDLA only'	CFANet
SAGA	✓		✓
MDLA		✓	✓
MAE	0.58	0.80	**0.40**
MSE	1.64	2.26	**1.49**
PCC@F	6.05	6.61	**8.00**
PCC@S	6.84	7.18	**8.16**
PCC@M	6.57	6.86	**8.02**

Effectiveness of the SAGA. When considering the parameters s and k in the SAGA module, the following factors are taken into account:

(i) The selection of s aligns with that of SWinTransformer [16], where a window size of 7 is used along with void padding. Given that $224 = 7 \times 32$, we opt for $S = 7$ to ensure it remains a divisor of the feature map size across all stages.

(ii) The selection of k is informed by the findings from KVT [17], which reveal that retaining approximately 66% of attention is sufficient. Gradually, we increase k to ensure a reasonable number of windows are attended to as the area size reduces in later stages. Our goal is to achieve a reduction of attention by nearly 30% $\sim$ 40% across the four stages. Accordingly, we set k to [1, 4, 4, -2] and use 2, 2, 6, and 2 blocks for the respective stages. This involves non-overlapping patch embedding, the initial patch embedding dimension set at $C = 96$, and the MLP expansion ratio of $e = 4$. Here, we conduct a comparison between SAGA and several existing SOTA sparse attention mechanisms [8,11,12] within the context of a classification task. To ensure a fair comparison, we follow the approach outlined in [8] by aligning the macro architecture designs with those of CSwin [8]. The results of this comparative analysis are presented in Table 3.

Through extensive evaluation, an interesting observation came to light: while crossformer achieves the best Mean Squared Error (MSE), our SAGA excedes in terms of other key metrics. Moreover, the difference in MSE between our approach and crossformer is quite small. This observation might be attributed to crossformer's consideration of neighboring window information. This observation serves to further validate our decision to focus on local window information.

Effectiveness of the MDLA. Our MDLA module contains DAF amd FFN blocks, inheriting dynamical convolutions to generate dynamic weights for better local feature aggression. To demonstrate the effectiveness of the proposed MDLA, we first verify the effectiveness of Multi-scale by comparing with Single-scale. Furthermore, as mentioned in the paper, depth-wise convolutional operations have shown the capability to model local attention. In order to further investigate the effectiveness of the proposed MDLA, we conducted additional experiments involving the 'depth-wise only' operation. This allowed us to assess the model's performance in capturing local attentions and evaluate the additional introduced by the MDLA module. Finally, we verify the effectiveness of DAF block and FFN block individually through experiments involving 'DAF only'and 'FFN only', respectively. Table 4 shows that using the MDLA achieves the best metrics of PCC-related, 'DAF only'and 'FFN only' have the best MAE and MSE, respectively. These strongly suggesting the effectiveness of the MDLA in enhancing gene expression prediction.

Table 3. Ablation study on SAGA.

Methods	DAT [12] CVPR2022	crossformer [11] ICLR2022	CSwin [8] CVPR2022	CFANet
MAE	0.50	0.45	0.60	**0.40**
MSE	1.64	**1.46**	1.88	1.49
PCC@F	5.76	6.49	5.63	**8.00**
PCC@S	6.62	7.17	6.40	**8.16**
PCC@M	6.26	6.93	6.08	**8.02**

Table 4. Ablation study on MDLA.

Methods	Settings				Results				
	Multi-scale	Depth-wise	DAF	FFN	MAE	MSE	PCC@F	PCC@S	PCC@M
Single-scale attention		✓	✓	✓	0.49	1.68	7.61	8.03	7.67
'Depth-wise only'	✓	✓			0.51	1.51	6.46	7.12	6.91
'DAF only'	✓	✓	✓		**0.36**	1.41	6.60	7.14	6.92
'FFN only'	✓			✓	0.47	**1.15**	6.32	7.00	6.80
CFANet	✓	✓	✓	✓	0.40	1.49	**8.00**	**8.16**	**8.02**

5   Conclusion

This paper proposes an CFANet to effectively and efficiently predict gene expression from each fine-grained spot on a tissue slide image. CFANet simultaneously considers on both the coarse and the fine levels to gain global (*i.e.*, external window) attention and local (*i.e.*, internal window) attention, respectively. Each CFAN Block contains the SAGA module and MDLA module. At the coarse level, a coarse-to-fine strategy is proposed to acquire sparse external window attention by adaptively filtering out the most irrelevant feature areas. At the fine level, a dynamically internal window attention mechanism is designed with dynamical convolutions, accurately capturing the locality of different windows. These two types of attention are then combined to predict gene expression. Through extensive experiments, we demonstrate the superiority of the CFANet over existing SOTA methods. CFANet holds the potential to facilitate studies novel treatments through effective and efficient gene expression prediction.

References

1. Marx, V.: Method of the year: spatially resolved transcriptomics. Nat. Methods **18**(1), 9–14 (2021)
2. He, B., et al.: Integrating spatial gene expression and breast tumour morphology via deep learning. Nature Biomed. Eng. **4**(8), 827–834 (2020)
3. Dawood, M., Branson, K., Rajpoot, N.M., Minhas, F.u.A.A.: All you need is color: image based spatial gene expression prediction using neural stain learning. In: Machine Learning and Principles and Practice of Knowledge Discovery in Databases: International Workshops of ECML PKDD 2021, Virtual Event, September 13–17, 2021, Proceedings, Part II, pp. 437–450. Springer (2022). https://doi.org/10.1007/978-3-030-93733-1_32
4. Yang, Y., Hossain, M.Z., Stone, E.A., Rahman, S.: Exemplar guided deep neural network for spatial transcriptomics analysis of gene expression prediction. In: Proceedings of the IEEE/CVF Winter Conference on Applications of Computer Vision, pp. 5039–5048 (2023)
5. Yang, Y., Hossain, M.Z., Stone, E., Rahman, S.: Spatial transcriptomics analysis of gene expression prediction using exemplar guided graph neural network. bioRxiv, pp. 2023–03 (2023)
6. Dosovitskiy, A., Beyer, L., Kolesnikov, A., Weissenborn, D., Zhai, X., Unterthiner, T.: Transformers for image recognition at scale. arXiv preprint arXiv:2010.11929 (2020)
7. Avsec, Ž, Agarwal, V., Visentin, D., Ledsam, J.R., Grabska-Barwinska, A., Taylor, K.R., Assael, Y., Jumper, J., Kohli, P., Kelley, D.R.: Effective gene expression prediction from sequence by integrating long-range interactions. Nat. Methods **18**(10), 1196–1203 (2021)
8. Dong, X., et al.: Cswin transformer: a general vision transformer backbone with cross-shaped windows. In: Proceedings of the IEEE/CVF Conference on Computer Vision and Pattern Recognition, pp. 12124–12134 (2022)
9. Cao, Y., Xu, J., Lin, S., Wei, F., Hu, H.: Gcnet: non-local networks meet squeeze-excitation networks and beyond. In: Proceedings of the IEEE/CVF International Conference on Computer Vision Workshops(2019)

10. Fu, J., et al.: Dual attention network for scene segmentation. In: Proceedings of the IEEE/CVF Conference on Computer Vision and Pattern Recognition, pp. 3146–3154 (2019)

11. Wang, W., et al.: Crossformer: a versatile vision transformer hinging on cross-scale attention. arxiv 2021. arXiv preprint arXiv:2108.00154

12. Xia, Z., Pan, X., Song, S., Li, L.E., Huang, G.: Vision transformer with deformable attention. In: Proceedings of the IEEE/CVF Conference on Computer Vision and Pattern Recognition, pp. 4794–4803 (2022)

13. Zamir, S.W., Arora, A., Khan, S., Hayat, M., Khan, F.S., Yang, M.H.: Restormer: efficient transformer for high-resolution image restoration. In: Proceedings of the IEEE/CVF Conference on Computer Vision and Pattern Recognition, pp. 5728–5739 (2022)

14. Lee, Y., Kim, J., Willette, J., Hwang, S.J.: Mpvit: multi-path vision transformer for dense prediction. In: Proceedings of the IEEE/CVF Conference on Computer Vision and Pattern Recognition, pp. 7287–7296 (2022)

15. Chen, S., Xie, E., Ge, C., Chen, R., Liang, D., Luo, P.: Cyclemlp: a mlp-like architecture for dense prediction. arXiv preprint arXiv:2107.10224 (2021)

16. Liu, Z., Lin, Y., Cao, Y., Hu, H., Wei, Y., Zhang, Z., Lin, S., Guo, B.: Swin transformer: hierarchical vision transformer using shifted windows. In: Proceedings of the IEEE/CVF International Conference on Computer Vision, pp. 10012–10022 (2021)

17. Wang, P., Wang, X., Wang, F., Lin, M., Chang, S., Li, H., Jin, R.: KVT: K-NN attention for boosting vision transformers. In: Computer Vision-ECCV 2022: 17th European Conference, Tel Aviv, Israel, October 23–27, 2022, Proceedings, Part XXIV, pp. 285–302. Springer (2022)

STFM: Enhancing Autism Spectrum Disorder Classification Through Ensemble Learning-Based Fusion of Temporal and Spatial fMRI Patterns

Ziyu Zhou[1], Yiming Huang[1], Yining Wang[1], and Yin Liang[2]([✉])

[1] Beijing University of Technology, Beijing, China
yiminghuang2002@gmail.com
[2] Faculty of Information Technology, School of Computer Science and Technology,
Beijing University of Technology, Beijing, China
yinliang@bjut.edu.cn

Abstract. This paper presents the novel spatial and temporal fusion model (STFM), an effective approach for Autism Spectrum Disorder (ASD) detection and classification tasks using foundational machine learning models. Utilizing ensemble learning principles, STFM improves the classification performance by integrating weak classifiers. The process begins with the sliding window method applied to fMRI data, constructing brain networks through Pearson correlation calculation between brain regions. This infuses the network with both temporal and spatial patterns. Then, bidirectional LSTM (Bi-LSTM) and 2DCNN are applied for temporal and spatial feature extraction respectively. The model further ensures smoother data variations between patterns through interpolation, and utilizes a basic cross attention mechanism for fusion of patterns. The fused patterns are then classified by a simple SVM classifier. The presented STFM model demonstrates a remarkable classification accuracy of 70.42%, surpassing most fundamental machine learning models in ASD detection.

Keywords: Machine Learning · Autism Spectrum Disorder · Classification · Spatial Temporal Pattern Fusion · Ensemble Learning · Cross Attention Mechanism

1 Introduction

Autism Spectrum Disorder (ASD) is a complex neurodevelopmental condition defined by social interaction impairments and restrictive, repetitive behavioral patterns [1]. The disorder's prevalence has surged recently, affecting about 1 in 54 children in the U.S. [2]. Early detection and intervention are pivotal for improved long-term results, underscoring the need for precise, efficient diagnostic tools [3].

Z. Zhou, Y. Huang and Y. Wang—Equal contribution.

© The Author(s), under exclusive license to Springer Nature Singapore Pte Ltd. 2024
F. Liu et al. (Eds.): PRICAI 2023, LNAI 14327, pp. 409–421, 2024.
https://doi.org/10.1007/978-981-99-7025-4_35

Magnetic Resonance Imaging (MRI) has become a significant tool for exploring ASD due to its noninvasive assessment of brain structure and function. Many studies highlight ASD-related structural and functional brain changes, like gray and white matter volume discrepancies, variations in cortical thickness, and functional connectivity [4]. This has spurred increased interest in creating MRI-based ASD diagnostic algorithms. As AI and ML technologies advance, their potential to improve diagnostic accuracy in conditions like ASD is increasingly recognized by the medical and research community. Recent studies have indicated that machine learning algorithms can be particularly effective in analyzing and categorizing neuroimaging data related to ASD, revealing patterns that might not be immediately discernible to human experts [5]. Additionally, there is growing evidence that AI-enhanced diagnostic tools, when utilized alongside traditional assessment methods, can significantly enhance the precision and timeliness of ASD diagnosis [6].

In this paper, we propose spatial temporal feature fusion model(STFM), an effective autism detection and classification model based on the fusion of temporal and spatial patterns of brain network. The model is designed with the inspiration of ensemble learning, which aims to improve the overall classification performance by integrating temporal and spatial patterns. Firstly, we process the preprocessed FMRI data using the sliding window method and construct brain networks within each window by calculating the Pearson correlation between brain regions. Secondly, we employ bidirectional LSTM(Bi-LSTM) and 2DCNN to extract the temporal and spatial patterns of the brain networks separately, achieving effective reduction on dimension while preserving feature information to the greatest extent. We conduct ablation experiments to demonstrate the effective extraction of two types of patterns. Subsequently, we employ bilinear interpolation to result in smoother data variations between patterns. Finally, we employ the basic cross attention mechanism for fusion of patterns and choose a simple SVM as the classifier in experiments. We conduct systematic experiments on the large ASD fMRI dataset, and achieve a classification accuracy of 70.42%. In comparison with relevant studies using basic machine learning classification models, STFM achieves the best classification results. The contributions of STFM are summarized in three folds:

- We propose a spatial and temporal fusion model (STFM), which unveils a new pathway in autism detection classification tasks using fundamental machine learning models.
- We employ deep learning models to separately extract the temporal and spatial patterns of brain networks, and effectively integrate both by cross attention mechanism.
- STFM achieves a classification accuracy of 70.42%, surpassing most fundamental machine learning classifier models.

2   Related Work

Machine learning (ML) and deep learning (DL) techniques have shown significant advancements in areas such as image classification, natural language processing, and speech recognition [7]. These methods have also been effectively applied to MRI data for ASD classification. Algorithms like support vector machines (SVM), random forests, and k-nearest neighbors are commonly used with both structural and functional MRI data for this purpose [8–10]. Moreover, DL techniques, including convolutional neural networks (CNN) and recurrent neural networks (RNN), have demonstrated potential in ASD classification [11,12]. The Autism Brain Imaging Data Exchange (ABIDE) provides an essential public dataset containing neuroimaging data from ASD individuals and controls, aiding the development and validation of new classification models [13,14]. Recently, the fusion of temporal and spatial features for MRI-based ASD classification has emerged due to its enriched representation of brain patterns [15,16]. For instance, Meng et al. [17] proposed a multi-kernel SVM that integrates these features, showing improved performance. Chen et al. [18] combined features using a deep belief network, and Zhang et al. [19] introduced a spatiotemporal convolutional network. However, there's still a need to better understand the fusion techniques and ensure model consistency across diverse datasets. In this regard, a comprehensive review by Rahman et al. [20] provides insights into machine learning methods of feature selection and classification for autism spectrum disorder, emphasizing the importance of feature engineering in achieving robust model performance.

3 Methodology

3.1 The Overview of Our Method

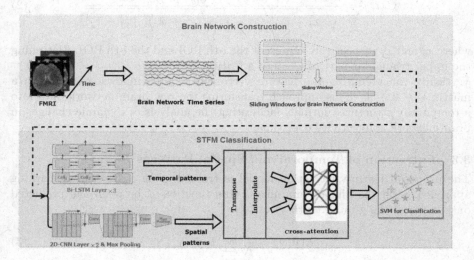

Fig. 1. Framework Overview of the Spatial Temporal Fusion Model (STFM)

The STFM is divided into four main components: brain network construction, pattern extraction, pattern fusion and classification. Initially, we employ a sliding window approach to construct the brain network and compute the Pearson correlation between brain regions. Subsequently, we use Bi-LSTM and 2DCNN independently to extract the temporal and spatial patterns of the brain network, and employ cross attention to merge these two types of patterns. Ultimately, we classify the fused features using Support Vector Machine (SVM). The overview of the model is illustrated in Fig. 1.

3.2   Brain Network Construction

First, we employ fMRI imaging to model brain networks, where fMRI can be abstracted as a time series. Next, a sliding window model is employed to process raw brain network data and incorporate temporal aspects [21,22]. The methodology involves: Defining a sliding window of width w and step size s. Segmenting the data into overlapping windows, with a total number of windows calculated as

$$N = \left\lfloor \frac{T-w}{s} \right\rfloor + 1 \tag{1}$$

where T represents the total length (or duration) of the data, w represents the width of the sliding window, and s represents the step size by which the window is moved in each step. Calculating the Pearson correlation coefficient between each pair of regions of interest (ROI) within each window, resulting in a symmetric correlation matrix C, in which the Pearson correlation coefficient C_{ij} between the ROIs i and j is:

$$C(i,j) = \frac{(x_i - \bar{x}_i)^T (x_j - \bar{x}_j)}{\sqrt{(x_i - \bar{x}_i)^T (x_i - \bar{x}_i)} \sqrt{(x_j - \bar{x}_j)^T (x_j - \bar{x}_j)}} \tag{2}$$

where x_i and x_j respectively represent the i-th ROI and the j-th ROI. Flattening the upper triangular part of C_{ij} into a feature vector v_k.

Vertically concatenating the feature vectors from all windows, resulting in a matrix $V \in \mathbb{R}^{N \times M}$. This approach transforms the raw brain network data into a temporally structured format, facilitating the analysis of dynamic changes in brain network connectivity over time.

3.3   Extraction of Temporal and Spatial Patterns

The proposed feature extraction model is trained using a supervised learning approach, with the aim to minimize a loss function $\mathcal{L}$ between the predicted output $\hat{\mathbf{y}}$ and the ground truth $\mathbf{y}$:

$$\mathcal{L}(\hat{\mathbf{y}}, \mathbf{y}) = \frac{1}{N} \sum_{i=1}^{N} L(\hat{\mathbf{y}}_i, \mathbf{y}_i) \tag{3}$$

where N is the number of samples, and L denotes a suitable loss function, such as the mean squared error for regression tasks or cross-entropy loss for classification tasks.

Temporal Patterns. We present our methodology for extracting temporal patterns from time series data using a bidirectional Long Short-Term Memory (Bi-LSTM) model. The architecture of an LSTM-based neural network allows for efficient learning of long-range dependencies in sequential data, making it suitable for time series analysis tasks [23].

Given a time series $\mathbf{X} = x_1, x_2, \ldots, x_T$, where $x_t \in \mathbb{R}^d$ represents the feature vector at time step t and T denotes the length of the series, our goal is to capture the temporal patterns and dependencies within the data. We employ a Bi-LSTM model, consisting of two separate LSTM layers, one for processing the input sequence in a forward direction and the other for processing it in a backward direction. The forward LSTM layer computes the hidden state $\mathbf{h}_t^f$ for each time step t as follows:

$$\mathbf{h}_t^f = \mathrm{LSTM}^f(\mathbf{x}_t, \mathbf{h}_{t-1}^f) \tag{4}$$

where LSTM^f denotes the forward LSTM function. Similarly, the backward LSTM layer computes the hidden state $\mathbf{h}_t^b$:

$$\mathbf{h}_t^b = \mathrm{LSTM}^b(\mathbf{x}_t, \mathbf{h}_{t+1}^b) \tag{5}$$

The bidirectional output at time step t is obtained by concatenating the forward and backward hidden states:
$$\mathbf{h}_t = [\mathbf{h}_t^f; \mathbf{h}_t^b] \tag{6}$$

where $[\cdot; \cdot]$ denotes concatenation. The resulting sequence of bidirectional outputs $\mathbf{H} = \mathbf{h}_1, \mathbf{h}_2, \ldots, \mathbf{h}_T$ captures the temporal patterns in both forward and backward directions.

The Bi-LSTM model has been widely used for various sequence-to-sequence learning tasks and has demonstrated its effectiveness in capturing complex temporal patterns [24,25]. In our work, we leverage this powerful architecture to extract meaningful temporal features from time series data for further analysis and interpretation.

Spatial Patterns. We present the methodology employed for the extraction of spatial patterns from brain networks using a 2D Convolutional Neural Network (2DCNN). The architecture of the proposed 2DCNN model is designed to effectively capture the spatial features within the brain network data [26].

Given a brain network represented by a matrix $\mathbf{X} \in \mathbb{R}^{m \times n}$, where m and n denote the number of nodes and features, respectively, the 2DCNN model learns to extract spatial patterns by applying a series of convolutional, activation, and pooling layers. The convolution operation is defined as follows:

$$\mathbf{Y} = f(\mathbf{X} * \mathbf{W} + b) \tag{7}$$

where $\mathbf{Y}$ is the output feature map, f represents the activation function (ReLU), $\mathbf{W} \in \mathbb{R}^{k \times k}$ is the convolutional kernel with size $k \times k$, b is the bias term, and $*$ denotes the convolution operation. The kernel slides over the input matrix $\mathbf{X}$, computing element-wise products followed by a summation, which results in a scalar value at each position of the output feature map $\mathbf{Y}$.

The extracted feature maps are then passed through a pooling layer, which aims to reduce the spatial dimensions and capture the most prominent features. Two common pooling methods are max pooling and average pooling. In this study, we employ max pooling, defined as:

$$\mathbf{Z}_{i,j} = \max{(p,q)} \in \mathbf{P}_{i,j}\mathbf{Y}_{p,q} \tag{8}$$

where $\mathbf{Z}$ is the pooled feature map, $\mathbf{P}_{i,j}$ represents the pooling window with size $r \times r$ centered at location (i,j), and $\mathbf{Y}_{p,q}$ is the element of the feature map $\mathbf{Y}$ at position (p,q). The effectiveness of 2DCNNs in extracting spatial features from brain networks has been demonstrated in various studies, such as BrainNetCNN and the identification of autism spectrum disorder using deep learning [27]. In this work, we follow a similar methodology and adapt the architecture of our 2DCNN model based on the specific characteristics of the brain network data under investigation.

3.4   Fusion of Patterns

Dimension Adjustment. To effectively process the extracted neural network data, it is necessary to increase the dimension of the feature representation from 16 dimensions to 512 dimensions. This dimension increase can enhance the expressiveness and granularity of the feature representation, thereby enabling the model to capture more complex and subtle patterns in the data. To achieve this goal, we employ a bilinear interpolation technique, which is a widely used method for increasing the resolution of images and other data structures in computer vision and related fields.

Cross Attention. We introduce the basic cross attention model for fusing temporal and spatial features extracted from brain networks. The cross attention is a powerful mechanism that calculates the attention scores between two input sequences and uses these scores to weigh the importance of features from one input sequence when processing the other sequence. It is widely applied in many fields like Visual question answering (VQA) [28]. Given two input sequences, $X \in \mathbb{R}^{B \times L_1 \times H}$ and $Y \in \mathbb{R}^{B \times L_2 \times H}$, where B denotes the batch size, L_1 and L_2 represent the sequence lengths, and H is the hidden size, the Cross Attention model computes the attention probabilities and the output as follows:

$$A = softmax\left(\frac{X \times Y^T}{\sqrt{H}}\right), \quad O = A \times Y \tag{9}$$

Here, A denotes the attention probabilities, and O represents the output of the cross attention model. This model enables the efficient fusion of temporal and spatial patterns extracted from brain networks, which can be applied in various brain decoding and analysis tasks. Specifically, our choice of cross attention for this fusion process, ensures a parameter-free and lightweight approach, differentiating our methodology from typical MLP-based solutions.

3.5   Classifier

The Support Vector Machine (SVM) classifier [29] is used for feature classification. Given labeled training data $(\mathbf{x}i, y_i)i = 1^N$, it finds a hyperplane that separates two classes maximally. The optimization problem is:

$$\underset{\mathbf{w},b,\xi}{\text{minimize}} \quad \frac{1}{2}|\mathbf{w}|^2 + C\sum_{i=1}^{N}\xi_i \qquad (10)$$

subject to

$$y_i(\mathbf{w}^\top\mathbf{x}_i + b) \ \geq 1 - \xi_i, i = 1,\ldots,N \quad \xi_i \geq 0, \quad i = 1,\ldots,N \qquad (11)$$

Here, $\mathbf{w}$ is the weight vector, b is the bias term, ξ_i are slack variables, and $C > 0$ is a regularization parameter [30]. For non-linearly separable data, we use the RBF kernel with the kernel function $K(\mathbf{x}_i, \mathbf{x}_j)$ as:

$$K(\mathbf{x}_i, \mathbf{x}_j) = \exp\left(-\gamma\|\mathbf{x}_i - \mathbf{x}_j\|^2\right) \qquad (12)$$

Here, $\gamma > 0$ is a parameter that impacts the shape of the decision boundary. Optimal C and γ are typically found using cross-validation techniques, which is a standard practice in machine learning to ensure optimal model performance.

4   Experiments

Dataset. In the process of processing data using a sliding window, we choose a window size of 30 and a window moving step size of 1, preserving the first 100 windows [31]. We discard samples with fewer than 100 windows, leaving a total of 706 samples. Detailed information is summarized in the Table 1.

Table 1. Summary of ABIDE Dataset for Research

	Age(average)	Gender(Male/Female)
Autism	19.62	270/151
Health	18.30	160/125

The raw fMRI data is preprocessed by the standard CPAC pipeline, and the AAL brain atlas is employed to automatically divide the whole brain onto 116 ROIs. Pearson correlation is calculated between every two ROIs. The symmetric matrix is then expanded into the upper triangle, resulting in a dimension of

$$\text{Dim} = \frac{N * (N-1)}{2} \qquad (13)$$

Here, 'Dim' refers to the dimension of the constructed brain network. As such, the final dataset size comes out to be $(706, 100, 6670)$, representing the (number of samples, number of windows, Dim), respectively. In our research utilizing the ABIDE dataset, we have thoroughly examined the distribution of cases, and we can affirmatively state that the dataset presents a balanced representation of both autism and control cases, thereby mitigating concerns related to imbalanced data-driven biases in our evaluation metrics.

Result and Analysis. To provide a more intuitive representation of the model's performance and stability, we construct a confusion matrix and performed 5-fold cross-validation. We measure model performance using the following metrics: True Positives (TP), True Negatives (TN), False Positives (FP), and False Negatives (FN). They represent correctly identified positives, correctly identified negatives, incorrectly identified positives, and incorrectly identified negatives, respectively. The key performance metrics are Accuracy, Sensitivity, and Specificity, computed as:

$$\text{Accuracy} = \frac{TP + TN}{TP + TN + FP + FN} \tag{14}$$

$$\text{Sensitivity} = \frac{TP}{TP + FN} \tag{15}$$

$$\text{Specificity} = \frac{TN}{TN + FP} \tag{16}$$

The results indicate that our model is slightly lacking in stability, which is an area that needs improvement in our future work. The confusion matrix and Receiver Operating Characteristic (ROC) Curves are as shown in Fig. 2.

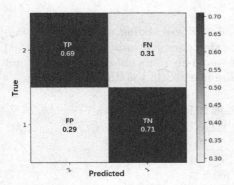 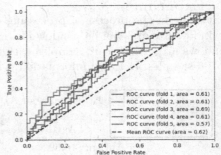

(a) Matrix of Classification Outcomes: A Detailed Confusion Matrix Illustrating True Positive, False Positive, True Negative, and False Negative Results

(b) The ROC curve illustrates the relationship between the sensitivity and specificity of a model. The X-axis represents 'False Positive Rate' and the Y-axis represents 'True Positive Rate'.

Fig. 2. Visualization of Model Evaluation: Confusion Matrix and Receiver Operating Characteristic (ROC) Curves

In order to verify the effectiveness of our model in the classification task on this dataset, we compare it with several classical supervised classification models in machine learning, including LDA (Linear Discriminant Analysis), KNN (K-Nearest Neighbors), SVC (Support Vector Classifier), Decision Tree, and Logistic Regression. In addition, we also include some deep learning models with larger parameter sizes, such as LSTM (Long Short-Term Memory), DNN (Deep Neural

Network), CNN (Convolutional Neural Network), and AutoEncoder. For the sake of fairness and reliability, the parameters for the comparison methods including LDA, KNN, Decision Tree and Logistic Regression, are optimized experimentally. Results for SVC, DNN, LSTM, CNN, and AutoEncoder models are taken directly from existing literature (references 33 to 37 in Table 2). Specifically, the ML models referenced in the table were trained directly on the data without any prior feature extraction using the STFM pipeline. The comparison of classification performance of STFM with other models is summarized in Table 2.

Table 2. The comparison of classification performance of STFM with other models

References	Methods	Performance		
		Accuracy	Sensitivity	Specificity
–	LDA	63.38	65.06	61.02
–	KNN	53.52	71.08	28.81
[32]	SVC	66.8	61.00	72.30
[33]	DNN	70.00	74.00	63.00
[34]	LSTM	66.80	–	–
[35]	CNN	70.20	77.00	61.00
[36]	AutoEncoder	67.50	68.30	72.20
–	Decision Tree	45.07	48.19	40.68
–	Logistic Regression	65.49	68.67	61.02
Our Method	**STFM**	**70.42**	**71.08**	**69.49**

In reviewing the classification performance comparison summarized in Table 2, it is evident that the proposed STFM outperforms the other models on multiple metrics. When considering accuracy, the metric most intuitively associated with model performance, STFM achieves a score of 70.42%. This represents an obvious improvement over the next best model, the CNN, which achieves an accuracy of 70.20%. Moreover, STFM notably demonstrates more balanced performance in terms of sensitivity and specificity, achieving 71.08% and 69.49% respectively. This surpasses the CNN, which, while having a higher sensitivity of 77.00%, lagging behind in specificity, scoring only 61.00%. The balance between sensitivity and specificity is vital, as it signifies the model's capacity to accurately identify both positive and negative classes. Among other models, the LDA, SVC, and DNN also display notable performance. However, none achieves the balanced efficacy of the STFM across all performance metrics. **Ablation Experiments.** During the temporal patterns extraction process, we set the hidden_size to 4096 and the number of LSTM layers to 3 in the Bi-LSTM model. For spatial patterns extraction, the parameters of our 2DCNN are kernel_size = (25, 25) and pool_kernel_size = (5, 5). The learning rate is set to 0.0001 for both processes. Our strategy involves using the dataset's provided labels for supervised learning to optimize the model parameters. After the training process, both feature extraction models have converged in terms of loss, and there has been a notable improvement in their classification accuracy, which are illustrated in Fig. 3. The results show that the classification accuracy of both types of patterns is higher than that of the original data. The classification accuracy for the temporal patterns is 69.72%, while the spatial patterns achieve a classification accuracy of 68.31%, both presenting an improvement compared to the original data (67.61%). The spatial temporal patterns integration introduced in STMF surpasses the classification performance when only temporal or spatial patterns are present, demonstrating the effectiveness of our proposed pattern fusion mechanism. The results are presented in Table 3.

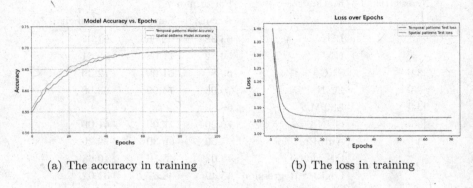

(a) The accuracy in training   (b) The loss in training

Fig. 3. The accuracy and loss in training

Table 3. Result of Ablation Experiment

Methods	Performance		
	Accuracy	Sensitivity	Specificity
Original Data	67.61	66.06	67.02
Temporal Patterns	69.72	79.52	55.93
Spatial Patterns	68.31	77.11	55.93
STFM	70.42	71.08	69.49

5   Conclusion and Future Work

This paper presents the STFM as an autism detection model, drawing on the concept of ensemble learning. We separately extract temporal and spatial patterns of brain networks and employ cross attention to integrate these patterns into a more complex classification model, effectively detecting autism. Experimentally, we compare our model with studies using basic machine learning classification models, and our model achieves the highest classification accuracy. In future research, we will focus on modifying the classifier component, attempting to use more sophisticated classification models to improve classification accuracy and fully exploit the hidden information in the patterns extracted by the STFM. Furthermore, as we progress in refining and implementing AI-based models like STFM, it's crucial to address ethical considerations, ensuring that patient data is protected and the application respects privacy and non-discrimination standards.

Acknowledgement. This work is supported in part by the R&D Program of Beijing Municipal Education Commission KM202310005026.

References

1. American Psychiatric Association: Diagnostic and Statistical Manual of Mental Disorders (DSM-5). Washington, DC (2013)
2. Centers for disease control and prevention: Data & statistics on autism spectrum disorder (2020). https://www.cdc.gov/ncbddd/autism/data.html. Accessed 1 May 2023
3. Ozonoff, S., et al.: A prospective study of the emergence of early behavioral signs of autism. J. Am. Acad. Child Adolesc. Psychiatry **49**(3), 256–266 (2010)
4. Amaral, M.E.A., et al.: The structural neuroimaging of autism spectrum disorder: a systematic review and meta-analysis. Front. Psychiatry **11**, 565164 (2020)
5. Deshpande, G., Libero, L.E., Sreenivasan, K.R., Deshpande, H.D., Kana, R.K.: Identification of neural connectivity signatures of autism using machine learning. Front. Hum. Neurosci. **7**, 670 (2013)
6. Bone, D., Bishop, S.L., Black, M.P., Goodwin, M.S., Lord, C., Narayanan, S.S.: Use of machine learning to improve autism screening and diagnostic instruments: effectiveness, efficiency, and multi-instrument fusion. J. Child Psychol. Psychiatry **57**(8), 927–937 (2016)
7. LeCun, Y., et al.: Deep learning. Nature **521**, 436–444 (2015)
8. Chen, C.K.J., et al.: A support vector machine classifier for the prediction of autism spectrum disorder based on structural magnetic resonance imaging. In: 2016 IEEE International Conference on Bioinformatics and Biomedicine (BIBM), pp. 934–937 (2016)
9. Jiao, X., et al.: Prediction of autism spectrum disorder based on eigen-connectivity patterns in functional magnetic resonance imaging. In: 2016 IEEE International Conference on Bioinformatics and Biomedicine (BIBM), pp. 917–921 (2016)
10. Li, Y., et al.: A machine learning approach to autism spectrum disorder detection based on structural magnetic resonance imaging. In: 2016 IEEE International Conference on Bioinformatics and Biomedicine (BIBM), pp. 922–927 (2016)
11. Mahbub, B.S., et al.: Deep learning-based identification of autism spectrum disorder using neuroimaging data. In: 2018 IEEE International Conference on Bioinformatics and Biomedicine (BIBM), pp. 1614–1618 (2018)
12. Supekar, Y., et al.: Combining MRI data and deep learning to predict autism spectrum disorder: a preliminary study. In: 2019 IEEE International Conference on Bioinformatics and Biomedicine (BIBM), pp. 1144–1148 (2019)

13. Di Martino, A.M., et al.: The autism brain imaging data exchange: towards a large-scale evaluation of the intrinsic brain architecture in autism. Mol. Psychiatry **19**(6), 659–667 (2014)
14. Craddock, C., et al.: The neuro bureau preprocessing initiative: open sharing of preprocessed neuroimaging data and derivatives. In Neuroinformatics. Stockholm, Sweden (2013)
15. Gliga, A.G., et al.: A review of MRI-based autism spectrum disorder classification using machine learning techniques. In: 2020 IEEE International Conference on Bioinformatics and Biomedicine (BIBM), pp. 1437–1441 (2020)
16. Subbaraju, N., et al.: Deep learning approaches for autism spectrum disorder detection: a review of advances using neuroimaging data. In: 2021 IEEE International Conference on Bioinformatics and Biomedicine (BIBM), pp. 1783–1787 (2021)
17. Meng, C., et al.: Multi-kernel SVM based classification using temporal and spatial features in fMRI data for autism detection. In: 2019 IEEE International Conference on Bioinformatics and Biomedicine (BIBM), pp. 1020–1023 (2019)
18. Chen, W., et al.: A multimodal deep belief network for ASD classification using temporal and spatial features from fMRI data. J. Neural Eng. **17**(5), 056020 (2020)
19. Zhang, Y., et al.: Spatiotemporal Convolutional Neural Networks for ASD classification using fMRI data. Neurocomputing **329**, 103–111 (2019)
20. Rahman, M.M., Usman, O.L., Muniyandi, R.C., et al.: A review of machine learning methods of feature selection and classification for autism spectrum disorder. Brain Sci. **10**(12), 949 (2020)
21. Ozonoff, S., et al.: A prospective study of the emergence of early behavioral signs of autism. J. Am. Acad. Child Adolesc. Psychiatry **49**(3), 256–266 (2010)
22. Preti, M.G., Bolton, T.A., Van De Ville, D.: The dynamic functional connectome: state-of-the-art and perspectives. Neuroimage **160**, 41–54 (2017)
23. Hochreiter, S., Schmidhuber, J.: Long short-term memory. Neural Comput. **9**(8), 1735–1780 (1997)
24. Schuster, M., Paliwal, K.K.: Bidirectional recurrent neural networks. IEEE Trans. Signal Process. **45**(11), 2673–2681 (1997)
25. Graves, A., Mohamed, A. R., Hinton, G.: Speech recognition with deep recurrent neural networks. In 2013 IEEE International Conference on Acoustics, Speech and Signal Processing, pp. 6645–6649. IEEE (2013)
26. Kawahara, J., et al.: BrainNetCNN: convolutional neural networks for brain networks; towards predicting neurodevelopment. Neuroimage **146**, 1038–1049 (2017)
27. Heinsfeld, A.S., Franco, A.R., Craddock, R.C., Buchweitz, A., Meneguzzi, F.: Identification of autism spectrum disorder using deep learning and the ABIDE dataset. NeuroImage Clin. **17**, 16–23 (2018)
28. Han, D., et al.: Cross-modality co-attention networks for visual question answering. Soft Comput. **25**, 5411–5421 (2021). https://doi.org/10.1007/s00500-020-05539-7
29. Cortes, C., Vapnik, V.: Support-vector networks. Mach. Learn. **20**(3), 273–297 (1995)
30. Vapnik, V.N.: The Nature of Statistical Learning Theory. Springer (2013)
31. Hutchison, R.M., Womelsdorf, T., Allen, E.A., et al.: Dynamic functional connectivity: promise, issues, and interpretations. Neuroimage **80**, 360–378 (2013)
32. Li, X., Dvornek, N.C., Zhou, Y., Zhuang, J., Ventola, P., Duncan, J.S.: Graph neural network for interpreting task-fMRI biomarkers. In: Shen, D., et al. (eds.) MICCAI 2019. LNCS, vol. 11768, pp. 485–493. Springer, Cham (2019). https://doi.org/10.1007/978-3-030-32254-0_54

33. Heinsfeld, A.S., Franco, A.R., Craddock, R.C., Buchweitz, A., Meneguzzi, F.: Identification of autism spectrum disorder using deep learning and the abide dataset. NeuroImage Clin. **17**, 16–23 (2018)

34. Dvornek, N.C., Ventola, P., Pelphrey, K.A., Duncan, J.S.: Identifying autism from resting-state fMRI using long short-term memory networks. In: Wang, Q., Shi, Y., Suk, H.-I., Suzuki, K. (eds.) MLMI 2017. LNCS, vol. 10541, pp. 362–370. Springer, Cham (2017). https://doi.org/10.1007/978-3-319-67389-9_42

35. Sherkatghanad, Z., et al.: Automated detection of autism spectrum disorder using a convolutional neural network. Front. Neurosci. **13**, 1325 (2020)

36. Eslami, T., Mirjalili, V., Fong, A., Laird, A.R., Saeed, F.: ASD-DiagNet: a hybrid learning approach for detection of autism spectrum disorder using fMRI data. Front. Neuroinform. **13**, 70 (2019)

Unified Counterfactual Explanation Framework for Black-Box Models

Jiemin Ji, Donghai Guan$^{(\boxtimes)}$, Weiwei Yuan, and Yuwen Deng

College of Computer Science and Technology, Nanjing University of Aeronautics and Astronaut, Nanjing, China
{archer_jjm,dhguan,yuanweiwei,dengyuwen}@nuaa.edu.cn

Abstract. Despite large-scale deployment in industry and daily life scenarios, the black-box nature of Connectionism-based deep neural networks is still criticized. Counterfactual explanation can shed light on the inner mechanism of arbitrary deep-learning model, thus being a preferable local interpretation method. There are a variety of methods for counterfactual generation, however, exist two defects: (1) Disunity. There is no agreement on model architecture and optimization methods of counterfactual generation. (2) Neglect of desiderata. There exist several desiderata for a good counterfactual sample, but most existing works only include a few of them. To address the above problem, we propose UNICE, a unified framework for counterfactual generations. UNICE models the counterfactual generation as a multi-task optimization problem on a dense data manifold learn by auto-encoder. Besides, UNICE addresses counterfactual desiderata to the best of our knowledge. What's more, one can custom UNICE components regarding specific tasks and data modalities. An UNICE implementation for tabular data is provided and surpasses state-of-the-art methods in five of six metrics, indicating the effectiveness of our proposed method.

Keywords: Interpretable AI · Counterfactual explanation · Multi-task optimization

1 Introduction

Algorithms based on deep neural network have achieved remarkable performance in various data modalities. However, concerns about trustworthy AI grow with its black-box nature. By European Union's General Data Protection Regulations (GDPR), not only personal privacy and data shall be protected, but also algorithms are required to be transparent and interpretable when applied in critical domains like finance [6], medicine [3], and autonomous-driving, etc [8]. Existing interpretations methods can be categorized by two criteria: ad-hoc vs post-hoc interpretation, in terms of interpretation time; global vs local interpretation, in terms of interpretation scope [4,19,21–23]. In this paper, we instead focus on Counterfactual Explanation [15] which is a post-hoc local interpretation method

F. Liu et al. (Eds.): PRICAI 2023, LNAI 14327, pp. 422–433, 2024.
https://doi.org/10.1007/978-981-99-7025-4_36

answers the equivalent "Why not" question in counterfactual conditional sentences. For example, Yonna's loan application was rejected by a dense-connected deep nerual network algorithm. An useful counterfactual explanation would generate a counterfactual individual with higher income or better credit records, whose application was approved. By comparing Anna and the counterfactual guy, The final explanation should be like "Have Yonna had a higher income up to 10000\$ per month, her loan would have been approved".

Existing counterfactual explanation methods vary a lot as an emerging research field of XAI. To give readers a brief understand about origin and recent trends in this field, We first review some representative literature as well as addressing common panic points.

Counterfactual, a concept originated from policy evaluation in economics [2], attempts to mimic parallel worlds where politicians make opposite policies and get different results. Casual Effect of a policy can be measured by compare results in parallel worlds with that in the real world. Inspired by the Comparison, the first Counterfactual explanation research [11] was proposed in 2017. However, counterfactual get a little different in AI explanation. Given a Dataset X, y, a data sample $x \in X$ and a black-box model f_{black}. A data sample x_{cf} is defined as **Counterfactual** when its corresponding decision made by f_{black} is different from that of the to-be-explained data sample x. Put it plainly, Counterfactual for XAI By comparison of Counterfactual data sample and the to-be-explained data sample, key features are identified to generate explanation, in that their changes result in different outcome of a local decision made by black-box models. Such an idea has been described in the above loan example.

In recent XAI research, it is consensus that counterfactual explanation is decided by a very important part, namely counterfactual sample generation in metric space. However, specific implementations of this key parts vary a lot.

Counterfactual Data Sample Generation: To generate feasible counterfactual data samples in metric space, one needs to first define a list of desired counterfactual properties as optimization goals, namely **Counterfactual Desiderata**. Afterwards, an optimization method is adopted to achieve these Desiderata. We find that a majority research [6, 7] in Counterfactual explanation recognized three Counterfactual Desiderata:

Validity is the minimum requirement of a feasible counterfactual. To enforce the generated sample x_{cf} to be counterfactual, researchers measure the distance between the predicted class $f(x_{cf})$ and the user-given class y_{cf}, where the cross-entropy loss is mostly used [5, 10, 18]

$$CEloss_{validity} = -y_{cf} \log \left(f\left(x_{cf} \right) \right) + (1 - y_{cf}) \log((1 - f\left(x_{cf} \right)) \tag{1}$$

Other work leverages hinge loss function to calculate distance [16].

Proximity is another basic principle for the counterfactual generation. Measurements for distance vary, such as L_1 norm, L_2 norm and cosine distance. For continuous tabular data, L_1 norm or L_2 norm is the most commonly used. To normalize features of different values, DiCE [16] add mean absolute deviation as the denominator, such that

$$Conloss_{proximity} = \frac{1}{m} \sum_{i=1}^{m} \frac{\left| x_{cf}^i - x^i \right|}{\mathrm{mad}_i} \tag{2}$$

where m is the number of continuous features, and x_{cf}^i, x^i, mad_i are the ith feature of the generated samples, the ith feature of the raw sample, and the mean absolute deviation of the ith feature respectively. When it comes to categorical feature, an indicator function is used to calculate the distance, such that:

$$Catloss_{proximity} = \frac{1}{n} \sum_{i=1}^{n} I\left(x_{cf}^i, x^i \right) \tag{3}$$

where $I(\cdot \mid \cdot) = 0$ if $x_{cf}^i = x^i$, and $I(\cdot \mid \cdot) = 1$ otherwise.

Sparsity means fewer features are changed in the generated counterfactual samples, thus readability of interpretation is guaranteed [14]. To ensure the sparsity of the generated sample, the most commonly used way is to add L_1 norm to perturbations in feature space [20], such that:

$$loss_{sparsity} = \|\epsilon\|_1 \tag{4}$$

There also exist some other ways like post-processing to filter out samples that do not meet the sparsity requirement [16]. Such neglect and chaos will prevent the XAI community from leveraging existing work and making more advances.

However, existing approaches usually address only one or a few of the above three properties, among which validity and proximity are the most reported. What's more, model architecture and optimization methods vary when confronted with different data modalities and interpretation task types. Such neglect and chaos will prevent the XAI community from leveraging existing work and making more advances.

To address this problem, we propose **UNICE**, a **U**nified **C**ounterfactual **E**xplanation framework to generate counterfactual samples and interpretations in natural language. By **unified**, our method (I) Summarizes the commonness of existing research. (II) addresses major desiderata of counterfactual generation to the best of our knowledge. By **framework**, components of our method can be customized according to different task types. Besides, our method is model-agnostic, which can be applied to arbitrary black-box decision models or classification models.

UNICE consists of three components, namely data representation learner, counterfactual generator, and explanation generator. Before conducting perturbation and optimization to solve the counterfactual generation problem, the data representation learner leverages an auto-encoder (AE) or its variants to get a low-dimension latent representation of raw data [18]. Afterward, the counterfactual generator conducts a search or optimization on learned data representation. Last, the explainer generator maps factual-counterfactual samples pair to natural language explanation and bridges the semantic gap. Each component of UNICE is decoupled and can be customized, and a formula description of UNICE in detail will be given in Sect. 3.

To conclude, the contributions of this paper are three-fold:

(1) We propose UNICE, a unified framework for the counterfactual explanation, which is comprehensive and can be customized. To the best of our knowledge, UNICE is the first unified framework that handles the intractable counterfactual explanation problem.

(2) We give UNICE implementation for tabular data, where desiderata of counterfactual generation to the best of our knowledge are addressed. However, we leave the counterfactual explanation generation part as future work and it is not claimed as our contribution.

(3) We conduct comparative experiments with multiple metrics on two air combat datasets and the effectiveness of UNICE is identified.

2   Method

2.1   UNICE Framework

Recall UNICE in the introduction, our framework consists of three components, namely data representation learner, counterfactual generator, and explanation generator. To better understand the mechanism and interaction between the above components, consider a supervised binary classification dataset $D = \{X \in \mathbb{R}^{n*m}, y \in \mathbb{R}^{n*1}\}$ with a classifier $f := X \to y$ and a UNICE framework (L, O, E), among which: (1) data representation learner L aims to map feature space to a data manifold in hidden space, such that:

$$Z = L(X), L := \mathbb{R}^{n*m} \to \mathbb{R}^{n*p} p \ll m, \tag{5}$$

where Z is the data manifold in hidden space. Such design aims to prepare a low-dimension space with data manifold proximity, which is beneficial to proximity desiderata as well as reduces the time complexity of downstream optimization. (2) Optimizer O models generation process as a multi-objective optimization problem in learned data manifold Z, where n desideratum is treated as n loss function respectively, such that:

$$X_{cf}^{opt} = \underset{Z_{cf} \in Z}{\operatorname{argmin}} L^{-1} \left\{ \text{loss}_1 \left(L^{-1} (Z_{cf}) \right), \text{loss}_2 \left(L^{-1} (Z_{cf}) \right), \ldots, \text{loss}_n \left(L^{-1} (Z_{cf}) \right) \right\} \tag{6}$$

where X_{cf}^{opt} is the optimal counterfactual sample of X, Z_{cf} is the latent representation of generated samples X_{cf}, and L^{-1} is the decoder mapping from latent space to feature space.

(3) Explainer generator E maps factual-counterfactual samples pair to natural language explanation and bridging the semantic gap between counterfactual sample and counterfactual generation, such that:

$$NL = E(x, x_{cf}) \ NL \in \varrho \tag{7}$$

where NL is the generated natural language explanation, ϱ is a human-readable interpretation domain. Please refer to Fig. 1 for a sketch of the proposed UNICE framework.

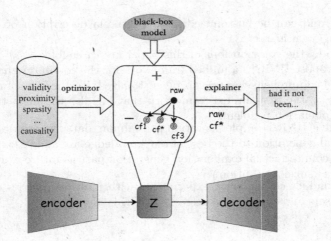

Fig. 1. A sketch of the UNICE framework. Z is the learned data manifold by auto-encoder; 'raw' is the given factual sample; cf_1, cf^* and cf_3 are representations of generated diverse counterfactuals, among which cf^* is the optimal one. Take the black-box model, the raw data point, and counterfactual desiderata as inputs, and multiple counterfactual representations are generated on the data manifold. Afterward, the optimal one cf^* is decoded to generate explanation text with comparison to the raw data point.

2.2 UNICE Implementation

The UNICE framework proposed above is conceptual and can be customized to arbitrary data modality. In this section, we give an implementation for tabular data.

Auto-Encoder for Tabular Data. One needs to handle various data types (continuous or categorical) and anomaly points when confronted with tabular data. We choose dfencoder [1], an auto-encoder variant for tabular data. The core idea of dfencoder is to separately train continuous features, category features, and binary features into three latent variables, and data points with large construction error are dropped to mitigate anomaly bias, such that

$$\operatorname*{argmin}_{L} \operatorname{dist}\left(L^{-1}\left(L\left(\{X_{\mathrm{con}}, X_{\mathrm{cat}}, X_{\mathrm{bin}}\}\right)\right), \{X_{\mathrm{con}}, X_{\mathrm{cat}}, X_{\mathrm{bin}}\}\right) \quad (8)$$

where L, L^{-1} are encoder and decoder respectively. We do not claim dfencoder as our contribution.

Desiderata as the Optimization Goal. Obviously that some frequently reported desiderata have mature design optimization goals, hence we follow the line and leverage some aspects of existing research. Specifically, we choose a part of our optimization goal as in Table 1.

Table 1. Optimization goals of validity, proximity, sparsity, and diversity. We use the existing goals directly due to less controversy.

Desiderata	Optimization goals
validity	$loss_{validity} = \sum_{i=1}^{n} -y_{cf}^i \log \left(f \left(L^{-1} \left(z_{cf}^i \right) \right) \right) + \left(1 - y_{cf}^i \right) \log \left(1 - f \left(L^{-1} \left(z_{cf}^i \right) \right) \right)$
proximity	$loss_{proximity} = \sum_{i=1}^{n} conloss_{proximity}^i + catloss_{proximity}^i$
sparsity	$loss_{sparsity} = \|\epsilon\|_1$
diversity	$loss_{diversity} = -\det(K), K_{ij} = \frac{1}{1+\text{dist}\left(x_{cf}^i, x_{cf}^j \right)}$

Where n is the number of generated counterfactual samples, L^{-1} as the decoder and z_{cf}^i as the latent representation of ith counterfactual. Please refer to Sect. 2.2 for detailed information on the above optimization goals. We disclaim the existing optimization goal as our contribution.

Our main concern is about the causal feasibility of counterfactual samples. Existing work, which sums up the difference between feature value itself and endogenous counterfactual feature value calculated by parent features, can impose causal constraints on the optimization process to some extent. However, we argue that simply summing up all differences is still far from enough. Violation of the causal constraint will accumulate in descendent nodes' value and should also be accounted for causality loss. We conduct a heavier penalization to take such accumulation into account. Let exogenous variables set in the ground truth SCM G as U, we calculate the causal feasible counterfactual as:

$$x_{cf}^{causal\_opt} = G \left(x_{cf}^1, x_{cf}^2, \ldots, x_{cf}^u, \epsilon \right) \tag{9}$$

where x_{cf}^i is the ith exogenous feature in x_{cf}, $G(\cdot)$ means calculating endogenous features in a breadth-first manner given desired SCM G and exogenous features. Last, we calculate the causality loss as L_2 norm between $x_{cf}^{causal\_opt}$ and x_{cf}, such that:

$$loss_{causality} = \left\| x_{cf}^{causal\_opt} - x_{cf} \right\|_2 \tag{10}$$

We also leverage a trick called counterfactual prototype [13] to guide the search process of the counterfactual sample. A counterfactual prototype is the representation of fact samples that have an opposite label to the given fact sample x. Such a representation could carry information about the decision boundary, hence guide the search process to a roughly right direction. Existing work show that a well-designed prototype can both speed up generation as well as improve fidelity [5,13], but they simply calculate the mean of k-nearest neighbors with an opposite label of given sample x. We follow this line and give a prototype implementation of more fidelity. Inspire by LIME's fidelity in neighborhood [19], we calculate a weighted prototype as:

$$proto = \frac{\sum_{i=1}^{k} z_{knn}^i * \exp \left(-\frac{D\left(z, z_{knn}^i \right)^2}{\sigma^2} \right)}{\sum_{i=1}^{k} \exp \left(-\frac{D\left(z, z_{knn}^i \right)^2}{\sigma^2} \right)} \tag{11}$$

where $\exp\left(-\frac{D\left(z, z_{knn}^i\right)^2}{\sigma^2}\right)$ is an exponential kernel defined on a certain distance with width σ, z, z_{knn}^i are the latent embedding of given sample x and its ith k-nearest neighbor embedding with an opposite label respectively. Our prototype loss is defined as:

$$loss_{proto} = \| \text{ proto } - Z_{cf}\|_2 \tag{12}$$

Finally, our optimal counterfactual is calculated by a multi-objective optimization:

$$x_{cf}^{opt} = argmin_{x_{cf}} \{loss_{validity}, loss_{proximity}, loss_{sparsity}, loss_{diversity}, loss_{causality}, loss_{proto}\} \tag{13}$$

We adopt NGSA-II, an improved version of the nondominated sorting genetic algorithm to solve the above optimization target.

3   Experiments

3.1   Experimental Settings

Datasets. We evaluate UNICE on two air combat datasets, DCS-AtoA and DCS-AtoG. Both datasets are collected from simulated scenarios of DCS-world, a digital battlefield game on the Steam platform. DCS-AtoA simulates an air-to-air dog fight scenario, with binary labels that (*0-no action, 1-ariel gun fire*), while DCS-AtoG simulates an air-to-ground attack scenario, with multiple labels that (*0-no action, 1-search, 2-aiming target, 3-attack, 4-disengage*). Both simulator scenarios are controlled by human pilots, and we take the labels as ground truth. Please see detailed feature information in Table 2 and, and causal constraints in Fig. 2.

Black-Box Models. We use a fully-connected neural network with five layers to build our air combat decision model on DCS-AtoA and DCS-AtoG. To guarantee our black-box models' performance, we conduct five-fold cross-validation and report an average AUC metric on two tasks, such that 0.93 for DCS-AtoA and 0.95 for DCS-AtoG. We believe such a performance can benefit downstream counterfactual generation and explanation.

Metrics. We compare different models on the following metrics:

Target-class validity is the percentage of counterfactual samples with opposite or user-defined labels. Target-class validity measures the basic standard that whether generated samples are counterfactual.

Proximity is the distance between generated counterfactual and raw sample. Since features in two datasets are all continuous, we implement a feature-wise L_2 distance normalized by mean absolute deviation.

Diversity averages the distance of every generated sample pair to measure how informative the generated counterfactuals are. When calculating one single distance, we reuse the distance definition in the proximity metric. Higher diversity is preferred.

Causal feasibility is the percentage of counterfactual samples conforming to causal constraints. Since there exists a precision error in floating-point numbers, we set an error tolerance $\delta = 0.1$ when measuring the distance between a causal feasible counterfactual and a generated counterfactual.

IM1 and IM2 are proposed by Van Looveren [13], among which IM1 is designed to measure the manifold closeness of generated counterfactuals, and IM2 is designed to measure the distance between generated counterfactuals and all factual instances.

$$IM1 = \frac{\|x_{cf} - AE_{cf}(x_{cf})\|_2^2}{\|x_{cf} - AE_{\text{ori}}(x_{cf})\|_2^2 + \epsilon} \quad IM2 = \frac{\|AE_{cf}(x_{cf}) - AE_{full}(x_{cf})\|_2^2}{\|x_{cf}\|_1 + \epsilon} \quad (14)$$

where AE_{cf} is the auto-encoder trained on counterfactual class (not counterfactual sample), AE_{ori} trained on origin class and AE_{full} trained on the full dataset (all classes). A lower IM1 means counterfactual can be better reconstructed by auto-encoder trained on the counterfactual class, thus close to the data manifold of counterfactual class. A lower IM2 means reconstructed counterfactual samples from AE_{cf} and AE_{full} are similar, thus counterfactual samples are avoided as outliers. Both lower IM1 and IM2 are preferred.

Baselines. Please see Table 2 for four baselines and their desiderata and optimization tricks.

Table 2. Desiderata and optimization tricks in four baselines and UNICE. Proto means whether a prototype is used to guide counterfactual generation, AE means whether the counterfactual generation is conducted in a data manifold learned by an auto-encoder. Only UNICE address all listed points.

Method	validity	proximity	diversity	sparsity	Causal feasibility	Proto	AE
DiCE [17]	✓	✓	✓	✓			
GRACE [12]	✓	✓	✓	✓			
MACE [9]	✓	✓	✓		✓		
ProCE [5]	✓	✓			✓	✓	
UNICE	✓	✓	✓	✓	✓	✓	✓

3.2 UNICE Performance

In this section, we first report the performance of four baselines and UNICE on DCS-AtoA and DCS-AtoG, then a thorough analysis is provided.

Comparison with Baselines. Performance measured by six metrics on two datasets is reported in Table 4 and Table 5. For the multi-classification task DCS-AtoG, we average performance on each class as the final result. The four baselines mainly differs in counterfactual desiderata they involves, which is detailed in Table 2. Among all six metrics, validity and Causal feasibility are expressed as a percentage, while others are in floating-point numbers. We add pre-defined causal constraints to MACE, ProCE, and UNICE. We do not compare sparsity because all our features are continuous and we find that none of them remain unchanged during optimization.

Table 3. Counterfactual generation performance of four baselines and UNICE on DCS-AtoA. Higher validity, diversity, and causal feasibility are preferred, while lower proximity, IM1, and IM2 are preferred.

Method	validity	proximity	diversity	causal feasibility	IM1	IM2
DiCE	100%	0.8524	6.7582	40.32%	0.6954	0.8082
GRACE	100%	0.8237	5.3252	38.95%	0.8299	0.9537
MACE	100%	0.9237	**7.5729**	66.85%	0.7237	0.7739
ProCE	100%	0.7850	N/A	65.40%	0.4362	0.6878
UNICE (ours)	**100%**	**0.6540**	6.5826	**78.50%**	**0.3667**	**0.5544**

Table 4. Counterfactual generation performance of four baselines and UNICE on DCS-AtoG. The setting are the same as those in Table 3.

Method	validity	proximity	diversity	causal feasibility	IM1	IM2
DiCE	100%	0.1893	**7.2819**	43.92%	0.5673	0.6529
GRACE	100%	0.1681	4.4733	45.28%	0.7032	0.8421
MACE	100%	0.2384	6.3812	82.96%	0.6742	0.6531
ProCE	100%	0.1536	N/A	85.32%	0.4441	0.7215
UNICE (ours)	**100%**	**0.1195**	6.1839	**94.30%**	**0.2879**	**0.5324**

Performance Analysis. As is shown in Table 4 and 5, we can find that:

(1) All models can provide 100% valid counterfactual samples. This is because the algorithm does not stop iterating until the counterfactual condition is satisfied.

(2) UNICE surpasses all other baselines in terms of proximity, causal feasibility, IM1, and IM2 metric, and achieves the second-highest performance when it comes to diversity.

(3) Taking a step further, the causal feasibility of UNICE outperforms ProCE and MACE which add causal constraints as well, by conducting a heavier penalization to unfeasible counterfactuals. Such a performance indicates the rationality of our design to consider error accumulation in a structured causal model.

(4) By IM1 and IM2 metrics, counterfactuals generated by UNICE are obviously more interpretable, or say, closer to the data manifold. A plausible explanation is because UNICE conducts optimization in data manifold representation learned by dfencoder. Besides, our prototype's guidance may also contribute to more realistic counterfactual samples. We will discuss what contributes to a more interpretable counterfactual later in Sect. 4.3.1.

3.3   Analysis and Discussion

Ablation Study. We use UNICE to conduct an ablation study where (1) optimization is conducted on raw feature space and (2) prototype loss is dropped from the optimization goal. Please see Table 6 for our UNICE's performance in two datasets:

Table 5. Ablation results on DCS-AtoA. 'Drop AE' means conduct optimization directly on raw feature space. 'Drop proto' means counterfactual generation is not guided by a prototype.

DataSet	Ablation operation	IM1	IM2
DCS-AtoA	drop AE	0.4231	0.6145
	drop proto	0.3701	0.5832
	None	0.3667	0.5709
DCS-AtoG	drop AE	0.3701	0.5866
	drop proto	0.3573	0.5392
	none	0.3542	0.5324

It is found that IM1 and IM2 on both datasets increase slightly when the optimization is not guided by a prototype. However, whether the optimization is performed on a dense data manifold representation has a greater influence on two metrics. Based on the above comparison, we strongly suggest adding a task-specific auto-encoder or its variant as an optimization device for the counterfactual generation.

Robustness Experiment. To validate the robustness of data representation, we study UNICE's performance under different embedding sizes of dfencoder. We report results on two datasets with embedding sizes of 32, 64, 128, 256, and 512 as in Fig. 2:

It is shown that IM2, proximity, and causal feasibility are stable on DCS-AtoA when embedding size varies from 32 to 512. Meanwhile, a larger embedding size causes a lower IM1, a plausible interpretation is that we need a latent space with a larger size to learn the overall pattern of tabular data. However, things are different when it comes to the AtoG dataset. We observe that all metrics are stable with different embedding sizes. Such a phenomenon might be related to the data distribution and remains to be explored.

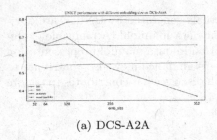
(a) DCS-A2A

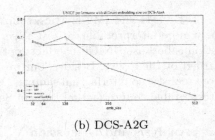
(b) DCS-A2G

Fig. 2. UNICE performance with different embedding sizes on (a) DCS-AtoA and (b) DCS-AtoG. Most of the metrics are stable with the change of embedding size.

4   Conclusion

We propose a conceptual framework, called UNICE, to address the disagreement and neglect in the counterfactual explanation domain. Consisting of a data representation learner, counterfactual generator, and explanation generator, UNICE addresses desiderata of a counterfactual sample and achieves competitive performance on two air fight datasets.

Currently, UNICE models the counterfactual generation as a multi-object optimization task, where optimizations are performed once for each sample. To speed up the generation process, we plan to integrate reinforcement learning into the counterfactual generator. Meanwhile, how to bridge the semantic gap remains an open question. We leave the above points for future work.

References

1. AlliedToasters: Dfencoder - autoencoders for dataframes (2022). https://github.com/AlliedToasters/dfencoder
2. Cartwright, N.: Counterfactuals in economics: a commentary (2003)
3. Chudik, A., Mohaddes, K., Pesaran, M.H., Raissi, M., Rebucci, A.: A counterfactual economic analysis of COVID-19 using a threshold augmented multi-country model. J. Int. Money Financ. **119**, 102477 (2021). https://doi.org/10.1016/j.jimonfin.2021.102477. https://www.sciencedirect.com/science/article/pii/S0261560621001285
4. Dubey, P.: On the uniqueness of the shapley value. Internat. J. Game Theory **4**(3), 131–139 (1975)
5. Duong, T.D., Li, Q., Xu, G.: Prototype-based counterfactual explanation for causal classification. arXiv preprint arXiv:2105.00703 (2021)
6. Grath, R.M., et al.: Interpretable credit application predictions with counterfactual explanations. ArXiv abs/1811.05245 (2018). https://api.semanticscholar.org/CorpusID:53293518
7. Guidotti, R., Monreale, A., Ruggieri, S., Pedreschi, D., Turini, F., Giannotti, F.: Local rule-based explanations of black box decision systems. ArXiv abs/1805.10820 (2018). https://api.semanticscholar.org/CorpusID:44063479

8. Hoofnagle, C.J., van der Sloot, B., Borgesius, F.Z.: The European union general data protection regulation: what it is and what it means. Inf. Commun. Technol. Law **28**(1), 65–98 (2019)
9. Karimi, A.H., Barthe, G., Balle, B., Valera, I.: Model-agnostic counterfactual explanations for consequential decisions. ArXiv abs/1905.11190 (2019). https://api.semanticscholar.org/CorpusID:166227893
10. Karimi, A.H., Barthe, G., Balle, B., Valera, I.: Model-agnostic counterfactual explanations for consequential decisions. In: International Conference on Artificial Intelligence and Statistics, pp. 895–905. PMLR (2020)
11. Laugel, T., Lesot, M.J., Marsala, C., Renard, X., Detyniecki, M.: Inverse classification for comparison-based interpretability in machine learning. arXiv preprint arXiv:1712.08443 (2017)
12. Le, T., Wang, S., Lee, D.: Grace: generating concise and informative contrastive sample to explain neural network model's prediction. In: Proceedings of the 26th ACM SIGKDD International Conference on Knowledge Discovery and Data Mining, KDD 2020, pp. 238–248. Association for Computing Machinery, New York (2020). https://doi.org/10.1145/3394486.3403066
13. Van Looveren, A., Klaise, J.: Interpretable counterfactual explanations guided by prototypes. In: Oliver, N., Pérez-Cruz, F., Kramer, S., Read, J., Lozano, J.A. (eds.) ECML PKDD 2021. LNCS (LNAI), vol. 12976, pp. 650–665. Springer, Cham (2021). https://doi.org/10.1007/978-3-030-86520-7_40
14. Miller, T.: Explanation in artificial intelligence: insights from the social sciences. Artif. Intell. **267**, 1–38 (2019)
15. Moraffah, R., Karami, M., Guo, R., Raglin, A., Liu, H.: Causal interpretability for machine learning-problems, methods and evaluation. ACM SIGKDD Explor. Newsl. **22**(1), 18–33 (2020)
16. Mothilal, R.K., Sharma, A., Tan, C.: Explaining machine learning classifiers through diverse counterfactual explanations. In: Proceedings of the 2020 Conference on Fairness, Accountability, and Transparency, pp. 607–617 (2020)
17. Mothilal, R.K., Sharma, A., Tan, C.: Explaining machine learning classifiers through diverse counterfactual explanations. In: Proceedings of the 2020 Conference on Fairness, Accountability, and Transparency, FAT* 2020, pp. 607–617. Association for Computing Machinery, New York (2020). https://doi.org/10.1145/3351095.3372850
18. Pawelczyk, M., Broelemann, K., Kasneci, G.: Learning model-agnostic counterfactual explanations for tabular data. In: Proceedings of the Web Conference 2020, pp. 3126–3132 (2020)
19. Ribeiro, M.T., Singh, S., Guestrin, C.: "Why should i trust you?" explaining the predictions of any classifier. In: Proceedings of the 22nd ACM SIGKDD International Conference on Knowledge Discovery and Data Mining, pp. 1135–1144 (2016)
20. Rodríguez, P., et al.: Beyond trivial counterfactual explanations with diverse valuable explanations. In: Proceedings of the IEEE/CVF International Conference on Computer Vision, pp. 1056–1065 (2021)
21. Rodríguez-Pérez, R., Bajorath, J.: Interpretation of machine learning models using shapley values: application to compound potency and multi-target activity predictions. J. Comput. Aided Mol. Des. **34**(10), 1013–1026 (2020)
22. Roth, A.E.: The Shapley Value: Essays in Honor of Lloyd S Shapley. Cambridge University Press, Cambridge (1988)
23. Winter, E.: The shapley value. Handbook Game Theory Econ. Appl. **3**, 2025–2054 (2002)

VIFST: Video Inpainting Localization Using Multi-view Spatial-Frequency Traces

Pengfei Pei[1,2], Xianfeng Zhao[1,2]([⊠]), Jinchuan Li[1,2], and Yun Cao[1,2]

[1] State Key Laboratory of Information Security, Institute of Information Engineering, Chinese Academy of Sciences, Beijing 100083, China
{peipengfei,lijinchuan,caoyun,laixuyuan,zhaoxianfeng}@iie.ac.cn
[2] School of Cyber Security, University of Chinese Academy of Sciences, Beijing 100083, China

Abstract. Video inpainting techniques based on deep learning have shown promise in removing unwanted objects from videos. However, their misuse can lead to harmful outcomes. While current methods excel in identifying known forgeries, they struggle when facing unfamiliar ones. Thus, it is crucial to design a video inpainting localization method that exhibits better generalization. The key hurdle lies in devising a network that can extract more generalized forgery features. A notable observation is that the forgery regions often exhibit disparities in forgery traces, such as boundaries, pixel distributions, and region characteristics, when contrasted with the original areas. These traces are prevalent in various inpainted videos, and harnessing them could bolster the detection's versatility. Based on these multi-view traces, we introduce a three-stage solution termed VIFST: 1) The Spatial and Frequency Branches capture diverse traces, including edges, pixels, and regions, from different viewpoints; 2) local feature learning via CNN-based MaxPoolFormer; and 3) global context feature learning through Transformer-based Interlaced-Former. By integrating local and global feature learning networks, VIFST enhances fine-grained pixel-level detection performance. Extensive experiments demonstrate the effectiveness of our method and its superior generalization performance compared to state-of-the-art approaches. The source code for our method has been published on GitHub: https://github.com/lajlksdf/UVL.

Keywords: Video inpainting localization · Spatial-frequency joint learning · Multi-view forgery traces · Generalization analysis

1 Introduction

Malicious video inpainting techniques have raised significant concerns due to their potential for misinformation and deception [4,13,20,22]. Existing video inpainting localization methods heavily reliant on specific data-related features encounter challenges when dealing with unknown forgery instances, leading to

F. Liu et al. (Eds.): PRICAI 2023, LNAI 14327, pp. 434–446, 2024.
https://doi.org/10.1007/978-981-99-7025-4_37

diminished performance in their detection. Similarly, prevailing video inpainting localization techniques tend to lack precise pixel-level outcomes in intricate sections of the manipulated areas, such as limbs or smaller components. Furthermore, the widespread utilization of social media platforms introduces challenges to the robustness of forgery detection, as various video processing operations like compression and cropping can disrupt the forgery traces present in videos [4]. Therefore, improving generalization performance and extracting forgery-independent features are crucial.

To address these challenges, we focus on identifying common characteristics among tampered videos. We observe that the pixel distribution of generated forgery regions using deep learning differs from natural distributions, and forgery regions inevitably leave traces on their boundaries. Moreover, the forgery and real regions in videos often have different sources, resulting in inconsistent region correlations [10]. Harnessing these generalized features is vital to bolster the method's overall robustness and generalization capabilities. We accomplish this by jointly learning multi-view forgery traces encompassing edges, pixels, and regions, as these features are prevalent in diverse object inpainting videos and transcend specific inpainting methods.

We introduce an innovative approach for localizing Video Inpainting Forgery using Spatial-Frequency Traces (VIFST). VIFST encompasses three key stages. In the first stage, we leverage the spatial branch, employing Sobel and Laplacian operators to extract boundary artifacts and the Spatial Rich Model (SRM) operator to capture pixel distribution features. Simultaneously, recognizing that frequency domain alterations can unveil characteristics that are hard to discern in the spatial domain, we utilize the frequency branch to capture region-level forgery cues [10]. In the second stage, as CNNs are effective in capturing local data patterns, we have developed a MaxPoolFormer that is grounded in CNNs and MaxPooling. This architecture aids in extracting local forgery features. In the third stage, recognizing that Vision Transformers (ViTs) excel in capturing sequential data patterns, we have employed the InterlacedFormer [18] to glean global features. The InterlacedFormer breaks down the dense affinity matrix into two sparse matrices: a short-range matrix and a long-range matrix. This sparse matrix structure, compared to the traditional self-attention approach, results in an almost $2\times$ acceleration in processing speed while maintaining effectiveness [18]. The ultimate outcome is the identification of pixel-level forgery regions.

The primary contributions of our work can be summarized as follows:

- We introduce an innovative multi-stage network that proficiently captures forgery traces in both spatial and frequency domains, thereby enhancing the effectiveness of our method in detecting unknown video forgeries.
- Leveraging CNN-based MaxPoolFormer and ViT-based InterlacedFormer, our model seamlessly integrates local and global features, significantly enhancing detection accuracy.
- Extensive experiments demonstrate that our approach outperforms state-of-the-art methods, exhibiting robustness and superior generalization.

2   Related Work

2.1   Object Inpainting Localization

Object inpainting has found wide applications in real-world scenarios, including object removal [6,16,20]. However, methods relying on 3D CNNs have shown limitations in video inpainting. To address this, recent approaches have incorporated optical flow into the inpainting networks [6], which helps alleviate temporal issues but can introduce temporal artifacts in the generated results. Corresponding to these detection methods, VIDNet [22] uses LSTM-based Error Level Analysis (ELA) and temporal structures to localize video inpainting. Wei et al. [13] utilize spatial and temporal traces, which encompass enhanced residuals and a dual-stream network with bidirectional convolutional LSTMs, to effectively localize inpainted regions. Zhang et al. [20] presents an efficient feature enhancement network for detecting inpainted regions in digital images. However, these methods often experience a substantial decline in performance when confronted with novel forgery techniques.

2.2   Vision Transformer

Currently, ViT-based networks are considered effective structures for feature extraction in sequential data, making them suitable for capturing temporal features in videos [2,3,18]. However, early versions of ViT require training on large-scale datasets and incur significant computational and memory costs. To address this, several approaches have been proposed. HRFormer [18] leverages the multi-resolution parallel design from high-resolution convolutional networks and performs local window self-attention on small non-overlapping image windows, enhancing memory and computational efficiency. PoolFormer [3] refines the self-attention-based ViT structure into a hybrid architecture combining CNN and ViT, resulting in significant reductions in computational costs. This hybrid architecture of CNN and ViT has gained considerable attention [2].

3   Method

Figure 1 presents an overview of the VIFST framework, while Algorithm 1 provides a detailed procedural outline. The VIFST method encompasses three distinct stages. In Stage 1, the spatial branch incorporates SRM, Laplacian, and Sobel operators, yielding outputs labeled 'a', 'b', and 'c', respectively. The frequency branch employs Discrete Cosine Transform (DCT) filters of varying sizes to capture region features. Notably, spatial features maintain the original frames. Additionally, the frequency branch generates outputs denoted as 'd', 'e', 'f', and 'g', corresponding to filters of full, high, middle, and low sizes, respectively. Moving into Stage 2, MaxPoolFormer blocks are harnessed to learn local features, building upon the spatial and frequency features from the previous stage. In Stage 3, InterlacedFormer blocks are employed to capture global contextual

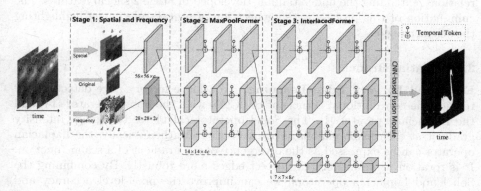

Fig. 1. Architecture of the proposed VIFST. It consists of three stages: Stage 1 extracts multi-view features from spatial and frequency branches. Stage 2 focuses on learning local features, and Stage 3 captures global context relations. The final output is a grayscale image indicating the detected forged regions.

Algorithm 1: Pseudocode for the detailed processing flow of VIFST.

Input : Video frame sequence *frames*
Output: Detected forged regions *detected_regions*

1 **Stage 1: Multi-view Features Extraction**

   // Spatial Branch: Extract edge and pixel features
2 *sobel_edges, laplacian_edges, srm_pixels* ← OperatorFilters(*frames*);
3 *spatial_56* ← CNN(*sobel_edges, laplacian_edges, srm_pixels, frames*);

   // Frequency Branch: Extract region features
4 *low* ← DCTFilter(0, *image_size*//16);
5 *middle* ← DCTFilter(*image_size*//16, *image_size*//8);
6 *high* ← DCTFilter(*image_size*//8, *image_size*);
7 *all* ← DCTFilter(0, *image_size* * 2);
8 *frequency_28* ← CNN(*low, middle, high, all*);

9 **Stage 2: Learning Local Features**

10 *local_s_56, local_f_28* ← MaxPoolFormer(*spatial_56, frequency_28*);
11 *local_sf_14* ← MaxPoolFormer(CNN(*spatial_56, frequency_28*));

12 **Stage 3: Learning Global Features**

13 *global_56, global_28, global_14* ←
    InterlacedFormer(*local_s_56, local_f_28, local_sf_14*);
14 *global_7* ← InterlacedFormer(CNN(*local_s_56, local_f_28, local_sf_14*));

15 *detected_regions* ← Fusion(*global_56, global_28, global_14, global_7*);

16 **return** *detected_regions*;

relations, extending the understanding developed in Stage 2's local features. The culmination of this process is the generation of a grayscale image highlighting the suspect regions.

3.1   Spatial Branch

Enhanced Forgery Edge Learning. To achieve forgery edge detection, we replace the convolutional kernels of the CNN with the Sobel operator [14] and the Laplacian operator [1]. The Sobel operator calculates the image intensity gradient at each pixel, enabling edge detection. Mathematically, the Laplacian operator can be expressed as the divergence of the gradient of a scalar function. It is rotation invariant and can detect edges more robustly. By combining the Sobel and Laplacian operators, we can improve the pixel-level accuracy and robustness of edge detection.

Pixel Non-natural Distribution Learning. Deep learning-based video inpainting methods often create forged regions with pixel distributions that deviate from natural patterns, thereby disrupting the original pixel distributions. To detect these forged traces, we substitute the traditional convolutional kernels of CNN with the SRM operator [12]. We compute SRM features based on neighboring pixel statistics. For a pixel block $X = (x_1, x_2, ..., x_n)$ of size n, the SRM feature $S(X)$ is represented by $S(X) = \frac{1}{n} \sum_{i=1}^{n} (x_i - \bar{x})^k$. Here, x_i represents individual pixel values in the block, $\bar{x}$ is the mean of the pixel values in the block, and k is a chosen positive exponent. This calculation helps in capturing the statistical characteristics of neighboring pixel values, which can then be used to analyze and characterize disrupted pixels.

Original RGB Information Learning. To preserve the details of the forgery while minimizing disruption to the original video information, we directly input frames into the spatial branch. The comprehensive spatial feature representation is denoted as $Y_{\text{spatial}} = \text{Concatenate}(Y_{\text{frames}}, Y_{\text{sobel}}, Y_{\text{laplacian}}, Y_{\text{SRM}})$, where Y_{frames}, Y_{sobel}, $Y_{\text{laplacian}}$, and Y_{SRM} represent the original video frames, Sobel features, Laplacian features, and SRM features, respectively.

3.2   Frequency Branch

The frequency branch implements DCT filters using CNN, as illustrated in Algorithm 1. The DCT filters are designed in four distinct scales, emphasizing details and capturing broader spatial information. Through frequency domain analysis, the method discerns compression artifacts, anomalies in specific frequency components, and manipulated effects. DCT partitions the image into various frequency-based blocks while preserving low-frequency components for later reconstruction. The inherent correlation features of DCT enable the identification of forgery traces that could be elusive in the spatial domain. This enhances the overall accuracy and sensitivity of forgery detection in manipulated videos.

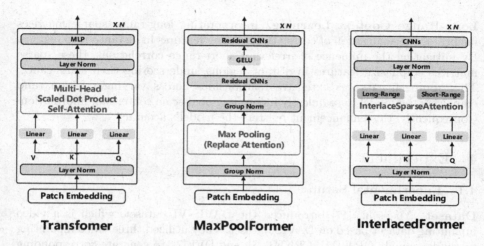

Fig. 2. This displays the structures of different Transformers. While the Transformer is based on the mutual computation of (Q, K, V) matrices, MaxPoolFormer relies on CNN and max-pooling operations, and InterlacedFormer decomposes the (Q, K, V) matrix into two identical short-range (Q, K, V) and long-range (Q, K, V) matrices.

3.3 Learning Local Features

As shown in Fig. 2, the MaxPoolFormer architecture is a CNN-based structure specifically designed for learning local forgery features. It incorporates a residual CNN to capture local image characteristics such as edges, textures, and shapes. By replacing the self-attention modules based on (Q, K, V) matrices with max pooling operations, MaxPoolFormer effectively extracts local regions of forgery while reducing computational complexity and memory usage. By leveraging the CNN's sensitivity to local features, the model progressively learns high-level features, resulting in enhanced pixel-level detection within regions.

3.4 Learning Global Contextual Correlation Features

Figure 2 illustrates the structure of InterlacedFormer [18]. The interleaved design of InterlacedFormer allows the model to learn short-range and long-range contextual features concurrently, resulting in the effective capture of essential information within the video.

Short-Range Context Learning. The short-range matrices capture intricate details at the pixel level within forgery regions, such as arms, legs, or wheels. This enables the model to prioritize pertinent features within a short distance while filtering out irrelevant ones. By focusing on short-distance features like edges and textures, the model optimizes forgery localization performance and improves the detection of fine-grained details.

Long-Range Context Learning. Incorporating long-range sparse matrices facilitates the acquisition of correlations among features in distant video regions. By mitigating the influence of irrelevant short-range correlations, these sparse matrices emphasize features in distant regions, underscoring their significance. This approach captures extensive relationships across varying positions and empowers the model to seamlessly integrate global-scale contextual information. Consequently, this enhancement bolsters the model's accuracy.

4   Experiment

4.1   Experimental Setup

Dataset. Yu et al. [17] introduced the DAVIS-VI dataset, which is a video inpainting dataset based on DAVIS dataset. They utilized three video inpainting methods, namely OPN [11], CPNET [8], and DVI [7], to generate corresponding tampered videos. In order to expand the dataset, we included three additional video inpainting methods: FGVC [5], DFGVI [15], and STTN [19]. The DAVIS-VI dataset consists of 50 original videos and 300 tampered videos, comprising a total of 33,550 frames. The training set comprises 200 tampered videos, while the test set contains 100 tampered videos.

Evaluation Metrics. We employ several evaluation metrics, including mean Intersection over Union (mIoU), Area Under the Curve (AUC), F1-score, and pixel-level Precision, to assess the performance of our method. These metrics quantitatively measure the method's performance in terms of its overlap with the ground truth, similarity to the ground truth, accuracy, completeness, and pixel-level precision. Higher values of mIoU, AUC, F1-score, and pixel-level Precision indicate superior performance of the method.

Baseline Methods. We selected several recent methods, namely NOI [22], CFA [22], CosNet [17], HPF [9], GSR-Net [21], VIDNet [22], and FAST [17], as baseline approaches. To ensure a fair comparison and due to the unavailability of publicly available pre-trained models, we directly cite the results reported in the corresponding papers for these methods.

Implementation Details We train the model using a single 24 GB GPU. Each video is treated as a 4-frame input sequence, and we use a batch size of 10 with a learning rate of 1e−4. In order to increase the diversity of the training data, we apply various commonly used data augmentation methods. The mean squared error (MSE) loss function and the Adaptive Moment Estimation (ADAM) optimization algorithm are utilized for model training.

Table 1. Comparison experiments on the DAVIS-VI dataset with recent approaches that test on one subset and train on the remaining subsets (*).

Methods	VI* mIoU/F1	OP* mIoU/F1	CPmIoU/F1	VImIoU/F1	OP* mIoU/F1	CP*mIoU/F1	VI* mIoU/F1	OP mIoU/F1	CP* mIoU/F1
NOI	0.08/0.14	0.09/0.14	0.07/0.13	0.08/0.14	0.09/0.14	0.07/0.13	0.08/0.14	0.09/0.14	0.07/0.13
CFA	0.10/0.14	0.08/0.14	0.08/0.12	0.10/0.14	0.08/0.14	0.08/0.12	0.10/0.14	0.08/0.14	0.08/0.12
COSNet	0.40/0.48	0.31/0.38	0.36/0.45	0.28/0.37	0.27/0.35	0.38/0.46	0.46/0.55	0.14/0.26	0.44/0.53
HPF	0.46/0.57	0.49/0.62	0.46/0.58	0.34/0.44	0.41/0.51	0.68/0.77	0.55/0.67	0.19/0.29	0.69/0.80
HPF+LSTM	0.50/0.61	0.39/0.51	0.52/0.63	0.26/0.36	0.38/0.44	0.68/0.78	0.53/0.64	0.20/0.30	0.70/0.81
GSR-Net	0.57/0.68	0.50/0.63	0.51/0.63	0.30/0.43	0.74/0.80	0.80/0.85	0.59/0.70	0.22/0.33	0.70/0.77
GSR-Net+LSTM	0.55/0.67	0.51/0.64	0.53/0.64	0.33/0.45	0.60/0.72	0.74/0.83	0.58/0.70	0.21/0.32	0.71/0.81
VIDNet	0.55/0.67	0.46/0.58	0.49/0.63	0.31/0.42	0.71/0.77	0.78/0.86	0.58/0.69	0.20/0.31	0.70/0.82
VIDNet-BN	0.62/0.73	0.75/0.83	0.67/0.78	0.30/0.42	**0.80/0.86**	**0.84/0.92**	0.58/0.70	0.23/0.32	0.75/0.85
VIDNet-IN	0.59/0.70	0.59/0.71	0.57/0.69	0.39/0.49	0.74/0.82	0.81/0.87	0.59/0.71	0.25/0.34	0.76/0.85
FAST	0.61/0.73	0.65/0.78	0.63/0.76	0.32/0.49	0.78/0.87	0.82/0.90	0.57/0.68	0.22/0.34	0.76/0.83
Ours	**0.73/0.84**	**0.81/0.89**	**0.72/0.82**	**0.75/0.85**	0.72/0.83	0.82/0.89	**0.85/0.91**	**0.79/0.87**	**0.84/0.90**

Table 2. Robustness testing on the DAVIS-VI dataset. The OP subset is used for testing, while the remaining five subsets (FGVC, STTN, DFGVI, CP, VI) are used for training.

Processing	mIoU	F1	AUC	Precision
None	0.8233	0.8964	0.9601	0.9854
Compression	0.8235	0.8966	0.9599	0.9854
Detail	0.8231	0.8963	0.9596	0.9853
Gaussian blur	0.7931	0.8760	0.9478	0.9825
Blur	0.8028	0.8827	0.9549	0.9835
Median filtering	0.8140	0.8904	0.9580	0.9845
Flip	0.7816	0.8695	0.9481	0.9814

4.2   Comparison Experiments

Table 1 showcases the pixel-level detection performance of various models. Notably, the VIDNet-BN method exhibits exceptional performance on both the OP and CP subsets, outperforming all other methods. This can be primarily attributed to the robust within-dataset learning capabilities of VIDNet-BN. In comparison to baseline methods, our approach consistently achieves superior performance in most cases and particularly excels in detecting unknown forgeries. This can be attributed to our method's proficiency in extracting more comprehensive synthetic tampering features, which enhances its generalization capability. Our experimental outcomes substantiate that our approach surpasses existing methods and showcases superior generalization capabilities.

4.3   Robustness Experiments

To evaluate the robustness of our method in real-world social media scenarios, we assess its performance under various video processing operations. Table 2 presents the performance after applying different video processing operations. In most cases, these operations have minimal impact on the evaluation metrics. Nevertheless, a slight performance degradation is observed when applying

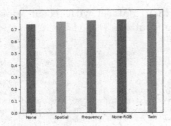
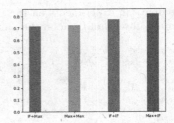

(a) Different branches.

(b) Different component combinations.

Fig. 3. Ablation studies with spatial-frequency branches and different component combinations. In the ablation experiments of the branches, 'Spatial', 'Frequency', and 'Twin' represent the results of the spatial branch, frequency branch, and twin branches, respectively. 'None' and 'None-RGB' indicate the results without any branch and without incorporating the original RGB information. In the ablation experiments of different components, the results are obtained by varying the combinations of MaxPool-Former (Max) and InterlacedFormer (IF) modules.

blur operations. This decline can be attributed to the disruption of pixel-level statistical features intrinsic to the forgery traces. These insightful experiments effectively underscore the robust nature of our method in addressing the challenges posed by videos circulated on social media platforms.

5 Ablation Study

5.1 Influence of Spatial and Frequency Branches

Figure 3a presents the analysis of the impact of the spatial and frequency branches. Compared to the baseline result of 'None', the 'Spatial' and 'Frequency' branches demonstrate superior performance, indicating the beneficial effect of spatial and frequency features on the detection task. The 'Twin' combines both spatial and frequency branches, achieves the best result. The 'None-RGB' result is only slightly inferior to the 'Twin' result. This suggests that incorporating the original RGB information is beneficial in preserving the original forgery information and improving detection efficiency. The joint learning of frequency and spatial features in the twin-bottleneck architecture proves to be highly advantageous for detecting forged traces from multi-views.

5.2 Impact of Different Component Combinations

As shown in Fig. 3b, the impact of different component combinations. The 'Max+IF' combination, which utilizes MaxPoolFormer in Stage 2 and Interlaced-Former in Stage 3, achieves the best performance and is recommended in this paper. Conversely, the 'IF+IF' combination, lacking local feature extraction,

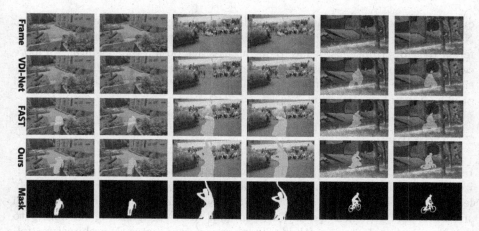

Fig. 4. Qualitative visualization results on the VI subset of the DAVIS-VI dataset. We present the inpainting frames in the first row. The last row is the ground truth mask of the input frame. The remaining rows are the results of comparison methods and ours.

exhibits significantly poorer performance. These results emphasize the importance of incorporating local feature extraction for effective tampering localization. Furthermore, compared to 'Max+IF', the 'Max+Max' combination, lacking the InterlacedFormer module, demonstrates a significant decrease in performance, indicating the significance of learning global features in improving detection performance. Moreover, swapping the learning order of MaxPoolFormer and InterlacedFormer in Stages 2 and 3 of the network ('IF+Max'), which learns global features before local features, performs the worst, even lower than the results with only one component. This finding further demonstrates the rationale and effectiveness of our component design, where learning local features before global contextual features aligns with common intuition.

6   Results Analysis and Discussion

Figure 4 illustrates that our method outperforms the baseline approach in achieving precise pixel-level detection, especially in regions like wheels and arms. The effectiveness of our method lies in its comprehensive multi-view feature learning. This advantage is attributed to our multi-stage design. Firstly, we learn forgery traces from various perspectives. Subsequently, we focus on learning local features, followed by analyzing these features from a global perspective to identify suspicious areas. This hierarchical feature extraction strategy enables us to better capture various forgery traces present in manipulated videos. This further emphasizes the effectiveness of our method in capturing subtle forgery features. Notably, our method demonstrates strong generalization performance across different data distributions, owing to our multi-stage design that facilitates a more comprehensive understanding of different types of forgery. Through these discussions, we underscore the importance and potential of our approach in the field of video inpainting detection.

7　Conclusion

In this paper, we propose VIFST, a novel approach for video inpainting localization. By jointly considering spatial and frequency traces, VIFST effectively learns more general features from multi-views, including edge artifacts, pixel statistics, and region frequency information, thereby enhancing its ability to detect unknown forgery methods. Furthermore, the network architecture follows a sequential order of local-to-global learning, combining the advantages of CNN and ViT to achieve fine-grained pixel-level detection. Experimental results confirm VIFST's superior generalization compared to existing methods and its robustness in handling processed videos on social media platforms. In the future, we aim to enhance the capabilities of VIFST, holding significant prospects for reinforcing content authentication on social media platforms within real-world scenarios. Furthermore, our efforts could empower law enforcement agencies to more effectively identify manipulated video evidence in legal proceedings.

Ethics-Related Considerations

In the evolution of video inpainting methods, concerns about their potential misuse for creating convincing forgeries have grown significantly, prompting ethical considerations. The purpose of video inpainting localization is to address the potential spread of misleading and deceptive content facilitated by video inpainting techniques. Simultaneously, the data used in this paper is sourced solely from publicly available datasets. It strictly adheres to all ethical guidelines without any violations.

References

1. Abbas, W., Shabbir, M., Yazıcıoğlu, Y., Koutsoukos, X.: Edge augmentation with controllability constraints in directed Laplacian networks. IEEE Control Syst. Lett. **6**, 1106–1111 (2022)
2. Chen, M., et al.: CF-ViT: a general coarse-to-fine method for vision transformer. In: Williams, B., Chen, Y., Neville, J. (eds.) AAAI, pp. 7042–7052. AAAI Press, Washington, DC (2023)
3. Diao, Q., Jiang, Y., Wen, B., Sun, J., Yuan, Z.: MetaFormer: a unified meta framework for fine-grained recognition. In: IEEE Conference on Computer Vision and Pattern Recognition, New Orleans, Louisiana, USA. IEEE (2022)

4. Dong, C., Chen, X., Hu, R., Cao, J., Li, X.: MVSS-Net: multi-view multi-scale supervised networks for image manipulation detection. IEEE Trans. Pattern Anal. Mach. Intell. **45**(3), 3539–3553 (2023)

5. Gao, C., Saraf, A., Huang, J.-B., Kopf, J.: Flow-edge guided video completion. In: Vedaldi, A., Bischof, H., Brox, T., Frahm, J.-M. (eds.) ECCV 2020. LNCS, vol. 12357, pp. 713–729. Springer, Cham (2020). https://doi.org/10.1007/978-3-030-58610-2_42

6. Ji, Z., Hou, J., Su, Y., Pang, Y., Li, X.: G2LP-Net: global to local progressive video inpainting network. IEEE TCSVT **33**(3), 1082–1092 (2023)

7. Kim, D., Woo, S., Lee, J., Kweon, I.S.: Deep video inpainting. In: IEEE Conference on Computer Vision and Pattern Recognition, Long Beach, CA, USA, pp. 5792–5801. IEEE (2019)

8. Lee, S., Oh, S.W., Won, D., Kim, S.J.: Copy-and-paste networks for deep video inpainting. In: International Conference on Computer Vision, Seoul, Korea (South), pp. 4412–4420 (2019)

9. Li, H., Huang, J.: Localization of deep inpainting using high-pass fully convolutional network. In: International Conference on Computer Vision, Seoul, Korea (South), pp. 8300–8309 (2019)

10. Li, J., Xie, H., Li, J., Wang, Z., Zhang, Y.: Frequency-aware discriminative feature learning supervised by single-center loss for face forgery detection. In: IEEE Conference on Computer Vision and Pattern Recognition, pp. 6458–6467. IEEE, virtual (2021)

11. Oh, S.W., Lee, S., Lee, J., Kim, S.J.: Onion-peel networks for deep video completion. In: International Conference on Computer Vision, Seoul, Korea (South), pp. 4402–4411 (2019)

12. Shi, X., Li, P., Wu, H., Chen, Q., Zhu, H.: A lightweight image splicing tampering localization method based on mobilenetv2 and SRM. IET Image Process. **17**(6), 1883–1892 (2023)

13. Wei, S., Li, H., Huang, J.: Deep video inpainting localization using spatial and temporal traces. In: ICASSP, pp. 8957–8961 (2022)

14. Xiao, X., Hu, Q., Wang, G.: Edge-aware multi-task network for integrating quantification segmentation and uncertainty prediction of liver tumor on multi-modality non-contrast MRI. CoRR abs/2307.01798 (2023)

15. Xu, R., Li, X., Zhou, B., Loy, C.C.: Deep flow-guided video inpainting. In: IEEE Conference on Computer Vision and Pattern Recognition, Long Beach, CA, USA, pp. 3723–3732. IEEE (2019)

16. Yang, W., Chen, Z., Chen, C., Chen, G., Wong, K.Y.K.: Deep face video inpainting via UV mapping. IEEE Trans. Image Process. **32**, 1145–1157 (2023)

17. Yu, B., Li, W., Li, X., Lu, J., Zhou, J.: Frequency-aware spatiotemporal transformers for video inpainting detection. In: International Conference on Computer Vision, pp. 8188–8197, October 2021

18. Yuan, Y., et al.: HRFormer: high-resolution vision transformer for dense predict. In: Advances in Neural Information Processing Systems, pp. 7281–7293. Virtual (2021)

19. Zeng, Y., Fu, J., Chao, H.: Learning joint spatial-temporal transformations for video inpainting. In: Vedaldi, A., Bischof, H., Brox, T., Frahm, J.-M. (eds.) ECCV 2020. LNCS, vol. 12361, pp. 528–543. Springer, Cham (2020). https://doi.org/10.1007/978-3-030-58517-4_31

20. Zhang, Y., Fu, Z., Qi, S., Xue, M., Hua, Z., Xiang, Y.: Localization of inpainting forgery with feature enhancement network. IEEE Trans. Big Data **9**(3), 936–948 (2023)

21. Zhou, P., et al.: Generate, segment, and refine: towards generic manipulation segmentation. In: AAAI, New York, NY, USA, pp. 13058–13065 (2020)
22. Zhou, P., Yu, N., Wu, Z., Davis, L., Shrivastava, A., Lim, S.: Deep video inpainting detection. In: 32nd British Machine Vision Conference 2021, BMVC, p. 35. Online (2021)

A Logistic Regression Classification Model to Predict ERP Systems Adoption by SMEs in Fiji

Sanmugam Goundar, Karuna Reddy[✉], and M. G. M. Khan

School of Information Technology, Engineering, Mathematics, and Physics,
Laucala Campus, Suva, Fiji
karuna.reddy@usp.ac.fj

Abstract. This study applies a popular data mining algorithm, as a branch of Artificial Intelligence (AI), to investigate the characteristics that influence the adoption of Enterprise Resource Planning (ERP) systems within SMEs in Fiji. A logistic regression classifier is utilised to identify the key determinants that contribute to the adoption of ERP systems. The study incorporates a comprehensive analysis of various demographic, organizational, technological and behavioral factors that provide valuable insights into the ERP-adoption patterns. From the model evaluations, the learnt model reveals that key influencing factors include SMEs knowledge and awareness, attitudes and beliefs, competitive pressure, perception of business process improvements, having high job specifications, and also having about 21–50 employees. All of these predictors have substantial effects on ERP adoption.

Keywords: Binary Logistic Regression · Classification · Machine Learning · ERP-adoption · Small and Medium Enterprise (SME)

1 Introduction

ERP systems bring the world's best practices that help streamline business processes and reduce costs by automating routine tasks and eliminating inherent process bottlenecks and redundancies. Furthermore, ERP systems provide a centralized platform for managing resources such as stocks, human resources, and organization finances, which can help to improve overall operational performance. With these benefits in mind, adopting an ERP system can be a valuable investment for SMEs who face enormous challenges and are always looking to improve their business processes and stay competitive in the current business context.

Business organizations in small developing countries like Fiji face enormous challenges in arriving at the adoption decision itself. While the penetration of ERP systems remains low among Fijian SMEs, there is a lack of in-depth research to guide them on the adoption and non-adoption of such systems. Given that an

© The Author(s), under exclusive license to Springer Nature Singapore Pte Ltd. 2024
F. Liu et al. (Eds.): PRICAI 2023, LNAI 14327, pp. 447–452, 2024.
https://doi.org/10.1007/978-981-99-7025-4_38

organization understands the strengths of ERP systems in terms of modern-day information management, the mere adoption can be construed as a success.

AI and machine learning models consist of algorithmic models (data mining methods) that are trained on historical data or human experiences to produce data-driven insights that assist an expert to understand the dynamics of relationships present in the data [1]. These algorithmic decision-making applications provide an opportunity for businesses to learn from data, make inferences and predictions, and identify relationships, which can guide businesses to make knowledge-based decisions [2,3].

This research presents the findings from an empirical study conducted among 405 randomly sampled SMEs in Fiji and tries to ascertain the key determinants that influence ERP systems adoption. It further analyzes the captured data and creates a classification model using the method of Binary Logistic Regression, which is a branch of AI and falls under the area of Supervised Learning Methods. The traditional ERP adoption determinants documented in the literature are used as a basis to develop the survey instrument for data collection and to conduct the analyses.

2   Literature Review

The existing body of literature has numerous outputs on ERP systems, their characteristics, implementations, usages, challenges, and future predictions. The ERP domain has attracted significant scholastic contributions in diverse and comprehensive forms [4]. In a study by [5], the authors assert that top management support, training of users, and quality of software are among the key determinants of ERP systems adoption. A similar study by [6] additionally indicates that firm maturity is a major determinant of ERP systems adoption where inherent factors like general organizational support, motivation of employees and receptiveness to change are major drivers. Similarly, [7] uncovered that ERP implementation success was very much dependent on top management support, robust communication, training and education, proper project management, and effective vendor support.

Highlighting the challenges in the adoption decision itself, [8], proposed a Decisions Making Model to help small and medium organizations to adopt ERP systems. Basing their assessment of construction companies, the authors went on to carefully review the existing technology models and incorporated new elements to formulate and project a new ERP adoption model. A similar study undertaken by [9] used earlier developed models and the concept of critical success factors to re-design the ERP adoption model. Combining the adoption of ERP and Business Intelligence (BI), [10] proposed a comprehensive model which incorporates factors like quality of the system, quality of service, quality of information, change management, communication, training, future vision and planning, competitive pressure, and the role of government.

3   Research Methodology

This study utilized the **Stratified Random Sampling** (StRS) survey design as the key methodology. The SME population data, i.e., sampling frame, was obtained from 8 Fijian towns spread across the main Islands of Fiji, namely, Viti Levu, Vanua Levu, and Ovalau. The eligibility criteria of a business with an employee number greater than 5 and less than 51 were used for SME classification. The sampling frame was stratified by location, which resulted in a representative sample from each of the main districts in Fiji. Using the sample size calculation suggested by [11], a sample size of 405 SMEs was obtained as a suitable sample size. A **structured questionnaire** was used to capture detailed quantitative information regarding business profile, knowledge and awareness, attitudes and beliefs, practices, adoption, impact, and theoretical model questions. In terms of the **mode of data collection**, each of the sampled companies was approached for a **face-to-face interview**.

The **Binary Logistic Regression (BLR) classifier** was utilized to predict the probability of the occurrence of adoption and non-adoption based on a set of predictors. The mathematical representation is given as $logit(y) = \beta_0 + \beta_1 x_1 + \beta_2 x_2 + \cdots + \beta_k x_k$, where β_i, $i = 1, 2, ..., k$ are the beta weights or the coefficient estimates of the model, $x_1, x_2, \cdots, x_k$ are the predictors, and y is a response to predict (adopter/non-adopter), and $logit(y) = ln(1/(1 - y))$. The model was created using the machine learning workflow whereby the classifier is learned using 75% training data with 10-fold Cross Validation and its model performance and evaluations were done on the 25% test data. This algorithm was carried out in **R** using the **tidymodels** framework.

4   Results and Discussion

The data showed that there were 41% adopters and 59% non-adopters. To model the classifier, predictors were selected systematically based on the assessment of the effects of the various combinations of predictors on the outcome. Table 1 presents the Odds Ratio (OR) which assesses the effect of a predictor variable on the response variable.

The OR for **Location** means that the odds of adopting an ERP for the SMEs in **rural** or **remote areas** is 0.45 times to that of those that are situated in **urban** or **city areas**. Alternatively, we could say that for SMEs in **urban** or **city areas**, there is $1/0.45 = 2.2$, or more than twice the odds of adopting an ERP compared to SMEs in **rural** or **remote areas**, after keeping all other predictors in the model constant. This effect is statistically not significant at the 5% level of significance. Similarly, for SMEs with more than 16 years of **Existence**, the odds for adopting an ERP is 2.4 times compared to an SME with ≤ 5 **years of existence**, after adjusting for other predictors in the model. Alternatively, **11–15 years** and **6–10 years** will have negative effects when compared with the reference category of ≤ 5 years. For the **11–15 years** category, the odds of adopting an ERP for SMEs with ≤ 5 **years of existence** is about 1.75 times

Table 1. Binary Logistic Regression Model Results

Predictor	Category	Odds Ratio	95% CI	p-value
Location (ref: Urban or City)	Rural or Remote	0.45	0.02, 8.58	0.6
Existence (yrs) (ref: <= 5 years)	6–10 years	0.88	0.01, 81.9	>0.9
	11–15 years	0.57	0.01, 51.2	0.8
	>= 16 years	2.36	0.04, 183	0.7
No. of employees (ref: 1–20)	21–50	4.98	0.48, 88.7	0.2
Job specification (ref: High)	Low	0.06	0.00, 0.87	**0.064**
	Others	0.43	0.03, 4.53	0.5
Competitive pressure (ref: No)	Yes	47.8	6.24, 874	**0.001**
State regulations (ref: No)	Yes	0.6	0.07, 4.37	0.6
Improve business process (ref: No)	Yes	31.5	4.14, 577	**0.004**
Knowledge and awareness	continuous	87.8	16.7, 1,117	**<0.001**
Attitudes and beliefs	continuous	172	10.4, 12,543	**0.003**

to that of **11–15 years of existence**. Similarly, for SMEs with ≤ 5 **years of existence**, the odds of adopting an ERP is about 1.14 times (or we could say 14% higher chance) compared to SMEs with **6–10 years of existence**, keeping all other predictors in the model constant. Looking at the **No. of employees**, for SMEs with **21–50 employees**, the odds of adopting an ERP is about 5 times to SMEs with <= **20 employees**, after adjusting for other predictors in the model. For **Job specification** in SMEs, employees having **high** job specification, the odds of adopting an ERP is about $1/0.06 = 17$ times compared to that of an SME with **low** job specification. For the **other** category of job specification, the SMEs with employees having **high** job specification, the odds of adopting an ERP is about 2.3 times to that of an SME with **low** job specification, keeping all other predictors in the model constant.

In terms of potential driving factors affecting the SMEs' intention to adopt an ERP in the future, the model found **competitive pressure** amongst SMEs, **state regulations**, and ERPs **improving business processes** to be statistically significant factors that influence the ERP adoption behavior of SMEs. The two behavioural predictors, **knowledge & awareness** and **attitudes & beliefs** reveal that both of these effects are so substantial that a minor increase could mean a high likelihood for the SME to adopt an ERP.

Figure 1 below presents the effects plot and the variable importance plot. The effects plot and the VIP plot reveal that the five predictors, in order of importance, are: knowledge and awareness, competitive pressure, attitudes and beliefs, improve business process, and job specification help predict the adoption behaviour very strongly.

4.1 Model Evaluation

Several evaluation metrics (accuracy, confusion matrix, precision, recall, roc auc) are utilized to measure the effectiveness of the model (presented in Fig. 2). From

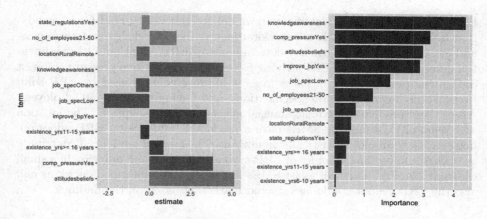

Fig. 1. LHS: Effects Plot; and RHS: Variable Importance Plot

| | **TRUTH** | |
| | *Adopt* | *Not Adopt* |

PREDICTION		
Adopt	TP = 42	FP = 3
Not Adopt	FN = 0	TN = 57

Measure	Value
Accuracy	0.993
F1 score	0.974
Precision	1
Recall	0.95
ROC auc	0.993

Fig. 2. The Confusion Matrix and its Measures

the model's confusion matrix, the accuracy of 0.993 signifies that the model makes about 99% correct predictions. A precision of 1 identifies the model can correctly predict 100% of the positive instances (i.e., ERP adopters) out of the total ERP adopters. A recall (sensitivity or true positive rate) value of 0.95 tells us that the model captures the 95% of the ERP adopters in the dataset. The F1 score of 0.94 indicates that the model is able to identify ERP adopters correctly (recall) and has the ability to avoid misclassifying the non-adopters (precision). The area (AUC) under the Receiver Operating Curve (ROC) was found to be 0.993, which indicates a very good overall measure of the model's discriminatory power and top-notch model performance.

5   Conclusion

From this empirical study of a representative sample of Fijian SMEs, we find that there are some key characteristics that strongly influence the adoption of

ERP systems. From the classification model created via 10-Fold Cross Validation techniques, we find that behavioral factors like knowledge and awareness, and attitudes and beliefs are key determinants of ERP adoption. Other influential determinants include ERP driving factors like competitive pressure amongst SMEs, the perception of business process improvements caused by ERP solutions, SMEs having high job specifications, and having about 21–50 employees. All of these predictors have substantial effects on ERP adoption. The location and years of existence for SMEs have a moderate influence on ERP adoption, however, they are not statistically significant. The learned model can contribute to understanding the dynamics of ERP-systems adoption and diffusion in a small economy like Fiji. This will assist SMEs in making more informed decisions and also the ERP vendors in doing targeted marketing based on the findings.

References

1. Mishra, S., Tripathi, A.R.: AI business model: an integrative business approach. J. Innov. Entrep. **10**(1), 18 (2021)
2. Wang, H., Huang, J., Zhang, Z.: Association for Information Systems Electronic Library (AISeL): The Impact of Deep Learning on Organizational Agility (2019)
3. Afiouni, R.: Organizational learning in the rise of machine learning (2019)
4. Moon, Y.B.: Enterprise Resource Planning (ERP): a review of the literature. Int. J. Manage. Enterp. Develop. **4**(3), 235–264 (2007)
5. Costa, C.J., Ferreira, E., Bento, F., Aparicio, M.: Enterprise resource planning adoption and satisfaction determinants. Comput. Hum. Behav. **63**, 659–671 (2016)
6. Rajan, C.A., Baral, R.: Adoption of ERP system: an empirical study of factors influencing the usage of ERP and its impact on end user. IIMB Manag. Rev. **27**(2), 105–117 (2015)
7. Dezdar, S.: Strategic and tactical factors for successful ERP projects: insights from an Asian country. Manag. Res. Rev. **35**(11), 1070–1087 (2012)
8. Negahban, S.S., Baecher, G.B., Skibniewski, M.J.: A decision-making model for adoption of enterprise resource planning tools by small-to-medium size construction organizations. J. Civ. Eng. Manag. **18**(2), 253–264 (2012)
9. Mayaram, U., Dussoye, A., Cadersaib, Z.: ERP acceptance model for SMEs based on CSFs. Paper presented at the 2019 Conference on Next Generation Computing Applications (NextComp), 19–21 September 2019
10. Aldossari, S., Mokhtar, U.A.: A model to adopt Enterprise Resource Planning (ERP) and Business Intelligence (BI) among Saudi SMEs. Int. J. Innov. **8**(2), 305–347 (2020). https://doi.org/10.5585/iji.v8i2.17395
11. Singh, A.S., Masuku, M.B.: Sampling techniques & determination of sample size in applied statistics research: an overview. Int. J. Economics Commerce Manag. **2**(11), 1–22 (2014)

Low-Resource Machine Translation Training Curriculum Fit for Low-Resource Languages

Garry Kuwanto[1]([✉]), Afra Feyza Akyürek[1], Isidora Chara Tourni[1], Siyang Li[1], Alex Jones[2], and Derry Wijaya[1]

[1] Boston University, Boston, MA, USA
{gkuwanto,akyurek,isidora,siyangli,wijaya}@bu.edu
[2] Dartmouth College, Hanover, NH, USA
alexander.g.jones.23@dartmouth.edu

Abstract. We conduct an empirical study of neural machine translation (NMT) for truly low-resource languages, and present a training curriculum fit for cases when both parallel training data and compute resource are lacking, reflecting the reality of most of the world's languages and the researchers working on these languages. Previously, unsupervised NMT, which employs back-translation (BT) and auto-encoding (AE) tasks has been shown barren for low-resource languages. We demonstrate that leveraging comparable data and code-switching as weak supervision, combined with pre-training with BT and AE objectives, result in remarkable improvements for low-resource languages even when using only modest compute resources. The training curriculum proposed in this work achieves BLEU scores that improve over supervised NMT trained on the same backbone architecture, showcasing the potential of weakly-supervised NMT for low-resource languages.

Keywords: Machine Translation · Low Resource Languages · Code Switching

1 Introduction

Neural Machine Translation (NMT) has witnessed remarkable advancements, especially in benefiting low-resource languages via unsupervised NMT methodologies. Techniques anchored by multilingual language models (LMs) pre-training offer promising improvements in translation capabilities [7]. Nonetheless, while large-scale LMs suggest that comprehensive pre-training can bolster low-resource NMT, these claims often falter when confronted with authentic low-resource scenarios. Traditional assumptions regarding abundant data and computational resources don't universally hold for these "left-behind" languages. As

---

G. Kuwanto, A. F. Akyürek, I. C. Tourni and S. Li—Contributed Equally.

a result, languages distinct from English frequently observe marked downturns in translation performance [5,6,8].

In this study, we introduce a training curriculum optimized for low-resource NMT. Focusing on Gujarati (gu), Somali (so), and Kazakh (kk), we employ strategies like code-switching LM pre-training and unsupervised NMT training. Additionally, we utilize comparable data training when accessible

2   Related Work

Low-Resource NLP. Recent studies indicate that a mere 6% of the world's 7000 languages feature in NLP research [5]. This work underscores the pressing need to focus on underrepresented and typologically varied languages. Echoing this sentiment, our research hones in on the under-explored languages: Somali (so), Gujarati (gu), and Kazakh (kk).

Unsupervised NMT. While unsupervised NMT thrives in settings with ample parallel data, its efficacy wanes in low-resource contexts [6,9]. We seek to invigorate its performance by coupling it with training on comparable text [7].

Mining Comparable Sentences. Research on extracting *pseudo*-parallel sentences is vast [3,4,10], yet its application for low-resource languages is scarce. Modern methods like CCMatrix and WikiMatrix often hinge on supervised systems or require hefty computational power [11,12].

Code-Switching. Our methodology leans on code-switching during LM training to amplify cross-lingual alignment, diverging from approaches like [16] but aligning with [15]. We spotlight monolingual data from low-resource languages, presenting a fresh perspective in this domain.

3   Proposed Methods

3.1   Dictionary Creation and Sentence Mining

Starting with the backbone architecture based on XLM [2], we first create a foundational word dictionary. This dictionary is seeded from crowd-sourced data via the Panlex's World vocabulary list, which we refer to as dict(Panlex). To enhance coverage, we train monolingual word embeddings for each language using fastText's skipgram model. Leveraging these embeddings, a linear mapping is learned between source and target languages with the MUSE methodology, using dict(Panlex) as initial translations. This process, depicted in Fig. 1, culminates in the creation of a high coverage dictionary, termed dict(Projected). For sentence mining, we access linked Wikipedia pages in distinct languages using the Wikimedia dumps. By translating source sentences to English using our word dictionary, and evaluating overlap through the Jaccard similarity score, we extract pairs with a minimum 0.1 Jaccard Similarity. This method of mining comparable sentences is illustrated in Fig. 2.

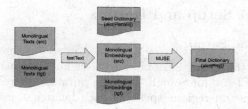

Fig. 1. Dictionary Creation Process

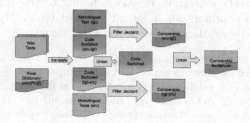

Fig. 2. Sentence Mining Process

3.2 Training Curriculum

The initial phase involves bilingual LM pre-training on monolingual corpora of both languages (e.g., so and en for en-so MT). A unique aspect of our method is the incorporation of a third "language" for pre-training, composed of code-switched sentences. These sentences merge English and the target foreign language, which, under the MLM objective, encourages alignment between the respective language embeddings. This method, as depicted in Fig. 3, emulates the Translation Language Modeling (TLM) objective in XLM but bypasses the need for parallel sentences. Following LM pre-training, we dive into unsupervised NMT training. Both the encoder and decoder leverage the pre-trained LM encoder block. We employ back-translation (BT) and denoising auto-encoding (AE) losses for unsupervised NMT, using the monolingual data from LM pre-training. The transition from unsupervised $BT + AE$ pre-training to $BT + MT$, where MT can either use supervised parallel data (MT_s) or our mined comparable data (MT_c), is illustrated in Fig. 3.

Fig. 3. Training Curriculum

4   Experiment Setup and Results

4.1   Experimental Setup

We evaluate using the WMT 2019 news test set for Gujarati and Kazakh, and DARPA's LORELEI [14] for Somali. Training durations were set based on average monthly incomes in regions speaking each language, using Amazon AWS EC2 rates, which allocated specific GPU-hours to each training step. Quick processes like lexicon induction were exempted. Our detailed training scripts can be found in supplementary materials, mostly adhering to the original XLM repository[1]. We utilize a common 60k subword vocabulary via Byte-Pair Encoding [13], with model configurations noted in the main text.

Table 1. BLEU scores for previous supervised and unsupervised results from [1] [8], [2] [1] and our models. Test and validation sets are from WMT19 for Gujarati and Kazakh and from [14] for Somali. *MLM*, *AE*, *BT* and *MT* stand for *MLM*, Auto-Encoding loss, Back Translation loss and Machine Translation loss, respectively. MT_s and MT_c utilize human-labeled parallel data and mined comparable data, respectively. MLM_{cs} utilizes both code-switched and original forms of monolingual data. Best results overall are **bolded** while best results in each section are underlined. All our models here use 1 (32GB) GPU. Parentheses in training objectives refer to two simultaneous losses while the ones separated with "+" are used successively.

Name	Supervision	en-gu	gu-en	en-kk	kk-en	en-so	so-en
Baseline (Time-Constrained)							
$(BT + MT_s)$	Supervised	<u>3.7</u>	<u>1.2</u>	<u>1.9</u>	<u>3.1</u>	<u>20.1</u>	<u>23.1</u>
$MLM + (BT + AE)$	Unsupervised	1.7	<u>1.2</u>	1.0	1.3	8.1	7.4
Ours (Time-Constrained)							
$MLM + (BT + MT_s)$	Supervised	6.8	3.0	5.6	8.4	23.1	29.4
$MLM + (BT + AE) + (BT + MT_s)$	Semi-supervised	11.6	6.9	7.2	10.7	23.5	29.2
$MLM_{cs} + (BT + AE) + (BT + MT_s)$	Semi-supervised, Code-switching	13.1	7.7	<u>7.9</u>	<u>10.7</u>	<u>23.6</u>	<u>29.3</u>
$MLM_{cs} + (BT + AE) + (BT + MT_c)$	Weakly-supervised, Code-switching	<u>15.0</u>	<u>11.8</u>	5.5	7.5	14.7	13.9
Ours (Best of Time-Constrained, ↑ batch size: 4k tokens per batch)							
$MLM_{cs} + (BT + AE) + (BT + MT)$	Semi/weakly-supervised, Code-switching	<u>16.3</u>	<u>12.8</u>	<u>9.7</u>	<u>12.7</u>	<u>23.7</u>	<u>29.7</u>
Ours (Best of Time-Constrained, ↑ batch size: 4k tokens per batch, ↑ time: MT trained to convergence)							
$MLM_{cs} + (BT + AE) + (BT + MT)$	Semi/weakly-supervised, Code-switching	**17.3**	**13.6**	**11.5**	**14.2**	**23.8**	**30.7**
Large Multilingual Models (MT trained to convergence)							
mBART25[1]	Supervised	0.1	0.3	2.5	7.4	–	–
XLM-R[2] $+ (BT + MT)$	Supervised	<u>13.2</u>	<u>7.8</u>	<u>6.0</u>	<u>8.4</u>	<u>22.5</u>	<u>27.5</u>

4.2   Results

Table 1 highlights BLEU scores for diverse NMT settings. Under time constraints, pre-trained LMs bolstered NMT performance, especially when enhanced with unsupervised MT goals and code-switching data. Training with vast comparable data proved beneficial when it surpassed available parallel data volumes, notably for Gujarati.

---

[1] http://github.com/facebookresearch/XLM.

Overall, merging code-switching LM pre-training, unsupervised NMT objectives, and vast comparable datasets can heighten MT results. Contrasted with power-intensive models like mBART and XLM-R, our approach yields better outcomes with fewer resources.

5 Conclusion

In our study, we investigate NMT techniques for low-resource languages, introducing a training curriculum optimized for low-data and low-compute scenarios. Notably, leveraging comparable data with strategic training objectives leads to marked gains. For instance, bitext mining produces quality comparable corpora, even for the low-resource languages studied.

The value of using comparable data varies by its size relative to supervised data; it greatly benefits Gujarati but is less effective for Somali. Pre-training models with a language modeling objective consistently enhances results across all languages. This effect is amplified when followed by unsupervised machine translation tasks before supervised/semi-supervised steps. However, starting with a large multilingual LM isn't always advantageous.

Incorporating code-switched corpora during LM pre-training significantly bolsters NMT performance (Table 1). As our methods don't rely on high-resource languages or parallel sequences, they provide a foundation for future exploration in other low-resource languages.

References

1. Conneau, A., et al.: Unsupervised cross-lingual representation learning at scale. In: Proceedings of the 58th Annual Meeting of the Association for Computational Linguistics, pp. 8440–8451. Association for Computational Linguistics (2020). https://doi.org/10.18653/v1/2020.acl-main.747
2. Conneau, A., Lample, G.: Cross-lingual language model pretraining. In: Advances in Neural Information Processing Systems, pp. 7059–7069 (2019). https://proceedings.neurips.cc/paper/2019/file/c04c19c2c2474dbf5f7ac4372c5b9af1-Paper.pdf
3. Grover, J., Mitra, P.: Bilingual word embeddings with bucketed CNN for parallel sentence extraction. In: Proceedings of ACL 2017, Student Research Workshop, pp. 11–16. Association for Computational Linguistics, Vancouver, Canada (2017). https://www.aclweb.org/anthology/P17-3003
4. Guo, M., et al.: Effective parallel corpus mining using bilingual sentence embeddings. In: Proceedings of the Third Conference on Machine Translation: Research Papers, pp. 165–176. Association for Computational Linguistics, Brussels, Belgium (2018). https://doi.org/10.18653/v1/W18-6317, https://www.aclweb.org/anthology/W18-6317
5. Joshi, P., Santy, S., Budhiraja, A., Bali, K., Choudhury, M.: The state and fate of linguistic diversity and inclusion in the NLP world. In: Proceedings of the 58th Annual Meeting of the Association for Computational Linguistics, pp. 6282–6293. Association for Computational Linguistics (2020). https://doi.org/10.18653/v1/2020.acl-main.560, https://www.aclweb.org/anthology/2020.acl-main.560

6. Kim, Y., Graça, M., Ney, H.: When and why is unsupervised neural machine translation useless? In: Proceedings of the 22nd Annual Conference of the European Association for Machine Translation, pp. 35–44. European Association for Machine Translation, Lisboa, Portugal (2020). https://www.aclweb.org/anthology/2020.eamt-1.5

7. Lample, G., Conneau, A., Denoyer, L., Ranzato, M.: Unsupervised machine translation using monolingual corpora only. In: International Conference on Learning Representations (2018). https://openreview.net/forum?id=rkYTTf-AZ

8. Liu, Y., et al.: Multilingual denoising pre-training for neural machine translation. Trans. Assoc. Comput. Linguist. **8**, 726–742 (2020). https://doi.org/10.1162/tacl_a_00343

9. Marchisio, K., Duh, K., Koehn, P.: When does unsupervised machine translation work? In: Proceedings of the Fifth Conference on Machine Translation, pp. 571–583. Association for Computational Linguistics (2020). https://www.aclweb.org/anthology/2020.wmt-1.68

10. Schwenk, H.: Filtering and mining parallel data in a joint multilingual space. In: Proceedings of the 56th Annual Meeting of the Association for Computational Linguistics (Volume 2: Short Papers), pp. 228–234. Association for Computational Linguistics, Melbourne, Australia (2018). https://doi.org/10.18653/v1/P18-2037, https://www.aclweb.org/anthology/P18-2037

11. Schwenk, H., Chaudhary, V., Sun, S., Gong, H., Guzmán, F.: WikiMatrix: mining 135M parallel sentences in 1620 language pairs from Wikipedia. In: Proceedings of the 16th Conference of the European Chapter of the Association for Computational Linguistics: Main Volume, pp. 1351–1361. Association for Computational Linguistics (2021), https://www.aclweb.org/anthology/2021.eacl-main.115

12. Schwenk, H., Wenzek, G., Edunov, S., Grave, E., Joulin, A.: CCMatrix: mining billions of high-quality parallel sentences on the web. arXiv preprint arXiv:1911.04944 (2019)

13. Sennrich, R., Haddow, B., Birch, A.: Neural machine translation of rare words with Subword units. In: Proceedings of the 54th Annual Meeting of the Association for Computational Linguistics (Volume 1: Long Papers), pp. 1715–1725. Association for Computational Linguistics, Berlin, Germany (2016). https://doi.org/10.18653/v1/P16-1162 , https://www.aclweb.org/anthology/P16-1162

14. Tracey, J., et al.: Corpus building for low resource languages in the DARPA LORELEI program. In: Proceedings of the 2nd Workshop on Technologies for MT of Low Resource Languages, pp. 48–55. European Association for Machine Translation, Dublin, Ireland (2019). https://www.aclweb.org/anthology/W19-6808

15. Yang, J., Ma, S., Zhang, D., Wu, S., Li, Z., Zhou, M.: Alternating language modeling for cross-lingual pre-training. In: Proceedings of the AAAI Conference on Artificial Intelligence, vol. 34, pp. 9386–9393 (2020). https://ojs.aaai.org/index.php/AAAI/article/view/6480

16. Yang, Z., Hu, B., Han, A., Huang, S., Ju, Q.: CSP:code-switching pre-training for neural machine translation. In: Proceedings of the 2020 Conference on Empirical Methods in Natural Language Processing (EMNLP), pp. 2624–2636. Association for Computational Linguistics (2020). https://doi.org/10.18653/v1/2020.emnlp-main.208, https://aclanthology.org/2020.emnlp-main.208

MARL₄*DRP*: Benchmarking Cooperative Multi-agent Reinforcement Learning Algorithms for Drone Routing Problems

Shiyao Ding[1(✉)], Hideki Aoyama[2], and Donghui Lin[3]

[1] Kyoto University, Kyoto-shi, Kyoto 606-8501, Japan
ding@i.kyoto-u.ac.jp
[2] Panasonic Holdings Corporation, 1006, Oaza Kadoma, Kadoma-shi,
Osaka 571-8501, Japan
aoyama.hideki@jp.panasonic.com
[3] Okayama University, Okayama-shi, Okayama 700-8530, Japan
lindh@okayama-u.ac.jp

Abstract. The use of drones as an efficient delivery solution is a promising technology, addressing the growing demand for deliveries. Unlike the traditional vehicle routing problem (VRP), we introduce a new drone routing problem (DRP) that considers distinct drone delivery attributes, especially the need for dynamic, collision-free routes in non-grid settings. To optimize team rewards in DRP, cooperative efforts of all drones are essential. Thus, we employ cooperative multi-agent reinforcement learning (MARL). We present MARL₄*DRP*, a comprehensive benchmark tailored for applying cooperative MARL to DRP. Our contributes to the optimization of drone delivery using MARL, offering a solid foundation for future research in this domain. All code is available at the repository: https://github.com/DING-1994/MARL4DRP

Keywords: Multiagent path finding · Drone routing problem · Multiagent reinforcement learning

1 Introduction

Delivering goods with drones poses logistical challenges [2]. As such, multi-drone delivery has become indispensable [5]. We define a novel drone routing problem (DRP) emphasizing the need for collision-free paths, drawing parallels to multi-agent path finding (MAPF). To identify optimal paths in DRP, cooperation among all drones is essential. This can be addressed through multi-agent reinforcement learning (MARL). While various MARL methods exist, there's a lack of a standardized DRP environment. To fill this gap, we introduce MARL₄*DRP* with key features: **Non-grid Map**: MARL₄*DRP* operates on non-grid maps, where each node can connect to multiple adjacent nodes from any direction, rendering traditional grid maps as specific instances. **Dynamic Goal**: Distinct from most MAPF problems, MARL₄*DRP* features dynamic start and end goals

F. Liu et al. (Eds.): PRICAI 2023, LNAI 14327, pp. 459–465, 2024.
https://doi.org/10.1007/978-981-99-7025-4_40

for drones. **Gym-standard Environment**: The DRP is formulated as a gym-standard environment [1], ensuring compatibility with multiple MARL frameworks. This has been confirmed with platforms like EpyMARL [3].

2   Drone Routing Problem

2.1   Definition of the DRP

Without loss of generality, we formulate the DRP problem on a non-grid map. Consider a group of drones $N = \{1, \ldots, i, \ldots, |N|\}$ moving on a two-dimensional non-grid map represented by $G = \langle V, E \rangle$. Here, $V = \{v_1, \ldots, v_{|V|}\}$ denotes the set of nodes, with each node v_k having a location given by $l_k = (l_k^x, l_k^y)$. Additionally, $E = \{(v_k, v_l) | \text{a link exists between nodes } v_k$ and $v_l\}$ symbolizes the set of edges. Each drone $i \in N$ is assigned a starting point $st_{epi}^i \in V$ and a goal $go_{epi}^i \in V$ for every episode epi.

For a finite episode of T steps, the path $path^i$ for each drone is described as: $path^i = (l^i[0], l^i[1], \ldots, l^i[T])$, where $l^i[0] = st^i$ and $l^i[t'] = go^i$ if drone i reaches the goal at step t'. Once the drone arrives at its goal, it stays there, i.e., $l^i[t]|_{t>t'} = go^i$. The cost function $cost$ for the moving path $path^i$ is given by: $cost(path^i) = \sum_{t=0}^{T-1} \|l^i[t+1] - l^i[t]\|_2$. The primary objective is to determine a set of paths for each drone i that arrives its own goal go^i while minimizing the total movement cost subject to the constraints such as collision-free, i.e., $\min \sum_{epi} \sum_i cost(path_{epi}^i)$, subject to $(\forall i \in N, l^i[T] = go_{epi}^i) \wedge (\forall t, \forall i \neq j, l^i[t] \neq l^j[t])$, where $l^i[T] = go_{epi}^i$ ensures that the drone remains at its goal go_{epi}^i at the terminal step T of episode epi.

2.2   Formulating DRP as a MAPF

In this section, we reformulate the DRP problem in terms of MAPF. We define its elements as follows:

State: We consider three state representations in this paper. One simple way is *coordinate-based representation*, designating each drone's position as (l^x, l^y). The another is *one-hot Representation*: each grid cell corresponds to a one-hot encoded vector. The length of this vector $s^i = [s_1^i, \ldots, s_j^i, \ldots s_{|V|}^i]$ equates to the total number $|V|$ of the nodes. It marks a node s_j^i with 1 if the drone occupies it, while the rest remain zero. For drones located on the edges, vector values are defined by: $s_j^i = 1 - \frac{len(loc^i - v_j^i)}{len(v_j, v_k)}$, $s_k^i = 1 - s_j^i$ when drone i traverses edge (v_j, v_k), and 0 otherwise. Here, $loc^i = (l^{x^i}, l^{y^i})$ represents drone i's current coordinates and $len(,)$ represents the distance. As drone i approaches node v_j^i, the value of s_j^i increases. An additional format is the *one-hot with Field of View (onehot_fov)*, which marks a node s_j^i in *onehot* with -1 if another drone occupies it.

Action: At each step, drones can choose a node to move. Consequently, we represent the action set A using the node set V. Actions available fluctuate based on the drone's current state s^i, i.e., $A(s^i)$.

Reward and Objective Function: Commonly in MAPF studies, the reward function $r^i(s, a, s')$ is structured based on: r^i_{move} when the drone moves (typically the inverse of the movement cost), r^i_{wait} when the drone remains stationary, $r^i_{collision}$ when a collision transpires, and r^i_{goal} when the drone reaches its designated goal go^i. Given that each drone i adheres to a policy π^i, the objective function is represented as: $J(\pi^1, ..., \pi^{|N|}) = \mathbb{E}_{\pi^1,...,\pi^{|N|}} \left[R(h) \right]$. Here, $R(h)$ denotes the discounted sum of immediate rewards received by all drones within a given timeframe, defined as: $R(h) = \sum_{t=1}^{T} \gamma^{t-1} \sum_i r^i(s[t], \mathbf{a}[t], s[t + 1])$.

3 Cooperative MARL for DRP

Cooperative MARL focuses on optimizing team rewards by considering actions from all agents. One method, independent Q-Learning (IQL), has each agent use a deep Q-Network, treating other agents' actions as parts of the environment. Another approach, such as value decomposition networks (VDN) [6], centralizes

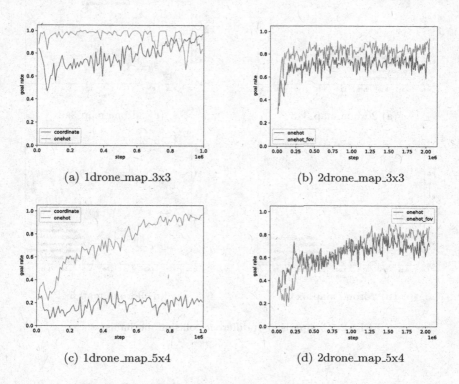

(a) 1drone_map_3x3

(b) 2drone_map_3x3

(c) 1drone_map_5x4

(d) 2drone_map_5x4

Fig. 1. Comparison of different state representations.

training but decentralizes execution. VDN combines individual Q-values to get a total Q-value, Q_{tot}, that reflects team rewards, aiming to ensure $Q_{tot}/Q^i = 1$. QMIX [4], similar to VDN, relates Q_{tot} to individual Q-values but employs a hypernetwork for weight adjustments. We'll explore three main considerations for applying cooperative MARL to DRP: 1) state representation, 2) collision mechanism, and 3) reward design.

State Representation. As described in Sect. 2.2, we test three state representations: coordinate representation, one-hot representation, and one-hot with FOV representation.

Collision Mechanism. Two primary mechanisms exist for collision handling: the *collision-bounce-back pattern* and the *collision-terminate pattern*. In the former, drones bounce back upon collision, receiving a penalty. In contrast, the latter terminates the current episode if any two drones collide.

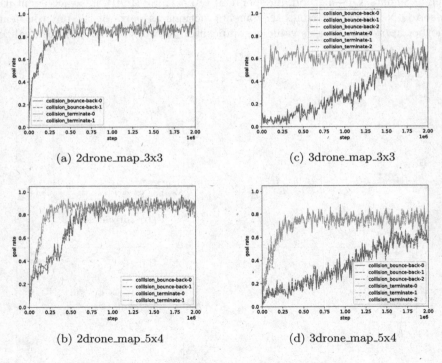

(a) 2drone_map_3x3

(c) 3drone_map_3x3

(b) 2drone_map_5x4

(d) 3drone_map_5x4

Fig. 2. Comparison of different collision mechanisms.

Reward Setting. The reward function, detailed in Sect. 2.2, plays a pivotal role in reinforcement learning. It steers the learning process, directing drones towards optimal actions. We evaluate different values for the four reward types in our model: r_{move}, r_{wait}, $r_{collision}$, and r_{goal}.

4   Evaluation

We tested on three maps: map_3 $\times$ 3 (9 nodes) and map_5 $\times$ 4 (20 nodes) for 1×10^6 steps in total (2×10^6 in some cases). The settings of the hyper-parameters are as follows: learning rate $= 0.01$ and discount factor $= 0.99$.

State Representation. In a single-drone test, both the coordinate and one-hot representations performed similarly. However, for larger maps, the onehot representation was superior, as evidenced in Fig. 1(a)(b). For the two-drone test, we compared only the one-hot and onehot-fov due to the inefficiency of the coordinate representation. As depicted in Fig. 1(c)(d), both representations yielded similar results on the larger maps. However, the one-hot-fov excelled on the 3×3 map. The smaller size of this map resulted in more collisions, rendering the fov information more critical for the drone. This suggests that on smaller maps, where collisions are more frequent, the fov information becomes invaluable for the learning process of the drone.

Collision Mechanism. We utilized the one-hot state representations for all drones. We then tested two patterns for the collision mechanism, with the results displayed in Fig. 2. In the scenarios involving two drones, as shown in Fig. 2(a)(b), both the collision-bounce-back and collision-terminate mechanisms had similar performance levels. Yet, with a higher number of drones, the collision-terminate mechanism was more effective than the collision-bounce-back, as illustrated in Fig. 2(c)(d). This can be ascribed to the fact that when a collision occurs, leading to the termination of the episode, there's an increase in the proportion of collision data. This surge makes it more efficient for the drones to learn collision avoidance strategies.

Reward Design. Using the one-hot representation, we examined three reward settings, which are depicted in Fig. 3: i) r_{move} =-0.005, r_{wait} =-0.005; ii) r_{move} =-5, r_{wait} =-5; iii) r_{move} =-5, r_{wait} =-50. The first setting achieved a nearly 100% goal rate but exhibited minor oscillations due to some drones choosing to wait near the goal. In the second setting, by penalizing both movement and waiting equally, the oscillations diminished, and a 100% goal rate was realized for the 3×3 map. In the third setting, by further penalizing waiting, we achieved a 100% goal rate across all map sizes.

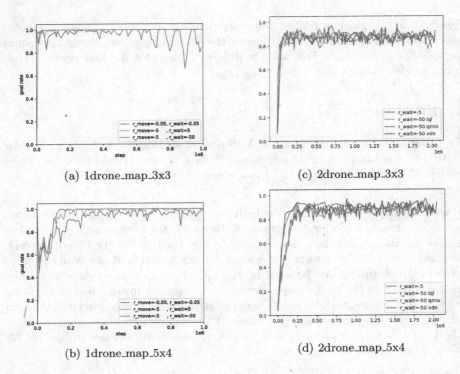

(a) 1drone_map_3x3

(c) 2drone_map_3x3

(b) 1drone_map_5x4

(d) 2drone_map_5x4

Fig. 3. (a)-(b): Comparison of different reward designs. (c)-(d): Comparison of IQL, VDN and QMIX

Cooperative MARL Comparison. Maintaining the one-hot representation, we conducted a comparative analysis of the value-based MARL algorithms: IQL, VDN, and QMIX. The comparative results are showcased in Fig. 3(c)(d). For the map_3 × 3 scenario, the performance differences among the algorithms were marginal. However, with an increase in map size, which necessitated enhanced cooperation, both VDN and QMIX surpassed IQL, highlighting their superior capability in fostering inter-agent collaboration.

5   Conclusion

In this research, we introduced a gym-standard environment for DRP, ensuring compatibility with cooperative MARL frameworks. This ensures easier benchmarking of MARL algorithms in drone routing contexts. We also examined three pivotal DRP settings, conducting extensive evaluations for each setting.

Acknowledgment. This research was supported by a joint research of Non-Grid Pathfinding Optimization in Continuous Time and Space from Panasonic Holdings Corporation and a Grant-in-Aid for Scientific Research (C) (23K11230) from the Japan Society for the Promotion of Science (JSPS).

References

1. Brockman, G., et al.: Openai gym. arXiv preprint arXiv:1606.01540 (2016)
2. Moadab, A., Farajzadeh, F., Fatahi Valilai, O.: Drone routing problem model for last-mile delivery using the public transportation capacity as moving charging stations. Sci. Rep. **12**(1), 1–16 (2022)
3. Papoudakis, G., Christianos, F., Schäfer, L., Albrecht, S.V.: Benchmarking multi-agent deep reinforcement learning algorithms in cooperative tasks. arXiv preprint arXiv:2006.07869 (2020)
4. Rashid, T., Samvelyan, M., Schroeder, C., Farquhar, G., Foerster, J., Whiteson, S.: Qmix: Monotonic value function factorisation for deep multi-agent reinforcement learning. In: International Conference on Machine Learning, pp. 4295–4304. PMLR (2018)
5. Rubenstein, M., Cornejo, A., Nagpal, R.: Programmable self-assembly in a thousand-robot swarm. Science **345**(6198), 795–799 (2014)
6. Sunehag, P., et al.: Value-decomposition networks for cooperative multi-agent learning. arXiv preprint arXiv:1706.05296 (2017)

Real-Time Event Detection with Random Forests and Temporal Convolutional Networks for More Sustainable Petroleum Industry

Yuanwei Qu[1(✉)], Baifan Zhou[1,2], Arild Waaler[1], and David Cameron[1]

[1] University of Oslo, Oslo, Norway
quy@ifi.uio.no
[2] Oslo Metropolitan University, Oslo, Norway

Abstract. The petroleum industry is crucial for modern society, but the production process is complex and risky. During the production, accidents or failures, resulting from undesired production events, can cause severe environmental and economic damage. Previous studies have investigated machine learning (ML) methods for undesired event detection. However, the prediction of event probability in real-time was insufficiently addressed, which is essential since it is important to undertake early intervention when an event is expected to happen. This paper proposes two ML approaches, random forests and temporal convolutional networks, to detect undesired events in real-time. Results show that our approaches can effectively classify event types and predict the probability of their appearance, addressing the challenges uncovered in previous studies and providing a more effective solution for failure event management during the production.

Keywords: Machine learning · sustainability · petroleum industry

1 Introduction

Background. Petroleum is dubbed as the "blood" of modern industry, as it is essential for a wide range of industries. The growing awareness of preserving a green planet for our future generations has prompted the petroleum industry to produce energy in a more sustainable practice [1]. However, the production of petroleum is still a complex and risky process that can have significant adverse consequences, if not managed effectively. During the petroleum production, accidents or failures, often resulting from undesired events, can cause severe environmental damage. For example, oil spills can lead to water pollution and habitat destruction, which will have long-term negative ecological impacts on our society and lead to economic losses. Therefore, it is vital to detect undesired events during production to minimise environmental damage and protect ecosystems. Additionally, detecting undesired events can assist engineers in performing accurate

F. Liu et al. (Eds.): PRICAI 2023, LNAI 14327, pp. 466–473, 2024.
https://doi.org/10.1007/978-981-99-7025-4_41

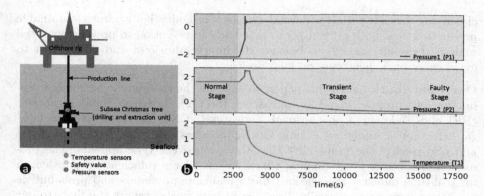

Fig. 1. (a) An offshore oil platform and production well (b) Undesired event detection: finding faulty stages via analysing sensor measurements. The illustrated fault is *Spurious downhole safety valve closure*, which means that the system reports that a safety valve has closed, while actually it has not. The subjective label provided by the domain expert indicates the faulty stage starts around 15000 s, but the actual fault should already start somewhere before 15000 s.

failure event management, which will optimise production processes, increase production efficiency, minimise energy consumption, and reduce maintenance costs. A safe and environment-sustainable production will help the petroleum industry to demonstrate social responsibility and addresses the concerns about ecological stewardship.

Related Work. The petroleum industry has adeptly incorporated AI into the production through the adoption of digitisation and Industry 4.0 methods. Due to the large data volume collected from oil well sensors, using AI techniques to assist undesired event detection is becoming feasible. Some studies [2–7] have investigated several machine learning (ML) methods for event classification on datasets such as 3W dataset [8].

Challenge. However, the previous studies have deficiencies in detecting and predicting failures. There are two *key challenges* (C) that should be addressed. (C1) the current classification and prediction methods are not performed in real-time, with large window sizes ranging from many minutes to more than one hour. This is insufficient for industrial needs. (C2) simple classification of faulty stages cannot give accurate information to engineers for when to take intervention: Although the event detection appears to be a classification task according to the labels in the dataset, it is not always so straightforward, because the labels are subjectively given by domain experts [8]. From Fig. 1b, it can be seen that some values in the transient stage between normal and faulty stages do not necessarily show drastic changes (Fig. 1): they are not normal but also not fully "faulty". There is no sharp separation between the transient stage and the faulty stage, which makes conventional classification not accurate enough. We argue that it is better to predict the probability of emerging failures, rather than simply classifying the time period as normal, transient or faulty. For having a sustainable production, it is both critical (1) to take early intervention to prevent potential undesired events, and (2) to balance the intervention cost and failure cost to avoid excessive expenditure on false positives.

Our Contributions. In this paper, to support the sustainable petroleum production, we propose two ML approaches (Sect. 2), based on Random Forests (RF) and Temporal Convolutional Networks (TCN), for *real-time probabilistic* detection of undesired events. Our approaches can classify the event type and also predict the probability that the given event type appears. The prediction is done for every minute, which we consider a sufficient window length for real-time industry applications. Both real-time prediction and probabilistic prediction have been limitedly discussed in past works; we are the first (to our best knowledge) to experiment with TCN for the undesired event detection task in the domain. The evaluation (Sect. 3) shows very promising results.

2   Data and Methodology

Data Description. We investigate the problem with the 3W dataset provided by Petrobras [8], which contains more than 20000 subsets of time series labelled with undesired events, amounting to in total 829,161 min (Table 1). The dataset consists of both data from real production platforms and simulated data generated from the OLGA system [9], which is an established tool in the petroleum domain for providing physically-realistic data. The data have labels of normal operation and eight undesired event classes (Event1-8). These undesired events are important events that can cause potential accidents or failures (for details, please refer to [8]). The data are acquired from eight different sensors per second, however, most subsets contain only five features, which are sensor measurements of downhole gauge pressure (P1), transducer temperature (T1) and pressure (P2), upstream choke pressure (P3), and downstream choke temperature (T2). The target value, in general, contains normal, transient, and faulty three stages in chronological order (Fig. 1b): the normal stage is always followed by the transient stage.

Methodology. Our methods are depicted as the data pipelines in Fig. 2. First, we select the meaningful features (non-empty, non-constant) as input data, then segment the input data (2D matrices) per minute and reshape them to 3D matrices. After that, the data is fed to (1) feature engineering (FE) and random forests and (2) to temporal convolutional networks for both event type classification and event probability regression. We choose feature engineering and RF because they are frequently used classic ML methods and have proven to be effective in past works [2], while TCN has been known as deep learning methods suitable for processing time series [10].

Time Series Decomposition: For the purpose of real-time prediction in every minute, the segmentation window length is set to 60, as raw data are collected each second.

Table 1. Statistics of the 3W dataset [8], including normal operation and 8 types of undesired events. The data number is counted by minutes.

No.	Event Name	#Real data	#Simulated data	#Total data
Normal	Normal operation	165860	-	165860
Event1	Abrupt basic sediment water increase	2177	150485	152602
Event2	Spurious downhole safety valve closure	2778	7991	10769
Event3	Severe slugging	9769	71619	81388
Event4	Flow instability	40961	-	40961
Event5	Rapid productivity loss	6215	214534	220749
Event6	Quick production choke restriction	1306	96583	97889
Event7	Scaling in production choke	5262	45345	50607
Event8	Hydrate in production line	2370	35966	38336

Probability Interpolation: The 3W dataset does not provide event probability. To allow probability prediction, we set the probability for normal stages 0, for faulty stages 1, and perform linear interpolation for the transient stages. This approach takes a naive assumption that the probability increases steadily as the production proceeds from normal stages to faulty stages. Although simplistic, it can already provide valuable insights.

Feature Engineering and RF: Before feeding the data to the RF model, we perform feature engineering to extract statistical measurements from the input data features. The extracted features are based on the work of [2], including mean value, standard deviation, skewness, kurtosis, minimum, maximum, median, and first- and third-quartile values in a window size of 60. The extracted features were normalised before using.

TCN: For the TCN model, there is no need for feature engineering, and the reshaped input data can feed directly to the model. Compared with ordinary convolutional neural networks that look at data both in history and the future two directions, the architecture of TCN uses causal convolutional layers to forces the model only look back to the history data to make a prediction, which fits the study task. The filter decides the receptive field of the network, and dilation (d) refers to the spacing between the values in the filter to increase the receptive field.

Benefits. In contrast to conventional classification approaches in previous works [2,3,5], our methodology offers two significant benefits. Firstly, the prediction window size has been reduced to 60 s. We recognise that continuous prediction every second is not always practical or feasible in the industry, as it may consume excessive time and resources and reduce prediction accuracy. We aim to achieve a more efficient and accurate prediction than past works [2,3,5] by predicting the event every minute. Secondly, our prediction method is based on a probabilistic approach, which provides a prediction of the likelihood of an undesired faulty event. This allows domain experts to make informed decisions

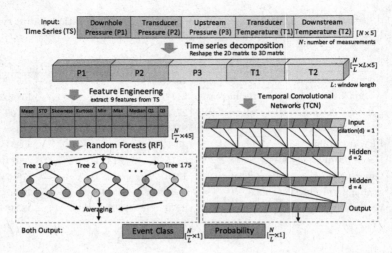

Fig. 2. We employ both RF and TCN with the illustrated workflow/architecture for event classification and probability regression, resulting in two RF models and two TCN models for each event, one of each for classification, and another each for regression. We adopt the window length so that we achieving real-time prediction (every minute) of event class and its probability.

about when to intervene and take preventive measures. The ability to make such decisions in advance can significantly reduce the potential damage caused by a faulty event, and reduce the economic and environmental impact of such incidents.

3   Evaluation and Conclusion

Experiment Setting and Implementation. We experiment with two RF and two TCN models for each event, with one RF and one TCN models for event classification and the other two for event probability regression. We choose separate models for each event than one single model for all events because of the uneven distribution of event data numbers, as evident from Table 1. Previous studies have tested a single classifier for all event classes, resulting in suboptimal results for some events (Event 2, 6, 7) [2,3]. For example, Event 1 has fifteen times as many data points as Event 2. This issue is critical for the industry, because the prediction for each event is essential, and inaccurate predictions can lead to severe consequences.

The proposed approach is then trained and tested with data from feature engineering for RF. Following common practice, we split 80% data to training set and 20% to test set. At the same time, the segmented data for TCN is divided into train-validation (for hyper-parameter tuning)-test data at 70%-10%-20%. We experiment with various hyper-parameter settings, adopting random search and partial grid search [3]. For the RF, a tree number of 175 and a maximum

Table 2. Results for classification (precision, recall, F1 score) and regression (rmse, mae) for the test set. The better results in comparison are underlined. M1 and M2 stand for our proposed methods Probability-RF and Probability-TCN, respectively. B: baseline of decision trees [3]).

Method	Event1			Event2			Event3			Event4			Event5			Event6			Event7			Event8		
	M1	M2	B	M1	M2	B	M1	M2	B	M1	M2	B	M1	M2	B	M1	M2	B	M1	M2	B	M1	M2	B
Precision	0.95	0.80	0.83	0.98	0.98	0.42	0.99	1	0.97	1	1	0.94	0.97	0.90	0.91	0.97	0.81	0.76	1	0.95	-	0.98	0.73	0.84
Recall	0.95	0.80	0.98	0.98	0.98	0.60	0.99	1	0.91	1	1	0.96	0.97	0.90	0.94	0.97	0.81	0.87	1	0.95	-	0.98	0.73	0.90
F1 Score	0.95	0.80	0.90	0.98	0.98	0.49	0.99	1	0.94	1	1	0.95	0.97	0.90	0.92	0.97	0.81	0.81	1	0.95	-	0.98	0.73	0.89
rmse	0.10	0.15	-	0.02	0.05	-	0.00	0.00	-	0.00	0.01	-	0.11	0.23	-	0.09	0.24	-	0.08	0.20	-	0.06	0.18	-
mae	0.06	0.10	-	0.01	0.02	-	0.00	0.00	-	0.00	0.01	-	0.04	0.14	-	0.04	0.15	-	0.04	0.12	-	0.04	0.15	-

tree depth of 10 shows the best result. For the TCN model in this study, we have set one stack of the residual block with a filter size of 3, dilations [1,2,4], and epochs 30 to get the best result. The Adam algorithm is selected as the optimizer for the TCN model.

We choose common metrics for binary classification, including precision, recall and F1 score, because they consider false positives and false negatives in uneven class distribution, providing more information than accuracy [2]. We choose root mean squared error (rmse) and mean absolute error (mae) for regression, as rmse is good to measure the differences between target and prediction, and mae is less sensitive to outliers.

Results and Discussion. According to our experiment results in Table 2, both random forests and temporal convolutional networks models have achieved promising results for the domain users, on the dataset in real-time classification and regression tasks. The RF model yields superior results to the TCN model (Event 1, 2, 5, 6, 7, 8), while TCN models show better results in Event 3 and 4. This is because Event 3 and 4 have only faulty targets and no normal or transient targets. Our experimental reproduction indicates that both real-time classification and probabilistic regression models generate good results, while the RF regression model yields the best results.

Figure 3 shows the probabilistic predictions of simulation and real train-test data made by the RF regression model for the undesired event 2. The predicted probability results are compared to the target probability labels in Fig. 3a, which show impressive good performance. In Fig. 3b, we plot the probability prediction using the 80%-20% train-test data split for both simulation and real data. The results show that the predictions almost overlap completely with the labels for simulation data. For real data, the predictions are also very close to the target labels. A comparison of the prediction results for simulation and real data indicates that the latter has lower accuracy. This is likely due to real data are more noisy than the simulation data. An example prediction of Event 2 (Fig. 3c) shows that our approach can indeed address challenge 2 (C2) deficiency of simple classification. Although the labels provided in the dataset show the faulty stage starts at 15000 s, our approach can regardless detect that the probability of Event2 is already very high at around 10000 s, which should be the actual case judging from the sensor data. Providing a probability of undesired events during the transient stage is crucial for the industry, as undesired events are typically labelled based on unfortunate consequences. With probabilistic prediction, early detection can perform more accurately to help avoid excessive expenditure on false positives and minimise the risk of actual undesired events occurring, which will reduce the environmental damage during the production. We also see that the probability prediction is not perfect as the second rise of predicted probability corresponds to no obvious sensor data change. This is due to the limitation of the simplistic interpolation strategy. A better prediction requires more sophisticated interpolation strategy.

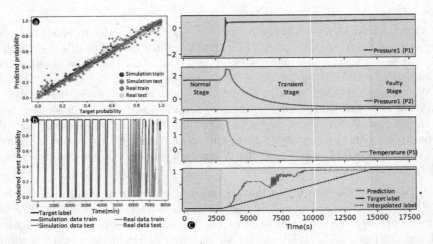

Fig. 3. Plots of probabilistic prediction of the *Spurious downhole safety valve closure* events by Probability-RF (a) scatter plot of prediction result and target. (b) line-plot of the no-shuffle data (partial). (c) an example Event2 (Fig. 1) stacked with the target labels and probabilistic prediction.

Conclusion. This paper proposes ML approaches with random forests and temporal convolutional networks for real-time undesired event detection during petroleum production, which can correctly classify the event type and provide a promising prediction of event probability. Our work contributes to a more sustainable petroleum production, by predicting event probability to engineers for performing event management and timely intervention to prevent undesired events. This proactive approach could help the industry to minimise ecological impacts, increase production efficiencies, reduce maintenance costs, and mitigate the growing concerns about industrial sustainable development. In future research, we plan to improve the probability prediction with better interpolation strategy and study the role of the work in the context of the digital twins.

Acknowledgements. This work is supported by the Norwegian Research Council via PeTWIN (294600), DigiWell (308817) and SIRIUS (237898).

References

1. Branson, D.: Sustainability in the oil and gas industry (2023). https://www.pwc.de/en/sustaina-bility/sustainability-in-the-oil-and-gas-industry.html. Accessed 06 Apr 2023
2. Marins, M.A., et al.: Fault detection and classification in oil wells and production/service lines using random forest. J. Petrol. Sci. Eng. **197**, 107879 (2021)
3. Turan, E.M., Jäschke, J.: Classification of undesirable events in oil well operation. In: 23rd International Conference on Process Control, pp. 157–162. IEEE (2021)
4. Carvalho, B.G., et al.: Flow instability detection in offshore oil wells with multivariate time series machine learning classifiers. In: 30th ISIE, pp. 1–6. IEEE (2021)
5. Gatta, F., et al.: Predictive maintenance for offshore oil wells by means of deep learning features extraction. Expert Syst. e13128 (2022)
6. Aslam, N., et al.: Anomaly detection using explainable random forest for the prediction of undesirable events in oil wells. In: ACISC (2022)
7. Machado, A.P.F., et al.: Improving performance of one-class classifiers applied to anomaly detection in oil wells. J. Pet. Sci. Eng. **218**, 110983 (2022)
8. Vargas, R.E., et al.: A realistic and public dataset with rare undesirable real events in oil wells. J. Petrol. Sci. Eng. **181**, 106223 (2019)
9. Olga dynamic multiphase flow simulator. https://software.slb.com/products/olga. Accessed 06 Apr 2023
10. He, Y., Zhao, J.: TCN for anomaly detection in time series. In: Journal of Physics: Conference Series, vol. 1213, p. 042050. IOP Publishing (2019)

SLSNet: Weakly-Supervised Skin Lesion Segmentation Network with Self-attentions

Songwen Pei[1,2,3(✉)] and Junjie Huang[1]

[1] School of Optical-Electrical and Computer Engineering, University of Shanghai for Science and Technology, Shanghai 200093, China
[2] State Key Laboratory of Computer Architecture, Institute of Computing Technology, Chinese Academy of Sciences, Beijing 100190, China
[3] Engineering Research Center of Software/Hardware Co-design Technology and Application, Ministry of Education, East China Normal University, Shanghai 200062, China
swpei@usst.edu.cn

Abstract. Computer-aided skin lesion segmentation with high precision is crucial to diagnose skin cancers in the early stage. However, the lack of pixel-level labels makes the skin lesion segmentation tasks challenging. To tackle this problem, a new weakly-supervised skin lesion segmentation network with self-attentions named SLSNet is proposed. SLSNet contains two modules and uses image-level labels as supervision information. One module named Intra-image Self-attention Seed Expansion (ISE) digs intra-image self-attentions with an expansion loss and a confidence loss to expand seed areas. The other module named Inter-image Affinity-based Noise Suppression (IAS) suppresses the noise pixels in attention maps via inter-image correlations. Extensive experiments conducted on ISIC-2017 dataset show that SLSNet achieves relatively high performance while reducing human labeling efforts.

Keywords: Healthcare · Skin Lesion Segmentation · Self-attentions

1 Introduction

Skin cancer [13] has become one of the most common diseases around the world. According to the American Cancer Society, over 100,000 new melanoma cases were diagnosed and more than 7,000 deaths [12] were recorded in the United States during 2021. With the rapid development of deep convolutional neural networks (DCNNs), methods like [2,3,9,10] have applied DCNNs to skin lesion segmentation. However, they need massive number of pixel-level labels to train for a high performance. It is labor- and time-consuming [15] for professional doctors to annotate pixel-level labels of dermoscopy images.

In order to reduce the pressure of labeling, researchers have proposed weakly supervised learning (WSL) methods for segmentation tasks. To increase useful

F. Liu et al. (Eds.): PRICAI 2023, LNAI 14327, pp. 474–479, 2024.
https://doi.org/10.1007/978-981-99-7025-4_42

semantic information with only image-level labels, methods like [4,8] explores self-attentions of images as extra supervision signals.

In this work, we propose a two-stage weakly-supervised segmentation network with self-attentions named SLSNet. It contains two modules. We propose an intra-image self-attention seed expansion module called ISE to expand initial seed areas. Inspired by [8], we enlarge the initial seed areas by extracting self-attention between original images and the corresponding image blocks cut from them. An expansion loss and a confidence loss are in use in ISE. Besides, an inter-image affinity-based noise suppression module named IAS is proposed to make the boundary of lesion areas clearer. We minimize the affinity of lesion features and normal features calculated in different images via a noise suppression loss to suppress the noise pixels, the lesion boundary will be clearer as well.

The main contributions are summarized as below.

1. We propose the ISE module who uses the image blocks and an expansion loss to expand the initial seed areas. Besides, a novel confidence loss is designed to decrease the unsure pixels.
2. We propose the IAS module with the novel noise suppression loss to suppress the noise pixels and obtain clearer boundaries of lesion areas.
3. Experimental results on public skin lesion dataset ISIC-2017 demonstrates that SLENet produces results comparable to fully-supervised methods while reducing human labeling efforts.

2   Lesion Expansion Network with Self-attentions

This section we mainly introduce the novel modules of ISE and IAS in SLSNet. The architecture of ISE module and IAS module is shown in Fig. 1. Section 2.1 and Sect. 2.2 are the detailed descriptions of Fig. 1.

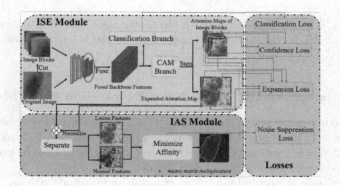

Fig. 1. The architecture of ISE module and IAS module.

2.1   Intra-image Self-attention Seed Expansion (ISE) Module

Given an input skin lesion image I_{ori}, We first cut the original image I_{ori} into N_s blocks. We define these image blocks as $I_s = \{I_1, I_2, \ldots, I_{N_s}\}$. The original image is cut equally in both the dimension of height and width. Note that N_s is a perfect square. To extract the intra-image self-attention contained in I_s, we design an architecture of Siamese network. I_{ori} and I_s are sent into the Siamese network as inputs. We fuse the features in the last two blocks of backbone network in a channel-wise way. The fused features of I_{ori} and I_s are sent into classification branch and CAM branch respectively. The classification branch includes a fully connected layer with a sigmoid function. We adopt BCE loss as the classification loss L_{class}. The CAM branch adopts Gradient weighted CAM (Grad-CAM) to obtain high-quality attention maps. In order to reduce the cost of computation, we choose to sum the CAMs of I_{ori} and I_s on channel-wise. Then we get the attention map of I_{ori} and I_s. We define them as $AttMap_{I_{ori}}$ and $AttMap_{I_s}$, respectively.

To spread the expanded semantic information of $AttMap_{I_s}$ back to the network, we design an expansion loss shown in Eq. 1 to realize this purpose.

$$L_{exp} = \sum_{a=1}^{N_s} \left\| AttMap_{I_{ori}}(a) - AttMap_{I_s}(a) \right\|_1 \tag{1}$$

where $\| * \|_1$ is the mean absolute error (MAE) loss. $AttMap_{I_{ori}}(a)$ is the image block in I_{ori}, which shares the same position with $AttMap_{I_s}(a)$ in I_{ori}.

We explore further and find that many pixels in $AttMap_{I_s}$ are uncertain to be either lesion pixels or normal pixels. We design a confidence loss defined in Eq. 2 to minimize Shannon entropy [14], thus eliminating the uncertainty.

$$L_{confi} = -\frac{1}{N_s}\frac{1}{N_p}\sum_{j=1}^{N_s}\sum_{i=1}^{N_p} Att^i log\left(Att^i + epsilon\right) \tag{2}$$

where $j \in [1, N_s]$. i is the i-th pixel in $AttMap_{I_j}$. Att^i is the attention value of the i-th pixel. N_p is the number of pixels exists in $AttMap_{I_j}$. $epsilon$ is used to prevent the value of Att^i turns into zero

2.2   Inter-image Affinity-Based Noise Suppression (IAS) Module

We observe that some pixels in $AttMap_{I_{ori}}$ are in the state of over-activated or under-activated. They are defined as noise pixels. Thus, the IAS module who explores extra semantic information between different images is proposed to acquire correct activation areas of skin lesions.

We first obtain the probability maps of lesion and normal features. The attention map $AttMap_{I_{ori}}$ is normalized with the range of $[0, 1]$ to transfer the attention value of $AttMap_{I_{ori}}$ to the probability scores of being the lesion areas. Then we obtain the probability maps of lesion features $PMap_{lesion}$ and normal features $PMap_{normal}$. After that we multiple them with F_{ori} to separate lesion features SF_{lesion} and normal features SF_{normal}. Next, we calculate the Affinity matrix of the i-th SF_{lesion} and the j-th SF_{normal} in the same batch in Eq. 3.

$$Aff(i,\ j) = \frac{SF_{lesion}(i) \odot SF_{normal}(j)}{\|SF_{lesion}(i)\|_2 \bullet \| SF_{normal}(j)\|_2},\ i \neq j \qquad (3)$$

where $\odot$ is matrix dot multiplication. $\| * \|_2$ is L2 normalization. The range of Aff is $[0, 1]$. Note that SF_{lesion} and SF_{normal} calculated in Eq. 3 are not from the same image since we need inter-image semantic information. Then, we design a noise suppression loss L_{ns} in Eq. 4 to minimize the $Aff(i,\ j)$.

$$L_{ns} = -\frac{1}{(N_{bsize})^2} \sum_{i=1}^{N_{bsize}} \sum_{j=1}^{N_{bsize}} log\left(1 - Aff(i,\ j)\right) \qquad (4)$$

where N_{bsize} is the number of images contained in a batch. i is the i-th image in the batch and j is the j-th image in the batch.

3   Experiments

3.1   Dataset and Evaluation Metrics

We evaluate the proposed SLSNet on ISIC-2017 [5] dataset. ISIC-2017 contains 2000 training images, 160 validation images and 600 testing images. This dataset has 3 types skin cancers, including MEL, NV and BKL. In order to improve the training efficiency, we adopt another 8917 images in the dataset of ISIC-2018 with only image-level labels during training.

During the evaluation process, We choose Dice coefficient (DICE), Jaccard Index (JA), Pixel accuracy (ACC), Specificity (SPE) and Sensitivity (SEN) as evaluation metrics.

3.2   Comparison with Other Methods on the ISIC-2017 Dataset

We have compared SLSNet to other state-of-the-art methods with various supervision types. The fully-supervised methods we adopt include [2,3,9,10]. The semi-supervised method is [6]. The unsupervised method is [11]. Besides, we also choose two weakly-supervised methods include [1,7]. The comparative results are shown in Table 1.

From Table 1 we observe that the highest metrics of JA, DICE, ACC, SPE are all achieved by fully-supervised methods. However, the results of SLSNet are very close or even higher to those methods. For example, the SPE of SLSNet is 1.33% higher than that of FrCN. When comparing the results with unsupervised method, the JA and ACC of our SLSNet are 14.04% and 5.21% higher than Only-superpixel, respectively. Furthermore, the results of our SLSNet also outperform other recently-proposed weakly-supervised methods. The JA, DICE and SPE of our SLSNet are 2.25%, 1.47% and 1.13% higher than the method proposed in [1], respectively. It can be concluded from the results that SLSNet achieves a slightly worse result compared with fully supervised methods, but it significantly reduces the workload in annotating pixel-level labels.

Table 1. Comparison with other advanced methods on ISIC-2017

Methods	Supervision	JA	DICE	ACC	SPE	SEN
FrCN [2]	fully	77.11	87.08	94.03	96.69	85.40
MB-DCNN [3]	fully	80.40	87.80	94.70	96.80	87.40
CSARM-CNN [9]	fully	73.35	84.62	95.85	99.40	80.22
UNet-SCDC [10]	fully	77.10	85.90	93.50	97.60	83.50
Ensemble-A [6]	semi	79.30	87.10	94.10	95.00	89.90
Only-superpixel [11]	unsupervised	60.60	–	86.90	–	–
CNN-SRR [7]	weak	73.00	–	90.20	–	–
Zaid et al. [1]	weak	72.39	83.30	93.76	96.89	87.07
SLSNet(Ours)	**weak**	**74.64**	**84.77**	**92.11**	**98.02**	**84.01**

4 Conclusion

In this paper, we propose a two-stage weakly-supervised segmentation framework with self attentions named SLSNet to improve the quality of skin lesion segmentation masks. SLSNet is mainly composed of two modules named ISE and IAS. ISE module digs the extra self-attention in image blocks of a single image to expand the seed lesion areas. IAS module suppresses the noise pixels by minimizing the affinity between lesion areas and normal areas in different images. Comparative experiments with state-of-the-art methods on ISIC-2017 show that SLSNet achieves a balance between high accuracy and low human efforts.

5 Compliance with Ethical Standards

This research study was conducted retrospectively using the open source dataset ISIC-2017. Ethical approvals were not required as confirmed by the license attached with the open access data.

Acknowledgment. The authors would like to thank the anonymous reviewers for their invaluable comments. This work was partially funded by the National Natural Science Foundation of China under Grant No.61975124, State Key Laboratory of Computer Architecture (ICT,CAS) under Grant No.CARCHA202111, and Engineering Research Center of Software/Hardware Co-design Technology and Application, Ministry of Education East China Normal University under Grant No.OP202202. Any opinions, findings and conclusions expressed in this paper are those of the authors and do not necessarily reflect the views of the sponsors.

References

1. Al-Huda, Z., Yao, Y., Yao, J., Peng, B., Raza, A.: Weakly supervised skin lesion segmentation based on spot-seeds guided optimal regions. IET Image Proc. **17**(1), 239–255 (2023)

2. Al-Masni, M.A., Al-Antari, M.A., Choi, M.T., Han, S.M., Kim, T.S.: Skin lesion segmentation in dermoscopy images via deep full resolution convolutional networks. Comput. Methods Programs Biomed. **162**, 221–231 (2018)

3. Bi, L., Kim, J., Ahn, E., Kumar, A., Feng, D., Fulham, M.: Step-wise integration of deep class-specific learning for dermoscopic image segmentation. Pattern Recogn. **85**, 78–89 (2019)

4. Chang, Y.T., Wang, Q., Hung, W.C., Piramuthu, R., Tsai, Y.H., Yang, M.H.: Weakly-supervised semantic segmentation via sub-category exploration. In: Proceedings of the IEEE/CVF Conference on Computer Vision and Pattern Recognition, pp. 8991–9000 (2020)

5. Codella, N.C., et al.: Skin lesion analysis toward melanoma detection: a challenge at the 2017 international symposium on biomedical imaging (ISBI), hosted by the international skin imaging collaboration (ISIC). In: 2018 IEEE 15th International Symposium on Biomedical Imaging (ISBI 2018), pp. 168–172. IEEE (2018)

6. Goyal, M., Oakley, A., Bansal, P., Dancey, D., Yap, M.H.: Skin lesion segmentation in dermoscopic images with ensemble deep learning methods. IEEE Access **8**, 4171–4181 (2019)

7. Hong, Y., Zhang, G., Wei, B., Cong, J., Xu, Y., Zhang, K.: Weakly supervised semantic segmentation for skin cancer via CNN superpixel region response. Multimedia Tools Appl. **82**(5), 6829–6847 (2023)

8. Jiang, P.T., Yang, Y., Hou, Q., Wei, Y.: L2G: a simple local-to-global knowledge transfer framework for weakly supervised semantic segmentation. In: Proceedings of the IEEE/CVF Conference on Computer Vision and Pattern Recognition, pp. 16886–16896 (2022)

9. Jiang, Y., Cao, S., Tao, S., Zhang, H.: Skin lesion segmentation based on multi-scale attention convolutional neural network. IEEE Access **8**, 122811–122825 (2020)

10. Lei, B., et al.: Skin lesion segmentation via generative adversarial networks with dual discriminators. Med. Image Anal. **64**, 101716 (2020)

11. Patiño, D., Avendaño, J., Branch, J.W.: Automatic skin lesion segmentation on dermoscopic images by the means of superpixel merging. In: Frangi, A.F., Schnabel, J.A., Davatzikos, C., Alberola-López, C., Fichtinger, G. (eds.) MICCAI 2018. LNCS, vol. 11073, pp. 728–736. Springer, Cham (2018). https://doi.org/10.1007/978-3-030-00937-3_83

12. Siegel, R.L., Miller, K.D., Fuchs, H.E., Jemal, A.: Cancer statistics, 2021. CA Cancer J. Clin. **71**(1), 7–33 (2021)

13. Siegel, R.L., Miller, K.D., Jemal, A.: Cancer statistics, 2019. CA Cancer J. Clin. **69**(1), 7–34 (2019)

14. Vu, T.H., Jain, H., Bucher, M., Cord, M., Pérez, P.: ADVENT: adversarial entropy minimization for domain adaptation in semantic segmentation. In: Proceedings of the IEEE/CVF Conference on Computer Vision and Pattern Recognition, pp. 2517–2526 (2019)

15. Zlateski, A., Jaroensri, R., Sharma, P., Durand, F.: On the importance of label quality for semantic segmentation. In: Proceedings of the IEEE Conference on Computer Vision and Pattern Recognition, pp. 1479–1487 (2018)

Trust and Reputation Management in IoT Using Multi-agent System Approach

Mohammad Al-Shamaileh, Patricia Anthony(✉)(iD), and Stuart Charters(iD)

Faculty of Environment, Society and Design, Lincoln University,
Christchurch, New Zealand
Mohammad.Al-Shamaileh@lincolnuni.ac.nz,
{patricia.anthony,stuart.charters}@lincoln.ac.nz
http://www.lincoln.ac.nz

Abstract. The Internet of Things (IoT) facilitates the provision of sophisticated services by linking an extensive array of diverse smart objects. As IoT devices become more intelligent, they will have the ability to communicate and cooperate with each other. As such, it is important to maintain effective cooperation among network deployed devices and ensure that they operate in a reliable and dependable fashion. In this paper, we describe IoT-CADM, an IoT agent-based decentralized trust and reputation model to select the best service provider for a particular service based on multi-context quality of services. We evaluated the performance of our model in a simulated smart factory environment against three widely-known models ReGret, SIoT and R-D-C and the result showed that our model outperformed these models.

Keywords: multiagent · trust and reputation · internet of things · trust calculation

1 Introduction

IoT is defined as a global infrastructure for information society which offers sophisticated services by linking virtual or physical intelligent entities (such as radio frequency identification (RFID) tags, sensors, and smart phones) through existing interoperable information and communication technologies. Applications running on IoT include e-health, smart homes, smart cities, and smart communities. These applications aim to help individuals make better decisions, ultimately saving them time and money [3,5].

IoT enables smart devices to communicate and cooperate with each other on behalf of human. To ensure that these devices operate in a trustworthy manner, Trust Management systems (TMSs) have been developed to determine the trustworthiness of these devices and to detect misbehaving actors in the system. However, existing TMSs largely use physical characteristics (such as memory rate, radio signal strength, delay factor and energy) to measure and evaluate

© The Author(s), under exclusive license to Springer Nature Singapore Pte Ltd. 2024
F. Liu et al. (Eds.): PRICAI 2023, LNAI 14327, pp. 480–485, 2024.
https://doi.org/10.1007/978-981-99-7025-4_43

trustworthiness [9,15]). Unfortunately, using physical characteristics is not sufficient to measure trustworthiness, especially when these devices become more intelligent and the IoT environments become more decentralized, dynamic, and open for each other. TMSs which rely on non-physical parameters have been developed but often have issues such as: how these systems gather the required information about entities, store information, score and rank the entities, and select entity. TMSs are used to evaluate the degree of confidence and the level of trust that should be placed on other parties before they cooperate [2,4,8,9,15].

In this paper, we describe IoT-CADM (Comprehensive Agent-based Decision Making) that can be used to select the best provider in a smart dynamic IoT environment based on the trustworthiness and the reputation of service providers. The model gather information from entities and calculate their trust scores using a trust and reputation scoring mechanism. The remainder of this paper is organised as follows. The background knowledge and the state of art are discussed in Sect. 2. Section 3 describes the design of IoT-CADM model. Section 4 reports the experimental evaluation and Sect. 5 concludes and presents future work.

2 Related Work

According to [11], trust encompasses the willingness of the trustor (evaluator) to embrace a certain level of risk based on a subjective belief that a trustee will consistently demonstrate reliable behaviour to maximize the trustor's interests in the face of uncertainty. On the other hand, reputation indicates the overall quality or character as observed or assessed by the general public [7]. It can be viewed as a collective assessment of trustworthiness based on the referrals or ratings provided by the members within a community.

To date, several studies have highlighted the importance of evaluating trustworthiness to maximize the satisfaction and the performance of the IoT applications especially, for applications that deal with the decision-making and partner-selection to maintain successful collaboration in the network [1,13–15]. In Public Reputation Systems (PRS), users rate each other in order to build trust through reputation. This kind of reputation system is based on a central unit (server) that aggregates up all the feedback after any event. [1] introduced IoT-TM (IoT-Trust Management) as a cluster-based approach to address the issues of IoT trust management such as countering bad-mouthing attacks and memory-efficient trust computation.

In [10], trust is evaluated by combining three main aspects "Reputation-Distribute-Conflict" about all the other parties in the environment during the trust evaluation process. The disrepute describes the negative opinions, while the conflict implements the consistency of the agent behaviours; where the reputation is used to indicate the positive opinions to enhance the process of selecting a trustworthy provider in multi-agent systems. The ReGreT system [12] is one of the earliest models that uses social interactions as a third source of information. ReGreT extends the capabilities of the agent to deal with trust and reputation in order to assist consumers to make rational decisions in a complex e-commerce environment setting. Kowshalya and Valarmathi [8] presented the Social Internet of Things (SIoT) trust management scheme that integrates IoT and Social Networking. They proposed a dynamic trust management model that takes into account direct observations (Dij), Indirect Recommendations ($CIij$), Centrality (Gij), Energy (E) and Service Score (S) to compute the trust score. The experimental results show that the model can also handle On Off selective forwarding attacks.

3   IoT-CADM

In this study, we simulated and implemented a smart factory supply chain which represents intelligent machines working together in supply chain during the manufacturing cycle. The IoT smart agents represent the intelligent machines in the supply chain as sellers and buyers. IoT-CADM consists of agent-based Service Consumer (aSC), agent-based Service Provider (aSP), Service Registry List (SRL)and Market Value Registry List (MVL). SRL provides a list of service of providers and the services they can offer. MVL contains the market value information for all service providers. The proposed model was developed and deployed using the JADE framework[1].

In this setup, all components are connected to the Open-IoT network and that they use the Suppliers, Inputs, Process, Outputs and Customers (SIPOC) supply chain approach to define business activities. In addition, aSP must provide at least one service. Services can be provided by different providers and aSC needs to select the best provider based on the multi-context QoS trust and reputation model provided by the model.

3.1   IoT-CADM Trust Evaluation and Selection Model (IoT-TESM)

IoT-CADM provides IoT-TESM (IoT-CADM Trust Evaluation and Selection model) that is used by aSCs to evaluate the trustworthiness of aSPs by combining information from different sources including Direct experiences ($DtSPi$), Indirect experiences ($IndtSPi$), and Market evaluation ($MrkVal$). The service consumer (aSC) selects service provider (aSP) by evaluating the IoT-TESM for every service provider aSP who provides a particular service $SRVi$. IoT-TESM is computed using Eq. 1, where the aSP with the highest evaluation value will be selected to perform the service. Here, α, β, and γ are weights and $\alpha + \beta + \gamma = 1$. The values of these weights are set manually by the system's user or automatically using the ASW (Auto-Scale Weights) which aims to give a balanced and fair values of the weights to increase the overall performance depending on what the agents see as important at that particular time.

$$Trust = \alpha DtSPi\% + \beta IndtSPi\% + \gamma MrkValSPi\% \qquad (1)$$

---

[1] https://jade.tilab.com/.

Direct experiences ($DtSPi$) is the main source of information, which reflect all the previous transactions between the aSC and aSP. Th Indirect experiences ($IndtSPi$ reflects the experience and relation between the same aSP with the others, and it indicates how the others think about the aSP. The Market evaluation ($MrkVal$) is used to increase the evaluation accuracy and reduce the risk of dealing with a new provider. MrkVal is the market value of the aSP. MrkVal provide more opportunity for new providers to be selected as $DtSPi$ and $IndtSPi$ are not available for new entrants.

4   Experimental Evaluation

The purpose of this experiment is to evaluate the performance of IoT-CADM against ReGreT [12], S-IoT [8] and R-D-C [10]. All models were implemented in the simulated smart factory environment.

We evaluated the performance of these models based on fourteen parameters which include quality of service, the quality of provider, total cash utility, and evaluation of trustworthiness. The trustworthiness score for each service provider is calculated using IoT-TESM. A high trust score signifies a high level of trustworthiness. We used TOPSIS, a multi-criteria decision analysis method [6] to rank the performance of these models.

The environment is populated with 230 agents. These agents may be active all the time during the simulation or only run for a specific period. Agents are distributed according to 4 different levels in the supply chain. L1 is service consumer only, L4 is the raw material providers. Between L1 and L4, the agents in L2 and L3 consume the services from the lower levels and provide services to the higher levels. These 230 agents are distributed across L1 (50), L2(55), L3(60) and L4(65). Here, when a consumer agent needs certain services, it collects the required information, evaluates and selects the service providers. The simulation is run for 10000 time ticks, which represent a duration of seven years where each time tick is equals to 6 h. In this experiment, we assume all agents are honest.

Figure 1 shows the performance of the four models across the fourteen parameters. It can be seen that our model, IoT-CADM is the top finisher for 8 out of the 14 parameters being evaluated. Using TOPSIS method, IoT-CADM is ranked as the best performer followed by ReGreT, SIoT and R-D-C. IoT-CADM and ReGreT are the top two performers since they use social information rather than just using physical behaviours.

Type	Seq.	Parameter	Weight (pw)	(Xi / SQR(SUM(X^2))) * 100				Ideal Best		Ideal Worst	
				IoT-CADM	ReGreT	SIoT	R-D-C				
Normalized Values	1	Context Aware	0.1	50	50	50	50	max	50	min	50
	2	Quality of Service (QoS)	0.1	57.7	57.7	57.7	0	max	57.7	min	0
	3	Quality of Provider (QoP)	0.1	100	0	0	0	max	100	min	0
	4	Number of Active Agents	0.1	61	48.3	48.1	40.3	max	61	min	40.3
	5	Number of completed transaction	0.1	65.2	44.7	44.2	42.4	max	65.2	min	42.4
	6	Total Cash Utility	0.1	65.3	44.6	44.2	42.3	max	65.3	min	42.3
	7	Avg.Evaluation and selection Time	0.1	24.1	67.2	66.9	20.8	min	20.8	max	67.2
	8	Avg. Number of SPs per Selection	0.1	52.4	57.1	56.6	28.3	min	57.1	min	28.3
	9	Total Comm_MSGs through the network	0.05	51.4	58.5	57.8	24.5	min	24.5	max	58.5
	10	Avg. Comm_MSGs per Transaction	0.05	38.5	62.4	62.2	27.4	min	27.4	max	62.4
	11	Avg. Eval. Trustworthiness DV1 (0 - 3000)	0.05	83	15.1	37.8	38.3	max	83	min	15.1
	12	Avg. Eval. Trustworthiness DV2 (3000 - ~)	0.05	64	49.8	42	40.8	max	64	min	40.8

Type	Seq.	Function	Models			
			IoT-CADM	ReGreT	SIoT	R-D-C
Ranking	1	Ideal Best (IB)	0.0156	0.1223	0.12	0.1276
	2	Ideal Worst (IW)	0.1367	0.0652	0.0658	0.0537
	3	Performance = IW / (IB + IW)	0.8976	0.3477	0.3541	0.2962
	4	Final Rank ==>	1	3	2	4

Fig. 1. TOPSIS performance ranking for all models

5   Conclusion and Future Work

In this paper, we discussed IoT-CADM, an IoT agent-based decentralized trust and reputation model to select the best service provider for a particular service based on multi-context quality of services. To ensure a successful and efficient collaboration among the IoT entities, they need to operate in a reliable and dependable manner. The IoT-TESM is used to evaluate the trustworthiness by combining information gathered from different sources including Direct experiences (DtSPi), Indirect experiences (IndtSPi), and Market evaluation (MrkVal). The proposed model aims to aid devices in the IoT environment to determine when, how and who they should collaborate with.

This work advances the state of the art by providing a trust and reputation model than can facilitate decision-making amongst agents in IoT environment such as smart factory, smart houses and smart city. The availability of such model can be beneficial to humans to provide better decision-making which indirectly saves time and money. In addition, the inclusion of artificial intelligence through the use of agents for decision making means that the IoT-CADM model can adapt to different environments when compared with traditional IoT trust and reputation models.

In this study, we assume that all agents are honest. It will be interesting to investigate the performance of our model in environments that are partially and fully populated with dishonest agents.

References

1. Alshehri, M.D., Hussain, F.K., Hussain, O.K.: Clustering-driven intelligent trust management methodology for the internet of things (CITM-IoT). Mob. Netw. Appl. **23**(3), 419–431 (2018). https://doi.org/10.1007/s11036-018-1017-z
2. Ben Saied, Y., Olivereau, A., Zeghlache, D., Laurent, M.: Trust management system design for the Internet of Things: a context-aware and multi-service approach. Comput. Secur. **39**, 351–365 (2013). https://doi.org/10.1016/j.cose.2013.09.001
3. Caminha, J., Perkusich, A., Perkusich, M.: A smart trust management method to detect on-off attacks in the Internet of Things. Secur. Commun. Netw. **2018**, 1–10 (2018). https://doi.org/10.1155/2018/6063456
4. Copigneaux, B.: Semi-autonomous, context-aware, agent using behaviour modelling and reputation systems to authorize data operation in the Internet of Things. In: 2014 IEEE World Forum on Internet of Things (WF-IoT), pp. 411–416 (2014)
5. Guo, J., Chen, I.R., Tsai, J.J.: A survey of trust computation models for service management in Internet of Things systems. Comput. Commun. **97**, 1–14 (2017). https://doi.org/10.1016/j.comcom.2016.10.012
6. Hwang, C.L., Yoon, K.: Methods for multiple attribute decision making. In: Multiple Attribute Decision Making. Lecture Notes in Economics and Mathematical Systems, vol. 186. Springer, Berlin, Heidelberg (1981). https://doi.org/10.1007/978-3-642-48318-9_3
7. Jøsang, A., Ismail, R., Boyd, C.: A survey of trust and reputation systems for online service provision. Decis. Support Syst. **43**(2), 618–644 (2007). https://doi.org/10.1016/j.dss.2005.05.019. emerging Issues in Collaborative Commerce
8. Kowshalya, A.M., Valarmathi, M.L.: Trust management in the social Internet of Things. Wireless Pers. Commun. **96**(2), 2681–2691 (2017). https://doi.org/10.1007/s11277-017-4319-8
9. Maddar, H., Kammoun, W., Youssef, H.: Effective distributed trust management model for Internet of Things. Procedia Comput. Sci. **126**, 321–334 (2018). https://doi.org/10.1016/j.procs.2018.07.266. knowledge-Based and Intelligent Information & Engineering Systems: Proceedings of the 22nd International Conference, KES-2018, Belgrade, Serbia
10. Majd, E., Balakrishnan, V.: A reputation-oriented trust model for multi-agent environments. Ind. Manag. Data Syst. **116**(7), 1380–1396 (2016). https://doi.org/10.1108/imds-06-2015-0256
11. Ruan, Y., Durresi, A.: A survey of trust management systems for online social communities - trust modeling, trust inference and attacks. Knowl.-Based Syst. **106**, 150–163 (2016). https://doi.org/10.1016/j.knosys.2016.05.042
12. SABATER, J.: Evaluating the regret system. Appl. Artif. Intell. **18**(9–10), 797–813 (2004). https://doi.org/10.1080/08839510490509027
13. Shayesteh, B., Hakami, V., Akbari, A.: A trust management scheme for IoT-enabled environmental health/accessibility monitoring services. Int. J. Inf. Secur. **19**, 93–110 (2018)
14. Sun, G., Li, J., Dai, J., Song, Z., Lang, F.: Feature selection for IoT based on maximal information coefficient. Futur. Gener. Comput. Syst. **89**, 606–616 (2018). https://doi.org/10.1016/j.future.2018.05.060
15. Yu, Y., Jia, Z., Tao, W., Xue, B., Lee, C.: An efficient trust evaluation scheme for node behavior detection in the Internet of Things. Wireless Pers. Commun. **93**(2), 571–587 (2016). https://doi.org/10.1007/s11277-016-3802-y

Author Index

Printed in the United States
by Baker & Taylor Publisher Services